Consumer Behaviour

Ray Wright

Australia • Canada • Mexico • Singapore • Spain • United Kingdom • United States

Consumer Behaviour
Ray Wright

Publishing Director
John Yates

Publisher
Jennifer Pegg

Developmental Editor
Laura Priest

Production Editor
Emily Gibson

Manufacturing Manager
Helen Mason

Editorial Assistant
David Barbaree

Typesetter
Gray Publishing, Tunbridge Wells, UK

Production Controller
Maeve Healy

Marketing Manager
Leo Stanley

Cover Design
Keith Marsh, Fink Creative Partners, Sanderstead, UK

Text Design
Design Deluxe, Bath, UK

Printer
Rotolito Lombardia, Milan, Italy

For more information, contact
Thomson Learning
High Holborn House
50–51 Bedford Row
London WC1R 4LR
or visit us on the World Wide Web at
http://www.thomsonlearning.co.uk

ISBN-10: 1-84480-138-1
ISBN-13: 978-1-84480-138-1

This edition published 2006 by Thomson Learning.

British Library Cataloguing-in-Publication Data
A catalogue record for this book is available from the British Library

Brief contents

Contents

10 The marketing mix, consumer behaviour and organisational buying behaviour 423

11 Present and future developments 461

Preface

Why the need to study consumer behaviour

There are over 60 million people living in the UK, over 400 million in the EU, 1.3 billion in China and over 6 billion in the world. All are potential consumers for one product or another as markets are opening up around the globe. Ultimately the majority of goods and services are produced for end individual consumption. It is true that many supply chains will involve one business selling raw materials, component parts and/or capital equipment to another, but eventually, whether the end product is a motorway, a more innovative fire engine, a holiday package, a pension scheme, a bathroom suite, fashion clothes or a new chocolate bar, the end consumer will be somebody within the 6 billion. So an understanding of customer or consumer behaviour, existing beliefs and attitudes and reasons for product/brand purchase or usage, becomes paramount, particularly in very competitive national and international markets. There is also the need to try to predict what might happen into the future. It is an essential and crucial part of marketing and not to understand the customer, not to understand their reasons for brand and retail outlet choice, must eventually cause the wrong product benefits to be offered resulting in loss of sales and corporate failure.

On a more personal level, I have always had a deep interest in trying to understand how other people think and what makes them behave in the way that they do. I feel that in doing this we come more readily to understand our own individual patterns of thought and ways of behaving. I have found many of the areas discussed and examined throughout the book, perception, learning, motivation, personality and so on, fascinating and complex and I am constantly learning. In some cases there are no cut and dried answers about human and consumer behaviour and I suppose this is what makes it so fascinating. Many students also comment on the subjects discussed throughout the book, saying that they were pleased to have had the opportunity to explore such interesting areas missed out in the past. My feeling is that a good and successful manager and well-rounded person should take the chance to examine both the natural and the social sciences, as this will enhance how they behave and interact with others, both in their private and business lives. I have to say that knowledge of the social and behavioural sciences has been invaluable to me in working for over 20 years in commercial sales and marketing and nearly 20 years in the educational sector.

After talking with the publishers it was felt that there was the need for a book on consumer behaviour with a European perspective rather then a US view and this I have tried to do. Toward the end of the book I have taken a little time to compare consumer behaviour with organisation behaviour as I felt that knowing the differences helps in overall understanding. The book consists of 11 chapters, all in colour, covering important areas and it should comfortably adapt to meet the needs of most courses. In every chapter in the book I have tried to take into account both theory and practice and examples of both are given throughout. I have tried to simplify the theories used hopefully categorising them in a logical and progressive manner so that one relates to the other and each relate to the issue of human and consumer behaviour. The general and marketing examples used are as relevant, up to date and as interesting as possible and many have questions attached that can be used by both student and tutor alike. These are enhanced by a series of colour diagrams and images. I have tried to take into account present and changing national and global consumer and market circumstances and hopefully the discussion that takes place will reflect this. Each chapter has ten more questions and two case studies at the end. More information, including suggested outline answers to all questions asked and other resources, are available online on a dedicated website: www.thomsonlearning.co.uk/wright.

Acknowledgements

I would like to specially thank the following people for their support and help over the many, many months of writing this book: Simon Wright for helping with the many problems and needs associated with the computer as well as helping with some of the photos and images used throughout the book; my wife for encouragement and suggestions; Hazel Pettifore for help with images; Dervogilla Elms for help with images and the editing and production teams at Thomson Learning, especially Laura Priest, Lisa Blackwell and Emily Gibson.

The publisher would also like to thank the following reviewers:

Charles Dennis
Brunel University

Sylvie Laforet
Sheffield University

Reinhardt Lohbauer
European Business College, Munich

Grace Mackie
Robert Gordon University

Frances Betts
University of Buckingham

Michael De Domenici
University of Greenwich

Mike Cant
UNISA, South Africa

Patricia Harris
Kingston University

Cathy Pickup
East Berkshire College

Walk-through tour

Learning objectives

Listed at the start of each chapter, these highlight the key outcomes covered in each chapter.

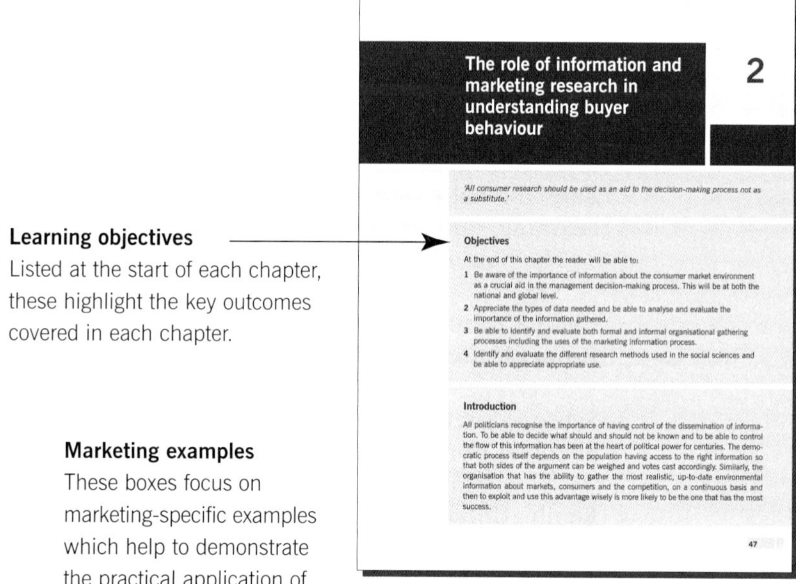

The role of information and marketing research in understanding buyer behaviour 2

'All consumer research should be used as an aid to the decision-making process not as a substitute.'

Objectives

At the end of this chapter the reader will be able to:

1 Be aware of the importance of information about the consumer market environment as a crucial aid in the management decision-making process. This will be at both the national and global level.
2 Appreciate the types of data needed and be able to analyse and evaluate the importance of the information gathered.
3 Be able to identify and evaluate both formal and informal organisational gathering processes including the uses of the marketing information process.
4 Identify and evaluate the different research methods used in the social sciences and be able to appreciate appropriate use.

Introduction

All politicians recognise the importance of having control of the dissemination of information. To be able to decide what should and should not be known and to be able to control the flow of this information has been at the heart of political power for centuries. The democratic process itself depends on the population having access to the right information so that both sides of the argument can be weighed and votes cast accordingly. Similarly, the organisation that has the ability to gather the most realistic, up-to-date environmental information about markets, consumers and the competition, on a continuous basis and then to exploit and use this advantage wisely is more likely to be the one that has the most success.

47

Marketing examples

These boxes focus on marketing-specific examples which help to demonstrate the practical application of marketing in a variety of business environments.

General examples

Examples are dispersed throughout the text to illustrate the practical application of key concepts.

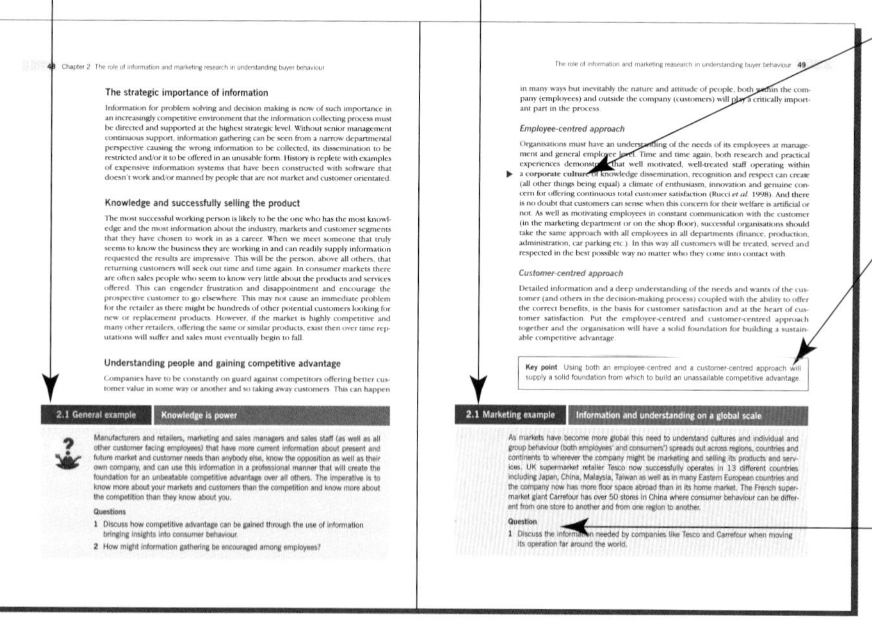

48 Chapter 2 The role of information and marketing research in understanding buyer behaviour

The strategic importance of information

Information for problem solving and decision making is now of such importance in an increasingly competitive environment that the information collecting process must be directed and supported at the highest strategic level. Without senior management continuous support, information gathering can be seen from a narrow departmental perspective causing the wrong information to be collected, its dissemination to be restricted and/or it to be offered in an unusable form. History is replete with examples of expensive information systems that have been constructed with software that doesn't work and/or manned by people that are not market and customer orientated.

Knowledge and successfully selling the product

The most successful working person is likely to be the one who has the most knowledge and the most information about the industry, markets and customer segments that they have chosen to work in as a career. When we meet someone that truly seems to know the business they are working in and can readily supply information requested the results are impressive. This will be the person, above all others, that returning customers will seek out time and time again. In consumer markets there are often sales people who seem to know very little about the products and services offered. This can engender frustration and disappointment and encourage the prospective customer to go elsewhere. This may not cause an immediate problem for the retailer as there might be hundreds of other potential customers looking for new or replacement products. However, if the market is highly competitive and many other retailers, offering the same or similar products, exist then over time reputations will suffer and sales must eventually begin to fall.

Understanding people and gaining competitive advantage

Companies have to be constantly on guard against competitors offering better customer value in some way or another and so taking away customers. This can happen

2.1 General example **Knowledge is power**

Manufacturers and retailers, marketing and sales managers and sales staff (as well as all other customer facing employees) that have more current information about present and future market and customer needs than anybody else, know the opposition as well as their own company, and can use this information in a professional manner that will create the foundation for an unbeatable competitive advantage over all others. The imperative is to know more about your markets and customers than the competition and know more about the competition than they know about you.

Questions

1 Discuss how competitive advantage can be gained through the use of information bringing insights into consumer behaviour.
2 How might information gathering be encouraged among employees?

The role of information and marketing reasearch in understanding buyer behaviour 49

in many ways but inevitably the nature and attitude of people, both within the company (employees) and outside the company (customers) will play a critically important part in the process.

Employee-centred approach

Organisations must have an understanding of the needs of its employees at management and general employee level. Time and time again, both research and practical experiences demonstrate that well motivated, well-treated staff operating within a **corporate culture** of knowledge dissemination, recognition and respect can create (all other things being equal) a climate of enthusiasm, innovation and genuine concern for offering continuous total customer satisfaction (Rucci *et al.* 1998). And there is no doubt that customers can sense when this concern for their welfare is artificial or not. As well as motivating employees in constant communication with the customer (in the marketing department or on the shop floor), successful organisations should take the same approach with all employees in all departments (finance, production, administration, car parking etc.). In this way all customers will be treated, served and respected in the best possible way no matter who they come into contact with.

Customer-centred approach

Detailed information and a deep understanding of the needs and wants of the customer (and others in the decision-making process) coupled with the ability to offer the correct benefits, is the basis for customer satisfaction and at the heart of customer satisfaction. Put the employee-centred and customer-centred approach together and the organisation will have a solid foundation for building a sustainable competitive advantage.

Key point Using both an employee-centred and a customer-centred approach will supply a solid foundation from which to build an unassailable competitive advantage.

2.1 Marketing example **Information and understanding on a global scale**

As markets have become more global this need to understand cultures and individual and group behaviour (both employees' and consumers') spreads out across regions, countries and continents to wherever the company might be marketing and selling its products and services. UK supermarket retailer Tesco now successfully operates in 13 different countries including Japan, China, Malaysia, Taiwan as well as in many Eastern European countries and the company now has more floor space abroad than in its home market. The French supermarket giant Carrefour has over 50 stores in China where consumer behaviour can be different from one store to another and from one region to another.

Question

1 Discuss the information needed by companies like Tesco and Carrefour when moving its operation far around the world.

Glossary terms

Glossary terms are highlighted throughout the text where they first appear and listed in a full glossary at the back of the book.

Key points

Highlight key issues to make it easier for students to recognise and remember them.

In-text questions

Short questions which encourage students to review their understanding of the main topics and issues covered in the chapter so far.

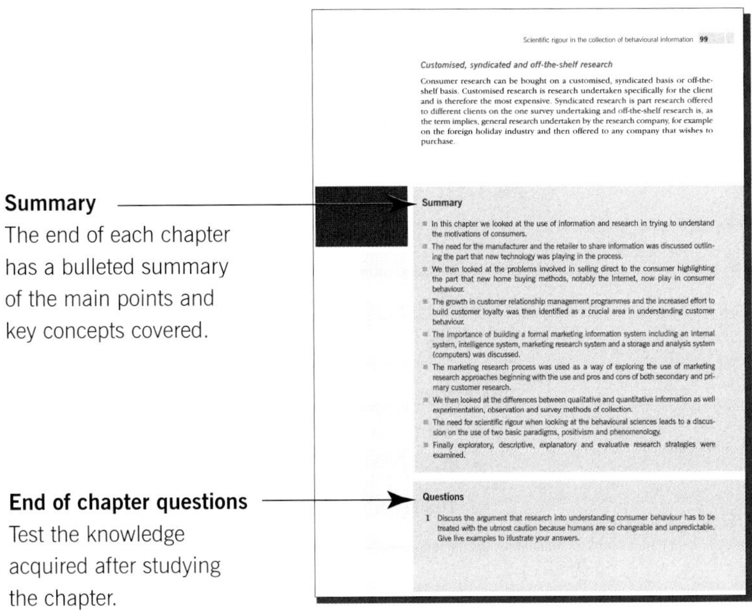

Scientific rigour in the collection of behavioural information 99

Customised, syndicated and off-the-shelf research

Consumer research can be bought on a customised, syndicated basis or off-the-shelf basis. Customised research is research undertaken specifically for the client and is therefore the most expensive. Syndicated research is part research offered to different clients on the one survey undertaking and off-the-shelf research is, as the term implies, general research undertaken by the research company, for example on the foreign holiday industry and then offered to any company that wishes to purchase.

Summary

- In this chapter we looked at the use of information and research in trying to understand the motivations of consumers.
- The need for the manufacturer and the retailer to share information was discussed outlining the part that new technology was playing in the process.
- We then looked at the problems involved in selling direct to the consumer highlighting the part that new home buying methods, notably the Internet, now play in consumer behaviour.
- The growth in customer relationship management programmes and the increased effort to build customer loyalty was then identified as a crucial area in understanding customer behaviour.
- The importance of building a formal marketing information system including an internal system, intelligence system, marketing research system and a storage and analysis system (computers) was discussed.
- The marketing research process was used as a way of exploring the use of marketing research approaches beginning with the use and pros and cons of both secondary and primary customer research.
- We then looked at the differences between qualitative and quantitative information as well experimentation, observation and survey methods of collection.
- The need for scientific rigour when looking at the behavioural sciences leads to a discussion on the use of two basic paradigms, positivism and phenomenology.
- Finally exploratory, descriptive, explanatory and evaluative research strategies were examined.

Questions

1 Discuss the argument that research into understanding consumer behaviour has to be treated with the utmost caution because humans are so changeable and unpredictable. Give live examples to illustrate your answers.

Summary

The end of each chapter has a bulleted summary of the main points and key concepts covered.

End of chapter questions

Test the knowledge acquired after studying the chapter.

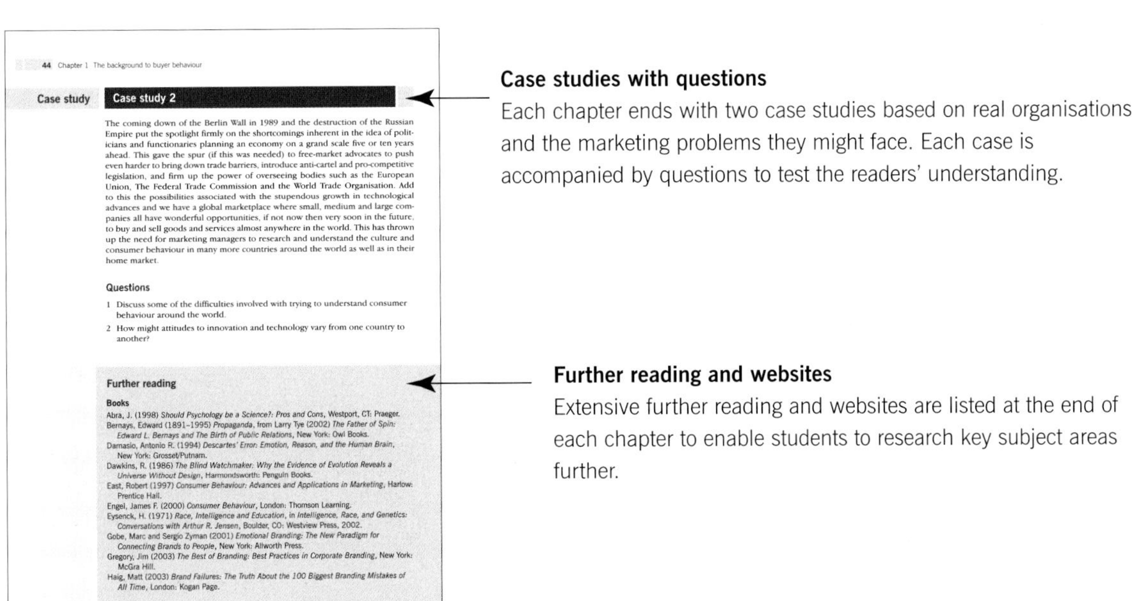

44 Chapter 1 The background to buyer behaviour

Case study

Case study 2

The coming down of the Berlin Wall in 1989 and the destruction of the Russian Empire put the spotlight firmly on the shortcomings inherent in the idea of politicians and functionaries planning an economy on a grand scale five or ten years ahead. This gave the spur (if this was needed) to free-market advocates to push even harder to bring down trade barriers, introduce anti-cartel and pro-competitive legislation, and firm up the power of overseeing bodies such as the European Union, The Federal Trade Commission and the World Trade Organisation. Add to this the possibilities associated with the stupendous growth in technological advances and we have a global marketplace where small, medium and large companies all have wonderful opportunities, if not now then very soon in the future, to buy and sell goods and services almost anywhere in the world. This has thrown up the need for marketing managers to research and understand the culture and consumer behaviour in many more countries around the world as well as in their home market.

Questions

1 Discuss some of the difficulties involved with trying to understand consumer behaviour around the world.

2 How might attitudes to innovation and technology vary from one country to another?

Further reading

Books

Abra, J. (1998) *Should Psychology be a Science?: Pros and Cons*, Westport, CT: Praeger.
Bernays, Edward (1891–1995) *Propaganda*, from Larry Tye (2002) *The Father of Spin: Edward L. Bernays and The Birth of Public Relations*, New York: Owl Books.
Damasio, Antonio R. (1994) *Descartes' Error: Emotion, Reason, and the Human Brain*, New York: Grosset/Putnam.
Dawkins, R. (1986) *The Blind Watchmaker: Why the Evidence of Evolution Reveals a Universe Without Design*, Harmondsworth: Penguin Books.
East, Robert (1997) *Consumer Behaviour: Advances and Applications in Marketing*, Harlow: Prentice Hall.
Engel, James F. (2000) *Consumer Behaviour*, London: Thomson Learning.
Eysenck, H. (1971) *Race, Intelligence and Education*, in *Intelligence, Race, and Genetics: Conversations with Arthur R. Jensen*, Boulder, CO: Westview Press, 2002.
Gobe, Marc and Sergio Zyman (2001) *Emotional Branding: The New Paradigm for Connecting Brands to People*, New York: Allworth Press.
Gregory, Jim (2003) *The Best of Branding: Best Practices in Corporate Branding*, New York: McGra Hill.
Haig, Matt (2003) *Brand Failures: The Truth About the 100 Biggest Branding Mistakes of All Time*, London: Kogan Page.

Case studies with questions

Each chapter ends with two case studies based on real organisations and the marketing problems they might face. Each case is accompanied by questions to test the readers' understanding.

Further reading and websites

Extensive further reading and websites are listed at the end of each chapter to enable students to research key subject areas further.

WWW

About the website

Visit the *Consumer Behaviour* accompanying website at www.thomson-learning.co.uk/wright to find further teaching and learning material, including:

For students

- 10 multiple-choice questions per chapter
- Related weblinks
- Preface
- Chapter learning objectives.

For lecturers

- Comprehensive teaching notes in instructor's manual
- Downloadable PowerPoint slides
- Further cases
- Answers to questions in the book
- Exam View testbank of multiple-choice questions.

The background to buyer behaviour

1

The conscious and intelligent manipulation of the organized habits and opinions of the masses is an important element in democratic society. Those who manipulate this unseen mechanism of society constitute an invisible government which is the true ruling power of our country. We are governed, our minds are moulded, our tastes formed, our ideas suggested, largely by men we have never heard of. This is a logical result of the way in which our democratic society is organized.

Edward Bernays (1891–1995), Propaganda

Objectives

At the end of this chapter the reader will be able to:

1 Examine the background to the study of **buyer behaviour** and be able to demonstrate the part that marketing, the market economy and the role of the customer play in this process.

2 Analyse, compare and evaluate the natural and social sciences and be able to show how this relates to the study of consumer behaviour.

3 Identify and examine all elements of the buyer decision-making process and demonstrate how it contributes to an understanding of consumer behaviour.

Introduction

As the world seems to shrink and many more markets are made available to small, medium and large organisations alike the need for knowledge and understanding, in both business-to-consumer (B2C) and business-to-business (B2B) markets, about customers and markets is crucial to the continuous success of the company. Only then can the correct products and services be offered that satisfy clearly identified needs. In this way sales and profits can be maintained and increased at a level that satisfies all relevant company stakeholders. Experience has shown that anything less can cause business disruption, the sacking of the Chief Executive Officer (CEO), acquisitions by more aware organisations and in extreme cases the closure of the firm. As more organisations market increasingly sophisticated products and services around the world, in an increasingly competitive environment, the need to have a deep understanding of customer/consumer behaviour will impinge on everybody.

1.1 General example

In 2004 key shareholders forced UK supermarket giant Sainsbury's chairman to resign because of falling market share and profit. An outdated distribution system, a portfolio of stores in dire need of refurbishment, and a growing perception among shoppers that Sainsbury no longer offered value for money was seen as the cause.

Question

1 Discuss why you think one retailer might be more successful than another. Give examples.

Key point The customer is the person (or persons) who buys the product/service and the consumer is the person who uses the product/service. They can be the same or different people. The term will be used interchangeably.

A market economy

At the beginning of a book on customer behaviour it is well to set the scene and establish the inextricable relationship between a market economy, the role of marketing and why there is this crucial need to try to understand customer and consumer behaviour at every possible stage in the decision-making process. There is no longer little doubt that in the debate between the various ways to successfully run and manage a modern economy the protagonists for a market approach now hold sway across most of the developed industrial world (Nikolai Smelev and Vladimir Popov in Heilbroner 2001; Osterfeld 1992).

In very simple terms free market economists and practitioners insist that markets will operate more effectively and efficiently if left to businesses and managers operating in the private sector where there are many competing companies. Free markets and the interplay between the demand and supply of products and services (known as the 'laws of supply and demand') are dictated by the needs of the consumer in a free populous marketplace where there is little or no government public sector interference (**Adam Smith** 1776; Hayek 1996).

A planned approach

Free market economists and practitioners go on to argue that a more planned economic approach, where politicians and civil servants make decisions about demand and supply, are much less successful. This is because they can breed national and local government interference causing decisions to be made for politic, bureaucratic and, in some cases, corrupt reasons rather than public and consumer needs. Under a planned system decisions made about what should and what should not be produced are decided on long-term demand forecasts which (because forecasting is looking into an uncertain future) are often unreliable in their outcomes causing shortages of some goods and an over abundance of others, e.g. not enough potatoes and fridges one year and too many apples and TVs another year.

Mixed economy

Of course no markets can be completely free, otherwise anarchy might ensue, and governments (to a greater or lesser extent) will, and do, step in to construct an acceptable social, ethical and legal competitively mixed economic framework within which businesses can then freely and effectively operate. The extent of government involvement will vary according to political and government policy. As a percentage of GDP it can vary from below 40 per cent in the USA to round about 60 per cent in Sweden (2002).

1.2 General example — Free markets – the dominant concept

Capitalism and the idea of free markets now dominate economic thinking across all developed economies. Organisations such as the G8, the World Trade Organisation (WTO) and the Organisation for Economic Co-operation and Development (OECD) now meet on a regular basis to bring down market barriers and to encourage unfettered trade between member countries. Consumer choice is the central part of the process and history has shown that in this way economies thrive and grow to the betterment of all participants.

The centrality of the consumer within the free market system

The central point to be made is that under a centrally planned economic system it is politicians, functionaries and administrators that decide what goods and services will be produced and this can lead to shortages and over production. Under a free, **liberal market economic** system, however, it is the **customer**, the **consumer**, through purchasing choices who will decide what goods, products, services, brands and benefits will be offered. Consumer acceptance and purchase will bring company success, while product rejection and dissatisfaction will inevitably lead to loss of sales, loss of profit and ultimate business and even industry shutdown.

Key point A planned and a free market economy
In simple terms:

In a **planned economy** it is politicians and governments that decide on what products and services will be produced and what markets and industries will survive.

In a free market economy it is the consumer who will decide what products and services will be produced and what markets and industries will survive.

This puts customer satisfaction and an understanding of their needs and wants and behaviour at the very heart of the economic and marketing process.

The role of marketing in understanding consumer behaviour

Marketing theory and concepts were originally developed in the USA well before the Second World War and did not really enter into business thinking as a compact and consistent approach in the UK and the rest of the modern world until much later. The business discipline of marketing was born, took shape and grew as a consequence of the pulling down of restrictive trade barriers, the opening of markets to competition and the imposition of legislation that outlaws anti-competitive behaviour and protects and supports the role of the consumer across all markets. So what is marketing?

Marketing definitions

Marketing is working on the concept that in operating in the types of markets discussed above making the customer continuously happy with the value and benefits offered by the company's products and **services** will lead to healthy business and through this to satisfactory profits. How these benefit satisfactions are achieved will differ according to the type of customer, the type of organisation and the type of market. In some markets after-sales service is important, in others innovative products, in others the use of technology and so on. What is crucial is that the supplier keeps pace with environmental and market changes, matches or beats the competition and always keeps close to and listens to customers' needs and wants. If an organisation fails in some way to follow this customer-centred mantra it will be inevitable some other company will, causing custom to be lost and sales to shrink and wither away.

So the simplest definition for those that are studying marketing is that concern for the wellbeing of the customer, consumer, client (however we might like to define it) must be at the very heart of the company's business model. The customer is 'the supreme sovereign', upset him or her at your peril. Shown here are three more formal basic definitions of marketing.

Key point Management definition of marketing
Marketing can be seen as a management process constantly identifying, anticipating, satisfying, exceeding! delighting! **consumer needs and wants** and expectations at a profit (or cost effectively) on both a short- and/or long-term basis.

Marketing as a philosophy

There is however another, broader way in which the concept of marketing can be viewed and this is as an underlying business philosophy. Ultimately the enlightened and dedicated marketer would want to see marketing, which is concern for ultimate customer satisfaction, expressed throughout the organisation as a philosophy of the heart as well as of the mind. Much easier said than done. An obsessive concern for the welfare of the customer should be imbued in all employees so that they truly believe this to be the correct approach and not just a slogan to be forgotten as soon as interactive customer contact begins.

Key point Marketing as a philosophy
Marketing is an obsessive concern for the wellbeing of the customer; it must be truly believed in the heart as well as the head and should permeate every action of all within the organisation and along the whole supply chain.

Strategic definition of marketing

It is now realised by successful companies that if marketing is to be successful and concern for the customer is to permeate all organisational functions it must be adopted, given support and driven by senior management at the strategic level. Long-term customer satisfaction is too important to be left solely to salespeople on the shop floor or to the sales representative in the buyer's office. Yes it is important to smile at customers, to be pleasant, helpful and friendly, and for a sales manager to follow up complaints and do what he or she says they will do is crucial to achieving buyer satisfaction, but these tactical marketing issues alone are not enough. There must be strategic support coming from the top of the organisation and this must be inherent in the strategic planning process. Organisational strategies, systems and structures, new product development, supply chain alliances, marketing research and so on should all ultimately be driven by customer demand. Only if a thorough market examination, looking at competition, markets, suppliers, publics etc. is taken into account at the strategic level, when developing internal resources (the marketing mix), will ultimate and lasting customer happiness be achieved. To this end we can now identify marketing as a strategic 'matching' process.

Key point A strategic definition sees marketing as a 'matching' process.
'Matching the resources of the organisation to the demands of the marketplace'.

Figure 1.1

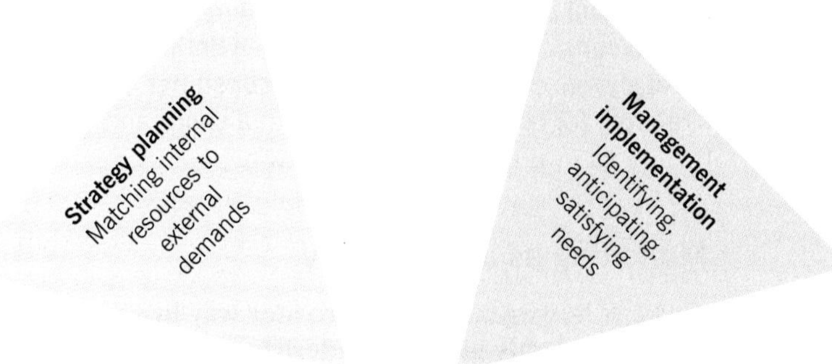

The marketing triangle: working together

Marketing used in every type of organisation

Marketing is now used in every conceivable B2C (business-to-consumer) and B2B (business-to-business) market and market sector across commercial, industrial, not-for-profit and governmental markets. For example:

- Dell computers market computer systems direct on the Internet to end consumers.
- Charities such as Oxfam buy B2B consultancy services to help organise their revenue gathering activities and have set up charity shops to sell in B2C markets.
- Supermarket retailers buy products and services from suppliers such as Nestlé and sell on to the end consumer.
- Government departments, such as social services have B2C marketing training courses on how to treat unemployment claimants and purchase office equipment from a B2B organisation.
- Banking corporations buy in advice from business consultants and sell financial retail services to the end consumer.

Understanding customer and consumer behaviour

We have seen above that the central part of the marketing process is to understand why a customer or buyer makes a purchase. Without such an understanding, businesses will find it hard to respond to the customer's needs and wants. The need to understand buyer or consumer behaviour and reasons for purchase is central to the concept of marketing goods and services to end consumers and business customers. Only in this way will an organisation be able to influence and predict reasons for purchase. If management can understand these customer responses better than the competition, then it is a potentially significant source of competitive advantage.

It is true that some businesses might still produce products and services without really knowing who the end customer might be or what might be the reasons for purchase. Known as '**product driven markets**' they tend now to be the exception rather than the rule. This is because as technology develops and markets open to customers around the world they inevitably become more competitive.

The days when an organisation could just produce a product and service in the hope that it might sell are rapidly disappearing. It is increasingly important for organisations to clearly understand the benefits wanted by customers as well as the reasons for purchase and, with some goods, repurchase on a regular basis, both in home and international markets.

Key point Understanding customer behaviour
In trying to understand customer behaviour we must identify the variety of internal and external influencing factors and problem-solving processes that will affect product, brand and service purchase decisions.

Buyer behaviour in business-to-business markets

Although this book will concentrate predominately on consumer markets it might be as well to establish here, in simple terms, the differences between **business-to-business markets** and **business-to-consumer markets**.

Business markets (or industrial markets) can be defined as markets where one business sells goods and services to another business *for use in that business* or to sell onto another business for its own use. For example capital equipment (buildings, transport), raw and manufactured materials (oil, wood, steel), component parts (windscreens, electrical fittings, nuts and bolts) and services (waste management, catering and utility services).

Buying will take place in the commercial, governmental and not-for-profit (NFP, charities, associations) sectors. Organisational buying behaviour in government departments and NFP sectors will be more rule-driven and transparent than in the commercial sector because money being spent comes from the taxpayer (government spending) and from many interested stakeholder subscribers. Purchases in these markets are by professional buyers purchasing goods and services for use by the employing organisation. So reasons for purchase tend to be predominantly rational and functional, linked to the purchase of goods and services for organisational and not individual use. (More detailed information on organisational buying behaviour is in Chapter 10.)

Behaviour in consumer markets

'When dealing with people, remember that you are not dealing with creatures of logic but with creatures of emotion.' DALE CARNEGIE

This book will therefore be predominately concerned with the purchase of goods and services in consumer markets. This can be defined as markets where individuals, families and small groups are buying goods and services for own, family or group use. Recent research has shown (Zajonc 1984; Bornstein 2004) that unlike B2B markets purchases are made for predominantly symbolic and emotional reasons and not so much for rational reasons. So, for example, it can be shown that a young man might purchase a particular type of car, not for the functional reason to drive from home to work, but for emotional reasons such as (hopefully) improving status, encouraging friendships and enhancing opposite sex attractiveness. Among other things, this is why the concept of the brand, name, logo, personality, etc., becomes so important in these markets both at home and in foreign markets.

Key point Consumer buyers are those who purchase items for their personal consumption. Business or industrial buyers are those who purchase items on behalf of their business or organisation.

The economic view on the market demand for goods and services

Market demand is defined by economists as the amount of goods and services that consumers are willing and able to buy over a particular time period. However, people have unlimited amounts of wants and needs and so demand in the national and global marketplace can only be effective where there is the ability to pay. For example millions of people in Africa live on a dollar a day and so cannot purchase everything they need. Latent market demand exists where economies are growing.

The law of supply and demand

The law of supply and demand sees an inverse relationship between the price of a product or service and the demand over a period of time. For normal goods, as the price falls demand expands and when the price rises demand slows down.

The rational consumer

Economists assume that consumers will tend to act rationally in their own self-interest when choosing what goods and services to buy. The lower the price the

Figure 1.2

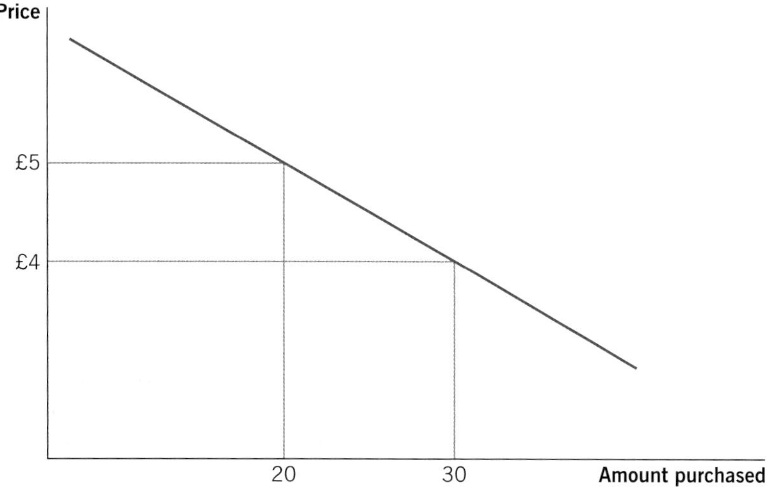

The law of supply and demand: the higher the price, the fewer sold; the lower the price, the more sold. The 'secret' of Tesco supermarket's original success – 'pile it high and sell it cheap'

more will be purchased and the higher the price the fewer will be purchased. For normal products they will be trying to maximise total satisfaction, taking into account the price they have to pay and the level of satisfaction gained from the purchase. Once a product has been purchased however (for example coffee, a holiday, a cinema ticket), demand will fall, as the need for another is less.

Elasticity of demand

For some products and services market demand will remain the same or only alter slightly as the price increases or decreases and this is known as **inelastic demand**. Examples here are petrol, alcohol and cigarettes. Demand for other products and services will fall or rise quite steeply after a price increase or decrease and this is known as **elastic demand**. Examples here might be all manner of grocery and vegetable products. Where there are substitute products a rise or fall in the price of one company's product or service, e.g. NTL telecommunications, will cause consumers to switch to a competitor, e.g. BT.

Other factors that will alter demand will include the following:

- A change in consumer income, e.g. more will be purchased, or there may be a movement from inferior to superior products, e.g. eating out rather than at home.
- A change in tastes and preferences, e.g. moving to healthier foods.

- Higher interest rates, e.g. postponing the purchase of a new car.
- Where products and services are complimentary, that is dependent on one another, e.g. an increase in house building will create an increase for building materials.

Marketing and the idea of the 'rational consumer'

Economists recognise that some luxury products (known as ostentatious goods), such as designer clothes, cosmetics, limited edition cars, have a higher price that will reflect a 'snob' satisfaction that comes from others knowing the price of a brand. However, many seem to put more emphasis on consumer rationality, rather than emotion, in comparing price and added value in purchasing products and services, than would the behavioural scientist. It also seems to be the case that an individual will give one reason (rational) for a purchase while the real reason (emotional) lies deeper within the mind often at the subconscious level. It might also be the case that what appears to be rational to one person might appear irrational to another.

Understanding the complex consumer

It is precisely because reasons for product/service/brand consideration and purchase are often based on complex and intricate **symbolic reasons** rather than fairly straightforward rational reasons that the study of consumer behaviour has become so widespread and intense. Managers will need to have knowledge and understanding of consumer behaviour at the general level as well as more detailed information about specific industry, markets and product brand areas. Organisations now spend billions of pounds a year attempting to discover reasons behind human behaviour, how the human mind operates and why one brand outsells another, why one product launch is successful while another is a failure or why one retail organisation outsells another. All this will be discussed in more detail in the next chapter on research.

The '5WH' acronym

Businesses now spend considerable amounts of money trying to learn about what makes the customer tick. The questions they try to understand are:

- Who buys?
- When do they buy?
- Where do they buy?
- Why do they buy?
- What do they buy?
- How do they buy? (5Ws and an H)

Beliefs and attitudes held

Similarly all consumers will hold some kind of belief or attitude about all areas of marketing and business including such things as: country of producing origin, industries, companies, product categories, **brands**, services, packaging, advertising, promotions and consumerism in general. Beliefs and attitudes held might range from warm appraisal or mildly interested through to total indifference, rejection and/or outright hostility. The strength of the belief and attitude will therefore determine the size of the task that faces the marketing manager. If the customer dislikes your company, your products marketed or the retail outlet offering them for sale and you are unaware of this then disaster can only but follow. At least if you are aware of the attitudes held, and can discover the reasons why this might be so, action can be taken to try to rectify and reverse the situation in some favourable way.

Key point The strength of the belief and attitude held by the consumer about your company and/or its brands will determine the level of marketing that needs to be undertaken.

The marketing mix and consumer behaviour

Organisations influence consumer behaviour through the use of an **integrated marketing mix**. Through the manipulation of its products (brands, packaging,

Figure 1.3

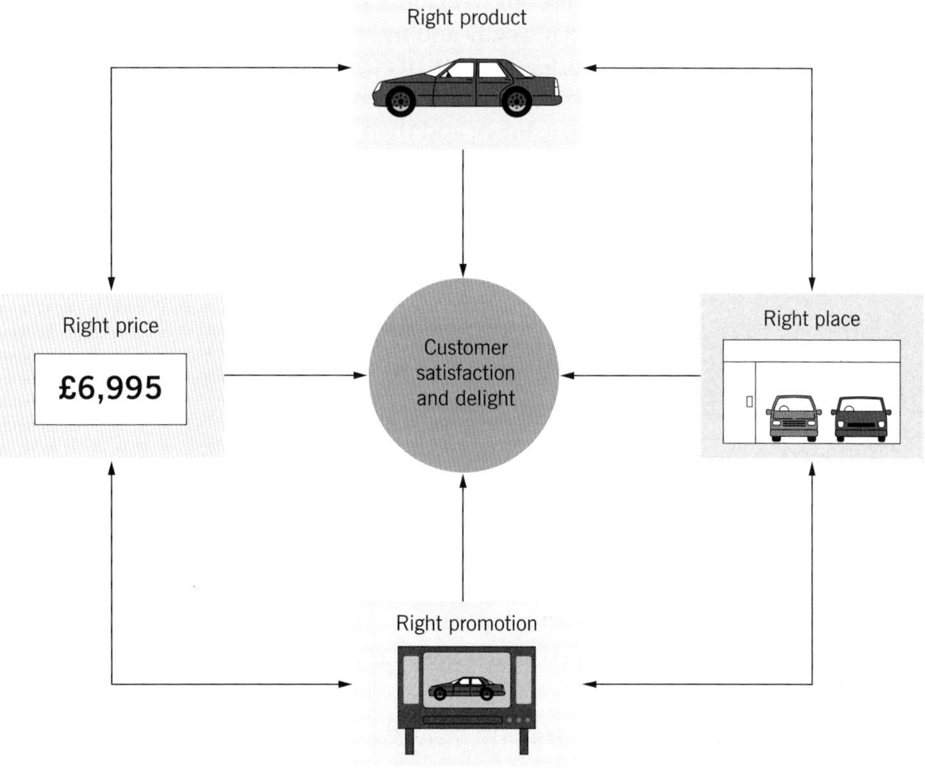

The integrated marketing mix: 'working together for success'

services, innovation etc.), prices, place (direct and indirect distribution) and promotion (the classical **'4Ps'**) the successful company is able to constantly offer benefits to satisfy changing customer needs and wants. This is discussed below.

1.1 Marketing example **Cutting the product/brand portfolio**

FMCG (fast-moving-consumer-goods) manufacturers Unilever, Procter and Gamble, Pears Soap, Cinzano Vermouth and Van de Kamp's frozen foods, have heavily rationalised the number of major packaged products in their product portfolio so that they can reduce consumer confusion and be more focused in promoting brand benefits. Unilever, the Anglo-Dutch group, has gone furthest by cutting its global brands from 1,600 to 400.

Question

1 Discuss why companies might reduce the number of brands in their product portfolio.

Corporate and product brands

Many producers and retailers are driven by the need to constantly grow and expand both nationally and internationally and absolutely crucial to this project is an intricate understanding of customers in all diverse and different markets. In this way company brand benefits, both functional and emotional, can be built in the mind of the consumer and then constantly advertised so that their 'personalities' will always be cherished, remembered and purchased. This brand building will need to take place at both the corporate and product portfolio level.

The cruise from hell – problems with corporate image

▶ Some organisations will follow a brand strategy where the **corporate image** and reputation become paramount and are used to market and sell all its products (Sony, Heinz, Kellogg's), while other organisations play down the corporate name preferring to market products under individual brand names (Unilever, Sara Lee, Procter & Gamble). There are many companies and brands that are known globally across the world and carry images and reputations within the mind of the consumer that have been painstakingly built up over the decades. Coca-Cola, McDonald's, Mercedes, Gillette, Microsoft, Nike, Wal-Mart, Manchester United all have a cache and 'personalities' that supporters want to be associated with because of the various feel-good emotions that this generates.

Product benefits wanted

Research has shown that benefits now demanded by consumers transcend mere functional capabilities moving heavily into the symbolic and the emotional (Jensen 2001). Affluence and a retail world of plenty seems to have created a buying environment were consumers insist on so much more out of the brands and services that they use. We buy sweets (Werthers Orginals) because they nostalgically remind us of long gone times when confectionary tasted so much better and life was much simpler. We are prepared to pay a premium for organic products such as eggs because they come with notions of farm life where chickens run free and eggs are collected where they lay. We buy houses, or take holidays, in the country, or abroad, because of the romantic, rustic belief that life there will be so much better, an escape that's away from the traffic and the hustle and bustle of town life. Video games and virtual reality now allow us to indulge and lose ourselves in a whole dream world of fantasy. Of course we may not admit or be able to articulate these reasons, preferring to give more obvious and mundane practical reasons.

1.2 Marketing example — The Dream Society

In his book, *The Dream Society* Rolfe Jensen argues that we will increasingly buy products and services that pander to our imagination and that can satisfy our hopes, aspirations and dreams. He predicts that the present information-based society will evolve into a society that values the stories behind products and services, which will fill the need for emotional wealth when material wealth has become commonplace. The demand for product stories will in turn increase the demand for imaginative storytellers who can artfully direct consumer emotions in a wealthy global culture where hard play replaces hard work. As wealth grows, so will the number of choices for consumer goods and emotional experiences (Jensen 2001, *The Dream Society*).

Creativity, design and innovation

Consumers' seemingly insatiable demand for choice, variety and new and exciting products puts incessant pressure on companies to constantly try to understand consumers' ever surfacing and more demanding needs and wants. They must constantly look for innovative products and concepts to match these needs and wants, knowing that complacency will inevitably lead to loss of sales, failure and eventual demise. This pressure is heavier in some areas such as hi-tech, e-business, e-tailing and fast-moving-consumer-goods (FMCG) industries where a culture of creativity and design has to be built into the fabric of the organisational culture itself so that all employees are always searching for new ideas that might be able to be turned into high-selling products.

Key point There is a continual need for companies to bring new and more innovative products to the market to satisfy ever-changing consumer demands.

The consumer and packaging

Customers' evaluations of products are greatly affected by appearances and design, including such things as touch, taste, texture and smell. In many cases the packaging that surrounds the product has become at least as important, if not more so in some cases, than the product itself and it continues to be an integral part contributing to the overall attractiveness of the product and becoming a quintessential ingredient in the emotive process of brand building. Companies will spend a fortune on consumer and packaging research, making certain that such things as materials used, colour combinations, wording and overall appropriateness match (or exceed) customer wants and expectations. This is especially so in the fast-moving-consumer-goods market (FMCG). Imagine Kit-Kat without its familiar red and white packaging, or Coca-Cola without the familiar tin or bottle, or Kellogg's cornflakes without the cockerel on the constantly busy box full of information, free gift and children's games and competitions.

Behaviour and price

Price will also have its emotive as well as functional content. It is well documented that the relationship between price and perceived value will always interplay in people's minds when choosing particular products.

price ← continuous movement → added value

Consumer concerns will pitch backwards and forward between price and added value depending on both functional and emotional concerns. It is mostly in the interest of marketing managers to push consumers toward the added value end of the spectrum where more customer satisfaction can be given, highest prices charged and greater profits made.

Place and channel of distribution (place)

▶ There are various **channels of distribution**. Some products are sold direct to the consumer, perhaps by an Internet website, direct mail, telephone or personal

1.3 Marketing example — Price confusion

British mobile phone firm Orange is overhauling its charges because of near market saturation and the intensity of the competition. But despite these changes to charges, many consumers continue to remain baffled by the plethora of payment options for phone services. This has led to market commentators making accusations against some mobile phone operators of deliberately distorting the price so as to cause confusion and restrict price comparisons. Mobile phone charges have now come under scrutiny by both government and European investigators.

Question

1 Discuss the pricing of the type of product and service identified above. Do you think that consumers should be protected from complex pricing that could cause confusion?

selling in the home; most however are sold through some kind of retail outlet. This will include supermarkets, departmental and chain stores, convenience stores, warehouses and individual outlets. All methods whether direct, in the home, or indirect through shopping malls, retail parks and retail and **factory villages** will give off an ambience that will have an effect upon consumer perception.

The consumer and corporate and brand communications

Last but not least in the marketing mix process is the role of communications and this will be discussed in great length throughout the book. Corporate and marketing communications are all the communications between the organisation and all of its stakeholders including customers, consumers, local communities, pressure groups, the media, financial institutions and so on. It is the way that organisations can influence customer and consumer behaviour and therefore its importance cannot be underestimated. Corporate communications includes everything from financial accounts statements, press releases, product recalls to the way that the fleet of vehicles is cleaned, maintained and driven and how the telephone is answered. All points of public and employee contact should promote a consistent corporate image. There is a large amount of crossover but in general terms marketing communications can be said to include all the traditional forms of promotion including advertising, **sales promotions**, direct response, **merchandising**, publicity, sponsorship, exhibitions and personal selling.

Key point The objective of corporate communications is to build and maintain a good image of the company with the customer and all other stakeholders. On the other hand marketing communications is about talking and listening to the consumer and generally promoting and selling the company's products and services.

Consumer behaviour evermore complex

The level of consumer needs and wants and the benefits demanded to meet and satisfy these needs and wants will vary from market to market from country to country and from continent to continent. In highly developed consumer markets such as the USA, the UK, France, Germany, Italy and Japan consumers have become extremely sophisticated with regard to their beliefs and aspirations and demand constantly upgraded personal attention from producers and retailers in terms of choice, product benefits offered and levels of service given. This has given rise to ever-tighter **market segmentation** and the movement from **mass-marketing** to so-called **customised or one-to-one marketing** that is offering a personalised product to match personalised needs across very large markets. This calls for an incessant deeper understanding of consumer behaviour at individual as well as group level.

Marketing research

Ever-evolving markets and complex and intricate changing customer reasons behind the purchase of products and services has put enormous pressure on marketers to collect and analyse more deeply information about its markets both at home and around the world. This has given dynamic impetus to an information gathering and a research industry that is worth over 18 billion euro in 2002 (ESOMAR) and now spans the globe. Using **secondary** (already collected), **primary** (first-hand) and both **quantitative** (numbers and statistics) and **qualitative** (opinion seeking) research methods marketing and research companies are constantly improving and updating methods of collection and analysis all hoping to understand their customers better than the competitor (marketing research is discussed in detail in the next chapter).

Inadequate and/or misleading information

What's important is that the research undertaken and the information gathered about consumer behaviour is as near correct as possible. It should be self-evident that if it isn't as near the truth as it should be then it will at best be misleading and at worse cause disastrous decisions to be made. History is rife with examples of customer information collected and then used, perhaps to launch a new product, which was later shown to be wrong in some way or another.

1.4 Marketing example — Failed products

A small example of products launched on the back of wrong information on customer behaviour that subsequently failed.

Dr Care: After much research and development and market and consumer research Dairimetics, Ltd. launched Dr Care family toothpaste, in a revolutionary aerosol container onto the US market. While the vanilla-mint flavoured product was advertised as easy to use and sanitary, many parents questioned the thought of letting their kids loose with an aerosol toothpaste and the product flopped (www.newproductworks.com).

The car model Ford Edsel is often cited as a classic marketing failure costing the company over US$200 million dollars in the late 1950s. The model was named Edsel, in spite of the fact that research clearly indicated that it was not an acceptable name by the consumer. Edsel was the name of Henry Ford's son.

Coca-Cola: In 1985 the Coca-Cola Company announced it would introduce a new Coke product to replace the old one, with its secret carbonated formula, a staple in the American marketplace since the late 1880s. Extensive market research had shown that, in taste test after taste test, the new Coke was favoured over the old Coke and its archrival Pepsi-Cola. To the amazement of senior Coke management, there was an enormous public outcry, leading to bad publicity and a massive drop in sales, forcing Coca-Cola to return, after six weeks, the old Coke to the shelves renaming it Coca-Cola Classic.

Global markets changing the need for buyer understanding

Markets around the world seem to be opening up and welcoming an influx of companies from around the world at a seemingly exponential rate. Governments and politicians in the Old, New and Developing World are now more or less committed to the philosophy and dictates of free, liberal world markets where the buying and selling of goods and services across nations is considered to be the most effective and efficient way of running the economy.

Developing markets

It must also be understood that new developing markets in Eastern Europe, Asia and South America are in different and early stages of marketing and are less sophisticated. Therefore the need for consumer understanding will still be at the larger group, larger segment level and the information wanted will be nowhere near as intense as in the one-to-one markets. These differences, however, could be rapidly disappearing as developing countries, such as China and India (with a combined population of nearly 2.5 billion) seem able to increase their economies by breathtaking amounts. Concomitant with economic development is the growth of wealthy, middle-class consumers with the buying power to be able to make similar demands exercised by consumers in old developed markets.

Market segmentation

▶ This leads us into the concept of **segmentation**, which is at the very heart of marketing. Manufacturers and retailers have known almost instinctively from early times that in most cases they cannot sell the same product in the same way to every customer. This has become increasingly so as we all become more sophisticated, wealthier and more aware of choice. So men will want different products to women, the young different from the old, the wealthy from the poor, people that enjoy adventure holidays different from those that would rather take a holiday cottage in the country, psychological introverts from extroverts and so on. In fact understanding consumer behaviour becomes more complex and difficult the more markets are segmented into ever smaller and intricate types of consumer groups. We will discuss this in more detail in Chapter 9.

> **Key point** Good segmentation, targeting and product positioning should lead to more satisfied customers and higher sales and profits.

Many people involved in the buying process

It needs to be understood that any one buying situation could involve many different people, all ultimately able to influence the final purchase. This is especially the case in business markets where goods and services being purchased might run to millions of pounds, euros or dollars and we can discuss this later in more detail. Even in consumer markets where money spent will be far less there are often two, three, four or more people all having a say in what product and brand to buy. In simple terms, as any good sales people will tell you, the customer and the consumer aren't always the same person. Mother might buy play and educational toys for her children, husband might buy perfume for his wife and first-time house buyers might take advice from the estate agent. This now broadens the scope in understanding individual customer behaviour into understanding group behaviour, because all or some of the participants in any one buying scenario might need to be included in the marketing approach depending on the amount of influence that might be exerted.

Anticipating consumer behaviour

Practice and experience shows that the organisation that has the most up-to-date information about its customers and markets is the one that will more than likely be the most successful. We only have to pick up a newspaper (preferably the more serious kind), turn to the business pages to read stories of retailer success and/or failure linked to management ability in keeping up with customer demands for ever-changing goods and services. We can also be certain in the knowledge that in today's marketplace competitors abound and all will be investigating ways of gaining competitive advantage through greater understanding of customers. This puts added pressure on managers to anticipate and try to understand earlier than others the direction that the demand for products might take. This implies almost knowing what features and benefits the consumer might be wanting in the future even before they might really know themselves. We will discuss how marketers are able to do this when we examine the whole area of marketing research in the following chapter.

The changing customer

The driving force behind the growth in the marketing and consumer research business (to emphasise, it is worth billions around the world) is constantly changing behaviour. Much of this is caused by world travel, watching TV 24 hours a day, reading magazines and newspapers and surfing the Internet. In this way people become constantly dissatisfied and bored with current offerings and so demand evermore value, benefits and innovative products and services often at the same or lower prices. And, of course, if one company is unable to accommodate another will.

Figure 1.4

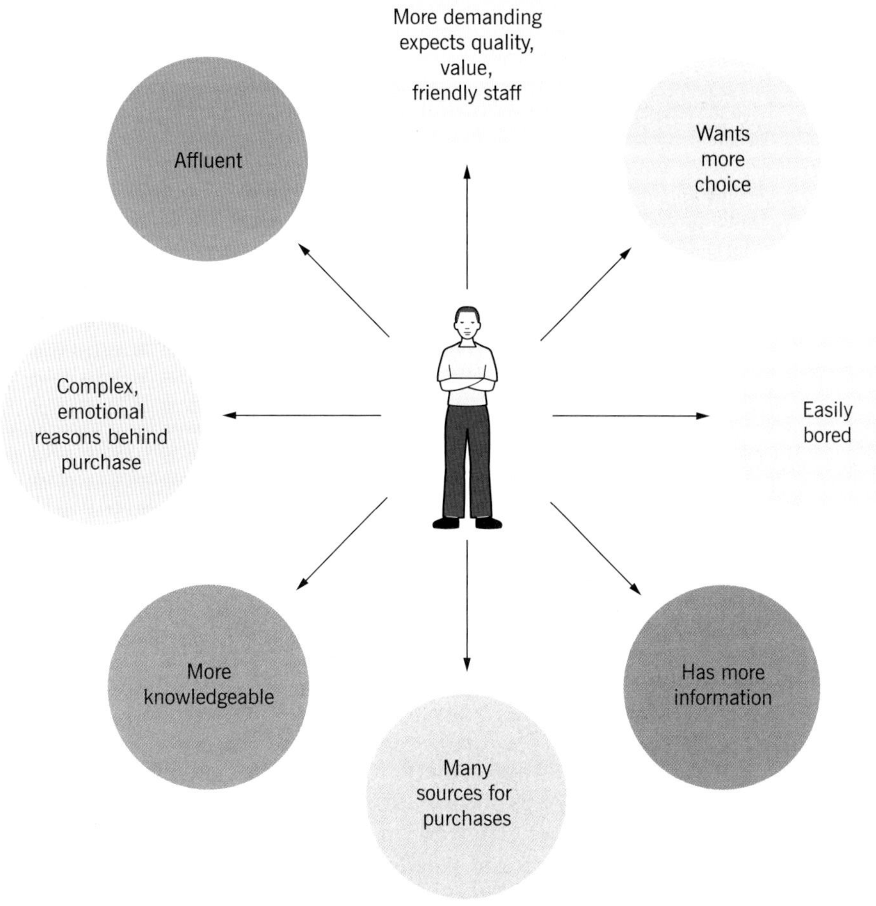

The modern consumer

Add to this the fact that in most modern economies income and wealth has increased on average by 2 per cent a year it can easily be demonstrated how much more affluent we all are when compared to 50 or so years ago. Having so much more **disposable income** to spend on discretionary products has opened up a whole range of new markets, holidays, cars, designer clothes, eating-out, to consumers across the whole social class.

Changing buying patterns

Instant communications seem to have increased the speed by which spending **culture**, trends, fads and consumer wants, demands and buying patterns change, both in the UK and around the world. So in the UK we see the craze for so-called 'house makeovers', 'garden makeovers', the 'cult of the celebrity', the obsession with organic foods and healthy eating and the concern for all things environmentally correct. This then puts unremitting pressure on marketing and consumer researchers to understand behaviour, stay ahead of the game and so be able to predict what consumer craze might be in decline and which will be the next to sweep the country.

1.5 Marketing example — Slimming Fad sweeps the UK

Unilever, the global FMCG branded goods manufacturer, unexpectedly failed to reach their sales targets for 2003 as more than 3 million weight conscious consumers ditched many of their high protein products, including the top-selling SlimFast, in favour of the low carbohydrate Atkins diet. Sales of the book have reached 3 million, knocking Harry Potter off the top spot in the UK book charts. Kellogg's, the breakfast food giant is watching the situation carefully seeing how it might affect the cereal market. Yougov.com the online research company found that approximately two-fifths of the population were currently dieting in some form or other and 58 per cent have tried to diet in the past five years.

Questions

1. Discuss the growth of the market for weight conscious foods. Do you think that this is just a fad or will it be more long lasting?
2. Do you think that Unilever should have foreseen this changing market and if so what measure might the company have taken?

Ethical problems

Some commentators argue that the easy availability of so much easy money is an **ethical problem** as it is forcing many families into debt from which they will never be able to recover. They go on to argue that the fault lies with organisations, financiers, marketers and retailers all encouraging people to relentlessly buy new products and upgrade the old, by appealing to consumers' emotional need for such things as status, self-esteem and social acceptance. The availability of credit exploded over the last 20 years with the latest figure showing that in the UK we are borrowing money at an ever-increasing amount to fuel the seemingly incessant need to continually spend on products, brands and services.

1.6 Marketing example — Ballooning debt

The rapid rise of consumer debt in the UK shows no sign of abating with the accumulative amount owed by individuals rising by 8 per cent to £109.37bn over Christmas 2003, according to new research by debt advice group Debt Free Direct. In January 2004, according to their figures, monthly borrowing on average was around £10 billion a month and around 18.3 million people, over a third of the adult population, owed an average of nearly £6000 each on credit and debit cards, loans and overdrafts. The research also found that about 4.1 million people who are not working owe £13.47bn – an average of £3,325 each. Back in 1971 only one type of credit card was available, compared to around 1,300 credit cards on the market now, and the amount of money owed on credit cards back then was worth £32 million but now it is over £49 billion. Figures across many other EU countries reflect the same sorts of growth in debt figures.

Questions

1 Do you think that consumers should be protected from taking on too much debt or should they be allowed to make their own mistakes?

2 How might the availability of so much 'easy money' affect consumer thinking, motivation and overall behaviour?

Health and overeating

There are also experts who are expressing concern about the health of the nation and the fact that more people, both young and old, are overweight, eat unwisely and lead a very unhealthy life, culminating in damaging and expensive health problems in later life. Conversely those who are accused respond by showing, on

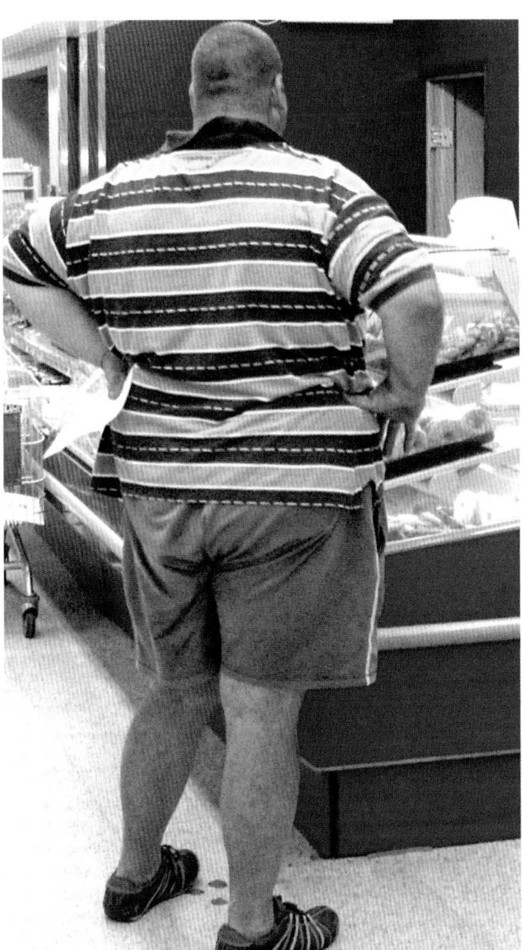

Overeating and obesity is now a health problem across the Western world

average, how more affluent, healthy and long lived we all are when compared with earlier decades and this has come about in a market economy by the interplay between free customer choice, competition and the continuous availability of new, innovative products, brands and services.

Green and ethical consumerism

Anti-consumerism movements have given rise to new markets such as 'Green Consumerism', where people purchase goods or services and invest in companies which operate in a manner that attempts to be 'friendlier' and less damaging to ecosystems and natural planetary defences. **Ethical consumerism**, which might be seen as a development of green consumerism, considers a variety of wider issues than just a product's green credentials, such as whether or not the manufacturer invests in the arms trade or has supported oppressive regimes. Through a comprehensive monitoring of the behaviour of modern business, ethical consumerism aims to encourage trade to be as responsible as is possible within the current economic system.

> **Key point** Constantly changing consumer behaviour puts enormous pressure on marketing personnel to anticipate and predict future buying patterns in markets across the world.

Buyer behaviour as a process

As global barriers have come down and competition grows across most industries and markets, companies and managers soon began to realise that unhappy and dissatisfied customers would be prepared to go to other players in the market if value wasn't continuously upgraded, complaints weren't addressed and service wasn't improved. It is now a fact of life that in today's marketplace benefits that used to be discretionary are now seen as an essential part of the product or service and more are forever being added. It is a truism that if you don't offer more and better benefits the competition will.

Before, during and after purchase

It is not enough, however, to offer benefits just at the time of the sale. Understanding customer behaviour should now be seen as a process and it has to be concerned with building relationships, before, during and after the sale if success is to be maintained. It's now what the customer expects. So called '***customer relationship management***' (**CRM**), '***customer retention programmes***' and '*customer loyalty schemes*' are about building long-term ongoing relationships with customers (in both B2C and B2B markets) secure in the knowledge that the cost of finding and persuading new customers can be many more times expensive then to hang on to existing customers. For example information technology has enabled all the large supermarkets to talk and listen to existing customers, on almost a one-to-one basis, and have many kinds of schemes that reward loyalty and constant use (usually the biggest spenders).

> **Key point** Understanding customer behaviour as a process
> Customer behaviour should now be seen as a process and has to be concerned with understanding customer behaviour and building relationships before, during and after the sale if sales and success are to be maintained.

The role of technology

It might be as well just to say a few words here about the role and use of technology in understanding buyer behaviour. There is no doubt that technology, like all other areas of business and marketing, has had a massive influence on how we study, understand and try to influence consumer behaviour. In fact, every chapter throughout the book will allude to this in some way or another. Technology has affected and, in the most part improved, how we collect consumer and market information, the amount we are able to store and warehouse, how we classify, analyse and cross-fertilise information, identify developments and trends at national and global level and how we then go on to use that information. Much of this can now happen in a convenient manner from a computer in the office of the marketing manager saving time, money and effort, allowing the competition to be beaten to the sale and customers to be satisfied more readily and effectively.

Behaviour and the role of the Internet

▶ The continuous growth of the Internet has put this relatively new form of **home shopping** at the top of the agenda. In the past particular consumer segments bought products and services in their own home through mail order, home catalogues, door-step salespersons and home party-plans. Buying on the world-wide-web now threatens to overtake all these methods combined in the type of products that can be offered and the size and number of market segments involved. Marketers must now try to understand how consumer behaviour will be affected and then develop marketing approaches that will be successful in different market segments.

Consumer decision-making and problem-solving processes

According to the definition of marketing discussed earlier the driving force behind the whole concept of marketing is this need to deeply understand customer needs and wants and motivations, at both the group level and, increasingly, at the individual level, even across mass markets. This must then involve the whole decision-making process including all the ground preparing that can take place, often many years before consumers might start to search around for information, through to interest, purchase and after sales service and (hopefully) life-time customer retention. Once there is working understanding and knowledge of the stages involved in the decision-making process the marketer can then attempt to inform and influence it at every stage, leading eventually to brand purchase and (depending on the type of product) repurchase on a long-term basis.

The consumer decision-making process

There are many factors that will influence human behaviour and the buying process, really beginning from early childhood through the teen years and into adult life. All this will be discussed in detail in later chapters and they are briefly described below.

The early years – external and internal influences

Years of research across all the social sciences described above seem to indicate that we are all, to a lesser or greater degree, influenced by the multitude of things that happened to us when we were first growing up. There seems to be clear evidence that both the stimuli from the external environment and human internal ▶ factors, the make-up of our inherited **biological gene-pool** and our **DNA**, will combine and interact to gradually mould and shape our thoughts, beliefs, attitudes and personality into the sort of person we then become. The relative strength and power of internal and/or external factors in shaping human beings is exceedingly complex and will vary from one culture to another and from one person to another. Expert opinion is also divided on the part and amount that either internal or external matters play in the process and it seems that the subject is constantly under review and changing.

Human experience and reflection Of course as we grow, develop and build cognitive mental abilities we are able, through experience and reflection to affect and influence many internal and external factors perhaps building on things that can be seen to be positive and possibly overcome those that are perceived as negative in some way or another. In this way the individual might eventually reach some kind of mental state of contentment. As with all elements of the human condition, however, there is no such thing as a definitive 'equilibrium' or 'non-equilibrium' mental state and most of us reside somewhere along a continuum being in neither one state nor the other. In extreme cases mental illness can ensue if there is a ▶ failure to solve mental contradictions (or **cognitive dissonance** as it is often known in the study of consumer behaviour) between one thought or idea and another.

Early influences and understanding consumer behaviour

Research has constantly shown that the environmental inputs, incessantly experienced during our formative years, that go on to shape our personality will also influence consumer behaviour in terms of the types of products, brands and services any one person might want to purchase at any one time throughout the whole of their life. The level, intensity and power of any one type of influence and how this might then affect purchasing decisions will vary quite markedly from one person to another, from one group to another and from one culture to another depending on the many factors that will be examined in every chapter as we move through the book. This will include such things as inherited dispositions, the nature of society, class structure and the culture we are all born into, our interaction and experiences with family, friends and acquaintances, how we learn and perceive the world, the evolution of our ideas, beliefs and attitudes, and the subsequent development of mind and personality. Researching, knowing and understanding all these factors discussed above are intrinsic to understanding consumer behaviour, developing and honing product benefits to meet identified needs and wants and then promoting and advertising to persuade purchase, re-purchase and life-long loyalty.

Organisations, marketers, the media

Of course all who have studied business and marketing (as well as many in the general public) are aware that businesses, marketers, marketing agencies and the media are all trying to influence people from the earliest possible age, either trying to get them to buy products now, think about buying in the near future and/or preparing the ground for purchase much later when grown-up and money is available.

Understanding and influencing decision-making behaviour

'Sociologists say the average person interacts repeatedly with approximately 250 other people, including neighbours, family, and co-workers; all can influence purchasing decisions.' JERRY WILSON, www.customerology.com

There will come a time when an organisation will be aware that there are customers in a particular market segment who are in the position of being able to buy particular products or services. This might be at almost any age and any stage in the human life cycle from the cradle to the grave. It might be a mother buying nappies for her new-born baby, grandparents buying toys for the grandchildren, parents clothes for schoolchildren, families doing the weekly shopping, groups of teenagers buying music, young couples looking for a house, a husband or wife purchasing a car, older couples wanting a holiday cruising in the Caribbean and so on.

Consumer decision making can be broken down into three major areas:

A The decision-making unit (DMU)

B The decision-making process (DMP)

C The **decision-making difficulty** (DMD)

A The decision-making unit (DMU)

The **decision-making unit** (DMU) is the concept that one, two or more people might be involved in the purchase of a product or service, that the customer might be different from the consumer. As a rule of thumb the more complex the purchase the more people will be involved in some way in the buying process. For example, both parents and the child might be involved in buying toys, especially if educational in some way and a husband, wife and even children might have an interest in buying a new car. Similarly the purchase of a new house might involve a young couple, parents, solicitor, estate agent and so on. Or the DMU might be just one person. This widens the need for consumer understanding across a whole group of people if marketing success is to be achieved (see Table 1.1).

Table 1.1 The DMU

An example of the DMU, the people (in this case the family) involved in buying a new car.

(acronym SPADE)

Suggester – grandfather and granddaughter

Purchaser – grandfather as a birthday present

Advisor – sales person, consumer association

Decision maker – daughter and parents together

End-user – daughter and children

A typical consumer decision-making unit

Key point There is the need for customer and consumer understanding across a whole group of people who could be involved in the purchasing decision if marketing success is to be achieved.

B The decision-making process (DMP)

When people are ready to buy things they will engage in some kind of decision making, where they will go through a process beginning with the realisation that they need or want to buy a product or service and ending with the purchase, usage and evaluation of the product or service benefits purchased. This we call the **decision-making process (DMP)**. Marketers must use all types of research so that they can understand the process that their customers (both in B2B and in B2C) are likely to go through so that they can influence, support and offer advice at every stage, hopefully ending with a thoroughly delighted customer.

> **Key point** Professional help and advice must be given at every stage of the decision-making process.

1 *Need recognition*

There will come a moment in time that will set off the decision-making process. This will be the realisation, gradual or immediate, by the potentially interested consumer that they have some kind of problem or need for a product or service. The need might be simple and caused by an internal stimuli, e.g. our stomach is rumbling, we are hungry and fancy a hamburger, we have a headache and must buy some pills. Or it might be in response to an external marketing stimulus, e.g. we pass Starbucks and are attracted by the aroma of coffee and chocolate muffins, or a billboard proclaims the delight of a premium larger and thirst gravitates us to the nearest pub.

More complex need recognition On the other hand the need recognition might be more complex. Perhaps the existing product, i.e. the cooker, is broken or worn-out and needs replacing, or perhaps a newer more modern product is now on the market. The chill of the winter might persuade a family to look for a holiday in the sun, or a special offer from Fords might convince them to forgo the holiday this year for a new car. In some cases the need might be more deeply hidden, perhaps within the subconscious, and be more to do with some sort of status anxiety or self-esteem problem.

> **Key point** The marketer has the ability to stimulate purchase of whatever product or service the consumer might need. Understanding customer behaviour will inform when the moment is right for purchase as well as the promotional methods that will be most effective for the task.

2 *Information search*

Having decided to look into the matter further the potential consumer (or consumers depending on how many people are involved in the buying exercise) will undertake a search for information on the products and services, talking to others, reading consumer magazines, going on the Internet, visiting retailers, looking for overall best value and benefits, the intensity of which will depend on the task in hand.

1.7 Marketing example — Information from many sources

Product and service information can come from many sources including the following: family, friends, neighbours, celebrity endorsement, recommendations; memory and past experiences, handling, trying, examining, using the product; trade associations, manufacturers, producers, retailers and salespeople; packaging, point-of-sale material and literature, in-store displays, Internet sites, search engines, publicity, newspapers, magazines, radio, television, consumer organisations; specialist magazines and product placement. Some sources of information are more valued than others, for example other customer recommendation and 'word-of-mouth'. The challenge for the marketing team is to identify which information sources are most influential in their target markets and why. This knowledge must be used to make the correct information readily available and then to guide and direct purchase and eventual customer satisfaction.

3 *Evaluation of alternatives*

After enough information has been collected options will be compared, questions asked and retailers, salespeople, websites, and literature visited and re-visited. When all doubts and objectives have been overcome the most attractive alternative will be purchased according to criteria such as value, design, features, emotional attractiveness, price and trustworthiness of the supplier.

Evaluation criteria The criteria used to decide to purchase will vary from each customer and from purchase to purchase. So for one customer price will be important, another value, another brand, another content and so on. To influence purchase at this stage the marketing manager must be aware of what benefits turn his or her customer segment on and be able to optimise organisational responses. Any uncertainty here could cause the customer to return to stage 2 to reconsider the information.

4 *Action and purchase decision*

There comes a time when the customer's mind is almost made up and purchase is about to take place. It is crucial that at this delicate stage of the decision-making process the task is made as easy as possible. Information will have been chewed over, benefits optimised, expert and others' opinions canvassed, and the customer is ready to buy. Complications such as unhelpful staff, improperly functioning systems, delays and lack of stock can scare off the customer and so destroy all the work that has gone on before. If this happens the customer could return to stage 2.

5 *Post-purchase evaluation*

The final stage of the decision-making process is something known as ▶ **post-purchase evaluation**. It is common for customers to experience some concerns after making a purchase depending on the importance and value of the decision. This arises from a concept that is known as 'cognitive dissonance' (conflict in the mind). The customer, having bought a product, may feel that it does not live up to their expectations or that maybe an alternative would have been preferable. In these circumstances the customer might find fault, complain, demand their money back or switch brands next time of purchase.

1.8 Marketing example — Managing customer dissatisfaction and post-purchase dissatisfaction

To manage the post-purchase stage, the marketing team must convince the potential customer that the product will live up to the benefit offerings made and so the salespeople must never 'over-promise' and so build too high expectations to obtain the sale. The customer should be constantly reassured that he or she has made the right decision both during and after the sale. Excellent products, quality processes and skilled staff with a deep knowledge of human nature will help overcome these problems. It's a fact of life that a dissatisfied customer will tell many others, a satisfied customer just a few.

Questions

1 How important is word of mouth recommendation or criticism?

2 How might the retailer minimise the risk of unhappy consumer post-purchase evaluation?

C The level of decision-making difficulty (DMD)

'Informal conversation is probably the oldest mechanism by which opinions on products and brands are developed, expressed, and spread.' JOHAN ARNDT

Depending on the consequences of making a wrong decision, the complexity of the decision-making process can range from careful analysis to pure impulse. While an impulse buy, such as buying a bar of chocolate, can take place instantaneously, complex purchases, such as buying a new car or a holiday will often stretch over a longer period of time. If we think about all the different things we purchase over the years we will see that some decisions are more difficult than others, some products we buy out of habit (FMCG from Tesco) others, such as buying a new drill, take a little more time and thought, while really important decisions, such as a new fitted kitchen, might stretch out over many months and cause intense soul-searching and conflict between husband and wife.

Buying a service rather than a product

Buying a service rather than a product can be extremely complex and risky and will add to the pressure. Unlike a product, it is **intangible** and cannot be seen. So the customer must make a decision based on more physical evidence such as the look and credibility of the sales person, the quality of the literature, the condition of the retail outlet or offices or recommendations by an existing satisfied client. On the other hand the supplier of the service must work hard to make certain that the same

Table 1.2 Decision-making difficulty (DMD)

- *Small levels of difficulty* – very simple routine evaluation processes, for example buying the weekly groceries. Problem-solving difficulties can vary even at this level according to whether the purchase is on impulse, a product or brand perhaps not bought before, or the use of a different supermarket.
- *Medium levels of difficulty* – this involves the purchase of relatively expensive products or services that are only needed occasionally, e.g. new refrigerator, carpet or three-piece suite. Consumer involvement level will vary according to such things as to whether it is a known brand or not, more features on offer and the price levels under consideration.
- *High levels of difficulty* – high expenditure, high emotional risk, high stress levels, e.g. buying a house, a car or making long-term large money investments. High-quality, reassuring information is needed on a constant basis, overcoming objections, countering competition offerings and spelling out benefit offering and default safeguards.

Figure 1.5

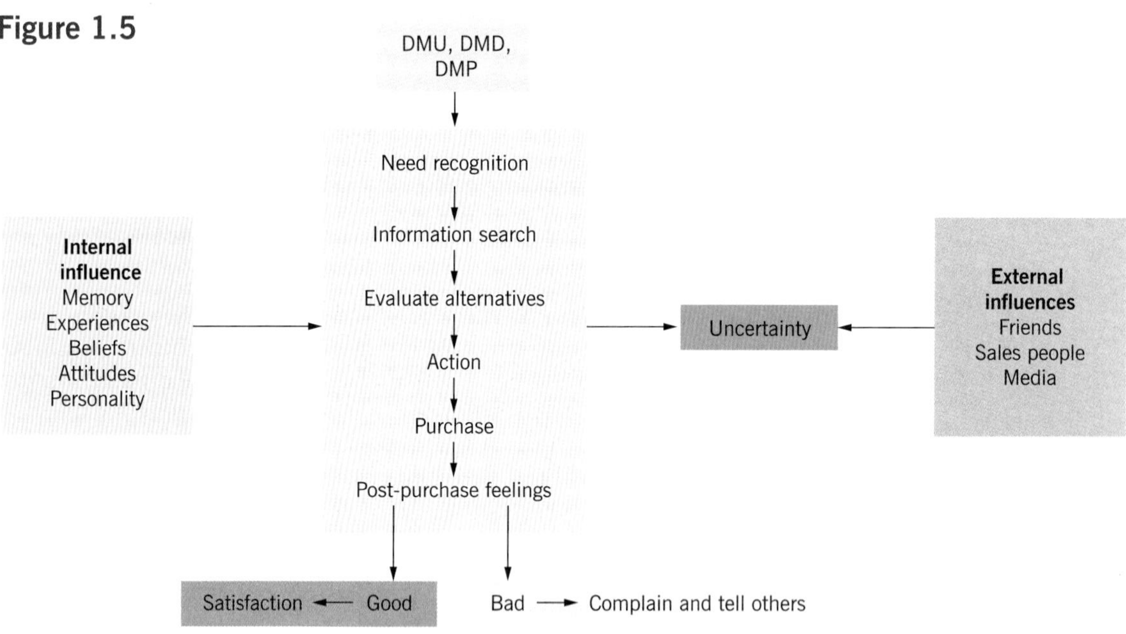

Aspects of decision making

quality is given every time the service is offered anywhere in the world. McDonald's has been able to do this by building in a whole raft of systems and processes that must be followed whether the fast-food outlet is in Hong Kong, New York or Berlin. (Services are discussed in more detail in Chapter 10.)

Key point All decisions have an element of difficulty and risk and this will vary from one type of purchase to another. It will also vary, however, from person to person as some consumers have a high-risk tolerance level while others have a low risk tolerance level, depending on personality and situation.

Situational influences

Situational factors have also been shown to influence the process. The time of day or night, the week, month or year, as well as such things as the weather and the place and circumstance of the purchase, have all been shown to have varying degrees of influence on the decision to buy. Some people are more able to make decisions in the morning rather than the afternoon and evening, some are more agreeable at weekends rather than during the week and some function so much better in the spring rather than in the winter. The urgency and necessity of the purchase will also have an affect. If the old freezer has irrevocably broken, or the TV no longer functions, then a replacement will need to be practically immediate. On the other hand if the purchase is for more leisurely reasons then the purchase will be more relaxed.

Table 1.3 Consumer perceived risk

Many products or services have varying levels of perceived risk. It will be more apparent if the purchase is complex, of high value or is difficult to understand. It will include the following type of risk:

- *Functional risk* – the product might not perform the wanted task adequately, e.g. a new computer system.
- *Money risk* – the product or service might not be worth the price and money spent. For instance, if a large amount of money is involved, e.g. a new house.
- *Social risk* – product or service might fail to reinforce self-esteem or status needs and so make the consumer look good in the eyes of others, e.g. jewellery, sports car, fashion clothing.
- *Psychological risk* – product or service might create inner feelings of guilt and/or mental disharmony, e.g. the money should have been spent elsewhere on school fees rather than on a holiday in the Caribbean.

The differences between the behavioural sciences and the natural and mathematical sciences

It is important at the outset to try to clearly identify the many problems involved when trying to understand consumer behaviour in an accurate, consistent and meaningful way. Although the study of human beings and, our concern, the study of consumer behaviour is now seen as the 'behavioural or social sciences' there are many that would contest that this is a misnomer because it is not strictly a 'science' in it purest form when compared with the 'natural' and 'mathematical sciences'.

They go on to argue that human behaviour cannot be studied in the same precise way as inanimate physical matter such as rocks, blood vessels, planets and chemicals and cannot therefore be considered a true science according to generally accepted definitions and principles. Others will refute this making the point that although there are stark and obvious differences between organic (people) and inorganic (physical) matter there are similarities that can be exploited in a truly scientific manner (Campbell Collaboration, Colorado). This is a debate that has been rumbling on for centuries in one form or another, it should serve as a warning to those interested in the study of consumer behaviour that the subject cannot be treated in exactly the same way as the natural sciences. This problem is discussed further below.

Relationship between variables

In the natural sciences the relationship between variables, the effect that one might have on another, can be positively established by eliminating, or holding steady, all other variables, except those under investigation. In this way a true and realistic picture can be created which can then be tested and retested by others.

1.3 General example — The litmus test – scientific experimentation

An example of scientific experimentation might be the simple 'litmus test' undertaken by schoolchildren throughout the ages. Scientists use red or blue litmus paper to determine if a substance is an acid or a alkali; blue litmus turns red if it is dipped in an acid and red litmus turns blue if it is dipped in an alkali (base). The litmus paper doesn't change at all if the substance is neutral, that is neither an acid nor an alkali. All other possible intervening factors can be isolated and eliminated or held steady so that the results can be seen as irrefutable. Consumers cannot be studied in this way.

With human beings it's impossible to get it right every time

It is not the case that results can be seen as irrefutable when studying individuals and groups of humans. There are so many factors that could be involved when trying to understand why people behave in one way rather than another, why one product launch might be successful and another fail, despite the fact that the initial consumer feedback was favourable on both. Respondents might say that they would buy a product if it came on the market yet not actually purchase when it comes up for sale. Conversely they might just as easily do the opposite, say they wouldn't purchase when in fact they do.

1.9 Marketing example | **Expensive flops – a non scientific approach**

So we have men telling Cadburys in the 1980s that they would be prepared to buy boxed chocolates for themselves, they weren't and the product failed; women saying that they would buy Uncle Ben's 'healthy' rice with calcium-enrichment in 1997, especially if launched with support from the American Dietetic Association, it too failed; and children and young adults liking Heinz's Funky Fries, a chocolate, cinnamon, sour cream and blue-coloured frozen fries, in research tests but changing their mind at launch time. So this product flopped while Heinz's green, purple and pink ketchup was a success.

What is a science?

In simple terms science is concerned with the search for truth and knowledge of our world and our universe in order that we may discover and come to an understanding of what exists and how it operates. It also refers to the organised body of knowledge that results from scientific study.

- Science involves standing back and observing particular phenomena in some kind of way, attempting to remove all subjectivity, and thus be as objective and unbiased as is possible.
- This should be undertaken in a systematic and orderly manner (known as the '**scientific method**') by first making empirical (by the use of our senses) observations about natural events and conditions, then collecting and classifying this data in a formulated and agreeable way, proposing hypotheses (assumptions), theories and models to explain those observations, and then testing and experimenting with these hypotheses in valid and reliable ways.
- The claimed-for results and the methods used must be clearly shown so that others may come along afterwards to experiment, measure and critically examine methods used and confirm and retest the results being claimed.
- In this way it may be hoped that laws and principles can be established and general truths or the operation of general laws can then be discovered.
- To make advances scientists must continually evaluate, and sometimes reformulate the very foundations of their field. They must be willing to reinterpret, and if necessary to abandon, old concepts for radically new ones.

1.4 General example | **Karl Popper (1902–94)**

Karl Popper (2001, *All Life is Problem Solving*) was a philosopher of science who promoted the theory that science moves forward by attempting to falsify hypotheses and theories. So every scientist should attempt, and has a duty to constantly try, to disprove his or her own theories.

Table 1.4 The scientific method

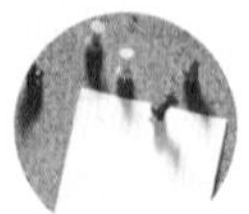

- Problem identification
- Observation
- Collection and classification of data
- Analysis
- Hypothesis or theory formulation
- Experimentation, measurement and testing
- Results announcement and constant retesting by other scientists

(If helpful we can reverse the 'analysis' and 'collection of data' around to obtain the memory aid (mnemonic) POACHER.)

The natural or exact sciences

Some argue (**Richard Dawkins** 1986) that physical reality, the material world and the material universe, is either all that exists or is all that can be really studied in the rigorous and systematic manner demanded by the scientific methods discussed above. All other areas such as consciousness, theology and God, the supernatural, telepathy and so on cannot and must be examined and explained in some other way. They go on to state that the natural sciences involved in the study of the physical aspect of the world and its phenomena, among other things will include such disciplines as physics, chemistry, biology, astronomy and earth science/planetary science.

Ontology

Ontology is the study of what exists (or doesn't exist) on the earth or in the universe. It includes the study of such things as the material and physical, consciousness and the mind, theology and the existence of a divinity (a God or Gods), telepathy, mysticism, fate, ghosts, goblins and fairies. Many scientists would want to argue that it is only the material and the physical aspects of the world that can be studied as a 'true' science and the rest should be dismissed as conjecture and the metaphysical.

Metaphysics

Metaphysics might be described as the study of the mind and consciousness rather than the study of matter. Whether we can study the mind and consciousness in the same way as we study the physical world is open to conjecture with some arguing that 'consciousness' is somehow different from matter, and so has to be looked at differently, while others argue that it can only be studied in a material sense, that's to say as part of the physical world.

The mathematical sciences – truth by agreement

'Mathematics: A tentative agreement that two and two make four.' ELBERT HUBBARD (1859–1915)

The mathematical sciences includes mathematics, geometry, algebra and calculus and can be said to be a science because we can, with absolute certainty, distinguish right from wrong because the numbers and symbols used and the relationships and attributes used are agreed by all and so become correct or incorrect by definition. It can be said to be a science because we can see that it follows the scientific method identified above. It consists of rigorous and systematic thinking, problems can be identified, information collected and classified, experiments made and hypotheses formulated, which can then be tested and re-tested by others.

Mathematics is in the mind – materialism is in the external world

There are, however, also differences between sciences that study the natural material world and mathematics, which exists in the mind and in the realm of pure reason studying abstract idealised objects, such as numbers, algebra and geometric objects that exist only in thought. Those that are interested can explore further.

The social and behavioural sciences

The social and behavioural sciences, on the other hand, are different from the sciences discussed above because they involve the study of the behaviour of individuals, groups (consumers), social organisations, cultures and society as a whole in the past, present and predicting into the future. Whether or not the study of these areas can be undertaken in the same rigorous and systematic manner as the natural and mathematical sciences is highly debatable with many commentators feeling that the subject matter, human behaviour, is so different from studying such things in the material world as chemicals, atoms and molecules that comparisons are superfluous.

Consumer and social research must reflect reality

Whatever side of the argument is adopted and whatever approach is taken, however, it is crucially important that the search for the 'truth' and realistic answers by marketers must mirror, as far as possible, the scientific method and so reflect reality and what is going on in the marketplace (as far as is humanly possible), otherwise the decision making will be flawed, mistakes made and sales and profits lost. Ultimately, however, students, academics and practitioners might have to accept the fact that, in many cases, there are strictly no right, wrong or straightforward answers, in marketing as it relates to consumer behaviour.

Key point The study of the social sciences must reflect, as far as possible, the scientific method if safe and realistic decisions are to be made.

1.5 General example **The most sensational charge of scientific fraud this century**

Until his death in 1971, the British educational psychologist **Sir Cyril Burt** was viewed as one of the most significant and influential educational psychologists of his time. Within a year of his death, however, the legitimacy of his research was being questioned. By 1976 he was officially accused of fabricating data and inventing facts to support his controversial theory that intelligence was largely inherited. A Dr Gillie set out to find two of Burt's research assistants, Miss Margaret Howard and Miss Jane Conway, who had supposedly undertaken a long-time (longitudinal) study looking at 53 sets of identical (monozygotic) twins, separated at birth and now in adulthood, to see if intelligence (nature) or upbringing (nurture) was the most influential. Despite a thorough search, he was unable to locate either, and was forced to conclude that they were fictitious names and the 'scientific' research was a sham (Gillie 1976).

Questions

1 Why do you think that Burt was able to get away with perpetrating such a fraud on the public and what does it say about the problems associated with the social sciences?
2 How might the fraud have been prevented in the first place?

The social 'sciences'

As with the natural sciences, the social sciences have been splitting into more and more separate disciplines the more sophisticated it has become and many of these are listed below. There is a danger with this development in that the 'big picture' might be lost.

Economics

Economic science is the study of the relationship between the production, distribution and consumption of wealth in a country and how seemingly infinite wants are reconciled in the best possible way with finite resources. It looks at such problems as scarcity, finance, debt, taxation, labour, law, inequity, poverty, pollution, war etc. This is probably the most successful of the social sciences in being seen as a 'science', although it still has many problems that arise because of the human (emotional) element in the calculations. Economist like to talk about the consumer as a 'rational' being making purchase decisions according to clear functional needs. However, as we debate throughout the book, this is not always the case and this has constantly caused problems when economists try to predict behaviour.

Sociology

Sociology is the study of people, groups, institutions and structures in society. It attempts to explain why societies develop in the way that they do and to predict future developments. In the study of consumer behaviour the household and the

1.6 General example — Economists get it wrong

One hundred leading economists surveyed in 'Blue Chip Economic Indicators' (Blue Chip Publications) in January 2001 estimated that gross domestic product (GDP) in the USA would grow 2.6 per cent that year. Yet 2001 was marked by three consecutive quarters of negative growth, and GDP grew by just 0.3 per cent. One study of 19 years of economic surveys found that economists failed to predict the right direction of long-term interest rates 71 per cent of the time. Probably the primary reason why predictions turn out wrong is unexpected developments that economists could not have foreseen. Common reasons include major world events, new legislation, and election outcomes and even weather patterns.

users of goods and services are examined in a domestic context. This context is seen as embedded in larger social structures, which are subject to social and cultural change.

Social psychology

Social psychology always used to be seen as an integral part of sociology and is the study of how individuals' thoughts, feelings and behaviours are influenced by the actual or imagined presence of both other individuals and groups. Heavily used in understanding behaviour.

Anthropology

Anthropology is the study of primitive groups of people, examining and comparing different races, ethnic groups and tribes across the world, looking at such things as culture, mores, rituals and ways of living. There is the hope that simple ways of living might explain and help us understand the more complex behaviour exhibited in the modern world.

1.7 General example — Anthropology at work

Margaret Mead lived with and studied many primitive tribes around the world in the 1920s and 1930s. In her best-selling books *Coming of Age In Samoa* and *Growing Up in New Guinea* she conducted fieldwork by living and studying the play, imaginations and experiences of young children as they were growing up. She showed that child rearing and individual developmental stages could be shaped by cultural demands and expectations as well as biology and that gender and other adult roles were often relative and varied from one society to another. She attempted to relate her findings to modern society.

Psychology

Psychology is relatively new and, as with all the disciplines identified above, covers a collection of academic disciplines concerned with mental processes and how individuals think and behave. It includes the conscious and subconscious parts of the brain, and what might be considered to be normal and abnormal, voluntary and involuntary, behavioural activity. This will be studied in much more detail later. Probably the greatest impact it has had in understanding human behaviour and motivation is the idea that reasons behind customer behaviour and brand purchases can be complex, and multilayered. In some cases, even dwelling in a subconscious area of the mind driving motivation and decision making.

Evolutionary psychology

Evolutionary psychology is based on the recognition that the modern human brain, and the human nervous system still has a large collection of inherited genetic problem-solving mechanisms, left over from our human and animal hunter-gatherer ancestors, that were created originally to meet the challenges of primitive environments. Adherents of this approach might therefore argue that if you want to discover the 'real' reason behind many aspects of human and consumer behaviour then study the behaviour, for example, of a group of baboons and extrapolate the reasons behind their interactions to people (and consumers) living in present times.

Political science

Political science studies the power relations, forms of government and how countries are run at local, national and international level. Areas examined will include different forms of government, businesses, trade unions, religion, pressure groups as well as looking at those with the wealth and ability to influence

We can learn about human behaviours by studying a group of baboons.
Source: istockphoto.com

power in some way or another. Many argue that corporate giants such as Wal-Mart, General Motors and Microsoft have too much power, as they are able to influence peoples' standard of living around the world. Others complain (particularly farmers) that the big supermarkets have unlimited power along the supply chain to constantly force lower prices from suppliers. Although political science attempts constantly to approach the subject from a scientific perspective many areas under investigation are still open to opinion and interpretation.

History

History is the study of peoples and institutions in times gone by. It attempts to describe the past and give reasons why events happened in the way that they did. Although we might agree on such things as dates of birth of prominent people and the place and time of great battles, reasons behind past great happenings such as why Julia Caesar was murdered or what were the causes behind the outbreak of the Second World War are more open to opinion and interpretation. In trying to understand consumer behaviour, history can inform us about such things as cultural changes over the decades as well as changes in stereotyping and prejudices, both in the UK and in countries around the world.

Linguistics

▶ **Linguistics** is the study of the structure, nature, development and modification of a language and its relationship to other languages. Important in understanding human thoughts and behaviour, as the things we might say in common could have differing meanings depending on such things as upbringing, culture, age and gender. To a child brought up in a working-class family 'dinner' is something taken between 12 and 1, while in a middle-class family 'dinner' is taken in the evening. Similarly ambiguity in the meaning of words will often lead to misunderstanding and false assumptions. For example words like happiness, goodness, beauty, justice, evil, terrorist, freedom fighter all have different layers of meaning to different people and cultures depending on learning, the use of language and approaches to interpretation. In marketing it is an ambiguity that can be misunderstood by the unwary and exploited by the more knowledgeable.

1.10 Marketing example

Legislators are constantly looking at the use of confusing ambiguous words on packaged products that seek to deceive, this includes such words as value, healthy, fat-free, low fat content, weight reducing, heart protecting, money-back, extra content. Retailers have long known that words will change and are now wary about using terms such as 'cheap', 'economy' and 'convenience' because they could have disparaging connotations in the minds of the consumer.

Figure 1.6

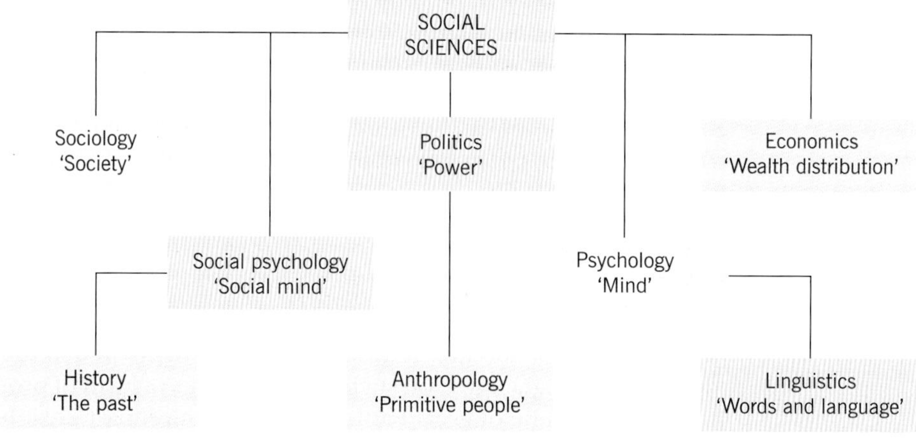

The social sciences

The 'nature' vs 'nurture' argument (or genetics vs environment)

Throughout history philosophers, sociologists, psychologists and other commentators have argued and debated about whether nature (genetics and biology) or nurture (upbringing and socialisation) is responsible for making us the people that we are. On one side of the argument are those that argue that our genes, our inherited DNA, our primitive past, is the biggest influence on such things as individual intelligence, emotions, good or bad behaviour, health and so on (**Eysenck** 1971; Jensen 2001) and on the other side are those who argue that the biggest influence is our family life, the way we have been bought up and the society and culture in which we live (**Carl Rogers** (1902–87) 1989). The answer probably lies somewhere between the two with opinions moving first in one direction and then the other over the decades. The enormous advances made in the study of human genetics, however, make the nature approach increasingly more scientific as experimental research undertaken can be more readily tested and replicated.

Research methods used in the social sciences

It is not intended to go into any great detail here about the possible research methods that might be used in the study of the social sciences, as the area of study is huge and would fill another book in its own right. However there is a brief discussion in the following chapter on marketing research. It is important to stress the point, however, that those that investigate, examine and attempt to explain and predict human nature must be as rigorous as possible in the approach taken, describing the methods used as well as detailing the weaknesses and limitations of the research undertaken.

The use of models

'All models are wrong but some are useful.' RAY WRIGHT, *Business-to-business marketing*

We shall be using **models** and diagrams throughout the book and it might be as well here to make the following points about the pros and cons behind this practice. It should be remembered that models are not a direct reflection of reality and the main reason for their use is to try to simplify, at times, very complex processes as well as to provide a means of stimulating discussion. For example we might try to explain the factors that might affect the consumer's decision-making process using only words but research has shown that understanding is made much quicker and easier if a simple diagram is drawn to assist the process. Models, diagrams and acronyms are also used for both memory purposes (mnemonics), making as certain as possible that important areas of concern are not overlooked. Students, practitioners and organisations may want to develop their own models and acronyms to suit their own needs, and many do.

Figure 1.7

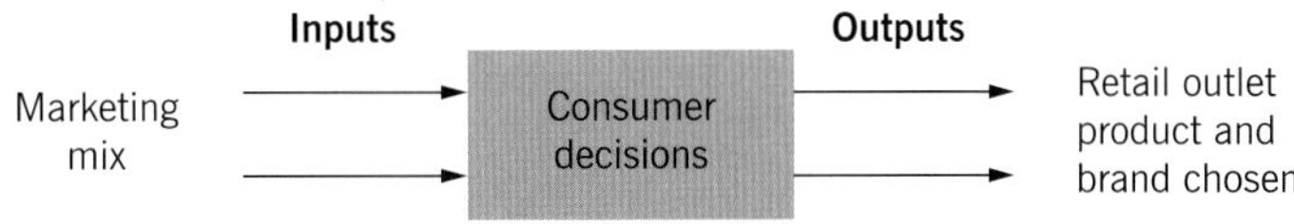

A simple example of a behavioural model

Table 1.5 **Pros and cons of using models and diagrams**

Pros

- Simplify complex problems
- Stimulate discussion
- Aid memory recall
- Support decision making

Cons

- Must never be confused with reality
- No guarantee that all marketing factors will be considered
- Measurement factors are subjective, and can be over or under generous.

Summary

- In this first chapter we have looked at the background to understanding the relationship between marketing and consumer behaviour.
- We then went on to give three definitions of marketing.
- The role of products, brands, services, pricing, distribution and promotions in consumer behaviour was then discussed.

- The changing customer, the role of technology, buying behaviour as a process, ethical problems, information gathering were outlined.
- We then looked at consumer problem solving and decisions making covering the decision-making unit (DMU), the decision-making process (DMP) and the decision-making difficulty (DMD).
- In the final part we looked in more detail at how the behavioural and social sciences should be studied comparing and evaluating the differences with the natural sciences.
- The natural, mathematical and social sciences where identified.
- The need for a rigorous and systematic approach was stressed arguing that care must always be taken when seeking information, researching, analysing and predicting consumer behaviour because people cannot be examined in the same way as the material world.

Questions

1. Discuss why one-to-one marketing or mass customisation has come about and explain its implications for the understanding of consumer behaviour. Give examples using real companies and brands.
2. Why do marketers need to constantly try to understand consumer behaviour and why might this be more complex and problematic in current times?
3. Discuss the proposition that companies manipulate the consumer into buying brands and products that they don't really want, are unhealthy or despoil the environment in some way or another. Give real examples to support your conclusions.
4. Why might calling the study of consumer behaviour a 'science' be considered controversial? Identify the major differences between the natural, mathematical and social sciences and give examples on how this might affect an understanding of the customer.
5. Describe the following social sciences and evaluate the role that each might play in helping to understand consumer and buyer behaviour,
   - **a** Sociology
   - **b** Social psychology
   - **c** Anthropology
   - **d** Evolutionary psychology
   - **e** Psychology
   - **f** Economics
   - **g** Political studies
6. Discuss the need to understand the intricacies of consumer decision making and identify and evaluate how the marketer might have an influence.
7. How might the decision-making process vary according to the purchase of the following product and services:
   - **a** A house
   - **b** A family holiday
   - **c** A pension scheme

8 What part might risk, money, self-esteem and inner mental feelings play in the consumer decision-making process? Give examples how different brands and products influence the process.

9 Discuss how constant technologically innovative products and services coming to the market affect consumer behaviour. What differences might gender and age make?

10 How, and why might consumer behaviour be different from one country to another? Use real examples to illustrate your answer.

Case study

Case study 1 Changing consumer perception – Skoda

Skoda had a monopoly in car manufacturing in Czechoslovakia until the 1989 'Velvet Revolution'. During this time it had developed a fearful reputation as possibly the worse built, worst designed car in the world. Jokes about its notoriety were ruthless, unremitting and widespread. The only place it sold in any number was in the country of manufacturer. After the fall of communism the Czech government started looking for a commercial partner in the West to revitalise its Skoda factories. Most respected commentators felt strongly that there would never be a business prepared to take on the acquisition because of the huge task of transforming the name from risible rejection to amiable acceptance. In 1991, however, Volkswagen took a 30 per cent stake in Skoda and started work in training and educating the workforce to Western quality standards in the hope of completely turning the business around, making the name of Skoda synonymous with quality and reliability. It invested over £2 billion in the plant, research, development and new models. It also undertook an advertising campaign, of momentous proportions, that excited the admiration of all in the promotion business. Ten years later, in 2001, VW took total control of the business and such was its success, Skoda had become one of the fastest-growing car brands in the UK motor industry, increasing sales in the first two years by over 60 per cent. Although sales in 2004 have fallen slightly, in line with other car manufacturers, the story is one of remarkable success, not least in being able to understand and alter and turn around such deeply ingrained consumer ridicule and opposition.

Questions

1 Discuss the part that an understanding of consumer behaviour played in the success of Skoda.

2 What were the major problems that VW had to solve to overcome consumer antipathy to Skoda?

Case study

Case study 2

The coming down of the Berlin Wall in 1989 and the destruction of the Russian Empire put the spotlight firmly on the shortcomings inherent in the idea of politicians and functionaries planning an economy on a grand scale five or ten years ahead. This gave the spur (if this was needed) to free-market advocates to push even harder to bring down trade barriers, introduce anti-cartel and pro-competitive legislation, and firm up the power of overseeing bodies such as the European Union, The Federal Trade Commission and the World Trade Organisation. Add to this the possibilities associated with the stupendous growth in technological advances and we have a global marketplace where small, medium and large companies all have wonderful opportunities, if not now then very soon in the future, to buy and sell goods and services almost anywhere in the world. This has thrown up the need for marketing managers to research and understand the culture and consumer behaviour in many more countries around the world as well as in their home market.

Questions

1 Discuss some of the difficulties involved with trying to understand consumer behaviour around the world.

2 How might attitudes to innovation and technology vary from one country to another?

Further reading

Books

Abra, J. (1998) *Should Psychology be a Science?: Pros and Cons*, Westport, CT: Praeger.

Bernays, Edward (1891–1995) *Propaganda*, from Larry Tye (2002) *The Father of Spin: Edward L. Bernays and The Birth of Public Relations*, New York: Owl Books.

Damasio, Antonio R. (1994) *Descartes' Error: Emotion, Reason, and the Human Brain*, New York: Grosset/Putnam.

Dawkins, R. (1986) *The Blind Watchmaker: Why the Evidence of Evolution Reveals a Universe Without Design*, Harmondsworth: Penguin Books.

East, Robert (1997) *Consumer Behaviour: Advances and Applications in Marketing*, Harlow: Prentice Hall.

Engel, James F. (2000) *Consumer Behaviour*, London: Thomson Learning.

Eysenck, H. (1971) *Race, Intelligence and Education*, in *Intelligence, Race, and Genetics: Conversations with Arthur R. Jensen*, Boulder, CO: Westview Press, 2002.

Gobe, Marc and Sergio Zyman (2001) *Emotional Branding: The New Paradigm for Connecting Brands to People*, New York: Allworth Press.

Gregory, Jim (2003) *The Best of Branding: Best Practices in Corporate Branding*, New York: McGraw-Hill.

Haig, Matt (2003) *Brand Failures: The Truth About the 100 Biggest Branding Mistakes of All Time*, London: Kogan Page.

Hayek, F.A. (1996) *Individualism and Economic Order*, Chicago, IL: University Of Chicago Press.
Jensen, Rolfe (2001) *The Dream Society: How the Coming Shift from Information to Imagination Will Transform Your Business*, New York: McGraw-Hill Trade.
LeDoux, J. (1996) *The Emotional Brain: The Mysterious Underpinnings of Emotional Life*, New York: Touchstone.
Mead, Margaret (2001) *Growing Up in New Guinea: A Comparative Study of Primitive Education*, London: HarperCollins.
Mead, Margaret (2001) *Coming of Age in Samoa: A Psychological Study of Primitive Youth for Western Civilisation*, London: HarperCollins.
Osterfeld, David, E. (1992) *Prosperity vs. Planning: How Government Stifles Economic Growth*, Oxford: Oxford University Press.
Popper, Karl (2001) *All Life is Problem Solving*, London: Routledge.
Ries, Al and Jack Trout (2001) *Positioning: The Battle for Your Mind*, New York: McGraw-Hill Education.
Ries, Al and Laura Ries (2003) *The 22 Immutable Laws of Branding*, USA: Profile Business.
Rogers, C. (1989) *The Carl Rogers Reader*, ed. Howard Kischenbaum and Valerie Land Henderson, Boston, MA: Houghton Mifflin and Co.
Smith, Adam (1776) *Wealth of Nations*, Sunderland, K. (ed.) Oxford: Oxford Paperbacks, 1998.
Solomon, M., G. Bamossy and S. Askegaard (2002) *Consumer Behaviour: A European Perspective*, Harlow: Prentice Hall.
Wright, Ray (1999) *Marketing, Origins, Concepts and Environments*, London: Thomson International Business Press.
Wright, Ray (2003) *Business and Marketing Dictionary*, Chelmsford: Earlybrave Publishing.
Wright, Ray (2004) *Business-to-Business Marketing: A Step-by-Step Guide*, Harlow: Prentice Hall.

Journals and articles

Blue Chip Economic Indicators, Randell E. Moore, New York: Blue Chip Publications, Aspen Publishers (www.aspenpublishers.com).
Bornstein, Robert (2004) 'Subliminality, Consciousness, and Temporal Shifts in Awareness: Implications within and Beyond the Laboratory', *Consciousness and Cognition*, 13: 613–18.
European Journal of Marketing, http://www.mcb.co.uk/ejm.htm.
Gillie, O. (1976) 'Crucial data was faked by eminent psychologist', *The Sunday Times*, 24 October.
Journal of Consumer Marketing, http://zerlina.emeraldinsight.com/vl=1159550/cl=22/nw=1/rpsv/jcm.htm.
Tucker, W.H. (1997) 'Re-reconsidering Burt: Beyond a Reasonable Doubt', *Journal of the History of the Behavioral Sciences*, 33(2): 145–62.
Zajonc, R.B. (1984) 'On the Primacy of Affect', *American Psychologist*, 39: 117–23.

Websites

BT website, www.btopenworld.com.
Campbell Collaboration Research and Development Center for Advancement of Student Learning at Colorado State University, www.cahs.colostate.edu.
Card Watch, www.cardwatch.org.uk.
Citizens Advice Bureau, www.citizensadvice.org.uk.
Competition Commission, www.competition-commission.org.uk.
Consumer Association, www.which.net.org.
Consumer Complaints, www.consumercomplaints.org.uk.

Consumer Gateway, www.dti.gov.uk/consumer_web/index_v4.htm.
Department of Trade and Industry (DTI), www.dti.gov.uk.
The Ethical Consumer, www.ethicalconsumer.org.
European Competition Commission, http://europa.eu.int/comm/competition/index_en.html.
Federal Trade Commission, www.ftc.org:
Heilbroner, Robert (2001) 'Socialism', *The Concise Encyclopedia of Economics*, www.econlib.org.
Office of Fair Trading, www.oft.gov.uk.
Organisation for Economic Cooperation and Development, www.oecd.org.
World Trade Association, www.wto.org.
Wright, Ray, marketing database, www.studentshout.com.

The role of information and marketing research in understanding buyer behaviour

2

'All consumer research should be used as an aid to the decision-making process not as a substitute.'

Objectives

At the end of this chapter the reader will be able to:

1 Be aware of the importance of information about the consumer market environment as a crucial aid in the management decision-making process. This will be at both the national and global level.

2 Appreciate the types of data needed and be able to analyse and evaluate the importance of the information gathered.

3 Be able to identify and evaluate both formal and informal organisational gathering processes including the uses of the marketing information process.

4 Identify and evaluate the different research methods used in the social sciences and be able to appreciate appropriate use.

Introduction

All politicians recognise the importance of having control of the dissemination of information. To be able to decide what should and should not be known and to be able to control the flow of this information has been at the heart of political power for centuries. The democratic process itself depends on the population having access to the right information so that both sides of the argument can be weighed and votes cast accordingly. Similarly, the organisation that has the ability to gather the most realistic, up-to-date environmental information about markets, consumers and the competition, on a continuous basis and then to exploit and use this advantage wisely is more likely to be the one that has the most success.

The strategic importance of information

Information for problem solving and decision making is now of such importance in an increasingly competitive environment that the information collecting process must be directed and supported at the highest strategic level. Without senior management continuous support, information gathering can be seen from a narrow departmental perspective causing the wrong information to be collected, its dissemination to be restricted and/or it to be offered in an unusable form. History is replete with examples of expensive information systems that have been constructed with software that doesn't work and/or manned by people that are not market and customer orientated.

Knowledge and successfully selling the product

The most successful working person is likely to be the one who has the most knowledge and the most information about the industry, markets and customer segments that they have chosen to work in as a career. When we meet someone that truly seems to know the business they are working in and can readily supply information requested the results are impressive. This will be the person, above all others, that returning customers will seek out time and time again. In consumer markets there are often sales people who seem to know very little about the products and services offered. This can engender frustration and disappointment and encourage the prospective customer to go elsewhere. This may not cause an immediate problem for the retailer as there might be hundreds of other potential customers looking for new or replacement products. However, if the market is highly competitive and many other retailers, offering the same or similar products, exist then over time reputations will suffer and sales must eventually begin to fall.

Understanding people and gaining competitive advantage

Companies have to be constantly on guard against competitors offering better customer value in some way or another and so taking away customers. This can happen

2.1 General example — Knowledge is power

Manufacturers and retailers, marketing and sales managers and sales staff (as well as all other customer facing employees) who have more current information about present and future market and customer needs than anybody else, know the opposition as well as their own company, and can use this information in a professional manner will create the foundation for an unbeatable competitive advantage over all others. The imperative is to know more about your markets and customers than the competition and know more about the competition than they know about you.

Questions

1 Discuss how competitive advantage can be gained through the use of information bringing insights into consumer behaviour.

2 How might information gathering be encouraged among employees?

in many ways but inevitably the nature and attitude of people, both within the company (employees) and outside the company (customers) will play a critically important part in the process.

Employee-centred approach

Organisations must have an understanding of the needs of its employees at management and general employee level. Time and time again, both research and practical experiences demonstrate that well motivated, well-treated staff operating within a **corporate culture** of knowledge dissemination, recognition and respect can create (all other things being equal) a climate of enthusiasm, innovation and genuine concern for offering continuous total customer satisfaction (Rucci *et al.* 1998). And there is no doubt that customers can sense when this concern for their welfare is artificial or not. As well as motivating employees in constant communication with the customer (in the marketing department or on the shop floor), successful organisations should take the same approach with all employees in all departments (finance, production, administration, car parking etc.). In this way all customers will be treated, served and respected in the best possible way no matter who they come into contact with.

Customer-centred approach

Detailed information and a deep understanding of the needs and wants of the customer (and others in the decision-making process) coupled with the ability to offer the correct benefits, is the basis for customer satisfaction and at the heart of customer satisfaction. Put the employee-centred and customer-centred approach together and the organisation will have a solid foundation for building a sustainable competitive advantage.

Key point Using both an employee-centred and a customer-centred approach will supply a solid foundation from which to build an unassailable competitive advantage.

2.1 Marketing example — Information and understanding on a global scale

As markets have become more global this need to understand cultures and individual and group behaviour (both employees' and consumers') spreads out across regions, countries and continents to wherever the company might be marketing and selling its products and services. UK supermarket retailer Tesco now successfully operates in 13 different countries including Japan, China, Malaysia, Taiwan as well as in many Eastern European countries and the company now has more floor space abroad than in its home market. The French supermarket giant Carrefour has over 50 stores in China where consumer behaviour can be different from one store to another and from one region to another.

Question

1 Discuss the information needed by companies like Tesco and Carrefour when moving its operation far around the world.

Figure 2.1

Company functions and employees must put customer understanding at the centre of all activity

Information gathering

Information gathering, storage and analysis, has to be driven by the needs of those managers, and other employees, that are seeking to comprehend both served and potential customers and markets and not by those who seek ownership for some personal objective aggrandisement. Informational objectives must be clear beyond doubt and there must be relevant information offered that demonstrably equates to organisational marketers' needs. It should always be presented in a client-friendly manner and the process must have feedback, monitoring and control systems built in. In this way the management and other users, at all levels in the company (and partner companies along the supply chain where this happens), can be encouraged to comment constantly on the quality, reliability and the relevancy of the data collected. If it is not helpful it should be dumped.

Key point Managers at the very top of the organisation must recognise and support the information collecting and analysing process, on served market segments and consumer wants, so that its vital importance is recognised by all and built into all aspects of strategic planning.

Information about the consumer sector

Enlightened companies and sales staff remember information for helping customers, not just information about them.

Much has been written over the last 50 years about marketing, its origins, concepts and practices and a large part of it tends to be focused on consumer markets, **consumer behaviour** and consumer purchases, rather than organisational buying and the business-to-business sector. In a way this is understandable because both basic marketing theory and marketing practice lend themselves more readily to the idea of marketing product and service brands to the domestic consumer, either in segmented groups or as individuals, rather than the industrial buyer. Empirical examples abound. We are all consumers and most of us are involved in some kind of retail expedition, seeking out, purchasing and using many different products and services on a daily, weekly and yearly basis. Consumer marketing is all around us constantly. Market researchers stop us on the street to ask questions about behaviour. Outdoor billboards, corporate images, retail outlets and shop windows, merchandising and point-of-purchase material, stock displays and sales people attempt to seduce us into spending our money. Adverts hit us every time we drive our car, walk down the high street, watch TV, listen to the radio, go to the cinema or view an Internet website.

There is no escape – a mass of advertising information hits the consumer everywhere in the world.
Source: Simon Wright

Sophisticated and unsophisticated consumer markets

The more sophisticated the market and the more consumers want **customised products** the greater the amount and depth of information that is needed. Similarly, the information needed in these customised markets is more about micro individual behaviour, while in more basic markets the information needed is more about macro-market and mass behaviour.

Understanding consumer behaviour

Producers, retailers and marketing and research agencies spend many billions of pounds each year in attempting to understand complex consumer behaviour in

Figure 2.2

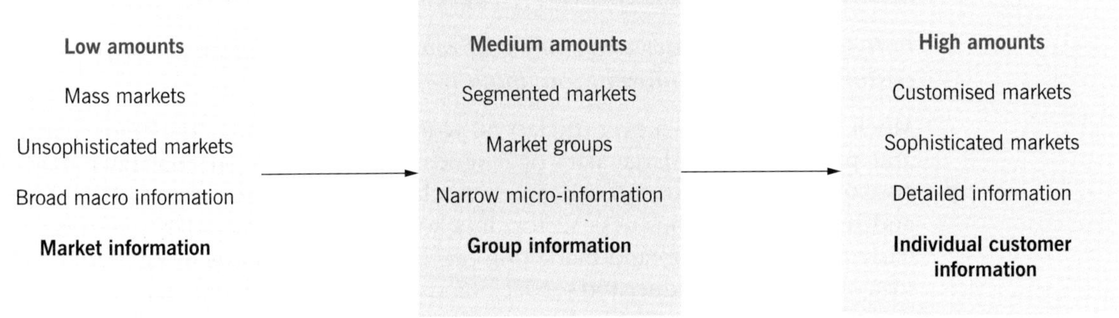

Level, degree and detail of market information needed

thousands of business-to-consumer markets across the world. Researching hundreds of millions of people all demanding products and services that will satisfy needs and wants that could vary from region to region and from country to country. The more sophisticated the market the more complex will be the group and individual benefits wanted and the quicker these wants will change. Marketers know that if they fail to identify and anticipate what it is that different markets want, their competitors will and markets will be lost. In consumer markets purchase decisions are driven by emotional (hopes and desires) as well as just functional needs. Products and brands must offer these kinds of benefits and be advertised and promoted in ways that stimulate the imagination. Information about human behaviour becomes the basis for success.

Key point Know the value of customer groups
The **Pareto 80/20 rule** tells us that 80 per cent of our business comes from 20 per cent of our customers or 80 per cent of our profits are made from 20 per cent of our customers and so on.

Understanding the business-to-business (B2B) sector

Conditions are different in B2B markets. Although individuals or groups are involved in the decision-making process, it is for the wellbeing of the organisation that the purchase is being made and the area of study is *organisational behaviour* rather than *consumer behaviour* and, to many, it is not nearly so exciting. Information needed would be more about economies, industries, markets and company development and not about individual desires. Unlike business-to-consumer markets (B2C) decision making is often complex and could involve many employees and managers throughout the organisation. Decisions are made for rational and functional rather than emotional reasons and the products and services wanted could be considered prosaic and mundane (although capable of producing vastly more sales). Promotional strategies lack the drama and exhilaration when compared with B2C markets.

Figure 2.3

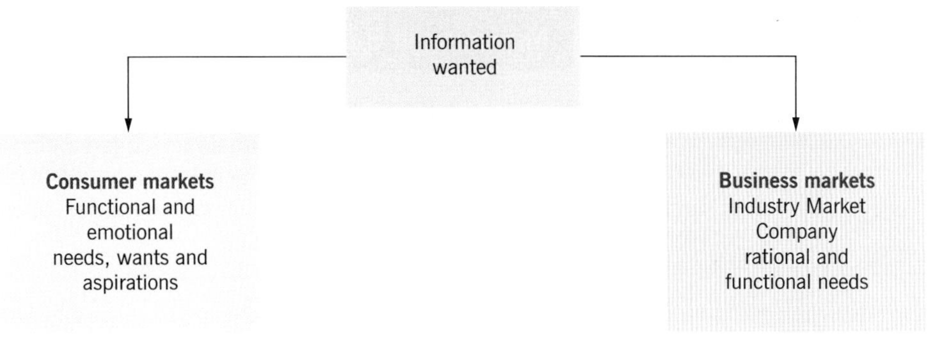

Information needed when looking at B2C and B2B organisational needs

Understanding the business-to-consumer (B2C) supply chain

Unlike the B2B market, the business to consumer (B2C) market will involve organisations that have a direct interest in the consumer. This will include manufacturers such as Kellogg's, Unilever, Cadburys, Colgate-Palmolive, Coca-Cola, Heinz, Walkers, Nestlé, Mitsubishi, Sara Lee, Sony, all of whom produce consumer brands that they then sell on to retailers such as Walmart, Dixon's, Debenhams, Next, B&Q, McDonald's, Amazon etc. All of these organisations are major collectors and users of information and marketing research about markets and consumers on a national and, increasingly, on an international basis. All have to constantly scan and monitor the environment so as to anticipate and be aware of any changes in consumer living, leisure, working, buying, drinking and eating habits. Because of the enormous influence they have on the consumer, both brand manufacturers and retailers should be seen as an essential part of the consumer buying behaviour process.

Understanding the role of the consumer brand manufacturer

Manufacturers in all retail sectors will be researching and monitoring consumer reaction to their existing portfolio of products making certain that satisfaction is constant and at the highest possible level. Each company will be continually looking toward bringing creative and innovative new products to the market certain in the knowledge that this is what consumers demand and competitors will supply if they slow down in this area of activity. Built-in market monitoring systems are a must if manufacturers are going to pre-empt or react in time to market threatening product add-ons or new product launches. Consumer brand manufacturers have the greatest influence on consumer behaviour through the enormous amount of TV, press, outdoor, radio, Internet etc. advertising and promotion that they undertake on a daily, weekly and yearly basis. For example FMCG brand manufacturer Procter & Gamble is the top US advertiser spending nearly $3 billion in its home market and nearly $5 billion around the world in 2004 (TNS Media Intelligence).

2.2 Marketing example **Marketing in B2C markets**

Sara Lee Corporation is a global manufacturer and marketer of high-quality, brand name products for consumers throughout the world. With its headquarters in Chicago, Sara Lee has operations in 55 countries and markets products in nearly 200 nations. The corporation employs 154,900 people world-wide. Information needed about customer and consumer behaviour is truly on a wide-world scale.

Understanding the role of the retailer

The small, medium and large retailers will also be diligently and enthusiastically searching for any piece of information that will enable them to serve their customers (and entice new ones) more effectively than at present. They will be well aware, as with manufacturers that consumers are now more discriminating than in the past and will quickly change retail allegiances if standards start to decline. Retailers are in a much better position than brand manufacturers to monitor and research customer behaviour. This is because they have direct contact on a regular daily or weekly basis and so have the opportunity to be right up-to-date on finding out needs and wants. They can do this by talking to and observing individual consumers as they enter and move around the store. More importantly they can obtain information through the EPOS system and loyalty cards and this is discussed below.

Building customer relationships

In many cases retailers are able to make and build two-way ongoing relationships with customers and if they are always on their guard (and as it happens many aren't) they should be able to discover any problem or complaint concerning product choice or service that might arise and they can then respond accordingly almost instantly. On the other hand manufacturers have to collect information in others ways, such as commissioning research through commercial research companies. Some also try to collect information and form relationships directly with their end consumers, by using direct mail, free consumer magazines and increasingly through the use of company-owned websites.

2.3 Marketing example

Serving over 14 million customers a week in 2004 in the UK alone, supermarket giant Tesco now has unprecedented access to **consumer buying behaviour information**, which can be used to constantly improve and upgrade its products and services.

Table 2.1 **Information wanted by retailers on consumer reactions to:**

- The **corporate image and brand positioning** compared to the competition.
- The approach to the store including car parking and overall ease of entry and exit.
- The ambience of the retail outlet in terms of welcome, layout, colours, music, ambience and overall friendliness.
- Ease of movement around the store.
- Merchandising and choice and range of products on show.
- Customer service, before, during and after transactions.
- Overall value for money.

> **Key point** Business-to-consumer marketing, B2C definition
> Business-to-consumer marketing is where one business markets products and services either to another business, i.e. a wholesaler or a retailer, to sell on to the end consumer, or sells on to the end consumer direct.

> **Key point** Business-to-business marketing, B2B definition
> Business-to-business marketing is where one business markets products or services to another business for use in that business or to sell on to other businesses for their own use.

Sharing information

The last decade has seen the growth in more partnership and collaborative schemes between retailers and manufacturers sharing information and working together to bring about better end customer satisfaction. Schemes such as **Efficient Consumer Response** (**ECR** see marketing example 2.4) have come about because of the realisation that a supply chain (or a demand chain if looked at, as it should be, from the standpoint of the consumer) that cooperates and works together will be more effective, efficient and economic in bringing ultimate customer value. Of course, as with all relationships there must be trust if sensitive information is to be shared and there are bound to be limits on the quality and quantity shared.

2.4 Marketing example **Efficient Consumer Response (ECR) www.ecrnet.org**

ECR-Europe is a large group of suppliers, manufactures and retailers working collaboratively together along the supply chain driven by the overriding need to understand and to serve consumers better, faster and at less cost offering the right product, at the right time in the right place. At the heart of ECR was a business environment characterised by dramatic advances in information technology, growing competition, global business structures and consumer demand focused on better choice, service, convenience, quality, freshness and safety and the increasing movements of goods across international borders aided by the internal European market. Its main concerns are to constantly create value, optimise choice of products and new product introduction and to optimise promotional effectiveness.

Questions

1 Using the giant supermarkets (Tesco, Asda, Carrefour) as examples identify how they all try to run their businesses driven by the needs of their customers. Give examples of this happening across the retail marketing mix.

2 Identify and evaluate the concept of ECR.

Table 2.2 **Shared customer/consumer information needed will include both the macro and micro**

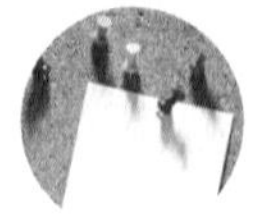

- Which consumer market segments are the most important in terms of sales, growth and profit?
- Which segments are growing, declining or static?
- The major competitors in each segment as well as their strengths and weaknesses.
- Type, brand and amount of goods and services purchased over a prolonged period.
- The turnover rate on brand, products and services.
- Reasons behind the purchases.
- Where customers would like to purchase goods and services.
- How retailer and the customer would like to see merchandise displayed.
- Features and benefits used and wanted.
- Ease of packaging usage, quality of product.
- Levels of price, value, service, sales promotion and special offers expected.
- Reaction to the product packaging in terms of materials used, colour combinations, ease of use.
- Problems/complaints about retail outlets or goods and services purchased.
- What might be expected on service, value, benefits, features and delivery etc. in the future.

Information along the supply/demand chain

Information gathering in consumer markets will be carried out by both manufacturers e.g. Cadburys, and retailers e.g. Sainsbury, all along the supply chain and, depending on the partnerships and working practices in place, shared so that ultimate customer satisfaction is constantly assured. The quality and quantity of information is more important to some organisations than others, depending on organisational type, products and services sold and markets served. A supplier making **own label products** under contract solely to one of the big supermarkets will not need as much information on the end consumer as the company selling direct to the customer in the continually changing communications market.

Figure 2.4

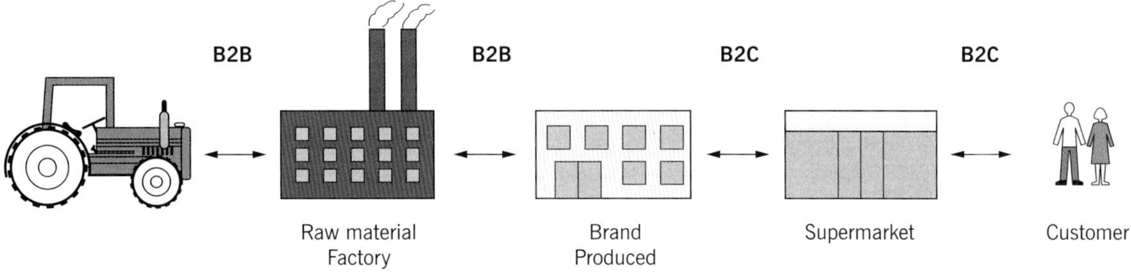

B2B and B2C information flows backwards and forwards along the supply chain

Information sharing techniques

To help in the process of understanding consumer behaviour and so better serve the customer supply chain initiatives have been introduced that are constantly being updated and improved, that offer many information-sharing techniques including the following.

Electronic data interchange (EDI)

EDI allows computer-to-computer information to be shared, in real time, between all trading partners in the supply and demand chain partnership. For it to work properly and efficiently there must be shared standard computer hardware and software programs as well as uniform usage development and training.

Extranet

The **extranet**, is an extension of the **Intranet**, and is a private link-up using Internet technology that allows access between the retailer and its permitted group of member suppliers. On-line information about such things as the hourly movement of stock (crucial in such areas as sales promotions) off the retailer shelves allows just-in-time constant replenishment by the manufacturer. As part of the process, Computer Assisted Ordering (CAO) is a system that automatically generates replenishment orders when shelf levels fall below an agreed pre-determined level.

Electronic point of sale (EPOS)

This is something we are all familiar with. It is the method of recording store sales by scanning product bar codes at the checkout. Electronic fund transfer point of sale

Figure 2.5

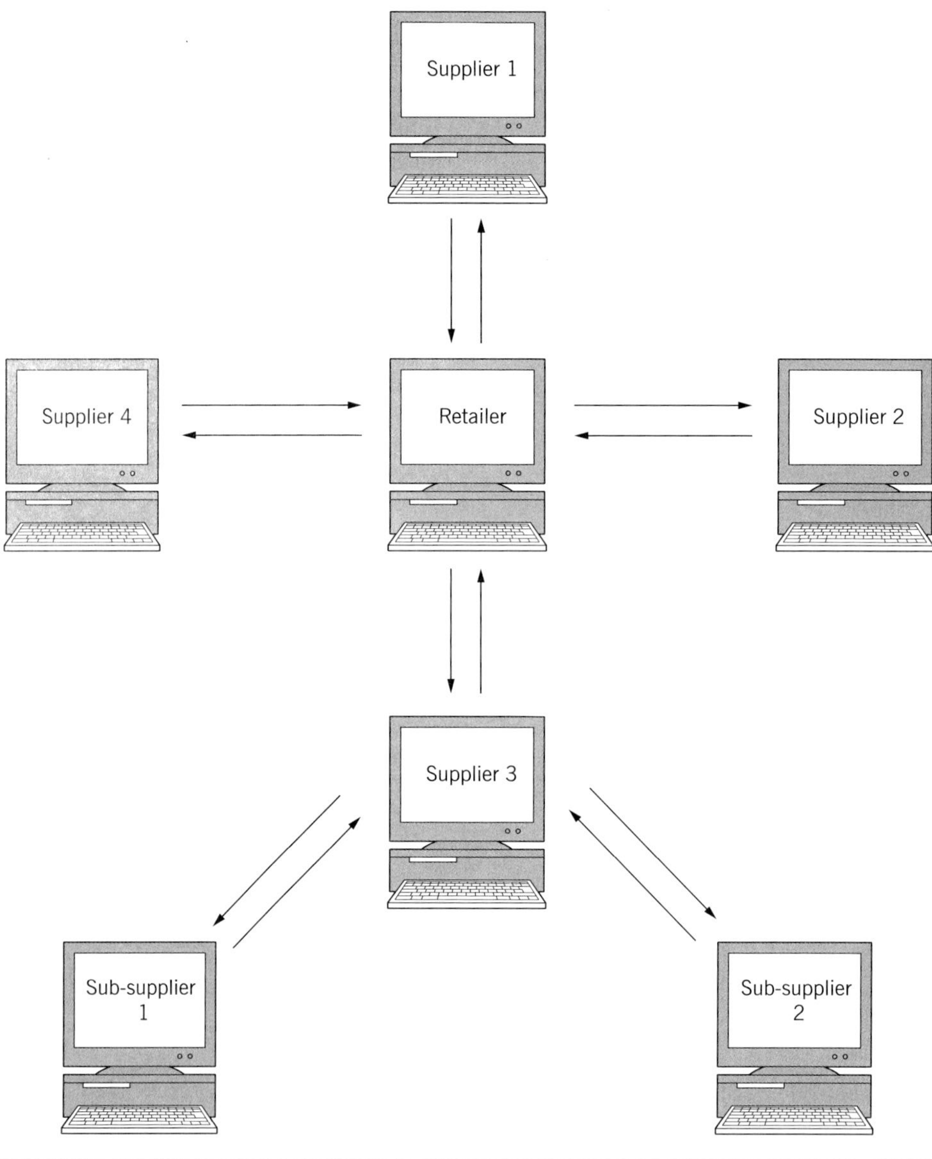

Electronic data interchange (EDI): all companies partner-sharing compatible software and hardware (sometimes using an extranet)

(EFTPOS) allows customers to have the payment of goods to be deducted immediately from their account using a standard credit card. It also allows the store to collect, store and use infinite amounts of information on the customer so enabling the customisation of product and service offerings. Merchandise can also be efficiently replaced.

Loyalty cards

When allied with the loyalty card scheme, used by many of the big retailers, EPOS systems give the retailer access to an inordinate, and highly valuable, amount of

Figure 2.6

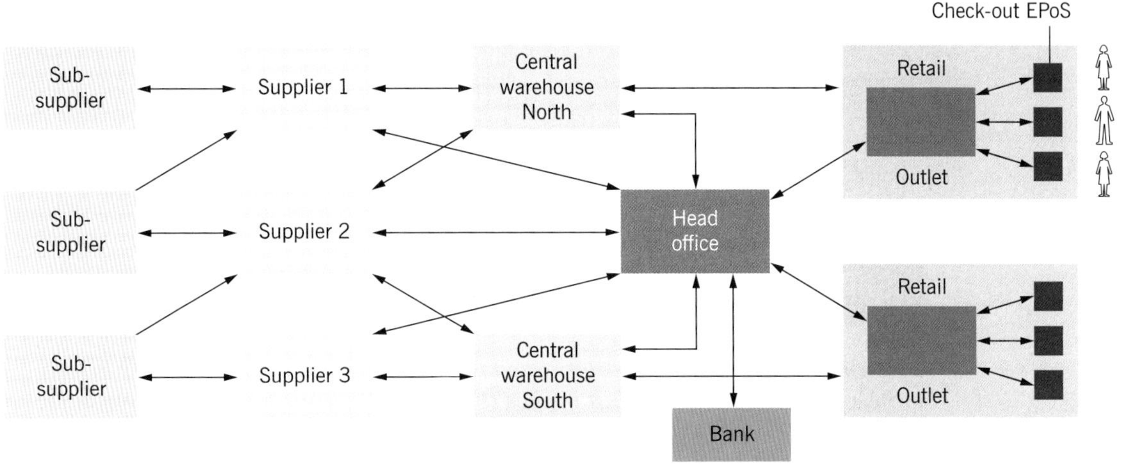

EPOS and EDI information flows

Speeding customers through the checkout. The latest technology, RDIF, allows a whole trolley full of products to be scanned at the same time without removing the products.
Source: Trolley Scan (pty) Ltd, South Africa and the University of New South Wales, Australia.

consumer information including, name and address and the weekly, monthly and yearly amount spent, as well as the kinds and numbers of products purchased. Some, but not all of this information may be shared with partner retailers and suppliers. The importance of this customer information cannot be overvalued and we will revisit this subject later in the chapter when we look at the use of the customer database. (In the UK a 2002 Mori poll showed that more than half of UK adults use loyalty cards.)

2.5 Marketing example — Category management

Category management is a retailer/supplier process that has developed through a three-way dialogue between retailers, suppliers and customers. How customers would like to see goods displayed in supermarkets became the driving force. This has resulted in the putting together of categories of products that can now be managed across the supply chain as strategic business units producing enhanced results by focusing on delivering constant consumer value.

Selling into retailers

'Humanize the brand – retailers need to remember that the corporate brand is their personality, it is what makes them lovable, unique and be seen as an old trusted friend.' ANON

It can sometimes be forgotten that, unless selling direct, producers will also need to sell into the retailer before their products can then be sold on to the end consumer. It should therefore be recognised (and most good sales people do) that retailers buy for different reasons than the end consumer and so their needs and wants should be part of the behavioural understanding process. In this way appropriate responses can be identified and developed so that orders are obtained and valuable 'shelf space' is achieved. A selection of the main differences between retailer and consumer buying needs is shown in Table 2.3.

Table 2.3 Differences between retailer buyer and consumer behaviour

The retailer buyer

- Mainly rational reasons for purchase as buying for the organisation.
- Interested in moving stock as quickly and as profitably as possible.
- Will often only be interested in the number 1 or number 2 brand in the market.
- Can be many people involved, depending on product or service.
- Partner relationships can be developed although buyers can change.
- High-value contracts on offer.
- End user will probably not be the decision maker.

The consumer

- Buying for self, family or friends.
- Few people involved.
- Mainly emotional reasons for purchase.
- Reasons for purchase can be complex.
- End user more often than not the decision maker.
- Short time to make decisions.
- Relatively low-value products when compared to retailer.

Key point Most producers must first sell into the retailer before reaching the end consumer.

Consumer behaviour when using multi-channels

There is now a multiplicity of channels, both direct and indirect, that products and services go through before they reach the end consumer. Most consumers now use many different methods of purchase destination (multi-channels) when seeking to find information and make decisions about buying products and brands. This is throwing up ever more issues with regard to human and customer behaviour as individuals attempt to come to terms about which channel choice will offer the best all-round value. There is no doubt that shopping patterns are changing as choice availability escalates and people become less loyal in their behaviour.

Keep up-to-date

This puts enormous pressure on marketers and researchers to keep up-to-date, be able to predict future shopping behaviour and so build marketing programmes that will help them encourage consumers to use their outlets and buy their brands rather than those of the competitor.

Buying through conventional retailers

Even buying in the conventional way (through so-called bricks and mortar retailers) on the high street, shopping mall, edge-of town retail parks, shopping village, factory villages, hypermarkets or supermarkets, has changed quite drastically over the last 20 years. This has thrown up new challenges for consumer researchers as they seek to continuously anticipate and predict how behaviour might adjust to these exciting new ways of shopping. Research has shown that many consumers will use a range of different destinations to shop at depending on such things as type of products wanted and level of decision-making difficulty involved, choice of retailers wanted, emotional state and situational factors like weather, amount of time available, and the time of day, week or month.

Reasons why we need to shop

Behavioural researchers (Jim Pooler 2003) have shown that there are lots of individual reasons behind shopping expeditions and many will be used for examples of human behaviour throughout the book. The major reasons will include the following:

Functional reasons: such as the need for the main weekly and daily top-up grocery type products at supermarkets and convenience stores or because the washing machine has broken down and another is needed.

Social reasons: to satisfy the need to meet and socially interact with others.

Emotional reasons: perhaps to alleviate boredom or just get out of the house. Increasingly, it has also become a form of entertainment with families going out for the day looking for pleasure and excitement.

Psychological reasons: obsessive buying can seem to give some sort of respite from inner feelings of depression or low **self-esteem**. Products bought might also generate feelings of safety, status and wanted approval of others.

Marketing research (research company Mintel 2002) has identified the following factors wanted by shoppers from retailers:

- Easy parking
- Choice of shops
- Choice of merchandise
- Convenient opening hours
- Helpful – knowledgeable staff
- Value for money
- Short wait
- Pleasant, exciting surroundings
- Exciting experience.

Buying from home

Although the vast majority of products and services are marketed and sold through intermediaries (retailers and occasionally wholesalers) there are many occasions when the products are sold direct to the home of the customer. Consumers are now spoilt for choice as so many ways are now available for people to purchase from home and more of us, of all ages, are now using this option. Although always popular through the use of home parties, catalogues and direct mail, this manner of purchasing has really taken-off over the last few years, mainly due to the increase in the use of the Internet.

Selling indirect and direct into the home

If we use as our definition of direct marketing 'the producer/manufacturer selling direct to the end buyer' then many products marketed to the home would not fall into this definition. For example some retailers market goods and services direct to the home either in tangent with a conventional retail outlet or as an exclusive channel method to their customers. So for example, Tesco, Currys, B&Q, use both the retail outlets and the Internet while Dell computers and easyJet chose to use website only access. The former group of companies could be said to be selling indirect (other producers' products) while the latter group of companies could be said to be selling direct (their own products and services).

2.6 Marketing example — easyJet business model – booking from home

easyJet is not afraid of competition, simply because it has developed a business model that ensures a built-in business advantage. Every effort is made to cut unnecessary costs. Travel agents are considered an overhead, so passengers must book directly by telephone or on the web, where additional discounts on the ticket price may be obtained. The end result is an airline operating on sound and competitive business principles that has simply learned to think 'outside the box'. What makes it operate so successfully is the way that the Internet has been strategically incorporated into the easyJet business model (www.AATL.com).

Questions

1 Discuss how the Internet has been used to sell products and services into the home. Give examples.

2 Why are some products sold more easily than others over the Internet?

Problems associated with selling into the home

All home buying behaviour has to be a subject for research and investigation if the correct marketing mix is to be developed. This is because buying behaviour is often different than when buying through conventional outlets and different problems and difficulties will arise. People are often apprehensive when buying from home, and this is especially so if the selling company is either unknown or is not well known. It can cause problems with questions of corporate reliability and trust, product risk and value level as well as the security worries associated with buying by credit or debit card. These problems have multiplied over the last few years as more people use the Internet for buying goods and services and examples of fraudulent and underhand practices increase.

Marketing direct from producer to consumer

The problem, however, is more acute where consumers are dealing direct in some way, without the comfort of a retailer between the manufacturer and themselves. This means that the producer has to research and undertake the whole marketing exercise themselves and cannot rely on any intermediary for help. To add to the problem, when confronted with direct selling companies, consumer behaviour will sometimes be different in many major ways and this must be researched and understood if satisfaction is to be obtained and sales and profits are to be made.

Consumer information needed when selling direct

In most cases, organisations that want to sell direct to the end consumer, will need similar information to retailers in terms of geo-demographic, social, behavioural and life style segmentation categories. They will also need information on individual and group customer reactions to being sold to in this way, especially when this can vary in many significant ways to when being sold to through an intermediary.

2.7 Marketing example — Products and services sold direct

Almost anything can be sold direct including: financial, leisure, communication and health services as well as products as diverse as cars, boats, houses and holiday homes, computers, electrical products, clothes, cosmetics and food and drink. Direct selling companies include Avon Cosmetics, Amway household, Dell computers, Kirby vacuum cleaners, Direct Line insurance, Tupperware household; the list seems endless. Direct selling methods include direct mail, the Internet, telesales, TV, door-to-door, home parties and exhibitions and seminars, producer workplace and factory shops. All these different methods must be researched to identify differences in consumer decision-making behaviour. There is a direct selling organisation at www.dsa.org (US) and www.dsa.org.uk providing information and ethical and working codes of conduct for its members.

Questions

1 Identify the problems associated with selling in the home.

2 What might be the future for home shopping?

Key point Marketers have to research and try to understand consumer home buying behaviour. The enormous changes in home shopping bought about by the growth in the Internet makes this essential for all organisations, whether or not they presently use home shopping channels.

Information and customer relationship management

'Quality is when your customers come back, not your products'. MARGARET THATCHER

Both retailers and producers in almost every sector have been building customer relationship management (CRM) and customer retention programmes (CRP) in order to keep existing customers contented. They also use such programmes to encourage the use of more products and services across the whole product portfolio and to introduce new products as they come to market. It has been consistently demonstrated that it costs very much more to cultivate new customers (anything from 5 to 10 times as much) than it does to hang on to the existing ones (Reicheld and Teal 2001). Add to this the fact that, increasingly, competitors will attempt to take customers away with more value added products and we can see why this area is so important.

The aim of CRM programmes

The aim of CRM programmes is to hold on to a customer for as long as possible by constantly researching individual behaviour and needs and wants as they grow and change. Using one or more of the many commercial IT CRM software programs now available, a business can create several communication and feedback processes throughout the customer lifecycle, so that they always have the insight needed to satisfy the right benefit changing wants as and when they arise. Services include inbound and outbound customer service support programmes using telephone, email, websites, mail and so on, covering such things as product information, promotions, after-sales service and complaints. (CRM programmes are examined in more detail in Chapter 9.)

Figure 2.7

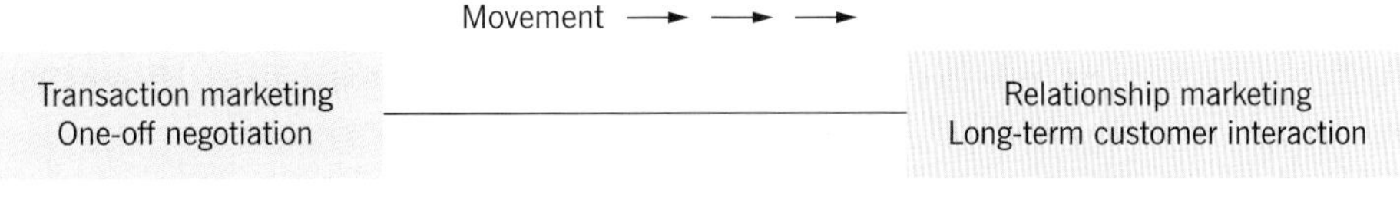

The movement is away from one-off negotiation meetings towards building networks of long-term customer/retailer interactions

Human behaviour and customer loyalty

Over the years many academics have researched behaviour attempting to prove the link between **consumer loyalty** and business profitability, and the evidence is quite compelling (Hughes 2003). On the one hand, there are commentators who argue that customer loyalty is often illusory and fleeting as people move from one store to another, one brand to another and one loyalty card to another depending on value, price and promotions on offer. Others argue that there is not necessarily a relationship between customer loyalty and profitability and it will depend on definitions and how the process is managed (Woolfe 2001). They go on to say that different approaches will be more suitable to different businesses, depending on the profiles of their customers and the complexity of their distribution channels. What seems to be important is to know the customer and then develop an appropriate personalised strategy. The multi-channels now available for shopping seem to suggest that questions about loyalty will become more problematic as the number of shopping options increases. This raises several obvious questions for any business such as:

- What do we mean by loyalty and how might it be measured?
- Is the lifetime value, in terms of sales and profits, of each customer known to the business (my wife and I have worked out that in the 25 years we have been using Sainsbury's we have spent approximately £130,000).
- Is information known about the number of existing customers (and new customers) that stop coming to the store every, day, week, month or year?
- Does the company know why they stop buying? And does the company know how many people, by word of mouth, influence others, to come or not to come?

2.8 Marketing example — Know your customer value

Business writers, Reinartz and Kumar (2002) argue that much of the common wisdom about the value of customer retention is not true. They say that they have discovered little or no evidence to suggest that customers who purchase steadily from a company over time are necessarily cheaper to serve, less price sensitive, or particularly effective at bringing in new business. Instead of focusing on loyalty alone, they advise companies to 'find ways to measure the relationship between loyalty and profitability so that they can better identify which customers to focus on and which to ignore'. As a result of their study, they have developed a customer matrix based on a combination of the length of relationship and profit generation. For example, they have defined four different customer groupings, described as:

- Butterflies – customers who are highly profitable but over a short term.
- Strangers – low profit yielding and short-term relationships.
- Barnacles – low profit yielding but long-term relationships.
- True friends – customers who generate high profitability over a long term.

Questions

1 Do you think consumer loyalty is a reality or is it just wishful thinking on the part of the brand manufacturer and retailer?

2 How can consumer loyalty be increased and maintained?

Behavioural information at the tactical level

It must be remembered that information is also needed for tactical decisions and programme implementation. There has been a danger in the past that strategy has become divorced from the tactical implementation and the two processes come to be seen as almost separate in some way. Customer retention processes may be in place, e.g. never allowing long queues to build up at the retail checkout or how to reply to customer complaints, but if front-line staff aren't actually implementing them, or customers are still finding areas of frustration with the implementation then dissatisfaction will follow. While successful organisations recognise the need for long-term thinking they will not neglect the information needed about putting the idea of customer satisfaction into operation.

Consumer information needed at the tactical level includes the following:

- Product benefits and level of service needed by each customer segment and individual.
- That staff responsibilities are clearly allocated.
- That staff are adequately trained.
- That performance indicators are agreed.
- Support resources needed.

- CRM systems in place and working.
- Monitoring, feedback, evaluation and control systems in place.

The information gathering process

The information gathering process can be formal, informal or a mixture of the two and it will vary between organisations, depending on size, wealth, style, management inclination and the industry itself. It will also depend on the operating climate. The more turbulent the environment and the more open to change and competition the product or service the greater will be the need for a continuous stream of relevant up-to-date information about markets, competitors and consumers.

Informal research

Much information gathering is done on an informal basis and tends not to be seen as marketing research, but its value cannot be underestimated. It was argued above that the successful person is the knowledgeable person who has an inquisitive and enquiring mind, always talking and listening to customers, observing their behaviour and asking questions about markets, competition and products and storing the data in their long-term memory for later use. The wise marketing and retail manager is the one who generates this sort of culture, encouraging employees to seek out and report back any relevant market information that might have an influence on, and be beneficial to the running of, the business.

Using the whole workforce to constantly look at what is happening locally, nationally and around the world will motivate all to feel that they are part of the company set-up and, more importantly, provide marketing strategists with a valuable source of informational supply. This process can be semi-formalised by building in some sort of reward system for information that proves to be the most useful. It's crazy if an organisation is unaware that a competitor is researching a new product range or is thinking about moving out of a particular market segment and/or moving into another when a sales person might have picked up this useful information but found little management interest.

Key point All members of staff should be encouraged to collect information on customers and markets and feed it back to senior staff.

The marketing information system (MIS)

Eventually the information gathering process will need to be viewed from a strategic perspective and put on a formal footing. This will help communicate to all employees the importance that the company places on using good information when making important decisions and about customers, markets and sales forecasting.

With the advent and development of information technology any organisation, whatever its size and financial situation, can now afford to have access to information technology, data storage and analysis equipment and services either by purchase or alternatively through leasing, rental, outsourcing and sharing. This will apply to both retailers and B2C manufacturers. If the latter options are chosen there is usually an option to buy in on either a continuous or ad hoc basis.

A strategic approach in setting up the MIS

Whatever the approach taken, the long-term strategic importance of a **marketing information system (MIS)** to the wellbeing of the organisation should be recognised and direction and support should emanate from the very top, at director level. It should involve all potential users (not only in the marketing department but also across all departments) in its design, be tested and re-tested to make certain that both information in and information out is relevant to employee needs. Monitoring, feedback and control mechanisms must be instituted to see that 'what needs to happen actually happens'. The monitoring process should be such that if user access is difficult, if the information collected is of the wrong kind or if the data analysis is unhelpful the process must be changed. Marketing information systems must, in true marketing fashion, be driven by the needs of the internal customers and not by the agenda and objectives of the designers and operators.

The MIS process

The formal information gathering process for the MIS can be broken down into the following four areas

1 Internal information
2 Market intelligence gathering
3 Marketing research
4 Information storage and analysis.

1 Internal information

An organisation will have a whole range of internal quantitative and qualitative performance indicators within its many functions and this information is essential to the marketing manager (and others) in the successful performance of his or her job. It is surprising how often this source of information is not utilised as effectively as it should be. There are examples of marketing managers seemingly unaware that certain markets are declining and others are increasing, or uncertain about the financial contribution of one product over another and there cannot be any excuse for not having this information at hand.

Types of information obtained internally

The financial department can supply figures on sales and costs and profitability across the whole product/service portfolio, as well as figures on cash flow and accounts receivable and accounts payable. Costs can be supplied on which customers are the most profitable and which the most expensive, who is the highest risk and who isn't, which combination of products/services are the most profitable and which the most expensive and so on.

Production can supply figures on optimum production runs, inventory positions and future needs. Indispensable to the system are the sales force reports coming into the company. The salesperson is in the unique position of being the eyes and the ears of the company out in the marketplace. The information that they are able to collect on the customer, the competition, suppliers etc. must be given the recognition it deserves (this is the major reason why the salesperson's report should never be used as a method of policing and control). All employee contributions to the information gathering process should be encouraged by the use of some form of recognition and reward system.

Information needed on consumers The following are examples of information that can be obtained internally and will help in maximising the relationships with suppliers, buyers and consumers.

Internal information on buyers includes:

- Overall sales and profit figures across all consumer segments.
- Numbers of customers, who buys the most and the least.
- Number and types of consumer complaints.
- Which customers buy across the whole range and which buy selectively and why?
- Which consumers could be in the market to buy products and services not already purchasing?
- Which consumers make the company the most and the least amounts of profit?
- Which customers offer the best and the least potential?
- Which competitors are consumers using and why?

Information co-ordination

The marketing department will need to set up a system for collecting and analysing reports from all the different internal functional areas. Yearly and monthly trends can be monitored so as to identify how the market segments are performing and how they might perform in the future. Sales and pricing can be compared with the competition and comparisons made between outlets and distribution channels. Qualitative observations and suggestions should also be encouraged and rewarded if this is thought to be necessary.

2 Marketing intelligence gathering

It was stated earlier that for an individual or a company to be a success, information about the relevant industry must be collected in a systematic way. It was argued that the superior performer would know more about markets than any other participant. The marketing intelligence system is that part of the MIS where the environment is monitored on a 24/7/365 *continuous basis*, for any information that might have some bearing, present or future on the company's marketing performance.

Intelligence unit

The size of the intelligence unit collecting information is relatively important and will depend on the size of the organisation. It may be a whole department or just one person working part time. What is important is the motivating thrust. There should be an almost obsessional need to unearth and classify any snippet of information, no matter how small, that might relate to the company's particular industry, market and customer group and that can be used either immediately or stored for future use. As well as those that work directly for the intelligence unit, all staff will need to be motivated and trained in intelligence gathering techniques so that it becomes an essential part of the company culture. Because of the seemingly infinite amount of information available, skills needed should include the ability to sort the data wheat from the chaff.

In the large organisation, whole departments will spend all of their time scouring magazines, newspapers, the trade press, the world-wide-web and other relevant sources, pulling out articles on consumers and markets that might supply a vital insight into the workings of both the industry and the business, and so help improve performance. Trends in the marketplace can be analysed and compared over the months and years looking for significant changes that could effect environments and competitive advantage. Working in this way a database of information can be built up and then used to analyse and forecast movements in the immediate and wider environment.

3 Marketing research

The difference between marketing research and intelligence gathering is that marketing research is taken on for a special purpose while marketing intelligence gathering is something that goes on all of the time. Marketing research will be used where some kind of specific information seems to be unavailable from marketing intelligence sources. This might be information on target consumer reaction to new product/brand/packaging developments, buying intention on a new product launch, reaction to a new promotional campaign and loyalty levels to one store rather than another. The marketing research process is discussed in more detail below.

Market research expense

Care will be taken in setting up this kind or research because the costs can be extremely high. Depending on both the scale and the objectives of the marketing research it can be undertaken in-house or, as is much more likely, contracted out to one of the many large marketing research companies such as BMRB or Mintel that operate on both a national and global scale.

2.9 Marketing example — Market research cannot predict the future

Some market commentators argue that market research can never meaningfully predict future needs and wants because customers asked will not have the knowledge to really be able to comment. They go on to say that most people see the future as pretty much more of the same that is happening now, faster smaller computers, better cars, more TV channels, cheaper flights and so on. What they can't see however is the bigger picture, that is how life itself might change. Who would have predicted the Internet, DNA, genetic biology, the mobile phone, the lap-top computer, nanotechnology and so on. Perhaps a classic example is aircraft design. In the 1990s BA asked its business flyers what they would like and almost predictably were told that they would like more of the same, good food and wine, comfortable seats and personal TV and video screens. What most respondents failed to mention was things like data sockets for mobile phone and a power supply for PCs.

Questions

1 How might research predict future consumer trends for new products and services?

2 Discuss possible changes that might happen in retail.

Information from marketing research

Marketing research might be used for any of the following purposes:

- Analysing new market segments, at home and around the world.
- Identifying new markets and/or customers.
- Researching the existing market for a new product/service launch.
- Talking to consumers about future wants and needs and so on.

4 Information, storage and analysis

Information from all the sources identified above needs to be classified, stored, analysed and, where necessary, cross-referenced for ease of use. In the distant past this task would have been undertaken manually (probably through the use of a carded classification system) but now even the smallest of companies can have access to more sophisticated information technology methods.

Information technology (IT) and the use of computers enable large amounts of consumers' behavioural information to be stored in an information database, retrieved in moments, cross-informational comparisons made, cross-fertilisation exercises undertaken and statistical and computer models used to examine and test the scientific validity of research undertaken or assumptions formulated. One database can be compared with another so organisational spend might be evaluated against promotional activity or buyer behaviour compared to the level of personal contact made. **Networking** and the Internet will allow this to be done on both a national and an international scale.

Key point The value of internal information cannot be over-emphasised and its collection should be formalised, monitored and controlled and disseminated to the right people.

Database marketing

The increasing number of uses for IT has led to the development of so called '**database marketing**'. The amount of data now available has allowed organisations to build huge computer databases on their existing and potential customers and markets, full of detailed information that can then be used to accurately market products and services directly and personally to all end customers as and when needed. A whole range of customer characteristics can be entered into the database, products purchased over a period, buying cycle, benefits wanted and so on, and then cross-referenced so that customer profiles can be developed. This will enable the retailer or producer to identify potential customers and offer individual customised products and services, special offers and sales promotions, when and where needed, which exactly match customer needs.

2.10 Marketing example

The UK website insolvencyhelpline.co.uk surveyed 65 failed companies to try to discover the major reason for failure. Top of the list of reasons given was the failure to focus on a specific market because of poor research.

Question

1 Give reasons why it appears that some companies fail to undertake research or use the wrong research.

Data warehousing and data mining

Data warehousing allows large amounts of customer information to be collected, classified, analysed and held for current and future use. **Data mining** is a process of discovering previously unknown information from the data in a data warehouse, by performing clever searches. Using and exploring the company database looking for potential customer segments where more/new products and services might be marketed. Ever more sophisticated software programs can be used to discover more and more possible group and individual buying patterns within the database.

Database and customer relationship marketing

Building on the concept of relationship marketing discussed above the enhanced capability offered by database marketing enables the retailer and to a lesser extent the brand manufacturer to develop an ever-closer interactive relationship with existing or past customers on a *long-term continuous* basis. The development of IT capabilities has enabled constant, personalised, interactive contact in the form of direct mail, email, telephone calls and personal contact at the checkout to be built across millions of consumers.

Table 2.4 **If used properly database and relationship marketing should offer the retailer the following benefits**

At the strategic level

- Understand and predict customer needs
- Build valued and long-term customer relationships
- Identify heavy and light users and manage consumer profitability
- Plan, stock and merchandise more effectively
- Improve branding and customer loyalty
- Market, sell and constantly upgrade across the whole product portfolio

At the tactical level

- Provide better customer service across all functions
- Cross-sell products more effectively
- Improve sales and customer contact staff customer service
- Simplify marketing and sales processes
- Discover new customers
- Increase customer revenues

Figure 2.8

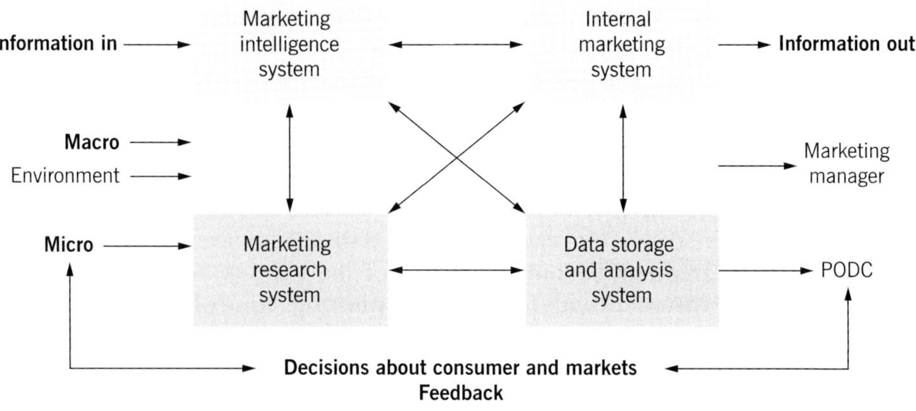

The marketing information system (MIS)

Secondary and primary information

There are two distinct types of research, secondary and primary research and the marketing and consumer researcher will probably use a combination of the two. We will look at each in turn beginning with secondary research.

Table 2.5 The role of the marketing manager

For simplicity and ease of understanding the role of the marketing manager can be identified under the acronym PODC

P Planning and forecasting – sales and the marketing and sales effort.

O Organising and co-ordinating – people and departments and partners.

D Directing (all the 'people things') – leading, communicating, motivating, empowering, decision-making.

C Control, feedback, monitoring and evaluating – to see what happens.

Secondary research

Secondary research concerns consumer information that has already been collected by others (hence also sometimes known as 'second-hand' research) and is available from many sources and in a variety of forms as long as the marketer knows where to look.

Internal sources of information

The first place to go for information will be within the organisation itself. This might be within one company or, if the company is global, from many divisions around the world. If there is an MIS, it is here that the first approach should be made. There might well be an Intranet (an internal Internet system) or an Extranet (an external private Internet system available only to a selective group of companies) online system in operation and again this resource should be the first port of call. The task for internal providers is making the right information immediately available when wanted in a form that matches the requirements of the internal customer. This task has sometimes turned out to be something of a problem because of the lack of presentation skills shown by the computer technicians who will have put together the computer programs. There should be a systemised approach to the collection, classification and dissemination of information based on the clearly agreed and identified needs of the various internal and partnering information consumers with feedback, monitoring, control and evaluation factors built in.

External sources of information

These include:

Government

Professional/trade associations

Commercial information gatherers

Government sources of consumer information

All countries operating in modern industrial markets will offer organisations access to information about the workings of government departments as well as access to specially collected information that might help the individual company in the more effective running of its business. This will include information on political, social and economic matters on a national and global level at both the **macro** and **micro environmental** level. As discussed in Chapter 1 most power brokers are now committed to the economic paradigm of the free market and politicians generally accept the need for easy access to all types of information, including of course the consumer, if businesses are to compete successfully on world markets.

The Office of National Statistics (ONS) (www.statistics.gov.uk) The **ONS** is an independent UK government department in its own right (supposedly free of government interference) and similar departments will exist in some way or another in all countries. Most of the information is collected for Government use but retailers and producers can purchase much of the information for commercial use.

Data produced by the Office of National Statistics Data produced by the ONS is enormous covering many areas of social, economic and business activity at both a macro and micro level include the following:

- Economic data, product data, general business statistics.
- Labour markets, employment and unemployment statistics.
- Gross domestic product (GDP) estimates on the movement of goods and services in the UK.
- Retail sales statistics, general household statistics, The Retail Price Index (RPI), the measure of inflation used to indicate movements and changes in consumer prices.
- Social and lifestyle changes.
- Demographic changes, movements, births, deaths and marriages.

The Government Statistical Service (www.statistics.gov.uk) The UK Government Statistical Service (GSS) is the main publisher of official business statistics in the UK. Most industrialised countries will have similar services and, as discussed in Chapter 1, there is movement to standardise procedures and publications across all government statistics so that methods can be harmonised and realistic comparisons made.

2.2 General example — Always scepticism about the use of statistics

The UK Commons Public Accounts Committee (PAC) questioned the 'accuracy' of results from the Office of National Statistics 2001 Census survey after it claimed the population of England and Wales was 900,000 lower than previously thought. The national census was also branded a wasteful and costly exercise by an influential group of MPs.

Professional/trade associations

Trade associations regularly issue market and consumer statistics and these are available on request. These cover most of the consumer-related industries including all areas of retail, leisure, tourism and electrical and domestic appliances. Examples include the British Retail Consortium (www.brc.org.uk), British Franchise Association (www.british-franchise.org) and the US Food Marketing Institute (www.fmi.org).

Commercial information gatherers

There are also many commercial research publishers offering a whole raft of consumer information both nationally and internationally. This might be in the form of a one-off research project or a continuous research programme that looks at markets, customers and competition in a particular industry. Much of this can be downloaded to the customer by the agency on a daily basis. Examples of agencies include: Kantar Group (UK) which owns Research International, Millward Brown, BMRB, Goldfarb, Kantar Media Research, IMRB (India) (www.kantar.com) and TN (Taylor Nelson) Sofres (UK), which has the quantitative research contract with Broadcasting Audience Research Board (BARB) with 4425 modems on TVs in UK households measuring TV viewing figures (www.tnsofres.com).

2.11 Marketing example ACNielsen research

ACNielsen's principal clients are manufacturers, retailers and brokers in the global consumer packaged goods industry. They also work with clients in a wide range of consumer product and service businesses, such as retail audits, financial services and the automotive industry. With over 9000 clients worldwide they offer information on such areas as: marketing, marketing research, product development, product management, sales, trade relations, retail purchasing, merchandising and space planning and category management. They answer such questions as: What is happening in the market? Why is it happening? What is likely to happen next? What is the best route for growth?

Question

1 Identify and discuss and evaluate the role that market research companies play in understanding consumer and organisation behaviour around the world.

Data protection

Many countries have enforced certain legal obligations with regard to the holding of information on individual consumers. This means that all business organisations must now follow a strict code of conduct with regard to the collecting, storing analysing and disclosing of information. Failure to conform can lead to prosecution and compensation awards (www.dataprotection.gov.uk).

The Information Commissioner (UK)

The **Information Commissioner** enforces and oversees the Data Protection Act 1998 and the Freedom of Information Act 2000. In the UK the Commissioner has a range of duties including the promotion of good information handling. Consumers can complain if retailers fail to make personal information available (www.dataprotection.gov.uk/commissioner).

The Statistics Commissioner (UK)

The Independent Statistics Commission was set up in response to concerns expressed by some about the independence and use of government statistics, especially by politicians. He or she has the responsibility to help ensure National Statistics are trustworthy and responsive to public needs (www.statscom.org.uk).

Difference between quantitative and qualitative research

In trying to understand consumer behaviour two basic approaches have evolved, quantitative and qualitative research.

Quantitative data

Quantitative research used to be the main method used by the large research companies because it uses numbers, logic, statistics and models and operates with large numbers of respondents. It attempts to use an objective scientific approach in the collection and analysis of data.

Qualitative data

However, as researching and understanding consumer behaviour became more complex, more subtle research methods were wanted and qualitative research was born. Researchers here use such techniques as: open-ended interviews and discussions, words, images, opinions, art, story telling, music and colours (right-brain-divergent reasoning). They operate with small numbers of people and are primarily concerned with getting a subjective 'feel' for the research topic, not a numerical, statistically

Table 2.6 Pros and cons of quantitative and qualitative research

- Quantitative methods will give limited information using only numbers and statistics but will be more scientific.
- Quantitative research can be fed into the computer and analysed objectively.
- Qualitative research will give more detailed information on respondent opinion, attitudes and beliefs but is considered less scientific.
- Qualitative research must be subjectively interpreted by experts and so bias could happen.

predictable (quantitative) measure. Both quantitative and qualitative research information will be available from secondary research sources on almost any subject under the sun. These two approaches are also used extensively in primary research and this is discussed in detail below.

Primary research

Despite the amount of secondary research information available there will always be circumstances where information that is needed is not available. When this is the case the company will have to instigate primary research. Primary research is new research undertaken by an organisation to help solve a problem that existing information cannot solve. It should never be undertaken lightly because of the possible high cost involved.

Consumer primary research can be broken down into three basic types:

1 Experiments
2 Observation
3 Surveys

1 Experimental research

Experimental research is widely used across a whole range of different markets from food, drink and cars to media, leisure and entertainment. Although different size companies might use this type of research it can be extremely costly, especially if undertaken by a research agency (perhaps £50,000 to £100,000 depending on the task) so it tends to be used by the largest companies, especially those operating in the FMCG market such as Sara Lee, P&G, Unilever and Nestlé to name but a few.

When performing experimental research the researcher tries to copy as closely as possible quantitative, experimental methods used in the natural sciences (and described in Chapter 1). Attempts are made to control and manipulate elements of the research environment to measure the impact of each variable. For example, a group of test subjects (who are consumers meeting certain criteria, such as frequent users of the particular product or service in question) is shown several television commercials, and after each one the group is asked questions designed to measure the likelihood that they'll purchase the product advertised.

Experimental research might be used to test the following:

- Consumer reaction to new products in trial and repeat-purchase research.
- Effectiveness of own and/or the competitor's advertising.
- How prices variation might affect the sales of a product.
- The effect of different package designs on sales.
- Taste tests, both open and blind.

Experimental research can be further divided into two groups:

- Laboratory studies
- Field research

Laboratory studies

Here there is an attempt to control virtually all variables other than the one being tested, and testing is generally done on the premises of the research company. However, it can take place at the client company, in a shopping mall or in a hotel. A representative sample belonging to the relevant target market might be asked to look at adverts, examine packaging and try out product brands. **Blind tasting tests** are often used with the control group knowing the brand (e.g. food, sweets, wine) being tasted and the experimental group not knowing. The results are then compared.

Laboratory tests are generally based upon a minimum of 100 to 300 test-respondents and can be very expensive, although this must be measured alongside the savings made against the launch of an unsatisfactory marketing campaign. In some cases it might be combined with field studies and the participants might take the product home to use. The researcher would then follow up with more questions on such things as likeability, how it compares with the competition, and repurchasing intentions.

2.12 Marketing example — The purchase laboratory

Researchers will even construct artificial retail settings for respondents to shop in. Using a purchase laboratory approach subjects are given money, script, or credit to purchase products in a simulated store. Researchers modify one variable at a time (for example, price, packaging, shelf location, size, or competitors' offerings) and determine what effect that has on sales volume. Internet based purchase labs (called virtual purchase labs) are now becoming more common.

2.13 Marketing example — Neuromarketing

Scientists working with marketing managers in the USA have started to adopt MRI (magnetic resonance imaging) scanners to probe into the mind of the shopper so as to track the deepest desires of consumers and adapt their advertising and sales promotions accordingly (2002). **MRI and PET scanners** were originally developed for medical use, diagnosing strokes, discovering tumours and identifying brain regions linked with movement or emotion. Now volunteers are put into the scanners to find out what happens to areas of their brain when pictures of consumer goods are shown. Researchers at the Brighthouse Institute of Thought Sciences at the Emory University Hospital in Atlanta, Georgia found that when volunteers say they 'truly love' something, the medial prefrontal cortex (linked to thinking) lights up on the scans. So if marketers can find what stimulates the medial prefrontal cortex they may have the basis of a successful branding and advertising campaign. However many question the validity (as well as the ethics) of the research and the jury is still out.

Smirnoff vodka – a blind taste test.
Source: Creative club/Smirnoff

Laboratory or field research

The researcher can further decide whether the experiment should take place in a laboratory or in the field, i.e. the 'natural' setting as opposed to an 'artificial' one. Laboratory research allows the researcher to control and/or eliminate as many intervening variables as possible. For example, the restaurant décor could possibly influence a response to a taste test, but a neutral setting, i.e. undertaking the taste test in a room in the research agency, would be seen as eliminating this extraneous variable.

2.14 Marketing example **Test marketing**

Marketing testing is done in the 'real marketplace' by test marketing the introduction of a new product (or advertising, sales promotions, sales push etc.) in a small but representative region of the country or in a few locations to see whether consumers will buy it. If successful a full countrywide launch can then take place. However, this is getting more difficult for large-scale testing as the big supermarkets, for example, are loath to give shelf-space as it disrupts their computer-operated range planning and stocking. If permission is given then the retailer will probably demand extra payment.

The pros and cons of laboratory or field research

For large and medium-sized companies, the best test of a product may often be actual market conditions and so some manufacturers go for a full product launch roll-out (based on solid research) which can be pulled if success seems not to be coming. Experts sometimes question how representative the test region might be when compared to the rest of the country, as there can be difficulties in controlling unwanted environmental influences as well as localised consumer behaviour and competition in these smaller markets. Even small businesses that cannot afford to hire outside consultants and researchers to provide an extensive product development programme can conduct its own 'in-house' controlled testing, or testing of new products or services with friendly cooperative selected stores. It will generate statistical sales information.

2 Observation

Individuals are not always able to clearly articulate their needs verbally and will often act differently to how they say they will behave. This is why observing consumer behaviour is often used as the favoured type of research. **Observation research** can be conducted in the customer's own home, out shopping (as they move around supermarkets etc.), in restaurants, at leisure and moving past adverts and outdoor billboards, etc. It can be a long- or short-term study depending on objectives and available resources. Observing consumer behaviour instead of asking for responses to set questions can take place by researchers personally observing, **CCTV** cameras, video and photo-cameras as well as mechanical devices for counting. The results can then be analysed by experts later.

Researchers can observe covertly (without the knowledge of the consumer), overtly (with the knowledge of the consumers) or as a participant. All these approaches might however cause problems.

Table 2.7 Advantages and disadvantages of observational research

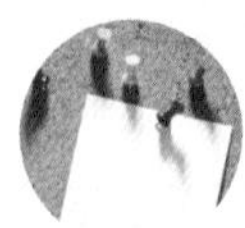

Advantages

- It measures behaviour directly, not reports of behaviour or intentions which can sometimes conflict.
- Flexible and relatively inexpensive.
- Can be used in both quantitative and qualitative studies depending on research design.

Disadvantage

- It is limited to behavioural variables and so cannot take into account consumers thoughts and feelings.
- It cannot usually be generalised from one situation to another.
- Covert observation could have ethical, or even legal, ramifications, overt observation can cause consumers to modify their behaviour and researcher participation can affect objectivity.

Many different observational methods used

There seems to be no end to the different observation type methods (mostly qualitative) used by researchers in the endless drive for greater consumer understanding. These include such methods as counting numbers of people, observing and tracking groups and individuals in the home, streets, work, at leisure, eating out and in shops as well as individual and small group interviews and psychoanalysis using therapy, handwriting and drawing. These are outlined and briefly discussed below.

Technology use

Ubiquitous technology has been utilised, as far as the law will allow, in continuously improving the process, so that our movements can be known and analysed by public and private organisations alike, restricted only by public opinion that is concerned with civil and human rights issues, and laws and rules and regulations that governments might care to introduce. Some of the methods discussed are quantitative and some qualitative.

Radio frequency identification (RFID) tags

Probably one of the most exciting, and at the same time frightening developments in the use of technology in monitoring human behaviour, is the use of **RFID tags**. These are 'silicon chip' transponders that are electronically programmed with unique information that can be read by a so-called transceiver. Antennas act as conduits between the tag and the transceiver, which controls the system's data acquisition and communication. The silicon chip transponder tags, filled with information come in a variety of sizes and can be built into almost anything including: credit (smart) cards; packaged grocery products; clothing; electrical products such as TV and washing machines, mobile phones; animals and even humans (under the skin). Antennas are available in a variety of shapes and sizes and they can be built anyplace where tag information might need to be tracked. This might be a door-frame, on billboards, on lampposts etc. to receive tag data from persons or things passing by the shop, through the door, or mounted on a tollbooth to monitor traffic passing by on to a motorway. In this way people and products can be programmed with almost unlimited amounts of information (some interactive) and then accessed and monitored wherever they might be.

Closed circuit TV cameras (CCTV)

CCTV cameras are now almost everywhere watching and monitoring everything that we do in all aspects of human behaviour. In high streets, shopping malls, retail centres, sports and leisure centres, on the highway, in museums and theatres, airports, bus parks and railway stations, in fact any place where people might congregate. We are watched and can be traced almost from the moment we enter a built-up area to the moment we leave.

Consumer shadowing

Competitive intensity pushes organisations to try to get ever closer to the reality of changing lifestyles, behaviour and attitudes and understanding contemporary issues that reflect the every day life of the average consumer. **Consumer shadowing** is a technique where a researcher will follow an individual, usually a mother, around all day (with their permission of course), starting off in the kitchen, going out shopping and then returning back to the home as the groceries are unpacked and put away. During this time behaviour can be observed and questions asked about the product brands selected in the supermarket and used in the home. This will all be analysed afterwards.

Tracking and measuring eye movements

Attitudes can also be measured through the use of physiological techniques. This includes measuring levels of eye pupil dilation (Hess 1965), heart rate (Westie and Defleur 1959) and skin resistance (Rankin and Campbell 1955) in response to relative stimuli.

Watching, evaluating and analysing consumer eye movement and pupil dilation (Hess 1965) for impact and appeal, using pupil meters, in response to marketing stimuli such as product, brand, packaging, shelf position, print or advertising images is another way of attempting to measure levels of interest and both qualitative (observation and interpretations) and quantitative (video and image analysis technology measuring size, time and speed of movement) methods can be used. It is a behavioural measure that documents what people actually see, as opposed to what they say or claim. It can take place in laboratory or field research conditions.

2.15 Marketing example **Eye tracking**

A major food brand decided to change its trademark purple packaging to a crisp white design. The company went through the usual route of bringing in focus groups to do qualitative tests and they absolutely loved it – it was a winning design. When the **eye-tracking** test was conducted, however, the crisp white packaging that everyone liked so much was completely lost against the competitors when placed on the supermarket shelf.

Table 2.8 **Observational information about consumers that can be discovered will include the following**

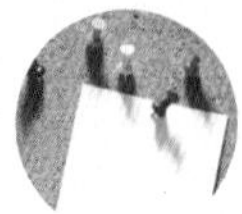

Observation in the car, car park and shop using cameras will highlight:

- Eye movement and adverts noticed.
- Parking and leaving problems in the car park.
- Socio-economic status of shoppers.
- Patterns on how the shopper enters and moves around the store.
- Eye and body movement when looking at products, packaging, sales promotions on the shelves.
- Time taken in product selection.

Observation in the home using cameras will highlight:

- How difficult it might be opening packaging.
- Problems putting together/operating product.
- Whether instructions are read, and conferring between household members.
- If company service department is contacted or not and if confusion arises.

Electronic point of purchase checkout scanners (EPOS)

We discussed earlier the EPOS the system that scans the products and records purchase behaviour (with the power to take the money straight out of our bank account if we wish) as customers move through the checkout. It is linked to a stocking and re-ordering process so that the store need never be out of stock. The technology is being constantly upgraded and linked to customer relationship loyalty management programmes (loyalty cards provide names and addresses) so that customised products can be offered in the store or linked directly to individual consumer behavioural needs.

Psychogalvanometer

A psycho**galvanometer** is an instrument that measures the skin response that accompanies the subject's interest or arousal. It measures galvanic, that is electrical conductivity, levels of the subject's skin in response to video or print adverts, pictures, film, packaging etc. (Rankin and Campbell 1955). There are machines that can measure heart rate responses in a similar way (Westie and Defleur 1959).

Voice pitch meters

Voice pitch meters are used in a similar way to the above but are linked to the voice and sound and in this way measure emotional reactions (including lying) to presented marketing stimuli.

Tracking television station watching

TV viewing statistics are obtained in two ways. One is by the use of surveys, where a sample number of viewers is asked about viewing behaviour. The other is by estimates obtained from a panel of television-owning households representing the viewing behaviour of all households. Small computer boxes, 'peoplemeters', are linked to every TV in the sample and every household member will press a designated button on a hand-held modem when they start and when they stop viewing. The TV is linked to the main computer at the head office of the research company and this allows market researchers to study television (and video) viewing habits on a minute-to-minute basis, seeing at exactly what moment a viewer changes channels or turns off their TV. The same system is used across Europe and the USA. The Broadcasters' Audience Research Board (BARB) is responsible for providing estimates of the households watching television in the UK at any one time. Similar methods are used for radio and the Internet.

Retail audits

Other ways used to track consumer purchasing behaviour is through the use of ▶ **retail audits** (examining the movement of stock through the store). It can be used to determine such things as the quality of service in stores, product selection and shelf space usage.

Trace analysis

Behaviour trace analysis studies involve finding things people leave behind and interpreting what they mean. It can include the following:

Credit card records Credit, debit, bank account history details hold an enormous amount of behavioural information on such things as purchasing preferences, eating habits, working and hobby practices and lifestyle.

Computer cookie (web bugs) records Web bugs are used as a tool for tracking Internet behaviour and where individual users go on the web and what they view. This way a profile of an anonymous user can be created over time, eventually providing rich detail about that user's preferences and interests. They can also be used to link web-surfing history with email. Advertisers can use this data to target advertising banners and information specifically to that user.

▶ **Garbology** Sounds pretty awful really but **garbology** is a type of research that consists of rummaging through people's garbage for evidence of purchase patterns, looking for such things as food preferences, waste behaviour and levels and types of alcohol consumption. It can also involve such things as detecting store traffic patterns by observing the long-term wear or dirt on the floor and tracks that people make in moving around pedestrian areas and utilising short cuts across lawns and gardens.

> **Key point** Care should be taken as much of the kind of research discussed above is dependent on individual's permission. If this is not obtained, researchers could fall foul of information laws as well as company and research association codes of conduct.

Content analysis

Researchers can become highly skilled at observing and analysing the content of magazines, television broadcasts, radio broadcasts, newspapers, articles, programmes, or advertisements etc., for evidence of future behavioural trends, and changes such as what might be the autumn fashion colours, or eating and drinking trends.

Narrative enquiry

Narrative inquiry is the process of gathering information for the purpose of research through story-telling. For example the researcher might live with a family for a time (a week, month or longer) and then write a narrative of the experience. Connelly and Clandinin (1990: 2–14) write that, 'humans are storytelling organisms who, individually and collectively, lead storied lives. Thus, the study of narrative is the study of the ways humans experience the world.' In other words, people's lives consist of stories that can then be analysed by a behavioural expert. Field notes, interviews, journals, letters, autobiographies, and orally told stories are all methods of narrative inquiry.

Focus groups and interviews

Traditionally, the most favoured method in qualitative research consists of focus groups and individual interviews. Focus groups can be thought of as 'group interviews' where a number of consumers in the target market (perhaps eight to twelve) are brought together in a room at the research building or in a hotel, presented with an idea, concept, or a prototype product, and asked to discuss their opinions with each other facilitated by a moderator. The whole process might be observed through a two-way mirror, videoed or taped and then analysed afterwards.

They are sometimes offered refreshment, perhaps a glass of wine or two, so that inhibitions will be reduced, perhaps emotions aroused, and participants' opinions therefore be nearer real feelings than if conventional survey methods were used.

A focus group in action.

Coloured drawings, cartoons and handwriting

Many of the techniques now used in qualitative research have been borrowed from the psychology and psychoanalysis profession. In an attempt to get into an individual's subconscious (where it is believed that true reality underpinning many of the decisions we might make might lie) group participants are given coloured pencils and crayons and asked to draw and colour patterns that might respond to their thoughts about a particular issue, concept, organisation or brand. Similarly they can be given a series of cartoons and asked to fill in the gaps that might be missing or asked to complete picture stories using their own words and drawings. Examining handwriting has for decades been another method used in the attempt to understand behaviour. An expert then attempts to psychoanalyse the results. In this way it is hoped to get behind the subconscious defence mechanisms and find out personality and what it is that people really think.

2.16 Marketing example | Rorschach inkblot test

There seems to be no end to the tests that are used in this form of qualitative research. In the **Rorschach inkblot test** a subject is given a piece of paper with a design print that looks like a giant inkblot. They are then asked to interpret and say what it is they 'see' in the pattern. Different people see different things. Those who believe in the efficacy of such tests think that they are a way of getting into the deepest recesses of the subject's psyche or subconscious mind. Those who give such tests believe themselves to be experts at interpreting their subject's interpretations.

Rorschach inkblot test.

Individual interviews

There are times when researchers may feel that talking one-to-one or in more intimate and sympathetic surroundings could yield more worthwhile results. These interviews would need to be carried out by a professional (perhaps with psychology training) and could be structured, semi-structured or completely unstructured.

3 Surveys

The use of the consumer survey questionnaire is probably the method most recognised by the professional and layperson alike. The image of the person in the high street, holding a clipboard and stopping passers-by is ubiquitous. It is the traditional marketing research method adopted and it can be used both on a grand scale with interviews involving hundreds and thousands of individuals taking place continuously or on a much smaller scale involving perhaps a few dozen people. Both governments and commercial organisations seek to get information on such things as living standards, leisure pursuits, health, retail store usage and satisfaction, buying intentions and so on. It can be used in both quantitative and qualitative surveys.

Surveys can be undertaken by:

- Person–person
- Home telephone
- Mobile phone
- Postal
- Internet
- TV

Quantitative surveys

Quantitative surveys will use closed ended, multiple-choice, levels of satisfaction or semantic differential-type questions that can be codified and then administered to a large stratified or random representative sample (e.g. a thousand respondents). The emphasis is on scientific accuracy using such things as algorithms, confidence levels and significant tests in an attempt to mathematically select a large enough sample of respondents that is as near as possible totally representative of the population as a whole. It is one of the main methods that comes closest to following scientific methods used in the physical sciences discussed earlier.

The ubiquitous personal interviewer. *Source*: Simon Wright

Qualitative surveys

Because closed ended, quantitative surveys lack the ability to measure the complexity of consumer behaviour, qualitative open-ended surveys are sometimes used. These allow respondents to give opinions and beliefs and demonstrate feelings and attitudes. Although capable of obtaining richer more detailed information on beliefs and attitudes, this type of survey will be much smaller than the survey discussed above (maybe even a few dozen people). The sample used will therefore not be a representative sample and the results will have to be interpreted in a subjective manner. Results obtained in this way can then be used as the basis for a larger, quantitative questionnaire survey.

2.17 Marketing example — Intercept interviews

Short, intercept or survey exit interviews are often used to measure levels of visitor satisfaction regarding shopping malls, **regional shopping centres**, factory villages, amusement parks, museums, festivals and other attractions. They can also be used to gauge the likelihood of consumers using a new location or new brands.

Marketing research process

As outlined above marketing research is research undertaken for a special purpose and the following factors need to be considered when using it to gather information.

Clear marketing objectives

The beginning of the marketing research process and arguably the most important part is to clearly identify what consumer and market information is needed. This may sound simple but often this part of the process is the most difficult, frequently characterised by confusion and ambiguity. If the real problem is not identified at the very beginning, the whole process will be distorted.

2.3 General example — Study failure as well as success

If you want to learn the secrets of success, it seems perfectly reasonable to study successful people and organisations. But the research of Jerker Denrell, an assistant professor of organisational behaviour at the Stanford Graduate School of Business, suggests that studying successes without also looking at failures tends to create a misleading, if not entirely wrong, picture of what it takes to succeed. He goes on to argue that information and research on successful companies is relatively easy to come by when compared with information on why companies fail. He argues that this information is just as important if we are to learn from our mistakes and the full picture is to be understood.

Question

1 Using examples of retailers show how failure in some way can be used to inform future activities.

Secondary and/or primary research

Secondary research sources should be investigated first to see whether any consumer information exists that could be of use in solving the identified problem. Most research projects will include some background secondary research to establish a framework for primary research for example identifying market size or customer numbers.

Setting a budget

A budget must be set indicating overall and intermediary costs. The method used for budget allocation should ideally be according to the objectives and task that need to be undertaken. It's axiomatic that no formal research should be undertaken if the cost of the research outweighs its end value.

Sampling frame

Rarely if ever will a company need information from everybody in the whole population, so most consumer research will be aimed at a selected target market. However it would be hideously expensive, impractical and unnecessary to interview everybody in this market so a **representative sample** is used. What is important is the sample used, known as the sampling frame, is as near a representation of the whole market, in terms of social class, gender, age, family life cycle, lifestyle etc., as is humanly possible (a metaphor might be the baking of a cake, as long as it is mixed properly tasting a small piece will give information on the taste of the whole).

Collection methods

The objectives of the market research will be determined by the overall objectives and the amount of money available. We have discussed earlier the use of primary and secondary research and it is very likely that this will be the first issue to be addressed. If primary research were to be used, both quantitative and qualitative methods would have to be considered. Methods adopted would then be chosen from the many discussed above.

Presentation of results

Information gathered will need to be interpreted and then presented to the commissioning organisation in as simple a way as possible.

Figure 2.9

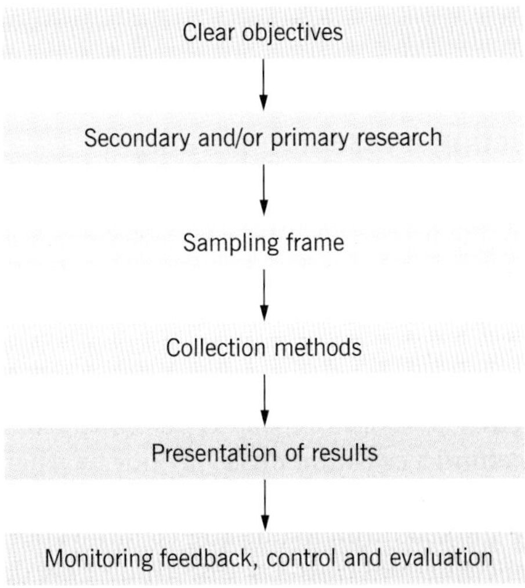

The market research process

Monitoring, feedback, control and evaluation

As with all planning, the control mechanism, consisting of the allocation of responsibilities and feedback reports, should be built in to monitor, regulate and keep on course the implementation of the whole market research programme. The overall results can then be measured against the objectives to ascertain levels of success or failure.

Scientific rigour in the collection of behavioural information

In Chapter 1 we discussed and compared the natural sciences and the social and behavioural sciences, pointing out and evaluating the differences. All research, no matter how undertaken, is looking for some kind of truth, facts about what exists, what happens in the world and why. Care, however, was cautioned when collecting information on behaviour because of the nature of humans and the differences when compared with collecting information about the physical world. Wrong or misleading information about customers, markets and human behaviour could cause a company to make misguided decisions that could turn out to be, at best very expensive and at worst so disastrous that they could put the company out of business. This puts huge demands on organisations, groups and individuals to be exceedingly careful and methodical about the approaches taken and the methods used when undertaking research of any kind.

Key point Wrong or misleading information can cause assumptions to be made about markets and consumer behaviour that could have a devastating affect on market decisions. Ultimately all information must be interpreted by managers and, in light of experience (and intuition), used as a guide to decision making not as a substitute.

Selecting a research paradigm

A research **paradigm** is about the different beliefs held about knowledge and how we might understand that knowledge. Academics and other commentators have been constantly arguing, over many hundreds of years, about the best way to study, report and understand such things as knowledge, learning, facts, values, beliefs, myths and human behaviour. It is a search in some way for where the 'truth' about human existence, and the world around us, might be found if indeed even this kind of discovery is possible. Can we, for example, deduce the real meaning behind a consumer's behaviour by what they say and don't say by asking closed end, yes and no type questions or must we also use open-ended questions for a more detailed understanding of motivations, beliefs and attitudes. We now know that people will also say one thing and do another, so maybe we must observe behaviour rather than just ask questions. These and other problems lead us to identify two basic research paradigms or approaches:

1 Positivistic
2 Phenomenological or interpretative paradigm.

1 The positivistic paradigm

In simple terms there are those who argue that the only possible way to understand people and their behaviour is by the use of a *positivistic paradigm of social science*. This approaches argues for objective **empirical** (using the senses) observation of the relevant consumer behaviour and the collection and use of large samples of quantifiable data that can be measured and then the results tested and re-measured by others using mathematical models and statistical analysis. It tries to operate as near the scientific approach used in the natural sciences as possible looking for causal, predictive laws.

Positivistic research methods will include the following:

- Experiments where variables can be controlled
- Quasi experiments
- Surveys using closed end type questions that can be codified (yes or no, multiple choice, satisfaction levels, semantic differential)
- Passive observation so as not to influence the results
- Content analysis – scientifically collected information (statistics) in literature, journals, books etc.

2 Phenomenological or interpretative paradigm (looking for meaning)

Others argue that there is too much emphasis on objective science and rationality and this doesn't take into account people's *feelings* and the *meanings* they put on to their actions that might be different in some way to behaviour observed. The interpretative paradigm of social research uses small samples and takes a subjective, qualitative perspective. It assumes that social reality is only partly observable as it also consists of beliefs, attitudes and motivations beyond the observable facts. This might be because the individual or group behaviour might be driven by reasons unknown, unavailable or not immediately obvious to the observer or needs, wants and desires that are not easily articulated by the respondent.

Methods used here include:

- Case study – observing, working or living with others over time
- Small sample studied over time (longitudinal studies)
- Ethnography – the study of ethnic group behaviour
- Focus/discussion groups
- One-to-one and group interviews
- Psychological techniques – experts interpreting respondent drawings, handwriting, innermost thoughts etc.
- Open-ended questionnaires – seeking out opinion, beliefs and attitudes

- Participant observation
- Text analysis: fiction, non-fiction and historical

Key point **Positivism** will tell us how many customers like, dislike or are neutral about shopping e.g. 60 per cent out of a sample of 1,000 people asked. On the other hand the interpretive approach will attempt to tell us the many different reasons (both conscious and subconscious) why people adopt the beliefs they have.

Post positivism – triangulation, the middle approach

In very simple terms a positivistic approach to research tries to follow the methods used in the natural sciences and argues that all investigation must be as objective as possible. This can only come about through observation (or the other senses where relevant) and measurement involving the constant collection of statistical data and reasoned analysis. Other methods are subjective and open to bias. On the other hand those adopting a **phenomenological or interpretative** approach argue that this crucially misses the workings of the mind and people's inner most thoughts and desires as these can't be observed and measured in the same way. Most commentators now take a post-positivistic middle view. They accept that there must be a rigorous scientific quantitative approach taken wherever possible but accept that there must also be room for respondent mind responses that cannot be measured in the same way.

Key point Positivism insists on measurable, observable data. Phenomenology argues for an understanding of the mind and people's emotions, feelings and beliefs. Triangulation is using a combination.

Strategic approaches to research projects

Research can be broken down into four basic types. In practice, however, there is bound to be overlapping and this should not cause any concern.

1. Exploratory research
2. Descriptive research
3. Explanatory research
4. Evaluative research

1 Exploratory research

As the term suggests, **exploratory research** is the initial research that will be undertaken if the problem has not yet been clearly defined and there is uncertainty about the exact customer behavioural activity that needs to be investigated. So it can be the starting point that enables the marketer, researcher or student to look further into a problem, without necessarily having any pre-conceived expectation, and so come up with clearer research objectives or, in some cases, even to formulate clearer assumptions that can be tested by other types of research discussed below. In more formal terms, once objectives have been established, it can help determine the best research approach, design and data-collection methods to use.

2.18 Marketing example

Inexpensive exploratory research approaches are often used to test basic concepts before more money is spent on development. Sample consumers are provided either with a written concept, e.g. on the use of loyalty cards, a cartoon storyboard, e.g. on an adventure holiday, or a prototype for a new, revised or repositioned product, e.g. a mobile phone upgrade, and asked to comment. If the result seems favourable, then further more conclusive research can be undertaken before deciding on a market launch.

Research design methods – informal or formal

Exploratory research can be quite informal as the purpose is to throw more light upon a subject of interest. An examination of secondary sources, current literature and archive material (libraries, Internet etc.) would probably be the best and most cost effective place to begin followed by inexpensive primary research using qualitative methods, such as observations or discussions with consumers, retailers, marketers, employees and so on. Even simple observation of consumer behaviour can be enlightening. Although beliefs are bound to harden in one way or another, sweeping generalisations and conclusions should be avoided at this stage because of the looseness of the approach. As the objectives begin to tighten up, more formal approaches can be used through in-depth interviews, focus groups, projective methods, case studies, pilot studies and so on. It can throw up interesting areas for others to investigate further.

2 Descriptive research

When the research objectives have been established the next stage might be to use ▶ some kind of **descriptive research**. This approach is taken so as to provide data about the problem being studied. This might be the number and characteristics of consumers in any given 'population' or 'universe' studied or the average or number of times something occurs as well as the intervening variables that might impinge in some way on the situation being researched. This lends itself to different levels of statistical analysis depending on the quality of the data collected. Descriptive research is used when the objective is to provide a systematic description that is as factual and accurate as possible. However, it can only describe the 'who, what, when, where and how' of a situation and not cause and effect.

Research design methods

Both secondary and primary research can be used, secondary research to get at relevant information such as numbers, figures and statistics and primary search to obtain more up-to-date and relevant information. The two most commonly used methods in the use of primary descriptive research design are observation, surveys and interviews.

2.19 Marketing example

It can be used in marketing, perhaps to describe numbers and types of consumers that use a particular supermarket, when is the most/least popular time, how shoppers move around the store and pick products off the shelves and what products are purchased.

3 Explanatory or causal research

The highest stage in the use of research methods will be **explanatory** or **causal research**. This seeks to understand the nature, relationship and the mechanism between one or more variables and so tries to identify causes or effects of social phenomena. From this we can seek to predict what might happen in the future.

Research design methods

The two most used methods here are experimentation and simulation. The experimentation method calls for the researcher to manipulate a specific independent variable in the experimentation group in order to determine what effect this manipulation would have on other dependent variables, while leaving a control group operating under normal circumstances.

2.20 Marketing example — Mail shot comparisons

Direct marketers will often compare the success of one form of direct mail offer with another. By altering the design of the mail shot to an experimental group of customers, perhaps in terms of promotional offer and/or content used, while maintaining the same design with the control group the greater or less response success rates can then be measured.

Simulation consumer modelling in marketing

Another way of establishing causality between variables is through the use of simulation. Using sophisticated software programs, computers can be used to simulate or imitate a real-life situation. By changing one variable in the equation, it is possible to determine the effect on the other variables in the equation. It is a quantitative research technique.

2.21 Marketing example — Simulation models in marketing

Computer software models can be set up simulating a company's particular market incorporating past, current and projected sales figures. Marketing mix variables such as pricing, distribution and sales promotions are then manipulated, e.g. lowering price, allowing for more distribution, increasing promotional spend etc., and then what affect this might have on consumer spending and sales figures is seen.

4 Evaluative research

The purpose here is to try to understand whether particular consumer policies and programmes help to alleviate a problem or are meeting the goals that have been set. This can be a one-off or a constant research programme. Increasingly, because of competition and changing customers' demands, companies are finding it necessary to be continuously researching and evaluating its effects in the marketplace.

Research design methods

A whole range of research methods might be used here, including mass surveys, observation and independent interviews depending on the nature of the task in hand.

2.22 Marketing example — Customer care programmes

Many organisations install some kind of customer care programme and then feel that the task is completed. Not so. There must be constant research to monitor and evaluate success or otherwise. The Finance Director of the most successful retailer in the UK, Tesco Supermarket Group, when asked how the company intended to defend their 30 per cent market share against the might of the competition replied that research has to be implemented that involved round-the-clock trips to all its stores (around the world) and its rivals, and most importantly, a 24-hour hotline to its customers.

Question

1 Evaluate the importance of retail consumer research, show how it might be undertaken and give reasons why you think that some retailers seem to be better at it than others.

Overall research design methods

Both positivistic (quantitative) and/or phenomenological (qualitative) methods can be used either singularly or in combination as can secondary and/or primary research. The choice will depend on such factors as the objectives of the research, pressure for scientific objectivity, the nature of the area under investigation, time and money involved, access to target sample and so on. Some research investigations lend themselves more readily to a quantitative approach, perhaps trying to discover the numbers of people in the population that use organic products. Other investigations will be better taking a more qualitative approach, for example seeking to discover consumer attitudes to the merchandising in a store.

Users of consumer research

Many different individual groups and organisations undertake an enormous amount of customer research around the world on a constant basis and it is constantly increasing. This includes students, academics, practitioners, consumer protection organisations, trade associations, manufacturers, producers, suppliers, retailers and

Figure 2.10

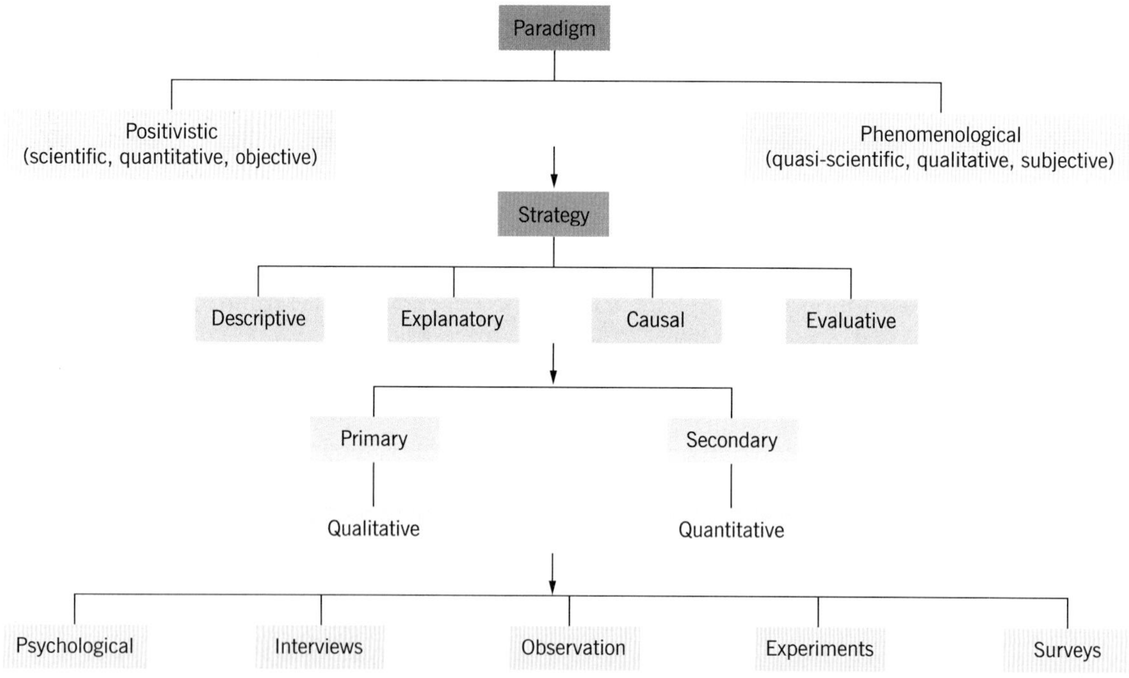

Overall research data process

market research commercial agencies. The level of accuracy will vary according to the purpose of the study, the amount of resources involved and the importance of the outcome. Much of the academic research undertaken in colleges and universities around the world is shared and used in conjunction with research undertaken by others, especially by the commercial sector. Some producers and retailers chose to undertake research themselves, especially at the informal level, while others will commission research from universities and research agencies.

The use of a marketing consumer research agency

The marketing researcher, whether working for his or her own organisation or for an outside agency, must develop skills in getting to the heart of the problem. This will involve talking to the client, going away and analysing the information and then returning with the 'brief' that sets out the client's needs as the researcher understands them. This process will be repeated, back and forth if necessary, until no one is in any doubt about the purpose of the marketing research. Many consumer research agencies exist to help producers and retailers with informational problems about the consumer on a national or global basis and they are used predominately because of the skills and professionalism offered. Because many retailers have access to large amounts of consumer information they will have the choice to either undertake the analysis themselves and use in-house facilities or outsource the whole operation to a specialist company.

Customised, syndicated and off-the-shelf research

Consumer research can be bought on a customised, syndicated basis or off-the-shelf basis. Customised research is research undertaken specifically for the client and is therefore the most expensive. Syndicated research is part research offered to different clients on the one survey and off-the-shelf research is, as the term implies, general research undertaken by the research company, for example on the foreign holiday industry and then offered to any company that wishes to purchase.

Summary

- In this chapter we looked at the use of information and research in trying to understand the motivations of consumers.
- The need for the manufacturer and the retailer to share information was discussed, outlining the part that new technology was playing in the process.
- We then looked at the problems involved in selling direct to the consumer highlighting the part that new home buying methods, notably the Internet, now play in consumer behaviour.
- The growth in customer relationship management programmes and the increased effort to build customer loyalty was then identified as a crucial area in understanding customer behaviour.
- The importance of building a formal marketing information system including an internal system, intelligence system, marketing research system and a storage and analysis system (computers) was discussed.
- The marketing research process was used as a way of exploring the use of marketing research approaches beginning with the use and pros and cons of both secondary and primary customer research.
- We then looked at the differences between qualitative and quantitative information as well as experimentation, observation and survey methods of collection.
- The need for scientific rigour when looking at the behavioural sciences leads to a discussion on the use of two basic paradigms, positivism and phenomenology.
- Finally exploratory, descriptive, explanatory and evaluative research strategies were examined.

Questions

1 Discuss the argument that research into understanding consumer behaviour has to be treated with the utmost caution because humans are so changeable and unpredictable. Give live examples to illustrate your answers.

2 How will an understanding of human nature help to bring about company success and competitive advantage? Look both in and outside of the organisation giving live examples where companies have achieved profitability through attention to this important area.
3 Identify important information that will be needed for meaningful market segmentation.
4 Discuss the difference between the research methods talked about in this chapter. What are the major pros and cons between the positivistic and phenomenological or interpretive approach to social and behavioural research?
5 Identify and discuss all the issues associated with the problem of 'information overload' and describe and evaluate how these problems might be overcome.
6 Describe and examine the use of the following and give live examples of how they are used by manufacturers and retailers to satisfy and create loyalty among consumers.
   a The marketing information system (MIS)
   b EPOS system
   c Data-warehousing, data-mining and data-based marketing
7 Discuss and evaluate the differences and methods used in the use of quantitative and qualitative research in understanding consumer behaviour. Why has there been such a growth in the use of qualitative research?
8 How far should technology be allowed to go in watching, monitoring and analysing human and consumer behaviour? Discuss and evaluate methods that are currently being used and speculate where it might be used in the future.
9 Identify a live product from those listed below and discuss the behavioural research that might have been undertaken before market launch.
   a A FMCG branded packaged product
   b A new automobile model
   c A range of men's fashion clothing
10 Identify and analyse all the factors that must be taken into account when undertaking information collection and research.

Case study

Case study 1 Information overload

One of the unhelpful side-effects of the information revolution has been the increase in pressure on employees through different forms of information overload. It should be recognised that just because the organisation has the capability for almost unlimited information collection and classification it is no reason for gathering and hoarding data that will not be of use in the foreseeable future. The availability of too much information can cause the prospective user to be so overcome by the quantity of information available that they cannot distinguish the good from the bad and the relevant from the not so relevant. At best this can cause frustration and withdrawal and at its worse it can cause illness and time off work.

The answer must be either some type of assistance and built-in filtering system and/or skills training that helps the user to judge what is and isn't usable data. The Institute of Management and PPP Healthcare published a report that shows that keeping up with hundreds of emails a day is one of the major causes of workplace stress for managers. Office email systems, leading to information overload, also contributed to the top two sources of workplace stress, constant interruptions and deadline pressures, which can damage performance at work as well as put personal lives at risk. The report by the Department of Trade and Industry found that workers take an average of 49 minutes a day to sort out their inboxes and many employees found that keeping up with office emails had become a logistical nightmare. According to the DTI, sick days as a result of stress cost business £7.11 million a week in the UK.

Questions

1 Discuss the problems caused by the seemingly unlimited supply of information. How might it be managed and controlled?

2 Do you think that there comes a time when too much information about the consumer could be unhelpful and what problems might it cause?

Case study

Case study 2 Neuromarketing

Dr Reed Montague, a neuroscientist at Baylor Medical School, re-created 'The Pepsi Challenge', the commercials from the 1970s and 1980s in which taste tests seemed to show that Pepsi was usually preferred over Coke. He wanted to find out why Coke sold more if it didn't taste any better. On examining the brain scans, he found that the people who chose Pepsi had a stronger response in an area deep in the brain called the ventral putamen, which triggers feelings of reward. He then repeated the test, but this time he told those taking part which of the sample tastes was Coke. The outcome was remarkable – almost all of the subjects said they preferred Coke. Their brain scans lit up a different area, not the ventral putamen, but the prefrontal cortex. This is the area of the brain that controls high-level cognitive powers. When participants were told which drink was which, they were thinking in a different way about the taste of Coke. Now the drink was associated with places and memories they had about Coke. Branding is about getting people to associate what is being sold with pleasant memories and their associations. In other words it was the brand, the image, which was more important than the taste. Scientists in The Baylor Medical School, Houston, Texas, used MRI scanners on men who were asked to rate the attractiveness of cars. Prestige cars such as Porsche and Ferrari showed activity in a brain region used for processing faces and linked to the main emotional centres. It seems that this could allow companies to discover through research whether their marketing, advertising products and brands are triggering vital responses in the minds of their consumers.

Questions

1 Discuss if you think that this kind of research has any ethical implications. Should there be any governmental controls on what research should and should not be allowed? Give examples.

2 How might this type of qualitative research help in building customised products and segmenting markets and how might other methods help in a research campaign?

Further reading

Books

Aaker, David A., V. Kumar, George S. Day (2000) *Marketing Research*, 7th edn, New York: J. Wiley and Sons.

Baker, M.J. (2000) *Marketing Theory: A student text*, London: ITBP.

Curwin, Jon and Roger Slater (2000) *Quantitative Methods for Business Decisions*, 4th edn, London: ITBP.

Hakim, C. (1987) *Research Design: Strategies and Choices in the Design of Social Research*, London: Allen and Unwin.

Hughes, A.M. (2003) *The Customer Loyalty Solution: What Works (and What Doesn't) in Customer Loyalty Programs*, New York: McGraw-Hill.

Kent, Ray (1999) *Marketing Research: Measurement, Method and Application*, London: ITBP.

Kumar, V. (2000) *International Marketing Research University of Houston*, Houston: Prentice Hall.

Peters, Glen (1997) *Beyond the Next Wave with Scenario Planning: Imagining the Next Generation of Customers*, Harlow: Prentice Hall.

Reicheld, F. and T. Teal (2001) *The Loyalty Effect: The Hidden Force Behind Growth, Profits, and Lasting Value*, Cambridge, MA: Harvard Business School Press.

Rogers, Carl R. (1980) *Way of Being*, Boston, MA: Houghton Mifflin, pp.115–17.

West, Christopher (2000) *Marketing Research*, Basingstoke: Palgrave Publishers.

Woolfe, B.P. (2001) *Loyalty Marketing: The Second Act*, Teal Books, www.brianwolfe.com.

Wright, R. (1999) *Marketing, Origins, Concepts and Environment*, London: ITBP.

Journals and articles

Connelly, F.M. and D.J. Clandinnin (1990) 'Stories of Experience and Narrative Enquiry', *Educational Researcher* 19 (5): 2–14. AER.NET.publications.

Gulati, R. and Garino, J. (2000) 'Get the Right Mix of Clicks and Bricks', *Harvard Business Review*, May–June: 179–88.

Hess, E.H. and J.M. Polt (1960) 'Pupil Size as Related to Interest Value of Visual Stimuli', *Science*, 132: 349–50.

Moe, W. (2001) 'Buying, Searching or Browsing: Differentiating Between On-line Shoppers In-store Navigational Slipstream', *Journal of Consumer Psychology*, 13 (1&2): 29–40.

Pooler, J. (2003) Why We Shop, Emotional Rewards and Retail Strategies, London: Praeger Publishers (www.whyweshop.com).

Rankin, R.E. and D.T. Campbell (1955) 'Galvanic Skin Response to Negro and White Experimenters', *Journal of Abnormal and Social Psychology*, 51: 30–3.

Rayner, K. (1995) 'Eye Movements and Cognitive Processes in Reading, Visual Search, and Scene Perception, in J.M. Findlay, R. Walker and R.W. Kentridge (eds), *Eye Movement Research: Mechanisms, Processes, and Applications*, New York: Elsevier, pp. 3–21.

Reinartz, W. and V. Kumar (2002) 'The Mismanagement of Customer Loyalty', *Harvard Business Review*, July: 86–94.

Rucci, A.J., Kirn, S.P. and Quinn, R.T. (1998) 'The Employee-Customer-Profit Chain at Sears', *Harvard Business Review*, January–February: 132–7.

Westie, F.R. and M.L. Defleur (1959) 'Autonomic Responses and Their Relationship to Race Attitudes', *Journal of Abnormal and Social Psychology*, 58: 340–7.

Websites

ACNielsen Research, www.acnielsen.com.

Association for Information Management (ASLIB), www.aslib.co.uk.

Association of European Market Research Institutes (AEMRI), www.aemri.org.

Association of Qualitative Research Practitioners, AQRP (UK), www.aqrp.co.uk.

British Market Research Association, www.bmra.org.uk.

BMRB (British Market Research Bureau), www.bmrb.com.

British Tourist Authority, www.visitbritain.org.

Broadcast Audience Research Board (BARB), www.barb.co.uk.

CACI: Marketing Systems Databases, ACORN (a classification of residential neighbourhoods), www.caci.com.

Efficient Response Europe, www.ecrnet.org.

ESOMAR, founded in 1948 as the European Society for Opinion and Marketing Research, ESOMAR now The World Association of Opinion and Marketing Research Professionals (but still known as ESOMAR) has 4,000 members in over 100 countries, www.esomar.org.

Euroquest, European Research Co., research companies from many European countries join together to offer pan-European marketing and social research, www.euroquestmrb.com.

Geodemographic information systems, computer maps offered on anywhere in the UK, www.geoweb.co.uk.

IMS Health (US), no. 2 in the world, almost a billion turnover, seems to mainly deal in health research, www.imshealth.com.

International Statistical Institute, ISI, 2,000 individual elected members, 133 countries, leaders in the field of statistics, www.cbs.nl/isi/.

Kantar Group (UK), no. 3 in the world almost a 700 billion pound turnover, owns Research International.

Mintel Research, www.mintel.co.uk.

NFO Worldwide, no. 5 in the world, part of the Interpublic Group, www.nfow.com.

Studentshout, general marketing site, www.studentshout.com.

TNS Media Intelligence, www.tnsmediaintelligence.co.uk.

Perception

3

'The best and most beautiful things in the world cannot be seen, nor touched ... but are felt in the heart.'

Helen Keller

Objectives

At the end of this chapter the reader will be able to:

1 Identify the main senses and explain and examine their role in the perceptual process.

2 Deconstruct the five main senses and demonstrate and evaluate how the various areas work in helping humans understand the world around them.

3 Illustrate how a critical understanding of perception and the senses can help marketing practitioners achieve successful consumer marketing programmes.

Introduction

If we are to understand why consumers behave in the way that they do, why they make the decisions in the way that they do and why they buy the products and the brands that they do, then we will need to look deeply into the whole manner of decision making discussed in Chapter 1. This will involve exploring the workings of the mind and the body, the factors and processes involved, and how interaction between all the parts can effect, to a greater or lesser extent, the eventual end result, the choice and purchase of the end product. We only have to think in a more focused way about our own purchases, from the simple (weekly shopping) to the more complex (a holiday) to begin to see how intricate and involving the whole process can be. This will include such things as **perception**, **learning**, genetic and social influences, **motivation**, **attitude**, **personality** and so on. However we will only be able to lightly touch on each of the areas addressed because of the vastness of the subjects involved.

Vastness of the subject

So much information has been written and argued over by so many great philosophers, scientists and academics that each single discipline could be (and is) a university degree course in its own right. In many cases some theories and assumptions are still the subject of fierce debate (nature versus nurture argument, Freud's theory of the subconscious) and so readers should be aware that, in many cases, there is still controversy about the veracity of the facts and the truth about any one approach over another. That said there is no doubt that we know more about customer behaviour than ever before, especially with the advances in the knowledge base and technology. It should also be remembered that, although each subject area is talked about individually, in reality all things interact and relate to everything else. So perception, experience, upbringing, **beliefs**, motivation and personality all affect and alter one another in a constantly interactive iterative way.

Perception

'One of the deepest problems in cognitive science is that of understanding how people make sense of the vast amount of raw data constantly bombarding them from the environment.' HOFSTADTER, 1995

We will begin by looking at the part that perception plays in understanding human and consumer behaviour. In simple terms perception can be seen as the way that humans (and animals) experience, try to understand and so make sense of the world around them. It begins with the moment of birth and then continues as we grow from children into adults and will only end at the moment of death. It includes all the senses: sight, sound, smells, touch and taste, that we use everyday in constantly interacting with the environment. The use of each will vary according to thoughts, emotions and the situation in hand as well as other factors such as culture, illness and disability, such as deafness or being blind.

Key point Perception can be seen as the way that humans (and animals) use their senses to explore, experience and try to understand the world around them.

Perception plays a critical part in marketing

It can easily be seen that perception plays a critical part in marketing programmes, where the use of pictures, images, spoken and written language, colour, noise, music, tastes and smells are used in such profusion, that an understanding of how it works is an absolute must for all managers that work in the business.

Perception – the process

'I am sure that if a fairy bade me choose between the sense of sight and that of touch, I would not part with the warm, endearing contact of human hands.' ANON

For many thousands of years many wise, learned and curious people have investigated and tried to understand how people come to know and understand what is happening in the world around us (Socrates, Aristotle, Descartes, Locke, Hume, Kant, Marx, Einstein to name but a few). Questions were asked about things that most of us now take for granted and seldom, if ever, question; on how the process actually works. Yet we only have to stop while in the town or in the country and think for a few moments to become aware of it happening. We look around and see objects we recognise immediately and other objects that take longer to bring into focus. We see familiar and not so familiar shapes and patterns of movement we see shades of light and dark and many colours of differing intensity, both near to us and far away. If we close our eyes and concentrate on noises, a similar rich pattern can be discerned. The sounds might be high or low, loud or soft, dominant or in the background, intermittent or continuous and near or far away. Similarly dissimilar smells, pleasant and unpleasant, strong and weak, recognisable and unrecognisable, will waft and drift around in the atmosphere and light, medium and strong breezes will cause pressure on our face and body. Even animals have abilities to perceive the world in similar sorts of ways, although the level and degree of perception will of course vary tremendously dependent on how primitive (chicken) or complex (chimpanzee) might be the particular animal.

Figure 3.1

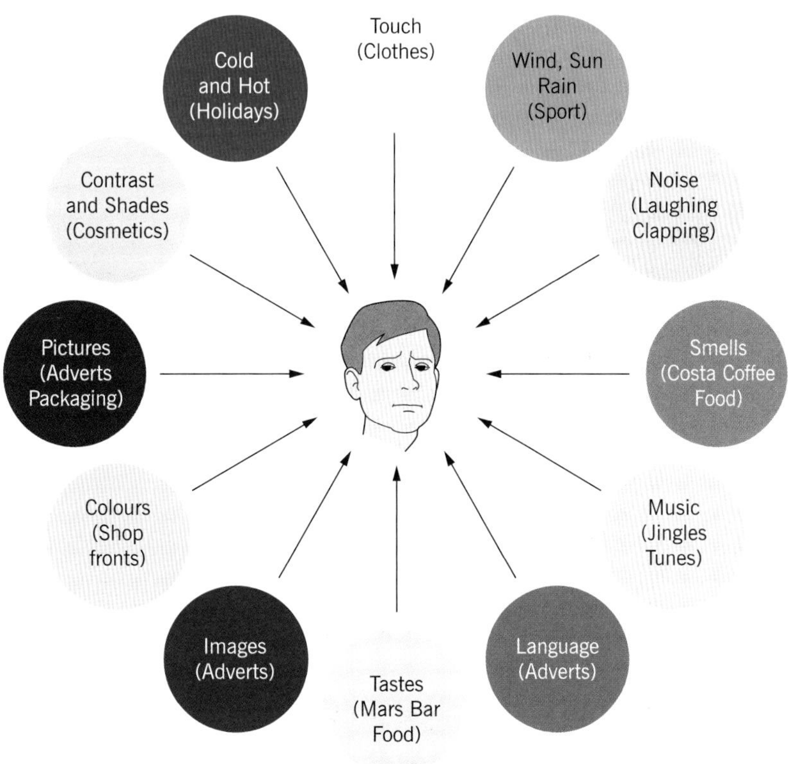

A mass of images bombarding the senses

Making sense of stimuli

'Photographic realism ... works to naturalize comprehension; it hides the work of perceiving meaning behind the mask of a "naturally, obviously" meaningful image.' BILL NICHOLS

The amazing thing is individuals tend to make sense of what is happening relatively quickly, often without even thinking very hard. The objects that attract might be people, a man, woman or a child; a car, a bus or a boat; buildings, a church, offices or a petrol station or perhaps trees, flowers, weeds or grass. It might also be a billboard advertisement, a retail outlet, shop windows, facia signs or shelves and shelves of products and brands, and it is recognised immediately.

Hear, smell and taste

The noises heard might be birds singing, a lawn mower grinding, a car starting up or a lorry chugging uphill in the distance. The smells might be of breakfast cooking, the scent of flowers, newly cut hay, cattle-manure or car exhaust fumes. Or it might be the smell of coffee from a Starbucks, beef-burgers from McDonald's or chicken from KFC. Of course this ability to quickly recognise surroundings will depend on how familiar a person might be with a particular environment. So a town person might have problems in the country and a country person problems in the town. Similarly a resident born and bred in Europe will have some difficulties in Asia and somebody from Asia will have similar difficulties in Europe. Having said this, strangers seem to be able to perceptually acclimatise themselves to unfamiliar surroundings fairly quickly.

Key point Upbringing including country of birth and residence, culture and whether living in the town, countryside, by the sea and so on will all affect perception.

3.1 General example — Social values and perception

In a well-known experiment conducted by Jerome Bruner and Cecile Goodman (1947), two groups of children were asked to judge the size of coins. One was a poor group from a slum area in Boston and the other was an affluent group from the same city. The poor group over-estimated the size of the coins far more than did the affluent group. Thus social values and individual needs can influence perception.

How the perceptual process works

A brand is a collection of perceptions in the mind of the individual consumer. To some it will mean nothing but to others, the target-market, it should mean value, quality, satisfaction and ultimately an over-all meaningful feeling of wellbeing.

The perceptual process can now be examined in more detail. It's known that stimuli of all kinds from the outside world, constantly bombard our bodies, and through the senses enter the inner world that is the nervous system, the brain and our **consciousness**. In this way individuals seem to have the ability to construct thoughts, mental pictures and concepts in the mind about what is continuously happening all around them. It will be at lightning speed with familiar stimuli and relatively longer with less familiar stimuli.

It can be a conscious and unconscious process as well as being a deliberate or habitual process or somewhere in between. We all tend to think that how we perceive the world is objective and factual but there is much evidence to show that this information is often more subjective and less a reality than people might imagine. This has important ramifications for marketing practitioners who must be aware that consumers might view brands and services benefit offerings, not only in different ways to the brand owners, but also in different ways from each other.

3.2 General example — Values and perception

There seems to be no such thing as an objective view of a football match. Our own experience will demonstrate that opposing fans will tell a different story of a match, depending on whom they support and whether they win or lose. In the European Cup in 2004, England had a disallowed goal that lost them the match. English pundits and newspapers were scathing of the Swiss referee, calling him unfair, biased (among other unprintable things) and fit only for refereeing games for schoolchildren. Unsurprisingly the fans of the opposing team disagreed as did the majority of the world's press who all saw the decision as skilful and correct. In a classic study in 1954, Albert Hastorf and Hadley Cantril interviewed opposing fans after a university football match with similar results. They concluded their study by stating that 'for these students, the perception and recall of what might seem to be "the same event" involved a very active construction of differing realities', they concluded by highlighting the crucial role of values in shaping perception.

Questions

1 How do you account for seemingly different perceptions of the same football match?

2 Can you recall from you own experiences examples of similar incidences happening?

Sensation and perception

'A rose by any other name would smell as sweet.' WILLIAM SHAKESPEARE

Although closely related, **sensation** and perception play two complimentary but different roles in how individuals interpret their world. Sensation refers to the process of sensing the environment through touch, taste, sight, sound and smell. This meaningless information is sent to the brain in raw form where perception comes into play. Perception is the way these sensations are selected, organised and interpreted as individuals attempt to make sense of everything around them. If initial perception and recognition is uncertain it can be an iterative process (backward and forward) undertaken at lightning speed, as checking and re-checking takes place against knowledge and past experiences.

3.3 General example — Perception and reaction through the nervous system

Some perceptual reactions can be driven more through the nervous system than the brain. If we unexpectedly 'see' a flash of lightning or 'hear' a clap of thunder we might 'jump' and react instinctively more through the nervous system than the brain. This will be returned to in more detail in the next chapter when Pavlovian classical conditioning and learning is discussed.

Table 3.1

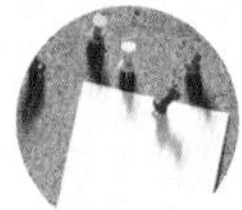

The senses

The senses of vision, hearing, taste and smell are located in the head. The senses of touch and movement are located in receptor cells throughout the body.

Sensation

The process of sensing the world through the major senses.

Receptors

Receptors are cells in the body and the head that react to external stimuli. Once the particular sense receptor is activated, information is sent through the nervous system to particular parts of the brain for interpretation.

Perception

Perception is the way these sensations are selected, organised and interpreted as individuals attempt to make sense of everything around them.

Figure 3.2

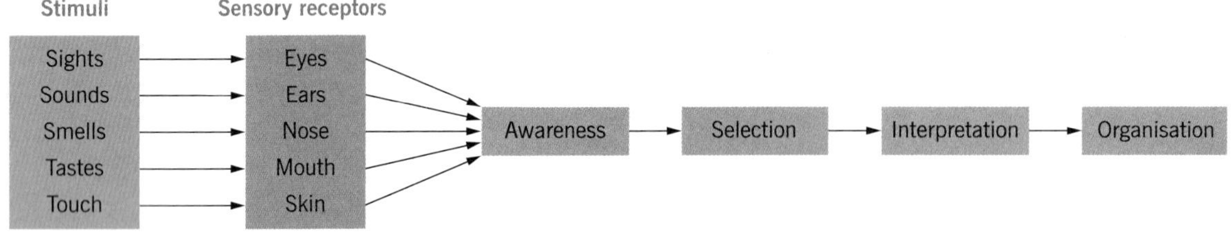

The perceptual process

Key point Definition of perception

The process of selecting, organising and interpreting sensory data into usable mental representations of the world.

Top-down and bottom-up perceptual processing

Perceptual processing can happen in an inductive (bottom-up) or deductive (top-down) way and by a combination of both.

Deductive, top-down processing

As we grow up we develop frameworks or 'perceptual sets' that can be seen as high order beliefs and experiences that determine how we view the world. With deductive, top-down processing sensations are identified and processed according to how they fit into an overarching framework of perceptual sets that would have been developed over time. Once established perceptual sets are difficult to change and some never do.

Inductive, bottom-up processing

New sensory information will be less as we get older but nevertheless will be coming in all of the time, especially with invention, innovation and change happening at such a tremendous pace. Inductive, bottom-up processing is the taking in of small amounts of original sensory information and building it into new perceptual sets.

A combination

Perception tends to be a combination of both top-down and bottom up processing. Individuals attempt to fit new sensations into existing mind-sets and reject or develop new mind-sets if unable to assimilate. This will vary from person to person and from group to group depending on beliefs, attitudes, dogmas, personality and the amount of exposure to new ideas.

3.1 Marketing example | Brand categories, perceptual sets

▶ It is believed that consumers build up mental product categories, or **perceptual sets**, over the years appertaining to negative (disliking the brand), positive (liking the brand) or neutral (having no feelings about the brand) attitudes to particular brands. When shopping, unless convinced otherwise, people will only purchase from the brands they have in their positive mental set. Heavily influenced by advertising and brand building it is obviously important for manufacturers and retailers to know exactly where they figure, in terms of attractiveness, in the mind of the consumer. This will reflect the amount of effort they might have to expend in moving a customer from one category (neutral) to another (positive).

Question

1 Identify your own perceptual set for a selective product.

Figure 3.3

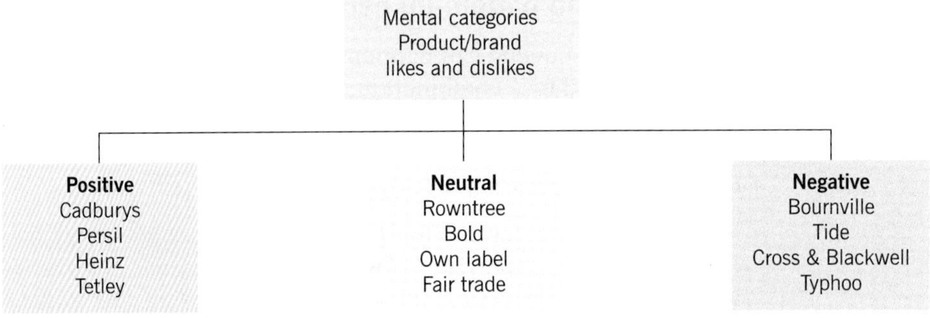

Perceptual sets – customers build mental perceptual sets about products and brands that are liked and disliked

> **Key point** Perception is a combination of top-down and bottom-up mental processing.

The use of the senses

'The way we see things is affected by what we know or what we believe' JOHN BERGER (1995)

People seem able to recognise people, animals, flora and fauna, buildings, products, brands, prices, advertisements often with the minimum of visual information. They can distinguish between multitudes of different smells, differentiate between hundreds of different colours and shades, feel the lightest touch of rain on their cheek or sand between their toes, and hear the faint and distant sounds of an owl hooting, a bird singing or a car starting up. It all seems to happen easily, automatically and in a moment. Yet everything that we see, hear, feel, smell, or taste requires billions of nerve cells sending messages back and forth from sense receptors to the brain, performing intricate calculations and usually making sense of the world in an instant.

The five main senses

▶ There are five main **senses** by which we make sense of the world. These are sight or vision, hearing, touch, smell and taste (shown opposite). Of these the main ones are vision or sight and sound. Each of the five senses activates a separate area of the cerebral cortex, the sheet of neurons that makes up the outer layer of the brain's hemispheres. Research has shown that if one area is damaged, for example sight loss causing blindness, then other areas can, in some cases, compensate, for example an increase in hearing ability (Ratey 2002). All the senses will be looked at individually but it should be understood that very rarely would any operate in isolation. Individuals see and hear at the same time or touch and see, or smell and taste or see, touch and taste. It is only when one or more of the senses might be malfunctioning that it can be shown how interdependent they all are.

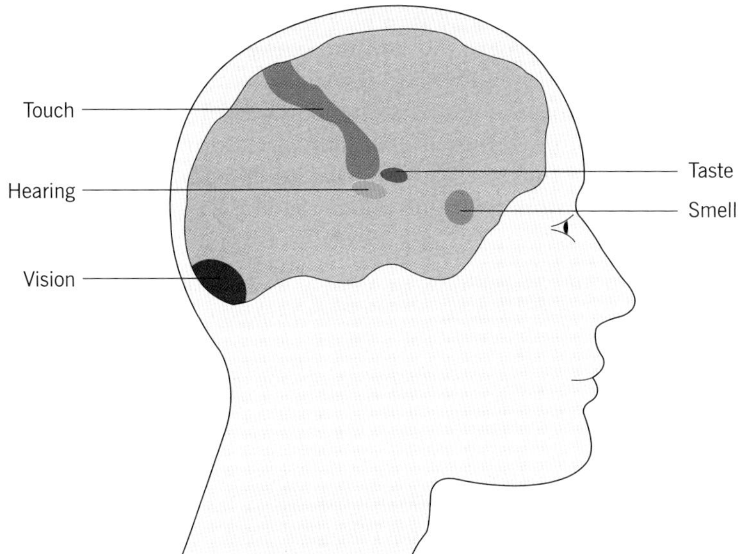

The five main senses

3.4 General example **Additional sensations**

Scientists now recognise that we have several additional kinds of sensations, such as pain, pressure, temperature, joint position, muscle sense, movement, but these can be included under 'touch' (the brain areas involved are called the 'somatosensory' area). In some cultures we talk about having a 'sixth sense' meaning, for example, that we can 'sense' in some way if we are being watched or somebody is walking up behind us yet we can't immediately see anybody. This might also apply to a sense of space that people need around them. This concept is important in retail outlet layout where room between aisles, through checkouts and in door openings is important. There is also the sense of balance control by an area in the ears called the 'vestibular'. Older people will have difficulty in walking, with the danger of falling over, if damage happens here.

Sight or vision

'A picture is worth a thousand words.' CHINESE PROVERB

Sight is probably the most developed sense in humans, followed closely by hearing and it seems to be the major way that both humans and animals come to know and understand the world around them. Most creatures begin their life by opening their eyes and seeing the immediate environment. Some information will have been genetically programmed and brought to the world by the animal or human while other information will need to be seen and understood in some way through the process of perception, learning and experience. We see people, objects, roads, cars, buildings, shopping malls, shop fronts and shop interiors, countryside, trains, the sea, boats, animals, the foreground and the background, colours, light and shade, movement and so on. We read books, newspapers, magazines, listen to the radio and watch TV. We see outdoor advertising billboards on the road, in the railway station and at airports. Some things are familiar and adopted in a habitual and automatic way, while other things are less familiar and demand more concentration as we seek to make sense of new or unfamiliar visionary experiences.

Key point Some sensory information we bring genetically to the world and will be programmed in our DNA, while other information is learned through interacting with the environment.

The process of seeing

It is self-evident that, unless we have a problem with our sight, we see and perceive the world through the use of our eyes. These are complex structures consisting of a transparent lens that focuses light from the environment on to millions of receptor cells contained within the retina. Here the light is turned into images. These images are then transmitted by the optic nerve connected to the back of the eye to the brain. The brain then adjusts and interprets these impulses in an attempt to make sense of what is going on in the world around us. We will see later that what the eye 'sees' and what our brain tells us and what we 'believe' can vary from individual to individual according to such things as upbringing, age, gender and culture.

3.5 General example — Current needs affect perception

Levine, Chein and Murphy (1942) presented people with a set of ambiguous line drawings and asked them to describe what they saw. One group was hungry while the other group had just eaten. The ones who were hungry more often perceived food items in the ambiguous drawings than those who had just had a meal. Current needs can thus affect perception.

Sight and colour

Individuals live in a world dominated by colour and it is an inherent element of sight perception. From the inside of the home, moving outside into the garden and onto the streets vision and perception is hit by a multitude of different and changing colours. The sky, plants, trees, traffic, road signs, shops, the workplace, the clothes people wear all interplay in a fantastic mixtures and shades of reds, greens, blues, yellows, pinks, purples and whites and blacks. Only when the sun goes down, evening comes and darkness erases all colours can we really appreciated the important part that it plays in our everyday lives, whatever the country we live in. Colours are rich in hidden meanings and symbolisms and over the centuries they have been shown to have a profound effect on people at all levels from the physical and mental to the emotional and the spiritual. They can affect and alter perception and moods and how we feel about ourselves, about others and about the world that we inhabit on a day-to-day basis.

How colour works

Taking a very simple approach, it can be shown that everything that exists in the world is made up of different combinations of electrons and atoms. Light, either from the sun or artificially constructed is made up of different electromagnetic energy wavelengths and frequencies. When light is shone on different materials the combination of these electrons and atoms and the way they absorb or reflect light, will determine the colour. Some materials absorb all light and energy and reflect back none (black and hot) whilst others absorb none and reflect back all (white and cool).

Colours and meanings

'I'm green with envy.' 'I saw red.' 'I'm feeling blue.' 'He turned purple with rage.' 'She was pink with embarrassment.' …

Many studies have been done with various groups of people showing the effects that different colours have on emotions and behaviour (Gerard 1958; Levy 1984). There are colours that stimulate the mind, others sedate, some depress, others are uplifting, some colours make individuals feel attractive and sexy while others drab and despondent and some encourage anger while others have a calming affect. All colours seem to have meaning associated with them and these meanings will vary according to such things as an individual's age, gender, culture and nationality. Meanings around the world have also changed and varied over time especially with exposure to commercialism and global marketing. Some (arbitrary) examples on colour meanings are given below.

> **Key point** Colour meanings can vary according to culture.

Table 3.2 **The meaning of colour**

Red – a powerful colour associated with anger, aggression, irritability, tension, as well as vitality, ambition, joy, sexuality, excitement and animal passion.

Pink – emotionally soothing and calming, gentle warmth, nurturing, unselfish love.

Orange – joyful, lifts the spirit, alleviates negative feelings, an antidepressant. Too much can cause agitation and restlessness.

Green – calming, comfortable colour of nature and the outdoors, it reduces anxiety and tension. Signifies freshness, regeneration and growth. Too much green can lead to lethargy, complacency and inactivity.

Yellow is a happy, bright, uplifting and optimistic colour, associated with sunny days. Stimulates the intellect. Too much can cause exhaustion, arrogance and conceit.

Table 3.2 (Continued)

Blue – is a cool, calming, tranquil, serene, protective, noble colour. It can inspire mental control, clarity, and creativity. Too much can cause coldness, sadness and depression.

Indigo – associated with the mysterious, the profound and the esoteric. It stimulates the intellect and gives a person a sense of courage, authority and inner calmness. An overdose can cause headaches and drowsiness.

Violet – powerful, calming, strong links with creativity. Those drawn to this colour are often shy. Excessive amounts can cause over-stimulation and feelings of inadequacy.

Purple – creativity, inspiration, sensitivity, spirituality and compassion.

Marketing and colour

Colour plays an essential part of business and marketing at both the strategic and tactical level and organisations will pay enormous amounts of money to build and upgrade, so that colours considered appropriate will be associated with both the company and its range of products. It can be so successful in some cases that a colour need only be shown for people to immediately guess the organisation in question.

Colour and images at the corporate level

Every major organisation will have developed and designed corporate colours that will reflect the values and products of the organisation in the minds of the consumer. Along with corporate slogans and images, colour thus becomes an essential part of corporate image to be clearly presented across every communicative object that may be associated with the organisation. In this way it will be hoped that customers will instantaneously recognise the organisation and perceive it as being efficient, modern, trustworthy and offer value and quality.

3.2 Marketing example — Corporate colours

Red white and blue is associated with Tesco, orange and blue with Sainsbury's, green with Asda, yellow and blue with Ikea, dark green with M&S, orange and white at B&Q, yellow and red at McDonald's, purple at Cadbury and so on.

Corporate images and colours often have a deep meaning for customers.

Colour at the product level

Just as important is colour at the product level in both the product and the packing and there are billions of pounds spent on both retail and business-to-business colour driven products every year.

3.3 Marketing example — Product ingredients and presentation

Imagine food being produced in non-expected colours. White tomatoes, green bread, orange cucumbers, black oranges, yellow lettuces, bright pink potatoes, purple ham, blue baked beans and so on. Much of the colouring in foods is artificially enhanced to make tomatoes and apples redder, cucumbers and beans greener, lemons more yellow and oranges more orange. Billions of pounds are spent every year on food biogenetic manipulation and added flavourings such is consumer demand for colour perfection. If the colour is perceived as 'not right' the customer will not purchase. Products selling colour are many and manifest. This will include indoor and outdoor household and industrial paint; coloured fabrics for curtains, furniture and clothes; coloured cosmetics for lips, eyes, face and body as well as colourings for the hair, fingernails and toenails. There is an enormous market in colouring for food and drink, for plants, shrubs, and trees and accessories for the garden. Colour fashion changes from one year to another and fashion 'experts' need to be able to make an educated guess on what the new colours might be for products as diverse as clothing, interior design and automobiles.

Questions

1 Discuss the importance of colour in products and store layout. How might it differ according to market segment and customer profile?

2 Identify some corporate identity colour uses and examine why you think that they have used the colours and designs chosen.

Packaging

Packaging is just as important and an enormous amount of time and money is spent on consumer perceptual research and packaging colour design, trying to get colour combinations that fit expectations. Computer technology has helped a great deal in all areas of product research as 3d images can be portrayed and colours and shapes manipulated on the screen to ascertain a respondent's reactions. Such is the power of colour that it would be extremely hard for us to imagine such well-known products in a different colour, such as a green Mars bar, a blue Kit-Kat, a yellow Coca-Cola, a pink Heinz baked bean tin and black Kellogg's cornflake packets.

Colour and lighting

We only have to go back to our brief outline on how colour works to see how crucial the role of lighting is in the process and it would be difficult, if not impossible to talk about one without the other. It's in shopping malls, airports, chain stores, departmental stores, fashion stores and so on, and looking at the lighting and colour arrangements we can see how innovative lighting affects can create dramatic colour images, shades of dark and light and illusions thus creating atmosphere, ambience and building a distinct, enjoyable shopping experience. Functional, bright and uniform lighting, for example, might be preferred by low-price supermarkets, such as Asda and Tesco, while a designer boutique such as Zara or Next will want to enhance brand image by using high-quality multi-coloured lighting that can create specific moods to match the needs of the target consumer.

Atmospherics – creating retail theatre through lighting, colour, music and display

In order to stay ahead of the competition and give consumers the shopping experience they crave **retail atmospherics** or so-called 'retail theatre' will play a crucial part in store positioning and consumer attraction. Retail theatre is the idea of transferring the effects, such as décor, varied colour hues, lighting, music, movement, technology and illusion from stage and theatre into the retail environment. It even encompasses the concept of major structural changes to both the inside and outside of the store on a regular basis so as to maintain interest and excitement. Colours, packaging, movement, music, images, range planning and choice of products act together to create a welcoming, exciting environment that customers will want to return to on a continuous basis (Bellizzi *et al*. 1983).

Retail atmospherics – the open door, lights, colours, images and music seduce the consumer.

3.4 Marketing example — Marketing sights are everywhere

Marketing will inevitably play a great part in the world of sight although it will vary depending on the area or country. In mature environments evidence of marketing can be seen everywhere. Shop fronts, shop interiors, billboards, bus stops, the sides of buses, TV and cinema screens, railway stations, airports, seaports and airships and air balloons. There are brand images and words, moving pictures, shapes and sizes and it is completely impossible to ignore.

Question

1 Discuss the possibility of perceptual overkill – too many adverts thus causing all to be ignored.

Sound and the ears

Hearing is largely considered to be secondary in terms of perceptual power when compared to sight. The auditory system (our ears), however, still has a tremendous capacity for picking up and conveying all kinds of information to the brain. The ears can also process sounds without concentrating on the source that produces it. For example we can still hear the sound of music, or traffic or birds singing in the background while concentrating on a major task such as writing, reading or shopping. It is central to learning language and gaining knowledge about the world. The ability to both think and talk in a shared manner with others is what makes us different from animals and has enabled the human race to grow in the manner it has. It would be impossible to imagine a world where there wasn't language, where people could only talk with signs. Although in serious decline there could still be as many as 6,000 different languages and dialects spoken around the world (Grenoble *et al.* 1998).

3.5 Marketing example | **Words become the ad**

'WHASSUP?!' is a word that haunted us in the late 1990s. Yelled to friends by schoolchildren and old trendies alike, it became a universal greeting. 'Whassup?!' was an advertising catchphrase (from a Budweiser ad) which worked so well because it was a real greeting used by the real guys who appeared in the campaign, rather than something dreamed up by a team of copywriters.

How hearing works

Hearing is caused by noises of some kind or another vibrating, disturbing and travelling through the air (sound waves), in a similar way to a stone that is thrown into the water, causing ripples that move out from the centre, gradually losing power and speed the farther they travel and move to the periphery. The ear receives these vibrations through very fine hair cells and these impulses are transmitted, through the auditory system, along various stages and connections to the brain. The stronger the force of the sound waves against the ear the louder will be the noise. We measure strength according to decibels (dB). The louder the sound, the more decibels there will be. In perception, sight and sound will more often than not work together.

Marketing and hearing

Along with sight, marketers, marketing agencies and sales people constantly use language to talk (and listen) to customers and other stakeholders about corporate and product benefits. Why customers should deal with one company rather than another, why they should shop at one shop rather than another and why buy one brand rather than another. Communication is an intricate part of marketing from talking to (and observing) potential and exiting customers about present and future benefits wanted, through to the use of complex methods of marketing research to communicate and promote brand benefits in the hope of continuous satisfactory purchases.

Table 3.3 Great slogans

Great ad campaigns over the last century become ingrained into our memory by constant repetition.

- Diamonds are forever (DeBeers)
- Think small (Volkswagen)
- Just do it (Nike)
- A Mars a day helps you work, rest and play (Mars)
- Let your fingers do the walking (Yellow Pages)
- The pause that refreshes (Coca-Cola)
- Drinka! Pinta! Milka! Day! (Milk Marketing Board, UK)
- We try harder (Avis)
- Good to the last drop (Maxwell House)
- The Bounty Hunters, they came in search of paradise (Bounty Bar)
- Anytime, anyplace, anywhere (Martini)
- Vorsprung durch Technik (Audi)
- The infamous 1970s 'choc-as-phallic-symbol' splendour of 'only the crumbliest, flakiest chocolate' (Cadbury's Flake)
- A million housewives every day pick up a tin of beans and say Beanz Meanz Heinz (Heinz Beans)

Music

'After silence that which comes nearest to expressing the inexpressible is music.'
ALDOUS HUXLEY, *Music at Night*, 1931

Music is used extensively throughout marketing more particularly in advertising and in the retail environment for a multitude of objectives. This might be to grab attention and increase awareness, create interest, atmosphere and mood, make people feel better more relaxed or feel more excited and so on.

3.6 Marketing example — Music and retail

Playing popular songs (for the target audience) for example should enhance shoppers' enjoyment causing them to spend longer in the store and feel less agitated about waiting to be served, whereas unpopular music might cause a hurried exit and agitation waiting at the checkout. Other research suggests (Milliman 1982) that music affects the amount of time that a couple might spend in a restaurant. Slow, romantic music keeps a couple longer (spending more on drinks), while fast music quickened departure times. Similarly playing Italian music in the supermarket might lead to more Italian food and wine being bought or playing German music more German products being bought (North 1997). Research by Yalch and Spangenberg (1988) suggested that music affects shopping times. In their study, clothing store shoppers were exposed either to a youth-oriented foreground music or adult-oriented background music. Interviews with shoppers as they were exiting the store revealed that younger shoppers felt they had shopped longer when exposed to background music, whereas older shoppers felt they had shopped longer when exposed to foreground music.

Questions

1 Discuss the use of music in retail outlets. Do you think it helps or hinders sales?

2 Identify how it's used in different stores you might have used.

Music and advertising

Music of all kinds, from baroque classical to heavy rock, plays an enormous part in most people's lives. Many of our most vivid and moving moments in life are shaped and put into memory by music of some kind. It seems to have the ability to affect every aspect of human emotion. Marketers are, of course, deeply aware of this and so music has become an intrinsic part of advertising around the world as they attempt to associate all manner of products and services with these intense feelings. We only have to view an evening's commercial TV offerings to see a range of adverts given drama, humour, nostalgia, romance, lust, excitement and an overall feel-good factor for the target audience by the background music. In fact the tunes behind certain adverts became so popular that they have entered the music hall of fame. Also popular, and still remembered by many, are **advertising sales jingles** using words and music in a repetitive and catchy way to aid recall.

Sight, colour, sounds, music and consumer segmentation

The choice of colours used across all the areas discussed above will be primarily dependent on the target market as well as the type of product being marketed. If the target markets are men then the products might be stronger colours, reds and blacks and if the target market is women then the colours might be softer shades of pinks and blues. If the customers are children then a mixture of bright, happy, attractive colours could well be the best approach. Music being played will relate to the age of the customer as well as the type of products on display. It is essential (and basic marketing) that retail interiors should be designed to meet the needs of clearly identified target consumer segments, so that individual shoppers feel at ease, get the buying feeling, and be tempted to linger.

Table 3.4 Great ads, great songs

- 'I Heard it Through the Grapevine', Marvin Gaye – Levi Jeans
- 'Search for the Hero', M People – Peugeot Cars
- 'Inkanyezi nezazi', Ladysmith Black Mambazi – Heinz Baked Beans
- 'Mercedes Benz', Janis Joplin – Mercedes Benz
- 'Stand By Me', Ben E. King – Levi Jeans
- 'Can't Take My Eyes Off You', Andy Williams – Peugeot 306
- 'Sarabande' (From Suite No. 4 in D Minor), Academy Of St Martin In the Fields – Levis TV Ad

3.7 Marketing example Whispering windows

Using a small attachable device 'Whispering Windows' transforms entire surfaces into audio speakers. This marketing tool allows retailers to emit music or advertising messages through a window, wall panel, display shelf or mannequin (www.whispering-windows.com).

Perception, the senses and positioning

All organisations attempt to position themselves in the market according to their target market and brand values against the products of their competitors. For example, Ford markets a range of cars for different target markets. The Ka is seen as a second car, the Range Rover is in the prestige conscious SUV market, the Jaguar is for the unassuming wealthy and so on. No matter that the Jaguar now has a Ford engine, as long as it still carries the kudos, glamour, status and wealth association of the Jaguar of old. Ultimately positioning has to take place in the minds of the consumer and it is all about perception.

> **Key point** Where a product is positioned in the market takes place in the minds of the consumer. It's about perception.

Other influences on sight and sound perception

As well as colour, lighting, sounds and music, sight and sound perception are highly influenced by such things as movement, size, position, contrast, repetition and the novelty of the stimulus all of which are constantly used in marketing and advertising. Take for example an advert in a newspaper or magazine. Much research has shown that a large advert will be more readily seen than a smaller one. Its position, back or front page, left-hand side or right-hand side, where exactly on the page and so on will play a large part in it being seen (and will cost more). Similarly a novel advertisement, perhaps showing a product in an unusual setting (a car on the top of a mountain) or movement of some kind (perhaps an optical illusion that shows the car moving) would more likely be seen than something mundane and commonplace. TV adverts will use contrasting black and white and colour in unusual circumstances. Unexpected sounds and music, repetitive, novel jingles, the use of celebrity endorsement all have the ability to create awareness, getting consumers to listen to or watch an advert, despite the multitude of competing stimuli.

> **Key point** Sight and sound perception are influenced by size, colour, position, repetition, novelty, movement, contrasts, celebrity and unexpected events.

Colour, image, shape and choice are so important in retail.

Touch

Touch, or tactile perception is another important means of gaining feedback from the outside world. Touch differs from that of sight and hearing as it is not localised to one area and we can 'feel', through the skin, with any part of the body. This might be through the hands and fingers, feet and toes, arms and legs, the head, face, chest or the bottom. Every day we rely on our sense of touch perception to do many everyday tasks such as sitting comfortably in an armchair, turning off the alarm clock in the dark, operating a mobile phone, changing gear in the car, typing on the computer key board or playing a musical instrument like a guitar or a piano. We are able to feel the wind on our face, the sun on our back, or the snow on the ground with or without the use of the other senses. We are also all aware that some areas of the body are more sensitive than other areas to the sense of touch and this will vary because of age, gender and between one individual and another.

Skin receptors

We feel through so called 'sensory skin receptors', internal small specific nerve endings on the surface of the skin that react to external pressure of some kind and send signals to the nervous system and/or to the brain.

Internal genetic response and homeostasis

Through a system called **homeostasis**, internal, genetically programmed skin receptors automatically respond to changes in cold and warmth and are driven by the internal need of the body to maintain an equilibrium temperature. Every organism with a nervous system can detect these changes in temperature and will act accordingly. Sweating cools us down when hot and goose pimples and shivering decrease heat loss when we are cold. Animals burrow underground or spray themselves with water to avoid the heat, and huddle together or puff out their feathers to maintain warmth. Stronger stimuli, such as intense heat or cold, a stubbed toe, knocked elbow or sunburn and cuts will also transmit signals to the brain that lead to pain. This in turn causes us to take some kind of avoidance action.

Cognitive touch responses

Other touch responses are more cognitive and purposively driven and, as with the use of the other senses, people usually seek out tactile encounters they find pleasurable while avoiding those they find painful in some way or other. When cold, individuals will actively seek out shelter, improved clothing of some kind or look to buy hot food. Similarly, if we feel hot, we take off clothing, look for somewhere to cool down or buy a cold drink. Pain avoidance action will include such things as wearing heavy shoes in the winter, protective clothing if in danger of scratches or bruises from a sporting activity and buying suntan lotion to protect from burning. Pleasure seeking tactile actions will include using seats that are deemed to be relaxing, wearing clothing that feels sensuous against the skin and sleeping on a snug mattress and walking on a comfortable surface. All areas for intense marketing activity.

Animate and inanimate touching

As well as just feeling pleasant, touch and tactile interaction have been shown to have many therapeutic and health-giving effects and we will discuss this in more detail when we look at social interaction. Far Eastern therapeutic balls (rolling around in one hand), Middle Eastern worry beads (constantly moving up and down) and the universal child's comfort blanket are examples. Both human and animal studies have shown the importance of touching, holding and cuddling, between parents and children and one person to another, as well as the health and calming properties associated with stroking small animals such as hamsters, rabbits, cats and dogs. Pressure allied to certain areas of the body (both animals and humans) either by hand or by acupuncture needles, have been used over thousands of years to alleviate all sorts of harmful conditions and improve mental and physical wellbeing.

3.6 General example — Chimps and touch deprivation

A research study investigated the long-term effect that removal from their mother and/or other chimpanzees has on chimpanzees' behaviour. Results indicated that 'deprived' individuals showed lower levels of activity, poorer social skills and higher levels of abnormal behaviour.

Key point The importance of tactile, touching relationships between parents and children as well as one person to another cannot be overestimated.

3.8 Marketing example

Regular consumers at a large supermarket were asked to recall particular checkout personnel over a set period of time. All remembered, favourably, one particular young woman. She was an experimenter who had been planted to deliberately touch every customer in a positive way during the course of each transaction. Looking for tactile 'buying signals', e.g. the prospective buyer running their hand over new furniture, feeling the luxury inside a new car, lying on a bed, walking on a new carpet with shoes off, trying out the remote on a new TV, salespeople will use touch as a way to close a sale. Research has shown that the comforting, pleasurable, even sensuous 'feel' of a mobile phone can be just as important as its looks.

Questions

1 Identify the sorts of products and services that are marketed to take advantage of cognitive touch responses including the need for tactile contact.

2 What new markets could be brought to the market?

Taste and smell

Food and drink companies are constantly researching consumer reaction to taste (and texture) and upgrading and introducing new products and new and different tastes on to the market in an attempt to gain competitive advantage. They have the added problem of having to work within a changing cultural, ethical and legal framework as food and drink products increasingly come under the scrutiny of pressure groups, politicians and legislators worried about unhealthy food, obesity and illnesses among both the young and the old. Constant pressure is put on food manufacturers to clearly label the chemical content in food and drinks as well as to outlaw certain harmful substances.

How the tongue works

The average adult person has about ten thousand taste buds that detect the chemical constituents of food and drink. Each taste bud has about a hundred taste receptors (special cells) and, although they are found mainly on the tongue they will also appear in other parts of the mouth. They seem to die and regenerate on a constant basis as well as reducing in number with the passing years. This can cause certain foods to taste stronger to the young than to the old.

3.9 Marketing example — Supertasters

It seems that a few people, so called 'supertasters' have many more taste buds than others. Some individuals who can taste more differences in such things as wine, coffee and tea than the rest of us have obtained interesting and lucerative employment working as professional tasters for producers and retailers.

Figure 3.4

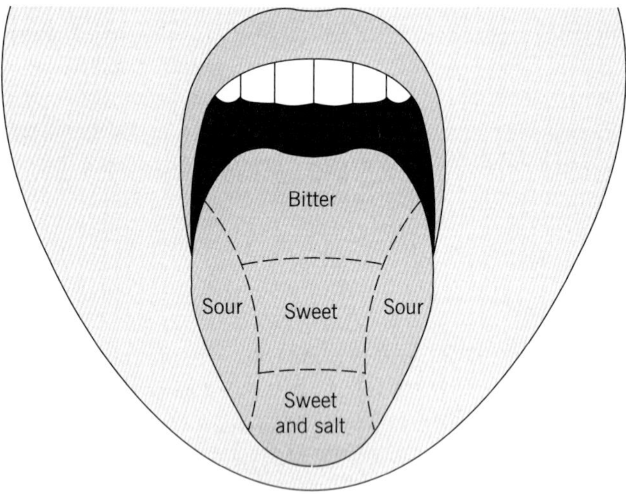

The mouth and four basic tastes

There are four basic human tastes, plus a fifth recently identified. These can be seen below:

Sour taste – Acids

Salty taste – Ionized salts

Sweet taste – Sugars, glycols, alcohols and aldehydes

Bitter taste – Alkaloids and many others

(plus Umami – monosodium glutamate, the main ingredient of soy sauce only recently discovered)

Taste, smell and olfactory receptors

As discussed earlier none of the senses appears to operate in total isolation from one or more of the others. Taste is no different and needs to work in conjunction with a sense of smell, to create the food flavour people love, or hate, so much. When individuals chew food chemicals are released into the mouth, react with taste receptors and instantaneously travel up the nose where they interact with the olfactory (sense of smell) receptors inside the top of the nose as odours. These connect directly to the brain thus creating the hundreds of different flavours and smells that consumers now enjoy (or hate) from living in a mature, sophisticated society. Colds, a blocked-up nose, allergies, infections and other illnesses can cause people to lose their sense of smell and sense of taste, either temporarily or for longer periods.

Taste and smell

Odours coming from the outside also work in the same way as those that come through eating, except that they travel directly up the nasal passages in the nose to these receptors and from there to the brain. This can take time especially with unfamiliar smells where messages are transmitted back and forth as attempts are made to understand the source. It is believed that there are only a few basic odours (perhaps about seven), and that all other odours are a combination of these and research continues in this area.

Key point Taste and smell senses need to function together.

Taste and smell – genetic or socially learnt

Although some children seem to be born hating brussels sprouts or cabbage or tomatoes and loving baked beans, ice cream and shredded wheat, to a great extent, perception of tastes as 'good' or 'bad' are socially learned behaviour. In some cultures, grilled octopus, sheep's eyes, jellied eels, pig's brains, snails and frogs legs are considered delectable, but in others, nauseating. Muslims will not eat pork products or drink alcohol, Hindus will not eat cows and Jews will not eat pork and shellfish and strict Buddhists are vegetarians. Many vegetarians cannot eat meat, fish or poultry products of any kind, the thought making them almost physically sick. There are individuals who love or hate peanut butter, Guinness, tomato sauce, garlic, onions, fresh cream, liquorice, seafood, chocolate or corned beef.

Key point As with sight and sounds, taste and smell likes and dislikes can vary from country to country.

3.10 Marketing example — Marmite and Shake n Vac

Over one hundred years ago, 'Marmite' savoury spread made from brewer's yeast was developed as a filling for sandwiches. Research showed the company that memories of the spread caused people to say, quite strongly, that they either liked or hated (no in-between) Marmite. Under the strap line 'Marmite – you either like it or hate it' the company, Bestfoods Ltd, through its advertising agency, created one of the most successful marketing campaigns of the last decade. One of the most popular products for almost 15 years was called 'shake n vac'. The idea was to shake a sweet smelling powder on to the carpet before vacuuming. In this way the room would smell of fresh flowers and the 'husband' would be aware that his 'house wife' had been working hard while he was at work.

Smell

Many animals (humans included) have to learn which foods are edible, and one of the clues they use is taste perception. Similar to taste, the sense of smell is a very basic drive and is connected to both genetic and social sources. In nature animals use smells to find a mate, seek out food and to sense danger, and newborn babies seem to be able to recognise their mother as well as a few good and bad smells. Although a universal reaction to bad foods, poisons and toxins still appears to remain, with the advancement of civilisation humans have lost much of the genetic content. We now have a comparatively weak sense of smell when compared with many other vertebrates, relying more on the senses of sight and sound when attempting to understand what is going on around us. Evidence seems to suggest that good or bad feelings generated by smells in humans are now more associated with upbringing, culture, learning, emotion and even psychology.

3.7 General example — The power of smell

Research collected by Tim Jacobs at Cardiff University (UK) indicates that dogs can distinguish between the smells of different people, even non-identical twins. Children can distinguish between the smell of their siblings and other children of the same age. Babies recognise their own mother's smell and mothers their own baby's smell. Emotion (fear) can be communicated by smell and heterosexuals and homosexuals can smell the difference between one another. It's even suggested that the human sperm may 'smell' their way to the egg. At the Monell Chemical Senses Centre in Philadelphia scientists have been developing the worst smell in the world, a 'stench soup' so disgusting it could be used as a weapon of war or for crowd control.

Smell and memories

So the smell of the farmyard, of animals, of wet fields, might have pleasant, nostalgic memories for somebody bought up in the countryside while smell awful for somebody bought up in the town. The smell of goat's meat cooking in the Middle East and the smell of pork cooking in the West will trigger off opposite reactions as will the smell of fish, spice, meat and vegetable markets in different places around the world. The smell of cut grass and perfumed roses in the park, breakfast cooking on a Sunday morning, the jumbled-up mix of sea, hot-dogs and suntan lotion at the beach, the smell of Christmas trees in December and rain on a summer day will all invoke different memories of days gone by.

3.11 Marketing example Good and bad smells

Thousands of products exist exploiting consumer reaction to smells. This is particularly so in the cosmetic, perfume, scents and fragrance markets as well as in some exotic food areas where smell plays such an important part. Good smells are linked to emotion and memories associated with good times. Supermarkets pump artificial smells of baking bread, restaurants smells of filtering coffee, and car showrooms smells of new leather, knowing that customers will be attracted and seduced into purchases. Consumers look for olfactory clues and scented stores can be associated with high-quality merchandise. Conversely bad smells will turn people off. So restaurants must guard against the smell of cooking, cinemas against musty odours and food manufacturers against a smell in a new product that is disliked.

Many products are now sold on the market to minimise bad smells. This will include products associated with the human body as well as public and private toilets and environmental waste cleaning and smell maintenance. Identify a bad smell and a product will exist which can minimise or eliminate the cause. Breath sprays, mouthwash, tongue cleaners, toothpastes, dental floss, underarm and foot deodorants, bath, body and hair fragrances, the list of products is endless. There are scents available, either natural or synthetic for the bathroom, toilet, kitchen, living room, bedroom, garage, car, garbage area, for animals, for smoke, for must and mildew.

Questions

1 Explain the enormous growth in consumer products that make people and situations smell better.

2 Examine why likes and dislikes exist between people, especially between men and women and different cultures.

Inhalants

Unfortunately some people become addicted to the smell of such things as glue and gasoline, lighter fluid, paint and paint thinner and aerosols that contain hairsprays and deodorants, cooking oils, and spray paint. Inhaling can cause similar effects to alcohol, initial elation followed by dizziness, sickness and even unconsciousness.

Taste and sight

We discussed earlier the importance of packaging to the product and the same importance must be given to the appearance of food and its relationship to taste.

3.12 Marketing example **Taste, smell and imagination in marketing men's fragrance**

Higher EDT Spray for Men by Christian Dior is a fruity, citrusy, spicy blend of fruity notes of pear, basil and frosted citrus, with spicy notes.
Jacomo De Jacomo for Men 3.4 oz Eau de Toilette Spray is a sharp, oriental, woody fragrance, blending crisp greens, sandalwood and patchouli.
Minotaure by Paloma Picasso, 4.2 oz Eau De Toilette Spray, for men is a slight spice combined with a hint of musk. This dashing cologne is powerful, yet subtle and sexy.

Any restaurateur, chef or husband or wife cooking at home will know that poorly prepared, poorly presented, bad-looking food will turn off eaters and actually seem to have an affect on the taste. Fish cooked from frozen rather than fresh, meat that looks the 'wrong' colour, vegetables that are misshapen have all been used in taste tests, accepted as full of flavour when tasted blind and then rejected when presented openly for respondents to see.

Key point What we understand as taste will involve both mind and body. In a physical sense it is really a composite sense made up of both taste and smell. Psychology will also play a part and consumer research has shown us that texture and the look of the product will also play a part.

Manipulating tastes and smells

Using bio-technology scientists are working on identifying and manipulating human taste genes so that they will be able to, for example, eliminate bitter taste from medicines and improve the sweetness of chocolate while reducing the fat content. Research into textures has enabled manufacturers to increase the hardness, texture and crispness of some foods, such as vegetables, fruit, pastas, chocolate, snack foods and so on, more in line with consumer demands and reduce the hardness in other foods to make them easier to chew for older people, e.g. meats, breads and biscuits, without interfering with the flavour. Many tastes, flavours and smells are naturally produced while others are artificial and produced by scientists and some are a combination of both. Flavours and colouring enhancers are added to every imaginable product found on the shelf in supermarkets around the world. In the UK, as of 2002, some 3,750 substances could be legally added to the food; nearly 3,500 of these being flavourings.

Reacting to research manufacturers and retailers spend billions of pounds a year in developing and putting flavours into products that match consumer demand (a typical strawberry milkshake contains approximately 50 artificial ingredients to create that great 'strawberry' taste). The manufacturer's problem is that packaged foods would taste bland and lack any visual appeal without the additives. Conversely many consumers are often troubled at the thought of so many 'foreign and unnatural substances' going into the food they consume on a daily basis.

Textures and the senses

Research (as well as our own experiences) has shown that some textures, both natural and man-made, are much more pleasing to the senses, that feel good as well as look good, than other textures and consumers are prepared to pay premium prices for products that use these materials. There are thousands of different kinds and shades of texture, occurring both naturally and by the hand of man. Textures can be hot, cold, hard, soft, smooth, rough, wet, dry, stone, metal, plants, wood and both animal and human skin.

Marketing and all of the senses

Marketers have learnt that the more sights, sounds, smells, tastes and touches they can put into their promotional messages the more powerful the audience reaction. In the past most communication approaches would use sight and hearing (colour, shapes, designs, movement, images, words, sound and music) to build brand awareness. Now technology is enabling them to imaginatively use the other senses, touch, smell and taste, to press home the message in a more effective manner. Smells invoke memories and appeal directly to feelings without first being filtered and analysed by the brain. The smell of a new cosmetic, a new car or a foreign holiday resort, the taste of chocolate, of a cool lager, or Mocha Java Blend coffee, and the roundness of a mobile phone, the texture of silk in a new shirt and the smoothness of marble on a Spanish tiled floor can be recreated through the use of modern design and technological techniques.

3.8 General example | **Mixing up the senses**

Some people suffer from a neurological condition called synaesthesia which mixes up the senses. Words, letters, sounds and colours can invoke the flavours of different foods in the mouth. For the few individuals who suffer from this syndrome the word 'cinema' may conjure the taste of lemons, the word 'London' the taste of rhubarb, the number '7' the taste of vomit and the word 'grandmother' the taste of mint. The sight of colours will also elicit tastes so that some people might 'taste' onion from seeing the colour purple, beef from the colour red and vanilla from the colour pink.

Stimulus organisation

It would be impossible to take in all the environmental information that impinges on the senses so a filtering process takes place. Some stimuli go unnoticed, some are ignored and some make it through to the brain where they are immediately rejected, held for a very short time or taken into long-term memory. How this happens will change as a person grows from being a baby, to a teenager and finally an adult. Over the centuries some thinkers and philosophers believed that humans were born into the world with an empty mind and build all perceptual experiences by empirically interacting with the external environment. Others argue that survival perceptual organisational abilities are hereditary and are there at birth (it's the nature versus nurture argument again!).

Figure 3.5

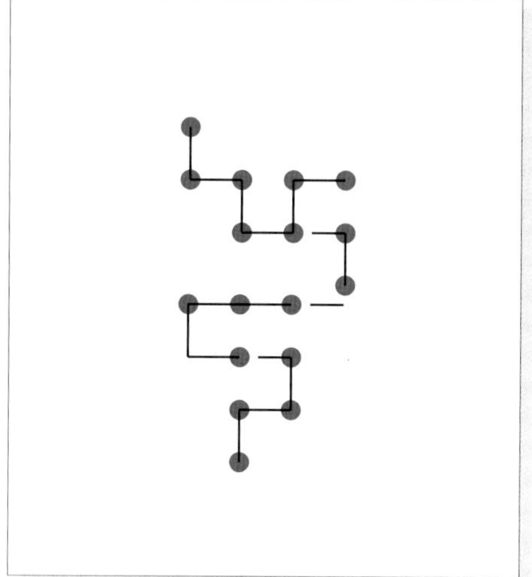

The human mind at birth – a blank sheet or genetically hardwired with some information?

Whatever the answer (probably somewhere in between) there has to be some type of perceptual organising process that takes place quickly because it would be impossible to function otherwise. Both conscious and unconscious factors will play a part in perception, as will levels of awareness, concentration, knowledge, intelligence and imagination.

Fit existing mind-sets

Research has shown that people tend to take in and process sensations that create cognitive harmony and coincide with already held interests and fit existing structures of beliefs and attitudes. Known as a **mind-set** or **schemata** they are ways of seeing the world already in the memory and are heavily influenced by socialisation and culture. Conversely individuals build mental defence mechanisms, and may reject information that contradicts beliefs that are unpleasant or distasteful. Too much constant exposure can also lead to '**habituation**' a situation where the stimulus is no longer noticed.

Perceptual organisation

'Gestalt theory holds that the whole is more than the sum of its parts.' KING AND WERTHEIMER (2005)

There has been an enormous amount of interest in how humans organise and make sense of sensory stimuli. Gestalt psychologists working in the 1930s researched the concept that animals and humans were born with genetic in-built ways of perceiving and organising the world. Because the world was a dangerous place babies (both animal and human) had to assimilate as quickly as possible the world around them if they were to survive in the wild when first born. This meant that limited information from exploring the immediate surroundings had to be quickly formed into understandable 'whole' patterns so that safety could be reached. An example would be the young turtles that when first hatched on the beach must climb out and make immediately for the sea otherwise they would be eaten by predators. It is argued that this organising ability is still genetically imbedded in the modern DNA after thousands of years and manifests in what the Gestalt school call 'universal principles'.

Gestalt universal principles

The Gestalt psychologists outlined what seemed to be several fundamental and universal principles (sometimes even called 'laws') of perceptual organisation and these are discussed below. The approach of Gestalt psychology has been extended to research in areas such as thinking and the mind, memory, and the nature of aesthetics.

▶ The use of **Gestalt** can be seen across a whole range of marketing concepts including packaging, merchandising and communications. Principles identified here include the following:

1 Closure
2 Figure and ground
3 Proximity
4 Similarity

1 The closure principle

▶ The principle of **closure** involves an individual's response to missing information. When viewing an object that is somehow incomplete, people automatically try to make sense of the image and supply the information that is missing to give a complete picture (perhaps that is why some people love jigsaw puzzles). Greatly used

Figure 3.6

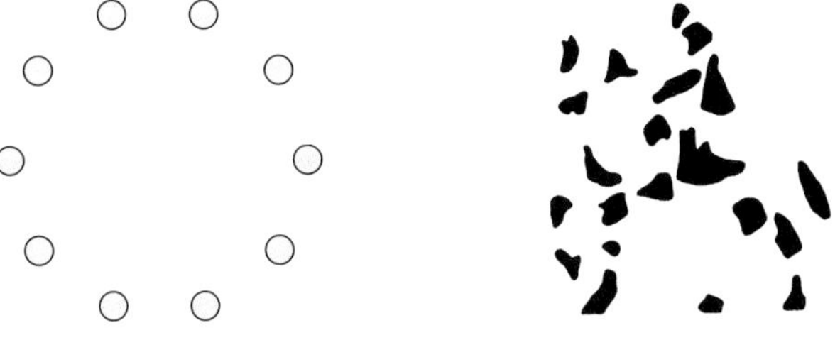

We automatically look for meaning and closure. Even though the circle is not joined together we still perceive a circle due to the principle of closure. We need to make sense of the other image

in advertising, marketers give only limited information in an advert seeking to encourage viewers to be drawn in and fill in the missing parts.

2 The principle of figure and ground

Confronted by a visual image, people have the need to separate a dominant shape (a 'figure' with a definite contour) from a 'background' (or 'ground'). In the diagrams below it seems impossible not to try to bring the 'white' image or the 'black' image to the front and push the other image to the back and so we constantly move back and forth from one to another.

Figure 3.7

Unambiguous figure and ground

Ambiguous figure and ground

Black on white or white on black?

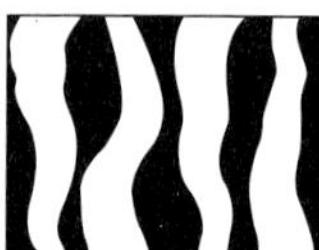

Figure and ground

Figure 3.8

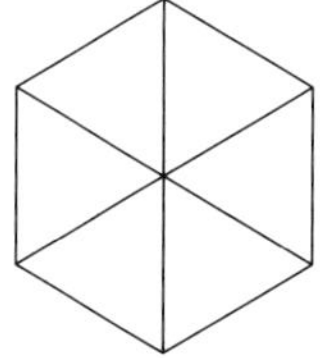

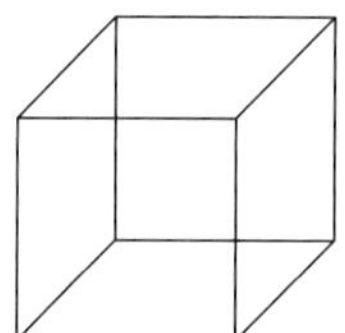

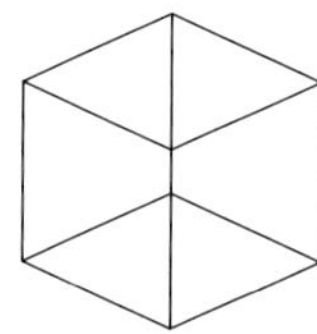

The Necker Cube. Strong and weak figure and ground – which is the front and which is the rear? It keeps switching back and forth

> **Key point** Figure-Ground Distinction; there is a need to determine what part of the visual picture is the background and what part stands out and is the foreground. Both images cannot be held at the same time.

3 The principle of proximity

According to this principle objects that are close together are perceptually organised as a unit. In Figure 3.9, we are likely to group the dots together in *rows* either downward (1) or along (2) not into just one square pattern. Objects not close together are seen as separate (3).

Figure 3.9

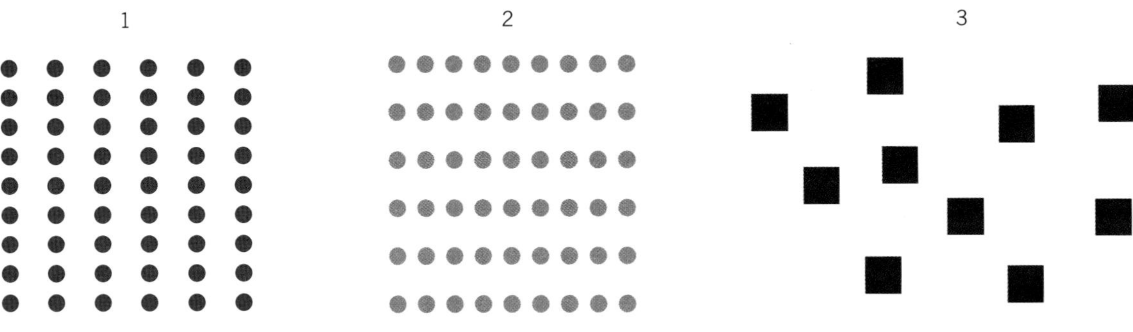

The principle of proximity

3.13 Marketing example **Proximity**

It is important to keep this law in mind when designing print and web-based materials. One should always focus on how the intended audience will interpret the graphics that will be employed. At the heart of sponsorship is the concept of proximity. Companies want their products to be associated with target market heroes such as David Beckham, Manchester United, The All Blacks, the World Baseball final and so on. Because of sponsorship and 'close proximity' marketers hope that values associated with iconic figures and organisations will attach themselves to the company and its brands.

Key point Proximity – figures, objects and images that are closest are grouped together.

4 The principle of similarity

According to the principle of similarity objects that are similar are organised together. In Figure 3.10, number 1 we see columns of squares or columns of circles, not rows. In number 2 all the dots are the same and we see an overall pattern.

Figure 3.10

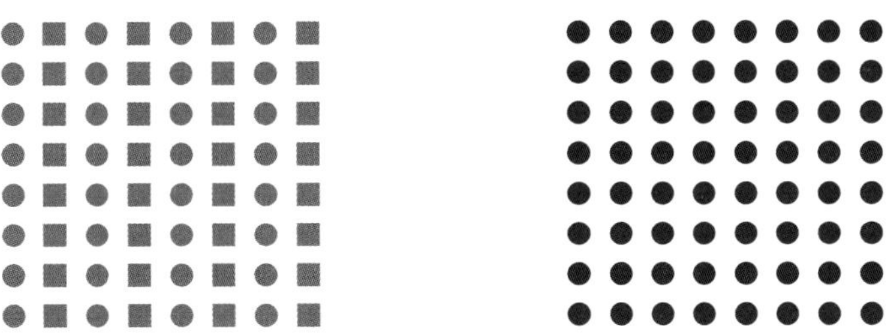

The principle of similarity

3.14 Marketing example — Similarity

The tendency to classify and group objects as a way of understanding the world is inherent almost in everything that humans do. Trees, plants, animals, insects, foods, houses, people, types of restaurants, types of shops, types of clothing, types of household goods and electrical goods, the list is endless. It is used constantly in retail range planning so that similar products are shown together. It's more pleasing to the eye to see it in this way rather than just an unconnected jumble.

Key point Principal of similarity, similar figures are organised and grouped together.

Perceptual constancy – our environment remains the same

Imagine waking up in the morning and the hands on the alarm clock had started to go backwards, or putting the light on in the room and the colour remains the same. Imagine that a car in the distance remained the same size the nearer it got, or the door seen at an angle stayed the same shape. People would be unable to function under such ambiguity and so people come to expect perception to be constant in some way or another. Perceptual constancy can be broken down into the following areas.

Size constancy

Object size remains constant despite the fact that the size of objects on the retina varies greatly with distance. A bus in the far distance looks to be the size of a thumb but an observer will have no doubt about its real size. One person near and one in the distance will again be thought of as normal size. Size constancy can be broken down into:

- *Relative size* – if two objects are of equal size, we perceive the smaller one as farther away.
- *Relative height* – below the horizon, objects higher in visual field are perceived as farther away; above the horizon, objects lower in the visual field are perceived as farther away.
- *Interposition* – if one object partially blocks our view of another, we view it as closer.

In Figure 3.11 we expect the line in the distance to be larger than the line on the same wall in the foreground because of perspective and inner and outer angles. According to Gregory (1990) because people in modern societies live with rectangular buildings, they perceive and interpret 'outward' or 'inward' pointing arrowheads at the end of the lines as a cue to the line's distance from them and so its length.

Figure 3.11

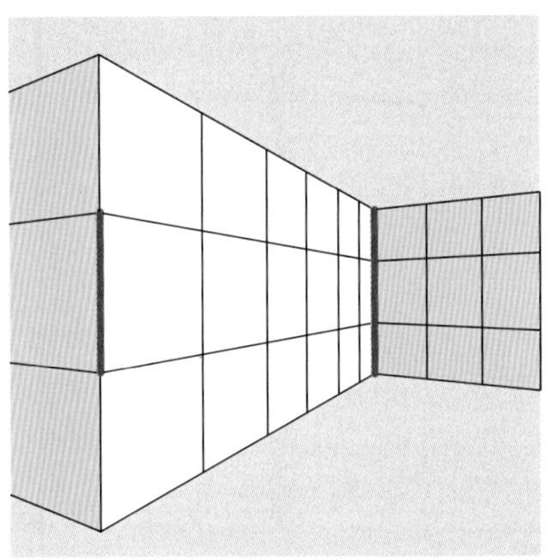

Perceptual constancy fooled. Measure and you will see the red lines are the same length

3.9 General example **Gestalt at work**

The anthropologist Colin Turnbull describes meeting a BaMbuti pygmy in the dense wide-open plains. Turnbull goes on to recount,

then he saw the buffalo, still grazing lazily several miles away, far down below. He turned to me and said, 'What insects are those?' At first I hardly understood, then I realized that in the forest vision is so limited that there is no great need to make an automatic allowance for distance when judging size. When I told Kenge that the insects were buffalo, he roared with laughter and told me not to tell such stupid lies. Because Kenge had no experience of seeing distant objects, he saw only trees, he had no way of making comparisons, he saw them simply as small.

(*Turnbull*, The Forest People, *1962: 217*)

Light constancy

People know that as light is obscured, becomes less, or is eliminated the appearance of objects change. With small amounts of information, however, whole objects can still be delineated and when light returns colours are expected to remain the same.

Shape constancy

Shape constancy allows the plate on the table to still be perceived as a circle even though the angle from which it is viewed appears to distort the shape. Similarly a door will be perceived as a door shape.

> **Key point** Perceptual constancy
> Size, shape and brightness of objects are expected to remain constant because our brains compensate for the relationship between size, distance, angles and brightness and darkness. We see what we expect to see: anything else would be de-stabilising.

Figure 3.12

A door appears to change shape as it is opened. Shape constancy ensures that we are not conscious of this. This will apply to everything that we see in nature

Stimulus confusion

Illusions reveal the brain's assumptions on how people expect to view the world. It seems that we all have perceptual 'mindsets' and attempt to see what we expect to see. When there are problems with the images confusion sets in. This can cause problems when individuals are asked feedback on what they have seen. For example research has shown that witnesses will give different descriptions when asked to recollect people that might have been involved in a crime of some kind (giving vastly different heights, ages and even type of background, Moushey 2005).

Figure 3.13

Stimulus confusion – how many legs on the elephant? An old woman or a young woman?

Key point Closure
We fill in the gaps from incomplete and imperfect forms so as to quickly perceive a whole. It should be remembered, however, that there are occasions when perception can be deceived.

3.15 Marketing example Closure, marketing and advertising

The principle of closure is constantly being used in advertising both in the use of words and images. Image research has shown that the use of a severely cropped image in a photo can result in greater involvement by consumers in the ad and even in a more positive response to the ad. This is because consumers have to use their imagination to fill in the incomplete pictures and end up being drawn into, and so thinking more about, the ad than they would if the images were not cropped. Cebrzynski (1998: 80) explained closure as being 'designed to make people disappear into the ad by forcing them to participate in the presentation of that ad'. Similarly we attempt to fill in the name of the company when presented with only a slogan or an image on the advert. For example the classic ads for Schweppes in the 1960s and 1970s ran for years with just the slogan 'schh you know who?'. Cigarette company Benson and Hedges ran billboards with just 'pure gold', Guinness used 'Pure Genius' and British Airways has 'The world's favourite airline'.

The concept of closure applies to story lines in films and plays. People like to see a unambiguous finish, usually with a happy ending. It has been used in advertisements as well. The classic example was for Maxwell House coffee. Neighbours kept meeting for coffee in romantic circumstances and viewers were kept hanging on over a series of five or six adverts to see whether it would end in love making (closure!).

Stimulus attention or awareness

Stimulus attention or awareness refers to the amount of time (if any) and level of concentration given in processing particular sensations. For example parents will be aware of the need to gain children's attention when asking them perhaps to tidy their bedroom or to do their homework. If they are not listening, because of so many other distractions, attention will not be given and no sensory processing will take place and the jobs will not be done.

Creating initial awareness has enormous implications for business and marketing communicators because of the need to communicate with many stakeholders, especially customers, about corporate values and brand benefits. The whole purpose of the £billions spent on media promotions and advertising around the world is to create awareness, stimulate interest, create desire and persuade purchasing action (the AIDA model) among target consumers. The difficulty for any one producer or advertising agency is how to successfully to do this when there are thousands of competitors trying to do the same thing.

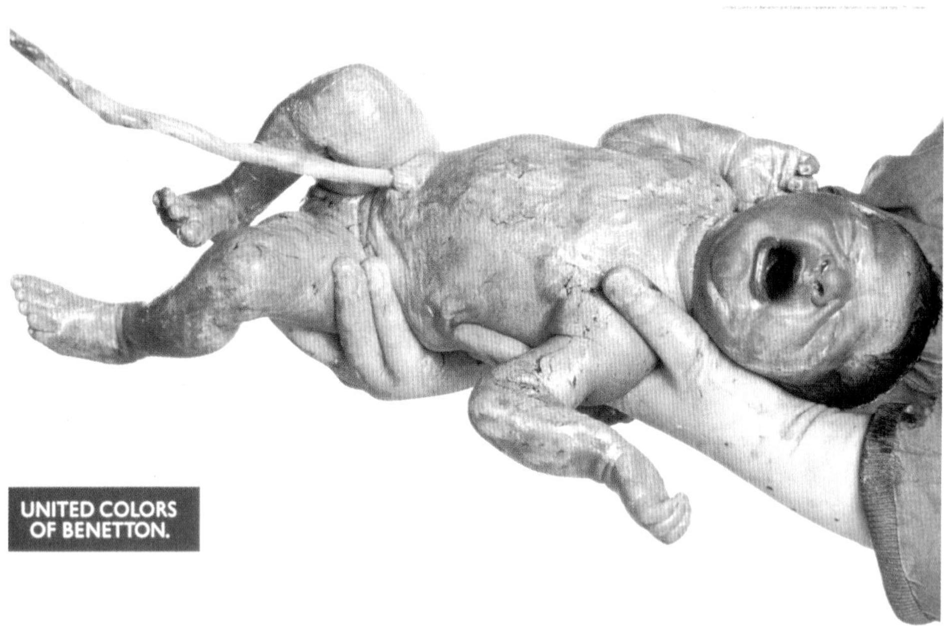

This advertisement created awareness of the brand through its shocking imagery. *Source*: United Colors of Benetton

Sensory overload

We now live in an age where there is access to almost unlimited amounts of information. **Sensory overload**, having more information than we are able to cope with, is without doubt the downside to this veritable mountain of information, such that there are instances of illnesses caused by working people unable to manage the process. Similarly, consumers are now exposed to more information then they are capable or willing to process. They can be so confused that they may either become very selective to what they are prepared to pay attention to or shut everything out completely seeing it all as boring, uninteresting marketing propaganda.

Sensory defence

We will look in more detail at defence mechanisms later in the book but research has shown that humans have developed **sensory defence** mechanisms to block out and filter all the information that is available. This is necessary if individuals are able to function properly as well as preventing eventual mental illness through too much stimuli. Sensory defence mechanisms enable people to selectively concentrate on particular stimuli while avoiding others.

Selective attention, comprehension, retention

Despite being exposed to over hundreds of random advertisements a day, through TV, in shop windows, newspapers, magazines, outdoor billboards, through the post, by telephone etc. consumers will selectively only pay attention to the adverts that interest them at that particular time.

Selective attention

Selective attention is the way that only certain messages are processed while others (the majority) are ignored. Messages that are selected will have caught the customer's attention in some way. This will be because the delivery method is eye-catching in some way or another. It is obviously in the interest of brand owners and their ad agencies to attempt to discover how this perceptual process works, who their target consumers will and will not listen to, how they like the message to be presented, so that they can then influence what is going on.

Selective comprehension

From the messages processed only a few are interpreted and understood in any meaningful way. If the message content is rejected it should be because whatever is being communicated isn't needed not because the message isn't understood.

Selective retention

Much information perceived will go into the short-term memory and be forgotten immediately after use. This could be because the message is confusing or of no long-term interest. Marketing people, however, would like its customers, and potential customers to transfer and retain information about their products, brands and services in their long-term memory, either for current or future use. The problem is that so would every other competitor in the market.

Attention, comprehension and retention are influenced by the following factors:

- *The communication method* The promotion methods used most must relate to the product, be eye-catching and stand out among hundreds of other ads. The message should be constructed so that it is retained in long-term memory.
- *The target market* The information must be relevant to the target market. Much information that emanates from the media on a daily basis is aimed at particular groups of people. As it is all paid for any that hits the wrong audience is money down the drain. Information about 18/30 holidays, for women's products or families with babies will immediately be rejected by the over sixty male thinking about investments and retirement.
- *Amount of personal involvement* It seems to be the case that we fail to notice old Volkswagen Beetles on the road until we require one. Similarly adverts for pregnant women will go unnoticed until a woman becomes pregnant and then she will see them all round her. We take up a hobby, golf, football, fishing, keep fit, playing the guitar and messages, thought irrelevant before, come to our notice and become part of our world.
- *Amount of exposure* Advertising agencies are well aware of the importance of widespread exposure in advertising campaigns. The more people hear a message, and from as many different sources as possible, the more they are liable to remember it. Of course this can be hugely expensive if a company has to pay for it.

- *Respect for the message sender* Research has shown that we are all more liable to listen to, and to certain extent believe, messages that are delivered by people (and companies) that we admire and respect in some way. That's why we see doctors (or people dressed as doctors) selling us medicines, ex-policemen selling car tyres, models extolling hair colouring as well as celebrities such as singers Michael Jackson and Madonna, footballer Thierry Henry, golfer Tiger Woods and actress Catherine Zeta-Jones.

3.16 Marketing example **Celebrity endorsement gone wrong**

After Magic Johnson went public with his HIV diagnosis, his Lincoln Mercury ads were pulled from the air and his endorsement deals were not renewed. Similarly Shredded Wheat pulled its ads featuring then England manager Glenn Hoddle and his family after he left his wife.

Sensory thresholds

The sensory threshold is the level at which individuals are able to detect or to lose the presence of a sensory stimulus. All people are different and so this will vary from person to person, probably getting worse as we get older. A young person might be able to hear the radio while the pensioner may not, some people are able to see a boat on the horizon while others cannot and there are individuals able to stand more pain than others and so on. **Sensory thresholds** are important in business and marketing because ultimate consumer enjoyment is totally dependent on whether the product feels, tastes, smells, looks, or sounds right to the particular target segment.

3.10 General example **Gender perceptual differences**

Many researchers have attempted to investigate undoubted gender differences with perception. Using ambiguous doodle-like black-and-white figures (see Figure 3.14 below), Coren, Porac and Ward (1978: 413) found gender differences in interpretation. Figure a, which was more likely to be viewed as a brush or a centipede by males, was more likely to be viewed as a comb or teeth by females. Figure b was viewed mostly as a target by males and by females mostly as a dinner plate. Figure c was seen by most men as a head and by most females as a cup.

Figure 3.14

a

b

c

Gender perceptual differences

Absolute threshold

The **absolute sensory threshold** is the point where something first becomes noticeable to the senses. It is the farthest distance we can see, the slightest sound we can hear, the faintest touch or hardness of bite we can feel, the smallest amount of flavour we can taste, or the lightest odour we can smell. It is the point at which a particular stimulus goes from being undetectable to detectable to our senses. Knowing how much sugar, garlic, salt, pepper, onion, flavouring, olfactory essence to put into the product, or knowing when a fruit is just ripe for picking so as to create the exact taste or smell that will accord to consumer demands, is an indispensable part of marketing. In a more abstract way it will also include important marketing emotional concepts linked to quality, value and brand positioning.

3.17 Marketing example — Absolute threshold and marketing

Absolute threshold in marketing could translate into the minimum quality of service and reputation one group of consumers might be prepared to accept before using a hotel (e.g. The Dorchester or the Hilton), the level of power another demands before considering a 'performance car' (e.g., a BMW or an Audi) and the reputation for 'coolness' before young fashion-conscious consumers would consider going to a particular nightclub or dance venue.

Recognition threshold

Although mostly lost on humans yet still strong in animals, the ability to discriminate, by sight, smell and taste, between good and bad foods, to know what might be poisonous or not, is part of animal and human genetic make-up. The recognition threshold is the level at which we are able to recognise the particular stimulus for what it is, naming the additive, distinguishing a sound, recognising an object by sight or touch and so on. Recognition threshold abilities vary between individuals, because of gender and culture and because of age. Practice, however, helps and if we take taste and smell for example, through repeated use, a ten-fold increase in sensitivity has been confirmed.

3.18 Marketing example — Recognition thresholds

Through practice and experience professional tea, wine and coffee tasters and perfumers are able to distinguish the smallest amount of difference between tastes, smell and flavours. In this way they seek to maintain brand consistency especially essential in premium products. They seem also to be able to identify the exact amount of every constituent, how much to add and how much to take away, so trying to give perfection. DNA testing to scientifically determine food and drink content is now commercially available and is being used by the Bordeaux growers of France in an attempt to expose fraudulent wines.

Marketing example and difference threshold

Academic and business and marketing practitioners are interested as well in how and when individuals recognise when a stimulus changes. How high might a night-club owner turn up the music before there are complaints from the neighbours, how brighter must lighting be before drivers are able to see the road clearer, how much additive must be used to drown out the noxious smell of a sewage farm and how much more salt must a chef add to the food before a customer's palate is satisfied? It also works in reverse with huge outcomes for the food industry in terms of health. How much can the manufacturer reduce levels of fat, salt, sugar and carbohydrates etc. without affecting the smell and the taste of its product? Similarly how much sweetener must be added to medicine to hide a particular foul taste? The difference threshold is the amount of change needed for us, the consumer, to recognise that a change has occurred. This change is referred to as the '**just noticeable difference**'.

3.19 Marketing example

The differential threshold seems to make a lot of difference to consumers when choosing cosmetics. A woman knows that she looks good in a particular shade of red lipstick. Choosing from different manufacturers' brands there will be levels of red below or above which she will not consider. It will be the same in considering the quality and price of clothes. Similarly in food. And companies have to be careful about changing content without informing the customer. For example, chocolate made sweeter or more bitter, curries too mild or too hot and too much salt in peanuts could turn the buyer off.

The just noticeable difference

'No matter how hard we look, we see very little of what we look at.' JAMES ELKINS (1997)

The amount of stimulus needed for the consumer to tell the difference, however, is not absolute and will vary according to the particular stimuli and the individual concerned. Imagine holding 5 kilos of shopping and half a kilo more were added. Most of us would not notice the difference. But if it was the other way around, holding one half kilo of shopping and 5 kilos were added then we are bound to notice the difference. If it was dark in a room and a 5 unit spotlight was switched on, the difference would be noticed. But if there was a 100 unit light on and a 105 unit spotlight replaced it the difference would not be noticed. Named after its original observer, Weber's law is a measurement of the percentage change needed (the just noticeable difference) before individuals can notice a difference.

Weber's law

Weber's law named after Ernst Weber, is the minimum amount by which stimulus intensity must be changed in order to produce a noticeable variation in sensory experience.

For example:

1 You presented two spotlights each with an intensity of 100 units to an observer.
2 You then asked the observer to increase the intensity of one of the spotlights until it was just noticeably brighter than the other.
3 If the brightness needed to yield the just noticeable difference was 120 then the observer's difference threshold would be 20 units, 20 per cent or a fifth. This would be the level of just noticeable difference.

Weber's Law can be applied to a variety of sensory inputs (taste, smell, brightness, colour, loudness, mass, line length, etc.). The size of the Weber fraction varies across activities but in all cases tends to be a constant within a specific activity.

3.20 Marketing example — Just noticeable difference (JND)

The idea of a 'just noticeable difference' is important in many areas. For example how much salt, sugar etc. would a manufacturer need to add to, or take away from, existing amounts before the consumer would be aware of the difference? How much larger must a newspaper advertisement be before the reader is aware? How loud must the music be before the audience reacts? How much more essence in a perfume before a change in smell is detected? More difficult to measure but just as important are questions about price increases, reduction in quantity, levels of customer service and so on. Rather than increase the price some manufacturers of things like chocolate bars would rather slowly reduce quantity hoping nobody will notice. The secret is to try to stay within the Weber law of JND, otherwise consumer dissatisfaction will follow.

Sensory evaluation

▶ Now seen very much as a science, **sensory evaluation** tries to measure, analyse and interpret consumer levels of sensory reaction to a whole range of products, brands and services. Used mainly in product upgrades and new product development it takes the five main senses, sight, sound, taste, smell and touch and, through research, tries to work out what consumer perception and sensory reaction might be to a whole range of possible original products. Scientists and researchers attempt to judge consumer reaction and behaviour in such areas as food, fashion, fragrances, cosmetics and drinks. Marketing agencies, such as 'flavour houses', exist to take scientific findings and help companies develop innovative consumer products (at a price of course). New convenience foods, healthier foods, new ways of packaging, are good examples of why we need sensory evaluation. Different sensory evaluation levels among consumers' offer producers ways of segmenting markets, e.g. some people like highly spiced food.

Sensory deprivation

Many experiments have been conducted over the decades that have looked at the problems caused when animals and humans have been deprived of one or more of the senses. Chimps that have been taken from their mothers straight after birth, fed by bottle, deprived of their mother's cuddles and left on their own have shrunk into the corner of the cage, refused to eat and eventually become seriously ill. Children that receive only diffuse light input in early childhood subsequently have difficulty in recognising light patterns. There seems to be a critical period in childhood for sensory receptor development and if missed can cause health and development problems later on. **Sensory deprivation** techniques have been used as a form of torture for years. Prisoners are hooded, made to stand for hours on end, exposed to silence/or constant loud noise after which confusion and destabilisation can cause individuals to confess to anything. Different levels of sensory deprivation among consumers, through upbringing or illness can affect reactions to products and brands later on in life. Organisations would like to encourage people to become hooked into their product/service brand, for example chocolate, cake, beer, music, film and theatre (even shopping). Advertising can be used to try to make the customer suffer feelings of sensory deprivation, and make them miss not indulging in some way on a continuous basis.

3.21 Marketing example — Sensory adaptation

Constant exposure to the same or similar stimuli will lead eventually to sensory adaptation. If we live on the main road we will eventually adapt to the noise and no longer be aware of it unless it is brought to our attention in some way. Similarly with the clock ticking away in the bedroom, it might irritate at first but eventually it will cease to be a bother. The same thing will happen with smells. Somebody working in a brewery will not notice the smell of yeast but a newcomer will. Marketers have to be mindful that consumers can adapt in the same way to products and promotions. Examples might be margarine advertised as a cheaper version of butter no longer tasting like butter, or using too many money-off promotion campaigns. The promotional messages no longer work in the same stimulating way.

Question

1 How might advertisers approach the problem of sensory adaptation? Give examples of live solutions in product development, packaging, sales promotions and advertising.

The role of symbolism in perception

It was the Swiss linguist **Ferdinand de Saussure** writing at the end of the nineteenth century who observed that a great deal of human communication happens, not through spoken language but by the use of symbols or as he came to define it, **semiotics**. He went on to study the methods that people used, various signals, signs, images, shapes and colours as well as through facial and body language, ways of dressing and behaving and so on, to find out if these 'life signs within society' were widespread and universal.

Examples of symbolism

Examples of 'semiotics' can be witnessed every day: thumbs up, thumbs down, shoulder shrugging, eyebrow raising, first finger tapping the nose, shake or nod of the head, hitting the forehead, arms raised or lowered, slow or fast movement of the body, legs crossed, shaking hands, bowing, one or two kisses on each cheek. Saussure also identified semiotics (some more consciously apparent than others) in colours (green for go, red for danger) in shapes, images, patterns and behaviour. Some of these are the same and some different across regions and countries.

3.22 Marketing example — Semiotics in advertising

Marketers and advertisers use semiotics extensively both as a complement to and a substitute for language. In this way they hope to get beneath the critical perceptual defences that people erect against the overtures of adverts. An Andrex puppy becomes a sign for caring motherhood and wiping your bottom; the Marlboro cowboy for an adventurous, vicarious, 'real man' lifestyle; purple becomes a symbol for Silk Cut cigarettes; the Kellogg's Cockerel sunny, early morning and breakfast; mountain streams represent freshness; green fields and cows, natural, organic products; spectacles represent intelligence; a white coat a scientific background; an umbrella security. Windsurfing becomes a euphemism for menstruation and a woman eating a slice of chocolate cake is used to sell constipation tablets.

Questions

1 Identify as many examples of semiotics as possible that you might use throughout the day.

2 Identify the use of semiotics in advertising.

Key point Semiotics and symbolism are heavily used in marketing and advertising.

Subliminal perception

Subliminal perception is supposed to occur whenever stimuli are presented below the conscious level of awareness and are able to influence thoughts, feelings, or actions. In recent years, the term has been applied more generally to describe any situation in which unnoticed, perhaps cleverly disguised, stimuli are perceived. **Subliminal advertising** involves infiltrating the subconscious with surreptitious visual or whispered messages. The idea is to bypass the stimulus-filtering mechanism, discussed above, of the viewer or listener. There is little evidence that it works (it's difficult enough trying to get through to the audience when they are conscious, let alone non-conscious). Truly unobservable subliminal messages are illegal in most developed countries.

Subliminal advertising

Many people still believe today that advertisers are able to pass messages into peoples' minds by slipping them in under the level of consciousness. This then triggers anxiety of some kind that can only be relieved by the individual buying a product or brand that he or she might not ordinarily want. In 1957 an unemployed market researcher named James Vicary contacted marketing and advertising managers of large companies through his company the Subliminal Projection Company, offering to instruct them in a new selling and marketing technique 'subliminal advertising'. Some time before Eastman Kodak had developed a device for use in high-speed photography, called a tachistoscope, that could emit an image at 1/60,000th of a second. This was so fast that it was imperceptible to the human eye but could be recorded by the brain below the level of consciousness. Using his secreted patented version of the tachistoscope Vicary claimed that experiments had taken place at an unidentified motion picture theatre at some unidentified time on over 40,000 unidentified picture goers. While watching a movie, the audience had been subliminally exposed to two messages. One said 'Eat popcorn', the other said 'Drink Coke'. According to Vicary the invisible advertising increased the sales of popcorn an average of 57.5 per cent and increased the sales of Coca-Cola an average of 18.1 per cent. Although Vicary was able to convince some advertisers and make lots of money, lack of concrete evidence, then and since, has convinced observers that his claims were fraudulent and the process a scam.

3.23 Marketing example Subliminal advertising

In the 1970s, Wilson Bryan Key rekindled the frenzy with his book *Subliminal Seduction*, which purported to reveal that ads for soap, alcohol, travel, clothes and other everyday products were riddled with embedded hidden messages and images such as male and female body parts, death skulls, snakes, volcanoes, the word 'sex' and so on. Unintelligible to the conscious mind, embeds were supposedly there to appeal directly to the consumer's primal instincts, manipulating an unwitting public into buying things they didn't need. Department stores and grocery store chains would play messages like 'stealing is dishonest' under background Muzak. Tens of thousands of consumers bought subliminal tapes and, later, videos and computer software that could be played in the background or while asleep attracted by the promise that a foreign language or school exam subject or driving a car could be learnt in this way. It was even suggested that playing tapes while pregnant would have a beneficial affect on the unborn child's intellect. There seems to be little or no evidence that any of this really works.

Question

1 Look at all forms of subliminal advertising and discuss whether or not you think that any of it works in a meaningful way.

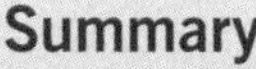

Summary

- In this chapter we discussed the concept of perception, including stimuli, sensation, processing and interpretation and its role in marketing and understanding consumer behaviour.
- The five main senses, sight, sound, touch, taste and smell were examined in some detail.
- Areas looked at under sight included the role of colour and light. Under sound it was words and music. Under touch it was textures and bodily impressions. Smell and taste were examined together.
- The role that both nature and nurture play in human perception was outlined.
- Gestalt perceptual principles including constancy, closure, figure and ground, proximity, similarity and confusion where outlined.
- Sensory awareness, differentiation, overload, defences, comprehension, selection, attention, retention, thresholds and deprivation were briefly examined.
- Semiotics, symbolism, sensory organisation and the role of subliminal advertising where identified.

Questions

1 Identify the factors and theories that are involved in the process of human perception. How might an understanding of how it operates help marketing practitioners in achieving marketing objectives?

2 Identify the five main senses and discuss the relevant importance of each.

3 How might sight and sound be used in developing successful consumer programmes? Give live examples to illuminate your answers.

4 Examine the importance of colour in packaging and merchandising. Give examples of brands that have successfully used colour to enhance presentation and discuss where this might go in the future.

5 Examine the importance of music to people and identify why it might, or might not work. Discuss how it is used in marketing giving live examples and evaluating good and bad practices.

6 There are some marketing commentators that feel that the senses of touch, smell and taste are underrated in marketing campaigns and an integrated understanding and use of all the senses would create more successful campaigns. Would you agree?

7 Identify the different mechanisms used by receivers to block-out or modify incoming sensations. What must advertisers do to try to make certain that the consumer is receiving their messages rather than those of the competitor?

8 Discuss the role of the following in understanding consumer behaviour giving examples of how they are used:
   - **a** Semiotics and symbolism
   - **b** Subliminal perception
   - **c** Celebrity endorsement

9 Discuss the Gestalt Universal Principles of Perception. How realistic are they in trying to understand how we organise the perceptual process? Give examples of how they have been used in marketing and advertising.

10 Discuss perceptual differences between male and female, the old and young, different social classes and the rich and the poor. Give examples where organisations have used differences, if any, in the marketing of products and services.

Case study

Case study 1 Perception, cultural and environmental factors

The argument about the degree of influence on behaviour of nature and nurture has been constantly discussed and argued over for centuries and seems to swing first one way and then the other. In a similar way, the idea that human perception is objective and universal, subjective and individual or a combination of the two has also been the centre of academic polemic, again for many hundreds of years. Visual perception is an interesting area where there are some that think that we all perceive the same thing while others think the visual perception is more subjective and relative to situation.

The Gestalt psychologists argue that there are organisational abilities such as, 'figure and ground', 'contrast', 'grouping', 'closure' etc. that are 'laws on the principles of perception' and might be universal and inbuilt in all cultures.

There are others that disagree and feel that this is too strong an approach. They argue that a picture is a pattern of lines and shaded areas on a flat surface that depicts some aspect of the real world. The ability to recognise objects in pictures is so common in most cultures that it is often taken for granted that such recognition is universal in man. Experiments have shown that people of one culture perceive a picture differently from people of another and that perception of pictures calls for some form of learning.

Questions

1 Discuss the differences that culture might make to the perceptual processes. Give examples of how and why it might differ around the world.

2 Identify the five senses discussed in this chapter and investigate how each might be different in Asia, the Middle East and in North and South America.

3 Give examples on how an understanding of perception will help marketers.

Case study

Case study 2 Marketing examples – the use of textures

- Wood textures are used extensively in furniture, floor and wall decorations in homes, offices and shops using different textured woods from around the world including: mahogany, maple, oak, beech, pine, walnut, redwood, olive, yew and rosewood.

- Many synthetic materials are used in household and clothing products including: plastics, nylons, rayon, Bakelite, polyester, acrylic and polyurethane.
- Animal and plant materials are used in car interiors using wool, leather, suede, cotton and rubber.
- Flooring is made of marble, rubber, natural and synthetic fibres.
- Jewellery and ornaments use gold, precious stones, diamonds, ceramics and glass.
- Metals such as iron, stainless steel, aluminium, copper, brass, gold, silver are used in a multitude of household products.

Questions

1. How many of the senses might be involved in the use of textures?
2. Discuss the use of textures in the marketing of products. What is its value in helping to sell one product rather than another?

Further reading

Books

Babbit, E.D. (1878) *The Principles of Light and Color*, in F. Birren (ed.), New York: University Books, 1967.

Berger, John (1995); *Ways of Seeing*, London: BBC and Penguin Books.

Block, J. Richard and Harold F. Yuker (1992) *Can You Believe Your Eyes?*, London: Robson.

Coren, Stanley, Clare Porac and Lawrence M. Ward (1984) *Sensation and Perception* (International edn), New York: Academic Press.

Dixon, N.F. (1971) *Subliminal Perception: The Nature of a Controversy*, New York: McGraw-Hill.

Doty, R.L. (revised ed. 2003) *Handbook of Olfaction and Gustation*, New York: Marcel Dekker.

Elkin, James (1997) *The Object Stares Back: On The Nature of Seeing*, Orlando, FL: Harcourt.

Gordon, I.E. (1997) *Theories of Visual Perception*. Chichester: John Wiley.

Gregory, Richard L. (1990) *Eye and Brain: The Psychology of Seeing*, 4th edn, Oxford: Oxford University Press.

Grenoble, Lenore A. and Lindsay J. Whaley (eds) (1998) *Endangered Languages: Language Loss and Community Response*, Cambridge: Cambridge University Press.

Hawkins, Del I., Roger J. Best and Kenneth A. Coney (1998) *Consumer Behavior: Building Marketing Strategy*, 7th edn, Boston: McGraw-Hill.

Hofstadter, D.R. (1995) *Fluid Concepts and Creative Analogies: Computer Models of the Fundamental Mechanisms of Thought*, together with the Fluid Analogies Research Group, New York: Basic Books.

Kelley, David (1988) *The Evidence of the Senses: A Realist Theory of Perception*, Baton Rouge, LA: Louisiana State University Press.

Key, Wilson Bryan (1973) *Subliminal Seduction*, New York: Signet.

King, D. Brett and Michael Wertheimer (2005) *Max Wertheimer and Gestalt Theory*, London: Transaction Publishers.

Korb, M.P., J. Gorrell, and V. Van de Riet (1989) *Gestalt Therapy: Practice and Theory*, 2nd edn, New York: Pergamon Press.

Myers, D.G. (1995) *Psychology*, 4th edn, New York: Worth Publishers.

Ratey, J. (2002) *A User's Guide to the Brain: Perception, Attention, and the Four Theaters of the Brain*, New York: Vintage Books.

Roberts, D. (2002) *Signals and Perception: the Fundamentals of Human Sensation*, ed. David Roberts, Basingstoke: Open University Press and Palgrave Macmillan. Chapters on smell and taste by Tim Jacob.

Segall, Marshall H., Donald T. Campbell and Melville J. Herskovits (1966) *The Influence of Culture on Visual Perception*, Indianapolis, IN: Bobbs-Merrill.

Sekuler, Robert and Randolph Blake (1994) *Perception*, 3rd edn, New York: McGraw-Hill.

Solomon, M.R. (2001) *Consumer Behaviour*, 5th edn, Upper Saddle River, NJ: Prentice Hall.

Turnbull, Colin (1962) *The Forest People*, New York: Touchstone Books, 1987.

Vernon, M.D. (1971) *The Psychology of Perception*, Harmondsworth: Penguin.

Wright, Ray (1999) *Advertising*, Harlow: Financial Times/Prentice Hall.

Articles and journals

Aaronson, B. (1970) 'Some Affective Stereotypes of Colour', *International Journal of Symbology*, 2: 15–27. As cited in D.T. Sharpe (1974) *The Psychology of Colour and Design*, Chicago, IL: Nelson-Hall.

Bellizzi, Joseph A., Ayn E. Crowley and Ronald W. Hasty (1983) 'The Effects of Color in Store Design', *Journal of Retailing*, 59 (Spring): 21–45.

Bone, P.F. and P.S. Ellen (1999) 'Scents in the Marketplace: Explaining a Function of Olfaction', *Journal of Retailing*, 75(2): 243–62.

Cebrzynski, G. (1998) 'Get Crazy: Reach Over the Borders of Reality in Advertising', *Nation's Restaurant News*, 32(23): 80.

Davies, G. (1981) 'Face Recall Systems', in Davies, Ellis & Shepherd (eds), *Perceiving and Remembering Faces*, London: Academic Press, pp. 228–50.

Gerard, R.M. (1958) 'Differential Effects of Colored Lights on Psychophysiological Functions', *Journal of Applied Psychology*, 43: 107–12.

Gorn, Gerald J. (1982) 'The Effects of Music in Advertising on Choice Behavior: A Classical Conditioning Approach', *Journal of Marketing*, 46 (Winter): 94–101.

Hastorf, Albert H. and Hadley Cantril (1954) 'They Saw a Game: A Case Study', *Journal of Abnormal Social Psychology*, 49: 129–34.

Jacob, T.J.C., C.S. Fraser, L. Wang, V.E. Walker, and S. O'Connor (2003) 'Psychophysical Evaluation of Responses to Pleasant and Mal-odour Stimulation in Human Subjects. Adaptation, Dose Response and Gender Differences', *International Journal of Psychophysiology*, 48: 67–80.

Kellaris, James J. and Anthony D. Cox (1989) 'The Effects of Background Music in Advertising: A Reassessment', *Journal of Consumer Research*, 16 (June): 113–18.

Kellaris, James J. and Robert J. Kent (1992) 'The Influence of Music on Consumers' Temporal Perceptions: Does Time Fly When You're Having Fun?', *Journal of Consumer Psychology*, 1 (4): 365–76.

Levine, Robert, Isidor Chein and Gardner Murphy (1942) 'The Relation of the Intensity of a Need to the Amount of Perceptual Distortion', *Journal of Psychology*, 13: 283–93.

Levy, B.I. (1984) 'Research into the Psychological Meaning of Color', *American Journal of Art Therapy*, 23: 58–61.

McConnell, J.V., R.L. Cutler and E.B. McNeil (1958) 'Subliminal Stimulation: An Overview', *American Psychologist*, 13: 229–42.

Milliman, Ronald E. (1982) 'Using Background Music to Affect the Behavior of Supermarket Shoppers', *Journal of Marketing*, 46 (Summer): 86–91.

North, Adrian C., David J. Hargreaves and Jennifer McKendrick (1997). 'In-store Music Affects Product Choice', *Nature*, 390: 132.

North, Adrian C., David J. Hargreaves and Jennifer McKendrick (2003) 'The Effect of Musical Style on Restaurant Customers' Spending', *Environment and Behavior*, 35: 712–18.

Peracchio, L.A. and J. Meyers-Levy (1994) 'How Ambiguous Cropped Objects in Ad Photos Can Affect Product Evaluations', *Journal of Consumer Research*, 21(1): 190–204.

Reingold Merikle, P.M. and E.M. Reingold (1992) 'Measuring Unconscious Perceptual Processes', in R.F. Bornstein and T.S. Pittman (eds), *Perception without Awareness* New York: Guilford Press, pp. 55–80.

Spehr, M., G. Gisselmann, A. Poplawski, J.A. Riffel, C.H. Wetzel, R.K. Zimmer and H. Hatt (2003) Identification of a testicular odorant receptor mediating human sperm chemotaxis', *Science* (March) 28: 299 (5615), 2054–8.

Spangenberg, Eric R., Ayn E. Crowley and Pamela W. Henderson (1996) 'Improving the Store Environment: Do Olfactory Cues Affect Evaluations and Behaviors?', *Journal of Marketing*, 60 (April): 67–80.

Walle, W. (ed.), *AMA Educators' Conference Proceedings*, Vol. 54, 106–110. Chicago, IL: American Marketing Association.

Yalch, Richard F. and Eric Spangenberg (1988) 'An Environmental Psychological Study of Foreground and Background Music as Retail Atmospheric Factors', in Alf.

Websites

Chandler, Daniel (1994) 'Individual Differences, Purposes and Needs' (www.aber.ac.uk/media).

Food Commission, www.foodcomm.org.uk.

Tim Jacob @ cardiff.ac.uk, School of Biosciences, Cardiff University, CF10 3US, UK.

Marketing database, www.studentshout.com.

Bill Moushey and Nathan Crabbe (2005), Pittsburgh Post-Gazette, bmoushey@pointpark.edu.

Nichols, Bill, US freelance photographer, www.sportsshooter.com.

Learning

4

'The illiterate of the 21st century will not be those who cannot read and write, but those who cannot learn, unlearn, and relearn.'

Alvin Toffler

Objectives

At the end of this chapter the reader will be able to:

1. Define the meaning of learning and be able to identify and evaluate the major different approaches taken by academics and commentators over the centuries.
2. Identify, examine and evaluate the many theories attached to understanding how both animals and humans learn and relate it to marketing and consumer concerns.
3. Identify the factors involved in the concept of memory and forgetting and demonstrate its importance underpinning the whole learning process.

Introduction

For hundreds of years writers, philosophers, psychologists and academics have been fascinated by the concept of learning, trying to define what we mean by learning, how it happens and what might be the most advantageous method to adopt to encourage both young and old to get the best from life. Even now the idea is never far from the minds of politicians (especially at election time), parents, educationalists, and business and marketing managers. No single subject has been more investigated, argued over and written about. Major different learning methods have been implemented, rejected, implemented (in some slightly different form) and then rejected again, in schools in countries all around the world as the search for the secret of successful learning programmes continues.

Learning and marketing

In marketing, marketing research, communications and retail, managers are interested in the learning process, particularly how consumers learn about products and services and corporate and brand values, which retail outlets to use, which products to chose and so on. They are also interested in understanding the mechanisms associated with short and long-term memory as well as the factors involved with forgetting, re-awakening and reminding customers about why they should repurchase particular products. In this way (along with perception discussed in the preceding chapter) they hope to be able to understand and influence the whole learning process and so clearly identify and satisfy consumer needs and wants.

> **Key point** Learning and perception
> It's worth a reminder that learning and perception (along with other factors) are inextricably entwined. How we interpret the world of our senses is dependent on social and cultural learning and experiences collected and honed throughout the whole of our lives.

Learning and knowledge

If you tell me, I will listen. If you show me, I will see. But if you let me experience, I will learn. LAO TZU, Chinese Philosopher

Learning can be defined as a relatively permanent change in behaviour (not through illness however) and ways of thinking, brought about by perceptual and cognitive (thinking) experiences. This can happen in a conscious, semi-conscious or non-conscious manner or as some kind of combination of all three. It can happen in the mind or it can be imprinted on to the nervous system so that, for example, we can't help ourselves feeling sick when we smell an odour associated with an unpleasant happening. It might be in a deliberate fashion, learning to drive a car, how to type or the benefits of one computer, one political party, one brand over another. It can happen in a less deliberate manner, which road to take to get to work, where the different products are in the supermarket, which butter tastes the best. Or it can happen unintentionally, perhaps feeling nostalgic when we hear the words of a favourite song, finding ourselves singing along when we hear jingles and sayings for well advertised brands or even shedding a tear when we see a programme about the early death of somebody such as Elvis Presley or Princess Diana.

> **Key point** Learning can be defined as a relatively permanent change in behaviour and ways of thinking, bought about by perceptual and cognitive experiences and social and cultural interactions.

Learning is an on-going process

People are continuously learning throughout their lives. Some of the things learnt will fit into similar patterns while other things will be different. Learning will happen by listening to and observing others and the world around us, reading, watching TV, and listening to the radio or by tasting different foods. It can be deliberate or habitual and unthinking. It happens when interacting with others, family, friends, it happens at school, university and work and it carries on through life into retirement and finally ends in death, reacting to stimuli, getting feedback, modifying behaviour in a ceaseless, iterative manner.

Culture and learning

Although globalisation, information technology and travel have brought people closer together there are still major differences in the things that are learnt and the things that people believe and this will have a great affect on thinking and behaviour. We only have to pick up a newspaper or listen to the radio or watch TV to see the huge differences in learning between nations, politics, religion, economic systems, values and priorities and the different ways that people chose to live their lives. In some societies citizens are encouraged to think for themselves and make decisions based on reasoned argument, while in others information and knowledge is seen as given and citizens are expected to inculcate without any discussion. Even within societies there are differences with learning capabilities, intelligence levels and knowledge amounts.

Marketing, consumer behaviour and learning

Marketers are interested in learning about the way that consumers learn, think and behave because they need to know how to communicate benefit messages that will persuade initial purchase and then build long-term loyalty. They want the customer to learn to love both company and product brand and learning to learn how people learn, memorise and retain relevant information is crucial to the process.

> **Key point** Learning how customers learn and retain relevant information is crucial if marketing managers are to be successful.

How we acquire knowledge – innate, reason and the mind or experience

There are different ways that humans are said to acquire knowledge and the truth about the world and the cosmos and some are more contentious than others. This is through **innate knowledge**, **received knowledge**, empirical observation and through rationalism and the use of the mind.

Innate, learned or a combination

Pivotal to the early debate about how humans acquire knowledge was whether or not it was acquired solely through the use of the senses or whether humans come to the world with some form of innate, hereditary knowledge.

- Some early thinkers argued that certain things such as morality and ideas of God and religion are examples of divinely innate (inherited) knowledge that humans bring to the world at birth (Herbert of Cherbury 1583–1648).
- Others argued that when we are born the mind is a blank slate and all knowledge we acquire comes though our senses empirically interacting with the environment (**John Locke** 1632–1704).
- David Hume writing in the eighteenth century developed the idea that cognitive (thinking) reasoning abilities and faculties were processes that could not be traced back directly to empirical experiences and so had to be partly innate.

Received knowledge – knowledge from God

Received knowledge is knowledge that is said to come to us from some divine source such as a God, a prophet or God's representative on earth. The Bible, the Koran, the Torah or individual prayer or visitations are all possible sources of received knowledge for Christians, Muslims and Jews. The belief that this was the only way that we could learn about the world held sway for over 1500 years and many great

Figure 4.1

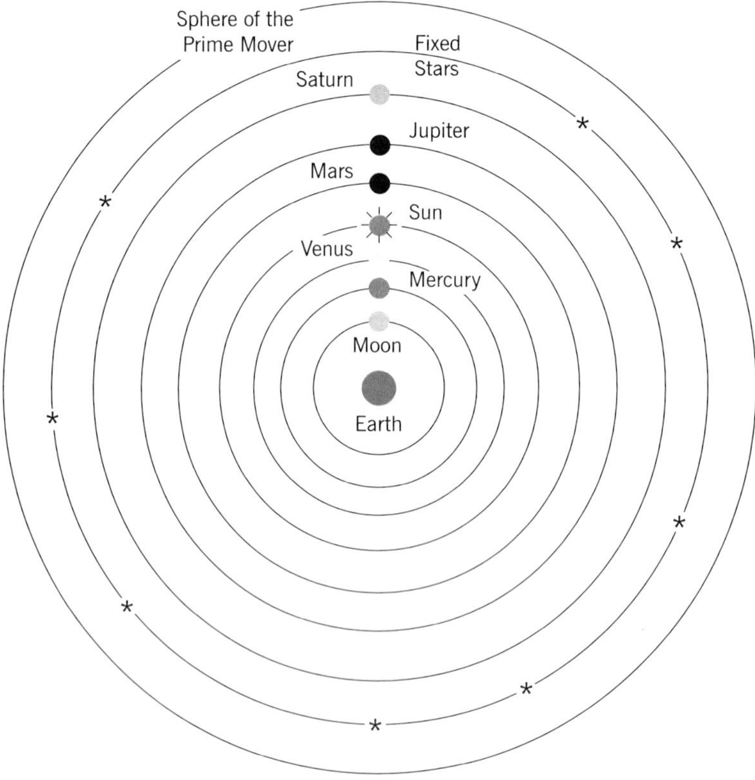

Greek philosopher Aristotle's view of the universe, with the earth at the centre, held sway for over 2000 years until Galileo (1564–1642) put the sun at the centre

philosophers and thinkers where imprisoned or put to death for daring to question received religious wisdom. It wasn't until the eighteenth century, in the period now known as the Enlightenment, that a rational, reasoned and systematic approach using observation and experimentation was generally accepted as the way to gain true knowledge about the world, the stars and the universe.

Rationalism – knowledge by reason

Rationalism or *a priori* knowledge ('prior to' experience) is knowledge about what is true or false in the world (known as propositional knowledge) that has been obtained by the working of the mind without observation and the use of the senses. It involves such non-experiential things as so called 'pure reason', 'intuition' and 'inner reflection'.

4.1 General example | Mathematics, geometry at the heart of pure reason

Mathematics and logic e.g. $2+2=4$, the fact that inside angles of a triangle add up to 180 degrees, the use of mathematics to uncover some of the secrets of the cosmos are examples because they are thought to come about by the use of the mind alone. The great scientist **Isaac Newton (1642–1727)** was able to predict the path of planets and comets with little or no observation using mathematics and reason.

Empirical knowledge – knowledge by observation

'No man's knowledge here can go beyond his experience.' JOHN LOCKE (1632–1704)

On the other hand empirical knowledge is knowledge about what is true or false in the world that is obtained after observing and interacting with the world through the use of the senses (sight, sound, smell, taste and touch). This is obtained either by our own direct observation or the direct observation and the testimony of others. There are some thinkers that argued that this was the only way that real knowledge can be obtained (John Locke, 1632–1704).

Our own observations

From early childhood humans learn how to talk, how to crawl and walk, how to behave in the company of others, how to shop and how to choose one product and one brand over another by observing the actions of others. Some of this information will be based on casual observation, conjecture and anecdote and some from more purposeful effort and have a more solid scientific foundation. We know empirically, that is by our own experiences, that rain will make us wet, the sun will dry us out, apples fall to the ground and some kinds of food are cheaper at one supermarket rather than another. I like the taste of one tea over another, and the smell of one perfume against another. Consumers buy one brand rather than

Figure 4.2

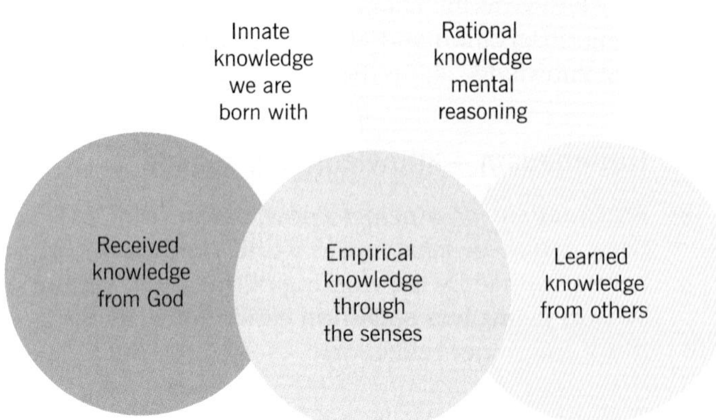

How people acquire knowledge

another because they like it better than any other brand. Similarly a person might have been on holiday to the south of England or to the south of France and prefer the south of France. Through constant use of the senses we build a mind-set, a whole series of experiences that is then used to interact with observations. In this way we build an enormous bank of knowledge that grows as we become older and as long as our short- and long-term memory remains active. (Of course, as we saw in the chapter on perception, sometimes our senses can be fooled and the information we think we are receiving isn't as it seems to be.)

The experiences of other people

Knowledge is also gained from discussing the experiences of other people both in person and from listening to them on TV and the radio and reading the print media. Whether information is believed or not will depend on how easily it fits into current beliefs and already held mind-sets. The problem for the layperson and the average consumer is telling the difference between what is true, what is partly true and what is untrue.

> **Key point** We learn from both our experiences and the experiences of others.

A combination of innate abilities, mental reasoning and observation

'Mother Nature has plainly not entrusted the determination of our intellectual capacities to the blind fate of a gene or genes; she gave us parents, learning, language, culture and education to program ourselves with.' (RIDLEY 1999: 77)

There seems to be little doubt about the critical importance of empirical information and it plays a central role in learning and the acquisition of knowledge. There

Formal learning beginning around the world. Young children learn by listening and watching the teacher

is also some evidence that, although we appear not to be born with conscious knowledge, there are innate genetically programmed reasoning faculties and abilities that enable such things as language, perception, problem solving and other skills (Pinker *et al.* 1999). So it seems that we use innate predispositions, mental reasoning and empirical observation to build knowledge of our environment.

Key point It is now generally believed that we use a combination of innate predispositions, mental reasoning and empirical observation to build knowledge about the world.

Marketing and consumer experiences and mental reasoning

There has been a large amount of research undertaken in trying to understand how consumers use both mental reasoning and practical experience when it comes to making decisions about the brands that they purchase. Bad experiences will no doubt cause non-purchase while good experiences should cause the opposite. Some products (FMCG) are bought out of habit with little reasoning and other, more expensive products (e.g. a car) will probably involve much more reasoning over a longer period (see the section on DMD in Chapter 1).

Intelligence and the capacity to learn

'The consumer isn't a moron; she is your wife. You insult her intelligence if you assume that a mere slogan and a few vapid adjectives will persuade her to buy anything.' A rebuke to advertisers about the sexist way that they talked down to women in ads – DAVID OGILVY

Inextricably linked to the study of learning is the concept of intelligence. People differ widely in intelligence from the non-literate to the genius (whatever is meant by that) and this will differ widely across the world. As with learning the study of intelligence and what is meant by intelligence as well as how it might be measured, has been the centre of argument and debate by academics and commentators for many hundreds of years. The **nature versus nurture argument** on learning ability also applies to intelligence. Are people born with levels of intelligence or do they acquire it in interaction with the environment? This leads to further questions about inherited brain capacity levels and the possible opportunities available through social relationships.

> **Key point** Central to the concept of intelligence and learning is the question of equal social opportunities and the inbuilt capacity to learn.

4.2 General example — Levels of intelligence

As early as 1843 the philosopher and writer **John Stuart Mill** theorised it was socialisation and the nurture of others that made the difference in defining levels of intelligence. On the opposite extreme psychologist **Sir Francis Galton** ('Hereditary Genius' 1869) postulated that intelligence was all genetics ('nature') and only loosely influenced by social interaction ('nurture') in a very limited way. Galton was one of the first in the field to try to measure levels of intelligence. Also known as the father of eugenics (selective breeding of humans), he went on to argue that for the wellbeing of society as a whole, only people with high levels of measurable, inherited intelligence should have children and breeding by others, especially the 'feeble-minded', should be restricted.

Questions

1. Examine the nature versus nurture argument about intelligence.
2. Discuss the dangers inherent in the discussion on intelligence levels. Do you think that particular problems arise when discussing race, gender and social class?

Measuring levels of intelligence

Throughout the whole of the twentieth century, psychologists, educationalists, politicians and others have tried to measure and compare levels of intelligence. The difficulty lies in trying to agree on what we mean by intelligence, crucial if it is going to be measured. In 1905, working for the French government **Alfred Binet** created the first '**intelligence (IQ) test**'. Taking a pragmatic approach he chose a series of

30 short tasks related to the everyday problems of life to try to discover intelligence levels among children.

Test now used in every walk of life

In the UK (and in many other countries around the world) intelligence tests of one kind and another have been used for school selection, universities, the armed services and many kinds of job interviews. Marketers, advertisers and retailers are interested in measuring consumer intelligence levels in different markets because of the affect it could have on marketing programmes. There have been attempts (controversially) to measure average intelligence between racial groups and sexes, attempting to try to explain the source and meaning of these differences (Eysenck 1971). The human genome project and the capability to measure many aspects of genetic make-up are having a huge impact on the part that physical and mental inheritance and development play in the intelligence and wellbeing of the individual.

4.1 Marketing example — The human genome project

The sales of new biotechnology products based on DNA discoveries alone are predicted to exceed $45 billion by 2009. Many other opportunities are constantly opening up. In medicine, recognising certain areas of the genome pertaining to diseases, doctors can provide for earlier and more accurate diagnosis of diseases. This information may also improve gene therapy treatments and influence new designs in drugs. Scientists now feel that they have a description of the entire human genetic code, identifying the 24 chromosomes and sequencing of 3 billion units of DNA that make up the human genome. Scientists believe having the genetic code will better allow doctors to tailor treatments specifically to individual patients and explore the genetic basis of human behaviour. A person's genetic sequence could one day indicate who has a predilection for a serious illness and perhaps be uninsurable, who might turn out to be a criminal, who should never consume alcohol, who might be a shopaholic, who will be the most emotionally 'turned on' by brands and so on.

Questions

1 Discuss the implications of the genome research on consumer behaviour.

2 Identify the possibilities for new product development.

Marketing, consumer behaviour and levels of intelligence

Many organisations have concerns about intelligence levels and measurement across two major areas.

The importance of employees

Marketing managers are aware of the importance of having the right person in the right job, at all levels, if they are to compete and maintain competitive advantage. As more demanding skills are needed, especially with the growth in the need for so-called 'knowledge workers' the cost of the wrong person in the wrong job can be heavy. Particularly important for marketing and sales is having employees that understand behaviour at the face-to-face customer level. Building great marketing programmes only to get it wrong in the retail outlet is the highest level of folly. The modern-day intelligence test measures a variety of different types of ability such as verbal, mathematical, spatial, knowledge levels, memory, problem solving, reasoning and decision making. They are often used in conjunction with psychometric personality type tests before individuals are employed.

Consumers and target markets

The need to know and understand the target market and the needs of the customer is fundamental to marketing and every student and practitioner in the business should learn this as a central part of any introductory course. This concept should remain an integral imperative throughout the career of any marketing and sales person. All customers in mature markets are now segmented according to such things as socio-economic, behaviour and group and individual psychology. Understanding target group and individual levels of intelligence must be seen as crucial because to get this wrong by either underestimating or overestimating consumer reactions to such things as new product offerings, brand values, price, advertising messages and promotional offers can lead to marketing campaign failure. The problem escalates for the international and global organisation, marketing products and services around the world to customers with vastly different levels of knowledge and understanding.

4.2 Marketing example — Never underestimate consumer intelligence

As one of the country's most successful entrepreneurs, Gerald Ratner built up a UK retail jewellery business with sales of £1.2 billion and profits of £121 million. In less than 10 years he had transformed the family business with 130 stores and sales of £13 million to a public company with 2,500 stores, 25,000 employees, owning the brands H. Samuel and Ernest Jones. But in a thirty-minute speech to 6,000 directors at the Royal Albert Hall he jokingly said that he sold earrings that cost less than a prawn sandwich at M&S, and that the sandwich would last longer and went on to describe a sherry decanter as 'total crap'. The next day there were disparaging headlines across the front pages of all of the tabloids accusing him of arrogance and insulting the intelligence of his customers. It cost him his personal fortune, his job and wiped an estimated £500 million off the company's value turning the profits into a £122 million loss and forcing the company to change its name to Signet. A lifetime's work catastrophically ruined overnight. Now, such is his infamy that 'doing a Gerald Ratner' describes any business gaffe that insults the customer in such a way.

Questions

1. Do you think that marketers and advertisers sometimes patronise and talk down to the consumer?
2. Discuss the importance of understanding consumer intelligence across different market segments.

Intelligence – culturally relative or universal

Similar to other human traits, whether intelligence is universal or cultural is another area of constant debate. Similar to other arguments about human attributes the answer appears to lie somewhere in the middle depending on the definition used. Albert Einstein and Isaac Newton might be considered geniuses universally along with Mozart but one may wonder how they might score in an IQ test. Some of the richest and brightest business entrepreneurs (Richard Branson, Alan Sugar) in the world have few academic qualifications. There is evidence that different societies and groups consider different abilities, skills and ways of behaving, as more intelligent than others. Is intelligence about making lots of money, having a house in the town and one in the country, owning lots of prestigious cars and taking expensive holidays or is it about living a non-materialistic, happy, healthy, spiritual life with lots of friends? It's these sorts of questions that make marketing and the study of consumer behaviour so fascinating for commentators and practitioners as they search for answers about customer satisfaction and benefits demanded from products, brands and services.

Key point The definition of intelligence is complex and a person could be intelligent in one area, academic, but unintelligent in another, perhaps interacting with others. It could also reflect relevant rather than universal values. However there seems to be agreement that it must involve knowledge levels, ways of behaving, reasoning abilities, learning from experience and both personal and interpersonal skills.

Learning and the study of human behaviour

How best to investigate and understand why people behave in the way that they do can be broken down into three simple areas and these are discussed below.

1. Genetic and biological influences.
2. Objective knowledge and the behaviourists.
3. Subjective knowledge and the role of the mind.

Genetic influences and the biologists

As soon as they are born all animals living in the wild have to adapt quickly to their environment if they are to survive. We have discussed early evidence that shows that most animals are born with some abilities or predispositions already 'learnt' and programmed into their hereditary genetic system (DNA). Other survival techniques have to be learnt by baby animals quickly by interacting with the environment. The same will apply to humans. It seems to be beyond any doubt that we bring some form of innate learning to the world as well as gaining knowledge by interacting with the environment. The disagreement is over how much and in what form.

4.3 General example **Genetic learning, 'imprinting'**

Many animals are born and, for safety's sake, able to move around and walk almost immediately. Linked to this is the innate concept know as 'imprinting'. Determined by hereditary formula inherent in a creature's chromosomes, imprinting necessitates the baby animal to immediately attach itself to the first thing it sees (the mother) and then to follow her wherever she goes. This was classically demonstrated by the Austrian scientist Konrad Lorenze who made himself the primary moving object that ducklings saw during a specific 'imprinting' sensitive period during their first few days of birth and as a consequence they followed him as if he were their mother. He went on to demonstrate that the ducklings could just as easily imprint themselves on to a toy truck, a coloured ball or bicycle.

Objective knowledge and the behaviourists

In very simple terms there have been writers and academics who think that all knowable things are objective, existing in the world independently of the individual and that these things can be understood by observation, experimentation and accumulated experience. Behaviourists do not study introspection (what people think) they only study behaviours. They argued that we couldn't know what people think so we shouldn't try to study it and make inferences; we should only study what we can observe. Animals were often used in their experiments and subsequent behaviour then extrapolated on to the reasons why humans behave the way that they do. This will be examined in much more detail later on in the chapter.

Key point Behaviourists believed that human behaviour could best be understood by watching (and experimenting) how animals behave and then using this information to learn about people.

Subjective knowledge and the cognitive psychologists

On the other hand, there are those who argue that understanding human behaviour is more complex than stated by the behaviourists. **Cognitive psychology** arose from a reaction to behaviourism because many felt that it did not take into account the role of the mind and rational, emotional and instinctive inputs into how and why people behave in the way that they do. For example if somebody opens a window a behaviourist could assume that this was because the person was hot. On the other hand, the cognitive psychologist might want to investigate mental possibilities such as having a fear of enclosed spaces.

Key point Cognitive psychologists believe that the human mind must be taken into account if behaviour is to be fully understood.

Figure 4.3

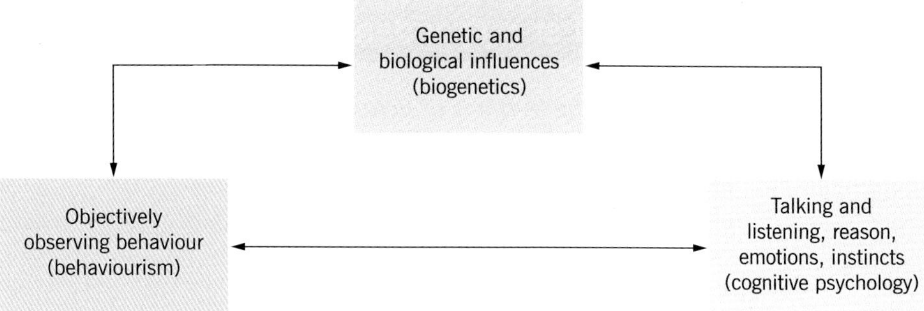

Three approaches in understanding behaviour

Behavioural learning theories

'It can be safely assumed that all animal and human behaviour is solely the result of reflex stimulus-response associations and the workings of the mind are irrelevant' IVAN PAVLOV (1927)

For the first half of the twentieth century the approach to understanding learning adopted by psychologists and others was to study how animals and humans behave, react and adapt to external events. Animals were used because they could be studied in a laboratory. It was believed at the time that all fundamental learning mechanisms were more or less the same and so results could then be used to show how humans learn. Behaviourism, as it came to be called, emphasised the observable aspect of behaviour looking only at inputs, the stimuli, and outputs, the responses. Known as the 'Black Box' model it ignored any mental processes that might be going on in-between the inputs and the outputs dismissing them as 'unscientific' because of their unobservable nature. Two major approaches, **classical and operant conditioning** will be examined. The second half of the twentieth century brought mental process into the equation and cognitive learning will be the third major approach discussed.

Figure 4.4

The behavioural black box stimulus (S) and response (R) model

Three major approaches to learning are:

1 Classical or respondent conditioning
2 Instrumental or operant conditioning
3 Cognitive (mental) processes

Classical or respondent S and R conditioning

'Only one thing in life is of actual interest to us – our physical experiences because that's the way we learn.' PAVLOV

Classical or respondent conditioning (also known as stimulus and response learning) is a form of passive, biological, involuntary, reflex learning that occurs when two or more events happen and are paired at the same time. Examples are many and widespread. If you have a pet and you feed it with tinned food, it will come running as soon as the tin opener is picked up, even if it is baked beans that are being opened. The animal has associated the sound of the opener with their food. Dogs will get excited if its owner just picks up the lead or says 'walk' or starts to put on walking shoes, associating this with actually opening the door and going for a walk. Perhaps we can remember, as a child, every time we heard the school bell for the end of the lesson instinctively sitting-up and unthinkingly preparing to leave. Many people experience heart palpitations or sweating if their phone rings in the middle of the night because of its association with bad news. A baby suffering pain by falling out of the pram early in life and taken to hospital in an ambulance may feel awful feelings of distress at the sound or sight of an ambulance later on in life.

> **Key point** Classical conditioning occurs when a person forms an involuntary reflexive association between two stimuli, so that encountering one stimulus makes the person think of the other. These feelings can be good or bad.

Classical conditioning – the original experiments

Many scientists examining human behaviour will work with animals, rats, rabbits, dogs, cats, monkeys etc. They are easy to work with and the results can then be examined and tested in more acceptable ways on humans. **Ivan Pavlov** (1849–1936) working over one hundred years ago was no exception and he used dogs in his original experiments on learning. He stumbled on the idea of classical conditioning almost by accident and an outline of his famous experiments is illustrated opposite.

Pavlov's experiments

Pavlov had a passive hungry dog in a cage (see Figure 4.5). He brought the food to the dog and when it saw the food it salivated (drools). This is a natural (it helps food digestion), uncontrolled, unlearnt, reflex reaction imprinted on to the dog's nervous system.

He called the food the *unconditioned stimulus* (UCS), meaning it's natural and unlearnt and the salivation the *unconditioned response* (UCR), also meaning natural and unlearnt.

He then paired the ringing of a bell (he called this a conditioned stimulus) with the food to see if he could alter the pattern of salivation (into a conditioned response). He did this for a number of times over a number of days and he found

Figure 4.5

Unconditioned stimulus and unconditioned responses

Figure 4.6

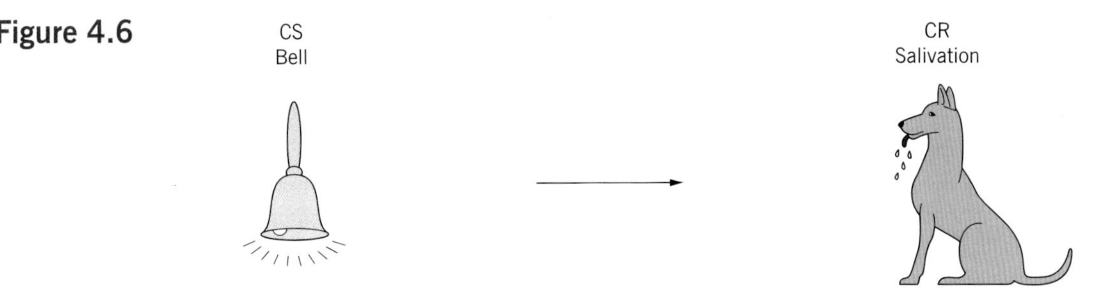

Conditioned stimulus and conditioned response

that the dog began to salivate at the sound of the bell before the food arrived. He could do this a number of times as the dog had, involuntarily, learned to associate the bell with the food. The bell had become a **conditioned (learned) stimulus**, and the dog's salivation to the sound of the bell Pavlov called the **conditioned (learned) response.**

Marketing and classical conditioning

The affect that classical conditioning has on consumer behaviour has to be understood throughout business, marketing and retail. Stimuli can be paired so as to create pleasant, happy feelings and this is heavily used in marketing and advertising. Successful retailers are aware that consumers are highly responsive to cues in their environment and will want customers to have a warm feel-good factor associated with visits to shopping centres and retail outlets. The smell of fresh flowers and fruit, of bread and cakes cooking, chicken roasting, a peeled tangerine and coffee percolating are all associated in many customers' minds with memories of childhood and other pleasant experiences throughout life. Equipment can now be bought that will inject these and other pleasant smells (new leather, a fire burning, scented candles, real Christmas trees) into the retail outlet artificially so as to stimulate associated feel-good emotions. Music will act in the same way and we must all have songs and tunes that as soon as we hear act as cues to send the memories flooding back. This is well known and again extensively used in all types of retailers' and advertising campaigns.

Extinction and advertising

Pavlov tried many variations of the experiment testing out the levels of learning and found that over a period of time, on hearing the bell on its own, without the presentation of any food, the dog unlearnt the association and did not salivate. This came to be referred to as extinction. Pavlov went on to measure the different and most effective ways of learning and food reinforcement, such as regular intervals, intermittent, little and often and large amounts at a time, to keep the association alive.

4.3 Marketing example — Extinction, good and bad feelings

The idea of extinction is particularly important in advertising where knowledge is needed about the most cost-effective way for mature brands such as Nescafe, Persil or Heinz beans to fight off extinction and so keep reminding consumers about the wonder of their products. For example are adverts more affective at maintaining audience interest in short bursts, in regularly small 'drips' or at irregular intervals? Where a brand is disliked or forgotten, associating it with something or somebody liked and admired by a particular consumer group can cause the extinction of negative feeling. Football star David Beckham was chosen to endorse the re-launch of the hair gel Brylcreem. He was seen as somebody that would be able to revitalise Brylcreem's old fashioned image among the new target audience of young males. Unfortunately, after endorsing the product, he shaved his head.

Questions

1 Examine the role that classical conditioning plays in understanding consumer behaviour.

2 Give examples of its uses in retail and advertising.

Spontaneous recovery

Pavlov found that, despite no reaction to the bell the day before, at the beginning of the next day and up to many days after, the bell and saliva association might suddenly begin again. The reappearance of an extinguished response after some time had passed he called spontaneous recovery.

4.4 Marketing example — Spontaneous recovery

Knowledge about spontaneous recovery can allow brand owners with seasonal products (Christmas, Easter) such as liqueurs, premium whiskys and food hampers (when as much as two-thirds of the sales are made) to use promotional money to carefully judge when the moment is right to start advertising and reawaken forgotten pleasant memories of Christmases past.

Other conditioning stimuli

Pavlov also tried using other stimuli instead of a bell, such as a buzzer and a torch. They were all found to work the same except some would take longer to condition than others. This he called higher order conditioning.

Figure 4.7

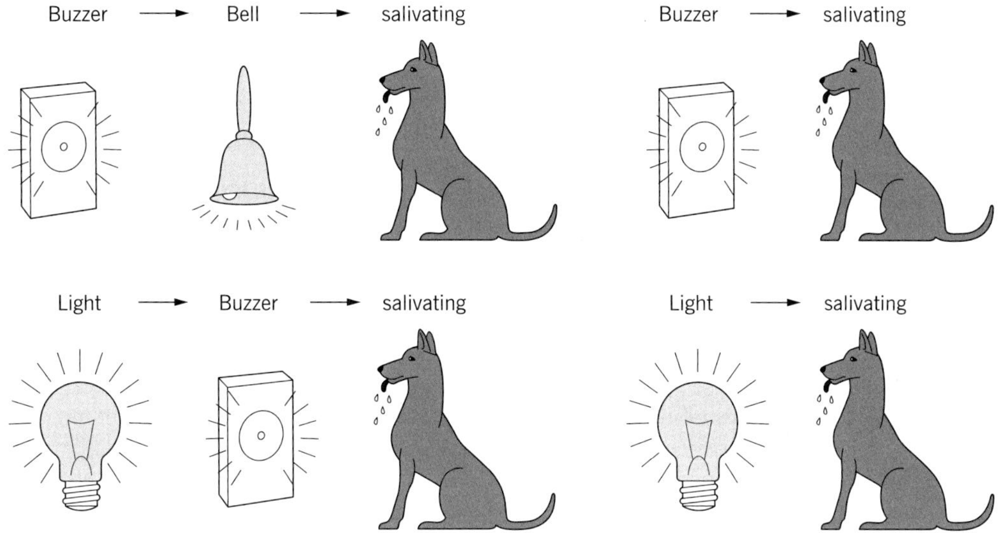

Higher order conditioning

4.5 Marketing example | **Higher order conditioning and brand extension**

As Pavlov used the power of higher order conditioning (buzzer using learning associated with the bell) so marketing practitioners have learnt the value of brand extension. This is using the customer awareness of and attraction to an existing brand's value to launch other products, for example Mars ice cream from the conventional Mars bar, Adidas into sports clothing and BIC disposable pens into disposable razors and lighters. It has been used increasingly as it's an effective and efficient way of maximising the power of the brand.

Stimulus generalisation

In some cases, the learned conditioned response to one stimulus, could also apply to a similar stimulus without further training. So the conditioned response of the animal to an electric bell could be transferred to similar stimuli, e.g. a church bell, or bicycle bell, in a way Pavlov called stimulus generalisation. This concept can be beneficial in some ways to markets, as the attractiveness that consumers might feel about one of the company's products might transfer to another. Called

- **brand 'extension'** it helps a company build a family of products all trading on the one brand name. An example might be Persil (soap powder, washing-up liquid, dishwasher powder). If the brand is strong enough, **brand 'stretching'** will allow the name to be used across a whole range of seemingly unconnected products. An example might be Virgin (insurance, cola, vodka, trains and planes). On the other hand, there can be problems if the attraction felt for one brand is transferred to the competitor's brand. For many years Brooke Bond PG Tips ran a series of adverts staring a family of Chimps, unfortunately when asked customers remembered and liked the ads, only many respondents thought it was for Tetley's. Similarly consumers can recall many wonderful car ads but are uncertain about which make it was for.

4.6 Marketing example — Own label copycatting

Because of the amount of resources tied into a well-known brand, manufacturers will fight anybody that attempts to take advantage and use their hard-won brand reputation for their own use. McVitie's took the supermarket Asda to court claiming that their own-label product Puffin chocolate bar was a copy, in name and design, of its own Penguin chocolate bar. The judge decided they could keep the name but must change the packaging. Coca-Cola also threatened Sainsbury's about its own label Classic Coke because its red and white colour and swirling logo looked too much like the Coca-Cola design. Sainsbury's backed down and changed the design. Research has shown the consumer can sometimes confuse manufacturers' brands with private retailer own label products (Mintel).

Stimulus discrimination

The opposite of generalisation is stimulus discrimination, in which an individual learns to produce a conditioned response to one stimulus but not to another stimulus that is similar. For example, a child may be afraid of dogs running free, but not when a dog is on a leash. So it appears to be to the advantage of a brand owner to try to clearly distinguish their corporate and product brand from the competitors' by clear product benefits and unmistakable marketing positioning.

4.7 Marketing example — Clear differentiation

Pepsi spent £500 million on a worldwide advertising campaign called 'Project Blue' with the aim of eliminating confusion and clearly differentiating Pepsi from its main rival cola and from other colas such as Virgin by changing the Pepsi can and bottles to electric blue.

Stimulus blocking

Leon Kamin discovered the concept of blocking much later in 1969. He found that blocking occurs when prior experience with one stimulus prevents later conditioning to a second stimulus. Research seems to suggest that stimulus blocking occurs because there might be only a certain amount of conditioning that can be sustained by any given stimuli. Later attempts at conditioning may be blocked simply because some limit has already been reached. This has important implications for marketers attempting to break the product benefits and alter brand loyalty away from the competition (for example Carlsberg lager trying to lure customers away from Kronenbourg or Estée Lauder cosmetics from Elizabeth Arden).

4.4 General example **Classical conditioning and animal training**

Classical conditioning is important to animal trainers because it is difficult to reward an animal with food at the time that the wanted behaviour is taking place. For example it's hard to throw a fish to a dolphin while it's in the middle of a jump or looking for a piece of equipment on the ocean floor a hundred metres below.

So trainers will associate the reward (fish) with something that is easier to deliver at the time. Marine mammal trainers use a conditioned whistle or a clicker at the time while reinforcing later with the food.

John Watson (1878–1958) – behaviourism

John Watson can be said to be the true father of '**behaviourism**' linking back to a paper he wrote in 1913. Watson took the work of Pavlov on animals and applied it to the development of humans, particularly children. As a result of his studies he concluded that all human behaviour could be explained almost entirely in terms of stimulus and response associations and reflexes. He rejected any idea that consciousness, introspection (or 'mentalism' as he called it) and terms such as desires and goals played any part in the process and even if they did they were not observable and so could not be measured. He went on to try to establish the idea of an objective psychology of behaviour called 'behaviourism' that would be seen as the 'scientific' study of people and be able to control and predict future actions.

Key point According to the 'behaviourist', mental processes cannot be seen and measured, observing animal behaviour and then relating it to human behaviour is therefore the only scientific way that learning can be measured.

Conditioning and controlling emotional behaviour

Watson went on to develop techniques to allow him to 'condition and control the emotions of human subjects'. His famous study for this was called the 'Little Albert' experiment in which he theorised that children have three basic emotional reactions; fear, rage and love. He wanted to prove that these three reactions could be artificially conditioned in children. Using a little boy named Albert to test his theory he repeatedly presented him with a white rabbit in conjunction with a sudden, loud noise to classically condition fear of the rabbit.

4.5 General example | **Watson's experiments – conditioning Albert**

John Watson conditioned a baby (Albert) to be afraid of a toy white rabbit by showing Albert the rabbit and then slamming an iron bar on the table behind little Albert's head (unethical or what!). This of course eventually made the baby unhappy. Watson went on to do it a few times thus conditioning Albert to cry every time he saw a white rabbit. He then went on to discover that stimulus generalisation had taken place and the baby cried when he saw similar white furry animals such as dogs, cats and guinea pigs. He even discovered that the baby cried when he saw cotton wool or a man with a white beard. We can envisage the consternation later on in life when Albert, now a child, cries at the sight of Father Christmas and nobody seems to know the reason why.

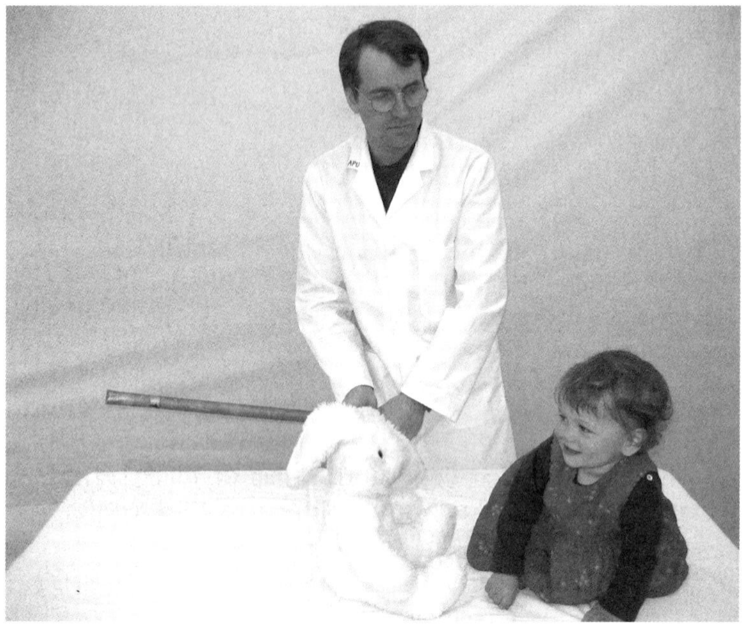

Conditioning fear of a white rabbit into the nervous system of a baby. The baby cries when the iron bar is slammed onto the table.
Source: Simon Wright

Working in advertising

After leaving university in the 1940s, Watson went into the relatively new business of advertising. He felt that he could use his scientific theories of behaviourism to manipulate and condition the 'animal' emotions of fear, rage and love to improve the effects of advertising in persuading consumers to buy particular products and brands. Some argue that manipulative means of emotional conditioning are still used to this day. Advertisers and agencies have become adept at researching target markets and then making certain that products and brands reflect emotional feelings that are welcomed by specific target consumers.

Conditioned good and bad feelings

Poor service (even in very small amounts) from a supermarket, bank, leisure centre or holiday etc. can eventually condition the consumer into having discontented feelings associated with the organisation such that they will then go elsewhere. Brand owners that become complacent and allow value offerings to gradually deteriorate can start up a conditioned chain reaction causing consumer dissatisfaction to build into eventual non-purchase.

On the other hand, many products that people initially dislike can become liked because of associated good feelings. For example tea, coffee and alcohol all have bitter tastes that are not immediately appealing to the palate. Individuals might come to like them, however, because of pleasant associated experiences, such as a tea break in between periods of hard work, or meeting good friends once a week in the pub or having a coffee abroad while having an exciting holiday.

> **Key point** Successful retailers are aware that consumers are highly responsive to cues in the environment and will want customers to have a warm feel-good factor associated with visits to shopping centres and retail outlets.

Conditioned fears and phobias

Watson's research was able to demonstrate how passive involuntary learning by classical conditioning and stimulus association could cause irrational fears, phobias, and obsessive ways of behaving. This is unwanted behaviour and, for example, a fear of spiders, fear of the outdoors, violent outbursts, inappropriate sexual activity, alcoholism and addictions can affect the quality of life of unfortunate sufferers. In some circumstances fear of school can cause very real illness symptoms such that a child is physically sick and just unable to go.

4.8 Marketing example — Conditioned painful experiences

A consumer who had a painful experience from food poisoning at a particular restaurant may have physical feelings of fear, trembling, sickness, just at the sight of the type of food eaten or even when passing the building itself. Getting violently drunk and sick on gin and orange or rum and coke as a young person can cause unpleasant feelings or even sickness just at the thought or smell of the offending drink, even much later in life.

Question

1 Describe experiences that you might have had from the type of painful conditioning described above.

Desensitising phobias

To treat phobias of specific objects, a trained therapist gradually and repeatedly presents the feared object to the patient while the patient relaxes. Through extinction, the patient loses his or her fear of the object. In one treatment for alcoholism or smoking, patients drink alcohol of some kind or smoke and then take a drug that produces nausea. Eventually they feel nauseous at the sight or smell of alcohol or cigarette smoke and stop drinking or smoking. Called **aversion therapy**, it's used to help in many other areas where people suffer from addiction or obsessive behaviour.

4.6 General example — De-conditioning Peter (Mary Jones 1924)

Mary Jones, a student of Watson, conducted a famous experiment in 1924 showing how conditioning can be reversed. Peter was a 2 year old, who for some unknown reason had been conditioned to fear fur and furry animals. He was shown a rabbit in a cage (which he hated) while he ate lunch (which he loved). This was repeated with the rabbit being placed nearer and nearer Peter, eventually being taken out of the cage. After 40 or so sessions Peter could eat lunch while stroking the rabbit. This study suggests that Peter's fear had been de-sensitised and had undergone extinction.

Conditioned response by observation and imitation

Edwin Guthrie's (1886–1959) experiments described how new skills could be learnt and adopted after one performance if the 'reward' is seen to be beneficial.

Figure 4.8

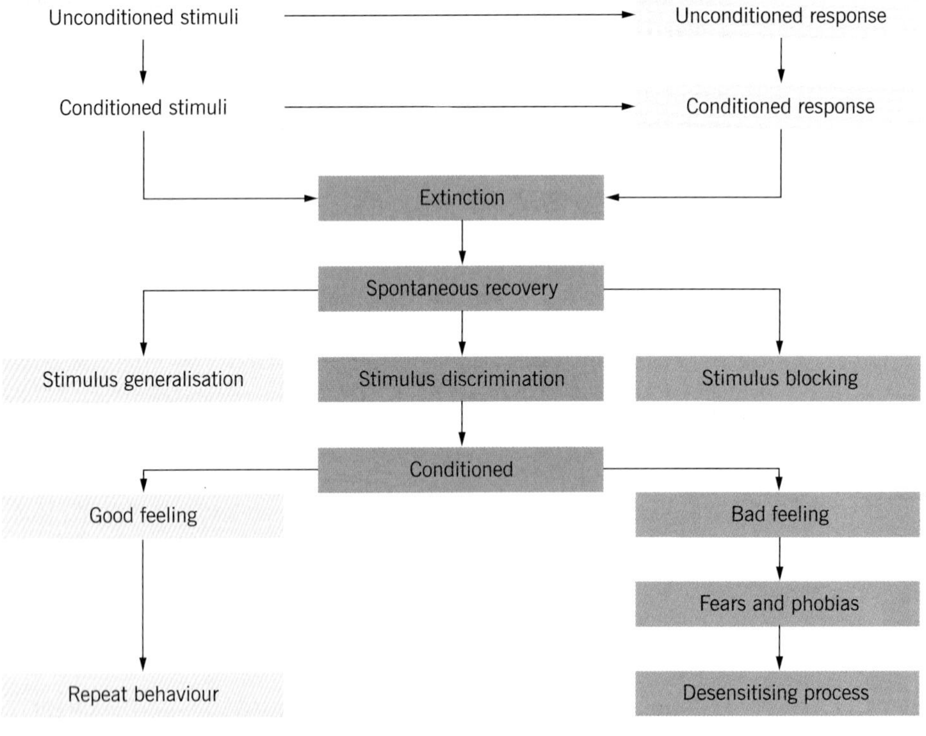

Aspects of classical conditioning

For example a child touching a red hot iron or nearly being run over by a bus will be conditioned not to repeat the experience. Albert Bandura (1925–) showed that conditioned learning also takes place through observation and imitation. In early experiments he was able to show that very young children could immediately copy adult behaviour. He had an adult enter a nursery classroom, pick up a plastic hammer and hit a large inflatable doll with a weighted bottom. This caused it to fall over and then return to the upright position. As the adult left, a watching child took the hammer and hit the doll in the same way. This new behaviour was displayed even though there had been no coaching or practice.

Operant conditioning and instrumental learning

Still a stimulus and response theory, operant conditioning works on the theory that when an animal (and subsequently humans) operates in the environment it will learn to seek out the things it finds rewarding (food) and avoid those things it finds painful or threatening (predatory enemies). This approach to learning came to be known as operant conditioning or instrumental learning.

> **Key point** Instrument or operant learning
> By trial and error animals learn to seek out those things they find rewarding while avoiding those things they find threatening. *Reward and punishment!*

Edward Thorndike – trial and error and reward and punishment

'When particular stimulus-response sequences are followed by pleasure, those responses tend to be "stamped in", responses followed by pain tend to be "stamped out"'. EDWARD THORNDIKE (1932)

▶ One the earliest researchers taking this approach was **Edward Thorndike** (1874–1949). He had heard stories of intelligent animals performing tricks in homes, zoos and in circuses and he set out to discover how this could happen and if it could be measured in some way. As a behaviourist, he argued that as the minds of animals could not be known, study should be about trying to understand and formulate laws based on the way that changes in external stimuli could mould and shape observable animal behaviour. Working at the turn of the century he constructed a series of so-called 'puzzle boxes'. These were small cages built so that animals placed inside could, through trial and error, get out if they could solve exit problems of varying degrees of difficulty. This involved pressing levers, latches or pulling a string and so on. Food, available on the outside, was used as the motivating stimuli.

> **Key point** Behaviourists believe that animal minds are unknowable and motivation can only be understood by observing behaviour.

Trial and error learning

Thorndike discovered that by chance an animal in the puzzle box would press the right lever that would give it freedom. The same animal would then remember what it needed to do next time it was in the same position. The reward associated with freedom/food acts to strengthen stimulus-response associations. Learning seemed not to involve any thinking or puzzling out and was purely mechanical in its application. He went on to show that constant practice strengthened the connection while disuse weakened the connection. His basic conclusion was that learning was simply the building of a connection between the situation (S) and a response (R) and that rewards strengthen the previous response and punishment weakens the previous response. It did not involve any mental or insightful learning. He went on to try to prove that this way of learning could also be applied to humans.

▶ **Key point** Thorndike was looking for a '**Universal Law of Effect**' that could be applied to all animal and human behaviour wherever in the world it might take place.

His 'law' stated that all basic learning takes place through trial and error and that actions that are rewarded (pleasurable) will be repeated and those that are punished (painful) will stop or be avoided. There is no mental involvement.

Key point Trial and error learning appeared not to involve any mental processes and was purely mechanical in its application.

Operant conditioning – reward and punishment and complex reinforcement

▶ The theory of **B.F. Skinner** built on the work of Thorndike. Again using the concept of reward (or reinforcement) and punishment he set out to discover how behaviour might change and learning take place in a more complex way in response to different types of stimuli. He went on to teach or train (he called it ▶ **shaping**) animals to behave in ways of his choosing and to predict how an animal might change. By trial and error the animal could learn that if it operated in the way Skinner wanted, it would be rewarded; if it didn't, it would either have the reward withdrawn or it would be punished in some way.

Key point With operant conditioning a reward (food) is given only after a certain response is made. The animal will continue to make the same response as long as the reinforcement continues. Conversely a response that produces punishment will be avoided.

The Skinner box

Don't listen to what people say about how they live their lives – see how they behave.

The Skinner box was a more complicated version of Thorndike's puzzle box. Skinner wanted to show how an animal, in this case a rat, could be manipulated, guided and even allowed to respond in its own way to change and learn new ways of behaviour in response to rewards and punishments of some kind. To help in the process, Skinner developed a range of positive and negative reinforcement techniques that enabled him to experiment with many different ideas about learning behaviour that could then be used to try to understand how humans learn and behave. Although much more subtle in the approach used when compared with Pavlov, Watson and Thorndike, he still asserted that human motivation and learning could best be understood by behavioural observation rather than seeking to gain access to mental processes.

Key point Skinner could be said to be the last of the great behaviourists arguing that behaviour could only be understood by observation and not through mental processes.

Skinner box – the experiments

The Skinner box contained a lever that an animal (rat) could operate and some means of delivering an outcome (food pellets or water) to the animal. He also had a light that he could pair with the food or water. The electric grid on the floor was used for aversion (punishment) reinforcement.

The box operated in the following way. As the rat moved around the cage it accidentally pressed the lever and a food pellet or water appeared. The operant is the ▶ behaviour just prior to the **positive reinforcer**, the food pellet, appearing. After a while the rat would learn that hitting the lever would make the food or water appear (reward). It would then furiously push away at the bar, hoarding his pile of pellets in the corner of the cage. Using the light as a positive reinforcer (reward) ▶ and the electric grid on the floor as a **negative reinforcer** (punishment), Skinner trained the rat to push the lever only after the light came on. He then went on to find out which method of reinforcement was the best and most long lasting.

Key point After a while the rat learnt that hitting the lever before the light came on produced an electric shock (punishment) and hitting the lever after the light came on produced the food and water (reward).

People and positive and negative reinforcement

Although Skinner generally used rats and pigeons for his experiments he went on to argue that operant conditioning was a science that could be used to explain the way that humans learnt and behaved (even the learning of language). He felt that it was possible to control people through manipulations of rewards and punishments. An infant made to feel clever because they can use a potty for toilet training, a pupil told that he or she has produced a good piece of work, and an employee given feedback and praised for the quality of work, will all feel better and try much harder. On the other hand, fear of a fine will make drivers fear speed cameras and drive more slowly, employees learn that slacking could lead to a loss of bonuses, students realise that assignments handed in late means that they lose 10 per cent of the marks and not paying bills on time can lead to services being cut off.

4.9 Marketing example — Consumer behaviour and positive reinforcement

We have seen that a positive reinforcer is any stimulus that strengthens the desired consumer response. A consumer who is told she is a valued supermarket customer will continue to use that particular supermarket. A hotel that gives high value, consistent personal service; branded clothes that cause others to compliment; and a perfume that is noticed favourably by husband or boyfriend will encourage repurchase and reuse. High customer expectations about the quality of after service on a new car, a holiday or the taste in a chocolate bar not met will turn positive reinforcement (reward) to adverse reinforcement (avoidance). We only need to refer back to marketing theory to know that consumers can have many changing different emotional and rational desires for buying products and services and companies and advertisers must use constant research (especially qualitative) to try to anticipate future needs.

Questions

1. Discuss how brand manufacturers and retailers implement programmes of positive reinforcement. Give examples and identify how they work.
2. What is meant by adverse reinforcement? Give examples.

Negative reinforcement and social marketing

Social marketing is used by charities and government agencies to try to stop the public behaving in anti-social and health threatening ways by using negative forms of reinforcement. We are told that drinking and driving, speeding and driving

Table 4.1 — Primary, secondary and generalised reinforcement

- *Primary reinforcement* These are basic reinforcers such as food and water and are unlearned needs that will occur naturally.
- *Secondary reinforcement* These are reinforcers (the light, buzzer electric shock) that are learnt when paired with the food or water (primary reinforcer).
- *Generalised reinforcement* These are general reinforcers learnt across a variety of situations linked to both primary and secondary reinforcers. They include such things as praise, money, fame and prestige. For example I like eating good food, money buys me good food – fame and prestige give me money ergo I associate fame and prestige and money with the basic pleasure of good food.

while on a mobile phone will lead to fines or imprisonment and health advertising campaigns give dire warnings on the dangers of smoking, eating fast foods and unprotected sex. Only if the negative reinforcements are strong enough will the campaigns be successful.

Skinner's reinforcement techniques

Skinner's research showed that reinforcement and avoidance techniques were the key to his learning theory. Over the years he built an impressive array of stimulus and response, reward and punishment tools and techniques to both understand and to shape the learning process. Similar schedules are used in advertising and shown in Table 4.2.

Table 4.2 Advertising and reinforcement schedules

Skinner's reinforcement techniques have been applied to advertising and there has been a great deal of research into the most effective schedules. Some of these uses are shown here:

- *Burst advertising* – scheduling a short period of heavy advertising, stopping for a time, and then coming back with another heavy burst. Based on trying to overcome audience apathy/inattentiveness.
- *Drip advertising* – scheduling an advertising campaign to be shown a little at a time across a longer time period – constant, slow repetition enters the long-term memory.
- *Pulsating advertising* – heavy advertising, a pause, followed by more intensive advertising, a pause, and so on.
- *Saturation advertising* – excessive advertising to make an impact on the market. Very expensive thus only for the very rich, e.g. Procter and Gamble.
- *Impact advertising* – the degree, power and depth of success of a campaign; the depth and number of consumers who see and remember the advertisement.
- *Wear-out advertising* – advertisements no longer have an affect on the audience and so should be changed.

Source: Ray Wright, *A Business and Marketing Dictionary*, Earlybrave Publishers

Marketing, extinction and spontaneous recovery

Skinner also encountered the problem with extinction, where people would gradually forget if reinforcement is ended. Similarly with spontaneous recovery, he found that in certain cases response rates could be reawakened after some time according to the stimuli and the degree of original learning. For example the smell of a tangerine will remind of times at Christmas and going to a pantomime, or the sound of seagulls will remind of holidays in the sun. Advertisers know that they must constantly advertise in some way or another if they are to maintain brand share in the market. Kellogg's recently ran an advertising campaign where they tried to awaken among older adults memories of eating cornflakes as a child so that they would start eating them again. If they remove the free toy from the Sugar Frosties children might lose interest and demand another cereal.

Strength of the reinforcement

Another important factor to consider is the strength of the reinforcement. For example if an animal is offered tree leaves as a food reward it will respond initially but then not bother (unless it liked tree leaves). A teenager will not continue to work delivering papers every morning if the pay is minimal, and a child will not continue to tidy his or her bedroom if praise is only given sparingly. Similarly consumers will learn not to respond to rewards considered unattractive. Conversely they will respond if the reward is considered worthwhile, e.g. the possibility of winning a cruise holiday or 50 per cent off in a sale.

Key point In classical conditioning the subject is conditioned to act in a certain way while passive. In operant conditioning the subject is active and is conditioned while acting on the environment. Both are stimulus and response theories of learning behaviour that take no account of mental or cognitive processes.

Aversion or avoidance learning

Research into avoidance or aversion learning looked at the role of punishment in more detail. In experiments, an electric grid beneath the floor is turned on causing the animal to try to escape into the safe cubicle next door. After a few trials it learns to jump to safety. The electrical grid treatment is paired with the light being switched on. After a while the animal learns to associate the light coming on with the imminent arrival of the electric shock and will jump every time the light is switched on.

Marketing, consumer behaviour and avoidance learning

In the same way consumers learn to avoid painful experiences by paying bills on time, travelling with reputable holiday companies, taking out extra guarantees and warranties and buying known quality products. Many marketers exploit this need by advertising that the consumer should avoid the so-called dangers of dealing with unscrupulous companies by buying from them; similarly trumpeting that their products will never break down while the competitors' might.

Figure 4.9

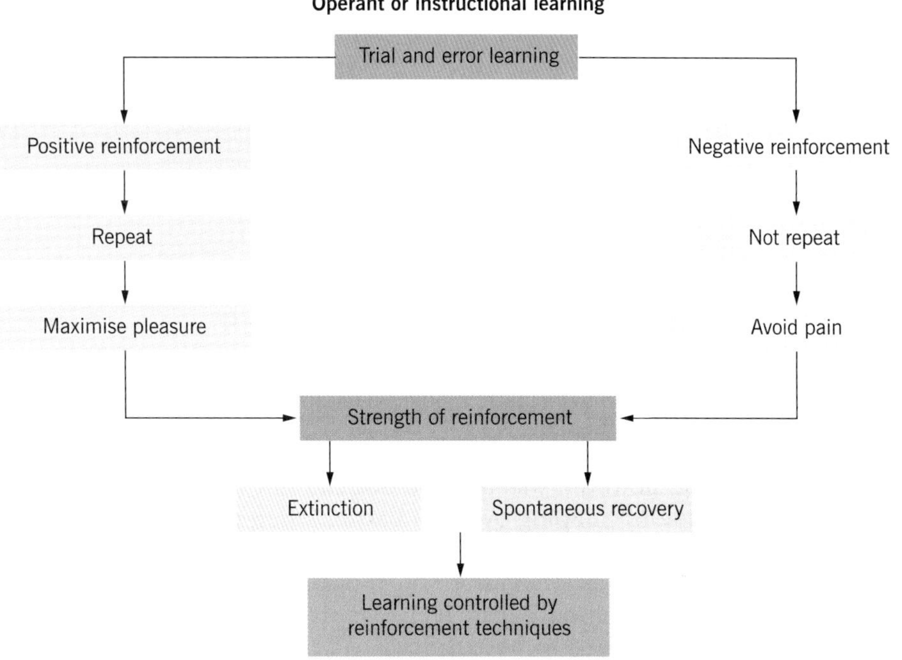

Aspects of operant conditioning

Cognitive (mental) processes and learning

'I not only use all the brains that I have, but all that I can borrow.'
WOODROW WILSON

The behavioural scientists discussed above were looking for universal laws of learning that could be said to be basic to both animals and humans in all parts of the world. Most of the investigatory work during this period, from the turn of the century to the 1970s, failed to take into account the part that cognition and thinking played in the process. There is no doubt about the importance of classical and operant conditioning but subsequent research has come to show that it was only part of the whole picture and the universal concept of behaviourism is now largely devalued.

> **Key point** Behaviourism was devalued as a universal law of learning when the importance of cognitive (thinking) processes was demonstrated.

Arguably the greatest contribution to the downfall of behaviourism as the dominant paradigm came about because of the experiments of **Martin Seligman** in the 1960s. Using an aversion cage, described above, a dog was placed into a harness and given the electric shock. It struggled but was unable to escape. After a while it

Figure 4.10

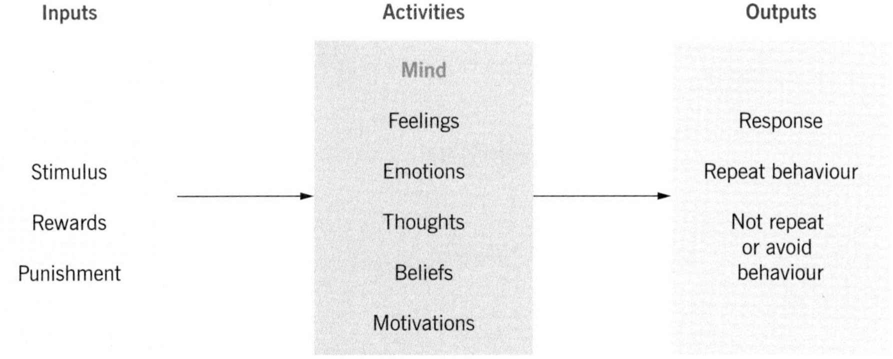

Stimulus–mind–response model. Mental activities and processes examined

ceased to struggle and seemed just to accept the punishment. The surprising thing, however, was that the dog did not try to avoid the pain of the shock and escape by jumping over the barrier when released from the restraining harness. These observations questioned the work of the behaviourists because according to the theory all organisms will repeat those actions that bring reward and avoid those that produce pain. It appeared that the dog believed that it could not escape, it had **learned to be helpless**, to be a victim. The behaviour was determined by what the animal was ***thinking*** and not by visible rewards or punishments.

These startling experiments were paramount in moving the argument away from the dominance of the stimulus and response behaviourist model into research into cognitive psychology and the role of the mind in learning behaviour.

Key point Cognitive psychology and the role of the mind began to replace behaviourism as the dominant paradigm.

Learned helplessness and explanatory thinking styles

Extending his findings to how humans behave, Seligman developed a cognitive model that attempted to explain how people think about bad and good situations in life. He built a model, he called 'explanatory styles' for explaining how some people appeared to be depressive and constantly taking a pessimistic approach to life while others were resilient and hopeful mostly taking an optimistic approach. He went on to say that we often learnt explanatory styles from our parents. Explanatory styles could be seen as a forerunner to psychographic and lifestyle segmentation, examined in Chapter 9.

Explanatory styles

Seligman classified the differences between pessimistic and optimistic type people and attempted to discover how the depressive might be helped to become more optimistic. As an example we can look at the reasons that individuals give for problems in life.

The pessimist 'I fail exams because I am stupid'; 'I don't have time to study'; 'I could never sing or play the piano because I have no talent'; 'I am an unlucky person'; 'it's always raining'; 'Ten years time I will be retired from work'; 'I am depressed'.

The optimist 'I know I can pass the exam if I try harder'; 'Anybody can sing and play the guitar if they want to'; 'I enjoy all the seasons'; 'I like myself and other people'.

4.7 General example **Always look on the bright side of life**

In his book *Learned Optimism* Seligman explains a self-help cognitive behavioural therapy that tries to help the depressive pessimist rationally address problems in the moment and look for alternative optimistic solutions. Many products and services are marketed and advertised on the idea of optimism.

Latent learning – mind and memory

Edward Toleman (1886–1959) was one of the first theorists to introduce the idea that the mind might play a part in the learning processes, although it wasn't recognised as such at the time he was writing. Working with students on experiments he discovered that there were occasions when animals seem to learn and store information in the memory without causing an immediate change in behaviour. Only later when a reward of some kind was offered would the **latent learning** become obvious.

Cognitive mapping

Using rats to explore a maze over a number of days, he clearly showed that when different routes to a food source were closed off the rats took the best route available that could only have been learnt through experience, memory and latent learning, called cognitive mapping. The function of reinforcement (food) seems to be to encourage animals to display what they have previously learned. Another line of evidence supporting the notion of cognitive mapping comes from chimpanzees. While a chimpanzee was passively watching in a cage, an experimenter hid pieces of fruit in various locations of a room. The animal was building a cognitive map and when the last piece of fruit had been hidden, the chimpanzee, when released, rushed immediately from one hiding place to another, uncovered the hidden fruits, and ate them.

Rats, a maze and experiments on latent learning

In Figure 4.11 rats take pathway 1, the shortest route to the food. Block pathway 1 at A and the rats take pathway 2, the next shortest route to the food. Block pathway 1 at B and we would expect rats to mechanically take pathway 2 as the pathway they last successfully took. But having a mental picture of the whole maze, they remember they would encounter the same blockage at B and so take pathway 3.

Figure 4.11

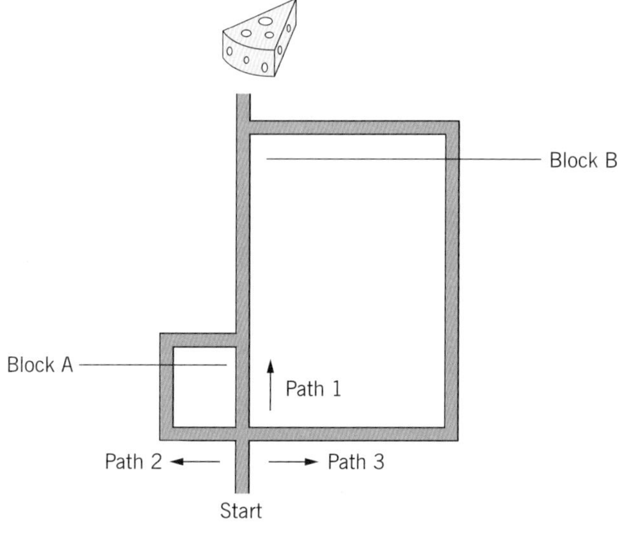

Rats, a maze and experiments with latent learning

Figure 4.12

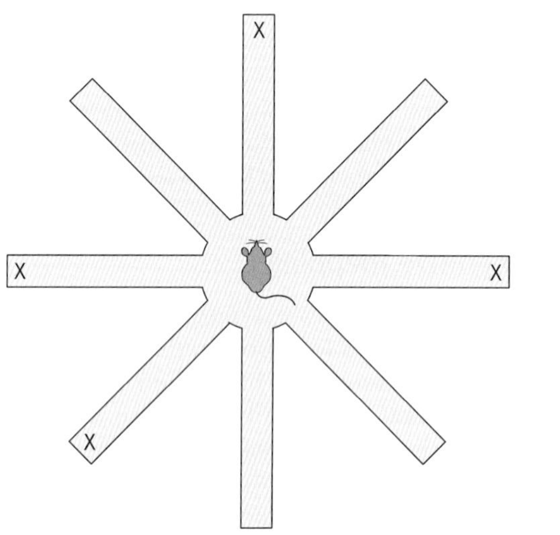

What way out?

In Figure 4.12 food pellets are put at the end of each pathway. The rat is introduced and finds some of the pellets. It's taken out and reintroduced later. It will not go down pathways where food has already been taken. The rats will stop running aimlessly in the maze when they know that the food is gone.

> **Key point** Experiments on latent learning challenged the view that learning can only be investigated by observable behaviour.

4.10 Marketing example — Latent learning

A great amount of the hundreds of billions of dollars spent on advertising and promotion around the world is spent on long-term brand building. A multitude of research has shown that building brand benefits in the mind and the memory of the customer take some time and it can be an expensive and frustrating business. This is because this type of advertising spend will not necessarily result in an immediate increase in sales especially when the product is high priced and purchased infrequently. However, evidence shows that people construct cognitive mind maps about attractive and unattractive companies and brands and will bring this into play later when products such as cars, electrical goods, furniture and financial services are needed.

Questions

1 Discuss the concept that much of what we learn is subsumed into the deep part of our memory and only comes into use when the motivation is sufficiently attractive.

2 Advertisers spend millions of pounds on advertising in the present knowing that results will not happen until some time in the future. Examine why this might be so and evaluate its worth.

Insight learning – more mental abilities brought into play

▶ Working with chimpanzees **Wolfgang Kohler** (1887–1967) set out to show that some animals appear to have intelligence and can demonstrate mental abilities in solving problems.

The experiments

In one of his studies, Sultan, a chimpanzee, was presented with a problem of having bananas placed above his head and out of his reach. Items available for use were some boxes and a pole. After some chattering and jumping unsuccessfully at the fruit the chimp walks away in frustration. He then spends a little time sitting and looking at the food, then at the boxes. There appears to be a sudden grasping of useful relationships and the chimp gets up and puts one box on the other and with the pole knocks the bananas to the ground. In a similar experiment a chimp, shut inside a cage, has a problem obtaining food outside the bars and beyond his reach. This time there are two sticks that will only reach the food if fixed together. After trying to use, in vain, first one stick and then the other to reach the food the animal seems to sit back and contemplate. After a short while the 'penny drops' and one stick is pushed into the other enabling the food to be dragged towards the cage, grabbed and eaten (see overleaf). With **insight learning** no trial and error experiments were involved.

> **Key point** Animals seem able to contemplate, think through and solve food-gathering puzzles without using trial and error methods.

Insight learning and problem solving

Thinking through the problem

After similar, as well as more difficult experiments, Kohler asserted that the chimps' ability to solve problems came about, not through blind trial and error or stimulus and response, but through them thinking through and working out the problem in an insightful manner. He went on to show that a correct response to a problem was remembered and so mistakes seldom made. He also showed that knowledge learnt in one task, using boxes, could be transferred successfully to other tasks, using ladders or chairs. Other experiments have shown that other, less intelligent animals such as dogs, squirrels and birds also demonstrate elements of insight learning.

> **Key point** Insight learning demonstrates that some animals learn by using mental processes.

Learning and doing

There is much evidence to show that the best skill-based learning experiences come by undertaking the task. For example a person can read how to drive a car, he or she can be shown how to drive a car, but actually getting in and driving it will be the ultimate method. Sales people will know that giving consumers a product to try for themselves will often close the sale. This is why many retailers will offer a customer the opportunity to try products, for example letting somebody test drive a new car for 24 hours, bring a TV or music system back if unsatisfied or eat a free meal at a restaurant (so good the consumer will come back). These have always been seen as successful types of sales promotions.

Learning sets and experiences

People build up mental sets or schemata in the memory which helps them to review problems or relationships in particular ways when confronted with unusual or new learning situations. Information that fits comfortably within these frameworks can then be easily slotted in with existing ideas and experiences. In experiments with baby chimps **Harry Harlow** (1905–81) used two trays with only one containing food. A square cover always covered the tray with the food and a round cover always covered the tray with no food. After hundreds of trials monkeys learnt to look only under the square cover and never bothered with the other tray. He then changed the covers to red and green triangles. As soon as the chimps discovered which cover the food was under (one or two trials) they no longer bothered to look under the other cover. They had built up a mental set of the process in their long-term memory.

Negative learning sets

There are occasions when people build up negative learning sets about the world that are misguided or just plain wrong. Examples cover such things as stereotyping people, religions, cultures, health practices and food quality, as well as company and brand values. In many cases it is in the interest of power groups such as politicians and company spokespeople to deliberately disseminate propaganda and mistruths about activities so as to gain public support.

4.11 Marketing example — Wrong paradigms

History is replete with examples of paradigms, mental views of the world that have proven to be wrong. Frenchman Louis Pasteur, had to fight the whole medical world to disprove the accepted scientific paradigm about the cause of some illnesses and establish his germ theory on how diseases spread. Many innovative new product developments have come about through creative individuals having the ability to challenge existing mind-sets. Examples that come to mind include the Dyson vacuum cleaner that uses revolving suction power and needs no bags, cameras that use a hard disc and need no film, cooking using microwaves.

Question

1 Examine ways that management trainers can break down existing restrictive mind-sets and coach marketing people into thinking in more innovative ways about new products and services.

Higher levels of learning

In further experiments Harry Harlow and others have shown that chimps and other primates are able to learn to solve relatively complex abstract problems sorting objects of differing shapes and colours into wanted patterns. The experiments also revealed that primates were often motivated by a range of emotions, including curiosity and affection rather than just food, to learn new ways of behaving.

Key point Baby chimps, and by extension baby children, are motivated to learn by a range of emotions, including curiosity, affection and wonder rather than just the reward of food.

In a series of experiments, Herbert S. Terrace (Duke University, Colombia) trained monkeys to recognise and touch on the screen the same sequence of seven objects that were changed after every test. Up to the present time there have been many experiments, with limited success, that have tried to teach chimps signs and the English language.

Learning and the subconscious

The idea that the mind has a conscious and a subconscious level came about through the work of the psychoanalyst **Sigmund Freud**. Working at the end of the nineteenth and into the early part of the twentieth century, he argued that a great deal of what we learn, fears and unacceptable desires, could be a danger to our wellbeing and so it is repressed into the subconscious. Here this learning sits, shut out of our awareness because of its anxiety-causing nature but able to drip through and influence our feelings, thoughts, beliefs and behaviour in all kinds of ways (the theory of the subconscious will be discussed in more detail in Chapters 8 and 9).

Table 4.3 The way we learn

There are many ways that people learn about the world. Including the methods identified below. (They are not all mutually exclusive.)

- *Genetic* – hereditary predisposition to learn in some way, e.g. language.
- *Stimulus and response* – an involuntary or voluntary response by the animal or human to a stimulus of some kind from the environment.
- *Reward and punishment* – seeking out rewarding experiences and avoiding those that are painful.
- *Trial and error* – trying different approaches and learning what works and what doesn't.
- *By association* – a fire burns, ice cream tastes good.
- *Reinforcement* – the stronger the reinforcement the stronger the performance.
- *Learning by imitation* – watching others.
- *Cognition* – thinking things through.
- *Rote* – learning things mechanically by constant repetition.
- *Learning by doing* – let somebody solve the problem themselves.
- *Experience* – building on past happenings.
- *Subconscious* – learning that takes place below the level of consciousness.

Conventional classroom learning – watching, listening, questioning and thinking things through

Memory and learning

▶ **Memory**, the ability to retain information over a period of time, is essential to learning. Without any memory, both short and long term, we would be unable to function and life as we know it would be impossible. Imagine never being able to take things into the memory. We would not be able to remember if we were getting up or going to bed, going upstairs or downstairs or what it was we had done the day before. Without long-term memory we would not know how to drive the car, read the newspaper or remember the names of friends and relatives. In fact there have been cases where, through illness, some people have lost their short-term memory, long-term memory or both. It almost goes without saying that memory is a crucial part of consumer behaviour. Companies like Procter and Gamble spend billions of dollars a year worldwide on advertising its hundreds of brands and they rely totally on customer memory and recall of brand values when out shopping and choosing one product over another.

> **Key point** Memory is the retention of information over different time periods. Without memory there would be no learning.

4.8 General example — Ebbinghaus experiments

Herman Ebbinghaus is seen as a pioneer in the study of memory. Working in the 1880s, he wanted to discover as much as he could about human memory and the part that it played in rote learning and the higher mental processes. He was the first person to approach the problem from a methodical, mathematical, experimental, scientific perspective. He came to the conclusion that information retention was better according to the ◀

following criteria: memorising over time rather than in a single session; continuous practice, rehearsal; early and late items remembered more than those in the middle; meaningful items take one-tenth the time to remember than nonsense items; greatest loss of data came during the first hour and recall after the first day compared to the end of the week was virtually the same.

Sensory, short- and long-term memory

While Ebbinghaus studied retention and memory over long periods of time, later experimenters (Broadbent 1958) studied stimulus selection, retention and memory loss over periods of time ranging from seconds, minutes and hours as well as for much longer periods. The idea of people having a more limited 'sensory' and 'short-term' memory as well as long-term memory came about through this work.

Memory as a process

From research undertaken it could be argued that the concept of memory is more ▶ a process (see **memory process**) than a series of compartmentalised happenings. In Chapter 3 on perception we identified the process by which external information is selected by the senses, interpreted by the brain and if necessary acted upon. Here we are interested in how and why information is selected for immediate or short-term use and how and why information is stored into long-term memory for later use. It seems that information passes through a three-stage process. Some of the information is rejected by the brain at stage one, so called sensory-memory, some at stage two, short-term memory and some information ends up being stored, potentially indefinitely, in long-term memory.

Figure 4.13

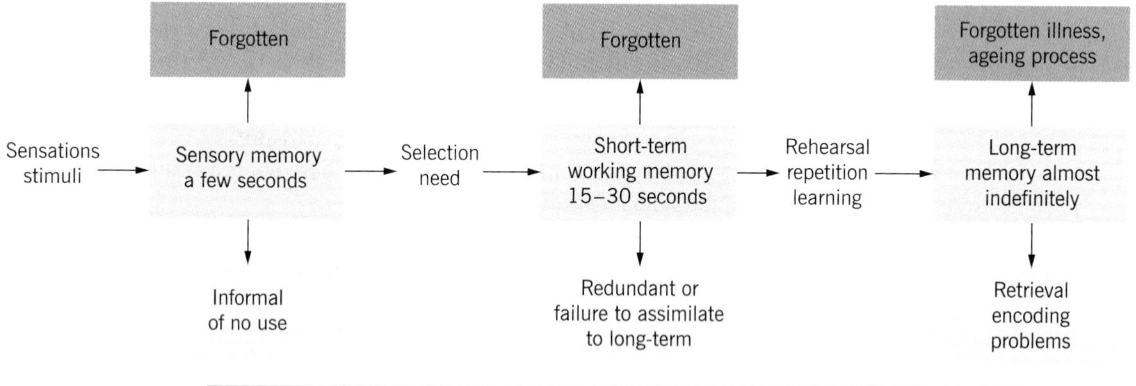

Memory as a three-stage process

Sensory-memory

In order for any information (read, seen, smelt, tasted or touched) to be eventually learnt it must first pass through the sensory memory. It's very difficult to measure the amount of information that fleetingly impinges on sensory memory as most of it is primitive and unanalysed and barely lasts for a few seconds before being automatically rejected. There's no doubt that the amount of information at this initial stage is enormous, much of it hardly at conscious level. We only have to imagine the incessant level of information throughout the day that momentarily flashes across our minds and then is immediately forgotten. This is especially so with advertising where hundreds of company and brand images fleetingly hit our peripheral vision and are gone. If deemed necessary, some information will make it through to the short-term (or working) memory.

Short-term or working memory

It appears that a small amount of sensory information will be selected in some way to move into short-term memory, or working memory. There is more conscious thought here and information is used by individuals to think, speak, solve problems, ask questions and do all the things that people do while moving through the day. Storage time is round about 15 to 30 seconds depending on the task in hand and the amount individuals are able to hold here at any one time appears to be seven of eight items (or 'chunks') give or take two items each side (Miller 1956). Information will be taken from both the external environment and the long-term memory in an iterative problem-solving process. For example, when driving we will be continuously aware of other road users; prices on washing machines are compared as the consumer moves from brand to brand along a range of washing machines, as is the quality and design available in a fashion outlet as a woman looks for a new dress; and the assorted drinks wanted by a group of people as one person queues to purchase at a bar must be temporarily remembered if mistakes are not to be made.

4.12 Marketing example — Amount held in short-term memory

Extensive research demonstrates that most individuals are able to hold between five and nine separate items of information in their short-term memory at any one time. This is one of the reasons why companies will 'chunk' their phone numbers so instead of 012067 7982367 (potentially 13 chunks) the customer will more easily remember 0800 00 66 00 33 (potentially 5 chunks). We can increase also the absolute capacity of short-term memory by combining bits of information into meaningful units.

Short-term memory – rote or maintenance rehearsal

Items can be remembered longer than 30 seconds in short-term memory by using what is known as 'rote rehearsal'. This involves repeating over and over again in our head the telephone number, the name and address, the prices and makes of TVs or anything else we want to remember for just a short period. (This will be unnecessary, of course, if we have managed to transfer it to long-term memory.)

Rote rehearsal, however, can easily be interrupted by lack of attention or a distraction of some kind and then the information has gone forever.

4.9 General example | **Infantile amnesia**

Infantile amnesia is the general inability of people to remember specific events from the early years of their lives. On the basis of both free recall studies and studies for memories of notable and datable early events (the birth of a sibling, hospitalisation) psychologists (Goleman 1993) have concluded that there are very few memories from before the age of 3 years.

Long-term memory

Long-term memory is that part of the brain where permanent information is stored and many believe that once information is there it is there forever (Higbee 2001). Capacity and storage duration appears to be almost limitless. If there is a problem with remembering things that have happened in the recent or distant past it's probably because of retrieval difficulties rather than problems of irreversibly lost material. The problems associated with retrieval are inextricably linked to how the information is encoded and originally taken into long-term memory in the first place.

4.13 Marketing example | **Rote learning**

Perhaps the simplest way that marketers attempt to influence consumers is by the use of rote learning. Rote is learning about things in a mechanical mostly unthinking manner. Marketers and advertising people repeatedly bombard their target markets with simple jingles, slogans, brand names and information about benefits which consumers then memorise without paying any attention. Many older people can still remember from 25 years ago such things as 'for mash get smash' (Cadburys mash potato), 'A million housewives everyday pick up a tin of beans and say beanz, meanz, Hienz', 'The Esso sign means happy motoring, the Esso sign means happy motoring, call at the Esso sign'.

Questions

1 Identify as many advertising slogans and jingles that you can remember that have used repetitive rote learning as a form of communication. Do you think that constant repetition can actually turn consumers off?

2 Discuss methods that marketers can use to help consumers memorise their product brands and services.

Encoding, storage and retrieval

The memory process can be broken down into three parts, encoding, storage and retrieval.

Encoding

Current studies in neuroscience strongly support the notion that a memory is a set of encoded neural connections. Encoding is the way that we put data into our memory and how it goes in will affect how easy it is to get out. The stronger the connections the stronger will be the memory. If data is learnt and encoded effectively it can be stored (and retrieved) for a lifetime, if not it may be forgotten within seconds, minutes or hours. Some data will be encoded and stored subconsciously while other information will need a deliberate concentrated effort.

> **Key point** Memory is a set of encoded neural connections. The stronger the connections, how effective the data is learnt and encoded, the stronger the memory.

Storage

How and where information is stored will enable good or bad retrieval, good or bad memory. Imagine how a search engine such as Google operates and we have an excellent metaphor. Data is given meaning and classified into compartments, similar items are filed together, crosschecking can take place and when looking for pieces of information one thing will lead to another making retrieval easier. Often in seconds if we understand the system.

Retrieval

This is how easily we can access the data. Information used regularly will just seem to 'pop' out whenever needed while other information can take longer. This might mean using associated reminder clues and cues used to encode as well as relaxing and allowing the answer to, again, 'pop' out in its own time. Sometimes our inability to retrieve long-term memories is only temporary, this 'tip-of-the-tongue phenomenon' is known as blocking.

Table 4.4 Marketing and retrieving information

Brands will be more easily remembered or forgotten according to the following:

- If they are first into the market.
- If there are a limited number of brands in the market.
- If it's been on the market for a long or short amount of time.
- If it's a descriptive brand, with a distinct or short easily encoded name.
- If the brand name is understood across countries and cultures.
- If there are large or small amounts of advertising, promotion and publicity on a national and global scale.
- If both corporate and product brand name are known.

Figure 4.14

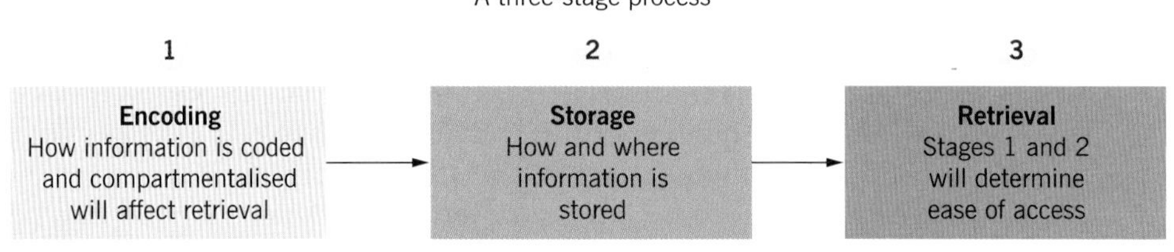

Long-term memory – encoding, storage and retrieval

Elaborate rehearsal

Elaborate rehearsal is consciously focusing on the meaning to be learnt and then relating it in some way to information already in long-term memory, this is known as the 'construction of knowledge'. In this way individuals are able to store and retrieve information more easily. There are many 'tricks' that can be used. Some can be picked up through experience and the learning process, for example associating rain with getting wet, the easiest way to drive to work, or where the bread and jams are displayed in Asda. Other information people will want to make a deliberate attempt to remember and so encode using some kind of associative memory strategy.

Types of long-term memory

Long-term memories are not all the same and they can be classified into different types according to content. **Daniel Schacter and Endel Tulving** (1994) introduced the terms **explicit** and **implicit memory**.

Explicit or declarative memories

Explicit memories (or declarative memories) are memories that are learnt and accrued throughout our lives and that are constantly in and out of the mind, sometimes gaining high levels of conscious awareness, other times receding into the background depending on circumstances. These are memories we know we know. They can be broken down into three parts:

Semantic memories are memories about words, ideas and concepts such as the capitals of the world, important dates in history, abstract concepts about how things work, laws, rules and regulations and different cultures and political systems. We might know (or think we know) the capital of Brazil, the population of Nigeria, the makeup of the European Union, the political system in China and how to cook an Italian dish (of course we might have problems associated with retrieval).

Episodic or autobiographic memories are personal things such as remembering our first day at school, a particular sports day, meeting the first boyfriend or girlfriend and the wedding of Uncle Jim in 1953. The important feature here is that the entire context surrounding the event is remembered with ourselves as an actor in the memory.

Procedural (skills) memories are memories about skills and how to do things, such as how to swim, play tennis, ride a bike, or drive a car. Some of these things, quite amazingly, we never seem to forget no matter how long it might have been, for example, since we last rode a bicycle.

Learning to play tennis by instruction

4.14 Marketing example — Brands into explicit memory

Brand owners would like to be part of this world and work constantly to make their products and services part of our semantic and episodic memory. They promote incessantly trying to inculcate into our memory brand names, brand benefits over competitors, logos, jingles, catchphrases, prices and retail outlets that hold stock. More importantly they want their brands and services to become an inextricable part of our autobiographical memory so that we remember the first time our parents took us to McDonald's, Disneyland or Sainsbury's. They would like their brand to be part of our lives including memories. Washing day smell and mother using Persil. Smarties for being a good girl, the Mars won at the school sports and Marmite sandwiches after swimming. The candle lit anniversary dinner at Harvesters, the day we bought our first (Ford Fiesta) car and the holiday with Thomson's.

Key point Brand owners promote constantly to make brand experience a positive and integral part of our lives. Their biggest nightmare is for any one of these memories to be for bad service rather than good.

Implicit or non-declarative memories

'What touches the heart is engraved on the memory.' VOLTAIRE

Implicit memories on the other hand, are memories that exist in our pre-conscious or sub-conscious and are able to influence behaviour.

Weak, or non-encoded implicit memories might occasionally come into conscious memory but only in a disjointed, hazy and obscure manner. For example I might have a distant and faint recollection of the death of a grandparent or an uncle teaching me to swim when I was about two or three. Over time this type of memory can distort and be difficult to distinguish between fact and fiction.

Conditioned memories are those that are formed more or less automatically through the processes of classical and operant conditioning, discussed earlier in the chapter. These kinds of implicit memory are more difficult to understand, sometimes only available through some kind of psychoanalysis, but there seems to be little doubt that they will influence behaviour. Examples include an irrational fear of water brought about through a hidden memory of an accident when an infant or the hatred of some type of food because of the actions of over strict parents forcing a child to eat.

4.15 Marketing example — Implicit memories

In a similar way to explicit memories marketers would love the brand to be implicitly embedded in our memories so that any response is emotional, habitual and unquestioningly positive. Children as well as adults automatically operate a Sony Playstation, move around Microsoft products and work an Orange mobile phone. For some the name of Porsche or BMW sends shivers down the spine, the mere mention of John Smith's bitter evokes pleasurable emotions about nights out with the boys and the name of De Beers causes many a woman to drift into reveries over diamonds, sumptuous nights out and romantic dreams.

Figure 4.15

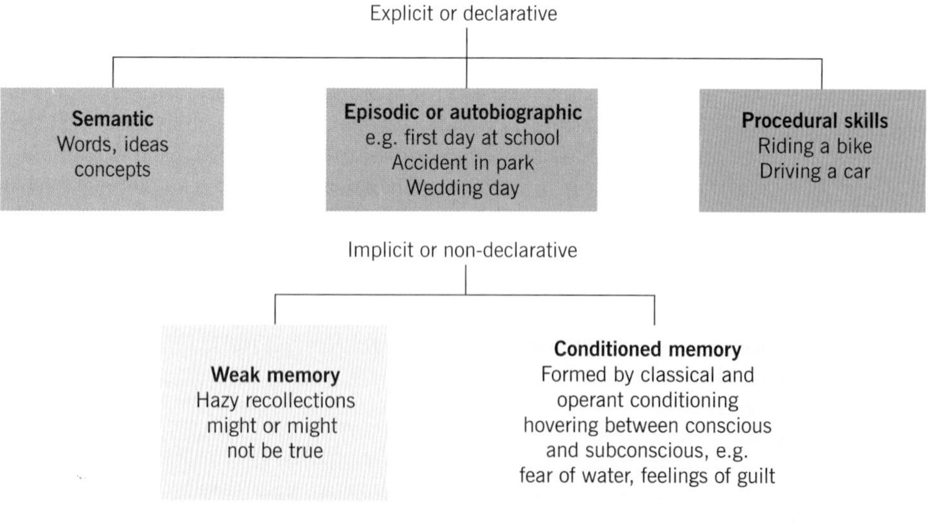

Components of long-term memory

Factors affecting memory and learning capacity

Many factors come together to either enhance or prevent memory and learning capacity.

Concentration and attentiveness

Concentration is often said to be the major way that information is engraved into memory. This is why attention deficits can radically reduce memory performance. Experience demonstrates, for students and others alike, how memory capacity can be improved by making a conscious effort to frequently repeat and integrate information (often with the help of mnemonics and memory aids of some kind).

Motivation

It's easier to learn when there is an interest in the subject or the subject is interesting. We can all think back to the difficulty of learning mathematics and sciences especially if taught in a boring manner. Yet ask the same people to statistically analyse the football results or work out ways to score in darts or to play an intricate computer game and the learning comes tumbling out.

The use of the senses

Many experiments indicate that memory storage and recall is increased if more than one of the senses are involved. Sight accompanied by sound and smell will mean easier encoding and any one might trigger off a memory. High and low, soft and loud speech, written words with different fonts and sizes, colours and pictures, novelty and distinctiveness all work to enhance memory. Education and levels of literacy will sometimes dictate which of the senses is best used in getting over particular messages, e.g. pictures where people are unable to read or write.

4.16 Marketing example — Attractive words in adverts

It's well recorded that in advertisements, in as many as 90 per cent of the cases, pictures are noticed before words, large type before smaller type, one font rather than another font and so on and all this is used to attract attention and draw people in to read the detail and so encourage the brand to become part of long-term memory. Some words, such as free, special offer, sale, one week only, are more emotive than others and more likely to be remembered.

Emotional state

Memories are often accompanied by feelings and emotions and they can have both a beneficial and harmful affect on memory. In some cases, when remembering an emotional event, individuals can recall not only what happened, but also how they felt at the time. The concept of 'flashbulb memory' is people having a vivid emotional memory of a particular traumatic incident. For example people of a particular age knowing where they were and how they felt on hearing about the assassination of John F. Kennedy, or of Martin Luther King and for younger people it's been incidents such as the death of Princess Diana, or the 9/11 Twin Towers disaster. Conversely emotion can cause people to forget and this is outlined in a little more detail below.

Situational factors

Situations can affect memory. For example hard times experienced when young, the first day at school, a particularly exciting holiday, the birth of a child and a car crash, can all have a lasting affect on memory recall. Of course it's the task of the marketing manager to make a service offered (a wedding, a holiday, a night out) such a momentous event that the consumer will not only never forget but be constantly telling others. In fact research seems to show that happy experiences can become exaggerated over time. Unfortunately so can unhappy experiences.

4.17 Marketing example — Learning while in the womb

Many anecdotal claims have been made that unborn babies react to being played Mozart. There might now be some more scientific supporting evidence, however. A small study by Leicester University (UK) found that babies can recognise pieces of music played for three months before birth, a year after birth. According to another study by doctors in the Netherlands on 25 unborn babies between 37 and 40 weeks' gestation, babies were able to learn and remember while still in the womb. They applied an acoustic sound to the womb and directed it above the unborn baby's leg. They determined whether the unborn baby had 'learnt' not to react to the sound if their body no longer moved, after four consecutive sounds. From their experiments they concluded that foetuses have a short-term memory of at least 10 minutes and a long-term memory of at least 24 hours. The results were published in *The Lancet*.

Question

1 Can you recall your earliest memory? Was it happy, sad or neutral?

Accuracy of memories

Some experiments also show that our memories can sometimes be confused and even downright wrong. Many false memories involve confusing or mixing fragments of memory events, some of which may have happened at different times but which are remembered as occurring together. Past memories can sometimes be exaggerated or underplayed when being told over time perhaps to bolster one's importance, to leave out areas of embarrassment or because parts have just been forgotten. Studies also show that feelings of certainty are no guarantee that the memory is correct (Schacter 1996). Sometimes we actually fill in gaps in our memory trying to make a complete picture (remember Gestalt!) without even realising it. We are also susceptible to suggestions from others that help us fill in these gaps in our memories. This demands that police are careful about saying or showing anything to witnesses that might influence crime recollections.

Key point Memories can be constructions made in accordance with present needs, desires, influences, etc.

Hypnosis

Contrary to what many people believe, hypnosis does not appear to aid memory's accuracy. Because subjects are extremely suggestible while hypnotised most countries do not allow it as evidence in a court of law.

Forgetting

There are different reasons why we forget some information yet remember other information. This might be due to illness that can affect both short- and long-term memory or it might be due to problems of interference associated with recall (Ebbinghaus 1913).

Reasons for forgetting include the following:

- *Weak encoding* This is why we forget most things. Try to remember the dream you had last night that you remembered so vividly the moment you woke up.
- *Lack of retrieval cues* We seem to need a system to help pull out particular information.
- *Current interference* Interference of some kind comes in-between the stimulus and the memory process.
- *Proactive interference* Proactive interference is when older information interferes with newer information. Learning similar languages such as Spanish and Italian can cause confusion with the new shutting out some of the old.
- *Retroactive interference* Retroactive interference is when new information makes us forget, or changes in some way old information. A teacher has to constantly learn new names which can then (embarrassingly) cause the names of past students to be forgotten.
- *The need to stay sane* Brain overload would occur if we were to never forget anything.
- *Repetitive action* Unless something special happens we can never remember every day at university or work.
- *Reverie or daydreaming* Many of us have had experiences of driving to work and then having no memory of how we got there.
- *Lack of sleep* Not enough sleep seems to have a big affect on memory.

- *Illnesses and traumas* Amnesia caused by the effects of drugs/alcohol, brain injuries, or physical or psychological traumas.
- *Emotions* Many people have suffered the nightmare of sitting down in an exam, turning the page over and then nervous emotion makes them forget everything. Similarly actors can forget their lines through a rush of adrenaline.

Repressed emotional memories

Sigmund Freud believed that part of conditioned implicit memory was repressed to decrease anxiety and hidden as a means to keep painful memories out of the consciousness; he called these **repressed emotional memories**. It can be awful things such as a terrible accident or violent death in the family or it can be lesser happenings such as being lost as a child, or alone and frightened in a thunderstorm. Concomitant to this was the concept of recovered memory. This was the idea that repressed memories could in some way (perhaps through psychoanalysis) be brought to the surface, discussed and any latent anxiety expunged. There is, however, little scientific evidence to support much of his work.

4.10 General example — False memory or reality

'Despite the fact that we humans are great collectors of souvenirs, not one of these persons [claiming to have been aboard a flying saucer] has brought back so much as an extraterrestrial tool or artefact, which could, once and for all, resolve the UFO mystery.' PHILIP KLASS

Summary

- The chapters began with a discussion on the relationship between learning, marketing and knowledge encompassing the differences between observational, empirical, scientific and received knowledge. The meaning of intelligence was briefly outlined.
- We then looked at the differences between genetic, objective and subjective knowledge and the role that they play in an understanding of consumer behaviour.
- Theories of learning were examined beginning with the behaviourists and classical and operant conditioning.
- Pavlov's classical conditioning involving stimulus and response mechanisms was examined in some detail and marketing and consumer related examples given. This was followed with how John Watson took Pavlov's theories on animals and related them to how humans learn and also develop phobias. Edwin Guthrie and child imitation learning was briefly outlined.
- We then moved on to operant or instrumental learning, the other major behaviourist theory. We looked first at Thorndike's law of effect involving reward and punishment and trial and error learning with animals.

- The major behaviourist B.F. Skinner was examined in some detail and we examined how he used the so-called Skinner box to show how animals learnt and developed new ways of behaving. His comprehensive methods were discussed in some detail looking at how he related his experiments to how people (and consumers) learn and behave.
- Experiments by Martin Seligman in the 1960s lead us into talking about the neglected role of cognition, the mind and thinking in the learning process. We first looked at learned helplessness before moving on to look at Tollman and his experiments with rats in a maze that highlighted the fact that latent learning and memory seemed to be taking place.
- Insight learning experiments with animals were analysed and again related to how people learn both in their day-to-day experiences and when acting in the role of the consumer.
- Finally we looked at the essential part that short- and long-term memory and forgetting have in learning.

Questions

1. Empiricists argue that we are born with nothing and come to 'know' the world solely through our senses while rationalists argue that we are born with innate knowledge that helps us understand the world. Discuss.
2. Examine the concepts of learning and intelligence. Demonstrate how it might be measured giving examples of past and current methods used in business and marketing.
3. Discuss why you think that the study of learning is important to an understanding of consumer behaviour both at home and around the world. Give examples of it use in practice.
4. Identify the factors involved in classical conditioning and discuss its relevance to human and consumer behaviour. How might it relate to neurotic and phobic behaviour?
5. Discuss the differences between classical and operant conditioning and how both theories are used and manipulated by marketing and advertising. Give live examples.
6. Examine why behaviourism became discredited as a universal law of learning.
7. Identify and evaluate all the different ways that people learn to behave in the way that they do. Explain why it is important for marketers to understand the different methods and give examples where knowledge gained has been used in such things as advertising, merchandising and packaging.
8. Discuss cognitive psychology and examine its relationship with the behaviourist approach to learning. How much thought do you think goes into the purchase of different types of products including groceries, holidays, financial services and clothes?
9. Identify and evaluate the different forms of cognitive psychology. Illustrate how marketing and consumer behaviour might be affected by its assumptions and conclusions.
10. Examine the different aspects of memory and show how marketers can use the process in marketing products and services to consumers.

Case study

Case study 1 Consumer behaviour and religion

Religion is on the up in the US where now more than 60 per cent of the population have some kind of affiliation with one of nearly 1,600 registered religious groups; and it's big business. One of God's success stories has been the growth in the aptly named Mega-Churches. Southern Christian is an example. The church can hold 9,000 people and sitting through a service is like going to a middle-of-the-road pop concert. There is an orchestra and professional singers and everything is displayed on a giant video screen including the words of the songs. So successful is this religious country club that they take in $500,000 in donations every week. There's even a police escort for the collection. In the near future they intend introducing retail outlets including a McDonald's.

The five largest religious groups in the world are:

1 Christianity 2 billion
2 Islam 1.3 billion
3 Hinduism 900 million
4 Buddhism 360 million
5 Chinese traditional religion 225 million
6 Secular, nonreligious, Agnostics, Atheists account for 850 million.

Questions

1 How relevant is marketing and an understanding of consumer behaviour to religion?
2 What kinds of products, services and brands might be important to markets dominated by some kind of religious belief? How might this vary across the religious groups identified above?

Case study

Case study 2 True or false information

Consumers have a constant problem in trying to decide what is and what is not good for them to buy and eat. Over the decades, so-called experts have told them that bottle feeding baby is better than breast feeding, that certain types of mattresses can cause cot deaths, that alcohol, tea and sugar is bad for the health only to be told a while later that its better to breast feed, that laying baby on its front is probably one cause of cot death and that red wine, tea and a certain amount of sugar can support good health. Commentators might tell us that Asda is cheaper than Tesco, that organic food and alternative medicines are good for us, that cigarette smoking is bad for us, that global warming is causing the ice cape to melt and that obesity among children is increasing. In many cases it's in the interest of the communicator to have us believe one thing rather than another to encourage the purchase of certain products and services. Ultimately whether we decide this information is true or false will depend on our faith in the information source and our own experiences and scepticism.

Questions

1 Discuss the consumer problems associated with contradictory information.

2 How might the consumer be helped and protected from new information that too quickly seems to question accepted orthodoxy?

Further reading

Books

Abra, J. (1998) *Should Psychology be a Science?: Pros and Cons*, Westport, CT: Praeger.

Anastasi, A. and S. Urbina (1997) *Psychological Testing*, 7th edn, Upper Saddle River, NJ: Prentice-Hall.

Blum, D. (2002) *Love at Goon Park: Harry Harlow and the Science of Affection*, Philadelphia, PA: Perseus Publishing.

Boakes, R.A. (1984) *From Darwin to Behaviourism*, Cambridge: Cambridge University Press.

Broadbent, Donald (1958) in *Attention and Memory: An Integrated Framework*, Nelson Cowan Department of Psychology, University of Missouri-Columbia, New York: Oxford University Press, 1995.

Dacey, John S. and John F. Travers (1999) *Human Growth and Development for Educators*, New York: WIU, McGraw-Hill Companies, Inc.

Ebbinghaus, Herman (1913) *Memory: A Contribution to Experimental Psychology*, trans by Henry A. Ruger and Clara E. Bussenius, originally published New York: Teachers College, Columbia University, http://psychclassics.yorku.ca.Ebbinghaus.

Eysenck, H.J. (ed.) (1960) *Behaviour Therapy and the Neuroses*, Oxford: Pergamon Press.

Eysenck, H. (1971) *Race, Intelligence and Education*, London: Maurice Temple Smith.

Eysenck, H.J. and M.W. Eysenck (1985) *Personality and Individual Differences: A Natural Science Approach*, New York: Plenum.

Goleman, D. (1995) *Emotional Intelligence*, New York: Bantam.

Harrison P. (1998) *The Bible, Protestantism, and the Rise of Natural Science*, Cambridge: Cambridge University Press.

Higbee, K. (2001) *Your Memory: How It Works and How to Improve It*, New York: Marlowe & Company.

Howe, M.J.A. (1997) *IQ in Question: The Truth about Intelligence*, London: Sage.

Loftus, Elizabeth F. (1980) *Memory, Surprising New Insights Into How We Remember and Why We Forget*, Reading, MA: Addison-Wesley.

Markle, S. (1969) *Good Frames and Bad*, 2nd edn, New York: Wiley.

Ogilvy, David (1985) *Ogilvy on Advertising*, New York: Vintage.

Pavlov, I.P. (1927) *Conditional Reflexes*, London: Routledge and Kegan Paul.

Pinker, S. (1994) *The Language Instinct*, New York: HarperCollins.

Pinker, S. (1999) *How the Mind Works*, New York: W.W. Norton & Company.

Pinker, S. (2002) *The Blank Slate: The Modern Denial of Human Nature*, Harmondsworth: Penguin Putnam.

Ridley, M. (1999) *Genome: The Autobiography of a Species in 23 Chapters*, London: Fourth Estate Ltd.

Sacks, Oliver (1985) *The Man Who Mistook His Wife For A Hat*, London: Picador.

Schacter, Daniel L. (1996) *Searching for Memory: The Brain, the Mind, and the Past*, New York: Basic Books.

Schacter, Daniel L. (2001) *The Seven Sins of Memory: How the Mind Forgets and Remembers*, Boston, MA: Houghton Mifflin Co.

Schacter, Daniel L. and Endel Tulving (eds) (1994) *Memory Systems*, Cambridge, MA: MIT Press.

Seligman, Martin E.P. (1998) *Learned Optimism: How to Change Your Mind and Your Life*, New York: Simon & Schuster, reissue.

Skinner, B.F. (1971) *Beyond Freedom and Dignity*, New York: Knopf.

Thorndike, E. (1932) *The Fundamentals of Learning*, New York: Teachers College Press.

Tulving, Endel and F.I.M. Craik (eds) (2000) *The Oxford Handbook of Memory*, Oxford: Oxford University Press.

Wadsworth, B.J. (1996) *Piaget's Theory of Cognitive and Affective Development*, White Plains, NY: Longman.

Wright, Ray (2003) *A Business and Marketing Dictionary*, Chelmsford: Earlybrave Publishers.

Articles and journals

Doogan, S. and Thomas, G.V. (1992) 'Origins of Fear in Adults and Children: The Role of Conditioning Processes and Prior Familiarity with Dogs', *Behaviour Research and Therapy*, 30/4: 387–94.

van den Hout, M. and H. Merckelbach (1991) 'Classical Conditioning: Still Going Strong', *Behavioural Psychotherapy*, 19/1: 59–79.

Howe, M. and M. Courage (1993) 'On Resolving the Enigma of Infantile Amnesia', *Psychological Bulletin*, 113: 305–26.

Hunt, E. (2001) 'Multiple Views of Multiple Intelligence, [Review of Intelligence Reframed: Multiple Intelligence in the 21st Century]', *Contemporary Psychology*, 46: 5–7.

Jansen, A., B. Boon, H. Nauta and M. Van Den Hout (1992) 'Salivation Discordant with Hunger', *Behaviour Research and Therapy*, 30/2: 163–6.

Miciak, A.R. and W.L. Shanklin (1994) 'Choosing Celebrity Endorsers', *Marketing Management*, 3, 3: 51–9.

Miller, G.A. (1956) 'The Magical Number Seven, Plus or Minus Two: Some Limits on Our Capacity for Processing Information', *Psychological Review*, 63: 81–97 (available at www.well.com/user/smalin/miller.html).

Perner, Josef (2000) 'Memory and Theory of Mind', in E. Tulving and F.I.M. Craik (eds), *The Oxford Handbook of Memory*, Oxford: Oxford University Press, pp. 297–312.

Pillemer, D.B. and S.H. White (1989) 'Childhood Events Recalled by Children and Adults', *Advances in Child Development and Behavior*, 21: 297–340.

Rimm, D.C., L.H. Janda, D.W. Lancaster, M. Mahl and K. Dittmar (1977) 'An Exploratory Investigation of the Origin and Maintenance of Phobias', *Behavior Research and Therapy*, 15: 231–8.

Telch, M.J., J.A. Lucas, N.B. Schmidt, H.H. Hanna, T.L. Jaimez and R.A. Lucas (1993) 'Group Cognitive-Behavioural Treatment of Panic Disorder', *Behaviour Research and Therapy*, 31/3: 279–87.

Tulving, Endel (1999) 'Episodic vs Semantic Memory', in F. Keil and R. Wilson (eds), *The MIT Encyclopedia of the Cognitive Sciences*, Cambridge, MA: MIT Press, 278–80.

Weinberg, R.A. (1989) 'Intelligence and IQ: Landmark Issues and Great Debates', *American Psychologist*, 44: 98–104.

Websites

Klass, Philip, UFO researcher interview, www.pbs.org/wgbh/nova/aliens/philipklass.html.

Memory Techniques and Mnemonics, from MindTools, www.demon.co.uk/mindtool/memory.html.

www.studentshout.com.

Motivation

5

'If a man would move the world, he must first move himself.'

Socrates

Objectives

At the end of this chapter the reader will be able to:

1. Examine the meaning of motivation and show the part that it plays in understanding human and consumer behaviour.
2. Identify, examine and evaluate the forces that drive motivation.
3. Look at the many theories of motivation and evaluate their worth in modern times especially when applied to marketing.

Introduction

In everyday life we constantly seek to try to discover reasons why others behave in the way that they do. People say such things as 'he acted with the best possible motives' or 'she had high levels of motivation' or 'we did not understand his motivation'. We seem to have to know the reasons why others think and act towards us and towards others as they do and why they might take one action rather than another. We might try to impute motivational reasons for somebody's actions through behaviour, for example somebody running at a railway station is in a hurry to catch a particular train, an individual closes a window because he or she is cold or a young woman crying at a dance has man problems. Or it might be the things that people say as well as the things that they do. A lecturer will ask a student why they are at university and be given the reply that a degree will lead to a good job. At a job interview an applicant when asked why they want the job might say it's because of the attractiveness of the company and a supporter of hunting feels that it's a functional way of culling vermin. There are times, however, when people say one thing and then do another, and because we have problems trusting particular individuals or groups, assumptions are made about what might be the real motives rather than those given.

5.1 General example **Motivation and trust**

In research undertaken by many research companies over the years, politicians, estate agents, journalists and second-hand car salesmen are constantly at the bottom of the public esteem league in terms of those whose motives we trust the most. (YouGov.com 2003)

Understanding motivation is crucial in marketing

'I can live for two months on a good compliment.' MARK TWAIN

It's important for all those organisations, producers, retailers, marketing agencies and so on, involved in buying and selling to try to understand why people want particular products and services, why one holiday might be chosen over another, one company rather than another or one brand rather than another. If marketers can understand reasons behind purchase decisions, then they should be able to develop marketing programmes that can beneficially influence in favour of their company's products and services rather than the products and services of a competitor. In a wider sense, understanding motivation can also bring many other company benefits when dealing with employees, supply chain organisations, pressure groups, local communities and other stakeholders.

Key point There has been a great deal of research that seems to demonstrate that there is a link between customer satisfaction, retention and profitability and the level of employee motivation.

Definition of motivation

In very simple terms motivation can be described as a process that starts with some kind of motive or need, perhaps for a drink of water, the drive or action to satisfy that need, and the fulfilment of the need, obtaining the water.

Figure 5.1

Motive or need	→	Action or drive	→	Need fulfilment
Drink of water	→	Seek out source	→	Obtain the water

The motivation process – a simple model

Motivational reason complex

There is no doubt that motivations are often more complex than at first appears. Many decades ago it was seen in simple behavioural terms, i.e. equilibrium seeking and drive reduction. Now enormous amounts of research have shown that individuals can be uncertain or unaware about the real basis underpinning behaviour and so give one reason for an action when another reason, often more deeply embedded in the mind, is the real one. For example a student might go to university because of parental pressure, not for the given reason of hoping to get a better job. The prospective employee wants the job because of the money and not the attractiveness of the company. Similarly a huntsperson may really hunt for enjoyment but the idea of vermin culling is given because it seems to be a more acceptable reason for both the hunter and the wider audience.

Motivational strength and intensity

'I will prepare and some day my chance will come.' ABRAHAM LINCOLN

The motivation that drives the need can be weak or strong depending on the type and the strength of the motive. The strength of motivational drive to find a drink of water will depend on how thirsty the person might be. Similarly if we desperately need to go to the toilet then the motivation to find a toilet will be high and it will concentrate the mind on that almost at the expense of everything else. There are some individuals that appear to have the motivational drive, for example, to be successful or to earn more and more money that stays with them for the whole of their lives.

Consumer motivation and the hierarchy of motives

▶ **Maslow's hierarchy of needs** (developed by **Abraham Maslow** (1908–70)) is the most popular of the humanistic theories on motivation and although now distorted by many business commentators part of the basic premise is still widely adopted and considered useful by marketing practitioners. This is the idea that consumers are motivated by a series of different needs with differing strengths for ▶ different people. **Safety needs** may be of most concern to one group of consumers when buying products and services, social and 'needing to be wanted' the overriding concern for others. For some people it may be status and recognition ▶ that matters most, while for others it may be **self-actualising** and inner spiritual needs. The motivations driving the demand for products and services might also change from product group to product group as well as across the product life cycle; for example it might be safety needs when buying financial services and status needs when buying a holiday. Needs might also change from country to country; for example a bicycle might be bought for sport in the UK (self-actualising needs) but for transport and work (security needs) in China. Needs up and down Maslow's triangle might also change as consumers grow older and lifestyles change. Marketing research, product development and communications will have to reflect this veritable kaleidoscope of changing benefits demanded by differing target market groups and individuals.

The shopaholic – retail shopping satisfies many needs

> **Key point** Examples of how differing needs, physiological (basic food and water), security (insurance, mobile phones in case of car breakdown), social (alcohol, night-clubbing, holidays), status (premium priced cars, large house), spiritual (reading material, theatre), are used by advertisers to sell their products can be seen constantly in TV adverts everyday.

Primary and secondary needs

Human needs and motives, however, are not as simple as the examples given above. They can be broken down into the following categories.

Primary needs

Primary needs are innate or biological needs such as the need for food, water, warmth, to go to the toilet, security, sex and (maybe) curiosity. All animals, as well as humans, can be said to share these basic needs in order to stay alive in a hostile world and they are inherited through the DNA.

Secondary needs

Secondary needs are needs that have been socially and culturally acquired through interaction with others. Although some higher-level animals (such as chimpanzees and baboons) might have some of these needs we tend to associate most of them with humans. These include such things as the need for: social interaction, tactile relationships, love, recognition, **status needs**, prestige, power, achievement and so on.

(It is secondary needs that most interest us in marketing and this will be discussed in more detail below.)

Internal and external needs

Motives can be further broken down into internal and external needs.

Internal or intrinsic motivation

This is a desire or a need to act that originates within the individual. After much thought an author might decide to write a book. This would then motivate him or her to contact a publisher. The only problem is maintaining the motivation over the many lonely months of writing.

External or extrinsic motivation

This is the desire to act to obtain an external reward. Children will be good knowing that if they are their parents will take them to the cinema. Tennis fans are motivated to queue outside Wimbledon all night long so that they might get a ticket for the final.

5.2 General example — Motivation and the law

Nowhere are motives behind behaviour and action more thrashed out and intricately mulled over than in a court of law. For ostensibly the same crime, a guilty person might go to prison for life or be released immediately under a suspended sentence according to proven motives at the time of the offence.

Positive and negative motivations

Motivation can be positive or negative. We can act positively to obtain the fulfilment of a particular outcome need or, conversely, we can act negatively to avoid an unwanted outcome. Driven by negative fear/safety motives a famous Arsenal footballer refuses to fly to away games and is prepared to travel across Europe by train, even though this takes much longer. Conversely, an Arsenal fan, driven by positive feel-good motives, is prepared to spend hundreds of pounds flying to an Arsenal away game over a two-day period.

Marketing and negative reinforcement

Consumers are motivated into spending billions of pounds a year on products and services that help avoid unwanted outcomes. Sun-cream to avoid burning skin and cancerous sunrays, pills that prevent sickness and headaches, breakfast foods that are good for the heart and insurance policies in case we have an accident in the car, break a leg or even die.

There are thousands of avoidance products on the market to prevent unwanted outcomes.
Source: Simon Wright

Marketing and buyer purchase motives

The reasons behind buyer behaviour are a crucial and central part of marketing and selling and billions of pounds are spent around the world every year on research in an attempt to discover reasons behind retail usage and brand purchases. Marketers are interested in both consumer and organisational purchasing behaviour and individual and group motivation because they need to satisfy customer needs.

So the real motives behind needs and wants have to be clearly identified if the appropriate products and services are to be produced, promoted and repurchased by the target market. Just as importantly, however, there is now the demand on marketing managers to hold and maintain customer loyalty for the long term, building and motivating good relationships and customer retention schemes on a continuous basis. With ever-present competition ready to take away dissatisfied customers and knowing that it can be many times more expensive to get new customers than it is to retain existing ones this becomes a high priority on all successful company agendas.

Rational, emotional and instinctive motives

In very simple terms reasons for purchase can be broken down into three categories, rational, emotional and instinctive (see Figure 5.2). As with many categorisations, the motives for purchase are not mutually exclusive and so tend to be a certain combination of all three reasons depending on the product or service on offer. Similarly products and services might be said to have two attributes, the functional and the symbolic. A car for example might be bought for functional reasons, that is to get from home to work, or it might be bought for symbolic reasons, that is to increase personal attractiveness and self-esteem.

Rational motives

Relatively speaking rational reasons behind purchase decisions are fairly easy to understand so the car has a three-year warranty, is good on petrol and maintenance and costs are low. On the other hand symbolic reasons for purchase, such as sex appeal, raising self-esteem, feel-good factors and so on, can be much harder to expose and understand, often seeming to reside and hide below the level of customer consciousness.

The emotions

Emotions and feelings can be both positive and negative but all might play a role in consumer buying behaviour and so have to be researched and understood by marketers so that product benefits can be directly targeted and communicated. Motivating emotions include: anger, pride, jealousy, envy, gluttony, greed, love, affection and nostalgia.

> **Key point** All human emotions are extremely powerful and are used in some way or another by brand owners and advertising agencies to sell products and services.

Instinctive reasons

Sometimes we seem to act instinctively, that is without really being aware of what it is we have done until the **instinctive behaviour** is over. If frightened, we jump or run and if somebody attacks, we defend ourselves. On a more prosaic level compulsive obsessive behaviour of some kind, e.g. eating or drinking, can take place instinctively, for example a whole box of chocolates can be eaten by a 'chocoholic' before there is realisation.

5.1 Marketing example Plato's divided soul

The theory of Plato's divided soul (Wright 1999) works on the simple concept that customers 'think' with three basic 'brains', the rational (the head), the emotional (the heart) and the instinctive (the gut). When buying products and services we think with an element of all three brains but some individuals and groups think predominately more with one element than with another. Some products will be purchased for instinctive reasons – impulse purchases such as chocolate, alcohol, cigarettes; some for emotional reasons – perfumes, cars, fashion; and some for rational reasons – plumbing services, petrol or electricity supply.

Questions

1 Discuss Plato's divided soul theory and identify products and services that might be bought for each level.

2 Do you think it is a viable theory?

Figure 5.2

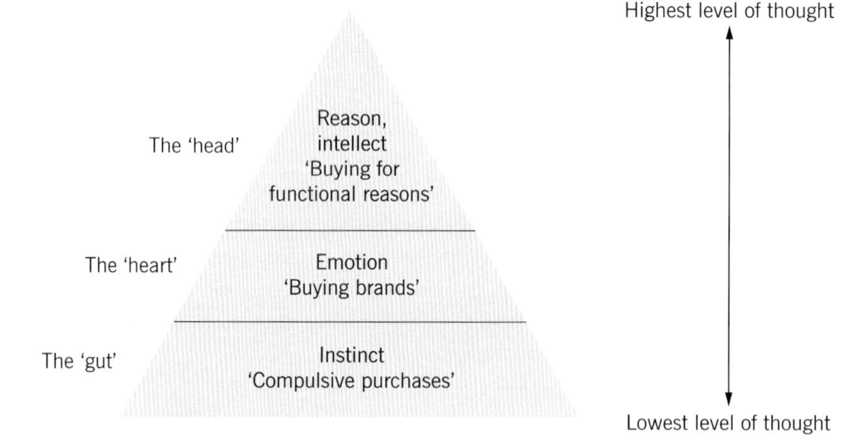

Plato's divided soul

Motivation, retail and business purchasing

Research seems to show that as much as 70 per cent to 80 per cent of all consumer products are purchased for emotional reasons particularly tied up in the concept of the brand (Zajonc 1984; Bornstein 1989). This is not the case when selling into the retailer. Here the professional retail buyer will be purchasing for the company and not for themselves and the decisions will be made mainly based on rational criteria. This will also be the same selling into the business-to-business market where one business is selling to another to use in the making of goods and services (see Table 5.1).

Table 5.1 Consumer, retailer and business buyer motives buying orange drink

Consumer purchase – emotional	***Retail purchase – rational***
Is it beneficial to health?	*Will it sell?*
Will I feel better after drinking it?	*Will it make a profit?*
Has it the right image?	*Will it fit on to the shelf?*
Does it taste nice?	*Will it fit on to the delivery pallet?*

Business-to-business purchase of goods and services – rational
Is the price low enough?
Will it do what I want it to do?
Is there continuity of delivery, after sales service?
Can I trust and build a partnership with the seller?

Key point Research seems to show that as much as 70 per cent to 80 per cent of all consumer products are purchased for emotional reasons, while rational reasons account for 70 per cent to 80 per cent of business-to-business sales. Companies recognising the existence of the three brains will need to communicate benefit messages that clearly reflect the relevant customer need.

Motivational conflict

Motivational conflict can occur when a person has to choose between different needs and different outcomes. We must all have experienced the conflict when faced with the problem of gaining immediate pleasure from eating a bar of chocolate and the nagging fear of putting on weight. There is the enjoyment that might cause us to stay up to the early hours of the morning drinking and the certain knowledge that we will feel awful in the morning. Then there is the problem of spending all our money now on immediately satisfying products, e.g. constantly eating out (instant gratification), or saving for something more substantial in the future, perhaps the down payment on a house mortgage (delayed gratification). It seems that the more affluent we become the more we have to constantly choose between different and competing needs and outcomes.

Key point Research has shown that some groups will spend money as soon as it is earned seeking 'instant gratification', while other groups seem able to save for more worthwhile products in the future known as 'delayed gratification' (Pooler 2003).

Cognitive dissonance

▶ It was **Leon Festinger** (1957) in his theory on 'cognitive dissonance' who argued that individuals could not comfortably hold competing values in the mind and so would develop defence mechanisms and strategies to solve these sorts of contradictions and dichotomies. In resolving these problems, people will do such things as exaggerating the benefits of one option while downplaying the benefits of the other, inviting evidence from others that support a particular option or even inventing reasons that might help resolve the uncomfortable conflict.

Marketing and types of motivational conflict

'Our life is frittered away by detail. Simplify, simplify.' HENRY DAVID THOREAU

▶ According to social psychologist **Kurt Lewin** (1890–1947) motivational conflicts arise when we experience in the mind wants and demands for benefits that are incompatible with each other. Four different conflicting mental states can be identified.

1. Pleasant versus pleasant conflict
2. Pleasant versus unpleasant conflict
3. Unpleasant versus unpleasant conflict
4. Complex pleasant/unpleasant conflict

Pleasant versus pleasant conflict

This mental conflict is when we need to choose between two pleasant outcomes. This might be between going on a holiday to somewhere exotic and buying a new conservatory for the house. This can cause high conflict levels, especially when there are two or more people involved in the decision. If marketers want to help solve the conflict in favour of their product or service they must make certain, as far as they can, that they have professional sales people and adequate and attractive information readily available in the marketplace. This should offer clearly targeted seductive benefits thus influencing the choice of their product/service over the product/service of the competitor.

Pleasant versus unpleasant conflict

There are occasions when we have to choose between wanting a product on the one hand yet needing to avoid the consequences of that product. We had the example of chocolate and putting on weight and drinking out late and feeling awful at work the next day. Other examples of possible pleasant and unpleasant conflict might be a mother wanting expensive cosmetics (feel-good factor) and spending all that money on herself rather than on her children (feel-guilty factor). In the same way a wealthy person may have problems buying an expensive motor-car, perhaps a BMW, and seeming to flaunt this wealth in front of poorer family members or friends. Again marketing people must first be aware of the conflict that might arise and then develop techniques to resolve and overcome it. In the case of food, many producers now produce less fattening versions, in the case of the cosmetics, promotion may be in terms of the prospective working mother being entitled to a special treat every so often, and advertising for the expensive motorcar may emphasise its quiet, un-flashy, unspoken elegance.

Unpleasant versus unpleasant conflict

'Out of the frying pan into the fire.'

This form of mental conflict comes about when an individual has to choose between two unpleasant alternatives. Examples might be having a toothache but hating the dentist or an unmarried pregnant schoolgirl having to decide whether to have the baby or an abortion. The consumer might be faced with two undesirable alternatives. The 5-year-old central heating boiler has broken down and the choice is between having it expensively repaired (in the knowledge that it might go wrong again soon) or to buy a new appliance. Reassuring words from the sales person might help solve this latter kind of problem.

Complex pleasant/unpleasant conflict

It's probably more realistic to think about situations where several types of motivational conflict are intermingled and the situation is not clear-cut. In this situation alternatives to be considered are more complex and have mixed pleasant and unpleasant qualities. On occasions like this we tend to be ambivalent about making decisions, vacillating back and forth between one decision and another, unable

Figure 5.3

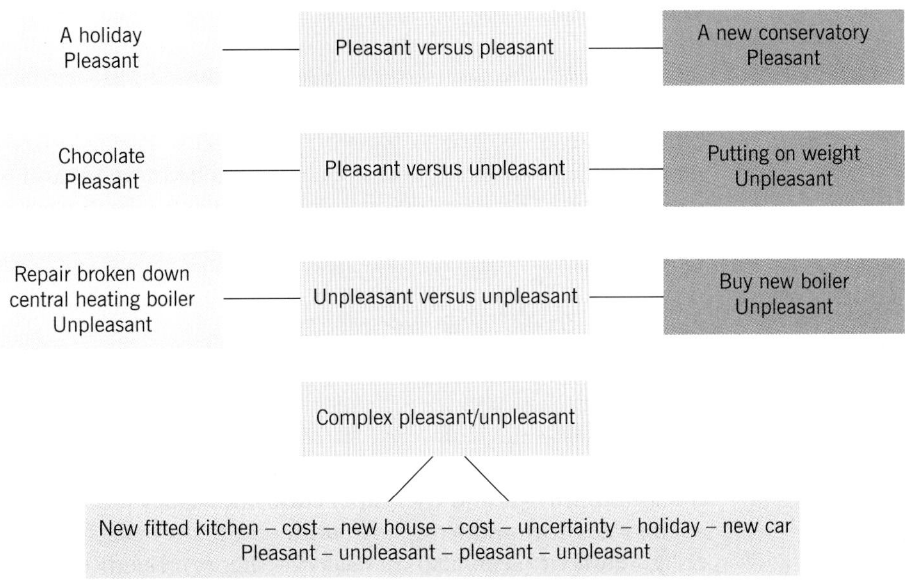

Pleasant and unpleasant motivational mental conflict

to make up our minds. The degree of vacillation and complexity will vary according to the importance of the decision (decision-making difficulty, DMD), the situation and our emotional and mental state at the time. For example everybody, at some time or another, will experience conflicting feelings about going out somewhere, perhaps to a party, the cinema or even college or university.

Key point All consumers will, at some time or another, experience inner conflict with regard to buying from a choice of products and services. It's the task of the marketing person to solve this problem making the customer choice comfortable and satisfying.

Motivational theories

Much has been written about motivation and many theories developed on the subject both at the academic and the business and marketing level. A broad cross-section, not all mutually exclusive, of these are outlined and discussed below relating the theories to business and marketing wherever possible. There seems to be broad basic concepts underpinning most of the work on motivation. These are identified below.

Biological genetic approaches

In the chapter on learning we discussed the very basic idea that many (if not all) motivating behaviours are biological in nature and have been built in to the nervous system (both animals and humans) over many hundreds of thousands of years. (This was discussed at some length in the previous chapter when we looked at the same concept under theories of learning.)

Nature versus nurture – constantly resurrected

This resurrects the nature/nurture argument – is our behaviour involuntary and motivated by inherited genetic factors or is it voluntary and motivated by learned social factors? There are many theories that argue both ways and in the middle. In the main it seems that we are safest adopting the position that motivation tends to include varying elements of both.

Needs and wants

We constantly talk about satisfying consumer needs and wants and it might be useful just to outline the difference in marketing terms. Physiological needs are basic inputs required to restore equilibrium to the human condition such as hunger, thirst, warmth, sex and (perhaps) curiosity. Higher level needs include social needs such as comfort and love, and more spiritual needs such as knowledge and self-enlightenment (seen also in Maslow's theory). Needs can be motivated internally, e.g. 'My stomach tells me I am weak with hunger', or externally, e.g. a billboard advertising a new film that I must now see.

5.2 Marketing example — Needs, wants and marketing

Wants are the products and services required by customers to satisfy the need requirement identified above. Wants required, however, are culturally and psychologically generated and can vary from region to region and from country to country: 'I am thirsty and need a drink of water' becomes 'I am thirsty and want a Budweiser lager': 'I need recognition' becomes I want a 'Mercedes Benz'. 'We need the company of others' becomes 'We want an 18/30 holiday'. It can be seen that the role of marketing, branding and advertising is to turn consumer needs into wants for their products and services rather than those of the competition.

Question

1 Examine why consumers seem to develop such an attraction to brands. Do you think that this is inherent in human nature or do you think that it's the marketing and advertising?

Drive reduction theory – push theory

Taking the pain versus pleasure ideas a little further Hull and others (Hull 1952; Spence 1951) argued that humans (and animals) are driven to action by the needs of the body and this has been the basis of many theories of motivation. All organisms have to be in a state of equilibrium. If the body has gone without something for a period of time, e.g. food and water, a need will arise that creates a tension or drive that will bring it back to a harmonious state. Once the need is satisfied, the drive is reduced and the organism is no longer motivated to act. **Drive reduction theories** can also be seen as a push theory of motivation because internal needs 'push' the organism to seek equilibrium.

Figure 5.4

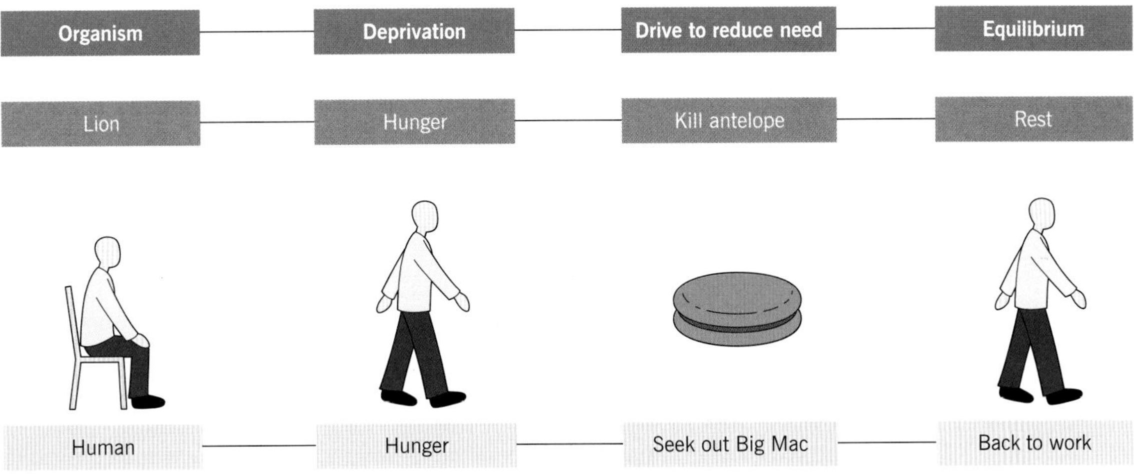

Drive reduction

> **Key point** A drive to reduce arousal or tension can be involuntarily genetically programmed into the DNA or it can be voluntary and more a matter of social learning and free choice.

Internal genetic stimuli

Homeostasis is the involuntary biological mechanism (the body's thermometer) that attempts to maintain the human (and animal) body at some kind of equilibrium. For example, if we are too cold, goose pimples will be activated to prevent heat loss. When we are too hot, sweating will be used to try to cool the body. If frightened, an adrenalin increase will prepare us to face the problem or run away (so called 'fight or flight' mechanism). However, if still too hot or too cold, we might voluntarily seek out a swimming baths to cool down or a hot drink (branded product) to warm up.

External stimuli

A feeling of internal deprivation can be caused by external rather than internal stimuli. The action of others, films, advertisements etc. can make us feel hungry, thirsty, cold, hot, frightened or sexually aroused. This might be a real or imagined need but we would need to take action in the same way as outlined above to reduce this tension and bring the body back to equilibrium.

> **Key point** Drive reduction theorists have argued that all actions are driven by the biological need to bring the body back to a natural, comfortable state of equilibrium.

5.3 Marketing example

Brand owners will want to convince consumers, ideally in a knee-jerk 'Pavlovian' way that bodily equilibrium will best come about by buying their products, e.g. a can of Pepsi, a meal at KFC, a Starbucks coffee, a coat from Gap, a Skol lager or an Orange mobile phone.

Question

1 Identify the motivating reasons why the products listed here might be purchased. How might they create body equilibrium?

Hunger and thirst

We have all experienced hunger pains in the stomach at one time or another and there is little doubt about its motivating strength, for without food, as with liquids, we would eventually die. As with many other issues discussed, hunger can be both biologically and socially driven: biologically driven both through an empty stomach (stomach contractions) and low blood sugar levels detected by an area of the brain known as the hypothalamus.

Marketing and socially motivated eating

Much eating, however, happens because of social demands. This might be at dinner parties at home, takeaways and in pubs and restaurants. This is an enormous area for marketing with billions spent every year in the UK alone, 24 hours a day seven days a week, on food and food-related products. There is also millions spent by organisations on marketing and promotional campaigns.

Illness and obesity

There is a downside to eating, however, with an increase in child and adult obesity in developed countries over the last 20 years now running at worrying levels. This growth in eating levels and health threatening weight increases has been blamed on food manufacturers, fast-food retailers and marketing and advertising. Manufacturers, such as Nestlé, for adding high levels of unhealthy ingredients, fast-food retailers such as McDonald's selling fattening foods, and advertisers for marketing the lifestyle and emotional benefits from eating particular brands.

5.4 Marketing example — Obesity and illness

According to a research report by Developing Patient Partnerships, UK education health charity, April 2005 (www.dpp.org.uk), most parents are uncertain about healthy and unhealthy foods and need support and information to tackle increasing levels of child obesity. Three-quarters of parents blamed the advertising and marketing of unhealthy snacks and drinks for making this job so difficult. In the UK two-thirds of adults and 20 per cent of children are overweight. Confectionery firms such as Mars, Nestlé and Cadbury are to withdraw some of their king-size chocolate bars and other companies such as Coca-Cola, Pepsi, Kellogg's and Kraft foods are to reduce sugar and fat content in their food in a bid to tackle obesity. Marketers are also blamed for promoting thinness and body shapes that are unattainable by most young girls. This can lead to comfort snacking, bulimia and anorexia.

Questions

1. Discuss the reasons behind so much obesity and overweight consumers in the world.
2. Do you think that manufacturers and retailers bear any responsibility for this phenomenon?

Curiosity as a motivator

The need that many individuals seem to have for stimulating experiences was outlined above. Much of this can be put down to a curiosity about the environment and history is replete with examples of people who have spent a lifetime investigating and exploring the world. Interestingly this urge to explore appears to have some linkage with countries and cultures and could therefore be seen as a social phenomenon.

Some research, however, seems to show that there might be a biological and genetic component for curiosity (Wilson 1975). The motive to explore and test-out the environment after birth appears to be important for survival. Newly born animals must become aware of dangers and where safety might lie as soon as possible if they are not to be eaten by a roaming predator. Baby salmon will seem to explore their birthplace before moving to the ocean knowing that they will have to come back to breed and die. Harlow (1958) found that monkeys will spend hours playing, opening and closing locks, rats have been shown to choose a novel pathway over one that is known and bears in zoos are happier if their food is hidden from them so they can spend time seeking it out.

The need for achievement and power

Falling somewhere between the nature–nurture argument sits the work of American ▶ **David McClelland** (1917–98). His research led him to believe that the **need for** ▶ **achievement** (and to a lesser extent power) is a distinct human motivation that can be isolated and clearly distinguished from other needs. He believed that this could be both a genetic disposition and be socially inculcated (see primary and secondary motivations outlined earlier). He went on to identify both high and low achievers and also the concept and role of power in motivation. He also felt that the need for achievement could be taught and he developed many programmes that attempted to pass this knowledge on.

5.5 Marketing example — High and low achievers

Marketers and advertising people have long recognised so-called high achievers and have segmented the markets accordingly. There are many advertisements for cars (Audi, BMW), for business flights (BT and Virgin), computer systems (IBM) etc. that are aimed at the high achiever segment of the market (both men and women) and these can be seen regularly on TV and in newspapers.

Key point The need for achievement and power might arguably be both an inherited characteristic and/or socially learnt.

Sexual behaviour

There is no doubt the sexual behaviour and sexual attraction is one of the most powerful motivators at both emotional and instinctive levels across most cultures. Its use as a central theme has now become dominant in marketing and advertising both in Europe and across the world. Never a day will go by without one major advertising campaign or another appearing in the media with sex as part of the major message. Although there are codes of practice on the promoting of alcohol through sexual attractiveness, most other product groups have no such restriction. So we see car, cosmetic, food, non-alcoholic drink, holiday and confectionary companies all using sex of some kind to market their product and service brands to men and women.

5.6 Marketing example

The Yves Saint Laurent Opium perfume billboard advert featuring Sophie Dahl attracted 730 complaints, making it one of the most complained about in the ASA's history. It was argued that it was sexually suggestive and degrading to women.

Satisfaction seeking, pain avoiding

It appears to be common sense that seeking out pleasurable experiences and minimising and avoiding those that are painful has to be a basic approach to understanding animal and human emotion. Many writers and philosophers down the ages have espoused this concept and it has a certain attractive simplicity that seems to fit the action of some consumers. As with many ideas about human behaviour, this approach can be both genetic and socially induced. Satisfaction seeking motivations are identified in more detail below.

Key point Pleasure versus Pain
In simple terms many writers (Watson, Skinner) believe that all organisms (in our case consumers) will be motivated to seek out those things they find satisfying and reject those things they find painful. We buy a product we like and so will repurchase. Conversely, we buy a product we dislike and we will not repurchase.

Stimulus seeking

A multitude of research has shown that not all behaviour can be explained by biological drive reduction discussed above. Most humans will actively seek out stimulation. We only have to be around young children for a while to see how they are constantly running around looking for things to play with. This forces parents and grandparents to make certain that cupboards are locked and fragile or dangerous implements are placed well out of reach from tiny probing hands. There are many examples of human activity seeking that positively encourage stimulation and movement away from the equilibrium.

5.7 Marketing example | **Deliberately seeking out stimulation**

Many people deliberately seek and indulge in all kinds of sports activity, some highly dangerous with high levels of arousal and excitement. These include such things as: motor racing, mountain climbing, skydiving, water skiing and bungee jumping. Others deliberately go to see scary films and take terrifying rides at a funfair. There are also many occasions, in affluent societies, when we eat when we are not hungry and drink when we are not thirsty. This might be out of boredom, low self-esteem, as a treat, on special occasions at parties and so on. Eating can make us feel better (even for a short while) and generate the so-called feel-good factor.

Question

1 Why do think that some people seem to be prepared to risk their lives in the sorts of extreme sports identified above; and why do you think that people eat and drink when they are not hungry?

5.3 General example | **Drinking alcohol and smoking cigarettes**

Drinking alcohol and smoking cigarettes might be said to be both push and pull, drive reduction and incentive forms of motivation depending on the individual level of addiction.

Arousal theory of motivation

The arousal theory of motivation suggests that individuals need some kind of optimum level of arousal and excitement. Too low and they seek to increase excitement and too high they seek to reduce excitement. The lowest level is sleep. Dr Marvin Zuckerman, proposed that individuals had different optimum arousal levels and these could be measured along a sensation-seeking scale. People in different professions were interviewed across the four dimensions shown below in an attempt to measure high, medium and low levels of sensation-seeking motivations.

1. Thrill, adventure seeking, risk taking – extreme sports, adventure travel.
2. Experience seeking – travel, walking, theatre, art and drugs, reading books.
3. Disinhibition – social stimulation, parties, drinking alcohol, many sex partners.
4. Boredom threshold levels – constantly needing to change circumstances, upgrading computer and video games, cinema.

All these areas are rich in the potential for segmenting product brands and services and companies will exploit all these needs so as to market and sell their benefit offerings.

Reinforcement

The use of reinforcement in the learning process was discussed in Chapter 4 and it can also be seen in understanding theories of motivation. Research has shown that both animals and humans will repeat behaviour that is positively reinforced (found to be pleasant) in some way and will not repeat behaviour that is negatively reinforced (found to be unpleasant) in some way

Figure 5.5

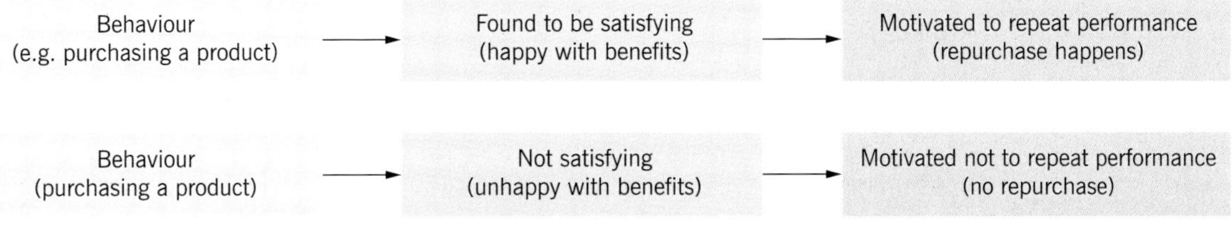

Reinforcement theory of motivation

> **Key point** Reinforcement can be positive or negative. Money, a word or praise, recognition of customer loyalty can all be seen as positive reinforcers and will motivate individuals to work harder or use particular retail outlets and buy specific brands. Bad customer service, unsatisfactory working conditions and brands that promise more than they actually give will have the opposite effect.

Intrinsic and extrinsic incentives

Incentives are rewards that encourage people to behave in particular ways and they happen throughout life. Children are offered sweets, toys and words and smiles of encouragement to act appropriately. Shoppers are offered sales promotions to buy particular brands and employees are offered bonuses to work harder. Schools and universities hold out the promise of a good job if exams are passed and health clubs offer longer life if a strict regime is followed. If the incentive is achieved and the need or want is satisfied then people (consumers) will be motivated to repeat the performance. Incentives can be extrinsic or intrinsic to the individual.

Extrinsic incentives

▶ ▶ **Extrinsic** incentives would be rewards external to the individual such as an ice cream, a holiday, salary or paycheque and so on. **Extrinsic rewards** such as these, however, seem to have a limited, short-term motivational value.

Intrinsic incentives

▶ **Intrinsic** incentives are rewards that are felt within the individual and include such things as feeling good about being able to play the piano, interesting and fulfilling work and a sense of achievement from exams and assignments passed. Intrinsic incentives, e.g. the pleasure that comes from undertaking religious work, tends to have longer motivational value, sometimes lasting for the whole of someone's life.

Figure 5.6

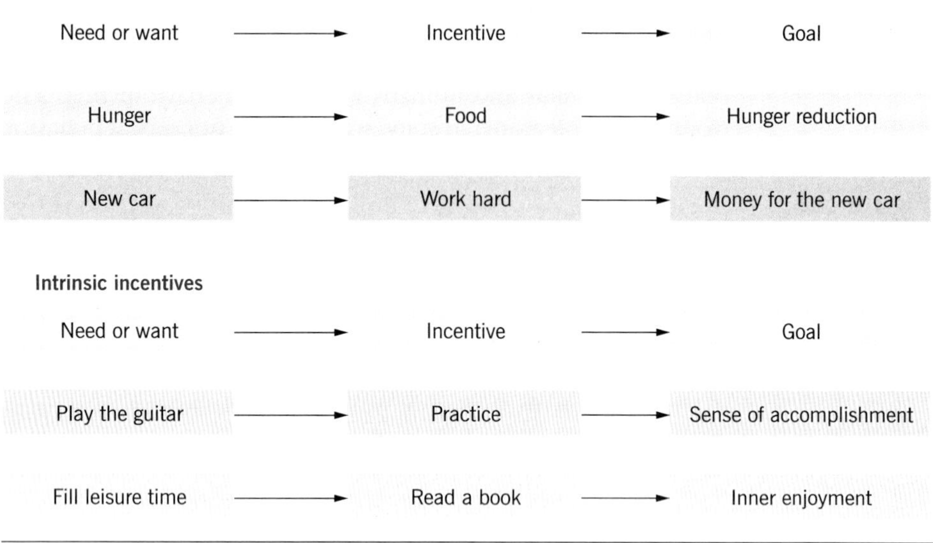

Extrinsic and intrinsic incentives

Identifying the right need

The difficulty is identifying the right need or want in the first place. We will see when we look at other theories on motivation (especially the Freudian theory of the subconscious outlined below) that these are not always as obvious as it seems. A consumer might say that the need is extrinsic, for example shopping at a store because of the choice of products, when in fact the need is intrinsic, for example the need to buy to compensate for feelings of low self-esteem. Qualitative research will help and this was discussed in some detail in Chapter 2. It should now be seen by the examples given above the opportunities that are available to producers and retailers in understanding the value of positive and negative reinforcement. If consumers are happy with the service and the products in a supermarket they will return again and again. Conversely if they are unhappy they will go elsewhere.

5.8 Marketing example — Incentives and reinforcement

A warm and welcoming reception, employees given recognition and rewards so that they are driven to give customer satisfaction, a choice of good merchandise, competitive prices, loyalty cards, adequate parking and so on, all play a part in reinforcing the consumer experience. Similarly branded products that live up to their promise, that have benefits that satisfy both extrinsic and intrinsic needs and wants and that alter to accommodate changing market and customer circumstances.

Question

1 Discuss the differences between intrinsic and extrinsic consumer satisfaction. Give live examples.

Satisfaction theories

We have discussed above that, in very simple terms, it can be shown that individuals are motivated to seek pleasurable satisfying experiences and avoid those that are found to be unpleasurable. This might be pleasure that is immediate or pleasure some time into the future. This can complicate things because somebody might be prepared to suffer some kind of unhappiness, pain or punishment now for happiness at some other time. For example a worker might hate working in a factory but enjoy the things that money can buy. In a similar vein it may be hard work bringing up a family but the satisfaction will come when the children are seen to benefit later on in life. In the main, products and services play an enormous part in peoples lives satisfying both intrinsic and extrinsic needs and wants.

Key point Both intrinsic and extrinsic products and services play an enormous part in satisfying consumers needs and wants.

Satisfied individuals are the most productive

Over the last decades many academics, scientists and other commentators have argued that contented and satisfied people are motivated to be the most productive and so they developed many theories about how best this might be applied to the world of work. Business people and marketers have since taken much of this work and attempted to apply it to understanding customer satisfaction. Some of these theories are outlined below.

Motivate by rewards or threats

'There are two things that people want more than sex and money – recognition and praise.' MARY KAY ASH, founder of mary kay cosmetics

Initially a social psychologist before becoming involved in academic management, ▶ **Douglas McGregor** (1906–64) is mostly known by management and marketing students ▶ for his work on **theory x and theory y**, seen as a 'reward or threats' approach. He maintained that there were some managers that felt that all employees were lazy, disliked work and would slack if not rigorously controlled ('x' types) and other managers that felt that this wasn't so and argued that employees would have wholehearted commitment if praised, given recognition and treated properly ('y' types). Theory x and theory y managers would thus treat staff according to these strongly held beliefs.

5.9 Marketing example — Behaviour and rewards or threats

Research has show that unhappy and discontented staff will have an affect on the levels of customer satisfaction, customer complaints and customer retention. There seems to be very little doubt that if employees are seen and treated in the way suggested by theory x, customer satisfaction would eventually suffer. The other problem is that managers (and others) who think that employees are basically untrustworthy and sly tend to think the same of working people, even in their role as consumers. This will then affect how they behave towards customers often seeing them (despite what they might say openly) more as a nuisance to be suffered than a valuable asset to be nurtured and respected.

Motivational incentives – money or recognition

'If you love your job, you'll never have to work a day in your life.' ANON

▶ **Hertzberg's Motivational incentive theory** was the first real effort by a researcher, ▶ **Frederick Hertzberg** (1923–2000), to systematically tease out the value of different motivators at both the extrinsic and intrinsic level. Up to this point most businessmen and many researchers (Taylor 1856–1915) felt that the overriding incentive to work was money and all that money could bring. Other considerations were often ignored.

Two sets of motivators – Hertzberg

'Words that enlighten are more precious than jewels.' ANON

After much research Hertzberg came to the conclusion that individuals were motivated by two separate kinds of motivators. The first set of motivators, he called 'hygiene factors' or normal level motivators. These would not in themselves lead to increased activity above the average level of effort that most employees contribute to the job (for example 70 per cent effort) but without them there are increasing levels of dissatisfaction and performance would fall below the given norm (70 per cent). The other set can be seen as higher-level motivators and if present can persuade up to 100 per cent total commitment.

Figure 5.7

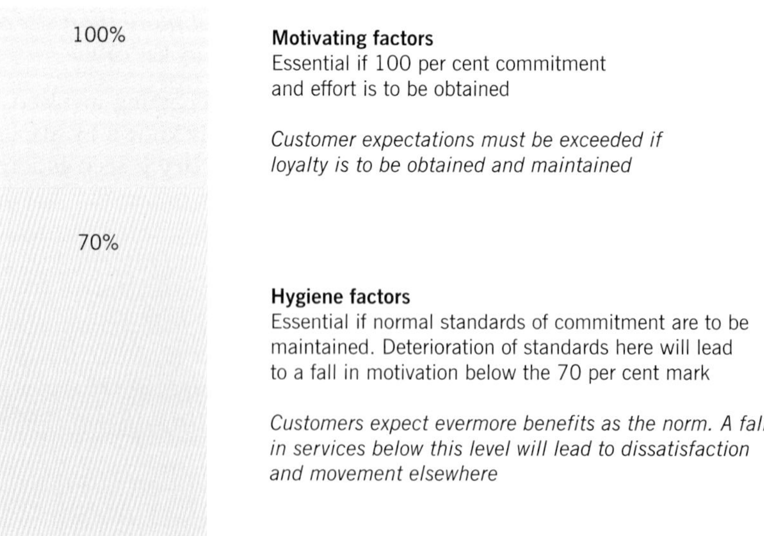

Hertzberg's theory of motivation

Table 5.2 **Normal and high-level motivators**

Hertzberg's hygiene and motivating factors
Normal level motivators or hygiene factors needed to maintain a healthy work environment – 70 per cent effort

- Working conditions, management approach
- Interpersonal relationships
- Salary, status and security

High-level motivators could persuade workers to operate above the norm and give 100 per cent commitment and effort.

- Achievement, recognition
- Growth and advancement
- Interest in the job

5.10 Marketing example **Hygiene and higher-level motivating factors**

Hertzberg can be applied to marketing and consumer behaviour in many different ways. We have already discussed the importance of contented and well-motivated staff to customer satisfaction, especially in retail where employees have direct contact with consumers. Applying Hertzberg's theory directly to the retail environment, consumers now expect much higher standards than in the past (these have become hygiene factors) and good service will not in itself encourage higher levels of loyalty (motivating factors). To achieve this retailers and manufacturers need to consider the motivating factors identified by Hertzberg such as one-to-one marketing, customer-relationship-management, recognition and making the customer feel important.

Questions

1. Discuss and give examples of customer benefits, once considered discretionary these are now demanded as part of the basic service.
2. Do you think that there is a limit to the amount of service that a retailer can offer? Will price become more important?

It was these findings that led to the idea of 'job enrichment', now an essential part of any work environment. (Frederick Hertzberg, *Work and the Nature of Man*, 1966).

Cognitive approaches to motivation

'There is no failure. Only feedback.' ANON

Other researchers see motivation more as a cognitive process, with individuals thinking through all the factors involved and then analysing the results and outcomes, both positive and negative, of different ways of behaving. The first to be discussed below is equity (or a social comparison) theory.

Equity theory

Equity theory (J. Stacey Adams 1965) puts forward the theory that, although initially satisfied, people will go on to compare various situations they find themselves in with others in the same or similar positions and will become unhappy if any unfairness or inequality is perceived. They will then attempt to modify their behaviour in some way so as to rectify these grievances. In the work situation this can lead to constant grumbling, increased absenteeism, lower productivity and quality and high staff turnover.

Consumers and equity theory

Consumers can develop feelings of being unfairly treated in many different ways. They may buy a product and find it on sale somewhere else at a cheaper price. They might have bought a product one day and discovered it has been reduced the next. Two people on exactly the same holiday may find that they have paid strikingly differing prices. Of course it could be argued that this is just bad luck, but if the level of grievance is high then the consumer might very well look minutely for things to complain about or just never buy from the seemingly offending retailer.

5.11 Marketing example — Bid TV

TV auction company Bid TV have customers bidding for a given number of a particular product on their TV show until all are gone. Under the old system individuals would bid at a price they were prepared to pay, some lower and some higher than others. This meant that when the auction was finished, and the limited number of products sold, participants would have paid different prices for the same object. Research showed, however, that this caused some sense of unfairness. They found that customers where happier, and would bid more often if they all paid the same price. This now happens and all successful bidders pay the one lowest price, no matter how high they might have bid, shown when the auction has finished.

Expectancy theory

Victor Vroom (1964) argued that motivational drives are the result of rational calculations made by people between anticipated rewards, the value of the reward and the costs/effort involved in achieving the rewards. He called this expectancy theory and it can be applied to almost everything we do in both our working and non-working time.

He goes on to say that if the cost/effort is too high in relationship to the value the individual places on the reward or the probability of actually achieving the reward is too high then motivation will be negatively affected.

5.12 Marketing example — Expectancy theory

Expectancy theory plays an important part in many areas of marketing. If sales people are given sales targets that they feel are too high and they believe that they are unachievable, they will be de-motivated and not really try. This will be the case even if the rewards are high. On the other hand if they are given a sales target that is low and easily achievable, they will not try if the reward offered is very low. In the same way if consumers are offered a sales promotion with a prize of £10,000 but the conditions of entry are long and tedious and there will be only one winner among perhaps a million participants then many might perceive the task to be not worthwhile. On the other hand if entry is easy, perhaps sending off a crisp packet, but the prize is small, maybe £5 then again customers might feel that is was not worth the effort. The task for promotional managers is to get the balance right for the consumer between incentives, expectancy levels and the work involved.

Table 5.3 — Expectancy theory – the three components

Vroom identified three elements of expectancy theory
Expectancy – the probability level that the reward might be achieved, e.g. offering the salesperson a bonus for increased sales. If it is thought that the sales target is too high, and therefore unachievable, no effort will be expended.
Instrumentality – the probability the performance effort needed will lead to the desired outcome.
Valence – the value the individual or group places on the desired outcome, e.g. the sales person is offered a reward for extra sales considered undesirable, perhaps a night out at the cinema.

Goal-setting theory

'Its better to travel hopefully than to arrive.' ROBERT LOUIS STEVENSON

Goal-setting theory states that people will perform better if they are working toward some type of goal or objective they would like to achieve (Locke and Latham 1990). They might set this by themselves or by working and agreeing with others. These goals will then affect behaviour and so direct and motivate efforts to achieve them. Widely used in industry, it led to the concept of management-by-objectives, MBO. It was then taken on in sports coaching where it was found that sportspeople perform better if they work to a constant improvement schedule. Interestingly enough it seems that it's not the goal itself that is motivating but the attempts to achieve the goal. Deficiencies and discrepancies appear to motivate people to worker harder until they get it right.

Key point Cognitive theories of motivation see the process as a series of often complex trade-offs that consumers make between the factors involved and the possible outcomes. This will include such things as our own experiences as well as the experiences of others, brand values and benefit promises and price.

5.13 Marketing example Goal setting

Goal-setting theory has been belatedly adopted and used in marketing and retail as another tool in the attempt to understand buyer behaviour. Some individuals set themselves goals, both short and long term, sometimes only in their own minds and sometimes in tandem with others. They then strive to buy the products and services that will help them achieve their tacit or implicit objectives. If groups of likeminded people, those with the same goals, can be identified, brand benefits can be offered and targeted to help the customer group in the process of goal attainment. Most of us have our own experiences of ambitions and goals that we set for ourselves. They can range from virtually unobtainable dreams, such as becoming a pop star or a premier footballer, to more down-to-earth ambitions such as changing jobs, learning to be a good cook, or walking five miles every day. What's important for marketing managers to understand is that the customer will buy products and services that will reinforce ambitions and support ideas about the ideal person he or she would like to be.

'The more goals you set – the more goals you get.' MARK VICTOR HANSEN

Unconscious motivations

Perhaps the most controversial, and certainly the most interesting of all the motivational theorists is Sigmund Freud. Although much of his work is now criticised and discredited there is no doubt that he has had a gigantic influence on Western thinking from the earliest part of the twentieth century to the present day, not least in the marketing and advertising industry, especially in the USA. To outrageously simplify an immense and detailed body of work, his great contribution to human understanding was to predict and discuss the concept of the unconscious mind an area of the mind below levels of thinking that could and did affect human motivation. His theory of human psychology makes life much more difficult because it argues that individuals will not necessarily know themselves what motivates or makes them feel happy as there are emotional forces operating below the level of consciousness, below the level of human awareness. For example an employee may say he or she only works for the money and has no concern for promotion when the truth might be that praise and recognition would be the more powerful motivating force.

Consumer behaviour and psychology

Although in a sense stolen from Freud's overall theory on the workings of the mind, the basic premise about their being an unconscious part of the mind has had tremendous consequences for all areas of marketing including new product development, packaging, merchandising and especially advertising and the sending of benefit messages. According to the theory, it meant that when asked why behaviour happened in a particular way, individuals either might not know, or might articulate one conscious reason thought to be the cause when in fact a deeper reason, buried within the sub-conscious, is the real truth behind the purchase motivation.

Figure 5.8

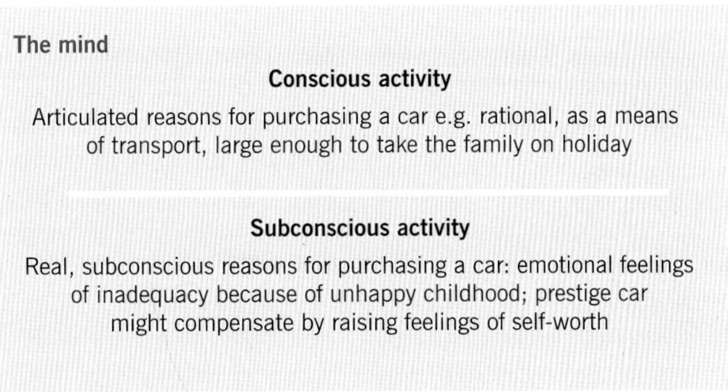

Freudian conscious and subconscious activity in the mind

> **Key point** Freudian theory on the levels of the mind is pervasive in trying to gain an understanding of human and consumer behaviour and we will return to it in more detail when we discuss its role in personality development in Chapter 7.

Humanistic motives – develop highest potential

'When I look at the world I'm pessimistic, but when I look at people I am optimistic.' CARL ROGERS

▶ **Carl Rogers'** (1902–87) theory was based on years of clinical experience dealing with clients and patients suffering from some form of physical and personality malfunctioning. He believed that the basic normal motivation for all humans was to develop their potential to the highest possible level. His theory is based on the concept that there is a single life force he called the *actualising tendency* that drives all living things, including plants, animals and humans, to make the best out of their lives.

He felt that good health and a positive attitude to life was the fundamental human state and mental ill health, depression, anxiety and social misbehaviour (such as disruptive behaviour and criminality) was a deviation from the norm. Rogers felt that the answer was to help and guide people back to mental health through non-judgemental discussions helping the client discover the way back to normality for themselves. His most famous writings were *Client-Centered Therapy*, and *On Becoming a Person*.

Key point Carl Rogers believed that the basic normal motivation for all humans was to develop their potential to the highest possible level.

Social motives – motivation learnt interacting in society

There is no doubt that man and most animals are social beings and have the need to be with others. Like many other characteristics this need appears to have both an inherited and socially learned content. We also like to be like specific other people and will copy the way they behave as well as behaving in a way that they might expect us to behave (we will discuss this in more detail in the chapter on social influences on motivation). In the chapter on learning, the work of Harry Harlow (1958) was discussed, where he took baby monkeys away from their mothers and bought them up in isolation. After a year they were placed back with other monkeys but were unable to socially interact in a friendly way, reacting viciously to the approaches of others. Other baby monkeys were given metal and cloth mother substitutes which were clung to incessantly. Eventually deterioration and early death would ensue.

5.4 General example — Social need and people

Other research has shown the deleterious effect on humans kept in solitary confinement and away from others. History has shown that one of the most punishing things that groups of people can do is to refuse to speak to another non-conforming individual in the group. Although there are times when people want to be alone there is no doubt that most of us seek out the company of others at some time or another. This might be because of the felt need to talk about experiences, show-off, flirt or alleviate the fear of being by oneself.

Motivation and aggression

While most people are driven by the desire to affiliate and be in the company of others, many people, especially males, are, at times motivated by aggression and violence. Husbands and wives, children and teenagers sometimes attack one another. So-called 'road rage', and 'shopping rage' is on the increase. We only have to look at programmes on the TV, read newspaper reports or visit the town centre on a Saturday night to see examples of drunkenness, threatening behaviour, fighting and other anti-social behaviour. There has been an enormous amount of research in to why this should be so and some of the possible reasons are outlined below.

Instinct

Again we come back to the possibility that the need for aggression is hereditary and instinctive. Charles Darwin, in the second half of the nineteenth century, argued that evolutionary change and development comes about through power, strength and the survival of the fittest animal and this is inbuilt into biological ▶ make-up. Writing at the present time **Richard Dawkins**, in his book *The Selfish Gene*, sees survival of one organism over another, and the propagation of the gene pool, as almost the sole purpose of life. Many experiments looking at the way packs of animals behave have identified aggression and the need to be top dog as an indispensable part of animal life. In the animal kingdom one male (for example, lions), will kill all the cubs of the defeated leader and then implant their own seed. Other experiments have tried to discover the part that the male hormone, testosterone might play in the process while others have emphasised the role of learning and society in male and female aggressive differences.

Key point Instincts are an innate inborn predisposition to act in a particular way probably for survival.

5.14 Marketing example — Behaviour and aggression

Many products can be bought that attempt to exploit this aggressive need of the consumer, some of which have now been banned. Spectator sports such as boxing, wrestling, bull fighting, football and rugby all market, exploit and make money out of individual, group, regional and national aggressive tendencies. Violence in books, films and computer games attract large readerships and audiences, and celebrities such as Arnold Schwarzenegger, Sylvester Stallone, Bruce Willis, *et al.* can be seen shooting up the world and are revered by the young as 'action heroes'.

Question

1 Examine the reason why there appear to be gender specific toys. Is this genetic or caused by social influences?

Frustration

Frustration is an emotional state that arises when individuals are prevented in some way from reaching a particular goal. It's a normal part of normal life and every day individuals encounter varying levels of frustration, at home, travelling to work, out shopping or in the pursuit of leisure. For example being stuck in a traffic jam, having an argument with one's partner, revising for an exam and being unable to obtain the relevant books, being unable to get others to understand one's argument and so on.

High and low frustration

The levels of frustration can be of varying strength levels ranging from high to very low. This strength will depend on the motivation and importance that people put on the goal, the intensity of the barrier, the ability to overcome the barrier and how near somebody is to success. Repeated frustrations can accumulate until a small irritation sets off an unexpectedly violent response or a giving up and a running away from the problem. This is known as the 'fight or flight' mechanism.

Positive and negative frustration

Frustration can be both a positive and a negative motivating force depending on the power of the barrier preventing goal obtainment. It can be a positive motivator when the frustration encourages us to work harder to overcome obstacles to success and this is a normal part of life. In fact many people enjoy and welcome the challenge of overcoming problems. This might be at work trying to get staff to work harder, playing sports, scoring a goal, and at home undertaking some kind of do-it-yourself activity. Frustration can develop into a negative motivator when the barriers to the goal attainment are too strong and too difficult to overcome. Extreme, intense levels of frustration can result in all kinds of defensive behaviour and these are discussed below.

Reaction to frustration

In many cases frustration can be constructive causing people to work harder or smarter to overcome problems and barriers to success. However it can be harmful and destructive in many ways if individuals are unable to eliminate the frustration. Below are examples of how individuals handle different types and different frustration levels and intensities.

> **Key point** Frustration can be both a positive and negative motivator. Positive and constructive if it makes us try harder to eventually overcome the barriers to goal attainment – negative and destructive if we are unable to overcome the barriers to goal attainment.

Frustration and aggression

Aggression tends to be the most persistent and frequent response to frustration. It can range from mild annoyance to uncontrollable rage. External causes of frustration can lead to verbal or physical violence against others. This will include differing levels of aggression such as a husband and wife or partners shouting at one another, throwing things, shouting at the children, children fighting in the playground, football violence and road-rage attacks.

Table 5.4 External and internal sources of frustration

External sources of frustration

External sources of frustration are caused by environmental factors outside the individual that block the way to a desired goal. Examples are:

- Overcoming problems – at work, at home or at play.
- Loss – losing credit cards, keys, papers.
- Failure – not passing the exam.
- Rejection – not getting the job.
- Delays – traffic jams, trains running late.
- Rules and regulations – staff sticking to the letter of the law, red tape.
- Unhelpfulness – working with others not so committed, unhelpful employees.
- Change – deviation from the norm and the expected.

Internal sources of frustration

Internal sources of frustration are caused by an individual's inner feelings even though failure may be attributed to external causes. Examples might be:

- Setting goals too high – feelings of self-doubt.
- Setting goals too low – boredom.
- Lack of skills and/or knowledge – unable to complete tasks.
- Low self-esteem – feelings of inadequacy, depression.
- Tiredness – unable to face up to problems.

5.15 Marketing example Consumer frustration

Marketers and retailers work constantly to minimise and eliminate negative frustration, knowing that too much will eventually motivate and encourage their customers to buy the competitors' brands and/or use the retail outlets of others. Supermarkets such as Tesco and Asda constantly research consumers to find out the factors that frustrate and annoy their customers and have put in processes and systems that will minimise or eliminate frustrating problems. Some of the most important ones are identified below.

Frustrating factor – lack of choice, products not in stock.

Answer – wide range of products, delivery systems driven by customer demand, working in partnership with suppliers.

Frustrating factor – waste of time queuing at checkout and at the deli counter.

Answer – system that guarantees, no more that one person in front at the checkout. Queuing ticketed system that ensures orderly and prompt service.

Frustrating factor – inadequate, difficult car parking.

Answer – all locations purchased and built with parking needs in mind.

Frustrating factors – products difficult to open, unattractive, difficult to store.

Answer – customer friendly, constant packaging technology upgrading.

Unfriendly packaging

5.16 Marketing example — Behaviour begets behaviour

All those working in marketing and retail need to understand that aggressive behaviour by one person can elicit the same response in others. I shout at you and you shout back. You shout at me and I shout back. When dealing with customers, however, the (trained) response to aggression should be calm and professional. It's axiomatic that customers seldom complain if no reason exists. The salesperson or switchboard operator may think the problem is minor but to the frustrated customer it may be of enormous importance. A measured composed response to pent up customer frustration, in most cases, will cause the anger to dissipate. Employee training should be given and organisational policies should be in place to pre-empt and deal with all likely sources of complaints.

Questions

1 Do you believe that the customer is 'always right'?

2 How do you think that customer complaints should be handled?

Anger displacement – taking out anger on others

When people are unable to get directly at the source cause of the frustration individuals will often take their aggression out on others, usually those that are the nearest and least likely to retaliate. This is known as **anger displacement** or redirection. A woman having had a bad day at work, cannot shout at the boss and might come home and take it out on her partner or the children. Students with bad exam results might show anger towards a boyfriend or girlfriend. We might drive aggressively and show anger to other car drivers, be rude to the shopkeeper or act impolitely to a supermarket checkout person. Psychologists attribute much hostility and destructiveness in our society to displaced aggression and long chains of displacement sometimes occur. For example when unemployment increases, so does wife beating, child abuse and violence on the streets.

Key point Passive–aggressive behaviour, indirectly making someone suffer rather than give open reasons, manifests itself in marketing when an upset customer does not complain at the time but never again buys a brand or uses a retail outlet from an offending organisation. Seventy-five per cent of consumers never complain. They just don't come back.

Scapegoating – blaming others

Scapegoating is holding other individuals or groups responsible for our own misfortunes and it appears to satisfy a universal need in human beings. It is similar to displacement except that this blaming of others usually has little or no foundation and is more long term and deep-seated. Those that have difficulty in finding a job might put the cause down to high levels of immigration and higher taxes are blamed on single-parent mothers on social security. On a grander scale scapegoating can be directed at religions, races and whole nations. All groups seem to have their favourite habitual blame-victims and so Jews, Muslims, gypsies, blacks, the Irish and so on have all been blamed by people for ill-fortune at one time or another.

5.5 General example **Scapegoating**

An oft-quoted example of scapegoating is the correlation between the price of cotton and the number of lynching of Blacks in the South between 1880 and 1930. Low price of cotton (blamed on black people), more lynching,

Stereotyping

Stereotyping is when people are expected to act and behave in predictable ways. In the main it's a normal part of everyday life helping us to understand quickly and automatically the world around us. So we expect other drivers to give way to us at a roundabout and to stop for pedestrians at a zebra crossing. We expect mothers to act in one way, fathers in another, young people to enjoy one kind of music, older people another, students are compliant and lecturers teach. Boys play with cars, girls with dolls, men drink beer and ladies wine and spirits. It becomes

Table 5.5 Anger displacement and scapegoating

Marketers must be aware of the need of consumers to blame others for their own shortcomings and try not to let such situations arise. One complaint not dealt with can cause the consumer to find fault with a whole series of smaller complaints:

Causes of consumer frustration can include the following:

- Implicitly being labelled a troublemaker or constant complainer.
- Customer making assumptions about the depth of feeling or caring of others.
- Situation exaggerated by customer.
- Injustice felt – when complaints are ignored or downplayed.
- Invasion felt – customer is asked too many questions about their private life.
- Feeling helpless or trapped when problems seem to be going around in circles.
- Unable to control certain situations – sales person is intimidating and aggressive.

unhealthy however when we stereotype in negative and role restricting ways. For example women cook and iron, men paint and decorate; men are better at senior management roles women less so; teenagers all drink too much and so on.

5.17 Marketing example Stereotyping

Media stereotypes are inevitable, especially in the advertising, entertainment and news industries, which need as wide an audience as possible to quickly understand information. With high time or space costs and little or no time to explain advertisers, for example on TV, must make their sales pitch within 15 to 30 seconds. Critics argue that to constantly depict women, children, men, ethnic groups, social classes, in stereotypical roles propagates and reinforces an unhelpful view of a changing society. Media awareness network (www.media-awarenessnetwork.ca)

Key point In many cases it is normal to stereotype as it helps individuals to quickly and automatically understand the world around them. It becomes unhealthy when its used to discriminate against others.

Persistence

It has been said that persistence or 'stickability' is one of the greatest of all human characteristics. It can be seen as a positive way of overcoming frustration and barriers to goal attainment. It is characterised by constant and vigorous effort and adaptive and variable responses. Many self-made businessmen and women entrepreneurs have been successful by always bouncing back no matter what the knock-backs they have suffered through life.

5.18 Marketing example **Persistence**

There seems to be widespread agreement that the ability to persistently seek out new sales opportunities can be one of the most productive of all sales skills. To keep making sales calls, despite the fear of constant rejection, when all others have given up and gone home has been shown to produce some of the most successful and highly paid salespeople.

Defence mechanisms

Many of the negative feelings people have, anger, frustration, envy, jealousy, unacceptable sexual desire, lust, and so on, are uncomfortable to hold in the mind, especially if somebody has been taught and indoctrinated that such feelings are unhealthy, disgusting or a sign of mental and personality weakness. To overcome such feelings, individuals are motivated into building mental **defence mechanisms** to protect the self-ego and some of these are discussed below.

Rationalisation – seeing both sides

This is a defence mechanism that uses reasoning to block out the emotional stress and conflict felt in the mind. Frustration builds up because I am late home from work and my wife and I are supposed to be going out to a restaurant for dinner. When the initial anger subsides I rationalise that it will be nice to get a takeaway and have a nice night in. Other examples might be where a person is angry being stuck in a traffic-jam because of a bad accident and rationalises that at least she is not the person injured; or waiting patiently at the airport as the plane is delayed knowing that ranting and raving will make no difference to the outcome.

Marketing and rationalisation

A consumer will sometimes have a particular product (or colour, or model) in mind and become frustrated because it seems to be unavailable. Marketing literature and/or the sales person can convince the consumer, through the use of reason, to consider an equally attractive substitute.

Intellectualisation – standing back

Very similar to rationalisation, a few people are able to detach themselves completely from their emotions and look in a totally objective, sterile way at the frustration-creating problem. It seems that this can be learnt through practice and often some kind of meditative process. There is no doubt that it is a useful skill for situations such as taking exams, working with computers, or working in stressful areas such as the social services, the job centre or even retail.

Marketing and intellectualisation

People who work in the front line between the company and consumers must try to act in a totally professional and detached manner, especially when dealing with constant customer enquiries and complaints.

Sublimation – positively re-directing energy

Sublimation could be seen as a healthy redirection of emotional needs. I want to hit my boss but can't so I go into the gym and work it off on the punch bag. I would have liked to become a professional footballer but I had an accident and couldn't play. Instead of bemoaning my fate for the rest of my life I take up golf. Similarly the wanted promotion at work may be blocked off in one direction so the employee takes another, second choice option, and happily directs all energy here.

Compensation – having to take second choice

With compensation, the benefits of the second option choice are exaggerated to 'compensate' for the loss of the first choice. It is similar to sublimation except that the original desire, i.e. to be a professional footballer, is never quite concealed and forgotten and is occasionally resurrected to nag for a while at the back of the mind.

Marketing, sublimation and compensation

We all maintain dreams about the ideal self that we would like to be in life. These dreams are normal and healthy in terms of sublimation, but not quite so with compensation. Marketers will therefore advertise and sell products and services benefits that pander to this dream concept of the ideal-self. Examples might be the dream of living in a house in the country and cosmetics that promise the romance that will never be.

Reaction formation – saying the opposite

This is defending against unacceptable feelings and behaviour by exhibiting the opposite of one's true wishes or impulses. A young man asks a girl out for a date and she refuses. Unable to live with the sense of rejection he tells his friends that he didn't really like her anyway. The student fails an exam and says that he or she didn't care anyway. Similarly we haven't the money for a Mercedes top of the range car so we condemn as pollutants those people that can afford the car saying we would never buy one.

Marketing and reaction formation

The problem here is that we can never take at face value the things that consumers might say. Qualitative research such as focus groups and one-to-one interviews can uncover true feelings.

Projection – blaming others

Projection is taking internal uncomfortable feelings and emotions and putting them outside on to others where we are more able to deal with them – blaming others for the faults we have. An individual has homosexual feelings but hates the thought so much that they vehemently attack all homosexual activity. One person might accuse others of jealousy, of unbridled ambition, of being overly critical, or always complaining, to hide the fact that he or she doesn't want to acknowledge these things about themselves.

5.6 General example | **Projection and religion**

Freud saw religion as a creation of the human mind, projecting the need for comfort, safety and certainty, once offered by parents through childhood, on to a God.

Denial – pretending it never happened

People are said to be in denial when they make excuses or refuse to accept that a problem exists rather than being truthful and realistic. Accused of drinking too much, an alcoholic in denial will just not accept that there is a problem saying that they could stop whenever they wanted too. Gamblers can be exactly the same. Men and women who cannot stop retail spending, usually on credit, are another example.

Marketing and denial

Problems like this can create ethical problems for marketing and the selling of products and services. When should a betting shop stop taking the money of a regular punter the manager knows to be up to their ears in debt? Should a barman continue to serve drinks to a known alcoholic? And should banks and shops constantly bump up the amount that individuals can spend on an increasing number of credit cards?

Repression – pushing out of consciousness

Similar to denial, with repression unacceptable experiences, such as childhood sexual traumas, playground bullying, painful accidents and the loss of a loved one are 'repressed' below the level of consciousness into an area Freud called the 'subconscious'. This can cause feelings of guilt, insecurity and low self-esteem later on in life that seem to have no explanation.

Marketing and repression

Many products are purchased because, emotionally, they seem to address and in some way satisfy many subconscious repressive feelings. Guilt feelings can be assuaged, be it over the short term, by advertisers telling their target market that they should indulge themselves occasionally by splashing out on expensive cosmetics. Buying a new car offering status symbol benefits might negate feelings of low self-esteem and buying insurance might help feelings of insecurity.

Escape or withdrawal – running away

'To love oneself is the beginning of a life-long romance.' OSCAR WILDE

Withdrawal or escape is a mental defence mechanism that can range from the minor to the severe. It involves individuals trying to remove themselves in some way from painful thoughts and feelings. This can be both physical and mental removal. Methods include avoiding all things that might resurrect bad thoughts and memories, including programmes on the TV, not reading newspapers, pretending not to care, acting in an uninterested manner, 'switching off', being apathetic and not speaking to other people. Others actually run away, perhaps from a failed marriage or large debts, sometime to another part of the country and sometimes going abroad. Sufferers might overindulge in excessive drinking and take all kinds of drugs to try to forget or block-out memories that cause extreme mental grief. This can ultimately lead to isolation, loneliness, loss of self-respect and illness.

Marketing and escapism

Most will want to escape from the problems of the world at sometime or another. This might consist of losing themselves in an adventure or romantic film, indulging in eating chocolates, reading a good book, going to a football match, going on holiday to Barbados and so on.

Fantasy and regression – making it up

If the pressure becomes too intense, however, pathological behaviour can set in and some people will build a whole fantasy world in which to escape. Mental illness will set in as all distinction between illusion and reality become lost. This can eventually degenerate into a regressive state where sufferers seem to lose all contact with the world and end up almost being unable to move, perhaps rocking back and forth on their haunches, thumb in mouth reminiscent of early childhood.

Marketing and fantasy

We all fantasise at some time or another and it can be a normal way of behaving, losing ourselves in problem-solving daydreams about holidays we might take, cars we might buy, and clothes we might wear. In fact we often purchase goods and services to feed these fantasies.

Key point Most defence mechanisms are healthy and a normal way of dealing with mental conflict. It's only when they begin to affect the wellbeing of the individual that they become unhealthy.

Figure 5.9

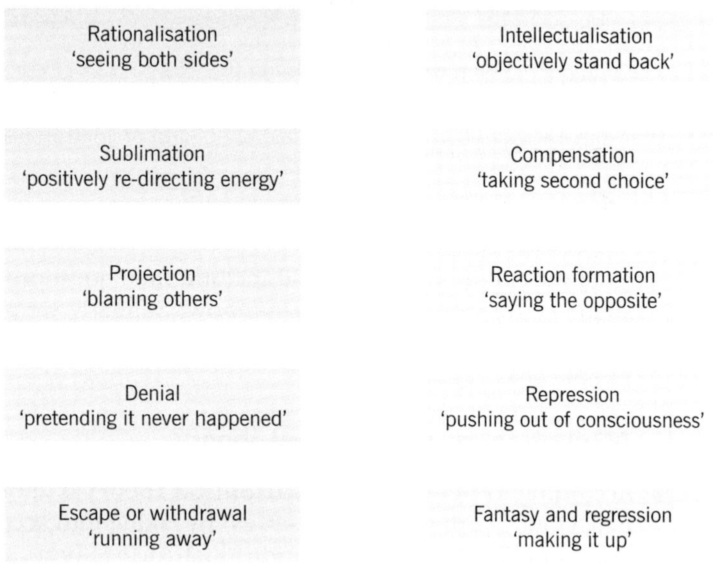

Mental defence mechanisms

Stress

'Today is the tomorrow you worried about yesterday.'

Reasonable levels of stress are a part of everyday life and most people learn to cope, many seeing it as a part of the motivating process. It tends to become stronger in times of change. This makes us adapt and adjust to different environmental circumstance. Illness, mental breakdowns and burnout can occur where stress levels become severe and long lasting. This is compounded where individuals experience a lack of control over stress-creating factors. Marriage, work, driving, travel, moving house, financial troubles, as well as chosen leisure pursuits, can all produce stress.

Marketing and stress

Many products and services are marketed with benefits that can take the stress out of everyday life. Fridge freezers, frozen dinners and microwave ovens allow busy working people to come home and quickly make meals for themselves and for the family; plane flights, holidays, car hire can be quickly and painlessly ordered through websites; and insurance companies offer an all inclusive package covering every possible contingency.

Understanding the behaviour of others

It seems to be part of the human condition to observe the physical world and the people in it and want to know what causes things to happen in the way that they do.

5.7 General example | **Social class levels and stress**

According to some research, workers on the lower rungs of the socio-economic ladder suffer more stress on the job than their superiors. The reason for this is the intense pressure that may be exerted coupled with having no kind of control over outcomes.

Examples in the physical world include such questions as: Why does it rain? What shape is the world? What is a rainbow? Similarly we ask questions about human behaviour and motivation not always accepting at face value the reasons that people give.

Attribution (or explanation) theory

▶ According to Heider (1958) **attribution theory** is about trying to understand the behaviour of others (and ourselves) by taking into account (attribute) two things. Forces or factors within the individual (disposition) and forces or factors in the environment (situation).

For example if somebody is walking along holding an umbrella and it's raining we say that factors in the environment, the rain (the situation), is causing the behaviour. If it is not raining however, and the same individual is walking along holding an umbrella we will probably attribute behaviour to the individual's eccentricity (disposition). Similarly when individuals think about motives for their own behaviour they sometimes adopt the same approach. Students who fail an exam might put it down to the weather, the personality of the lecturer, the quality of the questions (the situation). Or they might put it down to their own inadequacies, lack of ability, lack of effort or not really caring (disposition).

Key point It's important that marketers are able to understand the real reason behind purchase behaviour. Only then can they offer relevant benefits.

Complex human behaviour

Some academics argue (Vroom, Handy) that many of the motivational approaches identified above, responding to economic, social and self-actualising needs, are too simplistic and that individuals are much more complex than this. It is argued that the individual motives are liable to change over time according to the situation and relationships with other people. No single strategy, style and approach could thus succeed in understanding behaviour, improving worker performances or encouraging consumer loyalty, as individuals would respond differently according to intrinsic needs. To get the best out of people, business and marketing managers have the task of empathetically responding to all these complex needs on a person-to-person basis offering almost customised motivational solutions.

Motivation and cultural and religious differences

Social influences and culture can have a huge influence on motivation. In Japan there is enormous pressure on children, young adults and parents to achieve a good education. In some parts of India and Pakistan young couples are expected to marry partners chosen by the parents and in other countries, such as Turkey, young single men working abroad are expected to send money home to support their family. Australia has a culture of sports participation, in France it's cooking and in Holland it's travel. Religions have the ability to control behaviour from just a small amount to almost everything that people do. Strict Roman Catholics must go to confession at least once a week, Muslims must pray five times a day and not drink alcohol and Hindus must not eat beef. Motivational reasons for behaviour with most religions tend to be through received wisdom, often written down in a holy book (the Bible, Koran, Torah). The incentive to behaviour in one way or another is the promise of a spiritual after life of some kind. This will be discussed in more detail in Chapter 8.

Summary

- In this chapter we looked at motives that drive human and consumer behaviour.
- It was recognised that motivation can have both positive and negative effects and have varying degrees of strength and intensity.
- The differences in motivations between consumer and organisational purchases were then outlined.
- Theories discussed here included Leon Festinger's theory of cognitive dissonance and Kurt Lewin's identification of conflict.
- We then went on to talk about inherited genetic tendencies and socially learned motivational approaches.
- Other areas discussed in this part included the need for achievement and power, sex and curiosity and theories based on satisfaction seeking and pain avoiding behaviour.
- Other theories outlined included stimulus seeking, arousal roles and reinforcement processes and intrinsic and extrinsic human behavioural needs.
- Ideas based on contentment and end satisfaction as motivators were explained using McGregor's theory of incentives and threats and Hertzberg's normal and higher theory of motivation.
- Cognitive theories were then discussed using equity theory, expectancy theory and goal-setting theory as examples.
- The Freudian theory of the unconscious and repressed motives was touched upon as it was noted that more detail would appear in a later chapter.
- We then went on to look at the role of frustration and anger as both a positive and negative motivator as well as the concepts of scapegoating and stereotyping.
- Finally complex motivational behaviour, attribution theory and cultural influences on motivation where briefly delineated.

Questions

1. Examine the process of motivation and evaluate its importance in understanding consumer behaviour. Give live examples.
2. Discuss how motivation can be both internally and externally generated. Give examples of theories in this area.
3. Buyers purchase all manner of products and services at the rational, emotional and instinctive level. Explain why this might be so, giving live examples. Why might purchase motives be different at the consumer and organisational level?
4. According to social psychologist Kurt Lewin, motivational conflicts arise when we experience in the mind wants and demands that are incompatible with each other. Examine why this might be so.
5. How might frustration be both a positive and negative motivator? Identify and give examples at both the human and consumer behaviour level.
6. Discuss why and how frustration can lead to anger behaviour and why it might be that some individuals are quicker to be angry than others. Discuss and give examples of its affect on consumer behaviour and show how marketers and retailers should respond.
7. Many human defence mechanisms were identified, including intellectualisation, rationalisation, denial, projection, reaction formation, repression, sublimation, compensation and escape. Give examples why marketing practitioners need to understand all these processes.
8. Identify, examine and compare some of the motivational theories discussed throughout this chapter. Do you think that they are still relevant today in understanding consumer behaviour?
9. Identify and examine possible social motives behind human and consumer behaviour. Discuss how these might come about.
10. The father of psychology, Sigmund Freud, introduced us to the concept of the subconscious and hidden motives behind behaviour. Give examples in merchandising, sales promotions and advertising where product and service brand benefits are offered and aimed at this 'concealed world' of the consumer.

Case study

Case study 1 Retail motivational intensity

According to research (Mintel, Datamonitor) retail motivational intensity will vary from group to group with approximately one-third of us enjoying shopping (over 20 per cent confess to being obsessive 'shopaholics'), one-third dislike shopping and one-third are somewhere in the middle. Nearly 10 per cent of all shoppers suffer from compulsive shopping disorder (CSD). Over 50 per cent of people would seek out and buy brands rather than own label goods, while over 50 per cent of women confess they would rather shop than have sex and almost one in two girl teenagers are shopping 'enthusiasts'. Many consumers shop because it makes them feel better to be in the company of others. This might be because of feelings of fear or isolation if at home alone and/or the need to talk and be in the company of others. Thus many shopping malls and villages advertise a visit to their centre as a wonderful day out for the family in the company of other likeminded people. Many advertisements can be seen, particularly on the run up to Christmas, associating products and brands with this benefit need. A person is alone and when entering a nightclub or bar he or she orders a Barcardi rum or Tia Maria. Music with an infectious beat strikes up and happy, dancing people immediately surround them. People will also buy the same, or similar, products and services purchased by admired groups and revered individuals and even behave in similar ways. The levels of motivational intensity among different groups is regularly measured by the use of sophisticated quantitative and qualitative research techniques and these become the basis for ever tighter market and customer segmentation.

Questions

1 Discuss the part that motivation plays in retail behaviour. Identify some of the motivation theories that might apply.

2 Do you think consumers are cynically manipulated to behave in the way that they do?

Case study

Case study 2 Look at behaviour not at what people say

In his book *How Customers Think*, Harvard Business School professor Gerald Zaltman comments that there is a huge gap between what it is that customers say in focus group research and what their subsequent behaviour in the marketplace is. Eighty per cent of all new products fail within six months of launch despite the approval of rigorous consumer focus group testing. There is evidence to show that despite millions of people saying they don't like direct mail, 50 per cent of sales letters are opened and 75 per cent of these are read. While a majority of consumers say they wouldn't buy cosmetic products tested on animals, research shows that a majority never read the label to find out. Similarly research has shown that a stated intention to buy will not always translate into actual purchase. It seems that unconscious thoughts will more accurately predict behaviour rather than the things that people say.

Questions

1 Discuss the problems with attempting to understand consumer behaviour identified above. Where does that leave conventional research?

2 What methods of research might be used to try to overcome the problem?

Further reading

Books

Arnould, E., L. Price and G. Zinkhan (2002) *Consumers*, International Edition, 1st edn, New York: McGraw Hill.

Bolles, Robert C. (1976) *Theory of Motivation*, 2nd edn, New York: Harper and Row.

Cosmides, L. *et al.* (2004) *What Is Evolutionary Psychology: Explaining the New Science of the Mind* (*Darwinism Today*), New Haven, CT: Yale University Press.

Dawkins, R. (1976) *The Selfish Gene*, Oxford: Oxford University Press.

Festinger, Leon (1957) *Theory of Cognitive Dissonance*, Stanford, CA: Stanford University Press.

Hall, C.S. and G. Lindzey (1978) *Theories of Personality*, 3rd edn, New York: John Wiley & Sons.

Heider, F. (1958) *The Psychology of Interpersonal Relations*, New York: Wiley.

Hertzberg, F. (1966) *Work and the Nature of Man*, New York: World.

Hull, C. (1952) *A Behaviour System*, New Haven, CT: Yale University Press.

Locke, Edwin and Gary P. Latham & (1990); *A Theory of Goal Setting and Task Performance*, Englewood Cliffs, NJ: Prentice Hall.

Marrow, A.J. (1969) *The Practical Theorist: The Life and Work of Kurt Lewin*, New York: Basic Books.

Neal, Co, P. Quester and D. Hawkins (1999) *Consumer Behaviour: Implications for Marketing Strategy*, 2nd edn, New York: Urwin/McGraw-Hill.

Pooler, J. (2003) *Why We Shop: Emotional Rewards and Retail Strategies*, Westport, CT: Praeger Publishers.

Rogers, Carl (1995) *On Becoming a Person: A Therapist's view of Psychotherapy*, intro. Peter D. Kramer, Boston MA: Manner Book.

Rogers, Carl (1995) *Client-centered Therapy: Its Current Practice, Implications and Theory*, Philadelphia, PA: Trans-Atlantic Publications, repr.

Solomon, M. (1999) *Consumer Behaviour*, 4th edn, Upper Saddle River, NJ: Prentice Hall International.

Spence, K.W. (1960) *Behavior Theory and Learning*, Englewood Cliffs, NJ: Prentice Hall.

Taylor, Frederick W. (1991) *The Father of Scientific Management: Myth and Reality*, Chicago, K: Irwin Professional Publishing.

Vroom, V.H. (1964) *Work and Motivation*, New York: Wiley.

Vroom, V.H. (1999) *Management and Motivation*, Harmondsworth: Penguin Business.

Wilson, E.O. (1975) *Sociobiology: The New Synthesis*, Cambridge, MA: Harvard University Press.

Wright, Ray (1999) *Marketing, Origins, Concepts and Environment*, London: Thomson Publishing.

Zaltman, Gerald (2003) *How Customers Think: Essential Insights into the Mind of the Market*, Cambridge, MA: Harvard Business School.

Articles and journals

Adams, J. Stacey (1965) 'Inequity in Social Exchange', in Leonard Berkowitz (ed.), *Advances in Experimental Social Psychology*, Vol. 2, New York: Academic Press, pp. 267–99.

Bornstein, R.F. (1989) 'Exposure and Affect: Overview and Meta Analysis of Research, 1968–1987', *Psychological Bulletin*, 106, 2: 265–89.

Harlow, H. (1958) 'The Development of Affectional Responses in Infant Monkeys', *Proc. Am. Phil. Soc.*, 102: 501–9.

Marney, J. (1993) 'Making Sense of Consumer Motivation', *Marketing*, 98: 8–9.
Miller, N.E. and M. David Egger (1962) 'When is a Reward Reinforcing? An Experimental Study of the Information Hypothesis, *Journal of Comparative and Physiological Psychology*, 56: 132–7.
Sheppard, B.H., J. Hartwick, and P.R. Warshaw (1988) 'The Theory of Reasoned Action', *Journal of Consumer Research*, December, 15: 325–49.
Shimp, T.A., E.W. Stuart and E.W. Randall (1991) 'A Program of Classical Conditioning Experiments', *Journal of Consumer Research*, 18, June: 1–12.
Zajonc, R.B. (1984) 'On the Primacy of Affect' *American Psychologist*, 39: 117–23.
Zückerman, M. (2000) 'Are You a Risk-taker?', *Psychology Today*, Nov/Dec: 54–87.
Zückerman, M. (2002) 'Genetics of Sensation Seeking', in J. Benjamin, R.P. Ebstein and R.H. Belmake (eds), *Molecular Genetics and the Human Personality*, Washington, DC: American Psychiatric Association.

Websites

The DPP (doctor–patient partnership), www.dpp.org.
The National Obesity Forum, www.sussed.uk.net.
Marketing Database, www.studentshout.com.
Media Awareness Network, www.media-awareness network.ca.

Attitude

6

'The greatest discovery of our generation is that human beings can alter their lives by altering their attitudes of mind. As you think, so shall you be.'

William James, US pragmatist and philosopher (1842–1910)

Objectives

At the end of this chapter the reader will be able to:

1. Examine the meaning of attitude and show the part that it plays in understanding human and consumer behaviour.
2. Identify, examine and evaluate the forces that drive attitudes.
3. Identify and examine the many theories of attitudes and evaluate their worth in modern times especially when applied to marketing.
4. Evaluate some of the methods used in attitude measurement.

Introduction

Everybody has thoughts, beliefs and opinions about people, behaviour and the world around them. In fact it might be considered to be unusual if somebody said that they didn't have an opinion on some issue or another, whether it be wide questions about morality (such as abortion or stem-cell research) or politics (war and terrorism) or religion (Christianity or Islam) or more colloquial questions about football, TV soap operas or Sunday shopping. We only have to go into a pub or bar at any one time to hear people discussing and arguing about something they may have read in the morning's newspaper or saw on the TV the night before. Opinions and ideas will also vary around the world depending on nationality, culture and ethnic group. It seems to matter little if individuals have facts to back up arguments, often basing them on anecdotal evidence rather than scientific fact. As well as beliefs and opinion the idea of attitude is also part of the language and it's this concept that will underpin the discussion throughout this chapter.

Beliefs

All individuals and groups develop beliefs of one kind or another that helps them make everyday sense of their particular inhabited world. Not all beliefs are based on facts and will vary from nation to nation and culture to culture. Primitive societies might believe one thing and more modern societies another. Some beliefs will be based on localised day-to-day empirical experiences, while others will be based on learning and copying others that is perhaps passed down within the family and from generation to generation, often over hundreds of years. Beliefs might be based on religion, superstition and received wisdom and have little or no scientific substance behind them.

Many sources of belief

Beliefs can also come about through reading, watching TV, listening to the radio, discussing and arguing with others, the Internet, investigation and cognitive processes. For example there might be a generally accepted belief that a certain amount of rain is good and crops should be planted at a certain time of the year to obtain the best results; that there are two many cars on the road; that there should be the death penalty for murder; or that cigarette smoking is bad for the health. One group might believe in arranged marriages, while another that the young should be allowed to choose their own marriage partners. Some religious fundamentalists believe the world was created in seven days and is about four thousand years old, while secularists believe that it is billions of years old and came about through the 'Big Bang'.

Figure 6.1

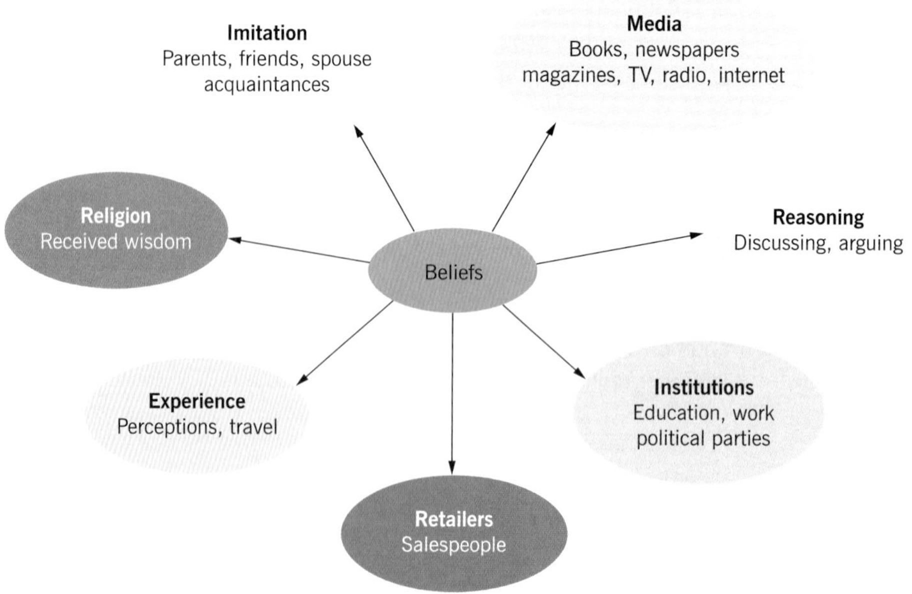

Origins of beliefs. Beliefs can come about in a number of ways

Strong or weak beliefs

As we can see, beliefs that people have can be varied and multitudinous, be learnt, acquired through experience, cognitive investigation and based on science, religion, superstition or just feeling. Not all beliefs are of the same strength and importance, however. I may believe that rats are used for medical experimentation, that women are paid less than men in similar jobs, or that a particular brand of toilet paper is better than another, yet not really care one way or another. Similarly others might feel strongly about such issues and so develop opinions, ideas and beliefs about such matters. Strong beliefs are often closely tied to a sense of identity and tend not to be changed that easily.

> **Key point** Not all beliefs are based on facts; they can be universal or vary from culture to culture; they can be learnt or acquired and can be weakly or strongly held.

Situation affects beliefs

Specific circumstances often influence consumer behaviour. For example, consumers in a rush are likely to take the most convenient product available and will want to be out of the store as soon as possible. Conversely those with plenty of time to spare will be quite happy to browse around and not be too bothered about queues at the checkout. Couples with plenty of money will want the highest quality products and will be prepared to shop around no matter the cost. Those with smaller amounts to spend will look for best value economy products. Buying while on holiday, away from home or for a special occasion (an anniversary or wedding) will all have an effect upon consumer attitude, as will the weather, the time of day and the time of the year.

Marketing, consumer behaviour and beliefs

'Your belief determines your action and your action determines your results, but first you have to believe.' MARK VICTOR HANSEN AND ROBERT G. ALLEN (2002)

▶ Capitalism and **consumerism** are such phenomena that nearly everybody, children, teenagers, young, middle-aged and older adults will all have good and bad opinions and beliefs about its pervasiveness and contribution to a healthy society.

Figure 6.2

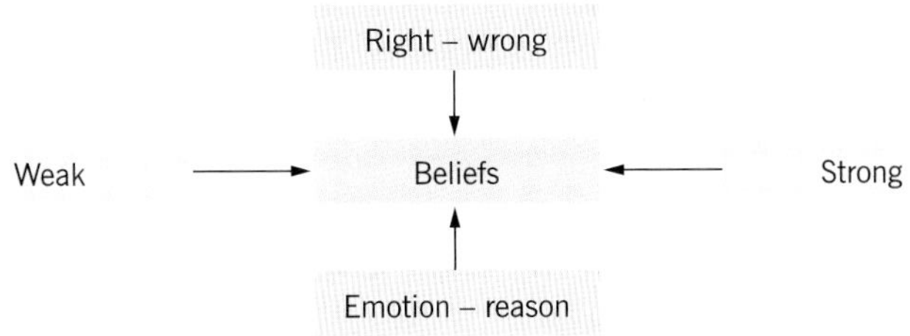

Content of a belief

This will be on such things as company responsibilities, environmental concerns, advertising, different products, competing brands, retailer choice and the role of marketing. Marketers therefore are tasked to make every encounter with the public such a rich and rewarding exercise that all its customers will believe that the organisation and its brands are so wonderful that they will always want to purchase its products and services.

> **Key point** A belief could be said to be an estimate of the probability that something is true.

Attitude

Unlike other behavioural concepts discussed earlier, it can be safely accepted that people are not born with an attitude. Attitudes are feelings and beliefs that people develop about objects, events, people and issues over a lifetime through learning and experientially interacting with people and the environment.

A belief can develop into an attitude according to the strength of feeling involved. The stronger the belief the stronger becomes the attitude and the more likely it will affect behaviour. Attitudes also imply a sense of generalisation and longevity. For example we might feel strongly about the noise coming from a party next door and believe that they should turn the sound of the music down. However, if it were a rare occurrence, the strength of the belief would be minimal and soon forgotten. If, however, it was constant over a period of months and years the belief in the need for quiet might become so strong that an attitude about all late night, noisy parties might become part of the way that we see the world.

> **Key point** Attitudes are feelings, beliefs and ways of behaving that people develop about objects, events, people and issues over a lifetime through learning and experientially interacting with people and the environment. Consumers may form, or have existing attitudes reinforced, before, during or after a purchase.

Components of an attitude

Many writers (e.g. Allport, Ajzen, Fishbein *et al.*), seem to agree that an attitude will consist of constant interaction between the following components:

1. Beliefs
2. Emotions
3. Behaviour

(Also known as the ABC model of attitudes – affect (emotion), behaviour and cognition (beliefs).)

Beliefs

If we take an issue like the death penalty, people will hold beliefs about whether they think it should be used or not. This belief will be based on such things as knowledge and information (right or wrong) on its use as a deterrent against violent crime and moral, humanitarian and religious issues, such as all killing of humans being wrong or it being right under certain circumstances.

Consumers and beliefs

Consumers hold beliefs about products and brands based on information from such sources as the manufacturer, the media, consumer organisations, friends and from own experiences. For example, a person might believe that the BMW (punch line 'The Ultimate Driving Machine') is the best-built car in the world because German manufacturers have a reputation for technical ability and design. This perception might be right or wrong, but it is obviously to the company's benefit to advertise and constantly supply information that reinforces this view.

Emotions

Using the same example, the issue of hanging also has the power to elicit strong emotional feelings such as anger, hostility, hate, loathing, vengefulness, contempt, remorse, pity, sympathy, love, empathy, guilt and so on. This seems to supply the energy that drives and maintains the particular attitude.

Consumers and emotions

Cars seem to engender deep emotional feelings in consumers. We only have to look any evening at adverts for cars on the TV. Most messages used promote emotional values such as pride, power, success, speed and sexual attraction, envy of others and so on. For whatever emotional reason, owners love their BMWs and probably no other consumer product epitomises the emotional power of the brand as well as the motorcar. It is possible to 'love' all the attributes of a particular brand and yet not own or even have access to the product. Many people around the world are deeply attracted to all things American but can only aspire to ownership due to lack of money and opportunity to purchase.

6.1 Marketing example — Emotions sell cars

Sex 'Cadillac Ladies Love to Play ... This one is really fun to drive ... feather light and sure to handle ... smooth and effortless on the move ... quick and nimble in the clutches' (1963 ad for Cadillac).

Adventure 'Go where no one has gone before – go farther than all the others ... A luxurious, and very personal, statement' (1992 Ford Explorer).

Romance 'We dressed in silence. And drove. Until four lanes became two. Two became one. And one became a tunnel ... Something that was there before was back.' (1992 Mercury Sable).

Behaviour

How we act about our belief on the issue of the death penalty will vary according to the strength of the belief and the emotional content. Some people with weak views might just discuss or argue at home or in the pub while others with stronger views might write or email the newspaper, their member of parliament or join pressure groups and go on public demonstrations.

The consumer and behaviour

Ultimately all marketing is about behaviour, persuading the consumer to go out and buy a particular brand, in this case the BMW. Owning a BMW will involve a particular life style, which might include joining a BMW owners club, washing and polishing it every Sunday, wearing the right clothes and being seen driving it around town.

Beliefs, emotions and behaviour and the hierarchy of effects

The three components of consumer attitudes, beliefs, feelings and behaviour, will all come together to influence the brands that are purchased, e.g. Maxwell House coffee, a Gillette razor, a Sony TV, and the retailers that are used to make those purchases, e.g. Tesco, Co-op, Dixon's. How consumers react to advertising campaigns and how their decision-making process works in practice along a hierarchy of effects, however, will vary and is still open to some discussion. For example will the consumer feel emotion first when first seeing an advertisement (stimulated feel-good factors drive motivation) followed by behaviour (a visit to the shop) followed by belief building (information from the salesperson), or will beliefs come first followed by behaviour followed by feelings and emotions? The alternatives are discussed below.

Figure 6.3

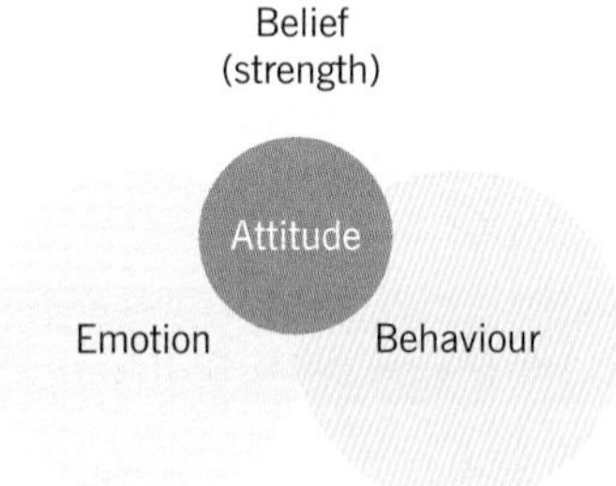

Components of attitude

Alternative consumer attitudes – hierarchy of effects models

It's important for marketing and advertising people to understand how consumer beliefs, emotions and behaviour interact together when forming attitudes about products and brands. This is because it will heavily influence how they go about building marketing and promotional campaigns.

Three approaches are identified below that might be applicable depending on the type of product and service and the personality of the customer.

1 High consumer involvement
2 Low consumer involvement
3 Emotional consumer involvement

High consumer involvement

Building beliefs

The standard or classical approach to attitude formation begins with the idea that consumers will want to have a high level of involvement in identifying and comparing companies' products and services. They take in information from TV, newspapers, radio and outdoor billboard adverts, analysing and evaluating this over time. In this way beliefs and attitudes about favourable and unfavourable products, services and brands will then be built and developed.

Reinforced by emotion

This will be reinforced by the development of an emotional attraction of some kind. This comes about through producer adverts that constantly emphasise a brand's ability to make purchasers feel better about themselves in some way or another (the 'feel-good' factor) when they have ownership. It could also involve consumers talking and listening to the advice of significant family members and friends.

Motivating behaviour

Behaviour will then follow as concrete beliefs, joined with strong emotional desires, motivate purchase, either directly from the manufacturer or indirectly from a retailer. Repeat purchase and continuous satisfaction will cement loyalty, making it very difficult for a competitor, unless they have a clear benefit advantage, to persuade the customer to switch brands.

Building belief → reinforced by emotion → motivate behaviour and action

Low consumer involvement

Limited beliefs

It could be argued, however, that consumers only have such a high level of involvement when buying one-off expensive products and services such as cars, holidays and life insurance. The low involvement approach to attitude formation begins in the same way as the standard approach but sees the consumer having limited knowledge and beliefs about products and brands and not really wanting to be as involved as manufacturers and retailers would like them to be. This is especially so with frequently purchased fast moving consumer goods, FMCG (all those products sold in the large supermarkets).

Motivating behaviour

Behaviour and the purchasing and trying of different brands will follow. Some brands will be known through mass advertising but not in the detail and to the extent that producers would like. For example the Andrex puppy might be remembered as something to do with toilet rolls, but little else. Point-of-purchase display material and sales promotions offering benefits like two for the price of one or 25 per cent off are useful here to encourage people to try one product brand rather than another.

Reinforced by emotions

Only after purchase and trial will emotions and feelings follow. If a brand is liked, an emotional loyalty attachment might be built. If the brand is disliked, another brand will be tried until a portfolio of liked and disliked brands are positioned in the mind of the customer. Again competitors will find it difficult to dislodge consumer preferences once emotional brand commitment has been established.

Limited beliefs → reinforced by emotions → motivating behaviour

Emotional consumer involvement

Emotions begin the process

There are occasions when it appears to be emotion that's the most powerful aspect in first stimulating consumer attitudes to a brand. Research seems to show that feeling plays as much as 75 per cent in the purchasing of consumer products. This is why emotion is such an important part of advertising, packaging and merchandising. So according to this theory on consumer involvement, consumers became interested in brands because they make them feel happy, or sexy, or important, or part of a group, or loved, or nostalgic, or proud and so on.

Motivating behaviour

Consumer emotions, stimulated by advertising will encourage the consumer to try particular products and brands. If the feel-good factor is reinforced, repeat purchase will take place.

Building beliefs

In this way beliefs about the pleasure-giving attributes of one brand over another will be thought through and translated into positive attitudes towards one product over another.

High emotional input → motivating behaviour → building beliefs

Figure 6.4

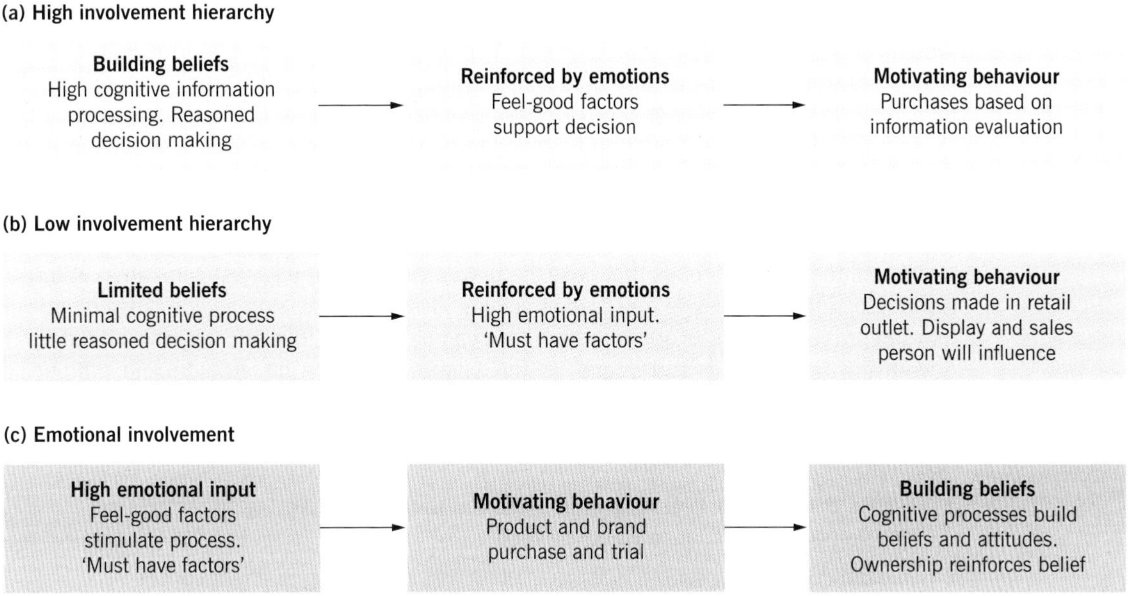

(a) High involvement hierarchy

Building beliefs High cognitive information processing. Reasoned decision making	→	**Reinforced by emotions** Feel-good factors support decision	→	**Motivating behaviour** Purchases based on information evaluation

(b) Low involvement hierarchy

Limited beliefs Minimal cognitive process little reasoned decision making	→	**Reinforced by emotions** High emotional input. 'Must have factors'	→	**Motivating behaviour** Decisions made in retail outlet. Display and sales person will influence

(c) Emotional involvement

High emotional input Feel-good factors stimulate process. 'Must have factors'	→	**Motivating behaviour** Product and brand purchase and trial	→	**Building beliefs** Cognitive processes build beliefs and attitudes. Ownership reinforces belief

High, low and emotional approaches to purchases

Key point Attitudes are weak to strong beliefs, emotional feelings and ways of behaving towards organisations, people, objects, events and issues that endure over time.

Belief + strength + duration + behaviour = Attitude

The relationship between attitude and behaviour

Many people assume that attitude will guide behaviour, that the things that individuals and groups say will subsequently affect the things that they do. However it could be that the reverse happens, and that behaviour affects attitude. For example if a customer uses the same supermarket or the same brand for many years they will begin to develop some kind of attraction to the company or brand and feel the need to adopt a positive, liking attitude to justify their behaviour. Similarly a person might have little or no nationalistic feelings toward their home country, town or even football club, but if he or she is abroad and somebody makes derogatory remarks about them they will probably find themselves adopting a defensive attitude. (This is discussed in more detail later when 'justifying principles' are discussed.)

Key point Attitude can affect behaviour and behaviour can affect attitude. Sometimes it can be a combination of the two.

6.2 Marketing example — The power of attitudes

We only have to listen to the news and the radio or read newspapers to see the power that attitudes can have over the way that people think and behave. Powerful belief systems dominate the different ways that groups of people perceive the world. People are prepared to commit outrageous acts and are prepared to go to prison or go to war and even to kill themselves in one cause or another. The growth of **pressure groups** propounding a whole range of values has magnified over the last twenty years. Environmentalism, animal rights, anti-vivisection, anti-use of animal fur, healthy eating, fair-trade and fair wages for third world countries are all groups that have the power to frighten the largest companies in the world into curbing excessive free market activity. Consumers develop a wide range of attitudes to products, services and brands. These can be both positive and negative attitudes. Advertising (and then brand usage) is the biggest influence on attitude and attitude change. The sender and the message vehicle will all influence how the brand is perceived.

Questions

1 Discuss the power of pressure groups. Do you think they have the strength to force companies to change working practices?

2 How difficult do you think it is for marketing and advertising to affect consumer attitudes?

Attitude strength – core and non-core values

Attitude strength will vary internally to the individual across the different attitudes held and externally from person to person. There are some issues that we might feel much stronger about than others. These can be identified as core and non-core values.

Core values

Core values are those values that become central to peoples' ways of behaving and thinking about themselves and they can be the bedrock of attitude formation. These core values will be relatively few in number, growing in strength over time, be resistant to attack and impact and inform most things that an individual will do.

Universal core values

Some core values will be universal and will have come about through cultural and social indoctrination. Western universal core values will include such things as concern for human rights, holding life sacred, freedom of speech, religious freedom, education for children and young people and the right for everybody to vote. 'Universal' core values could be different in different parts of the world and this will be discussed in more detail in the chapter on social influences.

Key point Consumers at the very heart of the economy
Politicians in most parts of the world now accept that a liberal free market approach is the most productive method of running an economy and is now a core value. This has enormous implications for marketing and understanding behaviour because it puts the consumer and freedom of choice at the very heart of the economy.

Individual core values

Individuals will develop, over time, their own core values that they use to define the sort of person they are. Most of these will be in agreement with the national universal core values but sometimes to a lesser or greater degree. For argument's sake, one person might believe that killing others is right under certain circumstances, that education is wasted on anybody over fifteen, that some religions should be banned and the ability to vote given only to those who have a proven level of intellect. Others might disagree. Each person will develop more personal individual core values that will be important to him or her but relatively unimportant to others. This might be a belief in compassion and helping others, having a commitment to work, vegetarianism, healthy living, animal rights, the sanctity of marriage and the family and so on.

The belief in God is a core belief for many

Non-core values

We hold other attitudes and values that are less strong and enduring than many of the core values discussed above. It is worth saying that some values might be core to one person lasting all their lives while non-core to another person lasting only six months, e.g. vegetarianism. Our non-core values might include some of the things above but without the strength and feeling of commitment. For example I might feel that it is wrong to shoot birds, to get drunk, to smoke and gamble but not care if others indulge. I might be polite, queue for services, be nice to others most of the time but be prepared to deviate according to circumstances.

6.3 Marketing example — Consumer behaviour and core values

Researchers are aware that many individuals develop strong and enduring attachments to products and services attached to lifestyle choices. Manufacturers will then use this information to offer clear brand benefits to groups of consumers that, depending on the strength of the attitude, and whether core or non-core, are often the heaviest and most loyal of all customers. Lifestyle choices such as: playing and watching sports such as football, sailing, fishing, golf; music of all kinds; dancing; watching TV and videos; healthy living and even shopping, will all be core to how one group or another live their lives. Markets and other markets like these are now worth billions of pounds and euros both in the UK and around the world.

Questions

1 How might markets be segmented by core and non-core values? Give live examples.
2 Discuss how core values might be different in countries around the world.

Key point Core and non-core differences
Core and non-core values can be differentiated and defined by the relative strength, longevity, resistance to change and the central part the attitude plays in the thinking and behaviour of the individual.

Positive and negative attitudes

Attitudes can be both positive and negative depending on the object of the attitude, the situation and the personality of the beholder. Everybody will have positive and negative attitudes at one time or another. These can be both core and non-core. For example one individual might have a negative attitude to the development of technology (never using the Internet) and another individual a positive attitude (loving it, spending many hours a day in exploration). This might have to do with the attitude object (in this case technology), a person's personality (pessimist or optimist), or the situation and circumstances (pressure of work). In many circumstances negative attitudes, refusing to obey parents, to work hard or not to drink and drive, will be punished in some way or another, e.g. refused sweets, money taken away or even going to prison. In the same way positive attitudes can be rewarded, e.g. praise, recognition and extra money. It may be discovered that a consumer has two attitudes (one positive and one negative) towards a product brand; in this case the marketer should downplay the negative, stress the positive, and allow the positive to overshadow the negative.

Positive or negative – the sign demonstrates the strong attitude of the writer

6.4 Marketing example **Polygamous consumer**

Studies indicate that few consumers are 'monogamous' (100 per cent loyal) or 'promiscuous' (no loyalty to any brand). Rather most are 'polygamous' (i.e. loyal to a portfolio of brands in a product category). From this perspective, loyalty may be explained as 'an ongoing propensity to buy the brand, usually as one of the several', Strategic Marketing.com.

Consumers and positive and negative attitudes

Customers develop positive and negative attitudes towards company and product brands. Obviously managers want their company to be seen in the best possible light and work hard to build positive attitude feedback. If, however, there is negative feedback, i.e. company and/or product brands are disliked, the job for the

Figure 6.5

Negative attitude	**Neutral attitude**	**Positive attitude**
Company and brand disliked	No strong feelings	Company and brands liked
Bad positioning	Indifferent positioning	Good positioning
Marketing task	**Marketing task**	**Marketing task**
Change customer attitude	Raise customer awareness	Constantly reinforce customer attitude

Customer attitude to corporate and product brand

public relations and marketing manager is much harder as they will have to try to change attitudes from disapproval into approval, usually a heavy and difficult task.

Attitude sources

Attitudes adopted might be strong or weak as well as positive and negative depending on upbringing, cultural mores and personality. Initially, early attitudes to things such as food likes and dislikes, going to bed, leisure activity, beliefs about others and so on will be learnt within the family. As we get older outside agencies will start to take affect and school, university, work, the church, the media will all have an input. Overlaying the process will be national, cultural and tribal influences and this will be examined in more detail in the chapter on social influences. Attitudes become more entrenched and more resistant to change the older we become. This is especially true of attitudes adopted early on in life.

Some attitudes are also nearer the surface of the memory and so more accessible than others. It can be the case that some people are unaware of the strength of a particular attitude because it remains inarticulated over time. Only when something or other happens to resurrect the particular attitude is its strength apparent.

> **Key point** Attitudes become more entrenched and more resistant to change the older we become.

Levels of commitment to an attitude

Levels of commitment to one attitude rather than another will vary according to:

- How it fits with identity and centrally held values and norms, e.g. 'Social welfare is wrong. People should stand on their own two feet', 'Being a vegetarian dominates my life'.
- How deeply entrenched and internalised is the attitude, e.g. 'We have lived in the country for five generations and would not move to the town'.
- The length of time the attitude has been held, e.g. 'I have supported Manchester United Football club for 40 years. They can do no wrong', 'My mother and I have drunk Robinsons Orange from since I was a little girl'.
- The ability to analyse and think things through, e.g. 'I have felt the same way about immigration for the last 40 years and nobody will change my mind', 'They will not convince me that drinking is bad for you, it's never done me any harm'.

Segmentation and attitude cluster

Attitude cluster is one of the most important methods used by marketers to segment markets. Segmentation and understanding the values that particular groups hold about issues and the consequent lifestyle adopted enables companies to develop products with customised benefits that will be attractive to all the different cluster groups.

Figure 6.6

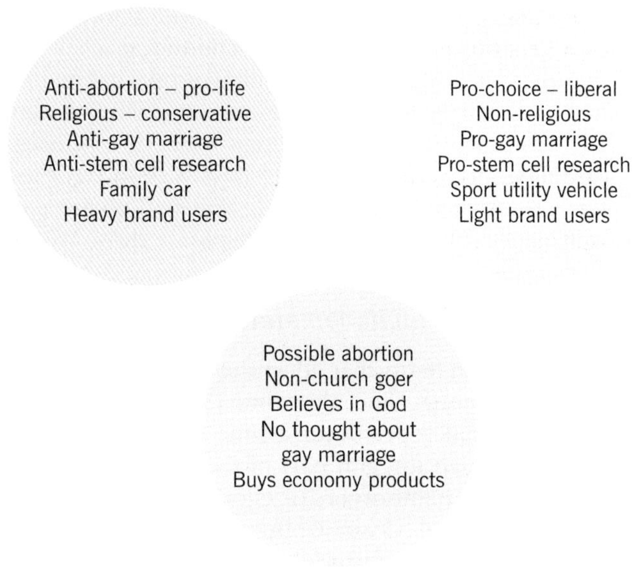

Attitude segmentation clusters

> **Key point** Segmentation, breaking the market up into like-mined groups of consumers is at the heart of marketing. In this way personalised benefits can be offered that satisfy individual customers.

Attitudes adopted for different reasons

'Life and work is either fun or drudgery. It depends on your attitude. I prefer fun'. COLLEN C. BARRETT, US President of Southwest Airlines

Attitudes of some kind are taken on by all individuals, some knowingly and others unknowingly, in all areas of life. Reasons why particular attitudes are adopted however will be different, as they seem to play different roles in the minds of individuals. Four reasons are given below:

1. **Utilitarian purpose**
2. **Value-expressive purpose**
3. **Ego defensive** function
4. **Knowledge function**

Utilitarian purpose – gain reward and avoid punishment

Some attitudes are adopted, from a very early age and then consistently throughout life, because they serve some practical, utilitarian purpose. We have discussed, when talking about both learning and motivation, the theory that people will want to maximise experiences that are rewarding and minimise those that are punishing.

The same idea can be applied to attitudes and can be aimed at a person, an object or a situation. It begins at early childhood where we learn that if we act in a way that pleases our parents we will avoid punishment, a smack or being put early to bed, and gain rewards, sweets, a smile or being allowed to stay up and watch the TV. Manipulating attitude to illicit wanted responses from others can be automatic or deliberately contrived. This stays with most of us for the rest of our lives as we learn positive ways of behaving that will please partners, spouses and friends as well as negative ways that will displease those we dislike.

Marketing and utilitarian attitude

Retailers soon learn that adopting a friendly, smiling persona will encourage consumers to return time after time. Nobody likes a miserable and constantly complaining shopkeeper. After a time this friendly approach can become ingrained and become an integral part of the retailer's personality. In the same way if consumers enjoy hamburgers or exotic coffee, they will develop a positive attitude to McDonald's and Costa Coffee. If, however they are health fanatics they will develop a negative attitude to all types of fast food considered unhealthy.

Never keep a shop unless you can smile

Value-expressive purpose – fit into an individual's life values

Value expressive attitudes are adopted because they chime with ideas about the sort of person that I think that I am, think that I would like to be or how I would like to be seen by others. Again from an early age children are told (by parents, religion and schools) how 'good' boys and 'good' girls should behave and many grow into adulthood holding fast to fundamental principles and central values. Others, of course will drop early value systems and adopt others as they interact with individuals, groups and gangs with different ways of living their lives that seem more exciting and attractive (for example heavy drinking, smoking marijuana, promiscuous sex).

Marketing and value-expressive attitudes

All consumers will have sets of value-expressive attitudes of varying strengths and will purchase products, brands and services that fit into these central values. For example some products are seen as 'English' and so groups might always try to buy these products first. Research has shown that there are groups of consumers who will only buy branded products, retail own label being seen as 'down-market' and inferior and not conforming to the image they want to project. In the same way, groups of young people will have different leisure pursuits (pubs, nightclubs, 18/30 holidays) compared with their parents (restaurants, dancing, gites in France) as well as from one group to another. The idea of segmenting and targeting the market according to activities, interests and opinions, AIO, has been an essential part of a marketing approach for many decades.

Ego defensive function – protect self-esteem

'No one', Eleanor Roosevelt said, 'can make you feel inferior without your consent. Never give it.'

We have seen that it is normal for humans to build defensive attitude mechanisms that protect their own sense of themselves, the inner reality that is the 'me' or the 'ego'. This involves defence against external threats, such as others belittling us, as well trying to manage negative internal impulses such as feelings of inadequacy, depression, anxiety and unacceptable impulses. Some are better at it than others. Attitude clusters are therefore adopted to take on this ego defensive role.

Status anxiety – 'My neighbour has a better car than me'

Excessive materialism, buying a big house in the 'right' area, mixing with the 'right' people, keeping up with the 'Joneses' to protect against feelings of low self-esteem are all good examples.

Marketing and ego defensive mechanism

There are many examples of new product launches that have taken much longer to reach full market potential because the concept damages consumer attitude value systems. Ready prepared cake mixtures, just needing hot water, were initially rejected because housewives felt they were not conforming to cultural norms (she was supposed to make and bake herself) expected as a wife and mother. Marketers overcame the problem by asking the housewife to 'add an egg'. Values were restored and the product sold. Similar problems where encountered with the use of microwave ovens, fridge freezers, ready prepared meals and instant coffee.

6.5 Marketing example — Automatic washing machines

Up until the beginning of the 1960s washday (usually Monday) for the average mother took all day. Using a boiler, electric wringer washing machine or a twin-tub (washer one side, spin-dryer the other side) the family washing was started early in the morning and finished late in the evening. When Hoover introduced the fully automatic Hoover Keymatic in 1963 it was expected to storm the market. Unfortunately this did not happen as quickly as expected, it took many years longer. The idea of not having to be there, leaving the automatic washing machine alone to get on with the washing threatened the housewife's concept of herself as a good mother, wife and home maker. A similar thing happened with the introduction of ready prepared meals and instant coffee.

Knowledge function – through knowledge and understanding

People also develop beliefs and attitudes by gaining knowledge about the world around them through experience and reason. In this way individuals obtain order, structure and a meaning to their lives, building a frame of reference for understanding and adapting to everyday events. The attitudes adopted, however, will not necessarily reflect reality because perception about things will most often vary from individual to individual, between male and female, young and old, from region to region and from country to country. We only have to take an issue like the Iraq war to see how politicians and commentators disagree about the information and the facts of the matter.

Marketing and attitude through knowledge

Although consumers buy predominately for emotional reasons, there is no doubt that the search for information and the reasoning process can still play a large part depending on the product or service under scrutiny. Potential customers will want practical, as well as emotional information on such things as features, quality, content, price, variations available, after sales service and so on. This information will then be examined and evaluated in the customer's mind, beliefs developed and, along with emotional input, positive, negative or neutral attitudes will gradually take root.

> **Key point** Although reasons are identified here under four distinct categories, it should be remembered that there will also be a fuzzy line between all of the reasons for attitude adoption discussed above with one area impinging on another.

Attitude formation will vary from person to person

The strength, importance and role played by the attitude functions discussed above would vary between individuals depending on personal characteristics and situation. For example somebody with low self-esteem might want constant praise and so adopt an 'ego-defensive' approach to attitude, while another person might seek constant material reward and so adopt a 'utilitarian' approach to attitude formation.

Attitudes and perception

Perception (discussed in Chapter 3) also has an affect on attitude formation. In 1954 Allport and Postman undertook a study to show that people would change how they perceive and interpret the world so as to maintain belief consistency and avoid internal conflict (Allport 1954). Subjects were asked to describe a picture that showed a white man arguing with a black man. The white man had an open razor in his hand. As the story was passed from one to another the details changed. Those who were prejudiced against blacks changed the details so that it was the black person who held the razor.

An interesting TV investigation into the reliability of eyewitness reports produced similar results. An actor in a shopping precinct carried out a mugging in broad daylight. He was white, middle-aged, reasonably well-dressed and wearing glasses and was clearly not a stereotypical mugger. In the eyewitness reports, everybody described him as a teenager or in his early twenties, rough looking and scruffily dressed. Many described him as black. No one mentioned the glasses.

> **Key point** Believing is seeing. Some people would change perception and their interpretation of the world rather than change beliefs.

Attitude and stereotyping

Everybody has attitudes about others in society and for the most part it's a normal, shorthand, way of understanding the world. We expect police, teachers, parents, young adults, children, shopkeepers, pop stars, politicians and civil servants etc., to act in particular ways and it would be disconcerting if they acted differently. Stereotypical attitudes held, however, can be weak to strong, right or wrong and positive or negative. The danger comes about when the attitude is strong, negative and wrong and is a cover for hiding personal insecurities by blaming others for particular ills in the world; for example, emotionally blaming young people for a perceived breakdown in the moral fabric of society and immigrants for high levels of unemployment without any rational investigation.

6.6 Marketing example | Stereotyping in the media

Media stereotypes are inevitable, especially in the advertising, entertainment and news industries, which need as wide an audience as possible to quickly understand information. Stereotypes act like codes that give audiences a quick, common understanding of a person or group of people – usually relating to their class, ethnicity or race, gender, sexual orientation, social role or occupation. Examples of stereotyping across all the following groups can be found in the media somewhere or other: ethnic and visible minorities, girls and women, boys, men and masculinity, gay and lesbians, whiteness and white privilege, older men and women, the disabled and so on (thanks to Media Awareness Network).

Questions

1 Discuss stereotyping. Give examples from personal experience.

2 How might marketing and advertising make use of stereotypical images?

Attitude change

There is no doubt that the older people get the more fixed in their ways they become and the more difficult it is for individuals to change their minds over strongly held views. Attitude change is more likely to happen if it has been adopted because of a knowledge or utilitarian function than a value-expressive or ego-protective function. Both knowledge and utilitarian functions are open to rational examination especially as individuals get older, travel more and interact with other people. For example a belief that all immigrants are in the country illegally, that all French people are unfriendly and eat frog's legs or that all dissenters are terrorists can be dispelled through travel, rational discussion and introspection. This is a problem, however, if these kinds of ideas are central to a person's value system and ego. In this case social and cultural upbringing and/or psychological wellbeing would prevent attitude change, especially if there was very little attempt at searching out relevant information and taking part in any serious discussion. In fact some people will refuse to change an attitude and would rather alter perception to avoid having to make this adjustment.

6.1 General example | Travel

Research from many sources suggests that over 80 per cent of adult Americans do not have a passport and have never travelled outside the US. The same numbers seem to have little or no idea where countries such as Germany, Spain, Japan, Iraq or Australia are in the world.

6.7 Marketing example — Discrepancy between consumer intention and reality

It's well known that customers overstate their intentions to purchase in marketing research focus groups and during simple concept testing. Generally, customer purchase intentions identified in research range from 30 per cent to 50 per cent. However, in the marketplace, only 5 per cent to 10 per cent actually make a purchase. Similarly research on TV advertisements appears to demonstrate the same thing, although there are suggestions that the questions asked could be more subtle so as to get better results. Other research has shown that a large majority of consumers say that they would not buy cosmetic products tested on animals while a majority never read the product labels to find out if this is the case.

Questions

1 Discuss the problems that could arise from the results of this kind of research.

2 Why do you think that consumers have a habit of saying one thing while doing another?

Ways of changing attitude

Attitude change can be less or more difficult according to the strength of the belief, its importance to the believer and the amount of time the attitude has been entrenched into a person's psyche. There is the need sometimes for attitude change both because of changes in society and changes in the marketplace.

Attitude change and society

There have been an enormous amount of changes in society over the last 50 years that have caused people to evaluate, adapt and change attitudes about the way that they think on a whole range of issues from marriage, eating and drinking to communications and leisure. In the UK 50 years ago over 95 per cent of all couples would not have contemplated living together before marriage, now over 75 per cent say they would live together before marriage. Fifty years ago most adults smoked and it was a central part of everyone's life, smoking in the cinema, the theatre, on public transport and at work. Now the figure is down to less then 25 per cent. Self-service supermarkets and frozen food were still to come and the nearest thing to a ready meal was going down the fish and chip shop. Much of this attitude change has happened gradually while other changes, especially over the last ten or fifteen years, have taken place much, much quicker. All this has been easier for younger people than for the old.

6.8 Marketing example — Social marketing

The UK government spends millions of pounds a year on social marketing and trying to change peoples' attitudes on health and anti-social behaviour activity. This includes advice on such things as pension provision, AIDS, sensible drinking and drink driving, healthy eating, and health and fitness. In 1987 in the UK, a leaflet about AIDS was delivered to every household, and the government also launched a major advertising campaign with the slogan 'AIDS: Don't Die of Ignorance'. In the summer of 2004 a £3 million ad campaign was set up to promote sensible drinking and warn people of the dangers of binge drinking. The theme of the campaign was to tell young people that 'it's not cool to get drunk'. A £4 m advertising campaign showing fat oozing out of a smoker's artery is one of the British Heart Foundation's most successful, it has said. The adverts, which appeared on television, billboards, and on pub beer mats, showed fat dripping out of cigarettes and arteries in a bid to force smokers to link cigarettes with the image of fat in their arteries.

Questions

1 Examine the part that social marketing plays in trying to change public attitudes.

2 Do you think that public money should be spent in this way?

Social marketing is marketing aimed at altering attitude
Source: Creative Club/Oxfam

Attitude change, consumers and markets

Marketing has played an enormous part in the process of changing people's attitudes both as a leading player and as a mirror that follows and reflects change as it happens. It has been a leading player in educating and changing people's attitudes across a wide range of markets and products. This includes attitude change to things like computers, the Internet and mobile phones as well as lifestyle changes with regard to the family, travel, holidays, retail 24-hour shopping and so on.

6.2 General example **Rogers innovation adoption curve**

The innovation adoption curve now used by marketers measures the length of time that it takes for attitude change to happen across the whole of society. This is discussed in more detail in Chapter 9.

Communications, influencing and changing attitudes

'I do not regard advertising as entertainment or an art form, but as a medium of information.' DAVID OGILVY, Advertising guru (1985)

Marketing communications are an essential part of influencing, building and maintaining positive consumer attitudes towards a company's product and service brands. To this end marketers bombard target segments 24 hours a day, seven days a week in an attempt to persuade customers to buy new products, change from one brand to another, use more of a product or use one retailer rather than another. Messages will come via TV, newspapers, magazines, roadside billboards, at airports and train stations, on transport, radio and the Internet. It will also come from personal communications of some kind. This might be by word-of-mouth (friends, acquaintances, family etc.) or by a sales person in the retail outlet, at an exhibition or by direct form of contact in the home.

Marketing communication to influence attitude

Promotional communication messages will emanate from manufacturers, e.g. Kellogg's, Mars, Toyota, retailers, e.g. Asda, B&Q, Dixon's, and through marketing and advertising agencies, e.g. Bartle, Bogle and Hegarty, Young and Rubicam, Olgivy and Mather. The persuasive task that they have will depend on the level of knowledge and loyalty that already exists among each target market. If an advertising agency is addressing a loyal target audience, for example for Persil, the persuasive objective will be one of reinforcing existing attitudes towards the product. If, however, the objective is to persuade consumer attitude brand change, for example from Bold (detergent and owned by Procter & Gamble) to Persil (owned by Unilever) then the task will be much harder.

Simple and complex behavioural approaches to communications

How customers behave in response to promotional campaigns developed by advertisers has been the subject of much research and two of the most important are discussed here under the concept of a simple and complex approach.

A simple approach to consumer communications The simple or classical approach to marketing communications identifies it as a linear, step-by-step hierarchical process. This can best be shown by the use of the classical hierarchical model known as **AIDA**. This stands for awareness (or attention), interest, desire and action (shown in Figure 6.7). There are many variations of this model but what it says in essence is that the task of the advertiser is to first initiate *awareness* (get the consumers attention) so that the audience is at least prepared to listen to the benefit message, then deliver the message in such a way that *interest* is created. This is then followed up by more targeted information that builds on this interest so as to inculcate *desire*. Finally the consumer is persuaded into *action* (going to the shop to purchase) by benefit offerings that seem too good to be ignored.

Complex approach to communications The communication process, however, can be seen as much more complex. The process identified under the simple approach can still be used but there is a difference. With the theory of a more complex approach to attitude building, consumer reaction is much less defined and harder to influence. At each stage of the process the effect might vary and the target audience react differently. For example at the awareness stage there could be different levels of individual awareness, one person might have paid less attention than another and so not be ready move on to the next interest stage. Interest may have been created but then pushed to the back of the mind of different sections of the audience as other factors impinge and become more important. A desire to purchase may have been inculcated but lack of opportunity and time erodes.

Action may be aborted as perhaps money problems arise or other choices present themselves. Add to this the possibility that consumers might, at any stage, regress to an earlier stage as memories, desires and intents fade in the light of new problems, and we can see how monumental is the task to influence attitude. The overriding consideration before, during and after expensive promotional campaigns is the need for research that will constantly inform on the consumer's state of mind.

Figure 6.7

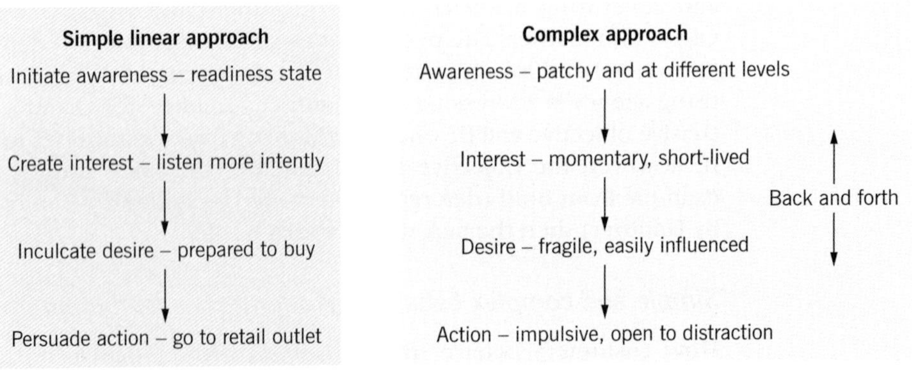

Communications hierarchy of effects models – simple and complex affects models

Factors in the communication process that influence attitude

Organisations that want to influence beliefs in some way should be aware of the factors that will influence consumer attitude. The following areas all affect the process.

a The message sender – source credibility and attractiveness It's important that the communicator (supplier, manufacturer or retailer) is respected and trusted by the end customer (the receiver). This is why it is so important for companies to retain the trust of its customers. In the main, people will be reluctant to buy products and services from companies they do not like. Often **celebrity endorsement** will be used to market an organisation and its products. In this way it is hoped that all the characteristics that the customer likes about the celebrity will then be associated with the company.

6.9 Marketing example — Celebrity endorsement

Organisations will use well-liked celebrities to promote their products knowing that this will convince customers and reinforce or change attitudes. After much research, British supermarket Sainsbury's used the young 'cool' chef Jamie Oliver to talk about their company knowing that he was admired by most of their core customers. Now Sainsbury's says he's responsible for a fifth of its profits. There have been celebrity failures however including Vinnie Jones promoting Barcardi Breezer (he was prosecuted for attacking another passenger on a plane flight and dropped), John Cleese and Sainsbury's (sales actually fell) and Billy Connolly and the National Lottery change to Lotto. All examples of communications that went wrong because they where a 'poor fit for the brand' in some way or another.

Key point The consumer must trust and respect the communicator's image, knowledge and expertise in the relevant area if the message is to be believed.

b Encoding and the message There should be a clear understanding of the difficulty of the task involved and this should reflect in the type of message that needs to be sent. Strong, negative attitude change will be a harder communication task than reinforcing already held positive attitudes among the target audience. One of the biggest problems for an ad agency is to get their message seen and understood by the target audience despite the thousands of other messages operating at the same time. To do so it must construct messages that will be clearly understood by the particular target segment with a message offering the relevant benefits. Get this wrong and time and money will be wasted and sales lost. Message methods will include rational and emotional appeal using repetition, words and/or pictures, novelty, colour, music, sex, humour, fear and nostalgia.

The arguments used might be one or two-sided depending on the sophistication of the target audience. Comparison with competitor products might also be used.

c The medium The message medium selected (face-to-face, TV, the press, radio, outdoors, direct response, the Internet etc.) must reflect the audience, listener or readership customer profile. For example, it's axiomatic that adverts placed in a magazine not read by the target market will be wasted. Normally, if the consumer likes an ad, the more likely they are to purchase the advertised brand. For a new product/brand, an ad has a stronger impact on brand attitude and purchase intention.

d Decoding If the customer has been researched and clearly understood, the message constructed in an appropriate manner and the correct medium selected, then there is every chance the message will be received and understood. If not, failure will follow.

e Receiver (customer and consumer) The receiver of the message might be face-to-face or on the other side of the world to the customer and there will always be the possibility of message distortion. Hopefully the customer will receive, understand and be prepared to act on the message received. Unfortunately this is not always the case and the following factors can all play a part in confounding the customer's ability to adequately perceive the message.

- Distraction may cause the viewer or listener to be otherwise occupied or to leave the room when the ad comes on, e.g. make a cup of tea, go to the toilet.
- It's a well-researched phenomenon that a person's emotional state, tiredness, anxiety, excitement and so on, can cause messages to be poorly digested or ignored.
- The message may be misinterpreted or ambiguous and confusing and so not be understood.
- Levels of literacy and education can be over- or underestimated thus negating messages.

f Barriers and interference to communications A message travelling through a communication channel (see Figure 6.8) will be subject to the influences of many different factors. Such interference and distortion is often referred to as *noise* or *clutter*. Some of these distorting affects have been identified above but probably the biggest problem of all is the presence of thousands of competitors' messages full of pictures, actions, colour, sounds, smells, all vying for customer attention, all attempting to gain that one moment of attention during which product and brand information can be imparted.

g Feedback, monitoring and control Feedback is crucial to any process where objectives need to be achieved and this is never more so than in the communications process. The sender must check in some way to see if the message has been received and understood in the manner intended. If this is not the case then monitoring, feedback and control mechanisms should allow misinterpretations to be corrected. In a face-to-face situation this is not too much of a problem for the skilled salesperson as linguistic, body and facial cues can be continuously read during the benefit presentation so as to identify any misunderstanding or concerns on the part of the customer, which then can be rectified as they happen. With other media such as TV, the press and radio, monitoring and feedback in this way is more difficult and some of the sophisticated research methods discussed in Chapter 2 will have to be used.

> **Key point** Good, well-researched and implemented communications are at the heart of all successful advertising campaigns.

Figure 6.8

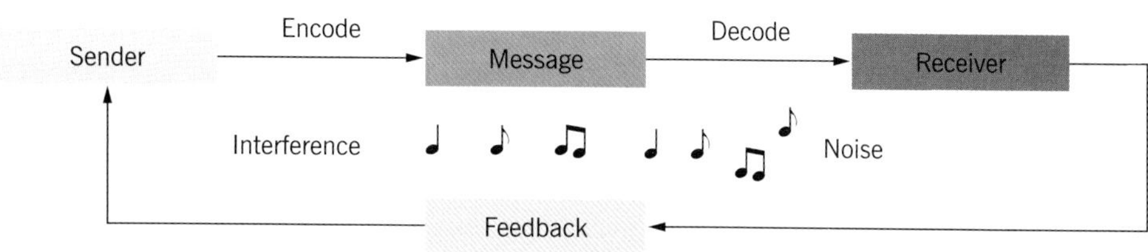

The basic communications model

Table 6.1 **Attitude change can come about by the following methods**

- Personal experiences.
- Watching and talking to others such as family, friends and acquaintances.
- Education, reading and introspection.
- Travel and observation.
- The media – TV, press, radio, outdoor advertising, merchandising and leaflets.
- Government sources.

High and low involvement in communications

It has been argued (Petty and Cacioppo, Elaboration Likelihood Model, 1986) that there are two routes of communication based on high or low levels of consumer commitment.

Central route – high involvement

The first level, the central route, assumes that the consumer has a high motivation and so high involvement in processing the communication message. For example if it's a premium product, a highly priced product or a product of great need or interest, the customer will spend time watching, listening, reading analysing and digesting the message content so that informed choices can be made.

Peripheral route – low involvement

The second, the peripheral route, involves low-involvement purchases and here the persuasion is affected more by the overall image and excitement created by the communication methods used rather than by the message itself. For example, Gap (US fashion clothes company) adverts contain images, music, and media that are cutting edge and in the forefront of young people's thinking. Its origins are in pop culture and its message is put across by cult celebrities. It uses little explicit messaging, only 'Gap' and, 'Denim' coming up at the very end. By association, however, it puts over the implicit message that 'denim' and 'Gap' are 'cool'.

6.10 Marketing example Comparative advertising

The jury is still out on the benefits or otherwise of comparative advertising or 'knocking copy', comparing a brand with the brand of a competitor. It can work where the comparison is based purely on price. However, research shows that, in many cases, every time the competitor's name is mentioned it could mean free exposure for them. This is because the target audience will spend little time examining the information and might only take in the name of the competitor. They might also put it down to competitor propaganda and exaggeration if they do happen to realise what's happening.

Attitude conflict

There are times when individuals are faced with beliefs and attitudes that have the ability to be in conflict with one another. For example, a restaurant used regularly has high status value but, at times, elements of the food have started to be of a lower quality than expected. This can cause problems as the consumer still wants to use the restaurant but has concerns about the food. In these kinds of circumstances uncomfortable feelings are caused by the mental conflict. Either the consumer must stop going to the restaurant (and forgo status) or they must make excuses or deny the meal deterioration (forgo quality). Decisions made will depend on the competing strength of the two options. Some theoretical approaches to this problem are discussed below.

Cognitive consistency – their need for harmony between attitudes

Everybody develops beliefs, attitudes and stereotypes about relationships, happenings and things that they come into contact with everyday. They are the bedrock upon which people build an understanding of themselves and the society that surrounds them. Very rarely, however do they question why and how this process takes place. We take for granted that there are some foods we dislike and were forced to eat as a child. That some music turns us on while other music we find appalling, that one person hates American policy around the world while another person believes that they can do no wrong. What most people fail to appreciate, because they've never given it much thought, is that the beliefs, opinions and attitudes that we use to make sense of reality are arrived at in a highly structured manner through the concept of 'cognitive consistency'. The following theories are discussed under the umbrella of cognitive consistency, and help to explain how humans attempt to order their world in an effort to obtain rationality and predictability in their lives.

The search for consistency

'Our attitude toward life determines life's attitude towards us.' ANON

Mental conflict will arise when there is an attempt to hold attitudes that are inconsistent or unstable. For example some Christians in the UK cannot entertain the ideas of gay bishops and same sex marriages, a ruthless business entrepreneur may find it difficult to be kind and compassionate and a vegetarian might have problems with hunting animals. (Many of the mental defence mechanisms used, denial, projection, rationalisation etc., were discussed in the preceding chapter on motivation.) We therefore tend to adopt attitudes that fit our existing mental schemata or patterns of thought developed through experience and knowledge attainment. For example somebody with left-wing political views might believe in extensive government social welfare, free hospital treatment and education and tight control of businesses. Conversely someone with right-wing beliefs will probably believe the opposite: little welfare, as this encourages laziness, paid for health and education, perhaps through insurance of some kind, and as little control as possible on businesses. We would not expect fitness extremists to eat cream buns, Church ministers to lead a promiscuous life, or students to read the Readers Digest magazine.

6.11 Marketing example **Consistency theory**

Marketers must remember that attitudes are not formed in a vacuum, they are dependent and must be consistent with already held beliefs about products and services. If consumers liked Mars Bars then it made sense that, as a similar product, they would go for Mars ice cream. On the other hand because customers liked and used BIC disposal razors it didn't follow that they would buy BIC disposal perfume. Perfume is a totally different product to a disposable razor, being at the premium end of the market. The launch was a failure.

Cognitive dissonance – inconsistency between held attitudes

According to Festinger's (1957) theory of cognitive dissonance (disharmony in thinking) there seems to be a need for individuals to seek consistency between their beliefs, opinions and attitudes. For example, it's mentally uncomfortable for smokers to believe on the one hand that smoking is pleasurable and on the other hand that it will kill you or for drivers of large SUVs (sports utility vehicles) that it gives status on the one hand and on the other hand it contributes to global warming. When this inconsistency between attitude and behaviour (cognitive dissonance) happens, there is an uncomfortable negative mental state that has to be eliminated. In most cases it seems that attitude will change to accommodate behaviour, although the relative strength of each would have an effect. So the smoker and the SUV driver will convince themselves that either the evidence is inadequate or those with vestige interests were distorting the picture for their own ends.

6.12 Marketing example — Advertising and cognitive dissonance

Government social marketing advertising has had limited success over the years in attempting to change the behaviour of young people. It ran a campaign instilling the dangers of AIDS in the late 1980s using an image of a cemetery and tombstones to try to frighten young people into using protection. It didn't really work, as the target audience continued to have sexual relations while convincing themselves that the government was overreacting and that AIDS could never affect them. They tried the same thing with smoking but toned down the use of the fear factor emphasising the less threatening, but nevertheless important, idea of sexual unattractiveness that comes about through smoking.

Question

1 Evaluate the use of emotional advertising in trying to change behaviour. Give examples and explain the pros and cons.

Balance theory – looking for consistency between attitudes

Heider's **balance theory** (1958) states that when uncomfortable conflicting views arise between two or more people they seek to reduce these tensions by either changing their own mind or trying to persuade others to change their mind. In this way mental balance and harmony can be restored to the relationship. There is also evidence to show that we are attracted to people who have the same or similar views to ourselves or we readjust our views to achieve the same outcome.

6.13 Marketing example — Consumer behaviour and balance theory

Marketers have to work hard to build balanced consistency between its products and consumer held beliefs and values. The task is to resolve any mental imbalance among consumers if and when this arises. For example companies can take advantage of the consumer's need for cognitive consistency by sponsoring events that have value for its target market, e.g. Manchester United, a Neil Diamond concert tour, horse of the year show, the Royal Ballet and so on. This enables the company to become associated in the minds of the consumer in a positive way, with the values particular events represent. If the target consumers have neutral or negative beliefs about a company, e.g. disliking Budweiser, Stella or Fosters, sponsorship by one of these companies of a favoured football team, e.g. Manchester

United, will initially cause an imbalance in the consumers mind, i.e. dislike of Fosters and liking Manchester United. If the strength of feeling about United is strong enough, Fosters will be liked because of pleasant associations and mental tension will be resolved, and balance restored. This mechanism is very similar to classical conditioning, a popular approach that is widely used in marketing.

Question

1 Discuss the use of sponsorship in entertainment and social events. Give examples and explain why failure and success might happen.

Figure 6.9

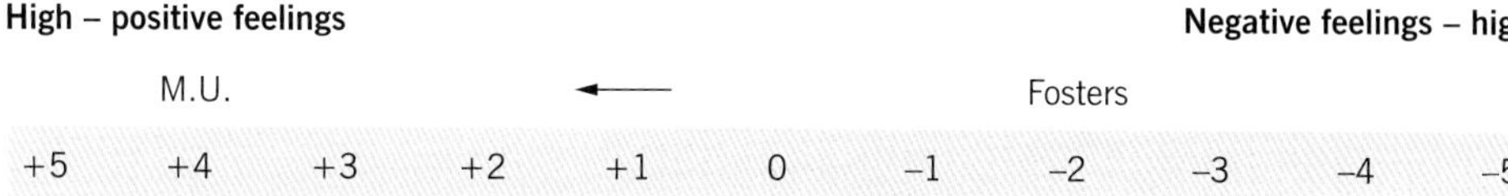

Feelings for Fosters will be transferred into positive feelings and balance is restored

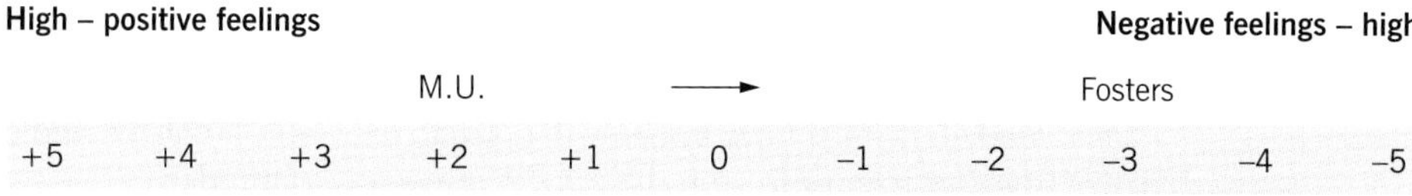

Feelings for M.U. are pulled from positive to negative and balance is again restored

Balance theory – the pull of weak and strong feelings. Osgood' theory of congruity (Osgood and Tannenaven 1955) states that the strength of opposing attitudes will determine the direction of attitude change. In the first example (in Figure 6.9) the stronger positive attitude (Manchester United) causes the weaker negative attitude (Fosters) to be changed to positive so that balanced harmony is restored. In the second example, the opposite is the case as the weaker positive feeling (Manchester United) is changed to the stronger negative feeling (Fosters) and mental balance is restored.

Key point Attitudes that reflect deeply held values or beliefs are less likely to change than ones that are less deeply held.

Justification principle – justify feelings and attitudes held

It has been argued that people can feel extremely uncomfortable with conflicting or negative feelings. This will cause them to adjust their attitude and justify the reasons for their behaviour so that it appears to make sense and be more positive (Aronson and Mills 1959). This is known as the **justification principle**. Some of the justification approaches are identified below.

Approval justification

Everybody seems at times to have the need to find approval in some way from other people (as well as self-approval) to justify the attitudes that they hold. It takes a very strong and convinced individual to hold on to views when confronted with views that are opposite. Many religious zealots will obsessively try to persuade others, driven by the feeling that the more members they convert the more the truth and certainty of the cause. On the other hand, a person might change attitudes to fit the general attitudes of a group where membership is valued. A couple selling-up and moving to Spain and finding the situation more difficult than they imagined might constantly tell others how wonderful the chosen move has been. In this way they seek to reinforce the decision made. They will often move from one reason to another to assuage doubts and dissonance only giving up when the problems seem insurmountable.

6.14 Marketing example — Post-purchase dissonance

Identified earlier post-purchase dissonance is the doubts that consumers sometimes feel after purchase. A woman buys a pair of shoes that she is sure she likes. Unfortunately her friends and family either ignore the purchase or show dislike. The woman is now unhappy, changes her view and takes the shoe back to the shop for a refund. There is a bigger problem with a purchase of a higher value. Buying a house, a pension plan or a car is usually a worrying process and doubts will creep in, especially if friends or family question the purchase. Marketers must have systems in place to deal with problems and complaints immediately they arise so as to stop the growth of negative attitudes.

Question

1 Identify in what ways organisations might counter the problems associated with post-purchase dissonance.

Minimal justification principle (MJP)

According to the MJP, dissonance would set in if the justification for performing a task of some kind appears to be minimal and silly. For example, it would be difficult to rationally justify working in a charity shop all day Saturday for only £5 saying that money (an extrinsic reward) was the reason for the work. Discomfort brought on by this dissonance would cause people to justify the work by convincing themselves that they wanted to work for charity because of compassionate feelings (intrinsic reasons). If the pay was £100 for the day's work, however, there would be no dissonance and money (extrinsic reason) could justifiably be given as the reason.

Over-justification effect

Over-justification occurs where attitude and behaviour are attributed more to extrinsic reward, such as money, or intrinsic reason, such as value in the work, depending on the situation. For example a footballer earning tens of thousands of pounds a week might have little or no loyalty to the club and pride in his work feeling that he played for extrinsic reasons. Conversely a footballer in the lowest level of the league, earning very little, might convince himself and others that he was only in football for the love of football and the club and the money were unimportant.

> **Key point** Justification principles cause us to reason in terms or intrinsic or extrinsic causes depending on the situation.

Marketing, consumer behaviour and justification

Marketers must be aware that consumers will often adjust and justify their behaviour to achieve cognitive balance. If a store such as Debenhams constantly has price cutting sales, the consumer might begin to justify visits only according to price (extrinsic reward) rather than the ambience of the store (intrinsic reward). This could well cause the store to be only used when there were special cut-price offers. In many instances smaller rewards that make the customer feel good, such as invitations and special offers, will gain more loyalty.

6.3 General example **Justification effect**

In 1976 Greene, Sternberg and Lepper played mathematical games with a group of schoolchildren, which the children seemed to enjoy. After a while, they started giving rewards for success. When they took away the rewards, the children quickly gave up playing the games. The explanation was that the children had decided that they were playing for the reward, not for the fun. Similarly observers were asked to look at two groups of carpenters, and give reasons that might motivate work behaviour. They were told that the first group was paid a very low amount of money while the second group was paid a large amount of money. Many of the observers made the assumption that first group worked for the love of the job and the second group for the money.

Self-perception theory

▶ **Self-perception theory** (Zanna and Cooper 1974) states that people make assumptions about their attitudes according to the behavioural outcomes. For example a person unexpectedly made redundant from a job will persuade himself or herself that it was the best possible thing that could have happened to them even though they didn't want to go in the first place. They now play the role of a fulfilled, active, retired individual. A supporter might have no feelings towards Ipswich Town football club. His son, a great supporter persuades him to go along. Caught up in the excitement and surrounded by die-hard fans he now takes on the same attitude as his son and is now a firm Ipswich Town supporter. In the same way a consumer, having spent a great deal of money on a holiday or a visit to the theatre and boasted to others, may convince themselves it was good even though there were initial feelings of doubt.

> **Key point** With self-perception theory, attitudes are adopted that support/justify behavioural outcomes.

Social judgement theory

Social judgement theory (Sherif and Hovland 1961) works on the premise that throughout their lives people construct a cognitive map of the world. This might be a simple or complex structure depending on intellectual capability and it will hold the sum total of all beliefs and attitudes held. Perceptual messages are then accepted, rejected or remain non-committed according to how they fit into this cognitive mind map or schemata. For example, if a person holds so-called right- or left-wing views about the world, he or she will accept or reject according to this principle. This will affect his or her views on such things as stem-cell research, abortion, euthanasia, gay marriages, environmental issues and so on.

Social judgement theory and consumer behaviour

Our cognitive schemata will affect our attitude to the different products and services that we might purchase. These include such things as: transport, cars and high or low petrol consumption, using a bicycle or public transport; food, fast foods, organic, health foods; leisure, watching or playing sports; holidays, sun worship or adventure and so on.

> **Key point** According to social judgement theory, attitudes adopted fit into existing mental schemata.

Measuring attitude

'Take the attitude of a student; never be too big to ask questions, never know too much to learn something new.' ANON

To be able to measure the strength, depth and longevity of an attitude is important to understanding human and consumer behaviour. We have shown throughout this chapter how difficult this can be. Some of the **attitude measurement methods** are discussed here.

> **Key point** We can ask people directly or indirectly about beliefs and feelings or observe behaviour and make assumptions in the difficult process of trying to understand and measure strength, depth and longevity of attitudes held.

The Likert, importance and satisfactory scales

The **Likert Scale** (Likert 1932; Anastasi 1982) presents a set of attitude statements. Subjects are asked to express agreement or disagreement on a five-point scale. Each degree of agreement is given a numerical value from one to five. Thus a total numerical value can be calculated from all the responses. It's a method that allows respondents to give answers that relate to positive and negative attitude strengths. The answers can then be coded and used in a quantitative manner.

The importance and satisfactory scale are similar to the Likert scale and examples are outlined below.

Figure 6.10

For each of the statements below, please indicate the extent of your agreement or disagreement by placing a tick in the appropriate box

1. Carrefour supermarket offers good value

Strongly agree	Agree	Neither agree nor disagree	Disagree	Strongly agree

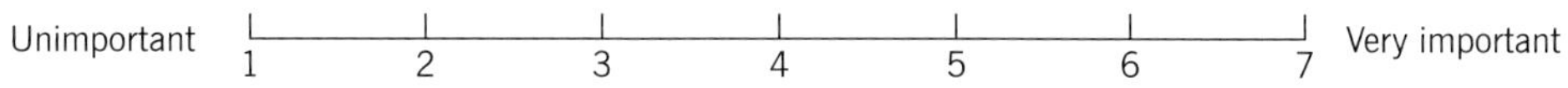

2. The supermarket offers a good choice of products

Strongly agree	Agree	Neither agree nor disagree	Disagree	Strongly agree

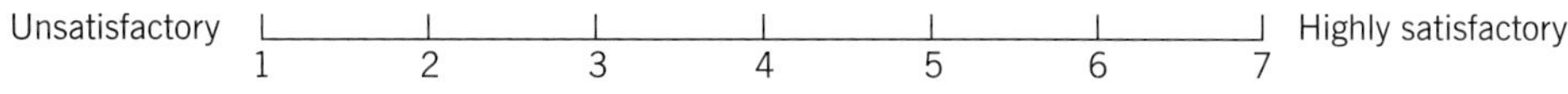

An example of the Likert agreement level scale

Figure 6.11

On a scale of 1 to 7, with 1 being very unimportant and 7 very important, how important would you consider car parking in a supermarket?

Unimportant 1 2 3 4 5 6 7 Very important

An example of the importance scale

Figure 6.12

On a scale of 1 to 7, with 1 being highly unsatisfactory and 7 highly satisfactory, where would you put the overall service of HSBC bank?

Unsatisfactory 1 2 3 4 5 6 7 Highly satisfactory

An example of the satisfaction scale

Semantic differential

'The meaning of a word is its use in the language.' WITTGENSTEIN

The **semantic differential** attitude measurement (Osgood and Tannenaven 1955) asks respondents to mark, with a cross, along a horizontal scale how they feel about descriptive opposites. Using as an example a group of hotels, the customer is asked to fill in a survey question across the following set of opposites; old-fashioned or modern; welcoming or unwelcoming; high price or low price; easy to get to or hard to get to; good service or bad service. All the crosses can be joined up revealing a company profile. This is shown in Figure 6.13.

The customer can be asked to go through the same process by looking at the nearest competitor to the initiating hotel group. Comparisons can then be made with the competitor's profile. In this way improvements can be carried out if the company is found to be lacking in any important customer service areas.

Figure 6.13

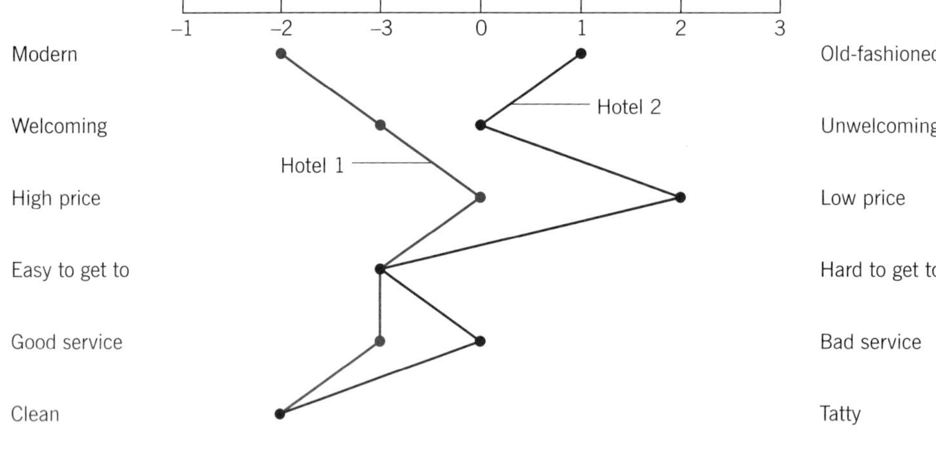

Semantic differential – how it might be used for assessing customer reaction to a retail store

Multi-attribute attitude models

The problem with the methods discussed above is that they fail to take into account mental complexities and the relative strengths and weaknesses of the beliefs and feelings that go to make up an individual's attitudes towards issues, companies, products, services and brands. 'Conjoined analysis' tries to weigh up the relative strengths and values that the consumer might hold towards a particular brand. For example the relationships between price, quality, consistence, kudos and so on. Multi-attribute models try to do the same thing with attitude. Fishbein's Multi-attribute Model (Ajzen and Fishbein 1980) is an example. It takes an individual's beliefs and feelings about a particular attitude object or issue that are then individually weighted and summed to yield an index of overall affect or attitude.

Example of a multi-attribute model

If we take for example the purchase of a new fitted kitchen, retail research should indicate the relative importance of the various attributes in the mind of the consumer. An example is given in Figure 6.14. The attribute scores will vary according to different buyer segments. The relative importance of the various attributes is identified on the left hand side. The important competitor scores are then shown against the attribute scores. The final results are then weighted.

The use of computers

If the research analysis is to be complex, one of the many available computer research software programs can be used to assist in the process. All questions are

Figure 6.14 **The scores for the different companies in the market are tabulated from left to right**

Fitted kitchens	Companies	1	2	3	4	5
Attributes	Importance Rating by customer out of 10					
Quality	7	6	8	9	6	3
Design	10	7	9	3	4	2
Customisation	6	5	3	6	2	2
Choice	9	8	5	8	3	4
Brand	8	7	5	9	7	2
Price	4	3	6	4	8	9
Availability	5	5	3	3	7	6
Fitting	3	8	8	6	5	5
Service	2	8	8	7	6	6
Delivery	1	8	8	8	8	8

Higher score signifies better standing. The task of the marketing and communications managers is to concentrate building on areas of strength and attempting to minimise and rectify areas of weakness

Multi-attribute model

6.4 General example — Having a positive mental attitude (PMA)

There seems to be little doubt that having a positive attitude to life contributes hugely to achieving happiness and building success. It's important in staff training and development and the following exercise is an example of the areas of importance. The following questions are asked on a scale of 1 to 10, 10 being a high positive attitude (like) and 1 being a low positive attitude (dislike). In terms of like and dislike how do you feel about the following? Yourself – other people – life – work – customers – the future.

coded in the questionnaire design. When the collection is complete the coded replies are put into the computer program. The program will then allow storage and all manner of complex cross-referencing to be done and comparisons to be made using the various coded pieces of information in many different ways.

Summary

In this chapter we looked at the following areas:

- Beliefs; origins of beliefs, strong and weak beliefs – components of an attitude; beliefs, emotions and behaviour.
- Consumer attitude and hierarchy of affects model; the interaction between low involvement, high involvement and emotional involvement.
- Attitude strength and core and non-core values – positive and negative attitudes; source of attitude, attitude cluster.
- Attitude function; utilitarian, value-expressive, ego defensive function and knowledge.
- Attitude, perception, stereotyping and change – marketing communication and attitude change.
- Cognitive consistency and theories; cognitive dissonance; balance theory; justification theory: social judgement theory; behaviour and attitude.
- Several attitude measuring models were identified.

Questions

1. Identify and examine the factors that go to make up a person's attitude. Evaluate the importance of the different elements and give live examples of how it might operate in consumer markets.
2. Discuss the way that beliefs, emotions and behaviour interact and operate in consumer decision making covering high involvement, low involvement and emotional involvement purchasing. Give examples using real products.
3. Our attitudes have varying levels of power to influence the ways that we behave. Discuss why this might be and how this power is different between people and how it changes as we go through the family life cycle from a toddler through to old age.
4. Examine the four reasons why people adopt an attitude to things and issues in the world, talked about in the chapter. These are utilitarian, value-expressive, ego defensive, knowledge.
5. Identify the role that an understanding of attitude and attitude development plays in the marketing concept of segmentation. Give live examples how marketers can segment markets according to attitudes adopted.
6. Discuss the need that we all seem to have for cognitive consistency and what might be the methods that are used to defend against dissonance and mental conflict. Identify and evaluate some of the theories behind this phenomena.
7. We all seem to have the need to justify why we behave in the way that we do. Justifications used can be realistic, unrealistic, rational and emotional. Identify methods used, discuss why this need is there and show how it is important in understanding consumer behaviour.
8. How might attitude affect perception and behaviour both at the individual and group level? Conversely how might behaviour affect perception and attitude and what is the role of emotion in the process?

9 Discuss the reason why attitudes seem to cluster into attitude groups that have a connection in some way or another. For example somebody that believes in hunting might also believe in the right to abortion, the importance of stem cell research, shorter prison sentences and so on. How is this occurrence used in marketing and understanding consumer behaviour?

10 Researchers are desperate to measure the strength and longevity of consumer attitudes. Discuss why this is so and identify and evaluate some of the methods used.

Case study

Case study 1 Positive and negative attitudes

Positive attitude

Most of the money spent on advertising is to build and maintain so called 'brand franchise'. Brand franchise is all the values, both emotional and functional, that customers perceive a brand to have. For example research has shown that a daughter will use Persil soap powder because her mother and her mother's mother have always used it. The feelings (attitude) that she has about the soap powder is that it could be trusted to look after the family wash and produce a whiteness second to none. In this way she was acting out the responsible role of a caring and loving wife and mother. Procter & Gamble, the owners of Persil are the largest advertiser in the fast-moving-consumer-goods market, spending over $5 billion a year around the world.

Negative attitudes

Ten years ago the German car manufacturer VW bought the Skoda car company from the Czech government. At the time, the name of Skoda was a constant joke, an example of everything about a car that was ugly, cheap, underpowered and always breaking down. Everybody thought that the VW management was mad keeping a name with so many negative connotations. Since that time, however, VW have achieved the marketing equivalent of a miracle by changing and reversing consumer attitudes. In a top ten poll conducted in 2004 by *Used Car Buyer Magazine* Skoda had its Octavia in sixth place and its Fabia model in eighth.

Questions

1 Discuss the influence that others have on our own attitude development. Give examples where your own experiences may have altered attitudes adopted from others and held for many years.

2 Identify the problems facing a company like VW when trying to reposition a brand having negative connotations. How might these problems be overcome?

Case study

Case study 2 Attitude and theory of reasoned action

There seems to be general agreement that an attitude has both emotion (affective) and belief components and that attitudes and behaviour should be consistent. In 1980, Ajzen and Fishbein took the argument further by publishing a *theory of reasoned action* which they claimed would improve the ability to predict people's behaviour from attitudes held. According to their theory, individuals made reasoned decisions about their actions and whether or not behaviour was likely to reflect attitude would depend on a combination of factors identified below.

Belief in strength of outcome For example one belief is 'drinking too much alcohol is bad for me'. Another belief might be 'drinking alcohol is fun' or 'drinking alcohol makes me more attractive to the opposite sex'. Each belief is then rated by strength on the likelihood that behaviour will produce the particular outcome, e.g. 'I will be ill', 'It will be fun' and 'I will be attractive to the opposite sex'.

Evaluation of outcome Each belief is then evaluated on how good or bad each might be. The belief strength and evaluation ratings are multiplied together for each belief and summed across beliefs to give a measure of attitude toward the behaviour.

Subjective norm The opinion of significant others are then taken into account. For example what might parents, friends, girl-friend, think about me giving or not giving up alcohol and how bothered would I be about their opinions.

Intention We then ask how likely the person is to engage in the behaviour. This will take into account behavioural influences such as social upbringing, personality and psychographics.

Perceived control In 1985 Schifter and Ajzen in their theory of planned behaviour included an additional variable, that of perceived person control, i.e. some behaviour is easier to control than others. For example if addiction has set there might be little or no perceived control over giving up alcohol.

Speed of access Some attitudes are nearer to the surface of memory than others. According to Fazio *et al.* (1984) and Fazio and Williams (1986) this makes these attitudes more readily accessible and action more likely than it will be with attitudes buried more deeply.

Key point The probability of an attitude affecting behaviour will depend on a weighted combination of the following factors: belief strength × evaluation of outcome × subjective norm × intention × control × speed of access = predictability of outcome.

Questions

1 How feasible are the theories outlined above? Are some parts in the process more important than others? If so which parts?

2 Do you think that consumers approach the purchase of products in the seemingly reasoned way outlined above? Give examples to illustrate your thoughts.

Further reading

Books

Ajzen, I. and M. Fishbein (1980) *Understanding Attitudes and Predicting Social Behavior*, Englewood Cliffs, NJ: Prentice Hall.

Allport, G.M. (1954) *The Nature of Prejudice*, Cambridge, MA: Addison Wesley.

Anastasi, A. (1982) *Psychological Testing*, New York: Macmillan.

Bandura, A. (1986) *Social Foundations of Thought and Action*, Engelwood Cliffs, NJ: Prentice Hall.

Berger, P.L. and T. Luckmann (1967) *The Social Construction of Reality*, Garden City: Doubleday.

Byrne, D. (1971) *The Attraction Paradigm*, New York: Academic Press.

Eagly, A. and S. Chaiken (1993) *The Psychology of Attitudes*, Fort Worth, TX: Harcourt Brace Joranovich.

Festinger, L. (1957) *A Theory of Cognitive Dissonance*, Stanford, CA: Stanford University Press.

Frijda, N. (1986) *The Emotions: Studies in Emotion and Social Interaction*, New York: Cambridge University Press.

Gilbert, T., S.T. Fiske and G. Lindzey (eds) (1998) *The Handbook of Social Psychology*, 4th edn, Vol. 1, New York: McGraw-Hill, pp. 269–322.

Graham, Bird (1986) *William James (The arguments of the philosophers)*, London: Routledge and Kegan Paul.

Hansen, Mark Victor and Allen, Robert G. (2002) *The One Minute Millionaire: The Enlightened Way to Wealth*, New York: Harmony.

Heider, F. (1958) *The Psychology of Interpersonal Relations*, New York: Wiley.

Hewstone, M. (1989) *Causal Attribution: From Cognitive Processes to Cognitive Beliefs*, Oxford: Blackwell.

Likert, R. (1932) *A Technique for the Measurement of Attitudes*, New York: McGraw Hill.

Nicolson, Ian A.M. (2002) *Inventing Personality: Gordon Allport and the Science of Selfhood*, Washington, DC: American Psychological Association (ASA).

Ogilvy, David (1985) *Ogilvy on Advertising*, New York: Vintage.

Sherif, M. and Horland, C.I. (1961) *Social Judgement: Assimilation and Contrasting Affects in Communication and Attitude Change*, New Haven, CT: Yale University Press.

Sherif, M., C. Sherif and R. Nebergall (1965) *Attitude and Attitude Change: The Social Judgment-Involvement Approach*, Philadelphia, PA: W.B. Saunders.

Solomon, M.R. (1999) *Consumer Behaviour*, 4th edn, London: Prentice Hall.

Stangor, C. and M. Hewstone (eds) (1996) *Stereotypes and Stereotyping*, New York: Guilford.

Stiff, J.B. (1994) *Persuasive Communication*, New York: Guilford.

Journals

Adams, J. Stacey (1963) 'Toward an Understanding of Inequity', *Journal of Abnormal and Social Psychology*, 67: 422–36.

Ajzen, I. and T.J. Madden (1986) 'Prediction of Goal-Directed Behaviour: Attitudes, Intentions, and Perceived Behavioural Control', *Journal of Experimental Social Psychology*, 22: 453–74.

Aronson, E. and J. Mills (1959) 'The Effect of Severity of Initiation on Liking for a Group', *Journal of Abnormal and Social Psychology*, 59: 177–81.

Bem, D.J. (1972) 'Self-perception Theory', in L. Berkowitz (ed.), *Advances in Experimental Social Psychology* (Vol. 6), New York: Academic Press, pp. 1–62.

Berkowitz, L. and J.A. Green (1962) 'The Stimulus Qualities of the Scapegoat', *Journal of Abnormal and Social Psychology*, 7: 202–7.

Bodenhausen, G.V. (1988) 'Stereotypic Biases in Social Decision Making and Memory: Testing Process Models of Stereotype Use', *Journal of Personality and Social Psychology*, 55: 726–37.

Boninger, D.S., J.A. Krosnick and M.K. Berent (1995) 'Origins of Attitude Importance: Self-interest, Social Identification and Value Relevance', *Journal of Personality and Social Psychology*, 68: 61–80.

Cooper, J. and R.H. Fazio (1984) 'A New Look at Dissonance Theory', *Advances in Experimental Social Psychology*, 17: 229–65.

Delia, J.G. and W.H. Crockett (1973) 'Social Schemas, Cognitive Complexity and the Learning of Social Structures', *Journal of Personality*, 41: 413–29.

Dick, A.S. and K. Basu (1994) 'Customer Loyalty: Toward an Integrated Conceptual Framework', *Journal of the Academy of Marketing Science*, 22(2): 99–113.

Fazio, R.H. and C.J. Williams (1986) 'Attitude Accessibility as a Moderator of the Attitude Perception and Attitude Behavior Relations: An Investigation of the 1984 Presidential Election', *Journal of Personality and Social Psychology*, 51(3): 505–14.

Fishbein, M. and I. Ajzen (1975) *Belief, Attitude, Intention and Behavior: An Introduction to Theory and Research*, Reading, MA: Addison-Wesley.

Gemmill, G. (1998) 'The Dynamics of Scapegoating in Small Groups', *Small Group Behaviour*, 20: 406–18.

Greene, D., Sternberg, B. and Lepper, M.R. (1976) 'Overjustification in a Token Economy', *Journal of Personality and Social Psychology*, 34: 1219–34.

Jones, E.E. and V.A. Harris (1967) 'The Attribution of Attitudes', *Journal of Experimental Social Psychology*, 3: 1–24.

Maas, A. and L. Acuri (1996) 'Language and Stereotyping', in C.N. Macrae, R.E. Petty and J.T. Cacioppo, (1986) *Communication and Persuasion: Central and Peripheral Routes to Attitude Change*, New York: Springer-Verlag.

Martin, N. and R. Jardine (1986) 'Eysenck's Contribution to Behaviour Genetics', in S. Modgil and C. Modgil (eds), *Hans Eysenck: Consensus and Controversy*, Lewes: Falmer.

Osgood, C. and P. Tannenaven (1955) 'The Principle of Cognity in the Prediction of Attitude Change', *Psychological Review*, 62: 42–55.

Schifter, D.B. and I. Ajzen (1985) 'Intention, Perceived Control, and Weight Loss: An Application of the Theory of Planned Behaviour', *Journal of Personality and Social Psychology*, 6: 649–744.

Sherif, M. and C.W. Sherif (1967) 'Attitudes as the Individual's own Categories: The Social-judgment Approach to Attitude and Attitude Change', in C.W. Sherif and M. Sherif (eds), *Attitude, Ego-involvement and Change*, New York: Wiley, pp. 105–39.

Taylor, S.E. and J.H. Koivumaki (1976) 'The Perception of Self and Others: Acquaintanceship, Affect and Actor-observer Differences', *Journal of Personality and Social Psychology*, 33: 403–8.

Tesser, A., L. Martin and M. Mendolia (1995) 'The Impact of Thought on Attitude Extremity and Attitude-behavior Consistency', in R.E. Petty and J.A. Krosnick (eds), *Attitude Strength: Antecedents and Consequences*, Hillsdale, NJ: Lawrence Erlbaum, pp. 73–92.

Thaler, R. (1980) 'Towards a Positive Theory of Consumer Choice', *Journal of Economic Behavior and Organization*, 1: 39–60.

Zanna, M.P. and J. Cooper (1974) 'Dissonance and the Pill: An Attribution Approach to Studying the Arousal Properties of the Pill', *Journal of Personality and Social Psychology*, 29(5): 703–9.

Websites

Media Awareness Network, www.media-awareness.ca.

www.changingminds.org

Personality

7

'Man's main task in life is to give birth to himself, to become what he potentially is. The most important product of his effort is his own personality.'

Eric Fromm (1941)

Objectives

At the end of this chapter the reader will be able to:

1. Explain the meaning of personality and identify the many factors that go to make up the concept.
2. Examine and evaluate the many theories discussed and show how the different approaches have changed over the years.
3. Demonstrate how an understanding of personality and personality development is used in the role of marketing and understanding consumer behaviour.

Introduction

That people act differently from one another is plain to see. We only have to look at friends and family to be aware of the differences in behaviour, in ways of thinking, talking, laughing and in general how each seems to have their own way of interacting with others and with the immediate environment. This also applies to people in general and everybody makes assumption about a person's personality by the way that they behave. The basic principles underpinning perception, learning, motivation and attitude and how and why people think and behave the way that they do in response to objects (brands), situations (shopping), issues and events (communications and sales promotions) are used to try to identify personality types and to segment people into like-minded group categories.

People act differently

People will not always act in the same way, however, even when faced with the same situation. If the service is bad in a restaurant, or the checkout at a supermarket is slow or a plane has been delayed causing long queues and seemingly interminable waiting, individuals will respond differently. One person might constantly mumble to themselves or to their partner, others might argue loudly with an employee, another might ask to see the manager and another might just sit back and wait patiently. Some people appear able to see the funny side of the situation while others find this impossible. The study of personality is aimed at understanding why people develop these different ways of behaving and ways of thinking to these types of situations.

Different people, different personalities, different behaviour

What is personality?

'A man's reputation is what other people think of him; his character is what he really is.' ANON

Personality seems to be a combination of lots of factors and many have already been discussed in previous chapters. In fact personality can be seen as the crucible for such things as perception, learning, motivation and attitude, as all these areas influence, overlap and are part of the personality construct. It includes how we think about ourselves and the world around us as well has how other people see us. So there are happy and sad people, intelligent and ignorant people, quiet and loud people, introverts and extroverts, angry and peaceful people, racists, saints, sportsmen and sportswomen, **optimists** and **pessimists**. Many like shopping, others hate it, brands such as Givenchy, Versace, Pierre Cardin, Vivienne Westwood, Christian Lacroix and Gucci are coveted by some and despised by others. In fact there are individuals who appear to define their personality by the brands they wear and are prepared to pay enormous amounts of money for the privilege.

Key point Personality is the repository of all the areas discussed throughout the book. How we perceive the world, our learning experiences, the beliefs and attitudes we adopt, what motivates us, both conscious and unconscious influences and the effect of social factors all intertwine to make up the personality of each individual.

Enduring personality

'Personality has proven to be a more important predictor of job success and personal happiness than one's education, age, gender and even job experience!' ANON

Although people have different moods, perhaps happy one part of the day and sad the next, we tend to think of personality as having characteristics or qualities that are long lasting. So when somebody is seen as being warm-hearted and friendly, it means that most of the time that is how he or she will appear to us. Of course people may be different in different situations but the overriding personality remains more or less the same. In some cases, personality may change, for example the fictional character Scrooge in the book *A Christmas Carol* written by Charles Dickens changes from a miserable, selfish curmudgeon to a warm, generous and happy person overnight because of a traumatic reflective experience. In the main, however, personality tends to stay more or less the same over one's life with small changes coming about through different experiences (Myers Briggs at Consulting Psychologists Press at www.cpp.com).

Key point Personality can be seen as a cluster of attributes or characteristics that remain more or less the same over time.

Inherited and environmental part of personality

As with all areas of understanding human behaviour, the nature versus nurture argument again comes into play. At the very least biological components determine such things as facial appearance, eye colour, hair, body type, size and height and there is no doubt that a person's appearance affects how they feel about themselves and through this their personality. Research has shown that some aspects of intelligence might have genetic content, as might characteristics such as melancholia, depression and anxiety (Eysenck and Eysenck 1985). It seems that people might also have an inherited predisposition to behave in certain ways. This could include the ability to be good at sports, playing music and mechanical aptitude. As with all areas of understanding human behaviour, many experiments have been carried out in an attempt to tease out biological and environmental influences. While these theories have yet to be proven one way or the other, they certainly constantly influence how the whole process of understanding personality is approached.

Key point How we look and feel about ourselves will have a high impact on our personality.

7.1 General example — Genetic inheritance and worrying undertones

One biological theorist, Hans Eysenck, believed that much of our personality, including intelligence was largely inherited and determined by inherited gene pools. Unfortunately this became very controversial at times, because of its implications with regard to gender, social class, nationality and race. To say that one group of people are born inferior in some way to another has, for some observers, worrying undertones, whether it could be true or not.

Personality, marketing and consumer behaviour

At the heart of marketing is the need to understand the individual needs and wants of every customer. Only in this way can products and services be produced that match exactly the benefits that are demanded. An understanding of personality is therefore crucial in the process, especially when it's known that customer needs and wants continually change and become evermore demanding. Many different personality groups have been identified over the years by marketing and advertising agencies recognising the need to communicate clear and relevant benefit messages to the right audiences. A typical theoretical example is briefly outlined in Table 7.1.

Table 7.1 General example of consumer personality types

Traditionalist – 35 per cent of the population. This group loves community, loves being with family and friends. Ford Mondeo. Holidays in France.

High Achiever – 5 to 10 per cent of the population. Power and physical wealth motivates. Workaholic. Lexus, BMW, Mercedes, Porsche. Very rarely holidays.

Socially Conscious – 20 per cent of the population. Environmentally concerned. Buys organic products and uses recyclable products. Drives small, fuel-efficient car.

Copycats – 15 per cent of the population. Loves all things flashy. Attempts to copy celebrities without the money. Buys fake Rolex watches, copied Louis Vuitton bags and counterfeit Armani suits. Drives a flashy, second-hand car.

Impulsives – 15 per cent of the population. Loves shopping, buying on impulse with little planning. Heavy credit card debt. Lavish spenders holidaying in Spain.

Personality types and traits

The fact that there seem to be many facets of human nature has fascinated researchers for thousands of years. This has driven many learned people to study personality including the idea of personality 'types' and personality 'traits'.

1 Type theory

One of the earliest approaches taken was the idea that personality was genetic, that humans were born with certain predispositions that would cause people to behave and act in different ways. These ways of behaving, types and traits would cluster and the end result would be the personality of any one person. Early theorists experimented with the idea that individuals could be classified into **personality types**. For example, happy people, sad people, angry people, natural criminals and so on. These are now discussed below, beginning with the Greek philosopher Galen.

Galen – personality from body fluids

One of the first theorists who held sway for many hundreds of years was Greek physician Galen working in the second century AD as physician to the Roman gladiators. He suggested that personality was made up of four types or temperaments caused by the balance of fluids, such as phlegm, blood and bile, in the body. The four temperaments were, melancholic, choleric, phlegmatic and sanguine. The basic idea behind his theory was that individuals were born with amounts of the various fluids that would affect personality in different ways. According to Galen, behaviour could be predicted by the combination of fluids that any one person might have in their body.

- A choleric personality would be violent, aggressive and irritable.
- A melancholic personality would be miserable, gloomy and depressive.
- A sanguine personality would be happy, cheerful and passionate.
- A phlegmatic personality would be sluggish, calm, cold.

Figure 7.1

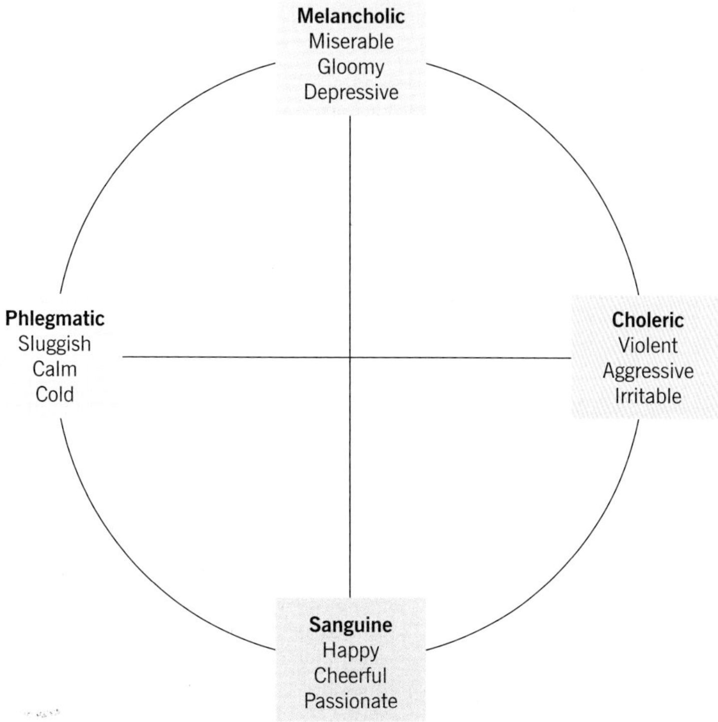

Galen's four personality temperaments

It was the forerunner to trait theory. Although Galen's theory hasn't survived under scrutiny, his idea of personality types has.

> **Key point** Type theory is based on the idea that behavioural characteristics can be grouped together to make up four different types of personality. There are subtle differences within each type to fit all persons.

Personality from physiognomy

Many academics and researchers have attempted to associate personality with outward appearance or physiognomy. The earliest-known systematic treatise on physiognomy is attributed to Greek philosopher Aristotle. He attempted to determine personality from facial features, hair, body, limbs, gait and voice. Others attempted to do the same thing by examining the shape and structure of the face (eyes too close together equals a violent and aggressive, criminal nature), the eyes, hands and the feet, in fact almost every part of the body in some way or another.

7.1 Marketing example | Iridology – personality and identification from the eyes

Researchers at the University of Cambridge, UK, compared over 2,000 iris images – a total of over 2.3 million possible pairs – and found that the chances of one person's iris being mistaken for another person's were extremely low. This makes the eyes useful in **biometrics** and as a means of identification at ATM machines, used with credit cards and as a supporting evidence for a passport. They go on to say that there is a popular belief that the iris systematically reflects one's health or personality, and even that its detailed features reveal the state of individual organs (iridology), but such claims have been discredited as medical fraud.

Questions

1. Discuss the potential for using biometrics in all types of marketing.
2. What might be the criticism in using these sorts of methods to identify consumers?

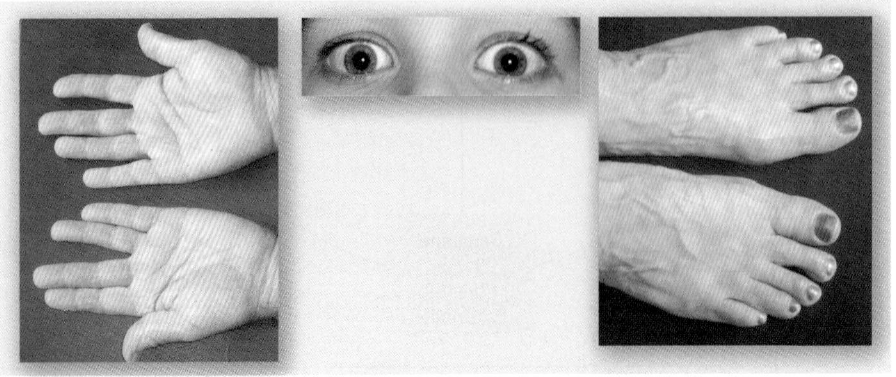

Personality can be assessed from examination of the eyes, hands and feet

Phrenology – personality from bumps on the skull

▶ In the nineteenth century **Franz Joseph Gall** introduced his so called 'science' of phrenology, the discipline of diagnosing disease or interpreting personality through the reading of the bumps on the skull. He believed that certain parts of the brain are compartmentalised with specific areas having specific functions (still true, although not in the way that Gall thought). For example humour might be at the back and depression at the front, passion on one side and rationality on the other. He also believed that as we grow parts of the brain would grow or shrink with usage causing indentation on the skull which could then be 'read', by an expert, using special equipment, who would then be able to determine personality. Although now discredited, he had a huge following at the time he was working with believers at the very highest levels in society.

Criminal personalities by face structure

▶ Italian physicist **Cesare Lombroso** (1836–1909) believed that criminal types could be identified by the make-up and structure of the face. For example eyes and eyebrows too close together, high cheek bones and so on. He spent many years studying the faces and skulls of dead criminals but, as with phrenology, his work is now universally seen as unacceptable. There are, however, still people who believe that people are born to be criminals but, despite constant DNA examination, the gene for criminality has yet to be discovered.

Physiognomy services

All of the above are still in use in some form or another by practitioners who try to determine and predict personality, to detect and help cure diseases and even to predict the future. All have their ardent followers who have belief in the efficacy of the various methods and they are prepared to pay money for personal readings. However none of the above has ever stood up to rigorous scientific investigation. Maybe this doesn't matter as long as user customers are happy.

Astrology and personality from the stars

Astrology is the study of the influence of the celestial bodies on the Earth and its inhabitants with particular reference to personality and future events. Astrologists have never been more popular and almost every newspaper and magazine around the world seems to have a section dedicated to star-sign future telling. The idea that personality can be determined by the conjunction of the planets has been with us for many thousands of years. There is no scientific evidence, however, to back up assertions made.

Personality from graphology (handwriting)

'Spoken words are the symbols of mental experience and written words are the symbols of spoken words. Just as all men have not the same speech sounds, so all men have not the same writing.' ARISTOTLE Fourth Century BC

7.2 Marketing example — Astrology

Horoscopes are big business. In the US over 2,000 newspapers carry daily horoscopes. According to research (Hastings and Hastings 1992) a quarter of Americans believe in astrology and nearly another quarter are not sure. The astrology business grosses several hundred million dollars a year. Professor Richard Dawkins, Charles Simonyi Professor of the Public Understanding of Science, Oxford University, described astrology as dangerous rubbish and star constellations as 'of no more significance than a patch of curiously shaped damp on the bathroom ceiling'. Experience has shown that people have a tremendous fascination with magic, the mystical, the supernatural and the paranormal. Reports on ghosts and hauntings, life after death, UFOs, funny men landing from another planet and so on are believed by large sections of society. Combine this with the use of alternative health cures and it's big business. It seems that some people feel better in believing and are willing to pay large amounts of money to be involved.

Questions

1 Discuss why it seems so many people are ready to believe in, and spend a great deal of money on, such things as astrology, the supernatural, the mystical and the use of alternative medicines.

2 How ethical do you think it is to market products and services to meet the needs of believers in the areas outlined above?

For centuries, philosophers and writers have made reference to the link between personality and handwriting. At the present time there are users of graphology who are convinced of its value. These organisations use handwriting analysis, along with other techniques, in determining the personality of existing and future employees. In this way they feel it can help them fit the right person to the right job. It's also used in counselling, vocational guidance, child monitoring and development and by dating agencies and in forgery detection. The task is made easier through the use of computers. However there still seems to be a lack of hard evidence of a link between handwriting, personality and future job performance (Ben-Shakhar *et al.* 1986).

for example, in developed countries such as the UK and USA, one of the main advertising media is through the TV. The main reasons for this are:
* Almost every home has at least one TV.
* Every target group watches TV.
* TV advertising is considered socially acceptable.
In developed countries, technology and innovation are moving very quickly therefore advertisers must keep up with this.
All forms of media are used in developed countries; TV, radio press and billboards, however in developing countries, the same

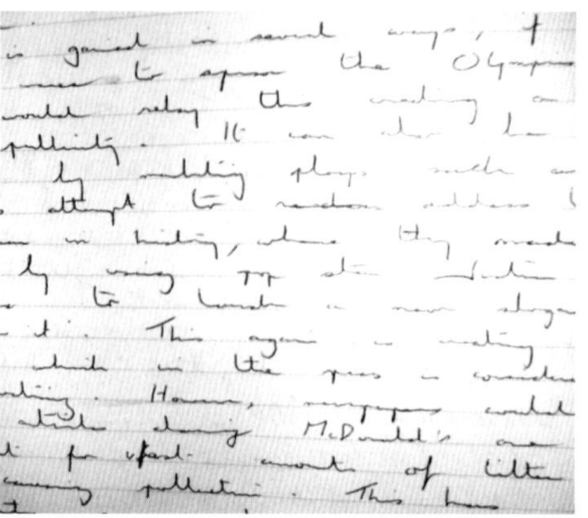

Handwriting depicts different personalities

Personality from body types

Another theory that is similar to Galen's is **William Sheldon's** body type theory (1898–1977). He proposed that the shape of a person's body could determine personality. Working in many US universities Sheldon took thousands of pictures of near naked students and through questioning came to the conclusion that there were three basic body types. Each body type could be associated with different personalities. These are shown in image below:

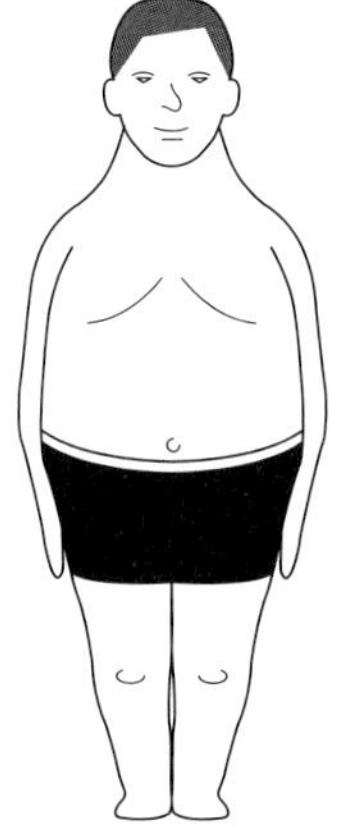

Endomorphs:
Fat, soft, round, not very aggressive, easy going, love comfort food

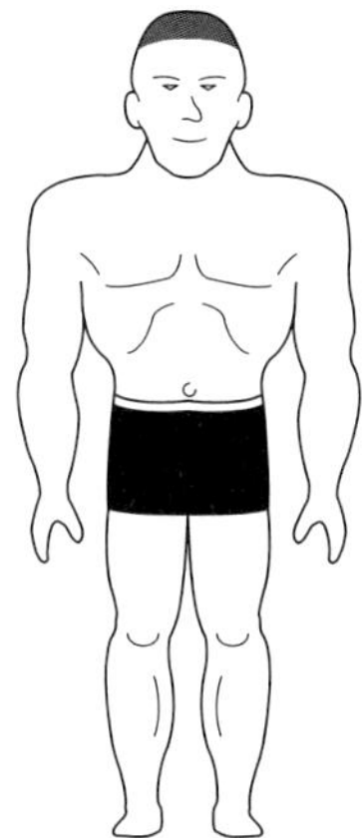

Mesomorphs:
Muscular, assertive, aggressive, active, personable

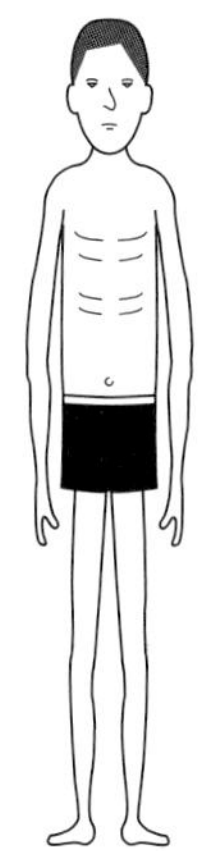

Ectomorphs:
Thin, restrained, socially inhibited, artistic, intellectual, highly-strung, loners

Sheldon's personality types

Criticism of body types The problem here might be one of stereotyping. We expect fat people to be jolly, a skinny person with glasses to be a swot and a muscular man to be good at sports. So the expectation of others caused people to conform and behave to body stereotypes. There very little evidence to support Sheldon and experience now informs that these broad theories are much too simplistic not least because people are often a mixture of the three body characteristics.

2 Trait theory – characteristic qualities that go to make up personality

The problem with type theory is that it is too simple a description of human personality. It doesn't give us enough information to more accurately describe the complexities in the way that people think, behave and deal with the problems of life. Because of this most of the theories outlined above have not stood the test of time and have been largely dismissed. This brings us to **trait personality theory** and one of the earliest proponents working in this field in the 1930s was the psychologist **Gordon Allport** (1897–1967).

Figure 7.2

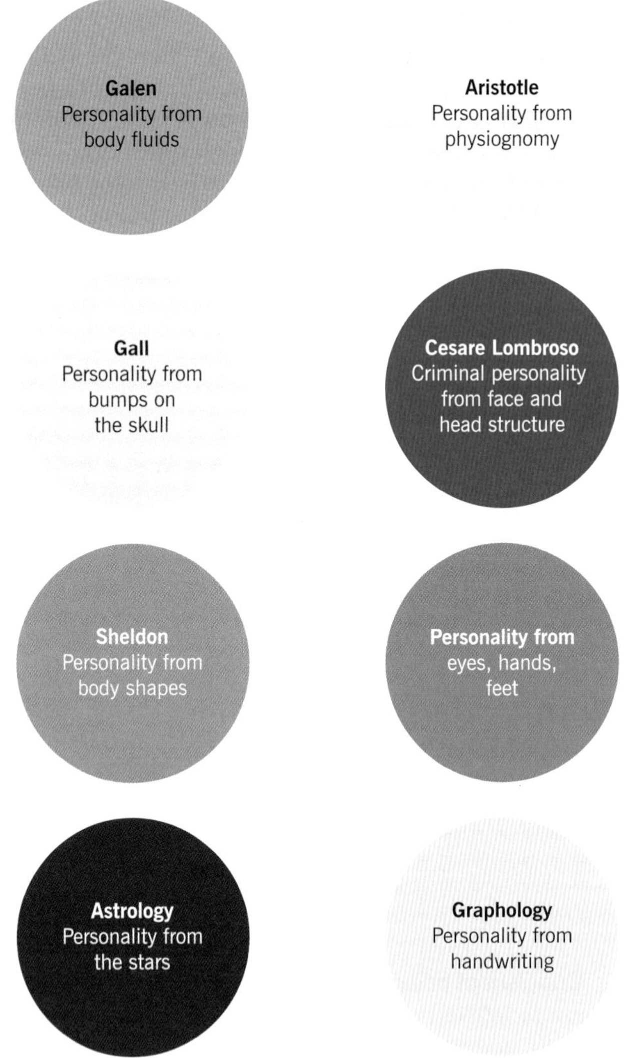

Dubious methods used to identify personality types

7.2 General example — Traits versus types

'Unlike traits, types always have a biosocial reference. A man can be said to have a trait; but he cannot be said to have a type. Rather he fits a type and types exist not in people or in nature, but rather in the eye of the observer. Type includes more than is in the individual. Traits, on the contrary, are considered wholly within the compass of the individual.'
GORDON ALLPORT (1937: 295–6)

Trait theory

Allport believed that individuals are more of a mixture of many traits (which he saw as the 'building blocks of personality') rather than being restricted to a broad category. For example one person might be rotund and melancholic by nature and another rotund and happy. Similarly a thin person might be submissive or dominant, tidy or untidy, imaginative or practical and so on. Members of the same family, even identical twins, might have some characteristics in common and other characteristics not in common.

> **Key point** According to Allport, traits are enduring characteristics and predispositions that determine how we perceive, think and act in a variety of situations. Personality can be viewed as a combination of these traits.

Allport's approach

Allport first identified 18,000 words that describe some aspect of personality. These he reduced to 4000 so that they were more manageable. He noticed that some traits, such as honesty, compassion, aggressiveness etc. were more or less dominant in one person than in another. He also saw that some traits, ambition, power seeking, competitiveness were more important and influential in people's lives than other traits such as modesty, attentiveness and sensitivity. He went on to categorise these into the following:

- **Cardinal traits**
- **Central traits**
- **Secondary traits or states**
- **Central and secondary traits reversed**

Cardinal traits These he saw as the most influential in affecting behaviour such that some individuals could become all consumed by them. They appeared to be deeply ingrained giving a long-term focused framework to people's lives. Cardinal traits would include such dominant, all-consuming things as ambition, the need for achievement, power, religious conviction and perhaps sexual orientation.

Central traits He noted that most people are not obsessed in the manner suggested under cardinal traits. Central traits are important to people's lives but they are not obsessed or consumed by them. These include such things as levels of intelligence, communications skills, honesty, fairness, pride, stubbornness, modesty, persistence, sociability, friendliness, humour, helpfulness and compassion. It is possible for a central trait such as pride, or compassion to be more consuming in some people's lives and so take on the mantle of a cardinal trait.

Secondary traits or states These can be seen as a temporary change in personality. These traits will not govern day-to-day reaction, and they are less important, less conspicuous, less generalised and less noticed by others and they will only come into play under particular circumstances. We typically use secondary traits or states to describe a person's reaction to something. For example people who are usually very calm and easygoing might become very excited, aggressive and anxious if threatened in some way. Similarly an individual might be meek and mild normally but become outgoing and verbose after a couple of drinks.

Central and secondary traits reversed Under certain circumstances a central trait can also be a secondary trait and vice versa. A person who has an outgoing central trait might be shy at first around new people. Similarly someone who is usually confident might exhibit fear or self-doubt when in a novel situation.

Figure 7.3

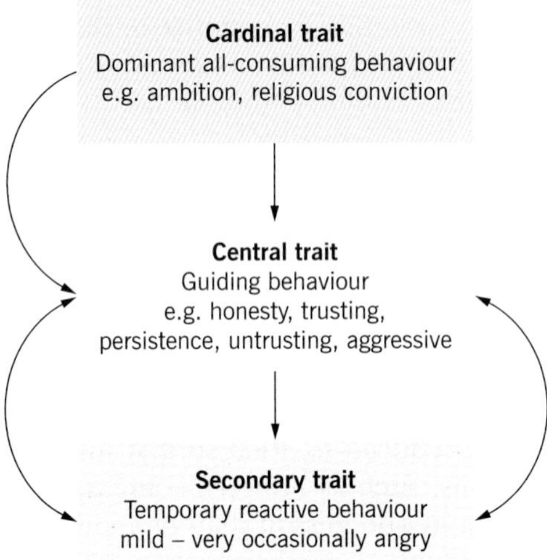

Cardinal, central and secondary traits

Unique personalities

Some of the traits identified above are common to everybody, e.g. intelligence, use of language, while others could be said to be more personal, e.g. artistic ability, sports skills, sense of humour etc. According to Allport, what makes people different from one another as well as unique is the level and degree of importance or otherwise of cardinal and central traits in their personality make-up. Using research he tried to cluster traits into similar personality types and compare one group with another.

7.3 General example **Unique personality**

Not all people have a sense of humour and the sharp wit, wealth of jokes or cutting sarcasm of a comedian such as Woody Allen, nor the intensity of compassion and concern for the poor and the needy of the world shown by Mother Teresa. Similarly the political ability of Mahatma Gandhi and the sports ability and personality of Muhammad Ali could be seen as unique personalities.

Inherited personality traits

There has been an enormous amount of research investigating whether personality traits have a strong inherited component. Evidence working with identical twins reared apart seems to suggest that there is, although this will vary from person to person and from trait to trait (Bouchard *et al.* 1990: 227). As we have found with all areas of human behaviour, how much is inherited and how much is the result of upbringing and society is still very much the subject of debate.

Traits and personality measurement

Building on the idea of trait theory, **Raymond Cattell** (1905–98) felt, first, that too many trait descriptions were in use and, second, to be really useful traits needed to be measurable so that differences between people could be assessed. For example people are honest or dishonest, submissive or dominant, serious or not across a range of possibilities. This led him to develop a classic empirical approach that is now seen to be seminal to the personality tests (such as Myers Briggs) that are in use to this day. Working over a number of years he was able to collect information on the behaviour and personality of thousands of people.

Factor analysis

Using a technique called factor analysis, a correlation procedure that identified and grouped together related variables (e.g. outgoing, extrovert, good company, gregarious and sociable might all be said to measure the same, or very similar personality traits) he was able to reduce the amount of variables to sixteen basic traits. From this he developed a questionnaire, the '16 Factor Personality Questionnaire' (see Figure 7.4). Cattell then went on to try to measure and compare the personality profile of individuals across an opposite word scale (similar to the semantic differential approach shown in Figure 6.13 in the preceding chapter).

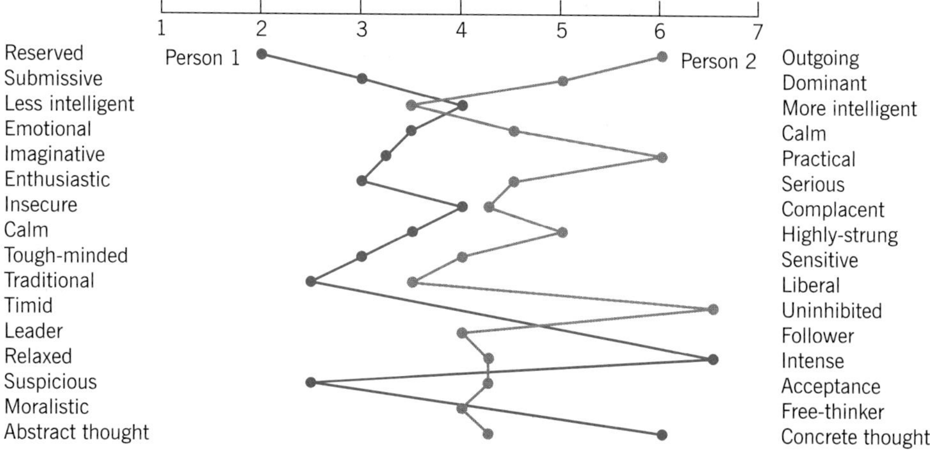

Cattell's 16 Factor Personality Questionnaire

Two personality factors – Hans Eysenck

Psychologist, Hans Eysenck, developed a similar model to Cattell's 16 factor analysis shown in Figure 7.4 also using factor analysis. After many years of research he concluded that all human traits could be broken down into two distinct categories: extraversion–introversion and emotional stability–instability (Figure 7.5). According to Eysenck, using a questionnaire (the Eysenck Personality Inventory or EPI) we should all be able to measure our personality somewhere around the circle. As a behaviourist, he believed that personality, to a large extent, was determined by our genes. He later added a third dimension to the EPI: psychoticism and impulse control.

Figure 7.5

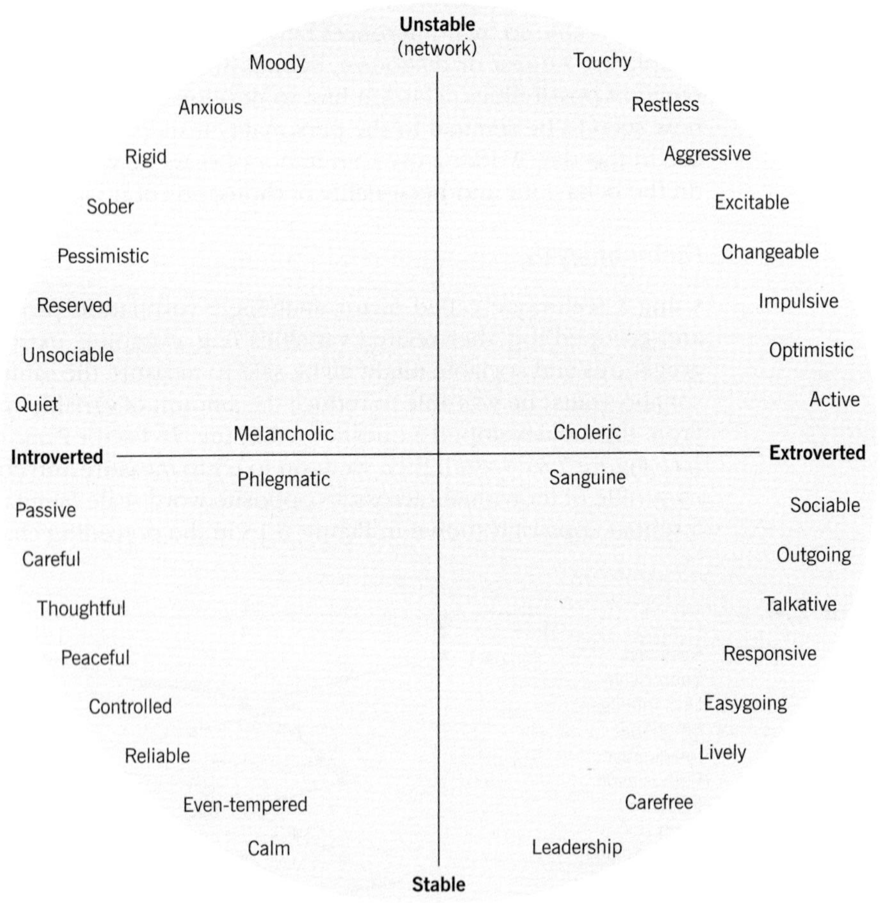

Eysenck Personality Inventory (EPI). Four distinct categories: extraversion–introversion and emotional stability–emotional instability are used to define specific personality traits. Personality is measured around the circular scale (Eysenck and Eysenck 1985).

The Big Five-factor Model of personality traits

Over the last few decades personality theorists have been working on and researching the number of traits that best qualify as descriptors of personality. In this way they hope to be able to control and measure in a more detailed and meaningful way. Building on the work of Raymond Cattell and Hans Eysenck, they have come up with the idea of a Big Five-factor Model of personality traits that are in use to this day. These five personality trait categories and their opposites are shown in Table 7.2.

Table 7.2 **The Big Five-factor model of personality**

All types of personality should be measurable using this model

1. Open or shut mind
2. Conscientious or negligent
3. Extrovert or introvert
4. Agreeable or hostile
5. Neuroticism – emotional stability or instability

1 **Open or shut mind** This includes levels of intellect and openness to new ideas and different cultures in business, the arts, humanities and the sciences. It covers such characteristics as curiosity, creativity, imagination and independence as against acceptance, conforming, practicality and control.

2 **Conscientious (the will to succeed) or negligent (uncaring)** It includes self-control, dependability, planning, thoroughness, and persistence paired with carelessness, negligence and unreliability. It is well correlated with educational achievement.

3 **Extrovert (outward going) or introvert (inward looking)** This includes someone who is active, sociable, talkative, self-confident and assertive on the one hand, and inactive, retiring, silent, timid and passive on the other.

4 **Agreeable or hostile** This includes someone who is friendly, altruistic, caring, helpful, trusting, soft-hearted and emotionally supportive on the one hand and suspicious, indifferent, selfish, ruthless and distrusting on the other.

5 **Neuroticism – emotional stability or instability** Here calm, secure, satisfied, composed, rational traits are measured against fearful, anxious, insecure, self-pitying, nervous, irrational and moody traits

OCEAN adapted from Digman (1990) and Goldberg (1990).

The value of the trait approach

The trait approach to personality is intuitively appealing and has become a popular method used in trying to understand personality development. This is because it seems that traits can be identified and the strength and degree of relevance of each trait can be measured, personality profiles built and one individual can then be compared with another.

The situation

The situation can play a large part in determining personality behaviour. For example a high-flying business man may be seen as assertive, ruthless and composed at work yet be retiring, caring and easy-going at home. Another person may be seen by everybody he or she knows outside work as placid and easy going but be the opposite in work because of the pressure and the strain of the job.

Figure 7.6

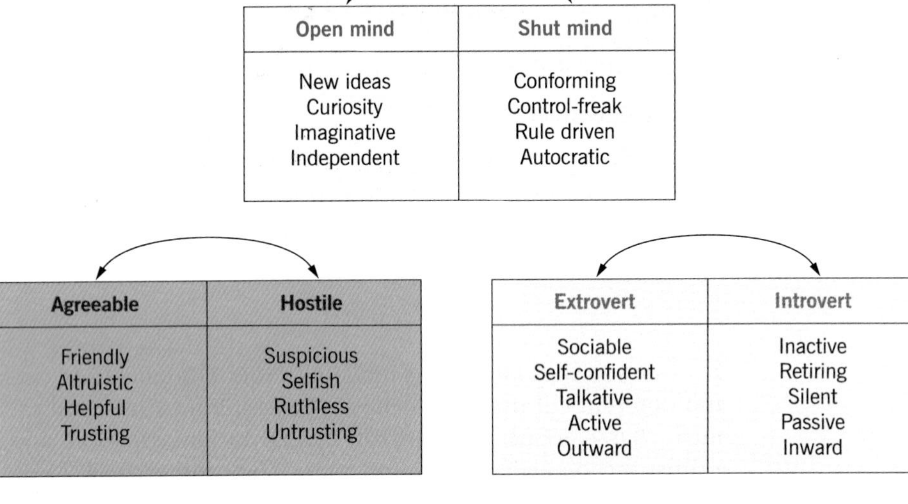

The 'Big Five-factor Model' of personality traits now used in modern personality questionnaires

7.4 General example — Assuming personality by behaviour

Personality is often assumed by behaviour. For example one of my sons is outward going, friendly, artistic (he writes music and plays the guitar) and open to new ideas. My best friend is agreeable to me but often aggressive and disagreeable to others. He is sociable, gregarious and has a great sense of humour but he can be ruthless when crossed. The difficulty, however, is that traits are not something we can really see or directly measure. We can only infer by observing behaviour or using questionnaires. This can be reasonably accurate if we have known somebody for a long time but problematic if we haven't. It may be that my son acts in a friendly way to me but he might be aggressive in other circumstances. I see my friend act humorously at times, usually when he has had a drink and assume he has a good sense of humour. He might be acting for my benefit and be melancholic most other times.

The use of personality questionnaires

The same problems can arise if questionnaires are used. Respondents will often misinterpret their own personality, sometimes inadvertently and sometimes because they prefer to err on the side of niceness. Research has shown that people who know us will often give a different personality reading than we will about ourselves.

Commercial questionnaires

Personality questionnaires are heavily used in the commercial world and seem to be quite successful. Managers feel that it is important to identify different personality types to fit into different kinds of jobs. The Myers Briggs model is one such questionnaire. It asks applicants a series of questions about their likes, dislikes, feelings and beliefs. From the answers a personality profile is obtained from 16 possible types. It accepts that everybody is different but works on the premise that there are general themes or similarities between people. From the way that the questions are framed, Myers Briggs argued that the questions cannot be anticipated and almost all respondents will answer truthfully. This type of technique would normally be used in conjunction with many other personality and competence techniques so as to get a rounded impression of job applicants.

7.5 General example — The Myers Briggs type indicator

The Myers Briggs type indicator is a typical example of a commercial personality measurement technique. Using four basic scales with opposite poles, it attempts to measure participant's preferences and from this their personality type. The four scales are: (1) extraversion/introversion, (2) sensate/intuitive, (3) thinking/feeling, and (4) judging/perceiving. They say that the various combinations of these preferences result in 16 personality types. Individuals taking part are asked to look at a whole series of word categories. Each category contains four, seemingly unrelated, words and they are asked to choose which words comes nearest to describing how they feel. There is a strict time limit so that the answers are spontaneous. This is so that the person taking part has little time to think and perhaps attempt to 'fix' the answers. At the end each answer is coded and from this a participant personality profile is constructed.

Questions

1 Discuss the value of intelligence and personality type questionnaires.

2 Do you think that they should be used to better understand consumer behaviour?

Psychodynamic theories of personality

Psychodynamic theories are concerned with the part that an individual's mind and thought processes (the '**psyche**') play in the development of personality from the moment of birth through to old age and death.

Psychoanalysis and Freud

Sigmund Freud (1856–1939) is important as the first major theorist to write exclusively about the role of the mind in trying to understand motivation and personality development. Arguably the one great contribution he made to an understanding of how people behave and think is the idea that there is a part of the human mind, the unconscious or sub-conscious that is beyond the grasp of normal consciousness. This 'unconscious' part of the mind contains motivations, thoughts, desires, lusts and fears that have been repressed since early childhood. This is because they seem to have the power to threaten, in some way or another, a person's mental wellbeing. They also contain inner feelings of such things as guilt, inadequacy, jealousy and low self-esteem that come to shape personality. For example a child might have been inadvertently made to feel unwanted as part of a large family, bullied by a brother, had parents that were too strict, had an accident or been abused in some way.

Psychoanalytical techniques Negative feelings and fears that lurk in the unconscious part of the mind have the power to leak through and influence the conscious part without individuals knowing how and why it has happened. This means that confusing and wrong reasons for behaviour are often given. According to Freud a trained person (a psychoanalyst) can get at the real motivating reason through the use of psychoanalytical techniques. Methods used included one-to-one discussions using therapy, free expression and analysing dreams.

7.3 Marketing example — The importance of the subconscious

The idea that there might be a subconscious part of the human mind that will influence the purchase of products and brands has had an enormous influence on marketing and the decision-making process. Prolific qualitative research has shown that the conscious reason that people might give for buying a product, for example a functional reason such as buying a car to get from A to B, perfume because it makes a pleasant smell, a premium ice cream for the taste, or a watch to tell the time, are often not the real reason. The real repressed subconscious reasons might be, a large car to compensate for inner feelings of inadequacy, perfume or a watch to raise self-esteem and fulfil dreams of romantic love, and premium ice cream to compensate for unfulfilled sexual desires.

Question

1 Identify six or seven different branded products and give possible subconscious reasons for purchase.

Unconscious, the preconscious and the conscious

Freud went on to say that there was a third part of the mind, called the preconscious, that sits between the unconscious and the conscious. Thoughts and feelings sit here, partly obscured, just before entering into the consciousness (e.g. trying to think about the name of the actor in a particular film and bingo! it just seems to pop out from nowhere). Personality and behaviour happens as a result of a constant interplay between conflicting psychological forces or energy across these three different levels of awareness.

Unconscious → preconscious → conscious → personality and behaviour

Sex sells. A Sloggi advert.
Source: Sloggi

The id, the ego and the superego – conflicting psychological forces

Human feelings and thoughts that operate at three different levels of awareness in the unconscious, preconscious and the conscious mind are generated by forces and energy that came to be known as the **id**, the **ego** and the **superego**. The id operates in the unconscious, the ego in the conscious and the superego partly in the conscious and partly in the unconscious part of the mind. Freud's theory of personality development encompasses this interplay between these three forces.

The id, the ego and the superego and personality development

We can now look at these areas in turn and discuss the part that each plays in affecting human and consumer behaviour, beginning with the role of the id (pronounced as one word).

The id – the wild animal or beast in us

'Greed is the bottomless pit which exhausts the person in an endless effort to the need without ever reaching satisfaction.' ERIC FROMM (1947)

The driving force in the subconscious is the id that Freud saw as the animal, primitive, instinctive part of our personality, left over from hundreds of thousands of years of development. The id is powered by the 'Libido' or the life force. This directs the mind to maximising pleasure and the replication of an individual's genes while avoiding pain.

Key point Id → the primitive part of the mind → powered by the libido that seeks pleasure, desires and lust fulfilment while avoiding pain.

The superego – sense of right or wrong, our conscience

The superego is the part that makes up our public and personal conscience, our moral sense of what's right or wrong. It is judgemental and gives us standards and principles and tells us how to think and how to behave. It's mostly concealed in our subconscious with a small part that moves in and out of consciousness. We develop a conscience through interacting with the outside world. First with our parents then through the many socialising agencies, such as school, church, work, friends, the opposite sex, the media that we come into contact with as we journey through life. We learn to behave appropriately in all manner of social, cultural and sexual situations. Morals and ethics will vary from nation to nation and from culture to culture and will be stronger in one group or individual compared with another. It can be seen that the superego will be in constant conflict with the id, morality on the one hand and urging primitive desires on the other.

Key point The superego → the conscience → powered by the demands of parents and other agencies.

The ego – the balancing force between the devil and the saint in us

The ego is the part of the mind that tries to balance the primitive urges of the id and the restraining morality of the superego. It again operates both in the conscious and unconscious parts of our mind (see Figure 7.7). The ego is driven by a common-sense realism about the need to live in the civilised world and becomes a mediator in the mind trying to strike up a compromise between unrestrained lust and barbarism and restricting and inhibiting morality. This might be to show self-control or to postpone gratification until the appropriate time or circumstance. For example the id might be trying to persuade me towards uninhibited alcohol drinking and drug taking, while my superego, my conscience, may be telling me my mother or the local priest will be angry and disappointed in me. My ego, the realities principle, will be trying to balance the two by telling me that a particular amount will be acceptable and that nobody will find out.

> **Key point** The ego → reality principle → balancing the force of the id with the moral demands of the conscience.

Figure 7.7

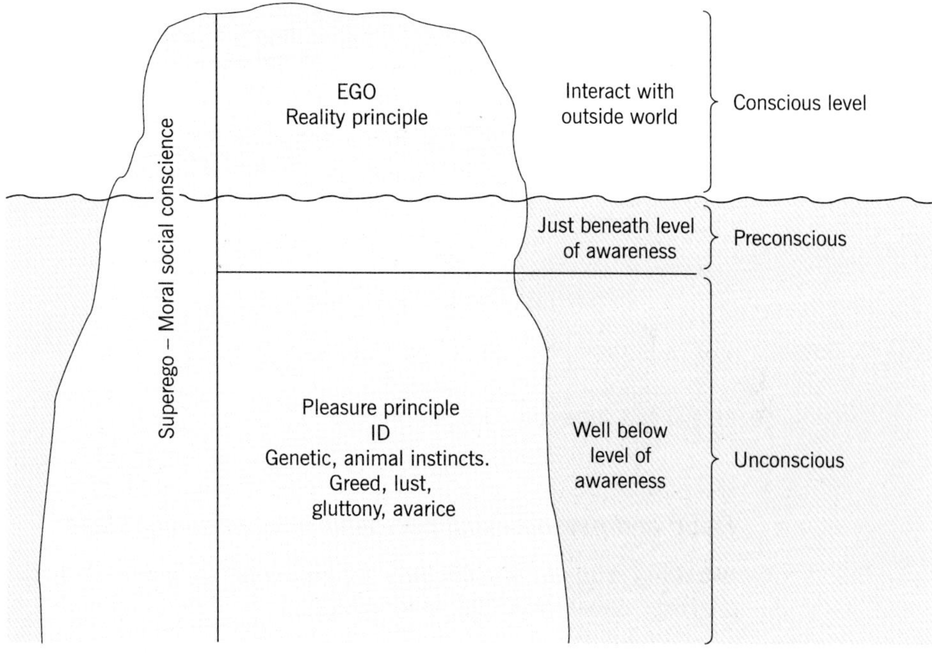

The conscious, the preconscious and the unconscious parts of the mind

7.4 Marketing example — Helping the consumer to balance the triple demands

Marketers and advertising people work hard to help the consumer balance up these competing demands. Some consumer groups seem to have little or no problem with being driven by the power of the id and grow fat and unhealthy on fast food, cigarettes and alcohol. Up to now this seemed to bother producers and retailers very little. Times, however, are changing and health, fitness and eating and drinking in moderation are firmly on the agenda. McDonald's, the devil of the health improvement lobby, have had to alter their menu to eliminate large portions and include salads and fruit because of falling sales. Governments have issued warnings to food manufacturers to clean up their products by reducing unhealthy ingredients. Advertisers must also constantly think up new ideas to persuade other more thinking consumers to ignore the pressure from their 'superego' and occasionally indulge themselves on possible guilt inducing products such as expensive cosmetics or luxury confectionary.

Question

1 Do you think that fast-food retailers should be more concerned about supplying healthy foods or should it just offer menus that its customers demand?

Figure 7.8

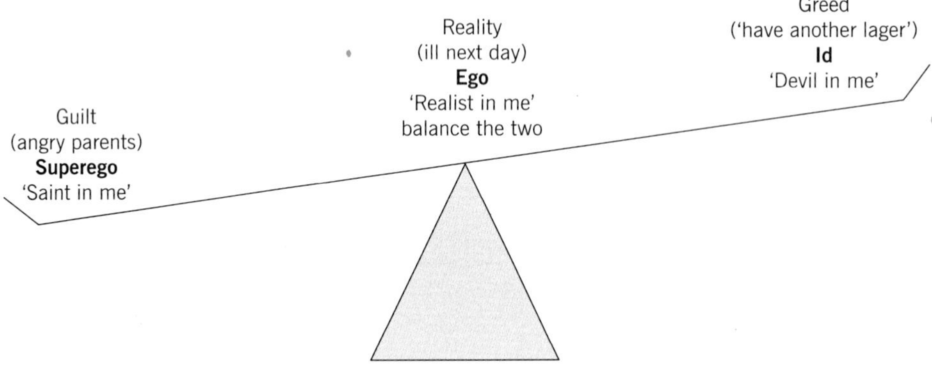

Id, ego and superego – a balancing act

Freud and psychosexual personality development stages

'We don't stop playing because we grow old; we grow old because we stop playing!' GEORGE BERNARD SHAW

Freud went on to link his theory of the mind to the theory of human development. Like many other theorists he saw human and personality development from birth to adulthood in terms of a number of clear stages. How each stage is negotiated before moving on to the next stage will have a lasting affect on subsequent personality development and behaviour. Growth is powered by a 'life force energy' (the libido) that, in the broadest sense, he saw as **psychosexual** and pleasure seeking.

Five psychosexual stages

Freud saw that as babies were growing different parts of their body seemed to give them the greatest pleasure. Theorists would later call these areas erogenous zones. Immediately after birth the greatest pleasure the baby has is sucking at its mother's breast (stage 1). Then around about one year old, pleasure moves to controlling the bowels (stage 2). By age three or four pleasure comes from playing with its genitalia (stage 3). This is followed by a period of latency until pleasure reawakens at adulthood with sexual intercourse (stages 4 and 5). This was at the heart of Freud's psychosexual development stage theory.

Conflict

Freud believed that at every stage, the baby or young child is faced with psychosexual developmental conflicts that must be successfully resolved in order to move on to the next phase. The early stages are the most important. Problems caused by parents' reaction at each stage, for example under- or overfeeding (stage 1) or too strict or too lenient toilet-training (stage 2) or making the child feel guilty or ashamed (stage 3), could have a severe affect on adult personality and examples are given in general example 7.6.

7.6 General example — Freudian personality characteristics

Freud considered the oral and anal stages as most important and examples of personality characteristics are given here.

Oral stage (0 to 1 year) Conflict can arise if the baby is over- and/or under-indulged in its feeding (breast or bottle) habits.

- *Orally dependent personality (over-indulged)* – selfish, over-dependent, immature.
- *Orally retentive personality (under-indulged)* – aggressive, argumentative, sarcastic, solitary, feelings of emptiness, untrusting.

Anal stage (1 year to 3 years) Conflict will arise if the child is too strictly toilet-trained, perhaps using punishment or humiliation, or too leniently toilet trained, perhaps being ignored or spoilt.

- *Anal-retentive personality* (strictly toilet-trained) – obsessively clean and tidy, a perfectionist, rule-driven, dictatorial, very stubborn, ungenerous and mean.
- *Anal-expulsive personality* (leniently toilet-trained) – untidy, messy and disorganised, over-generous with little self-control.

Key point The degree to which parents either frustrate or over-indulge the child's expression of pleasurable feelings will have a lasting affect. Problems will be pushed down into the subconscious and insidiously manifest themselves in different ways through personality development. This will affect buying behaviour.

Failings of psychoanalysis

In attempting to build a universal theory of the mind, Freud undertook much research and undertook many experiments. The big problem, however, was that he predominantly used interviews and observations with very small numbers of people making his work difficult to test. He relied on his own interpretations and his approach could not, in any way, be seen as scientific. Other disagreements focus around his negative approach to experiences, his insistence that it is really only early childhood that shapes adult personality and his failure to allow for the social, cultural and gender influences pervasive at the time of his writings. His idea that detailed analysis of dreams can get at ideas in the subconscious has also been largely debunked.

Many of his ideas adapted to modern thinking

That's not to say that some of his work hasn't been valuable. Although many of his findings and conclusions about the workings of the human mind have since been rejected or still remain open to argument, there is no doubt that he remains a giant of the twentieth century. His basic concepts about the nature of personality development (and mental disorders) still have resonance and they are constantly adapted to fit modern thinking.

Marketing, the subconscious and psychosexual theory of personality development

Freudian theory really began to be used seriously in marketing in the USA after the Second World War. Pent-up demand for consumer products and the growth of organisations to fulfil these demands created huge markets. As competition grew, emphasis shifted to the consumer's view on brands and services wanted rather that the view of the producers. This meant that one organisation had to try to understand their customer motivations better than another organisation if competitive advantage was to be maintained. The development of **motivational research**, under the leadership of Ernest Dichter in 1946, grew from this need for a deeper understanding of human buying motives. Dichter relied heavily on the psychoanalytical work of Freud and the neo-Freudians (exploring both the subconscious and personality development) adapting clinical or therapy methods and using qualitative research techniques, many still in use today (Ernest Dichter and motivational research is discussed in more detail in Chapter 9 on lifestyle segmentation).

7.5 Marketing example — Motivational research

Ernest Dichter (1907–91) founded the Institute for Motivational Research in 1946. He was a follower of Freud and used psychoanalytical techniques to analyse consumer behaviour. He believed that early life experiences (such as a caring or uncaring parental feeding programme and strict or lenient toilet-training) could be used to explain consumer-buying behaviour with regard to such products as alcohol, cosmetics, toothpaste, soap-powder, the level of giving to charities and so on. For example he argued that women associated baking with their role as wife and mother and childbirth and would not buy instant cake mix (just add hot water) because of feelings of guilt. He was right and the product didn't sell. However, when they were asked to add an egg to the mixture, guilt feelings were salved and the product sold. Similarly canned soup was marketed as being as warm and nutritious as mothers milk which again helped it sell.

The Neo-Freudians – adapt yet maintain the concept of the subconscious

Many theorists accepted the concept of the unconscious and the idea that suppressed influences can affect personality. Known as the neo-Freudians, they have all adapted his theories to come up with similar theories of their own.

Carl Jung's analytical psychology – the collective unconscious

Carl Jung accepted the concept of the unconscious mind but he argued that it operated in a different way to how it had been described by Freud. He believed that the repressed thoughts, fears and emotions came not from individual psychosexual conflicts but from an ***inherited collective unconscious***. He attempted to demonstrate that the things that subconsciously influence personality in children and adults are similar across cultures and across time. He felt that they had been genetically passed on from generation to generation, for thousands of years. To support his theory he spoke of the immediate attachment that all babies have to their mother as well as such things as fear of the dark, of spiders and snakes, of heights and so on. He also attempted to show how images, stories, myths and legends about the earth, the sun, the stars, the moon, gods and devils and good and evil all seem to be predominate themes across the world throughout history.

7.6 Marketing example — Analytical psychology

According to Jung's theory, people across the world could feel satisfied with similar sorts of products and services, everybody eating the same sorts of things and dressing in similar ways. Many global companies now market and sell practically the same products and services in almost every country and every continent. Coca-Cola states that their products are available in 95 per cent of possible outlets. McDonald's has 31,000 restaurants in 119 countries. Germany's Metro supermarket group has 20 stores in Russia. Swedish household and furniture retailer Ikea has successfully taken the same retail formula to over 30 different countries in Europe, China, North America, Russia and the Middle East.

Questions

1. Do you think that consumers around the world are now ready to buy the same or similar types of products?
2. Discuss the reasons why this might, or might not, be so.

Psychosocial stages

Theorist **Erick Erickson** (1902–94) also felt that a person's personality developed in stages from birth through to old age and that each stage had to be successfully negotiated if human potential was to be enhanced and vulnerability minimised. Failure at any one stage could lead to feelings of mistrust, guilt, inadequacies and lack of self-confidence and self-esteem. Unlike Freud, however, he felt that these stages were **psychosocial** in nature rather than psychosexual.

Social interaction forms personality

From the moment of birth, through early growth and into adolescence and adulthood, individuals interact with and learn about the world and their sense of wellbeing from other people. According to Erickson it's in this social interaction that conflict can arise. From the moment of birth, almost until puberty the most important relationships are between the child and its parents. It's through this relationship and later on with other relationships that a child builds its personality. It learns to trust its environment, become independent, is able to take the initiative and feel comfortable and confident in the world. Erickson identified a number of stages or milestones at different ages where conflict can arise and damage can occur, the early years being the most important.

Key point Erickson saw personality developing in a social setting – families and friends interacting with one another. This was unlike Freud who saw the stages as psychosexual.

Individual psychology – each person is unique and adjusts differently to the environment

Similar to Freud and Erickson, **Alfred Adler** (1870–1970) believed that both the role of parents in childhood development and our genetic make-up played a large role in the shaping of a personality. However he paid less attention to the role that growth stages might play in the process and more to the actual interactions and the development of the whole person what he termed **individual psychology**. He saw that the child would have problems growing up because he or she would be constantly interacting with more powerful others, particularly mother and father and older siblings, when forming personality. He recognised that this power could be used, inadvertently or otherwise, in a positive or negative manner. The areas that concerned Adler included such things as parental pampering, neglect, encouragement and abuse.

Birth order and personality differences

He also looked at the effect of birth order and its affect on personality. For example he found that the first-born might misbehave constantly wanting to regain favours lost with the birth of the next child. In a similar way, the second born might be more competitive wanting to catch up with the older sibling. Finally the youngest might fail to be independent and have an exaggerated opinion of his or her worth because of being over-indulged and spoilt.

Managing an inferiority complex

What particularly interested Adler was how individuals were able to manage the different outcomes that came about because of haphazard or bad parenting, particularly later on in life. He believed that, because of the unequal power relationship between a little child and a full-grown adult, inferiority complexes, usually repressed into the subconscious, were often inevitable. His research indicated that people dealt with these negative feelings in many ways. For example some people would be motivated to work harder, try more and think through harmful feelings. On the other hand others might give way and became apathetic, lazy and depressed. Others 'overcompensate' for feelings of inferiority by boasting about their wealth and success and getting wrapped up with power and excessive **materialism**. Overall he saw personality development as the constant need for self-improvement and the striving for superiority.

7.7 Marketing example Feelings of inferiority

Adler believed that the unequal relationship between adults and the child can cause a sense of inferiority and low self-esteem to develop, especially if parenting was bad. Of special interest to him in his studies was how adults strive for superiority and deal with problems of inferiority later on in life. Research seems to show that many products, bought by both male and females are purchased to compensate in some way or another for feelings of inferiority and low self-esteem. This includes everything from 'snacking' and comfort eating, drinking too much alcohol, needing to constantly shop for new clothes, buying bigger and better cars, having to have better things than neighbours and so on.

Key point Adler felt that individual personality developed in interaction with others and that this could often lead to feelings of inferiority because of the unequal relationships.

Feminine psychology – gender differences determined by society

'Women approach shopping as a stress reliever whereas men treat shopping as a stress creator.' ANON

Freud has constantly been accused of knowing very little about psychodynamics from a woman's point of view. It's argued that his theories mainly concern the male and his ideas on the development of the female mind and personality are clouded and biased by the Victorian culture pervasive at the time he was writing. **Karen Horney** was the first theorist to disagree with Freud and attempt to take the woman's perspective. She disagreed with Freud's view that men and woman were born with inherent differences in their personality potential. She argued that real gender differences came about through the interaction of females with culture and society. For her, gender inequalities were the result of male dominance, power relationships and the restrictions that men put on women. In this way she could be seen to be the mother of **feminine psychology**.

7.8 Marketing example Consumer behaviour and gender

Consistent research evidence (Mintel, Datamonitor) seems to suggest that men and women relate differently to shopping, consumption and material possessions. It's no surprise that overall more women than men prefer shopping. There are also gender differences in choice. Woman go for objects of sentimental value, like buying things for themselves, their husband and their children while men choose things related to leisure and finance. Women liked possessions that offered emotional comfort and the relationship with others they symbolised, while men preferred things they could use and were activity related. According to a study from Exeter University (UK 2003) the shopping habits of men and women will always be incompatible. Woman like to shop for longer than men and they should spend no longer than one hour and 12 minutes together, otherwise an argument will usually break out.

Question

1 Discuss consumer gender differences. Do you think that there is any truth in the assertion the generally woman like to shop but men do not?

Men wait while women shop

Existentialism – we have the freedom to decide our own nature

Existentialism is a difficult term to define and it has been related to a large body of thinkers of the nineteenth and twentieth centuries (Heidegger 1966; **Sartre** 1984). In very simple terms it might include the following concepts.

- Existence before essence – we bring nothing into the world and all we learn we learn from living in the world.
- We have the ability, the freedom and the responsibility to define and to decide our own nature, not by discussion but by living.
- There are questions, the existence of God, the meaning of life and death, of personal relationships, on introspection, that we as individuals must ask about living in the world.
- Individuals, if they choose, have the ability to create their own values and morality by living and acting in the world.

- Our free will, to choose or not to choose to behave in one way or another is paramount.
- In this way we are responsible for and develop our own personality.

7.9 Marketing example — Existentialism and consumerism

Existentialists argue (Elliot 1997) that humans do not have any special or unique essence and this emphasises the isolation of the individual in a hostile or indifferent world. It could be argued that people are constantly buying evermore expensive products and services to give meaning to an otherwise unmeaning existence. Unfortunately the meaning given by constant consumption is superficial, causing the consumer to be constantly looking for new shopping experiences.

The torment of freedom – fear of being alone in the world

'Customers hate having to make decisions, especially about high priced items, and a sales person is there to help the customer with this burden. Once a decision has been made a weight will fall from the consumer's shoulders and gratitude will follow.' RAY WRIGHT

▶ **Erich Fromm** was born in Germany in 1900 and was writing and studying predominately between the two world wars and living at a time that spawned the rise of National Socialism and the Fascist party. In his most influential work *Escape from Freedom* he argues that individuals live a painful existence, alone, insecure and powerless in a world free from social, cultural, religious and working structures that once provided clear identity and meaning to everybody's lives. This sense of freedom gives rise to anxiety and deep feelings of emptiness and loss of purpose. According to Fromm, in an attempt to escape empty, isolating freedom and alleviate anxiety, people will adopt different personality types and traits, shown below, that will provide the structure and purpose once offered by mummy and daddy.

Authoritarianism The authoritarian personality is attracted to authoritarian systems with powerful dominant leaders (e.g. Fascism). Individuals become submissive and passive or become an authoritarian figure themselves. The strong are admired and the weak despised. Either way a purpose is given to life.

Destructiveness Authoritarians will respond to negative feelings by striking out at the world in anger in an attempt to alleviate inner pain leading to brutish behaviour, crime and indiscriminate killing. There might also be an inner destructive response that can lead to alcoholism, drug use and suicide. The sadistic personality finds pleasure in hurting others, the masochist in self-hurt.

Conformity Others will escape from freedom by losing themselves in the crowd. In this way they can remain anonymous and not have to take on responsibility for their own actions.

7.7 General example | **Authoritarianism**

We look for structure everywhere and many people feel decidedly uncomfortable when it's not there. In lectures the students will demand structures and slides and the lecturer will stick rigidly to his or her notes no matter if the process works or not. In this way both feel safe and individual freedom is minimised.

7.10 Marketing example | **Booking holidays**

From the late 1950s the foreign package holiday grew and grew almost exponentially. From arriving at the airport and the flight out to the moment they were ready to come home everything was structured and catered for. There was food on the plane, a coach to the hotel, trips to see the sites, evening entertainment and a representative to look after any problems before catching the coach to the airport and the flight home. Everybody felt adventurous but nobody would stray far from the set itinerary and all felt safe. Few tourists ever enjoyed the freedom to arrange the whole process for themselves. The growth in the Internet now seems to allow them to do this. It's an illusion however as customised choices still remain firmly under the umbrella of an overseeing authority and few people still ever strike out entirely on their own.

Questions

1 Do you think that consumers are happy to travel around the world booking their own modes of transport and own hotels? Do you think that there are still opportunities for the packaged tour operator?

2 How might things change into the future?

Humanistic theories of personality development

According to the **humanistic theory of personality development**, most humans are driven to achieve their maximum potential in life and will always do so unless obstacles are placed in their way. According to this approach, the ultimate goal is a sense of inner, spiritual peace. Obstacles that detract as we move through life include hunger, thirst, sex, safety and security concerns, financial problems, social inclusion or anything else that takes our focus away from maximum psychological growth. Two of the most popular theories, those of Abraham Maslow and Carl Rogers, were discussed in Chapter 5 on motivation and interested readers can refer back. Marketers would argue that constant consumption would supply many of the answers to a full and contented life while others express doubts arguing that too much materialism confuses and clouds the really important things in life.

Key point Carl Rogers believed that all humans were unique, were basically good and everyone possesses a positive drive towards self-fulfilment.

Complex personality development

In later years many theories surfaced emphasising the more complex and intricate nature of personality development. The arguments stressed not only the role of genetic inheritance and social interaction but also the idea that individuals develop many concepts of 'self'.

Figure 7.9

Aspects of personality development

Self-concept theory

Self-concept is the thoughts, beliefs and concerns that individuals hold about their own attributes and characteristics and how they evaluate these qualities with regard to their own personalities. Many thinkers have written about **self-concept theory** and some of these ideas are identified below.

Three personality states – the good, the bad and the ugly

Unlike Freud who believed that anxiety and conflict was the driving force behind personality development (between the id, ego and superego), **Henry Stack Sullivan** (1892–1949) believed that it came about through social interaction. Beginning with early childhood, mental defence mechanisms such as *selective attention and selective inattention* are used to protect against levels of anxiety. In this way the child, the adolescent and later the adult, learns to ignore or reject uncomfortable anxiety producing feelings. He believed that personality developed through social interaction and selective attention well into adulthood. In this way individuals think and learn about themselves and others that they come into contact with. (This will be discussed more in the next chapter on social influences.)

The bad-me, the good-me and the not-me

Sullivan felt that there were three basic ways that we see ourselves: the bad-me, the good-me and the not-me. The bad-me is the negative side of my personality and contains those things that I don't like about myself. These will be hidden from other people and even, at times, from myself, because they can cause anxiety, guilt or embarrassment. The good-me is the positive side of my personality, these things I often think about and share with others. The not-me is the part I hate about myself and I will avoid by repressing into the subconscious. All three states will affect personality development.

Key point Henry Stack Sullivan builds on the idea of a three-part personality introduced by Freud (the id, ego and superego) but saw it as the 'bad-me', the 'good-me' and the 'not-me'. These personality states came about through social interaction.

Role playing – multiple personalities

'All the world's a stage, and all the men and women merely players. They have their exits and their entrances, and one man in his time plays many parts, his acts being seven ages.' WILLIAM SHAKESPEARE

Some writers argue that people have more that one personality and that they act out, usually subconsciously or unthinkingly, different roles depending on the situation known as **role playing**. This might be the role of a father or mother to the children, a son or daughter to their mother and father, a brother or sister to siblings, a friend to peers, a lover to their spouse, a teacher or solicitor at work, a student if taking night classes and so on. In fact some investigators believe that there is no 'core' self just a series of different roles adopted for different occasions. For example when playing the teacher a person might be formal, reserved, didactic and professional. When playing the father he might be informal, involved, responsible and sympathetic. When playing the husband and lover he might be sharing, devoted, intimate and loving and when with his friends in the pub he might be childish, comic and irresponsible.

7.11 Marketing example — Role playing and consumer behaviour

Research has shown that we will buy products according to the role we are playing at the time. For example it was shown that a woman buying ice cream or yoghurts would buy the branded packs in her role as a mother, the economy packs for the school fete in her role as a school helper, the small-sized premium pack for her and her husband and a single high-priced extra-premium single offering as a special treat for herself as an individual 'woman' (because she needs to feel special), eating it and telling nobody. L'Oréal used the catchphrase 'because you're worth it' around the world to minimise guilt feelings a woman might have as a mother in spending money on premium cosmetics for herself. 'Because you're worth it' is aimed at reassurance by reminding her that she deserves a special treat in her oft forgotten role as a 'woman'. This puts added pressure on marketers to not only segment markets in the usual way, e.g. age, gender, behaviour and so on, but also in terms of the roles being played.

Question

1 Discuss the idea that people play different roles in their lives and buy different products and services to match these roles.

The extended self – 'I am the material things I possess'

▶ The **extended self** consists of our actual self and the external objects that we gather around that we consider part of our self. This might be my house, my car, my holidays, the fitness club, the restaurant I regularly eat out in and so on. In many cases I, and others, define my personality by the money I've got, the golf club I belong to, and the brands that I purchase. This appears to be especially true of children and young adults where having the right brand of shoes, mobile phone and music player becomes the major thing in life.

Symbolic self-completion theory – brands compensate for identity gaps

Research has shown (Belk 1988) that some individuals will buy products to compensate for an incomplete definition of 'self'. Purchases will be for 'symbolic meanings' attached to the products and brands rather than functional benefits themselves. Consumption can thus raise a person's status, build self-image and improve the overall feel-good factor.

7.12 Marketing example — Playground respect and ring tones

Image and self-concept has an enormous impact on the types of goods, services and brands that people purchase. In fact there are many people, especially the young, who will only ever wear and use brands that bring the respect of others and are seen as 'cool'. Research has shown that infants as young as two years already recognise and covert particular brands. The launch of a chart for musical ring tones suggests that many young people remain addicted to the mobile phone as a self-defining product. Youngsters spend on average £4–£5 per month changing the ring tone on their phone so that they can have the latest and most cool version – it gives 'respect'. Marketers were taken completely by surprise by the demand and the market. In the year 2000 the UK market was worth £2.5 million. In 2004 it was worth over £100 million a year.

The actual, mirror and ideal self

Similar to that of role-play is the theory that individuals have different thoughts and beliefs about our own idea of self (Higgins *et al.* 1987). This can be broken down into three areas: the core or actual-self, the mirror-self and the ideal-self. It's argued that the closer the three are in characteristic content the healthier will be the overall personality.

The core or actual self – is the self that I believe is really 'me'. Individuals will like or dislike their core self to varying degrees across such areas as feelings of adequacy, self-esteem and security.

The ideal self – is the self that I think I would like to be. This would cover such qualities as confidence, dominance, attractiveness and acceptability by others.

Mirror or looking-glass self – is the self I think I portray to other people and some of us are more sensitive to this than others. I hope I come across as generous and trustworthy, always willing to listen to the views of others. Of course I may not be seen in this way and unless I ask (which we very seldom do) I try to make assumptions by judging the reaction of those I interact with.

Many people seem to spend some time in thinking about how they might bridge the gap between how things are and how they would like their personality to be. This will depend on how much individuals care and this varies from person to person.

7.13 Marketing example — Consumer behaviour and self-concept

Many people will also buy products and brands according to a mental concept of their 'core', 'idea', or 'mirror' self needs. Research has shown that 75–80 per cent of Nike sports products are purchased by people who never undertake any sport. This would be related in some way to both how they might like to be seen by others (mirror self) and the concept of how they would really like to be (ideal self). Many adverts try to influence the different concepts of self.

Key point Higgins developed the idea of three parts to personality – the 'core-self', the 'mirror self' and the 'ideal self'.

Intellectual and emotional development

Researchers constantly measure intellectual development, at school, in job interviews and at work but very seldom is emotional development measured. So somebody, perhaps the head of a large organisation, would have a proven track record as far as intellectual prowess is concerned but be very immature emotionally when placed in testing emotional circumstances. For example a normal staid, conservative individual might suddenly start acting like a child when confronted with unfamiliar situations, perhaps drinking too much alcohol. It seems that people develop intellectually and emotionally in separate ways.

Does personality change over time?

Personality by definition is long lasting, as compared to moods, which can change throughout the day. Our personality tends to be set by the time we leave our teen years although our ability to express personality can mature and strengthen over time. Most people intuitively feel that they are basically the 'same' person they were a number of years ago. Even people in their eighties say that, apart from physical ailments, they feel the same person that they were when they were 20.

Normal and abnormal personality

There is the danger that people talk about normal and abnormal personalities as if there is a black and white distinct difference. There are many definitions of what is normal but it seems that personality disorders, rather than just eccentricities, can be said to be abnormal when they become unhealthy and mentally restricting in some way. Obsessive compulsive disorder (OCD) is an example of this type of mental abnormality. Sufferers' lives are driven by obsessive behaviour such as having to check that the house is locked up, or that the taps are all turned off, or that their hands are clean twenty or thirty times before they are able to go out. Consumers are affected when they become addicted to certain activities. For example some people can't stop shopping, spending money on credit cards, collecting things, gambling and drinking alcohol. In the latter cases some blame retailers for encouraging this obsessive behaviour, others the customer, while others argue that governments should take some kind of legislative action.

Transactional analysis – adult, parent and child

Still in use on management courses around the world **transactional analysis** (or **TA**) was the brainchild of **Eric Berne**. He thought that human personality was made up of three '**ego states**' (mind sets). He called these three states 'Parent', 'Adult', 'Child'. Each ego state is an entire system of thoughts, beliefs, attitudes and behaviour and we switch back and forth between the three depending on our mood at the time, the situation and the interacting person. He called this the transaction, and transactional analysis is the attempt to understand the process. According to Berne the three ego states should be in balance. For example too much of one state (parent) and too little of another (child) creates a rigid, rule driven, up-tight personality without any sense of humour. Similarly too much child and too little adult will create an irresponsible personality, unable to adopt a mature approach to life.

Key point According to transactional analysis the three ego states 'Parent', 'Adult', and 'Child', should be in balance if mental harmony is to be achieved.

Parent, adult, child (PAC) ego states

The parent in me, our 'taught' concept of life. The nurturing parent and the critical parent. The critical parent is finger wagging, rule driven, lecturing, controlling, emotional and no fun. The nurturing parent is protective, often talking to a young son or daughter in a childlike way.

The child in me, our 'felt' concept of life. Acting in ways remembered as a child. The child in me will be playful, sulky, irresponsible, emotional, fun loving, curious and submissive with little thought for the future. Decisions made are not thought through.

The adult in me, our 'thought' concept of life. The grown up, mature person in me. The adult in me is objective, detached, rational and reasonable and attempts to see both sides of a problem. It's my ideal self.

Individuals will switch back and forth between the three ego states interacting with others and within their own minds. For example I take back a car under guarantee and expect to it be free. I am polite and reasonable (adult). The service engineer tells me I will have to pay (parent). I react in anger (child) and a row ensues. I storm out swearing. I phone back the next day pretending to be a customer and book an appointment I intend not to keep (child).

Conflict between ego states

Conflict can arise in transaction when PAC ego states are in conflict. For example my wife complains in a whining voice that she doesn't feel very well (whining child). I answer that it is because she drank too much the night before (critical parent) – she will adopt her parent ego response (parent to parent) – result conflict. If I had responded in the same way 'take the day off from work, you deserve it. I will phone in sick as well and we can go to the seaside for the day' (child to child) – result harmony.

Complementary transactions usually happen when both actors are at the same level, e.g. parent-to-parent, child-to-child or adult-to-adult, if both are thinking in the same way communication is easy. However this will depend on the ego state of the parent or the child. For example critical parent interacting with critical parent has the potential for conflict. More possibilities for conflict exist when transactions are *crossed* e.g. parent-to-child or parent-to-adult. Adult-to-adult is the most rational level.

Ego states interact internally as well as externally

Ego states will interact within the person as well as with other people. We must all be aware of constant internal dialogue between our parent and our child ego states. For example 'stay in bed for another hour' (child) or 'get up for a lecture or

Figure 7.10

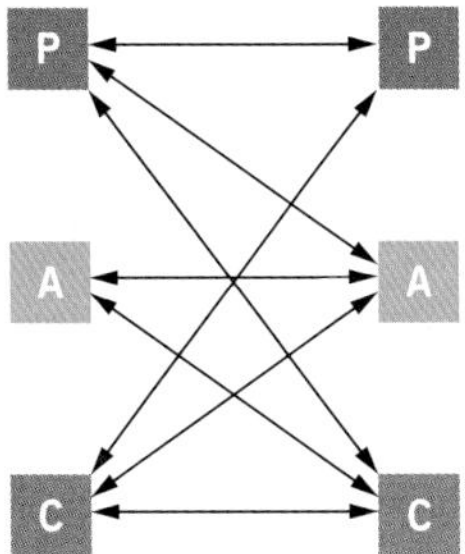

Transactional analysis. Constant interaction between the 'Parent', 'Adult' and 'Child in me' and the 'Parent', 'Adult', 'Child in others'. There is also internal interaction between the parent, adult and child within myself

work it's important not to miss' (adult). Similarly 'spend all my/your money on a new dress' or 'eat more chocolate' or 'have another drink' (child) against 'save for a holiday' or 'you will get fat' or 'you will get drunk and feel awful in the morning' (parent).

Key point Once again we have the concept of three-part personality states (TA) but now shown to interact in a more complex manner. It seems there should be a balance between the three ego states. Too little or too much of any one state can lead to personality dysfunction.

I'm OK – you're OK

Transactional analysis is used to help individuals obtain a healthy positive attitude towards themselves and towards other people. *I'm OK – You're OK* is the name of the book by Thomas Harris (1996) that identifies positive and negative personality states. He sees that liking one's-self and liking other people (I'm OK – you're OK) as the healthy state for most people. This and other negative states are identified below.

I'm OK – You're OK: high self-esteem, high regard for others – positive state

I'm not OK – You're OK: poor self-esteem compared with others – negative state

I'm OK – You're not OK: high self-esteem, low regard for others – negative state

I'm not OK – You're not OK: poor self-esteem, low regard for others – negative state

7.14 Marketing example — Ego state and products

Individuals will purchase products and services according to different ego states and the marketer and salespeople should be aware and respond accordingly. Customers can easily move from one state to another often according to the reaction they get from the retailer, salesperson or other company employee. A complaining customer 'parent' can be reconciled by an 'adult' response from the retailer or made more angry by an adverse anger-provoking response (rule-driven parent or child). All sales situations have the potential for success or failure based on an understanding by the salesperson of the different ego-state responses that might be adopted by the customer. Consumers will purchase different products depending on the different parent, adult and child personality.

Intellectual development of personality – childhood cognitive stages

Jean Piaget (1896–1980) conducted years of research into the way that children develop intellectually and his work is still of great importance today. He is similar to other theorists discussed here in that he describes this **intellectual development of personality** as a series of stages. A child must complete one stage before they are able to move on to the next stage. He was different in that he was more interested in how genetic and biologic changes affected intellect and abilities as the child grew rather than the psychological influences. Overall he believed that the child's mind and subsequent personality is constructed by constant interaction with the environment. As most teachers will know (if they can remember), Piaget identified four clear primary cognitive childhood development stages that all children pass through, though not necessarily at the same rate. Unlike the other theorists discussed above, Piaget was able to construct empirical tests to measure intellect development and could therefore be considered more scientific. He spent little time in looking at inherent biological affects on intelligence.

7.15 Marketing example — Intellectual development

Caveat emptor, 'Let the buyer beware', is the idea that consumers take responsibility for the products and services that they purchase rather than having protection and laws constantly being introduced by governments to meet each new situation. It works on the assumption that people are intelligent and have the ability to know when the items and services that they are buying are not of the standard expected. On the other hand there are retail commentators and pressure groups that argue that the relationship between organisations and consumers is unfair as retailers and manufactures have more power and access to so much more advice and information than the individual consumer. They go on to argue that the relationship is so unbalanced that governments have to step in to redress the balance. This is especially so as technology makes products and distribution systems so much more complex and mystifying.

Questions

1 Discuss consumer intelligence. Do you think that some consumer groups are more intelligent than others?

2 How much protection should governments and law makers give consumers?

Table 7.3 Piaget's intellectual and ability stages

His four stages are very briefly outlined here:

- *Sensorimotor* (0 to 2) At this stage he built tests to measure quite basic structures, motor actions such as sucking and grasping, eye movements, reaction to sound. He showed that children were able to do things in order, understand cause and effect and realise that objects continue to exist even when out of sight.
- *Preoperations* (3 to 7) At this stage a child could intuitively solve problems, such as realising that quantity doesn't change if shape changes. They have an egocentrism, the belief that everybody sees the world the way that they do.
- *Concrete operations* (8 to 11) Here the child is able to reason empirically and objectively understand subtle qualitative differences. They understand grouping, such as different breeds of dog are still dogs.
- *Formal operations* (12 to 15) Abstract thinking where ideas and theories about the world can be thought through and worked out in the mind detached from the thing under examination.

7.8 General example Fluid and innate intelligence

Raymond Cattell suggested that intelligence could be divided down into two basic types: ***crystallised intelligence and fluid intelligence***. Fluid intelligence is the ability to learn and think through new things. This ability initially grows as we grow but deteriorates into old age. Crystallised intelligence, on the other hand, is the sum total of all the things that we have accumulated throughout a lifetime, including knowledge and skills. It tends to be age and culturally centred. Fluid intelligence, the ability to think through new things belongs to the young and crystallised intelligence is predominately with the old.

Question

1 Discuss the meaning of intelligence, how it might be measured and its use in understanding consumer behaviour.

Key point Intellect is an essential component of personality.

Social comparison – learning and comparing ourselves with others

'Character is so largely affected by association, that we cannot afford to be indifferent as to who or what our friends are.' ANON

It would have been noticed that a great deal of personality development happens in society as we compare and adjust the way we think and behave and in interaction with others, peer groups, reference groups and so on. This is an enormous area for investigation and we will be discussing this in more detail in Chapter 8 on the influences of culture and society.

Personality, society, culture and psychographics

There are many cultural and sub-cultural differences in personality and personality development within countries and across nations. For example priorities and influences will be different from the north of England compared with the south and from the UK and the countries in the Middle and the Far East. Although many aspects of personality continue to be included in marketing strategies many now recognise how complex the process of personality is, geography, nationality, culture, and situational factors all play a part in consumer behaviour. We will return to personality when we examine the part that social and cultural differences play in it in Chapter 8 and the process and the role of psychographics and lifestyle in Chapter 9.

Summary

In this chapter we looked at the following areas.

- The meaning of personality, biological and social influences and its importance in marketing and understanding consumer behaviour.
- Theories of personality beginning with type and trait theories. These included: Galen's four personality temperaments, personality from physiognomy, phrenology, Sheldon's body types, graphology and the use of astrology.
- We then looked at the development of trait theory beginning with theorists Gordon Allport, moving on to Raymond Cattell, then on to five-factor analysis, showing how it is still used to identify and measure different personality categories.
- Psychodynamic theories of personality were then discussed beginning with Sigmund Freud. We examined his idea of the parts that the id, the ego and the superego play in activating the conscious and subconscious parts of the human mind and then went on to look at his theory of psychosexual stages in the personality development of the child through to adulthood.
- Neo-Freudian theorists were discussed including Carl Jung's analytical psychology and the collective unconscious, Erik Erickson's psychosocial stages, Alfred Adler's humanistic psychology and Karen Horney's belief in gender similarities.
- We looked at Eric Fromm's concept of freedom before, briefly, the role that theories of existentialism might play in personality development.
- Self-concept and role-playing theories were examined before moving on to talk about transactional analysis and possible ego conflict states, the games people play and 'I'm OK, you're OK' theories currently in use.
- Finally we briefly look at Piaget's theory of intellectual development.

Questions

1 Discuss what we mean by personality. Identify the factors that might be involved and give live examples of different personality types in the world of business, politics and entertainment.

2 Examine how an understanding of personality links in to marketing and consumer behaviour. Identify some of the ways that advertising agencies have used personality groups to build promotional strategies. Give live examples.

3 Discuss and evaluate some of the theories of personality linked to biological causes. How has the discovery of the human genome and DNA helped or hindered in this area of research?

4 Type and trait theory of personality are still in use to the present day. Discuss its development and outline how it's presently used in trying to ascertain personality differences.

5 Discuss the proposition that Sigmund Freud's theory of the subconscious mind is one of the most important discoveries for the development of marketing and understanding consumer behaviour. Give live examples of its uses.

6 There are many theories that talk about personality development in terms of a series of stages beginning from birth through to adulthood. Evaluate the differences between Freud's psychosexual stages and Erikson's psychosocial stages. Show how an understanding of both can aid marketers.

7 Theories of free will and existentialism sprang up during the early and middle parts of the twentieth century. It takes many forms but it appears to suggest that individuals are free to decide their own thoughts, beliefs and personality free of any outside interference. Discuss this concept giving examples were possible.

8 Identify the ideas and beliefs underpinning theories of self-concept. Examine how multiple personalities might be built and show what purpose they might play. How can marketers use an understanding here to help build marketing campaigns?

9 Examine the use of 'transactional analysis' and 'games people play' in understanding human and consumer behaviour. Evaluate its use today and show how effective it might or might not be in looking at personality development.

10 Show how personality contains elements of all the areas discussed throughout the book. Give examples of each area discussed.

Case study

Case study 1 Games people play

In his wide-selling book, *Games People Play*, Berne (1996) writes that people need constant recognition and comfort (he calls 'strokes') especially from a significant other (e.g. spouse). He sees it as a power game with each person using positive and negative methods to obtain 'strokes' from one another. These develop into favourite, habitual ways of interacting and communicating with one another. For example, I may be angry with my wife and say I am not going to a party that evening. I want her to persuade me to go and make me feel wanted (a mental stroke). She tries but I refuse wanting a little more. She then gets angry and the 'game' escalates. It ends up with her going to the party on her own and me sulking at home. Under certain conditions 'games' played can become unhealthy, poisonous and even violent over the years. Consumer products become an essential part of the process as people buy one another products and services that reflect recognition and comfort needs from the other person.

Questions

1 Discuss Berne's thinking behind the book *Games People Play*. Do you think that people in relationships behave in the way outlined above?

2 How might the behaviour shown above feed into consumer behaviour and the purchase of products and services? What part might human subconscious play in the process?

Case study

Case study 2

According to a report undertaken for a slimming magazine, in a survey of 4000 overweight women, all but 1 per cent said that they were unhappy with their body size and would use cosmetic surgery, slimming pills or starvation methods to solve their problem rather than using exercise of some kind. Over 90 per cent said that they were often depressed about the shape of their bodies and often had feelings of inadequacy and low self-esteem. They went on to say that they often felt that they were viewed as abnormal in some way and sometimes treated as second-class citizens. Seventy per cent said that they regularly had to face adverse comments from family, friends and work colleagues about their weight problem. Although not to the same extent, men are increasingly suffering the same sorts of problems especially as the media continues to portray ideal body images and shapes as the personality norm. Worryingly this obsession with body shape begins at a very early age with many young school children reporting concerns about their appearance and giving examples of verbal abuse and bullying because they appear to be different. Government agencies and charities run social marketing campaigns urging people to take on more responsibility for the things they and their children eat as well as taking regular exercise. However many argue that there are more complex reasons behind why there are so many overweight people which need to be addressed.

Questions

1 Discuss the reasons why being overweight could affect personality. Why is it such a problem in modern economies and how much of this is due to marketing and advertising?

2 Identify and evaluate the products and services that are aimed at this market.

3 Do you think there should be more laws and regulations to try to help solve the problem?

Further reading

Books

Allport, G.W. (1937) *Personality: A Psychological Interpretation*, New York: Holt and Company.

Arraj, T. and J. Arraj (1990) *Tracking the Elusive Human, Volume 1. A Practical Guide to C.G. Jung's Psychological Types, W.H. Sheldon's Body types*, Chiloquin: Inner Growth Books.

Berne, E. (1996) *Games People Play: The Basic Handbook of Transactional Analysis*, New York: Ballantine Books, reissue of *Games People Play: The Psychology of Human Relationships*, New York: Ballantine Books, 1964.

Cantor, N. and J.F. Kihlstrom (1987) *Personality and Social Intelligence*, Englewood Cliffs, NJ: Prentice Hall.

Cattell, R. (1983) *Structured Personality Learning Theory*, Westport, CT: Praeger Books.

Craik, K.H., R. Hogan and R.N. Wolfe (1993) *Fifty Years of Personality Psychology*, New York: Plenum.

Eysenck, H.J. and M.W. Eysenck (1985) *Personality and Individual Differences: A Natural Science Approach*, New York: Plenum.

Fromm, Erich (1941) *Escape from Freedom*, New York: Holt, Rinehart and Winston.

Hall, C. and G. Lindzey (1985) *Introduction to Theories of Personality*, New York: John Wiley & Sons.

Hall, Calvin S. *et al.* (1997) *Theories of Personality*, New York: Wiley: 4th edn.

Harris, Thomas (1996) *I'm OK – You're OK*, New York: Avon Books.

Hastings, Elizabeth Hann and Philip K. Hastings (eds) (1992) *Index to International Public Opinion, 1990–1991*, New York: Greenwood Press.

Heidegger, Martin (1966) *Discourse on Thinking*, New York: Harper & Row.

Mischel, W. (1993) *Introduction to Personality,* 5th edn, Fort Worth, TX: Harcourt Brace.

Mitchell, S. and Black, M. (1996) *Freud and Beyond: A History of Modern Psychoanalytic Thought*, London: HarperCollins Publishers, repr.

Robertson, Ivan T. and Dominic Cooper (1995) *The Psychology of Personnel Selection: A Quality Approach*, London: Routledge.

Sartre, Jean-Paul (1984) *Existentialism and Human Emotions*, New York: Philosophical Library.

Schultz, D. and S. Schultz (2004) *Theories of Personality*, CA: Wadsworth Publishing, 8th edn.

Journals

Belk, R.W. (1988) 'Possessions and the Extended Self', *Journal of Consumer Research*, 15: 139–168.

Ben-Shakhar, C.T. *et al.* (1986) 'Can Graphology Predict Occupational Success? Two Empirical Studies and Some Methodological Ruminations', *Journal of Applied Psychology*, 71.

Bouchard, T.J., D.T. Lykken, M. McGue, N.L. Segal and A. Tellegen (1990) 'Sources of Human Psychological Differences: The Minnesota Study of Twins Reared Apart', *Science*, 250: 223–8.

Digman, J.M. (1990) 'Personality Structure: Emergence of the five-factor Model', *Annual Review of Psychology*, 41: 417–40.

Elliot, R. (1997) 'Existential Consumption and Irrational Desires', *European Journal of Marketing*, 31: 285–96.

Goldberg, L.R. (1990) 'An Alternative "Description of Personality": The Big five-factor structure', *Journal of Personality and Social Psychology*, 59: 1216–29.

Higgins, E.T. (1987) 'Self-discrepancy: A Theory Relating Self and Affect', *Psychological Review*, 94, 319–340.

Higgins, E.T., R.L. Klein and T.J. Strauman (1987). 'Self Discrepancies: Distinguishing Among Self-states, Self-state Conflicts, and Emotional Vulnerabilities', in K. Yardley and T. Hones (eds), *Self and Identity: Psychosocial Contributions*, New York: Wiley, pp. 173–86.

Hogg, M.K. and P.C.N. Mitchell (1996) 'Identity, Self and Consumption: A Conceptual Framework, *Journal of Marketing Management*, 12: 629–44.

Lester, David (1981) 'The Psychological Basis of Handwriting Analysis: The Relationship of Handwriting to Personality and Psychotherapy', PhD, Nelson Hall, Chicago.

Smith, L. (1997) 'Jean Piaget', in N. Sheehy, A. Chapman and W. Conroy (eds), Biographical *Dictionary of Psychology*, London: Routledge.

Thatcher, M. (1997) 'A Test of Character', *People Management*, Vol. 3, No. 10, May: 34–5, 37–8.

Websites

British Academy of Graphology, www.graphology.co.uk/.

International Graphology Association, www.graphology.org.uk/.

North Dr Kathryn and Dr Michelle Mills, from The New Children's Hospital, Westmead, Sydney, The Science of Athletics the National Geographic channel Found on www.TimesonLine, 'Do genes play a role in sport?', 13 May 2002, Sanjida O'Connell.

Teamtechnology.co.uk, www.teamtechnology.co.uk (Myers Briggs Types).

Social influences on customer behaviour

8

'We are living in a world today where lemonade is made from artificial flavours and furniture polish is made from real lemons'.

Alfred E. Newman, US Cartoon Character

Objectives

At the end of this chapter the reader should be able to:

1 Describe and analyse the meaning of society, social class, culture and sub-culture and illustrate how they are changing around the world.

2 Examine the part that social agencies play in socialising norms and values into people from generation to generation.

3 Identify and evaluate the strength of social theories.

4 Identify the impact of groups on marketing and consumer behaviour.

Introduction

Throughout all the previous chapters the affect that social influences have on how people behave has constantly arisen. From the moment of birth, through the teenage years, into adulthood and old age, **society** and culture shape and mould people's behaviour. Society affects perception, learning, motivation, attitude, personality and the human mind. There have also been constant references on the part that social influences play compared with genetic, inherited characteristics. There is no doubt that how and where an individual is born and raised, into which family, which social class, in China, America or Russia will make a huge difference to a person's lifestyle and behaviour.

What is society?

Research has shown that people started coming together thousands of years ago for many reasons. Safety was a prime need because life was tough and difficult. Only by coming together could individuals and their offspring protect against dangerous animals and warring tribes as well as using the combined strength of others to hunt, tend animals and grow food. People also came together for social, religious and sexual needs. As family groups and tribes began to grow they started to build language, structures, frame works and collective ways of living together. The more sophisticated societies started to construct organisations, institutions and complex infrastructures including roads and means of transport. When 'society' is discussed nowadays it includes such institutions as governments, politics and law, the civil service, schools and universities, work place, heath, leisure and communication systems as well as the family, the police, the church, the armed forces and charities. Other aspects of human life that relate to how we live and cooperate together in social groups include history, culture, **subculture**, traditions, religions, mores and belief systems.

8.1 General example | Thomas Hobbes – Society protects individuals

Thomas Hobbes (1588–1679) is perhaps most famous for his political philosophy. In his writings he argued that men were fundamentally aggressive and if left living in a state of nature, that is a state without civil government, there would be constant war of all against all in which 'the life would be solitary, poor, nasty, brutish, and short'. There would be 'fear and poverty, no leisure nor industry, culture of the earth, navigation, nor commerce' (from the *Leviathan* in McNeilly 1968). For him, the only way out of this desperate situation was to make a social contract (form a society) and establish an authoritarian state to keep peace and order.

Jean Jacques Rousseau – society corrupts individuals

On the other hand French philosopher **Jacques Rousseau** (1712–78) believed that in a state of nature, individuals were inherently good and it was society that corrupts people by bringing out their aggression, selfishness and inclination to be evil to one another. He believed that laws and social structures were necessary but that they should be based on equality and democratic consent.

Questions

1. Do you agree with Thomas Hobbes, i.e. society protects individuals, or with Jacques Rousseau, i.e. society corrupts individuals?
2. Discuss how you understand the meaning of 'society' and identify how it might vary in countries around the world.

Society – systems or actions

The former British Prime Minister Margaret Thatcher once famously said that there is 'no such thing as society only individuals'. This caused a minor storm at the time and raised an interesting philosophical question about the nature of society. This is whether it's people that create society by interaction or whether it's society that creates people by imposing systems and expected ways of behaving. Or, as is most likely, are both of these important ways of understanding human behaviour. We only have to look at the strength of nationalism in sectarian violence, uprisings and wars around the world to see the power that a particular society has over its citizens. Elements (mainly harmless) of the same thing can be seen in football, basketball, athletics and other sports where nationalism and tribalism is heavily exploited by commercial elements earning billions of dollars for business organisations.

An example of UK nationalism. Many in the US, where the Stars and Stripes is almost worshipped, would consider such dress behaviour as a disrespectful treatment of the country's flag

Sociology

'In the lifetime of one person, we went from figuring out where we came from to figuring out how to get rid of ourselves.' JACK HORNER, on the 80 years between Darwin's *On the Origin of Species* and the nuclear bomb, in *Time*, 26 April 1993

Sociology is an area for investigation that looks systematically at the way that societies are organised and how they develop and change. This includes all of the factors identified above under our explanation of society. Along with most of the social areas of investigation, sociology attempts to be seen as a 'science' but has problems with the limitations associated with the investigation into human behaviour discussed in earlier chapters.

Sociology and the customer

Both the consumer and the business customer are legitimate areas for examination in sociology. Sociological studies look at family and group consumer cultures and sub-cultures and spending patterns, across social class, family life cycles, gender, age, occupation, income, lifestyle groups and so on. Customers and markets are also segmented according to all of these areas because of the different products and services wanted.

Sociology and the physical situation

Sociologists will want to also take into account the physical situation, for example looking at how people behave if they are poor or wealthy, in strong and in weak economic conditions, whether they are working or on holiday and when they are with crowds of people or just a few people. They will also want to know how buying levels differ if the weather is hot, cold, wet or windy and when products and services are in short supply or in surplus (for example during a recession or in an economic boom).

Social psychology

Key point To a lesser extent sociologists will also examine how business customers behave and we will look in more detail at this area in Chapter 10.

As with all the disciplines, sociology has split into more functional areas as information and knowledge becomes more readily available. Humans are social animals and their thoughts, feelings and behaviour usually happen in relationships with other people, with individuals and groups influencing one another. Social psychology is the discipline that studies the workings of the mass and group mind in a social setting (partly discussed in the preceding chapter).

Social psychology and the situation

Unlike the sociologist, the situation the social psychologists are interested in is the one perceived and interpreted by the individuals in it (known as phenomenology). In order words, it is the psychological interpretation of the situation, not the physical objective situation that is of interest. Social psychologists would look at phenomena such as group terrorism, the growth of the Mafia in Italy, the multiple murders that took place in the Columbine High School in Colorado in the US in April 1998 and the Hillsborough deaths in the UK where almost a hundred people were crushed at a football match. They will also look at more mundane happenings such as the feelings that people have on a crowded train in the rush hour, or queuing at the airport or supermarket checkout, or out on the town getting drunk with a group of friends or bidding for products at an auction.

Marketing, consumer behaviour and social psychology

On a lighter scale questions would be asked about the group thinking behind retail and product and service purchase activity. This would embrace such things as the affect of advertising campaigns and sales promotions, the attraction of brands, why there is a rush to buy one type of product rather than another, why stock market shares falling when all economic indicators suggest they should be rising and why it takes far longer for some innovative products to be taken up by the general public than others.

8.1 Marketing example — Christmas and the consumer group mind in the run up to Christmas

Sociologists (among others) are interested in trying to understand, and second-guess the group mind of the consumer in the run up to Christmas. A few years ago the pattern could be more or less predicted with consumers starting to shop at the end of November and increasing their spending towards the start of the holiday. The retailer would then begin the cut-price sale on New Years Day on January the 1st. Now this has changed. The consumer has become more astute and shopping behaviour is different. Many have started leaving the purchase of large ticket items to the January sales rather than before Christmas knowing that the prices would be so much cheaper. As sales started to fall prior to Christmas worried retailers began to start their money off sales much earlier, first to Boxing Day, then to a few days before Christmas and then a week before Christmas. Now nobody seems to be able to predict what might happen at this festive time of the year.

Question

1 Discuss consumer behaviour over the holiday period identified above. Why do you think shopping patterns are changing?

Social anthropology

Anthropologists study early human behaviour and cultural developments in primitive societies, ethnic groups and tribes. In this way they hope to identify social patterns of behaviour that can then be used to explain the more complex ways that groups behave in modern society. The reasoning behind this approach is that although present day relationships seem much more intricate and multifaceted the reality is that if we strip away the surface veneer, some of the same basic simple social structures exist. Similarly evolutionary psychologists go even further back in the evolutionary past and study the behaviour of groups of animals, such as baboons, and try to make the same sort of connection to behaviour in a modern social setting (discussed in more detail in Chapter 1).

The Christmas rush – braving the horror of the shopping crowds. Source: Alamy

8.2 Marketing example — Primeval instincts in the high street

Research conducted for Barclaycard at Exeter University (UK) in 2003 seems to suggest that both men and woman display primitive 'primeval instincts' when shopping in the high street. According to this study 70 per cent of men are likely to fit the traditional 'hunter' profile, while 80 per cent of women are more like 'gatherers'. Most male shoppers want to go straight for the 'kill', because they go with the aim of buying specific items and tend to be more decisive. Whereas women treat bargain hunting as a 'leisure pursuit' in itself and are generally categorised at 'gatherers'.

Questions

1 Do you think that men and women have different shopping motivations and patterns?

2 If so do you think that they are coming closer together?

Social class and stratification

Ever since society has existed people have come together in groups and given status according to the relative characteristics of each group. **Social class** or stratification has been defined by physical strength and power with the group, by family ties, by gender, by tribal connections, by race, by religion, by birthright, by education, by occupation, by the people you mix with and by wealth and ownership of land and property.

Ascribed social class

In some societies people are born (ascribed) into a high- or low-class system and movement is virtually impossible. In earlier times people could be born into slavery and would be owned for the whole of their lives as property by other people. Some ethnic groups were also seen as being much lower in social class than others and interrelationships and inter-marriages were forbidden. The 'caste' system found in India is a good example of this implacable system. In Hinduism social differentiation is stressed by the 'caste' that each individual is born into, e.g. the 'Brahmin' caste is the top caste and the 'untouchables' are the bottom caste. Caste membership in this life is the result of 'good' or 'bad' conduct in the previous life. Movement upwards in the next life can only happen if repentance and compensation takes place in the present life.

8.2 General example — Social class and economic determinism

According to the philosopher Karl Marx, writing in the 1860s and 1870s, social class and power has always been determined by the ownership (or non-ownership) of the means of production, i.e. who owns the factories, farms, coal mines, raw materials etc. He called them 'capitalists' (own the capital) and said they joined together to protect their own and family interests. Those who work for these capitalists he called the 'proletariat' (worker) class and despite working the hardest they suffered the most from hunger and deprivation. In his theory the workers would rise up and destroy the capitalists, just as they did in the distant past under an unfair master/slave and feudal lord/serf economic relationship, and the world would become a classless, social utopia.

Question

1 Discuss why society hasn't changed in the way that Marx predicted.

Acquired social class

'Society is composed of two great classes – those who have more dinners than appetite, and those who have more appetite than dinners.' SÉBASTIEN-ROCH NICHOLAS DE CHAMFORT

In an acquired social class system people are able to move from one class to another dependent on hard work, endeavour (and good fortune). So individuals are still born in to lower, middle and upper classes but those at the bottom (the working class) can aspire to higher things by study, getting a good job, saving money, buying a house and mixing with the 'right' people. There are many that argue, however, that it is infinitely more difficult to move from the lower classes if you are born into a poor family, live in a deprived neighbourhood, go to a sink school and have little chance of getting a decent job and have less choices overall.

> **Key point** Stratification and where people are in the social hierarchy can be **ascribed** (born into) or **acquired** (achieved in life).

The erosion of social class barriers

Research shows that an upwardly changing economy, multiculturalism and more freedom, wealth and awareness especially among the young are gradually eroding the British class system, although features of the system remain (Haralambos *et al.* 2004). The breaking down of class systems and privilege and wealth inequalities will vary in different parts of the world dependent on country wealth, political commitment, religious and democratic freedoms and availability of information and media systems. As social class barriers come down it throws up an opportunity for marketers to offer standardisation brands (with the concomitant savings from economies of scale) around the world.

8.3 Marketing example — Max Weber and class

The sociologist **Max Weber** (1864–1920), writing at the turn of the twentieth century, felt that Marx's ideas about social class were much too simple and many other factors needed to be taken into account. Where people live, went to school, took holidays, their life chances, friends, educational levels, leisure pursuits, in fact the whole of somebody's lifestyle would contribute to their social position. In fact his ideas are much nearer to how many might describe social class today. His concept of 'lifestyle' as a way of segmenting markets is of enormous importance to marketers and advertisers and it will be discussed in much more detail in the next chapter.

Questions

1 Do you think that social class distinctions are crumbling or no longer exist?

2 Look at the relationship between 'society' and consumer behaviour and discuss why you think Weber's concept of lifestyle is so important in marketing and retail.

Social diversity

All societies have a mix of people with different ideas about political, economic, social, religious and philosophical issues. They might have poor and rich people, religious and secular people, Christians, Jews, Muslims, Hindus, those who believe in individualism free from state control and those who believe in collectivism and lots of state control. These differences vary from one country to another and within one country compared with another. For societies to cohere and live in peace and prosperity these differences must be recognised, reconciled and absorbed both internally and externally and beliefs and values internalised so that social and tribal members feel an integral part of the whole. This will not happen where perceived unfairness and inequalities continue to exist. Nation forming and social cohesion can take many hundreds of years as with Europe and the so-called old world, be much quicker as with North America or still be happening as with Africa (although apartheid in South Africa seems to have been successfully dismantled) and the developing world. From a marketing perspective consumer spending cannot be maximised until and unless conflict is reconciled, compromise agreed and stability and rational economic policies implemented. In many parts of Europe multiculturalism, and the richness it can bring, has been the source of thousands of new products and services particularly across grocery, take-away, eat-in restaurants, cosmetics and music. Countries that feel comfortable with **social diversity** at home can also have advantages in dealing with global cultural diversity.

8.3 General example **Culture and social diversity**

Researchers at Duke University in Durham, North Carolina, have been involved in an international research project looking at the cultural behaviour of orang-utans. The animals' behaviour, the use of labels, signals, skills and symbols etc., appears to show that there is extensive social contact between these animals. It also suggests that human culture started to develop as long ago as 14 million years. Other researchers (Professor William Mcgrew, Chimp Studies, Miami University, Ohio at www.muohio.edu) have found more evidence that chimpanzees living in different parts of Africa have developed distinct customs demonstrating, in a similar way to humans, cultural diversity.

Social exclusion

'Beggars should be abolished. It annoys one to give to them, and it annoys one not to give to them.' NIETZSCHE

Within all societies there exists a sub-stratum of people that are deprived and poor and can come to be seen as **socially excluded**. Poverty and low living standards can restrict groups of people's access to good food, health, education, work, artefacts and all the opportunities and life's choices that are available to the rest of society. Caring governments will use social marketing as a way of communicating messages to these groups about available benefits that could help with the problem.

Services aimed at the lower income consumer

Public, private and non-profit organisations will all be involved at some time or another in developing social marketing strategies aimed at improving the health

Social diversity is now common across Europe: Camden Town, London. *Source*: Simon Wright

and wellbeing of the populations they serve. This will include campaigns aimed at informing poorer people of the availability of welfare programmes, stopping people smoking and drinking too much, reducing the risk of AIDS, stopping child abuse, understanding mental health, getting involvement in energy reduction and waste management and so on. The UK Co-operative Bank undertook research and found that the most pressing financial problems for people on low incomes were debt management, access to credit and current account facilities. They have responded by offering financial services working with Credit Unions. Credit Unions are member-owned, non-profit, financial cooperatives organised by consumers to encourage savings and to obtain loans at the lowest possible cost, set up specifically to help people excluded in the past from using these types of services.

Three main social class groups

It is often easier and more helpful to divide the class system (categorised according to occupation and income) into three main groups. These can then be applied to many countries around the world in both developed and developing countries. Social class is still used as a method to define the levels of demand in consumer markets especially in countries such as China, India and Brazil. The size of each social-class group will vary from country to country.

Social exclusion – down and out in a large city.
Source: Simon Wright

Upper class

The upper classes consist of people with great wealth, both inherited and accumulated, influence and power, and account for a very small percentage of the population. Their network of influential friends and acquaintances, type of education, leisure pursuits and pastimes, also defines them.

Middle class

The middle classes have a large disposable income and include industrialists, professionals, businesspeople and managers. They could have two or three holidays a year, two cars, with children at private school.

Working class

The working class are the unemployed or those working in menial unskilled jobs usually with low or restricted income. The persistence of class differentials in both mortality and illness is evidenced in regular reports provided by national statistical offices.

Objective and subjective social class

It should be remembered that individuals do not always see themselves in the social class identified by observers. For example by occupation, income and home address a family might be classified as working class but when asked it could well see itself as middle class.

Table 8.1 The UK National Readership Survey (www.nrs.co.uk) provides more detail in the following socio-economic groupings

The socio-economic scale

Social grade	Description of occupation	Example
A	higher managerial, administrative or professional	Company director
B	intermediate managerial, administrative or professional	Middle manager
C1	supervisory, clerical, junior administrative or professional	Bank clerk
C2	skilled manual workers	Plumber
D	semi- and unskilled manual workers	Labourer
E	state pensioners with no other income, widows, casual and lowest grade earners	Unemployed

8.4 Marketing example — Social class

Social class categories are of importance to marketers as long as it can be shown that groups of people buy products and services according to class position and in many instances this seems to be the case. It's also important for business to have some idea of the wealth spread and demand for its products both in home and foreign markets. For example India has a population of nearly one billion with many hundreds of millions of people still living on a dollar (US) a day. This might cause a manufacturer to think that a market for premium products, e.g. Mercedes cars, might be non-existent. However this is not the case as India also has its share of very wealthy people. According to Indiaonestop.com, in 1999 250 million people might be classified as high, middle and low middle class and this is growing between 1 and 2 per cent a year. Out of this 250 million, 40 million have an annual income of $600,000 US and 150 million have an annual income of over $20,000 US. By 2025 50 per cent of the population could be classified as middle class.

Questions

1. Discuss the issue of social class across global markets. Do you think it is still a relevant way of classifying consumer groups?
2. How might marketing be different across the social class groupings?

Key point Individuals and groups have a social class position in society according to birth, wealth, power and income. It's easier in some societies than others to move from one social class to another.

Culture

Culture can be described as the particular ways that people in different countries and regions across the world organise society and behave and live their lives. It encompasses language, a system of shared political, economic and social beliefs, values, morals, customs, myths and rituals, buildings and infrastructure, artefacts, food and drink, leisure activities and so on. Cultures are learnt and then passed on from one generation to another by all the many social institutions and organisations that exist in a society. Cultures will be different from country to country. For example in the United States morality deems that one should not be naked in public. In Japan, on the other hand, groups of men and women may take steam baths together without it being seen as improper. In Western countries ties for businessmen are perceived as arbitrary while turbans must be worn in some parts of Asia. Women can more or less dress how they please in Christian countries but must be completed covered or at least wear a headscarf in many Muslim countries.

8.5 Marketing example — Ethnic minority markets

Many manufacturers are now waking up to the fact that many markets for ethnic products, ignored in the past, are now worth many hundreds of millions of pounds. According to French company L'Oreal, black women in the UK spend six times more on hair-care than white women. In the past ethnic minorities would either purchase unsuitable products and convert them or spend time hunting out products that work for them. Now L'Oreal, has set up a laboratory in Chicago, an area with a large black population, to study differences in black, Asian and Hispanic hair, and skin needs and wants. The market research company ACNielsen says that, because of their purchasing power, ethnic segments across a whole range of markets can no longer be overlooked. In the US, African Americans account for 12.7 per cent of the US population and yield a purchasing power of over $650 billion.

Question

1 Identify and evaluate other ethnic minority markets.

Marketing, consumer behaviour and a blame or supportive culture

The culture of an organisation will affect retail employees and the way that they treat the customers. An unhappy, blame-ridden culture is characterised by too many rules, constant criticism, hidden agendas, an unwillingness to listen to others and excess dominance by managers. It could create fear, unhappiness and a reluctance to take decisions in support of customer satisfaction. In the same way it could stifle creativity and innovation with employees unwilling to experiment with new ideas and new product development or make instant decisions for fear of management condemnation and retribution. On the other hand a supportive culture could encourage the opposite by positively encouraging and empowering staff to communicate back and forth with one another and build the confidence to take customer service improvement driven initiatives. Job satisfaction will follow, as individuals get more involved with the job knowing that they will have backup and recognition even if problems arise.

Homogenisation and global brands

'English has become the world's dominant language. It is the language of economic globalisation and international organisations, and it is logical that it will take root in Central Europe, just as it did in Western Europe.' ANON

There is evidence to suggest that consumers in many countries are becoming similar to one another in the products that they buy and the lifestyles that they adopt. Travel and information through the media are encouraging individuals to want to be able to choose from the many global brands now available. This is especially true with US products and to a lesser extent other modern Western economies. Coca-Cola, McDonald's, Carrefour, Microsoft, IBM, Procter & Gamble, Nike, Unilever, Sony, Mercedes, Intel, Nokia, Marlboro, Ford, Disney, Levi and US films, videos and music are just a small example of global brands and products that have changed cultures and come to define the way that people live. In this way a global brand's value comes to mean the same thing for consumers whether they are in the United States, South America, the Middle East, Morocco, India, Russia or China.

8.6 Marketing example — Global branding

According to brand expert company Interbrand, Coca-Cola in the US is the most valuable and recognisable brand name in the world worth around 70 billion US$. The highest valued brand outside of the US is Nokia worth 30 billion US$. Both are sold in virtual every country on the planet. Procter & Gamble, the world's largest producer of branded package goods spends over 5 billion US$ on its portfolio of branded FMCG products, McDonald's fast-food products are now available in 30,000 outlets in almost every country around the world. The world's largest retailer, Wal-Mart, Starbuck coffee houses, Toys r Us are all global players spreading their philosophy in every corner of the world. Staggering numbers and amounts are linked to brands that are creating the same lifestyle wherever they are sold around the world.

Key point People all around the world sharing the same vision and set of values about a brand (loving it!) can be seen as the ultimate ambition for a global brand.

American cultural imperialism

Some people around the world welcome the onslaught of American products and brands linked to an American way of life and see it as economically healthy, others reject what they see as unacceptable **cultural imperialism**. In every continent in the world there are people who resent the fact that companies like Coca-Cola, McDonald's, Nike, Budwieser, Disney and Malboro can enter and dominate their markets and begin to destroy cultural ways of thinking and behaving that have existed for hundreds, if not thousands, of years.

Sub-culture

Cultures are made up from a large number of sub-cultures. Sub-cultures are small groups of people, within the common culture with shared beliefs and value systems based on common life experiences. Sub-groups could be formed according to many different criteria including such things as age, gender, ethnic origin, religion, beliefs and leisure pursuits. Membership of any one sub-culture is not necessarily all encompassing, for example a married person might be an avid Manchester United football fan adopting all the values of the sub-culture for part of the time but acting in a mainstream manner when engaged in normal family pursuits. Similarly acting within a sub-culture will probably not be for life and, depending on the strength of the attraction, people might move from one sub-culture to another and back into the mainstream as the passing years bring more conservative ways of behaving.

8.7 Marketing example — Sub-cultures and niche-markets

Sub-cultures have proven to be a healthy opportunity for marketing. Britain's diverse communities, including ethnic, religious and sexual minorities now make up a number of niche markets worth £120 billion. Minority groups, Chinese, African, Asian and Indians have spending power of 12 to 15 billion pounds a year. In the US there is estimated to be 14 to 16 million gay, lesbian and bisexuals over the age of 18 with a buying power of $610 billion ($200 billion for lesbians alone). Twenty-five million adults in the US care about green issues and put environmental and spiritual concerns at the centre of their beliefs. Afro-Americans are often trendsetters for young people and Hispanics have a major influence on the music market. Women and men between the ages of 50 and 64 have the highest incomes and spend more on fashion products and food and leisure than the rest of the population. Other sub-culture niche markets include: skate boarding, singing, kite surfing, countryside rambling, speciality gardening and all kinds of dancing. The list is endless and many niche markets are waiting to be exploited by innovative companies.

Questions

1. Examine some vibrant niche markets and give reasons why you think that they are successful.
2. Identify groups of consumers where a niche market might exist.

8.4 General example **Youth sub-cultures**

Youth sub-cultures, all with their own style of dressing, language, beliefs, attitudes and ways of behaving, seem a natural phenomenon for the young. It's a way that individuals can rebel against the mainstream and develop and express their own personality within a group of like-minded people. Groups that have come and gone over the years include such names as: Goths, Hip-Hop, Hippies, New Age, Punks, Skinheads, Rockers, Straight-edge, Skaters, Head Bangers and so on.

> **Key point** Culture consists of different ways of behaving, family living, sex and marriage, talking, eating, dressing, working, relaxing as well as infrastructures and artefacts that are passed down from one generation to another.

Socialisation

Every individual in every country around the world will be socialised into behaving in generally acceptable ways. In all cultures there will be central **value systems**, considered normal in that society, which will be inculcated into everybody from the moment they are born up to the moment that they die. This **socialisation process** happens first in a very informal way with the parents and possibly close relatives teaching the children how to eat, drink, go to the toilet, walk, talk and behave and interact with others around them in the same way that they were taught by their mothers and fathers. This will be reinforced and added to as the child grows older (now sometimes in more formal ways) by friends, both inside and outside of school and university, by schoolteachers, by the police, by people at work, neighbours, other parents and so on. People will also learn how to behave through observing and copying others, by watching TV, by looking on the Internet, listening to the radio, by reading books, magazines, newspapers and by deliberate studying. In this way the particular culture and/or sub-culture of each group is passed on to other members. Sometimes **socialisation** seems to break down and groups of people (especially the young) are accused by others of acting in anti-social ways.

> **Key point** As well as regulating people's behaviour, social norms are also deeply internalised so that they become inextricably part of the human psyche.

8.8 Marketing example **Social learning, Albert Bandura**

In his book on **social learning** theory (1977), **Albert Bandura** emphasises the importance of observing and modelling behaviours, attitudes, and emotional reactions of others in the social learning process. It seems we first copy our parents, then friends, peer group members and relatives. As we grow older we test out ways of behaving to measure the reaction of others. Behaviour deemed to be acceptable is adopted while unacceptable behaviour is dropped. As an example, many consumers will model their behaviour on TV commercials that suggest that drinking a certain brand of alcohol, using a particular hair shampoo or driving one make of car rather than another will make them popular and win the admiration of attractive people.

Question

1 How influential do you think that advertising is on long-term social behaviour?

Social agencies

Social agencies are the social institutions and organisations that teach group members the culture and ways of living and behaving in any one society. Social agencies can be formal and/or informal and ascribed (born into) or achieved (joined) and these are discussed below.

Informal agencies

By far the most important informal socialising agency is the family. There is evidence to show that the earlier the influence the stronger it becomes and the longer it lasts into adulthood. In this respect the mother can be considered the primary influencer because of the intimate relationship with the newborn baby and child in its early formative years. Next brothers, sisters and close relatives would follow the authority of the father. Of course the relative influencing strength of the family members on the development of the child would vary according to the culture and the lifestyle of the family group. Other informal socialising agencies include groups of school friends, acquaintances, work colleagues, the media and so on. In some countries the extent of religious involvement gives the church representative more influence at the informal level.

Key point The power of the mother/father influences on early child development was discussed in some detail in the preceding chapter on personality stage development.

Marketing and the family life cycle

The strength of the family on consumer behaviour has been well researched and described because it is arguably the greatest of all the socialising influences. This is especially so in decision making and the buying of consumer products and services. It has therefore become one of the foremost ways that marketers segment their markets for products and services in the world. This should take into account cultural differences and how **family life cycles** could differ from one generation to the next. Marketers spend millions on attempting to group family life cycles into meaningful (and profitable) segments that suit their own special needs. Below is a simple example of a family life cycle.

8.9 Marketing example — Family life cycle categories

Baby – toddler – child – tweenie (between 10 and 12) – teenager – couple living together or married, no children – young couple with children under six – young couple with children over six – single-parent household – single-person household – older couple with grown up children living at home – older couple with no children at home (**empty nester**) – older person living on their own.

Questions

1 Think of the different kinds of products that could be purchased at all the different stages of the life cycle.

2 Discuss the value of segmenting the market in this way.

Formal socialising agencies

There are other socialising agencies that have more formal expected ways of behaving. These will include: primary and secondary schools, university, work, the church, the armed services, the police, political parties and local and national government as well as clubs and associations such as the Boy Scouts, the Girl Guides, golf clubs and so on.

8.10 Marketing example — Family changes and new products and services

Of particular interest to marketers has been the change in family relationships. In the UK in the mid-1960s, only 5 per cent of single women lived with a man before getting married. By the 1990s, about 70 per cent did so and there is a large proportion of unmarried couples with children. In the UK one-parent families now exceed two million and nearly a third of all households are single occupancy. Although a very small percentage, there has been some growth in same sex couples living together and in some countries gay marriages are now allowed. All this change is a fertile ground for products and services that offer benefit solutions to meet new demands thrown up by these changes.

Table 8.2 — Formal and informal socialisation agencies

Socialising agencies teach us how to behave and include the following:

Family – parents, mother and father, siblings, relatives.

Friends – colleagues, acquaintances, peers, neighbours, girlfriend or boyfriend, spouse.

Education – infant, primary, middle, senior school, college, university.

Church – Christian, Muslim, Jew, Hindu, Sikh, Rastafarian, Buddhist.

Groups – peer groups, reference groups, social groups, work groups.

Mass Media – TV, newspapers, magazines, radio, cinema, Internet.

8.5 General example | The power of early indoctrination

St Ignatius Loyola, founder of the Jesuits and the Society of Jesus, is supposed to have said 'give me the child until the age of seven and I will give you the man', meaning that religious and superstitious values indoctrinated before this age on the impressionable young would be so deeply buried that they would be beyond the reach of any kind of change.

Question

1 Do you think that early socialisation has the power suggested above?

Social norms

▶ These normal expected ways of behaving are known as social '**norms**' and they will apply to every situation, in whatever role a person might find himself or herself. Like the associated concept of values, norms will often differ from group to group, and from society to society. Whereas values are very general guidelines for behaviour, however, norms compliment values because they represent very specific rules that govern people's behaviour in particular situations. It's the norms and the culture that come together to make up any given society, as life would be impossible for groups of people without known values and expected ways of behaving to give the concept understandable meaning.

8.6 General example | Un-socialised children

A California girl, Genie, was locked in a room alone from the age of about 1 1/2 years old until she was more than 13. A psychiatrist described her as 'un-socialised, primitive, hardly human'. Later, she learned to eat quite normally, was toilet-trained, and tolerated being dressed like other children. Yet her mastery of language never progressed beyond that of a 3 or 4-year-old. The 'Wild Boy of Aveyron', found in southern France in 1800, looked and behaved like an animal. An attempt to change him from 'beast to human' failed. The 'wolf children', Kamala and Amala, were discovered by Reverend J.A.L Singh in 1920 in a jungle in India having been bought up by wolves. Both died young and were never really bought back into human society.

Social norms and social roles

'Who am I then? Tell me that first, and then, if I like being that person, I'll come up: if not, I'll stay down here till I'm somebody else'. LEWIS CARROLL, *Alice's Adventures in Wonderland*

The idea that individuals play many different roles throughout their lives was discussed in some detail in the chapter on personality. The characteristics that go to make up the social role being played might be partly hereditary, for example male and female, and partly learnt through social interaction. All roles adopted will have learnt social norms attached that can be culturally variable. For example boys learn to play with toy cars and girls with dolls. Young people must learn the mating rituals relevant to their society. In some cultures women do all the cooking and cleaning and men the hunting and gathering (going out to work). Individuals learn how to be a good son or daughter, how to be a parent or husband or wife, how to be a pupil or student, how to behave at work and ultimately how to be a respectable citizen or tribal member. Many people will play many roles often switching from one to the other during the day. The sociologist, Ervin Goffman (1959) has argued that these roles can be real, sincere and honest or they can be false and contrived depending on the situation and the people we may be trying to impress (all markets for segmentation to the observant marketer).

8.7 General example | **Gender roles**

Many studies have found that gender roles are socialised by parents and others from a very early age often in an unconscious manner. In a study in 1986 Statham found that parents had great difficulty in combating patterns of gender learning. Nearly all the children in his study played with gender type toys given by relatives. In 1972 Weitzman *et al.* found gender differences in preschool children's books, toys and TV programmes. In 1976 another study by Will, Self and Datan showed that mothers practise gender stereotypes as early as five or six months. Nancy Chodorow found that boys break with their mothers at an early age to assert their masculinity and individuality while girls maintain an indefinite continuity based on emotion and feelings.

8.11 Marketing example | **Social norms and roles**

Lots of social roles have marketing and consumer considerations attached, many of them becoming stereotypical. An attentive husband or wife will buy presents and send cards at Christmas, Diwali, Ramadan and Jewish New Year and on anniversaries and birthdays. A young man wanting to impress a girl will want to have a particular motorcar and a young woman will be concerned about dress codes and fragrance smells. Middle-class aspirants must have upmarket kitchen equipment and household furniture, go on holidays to 'in' places, eat at the 'right' restaurants, and shop at high-class stores if they want to maintain an aura with friends and neighbours that befits their wanted role status.

Role models – people we would like to be like

It's argued that people have 'role' models, individuals that are respected, admired and copied in the way that they live their lives (Bandura and Walters 1963). **Role models** can come from mundane sources such as family, friends, work and so on

Selling to children. *Source*: Creative club/Mattel

or from the more exotic world of adventure, sport and entertainment. This can cause problems if the role model held in high esteem by young people disgraces himself or herself by perhaps taking drugs, being constantly drunk or misbehaving in some other unacceptable manner. Advertising people all around the world exploit this need for role models by associating their brands with people admired by a company's target market.

Status – people we would like to be or groups we would like to join

'The person with the most possessions at the end is the winner.' REAR WINDOW CAR STICKER

Status can be defined as the relative position that individuals, groups and roles have in a social hierarchy based on such things as money and wealth, occupation, education and breeding. Power and privilege often goes hand-in-hand. In most societies status is important, as most people seem to need and want the admiration and adulation of others. As with social groups, status can be ascribed, e.g. born into money, or it can be acquired, e.g. a pop star, premier club footballer, business entrepreneur.

Cars are status symbols

Not all people think in the same way about who has and hasn't high status but in general those with a high income, a large house in the 'right' district, exotic cars, and a glamorous lifestyle are admired and envied by groups with a more mundane existence. Professional occupations such as architects, lawyers, doctors and solicitors as well entertainers, sportspersons and other celebrities are also considered by many to be of a high status. The whole history of a society can be seen as one group of people attempting to raise their status in relationship to another. This could be one country, one class, one region, one tribe or one football team defining themselves by their superior position to others. Similarly it could be gender, how males and females relate to one another or it could be wanting to be seen as friends with the wealthy, the famous and aristocratic, joining a 'chartered institute', going to a prestigious university or having a grand sounding job title.

Key point Status would be an irrelevant concept for a person living alone on a desert island. A personalised number plate needs to be seen by others otherwise it's meaningless.

Figure 8.1

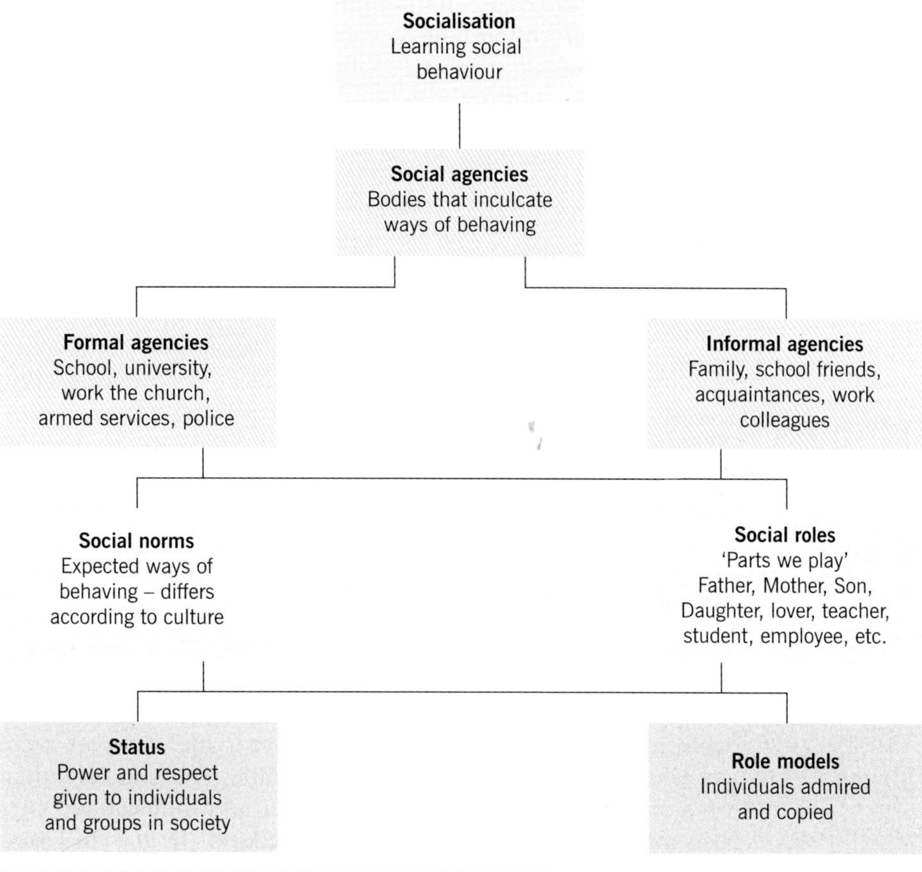

Socialisation

Weak, medium and strong norms

Basic norms vary along a continuum between the informal and weak to the formal and strong. At the weak end norms are known as 'folkways', in the middle are norms known as 'mores' (pronounced 'more-rays') or morals and at the end are laws, rules and regulations. Norms tend to be unofficial and passed down by generation to generation by family, friends and others in both an implicit and explicit manner, while the stronger norms will be officially brought into law by the government and written down and regulated. All manner of weak, medium and strong norms will vary across nations and cultures.

Folkways or conventions

Folkways or conventions are acceptable ways of behaving and will include the following: manners at the dinner table, shaking hands, bowing, rubbing noses, or kissing as a form of greeting others, how men and women should dress and react to one another, children being subservient and polite to their elders, working with others in groups, not constantly fighting with one another and so on.

8.12 Marketing example — Conventions and consumption

Over the years marketers have worked hard (with some success) to impose consumer concepts as conventions and folkways. Father Christmas dressed in red and white emanated from a Coca-Cola advertising campaign and is now firmly entrenched, along with the Christmas tree, lights, presents, the turkey and liqueurs as part of Christmas. Advertisers have invented or embellished 'mother's day', 'father's day', 'grandparents' day', 'Valentine's day' as well as 'exam passing', 'becoming well again', 'changing homes' and even 'death and bereavement'. They are marketed as opportunities for consumers to spend money on cards, gifts and tokens in love and remembrance or risk causing guilt and offence.

Rituals

Rituals are formalised repeated ways of behaving that help give structure and social cohesion to social life. Many rituals are the same or similar in many parts of the world and people of all cultures appear to gain satisfaction, comfort or security from the meanings that rituals help give to life. Many are sacred or religious and act as milestones through the journey of life. These include thanksgiving at births, rites of passage into adult life, marriages and homage and ceremony at death. It also includes making sacrifices of some kind (human in years gone by) such as Muslims visiting Mecca at least once in their lifetime, rites of cleaning or purification, processions, celebrations and festivities.

8.13 Marketing example — Rituals

All religions have rituals, as do nations, races, towns, villages, associations and clubs. As with conventions, commercial organisations have not been wanting in associating and encouraging consumer spending as a part of these rituals. Whether this is the sale of religious symbols and other merchandise or food and clothing, commercialism abounds. Champagne is a perfect example of a brand that has been successfully marketed as a 'must have' product at marriages and other congratulatory events and religious holidays throughout the year.

Myths and legends

Myths are stories that are fictional and are handed down through the ages and often believed by many people. All countries have them and they tend to be used to describe heroes, ancestors or supernatural or religious beings, or explain some historical happening usually in terms of national or ethnic glory or honourable characteristic trait. They can become an enormous source for commercial exploitation (movies, books, comics, toys) and examples will include stories about the Greek gods, Roman heroes, Nordic Vikings, Chinese warriors, American Indians, Celts, Robin Hood, William Tell and King Arthur.

Mores – moral ways of behaving

Mores are more deeply ingrained than conventions and are about morals and values that are expected for social group members. These will be to do with things such as types of government, e.g. democratic, autocratic, monarchy, religious conviction, sexual behaviour, the need or otherwise for marriage, beliefs about abortion, how children and animals are treated and so on.

8.14 Marketing example — Mores and consumption

The morals and values of any society are an enormous fertile breeding ground for encouraging consumption. As religious concerns diminish, commercial considerations increase. Outlandish stag and hen nights for men and women about to get married, lasting two or three days; marriages in exotic places around the world, holidays exploiting sun, sex and sangria for single young people, children elevated to the level of vicarious brand fashion totems, all mirror changing mores and the intervention of marketing.

Laws and rules and regulations

Laws and rules and regulations are ways of behaving that are obligatory and backed up by the force of civil or criminal law. This will apply to both consumers and business customers. In many cases there will be differences from one country to another, although community associations such as the European Union are constantly harmonising laws across all member states. All governments in developed markets now recognise the importance of the consumer as the final arbiter in what consumer goods should and should not be produced in the successful running of a free market economy. To this end we have seen the rise in so-called 'consumerism' and the power of the consumer. Politicians, recognising the unequal relationship between the customer and big business are constantly redressing the balance by introducing consumer laws that protect the consumer and reign in the ability of organisations to manipulate and restrict competition and consumer choice.

8.15 Marketing example — IBM a global company

'As a global company, IBM is committed to "following local laws and customs of the countries in which we operate." IBM marketing and communications materials present information in culturally appropriate ways. Our customers also need to rapidly reach new multilingual and multicultural markets, while minimizing entry costs and economic risks. Customers need products and services that support their languages and cultural conventions – today', IBM website.

Norms and forms of social censor

Normative expected ways of behaving in any given society are both formally and informally enforced and much of it is habitual or sub-conscious. Methods of enforcement will be passed down from generation to generation as a part of cultural inheritance. Informal social norms (conventions and folkways and to a certain extent mores) are often unspoken or only lightly touched upon and people learn by observation or by listening to others. Individuals find out that they have broken a 'norm' only when censored by others (initially the family and friends). Informal criticism or censor can be by a sharp rebuke by mother ('go and wash your hands before having dinner'), by a definite coolness in the way that a wife or husband might talk to one another, facial language such as father scowling or not smiling, by body language, e.g. friends turning their backs when we approach, or by family, friendship or work groups refusing to talk to us. In fact we are all trained very early on in life by informal censor when we have contravened a 'norm' and upset somebody or some group. Because nobody likes being ostracised (seeking pleasure and avoiding pain) learning to behave in socially expected ways happens very quickly.

The more important the norm that is broken the stronger will be the censor

Some expected ways of behaving are more important than others and so the criticism and censor imposed will be much stronger. In the most extreme cases, the breaking of a norm could mean banishment from the group, a monetary fine, imprisonment for a varying amount of time or even a death sentence in some way or another. The seriousness or otherwise of the norm breaking will vary in countries around the world (as well as changing in magnitude) according to political and religious cultures and systems. In the West homosexuality, fornication and adultery have, in the main, come to be accepted as part of life's rich pattern, while in other parts, notably some Muslim countries, it's still punishable by stoning, imprisonment and even death.

8.8 General example — Honour killings and culture clash

Indian law recognises inter-caste marriages, but certain communities, especially in rural areas, still consider them to be an insult. Cases of honour killings persist where parents and relatives of young men and women from different castes who have married or have been seeing one another have been killed in public. There have also been instances of young women born in European countries such as the UK being murdered by relatives because they refused to go back to India or Pakistan to marry, unseen, a man selected by their parents.

Figure 8.2

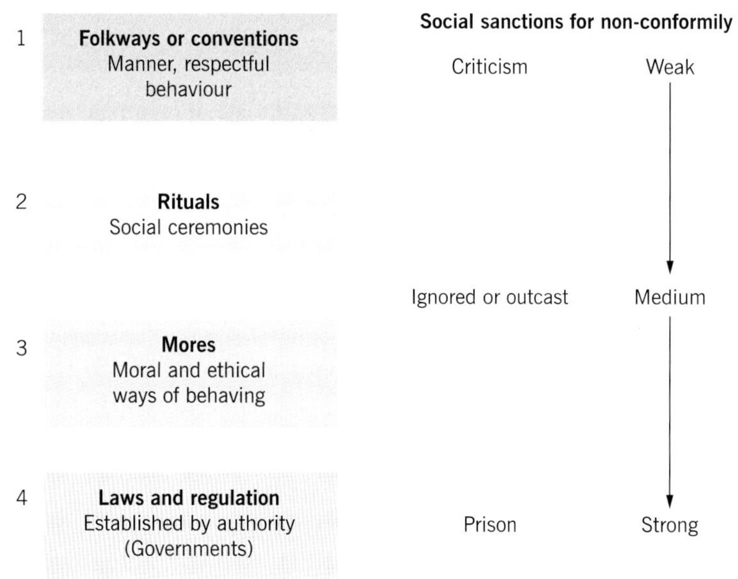

Weak, medium and strong sanctions for ignoring or not behaving in socially acceptable ways

Labelling theory – tell somebody they are a criminal and they will act like a criminal

A group of sociologists, later known as labelling theorists (Lemert, Cooley, Mead, Tannenbaum and Lemert), began exploring how and why some behaviour was seen as criminal or deviant and other acts were not and why some people were identified as criminals and others were not. They came to the conclusion that in many cases people were not criminal by nature, the label being attached by the community as a social reaction to particular ways of behaving. For example many ways of behaving once considered normal are now defined as deviant and ways of behaving once considered deviant are now considered normal. And this will vary from one country to another. This includes such thing as using marijuana, smoking in restaurants, animal hunting, drinking under the age of 21, homosexuality, divorce, smacking children and so on. In any conflict, one group could be defined as freedom fighters by one side and terrorists by the opposing side. In the twentieth century many individuals jailed for criminal offences against the state have ended up in positions of power when political circumstances have changed (e.g. Nelson Mandela in South Africa). **Labelling theory** thus becomes key to how many people define themselves as individuals, within groups and within society.

8.9 General example — Homosexuality – deviant or not?

Homosexuality was illegal in the UK until 1967 (it still is in most Muslim countries) and up to this time practitioners were seen as criminals and could be sent to prison. Famous novelist Oscar Wilde was vilified and locked up in Reading jail and died as an outcast for gay behaviour that is now considered a normal part of life in many countries around the world.

8.16 Marketing example Labelling theory

Marketers have to be extremely careful about how they react to labelling theory and the concomitant issue of stereotyping especially when marketing around the world. Research has shown that having an ethnocentric view of the world, believing that your own race, religion, nation or group is better than others, is more commonplace than people imagine. Standardising or customising products and services in global markets is a recurring problem in marketing and managers must make decisions based on empirical research rather than on unsubstantiated beliefs if disasters are to be avoided. Labelling social classes and ethnic groups in stereotypical ways, for example believing that working-class consumers are not interested in buying expensive, premium products, can also be mistaken and lead to lost sales.

Question

1 Discuss the relationship between labelling theory and marketing and advertising.

Key point Deviance is not a quality of the act the person commits, but rather a consequence of the application by others of rules and sanctions to an offender. The danger is that to tell a group of people that they are different or no good can cause them to behave as labelled.

Symbolic interaction – getting into the minds of people

▶ **Symbolic interaction** is the theory that to know how society works we should focus on how subjectively humans interact and continually adjust their behaviour to the action of other 'actors' in life. Theorists such as the German sociologist Max ▶ Weber (1864–1920) and the American philosopher, **George H. Mead** (1863–1931) believed that the meaning that people give to their lives was more important in gaining an understanding of social life than standing back trying to take an objective macro-structural aspect of social systems. For example the reasons behind such major issues as crime, suicide rates (or consumer buying behaviour) in a country could be understood by standing back and looking objectively at the statistics and the role of the major institutions. In the case of crime this would be the police, the courts and the prisons (a macro-structural approach). Believers in symbolic interaction, however, see humans not as passive, conforming objects of the socialisation process but as active creative participants who interact with others to construct their own world. They would argue that observing and talking to those involved would lead to a better understanding of criminal behaviour.

8.17 Marketing example Consumer behaviour and symbolic interaction

In trying to understand consumer behaviour we could take a macro-structural approach or a symbolic interaction approach. The former method would involve searching out secondary quantitative data on retail sales over a period of years across the different retail sectors. It would also involve looking at sales at different times of the year across different outlets as well as the effects of such things as advertising and distribution. From this type of information marketing decisions can be made. This approach might work in business markets where organisations buy for functional and rational reasons but would have severe limitations in consumer markets where emotion, indecision and change greatly affect purchasing behaviour. These differences have persuaded researchers to take a symbolic interaction approach using many different qualitative methods to try to understand the thoughts, motivations and meanings that millions of individual consumers give to their different shopping experiences.

Questions

1 Discuss the pros and cons of taking a macro-structural or a symbolic interaction approach to understanding consumer behaviour.
2 Which method might work better in B2B markets?

Key point Observing, talking and listening and getting into the minds of individuals to try to understand how they subjectively view buying products and services using qualitative methods is as important as using more quantitative methods of research in trying to understand the customers' reactions to marketing and retail operations.

Groups

The biological and social need that humans have to be with one another from the moment of birth was discussed in earlier chapters. It was shown how debilitating this can be if an infant is deprived of contact with its mother. To a lesser or greater extent this social need appears to stay with people throughout their lives. Throughout history people seem always to have gathered together for stronger protection, building shelter and hunting and growing and cooking food. They also meet on a regular basis to play, talk, dance, sing and enjoy one another's company on a regular basis and this need is still the same in modern times. The need for social interaction, as well as the need at times to be alone, is well documented by consumer behaviourists and is an essential part of many strategic marketing programmes. There are many other types of groups and some are described below.

Key point Whenever two or more people come together on a habitual basis and communicate with one another (whether this is regular or intermittent) gives us a simple definition of what constitutes a group.

Ascribed and acquired groups – born and/or moved into

Some groups we are born into, e.g. family, gender, peer, tribal, race and social class, and are known as ascribed groups. Other groups, known as acquired groups, we join as we journey through life, e.g. educational, work, membership, associational. Ascribed group membership will affect life's chances and the membership and quality of acquired groups. In some countries, because of inequalities and poor living conditions, there is little opportunity for overcoming deficiencies inherent in ascribed group conditions (Africa), while in other countries life adjustments can be made (Europe).

Voluntary and involuntary groups

In a similar vein as we travel through life we can choose to be a member of some groups, e.g. the scouts, girl guides, golf, fishing, social and dancing clubs, while other groups are involuntary and thrust upon us, e.g. old age pensioners, prison (if we commit a criminal act), jury service (obligatory in some countries), management committees and working groups.

The Scout Association, a voluntary, acquired membership group.
Source: The Scout Association

Key point Ascribed and acquired group membership will play an enormous part in consumer consumption behaviour.

Table 8.3 **People join groups for the following reasons:**

- Synergy (the whole is greater than the sum of the parts) leading to more productivity.
- Reward of some kind. Money, support, encouragement, commitment.
- Interpersonal needs – affection, friendship, building relationships.
- Leadership and control.

Peer groups – people of equal standing

Peer groups consist of people who come together on a regular basis and all have equal standing and share things in common. This might be social class, age, rank, occupation or a pastime of some kind. Apart from the family, the peer group will be the earliest group that a boy or girl will encounter when entering nursery or infant school. It's here that children first learn to mix with others in the same position as themselves. Successful participation is the prerequisite for the development of self-concept and personal and interpersonal skills and failure to assimilate can cause personality problems throughout a person's life. As the child grows older, he or she will be involved with peer groups all through life in primary, secondary and tertiary education, in marriage, as parents, at work, in retirement and in friendship, lifestyle and other groups.

8.18 Marketing example **Consumer behaviour and peer groups**

Peer groups are enormously important for marketers aware of the strength of peer group pressure in getting group members to conform in similar ways. Research has shown that product and brand ownership starts for many as early as three or four year old, with toddlers wanting the same as others at nursery school (Fischer *et al.* 1991). The need to fit in and feel like part of the group builds as the child grows older and peaks during early adolescence. So teens are more likely to conform to their peers' norms and behaviours, and be more susceptible to their pressure than at any other time of life. Anybody who has brought up children will know the importance of playground credibility and the need to be seen as 'cool' to the development of a healthy self-esteem. The adolescent who is a loner or who goes against the expectations of the peer group risks being ridiculed and regarded as strange. Peer groups will influence the choice of clothes, music, mobile phones, entertainment and leisure activities. Although influencing less, peer pressure to buy brands and adopt particular ways of living can affect individuals for the whole of their lives depending on intellectual and emotional development.

Questions

1 Give examples from your own experience of peer group pressure forcing you to conform in some way by having to have a product of some kind.

2 Do you still feel that peer group pressure affects your consumer behaviour in some way?

Reference groups – looked up to for lifestyle

▶ **Reference groups** are groups that people identify with and refer to in order to evaluate and regulate their beliefs, opinions and actions. A reference group might be the peer group or a small part of the peer group. We must all have memories of small groups of people at school that we might have admired and so copied them (as far as we could) in ways of behaviour. Like peer groups as a whole, reference groups are crucial for the marketing of products and services especially as people get older, more selective and more set in their ways.

8.19 Marketing example **The traditionalist**

Many advertising agencies have identified a large segment of the market as 'traditionalists'. This is a large group of people (as much as a third of the population depending on the particular research) who are conservative and traditional in their behaviour and their view of the world. Over 50, they prefer not to stand out from the crowd, feel secure with quality, middle of the road branded products, and would have the same type of non-adventure holiday every year. Members of this group will look towards respected, conservative groups in the community for direction, for example church members.

Associative reference groups – realistically belong

Associative reference groups are people who more realistically represent a person's current social position and status, for example college friends, neighbours, co-workers and members of clubs, churches and other organisations.

Aspiration reference group – would like to belong

▶ **Aspiration reference groups** are people that a person admires and would like to be like. This might be sportspeople, entertainers, politicians, the extremely rich and so on. In many Western countries there appears to be a cult of the 'celebrity' where many people (especially the young) obsessively admire the celebrity, not for any skill or aptitude, but just for being famous. They seek desperately to be in the same position and so have universal recognition. Knowing this it's easy to see why advertisers will use famous celebrities who are admired by their target audience to endorse products they want to market.

Disassociation reference group – would hate to belong

▶ The **disassociation reference group** is a group that others do not want to be like. More products for younger people recognise that adolescents want desperately to rebel against many family values and become 'themselves'. For example, the store literally named The Gap came about because many younger people wanted to actively dissociate from parents and other older and 'un-cool' people. It's crucial for marketing and advertising people to know what is street credible and what isn't, if they are selling in this market. Similarly a company marketing a 'young' fashionable brand, e.g. Levi, would be upset if older, unfashionable individuals started using it.

> **Key point** Disassociation reference groups are people that we would not want to be compared with, particularly with the brands used and clothes worn.

Contrived or emergent groups – formed for a specific purpose

Some groups are *contrived*, that is they are formed for a specific purpose. Organised clubs, associations, unions, or committees at both the work and social level are contrived groups. They tend to be formal, have objectives and meetings and might have rules and regulations and keep minutes. On the other hand, other groups *emerge* and form spontaneously. Groups can be ad hoc or happen on an intermittent or regular basis.

> **Key point** Groups discussed here are not mutually exclusive and an individual could well belong to more than one group at any one time.

Figure 8.3

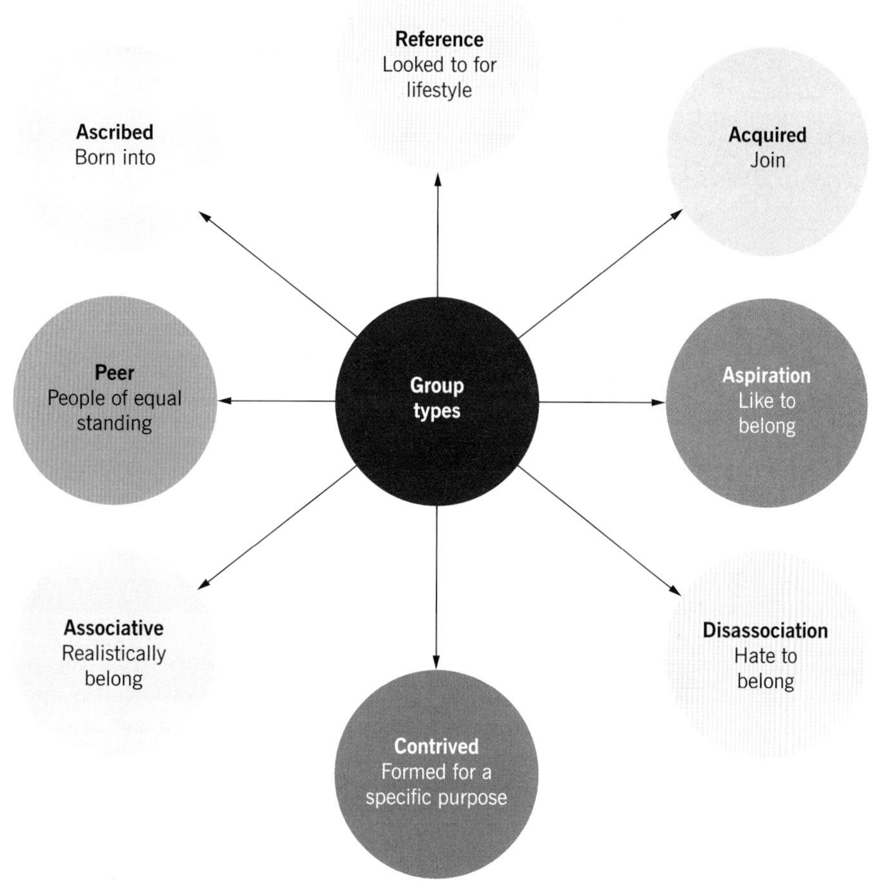

The many different types of groups

The power of groups

'Never doubt that a small group of thoughtful committed citizens can change the world; indeed it's the only thing that ever has.' MARGARET MEAD (1928)

Many researchers have investigated the phenomena and power associated with group membership and **group dynamics** (Brown 2000). There seems to be little doubt that individuals can and do act differently when in groups with other people than when alone. Differences in behaviour can also vary according to the size, type and purpose of the group.

8.20 Marketing example — The power of buying in groups

Over hundreds of years, farmers, producers, retailers, workers, and consumers found that they could accomplish more collectively than they could individually. This encouraged them to come together to form worker trade unions (workers), trade associations (organisations), voluntary buying groups (retailers) and worker **co-operatives** (small wine, milk, farm producers). Individual consumers in the UK, recognising the power of group action, first came together in 1844 and opened up the first co-op shop, selling basic food items, in Rochdale in the north of England. All users became part owners and shared in the profit. Now a worldwide movement, co-ops are involved in many areas of retailing including supermarkets, convenience stores, travel and leisure, financial services and funerals. Consumer pressure groups such as 'Which' now play an important role in protecting the rights of the consumer against the power of large producers and retailers. Some individual consumers recognising the advantages of buying larger amounts rather than single items, now use the power of the Internet to come together to purchase specific products collectively receiving a discount for the bulk purchase.

Questions

1 Discuss the power of consumer groups working together. Look specifically at the co-op movement and voluntary buying groups.
2 How might the Internet continue to work to the advantage of group consumer behaviour?

Conflict in groups – the inevitability

As soon as people come together there seems to be the potential for conflict of some kind. Whether there are two or two thousand it is inevitable that individuals will sometimes think and behave in differing ways and unless a compromise is reached disagreement could ensue. If managed appropriately, conflict can be good for the group, constantly sparking off new ideas bred in the cauldron of argument. In fact it can be disconcerting working with a harmonious group where disagreement seems non-existent. In a good group discussion, constructive argument will be expected, ideas and opinions from all will be encouraged and the more reticent members recognised and invited in.

Key point By exposing differences, group members can produce quality decisions and satisfying interpersonal relationships.

8.10 General example The value of conflict

The following is quote about the power of conflict from actor Orson Welles in the film the *The Third Man*.

'In Italy for 30 years under the Borgias, they had warfare, terror, murder, bloodshed – but they produced Michelangelo, Leonardo da Vinci, Brunelleschi, Machiavelli and the Renaissance. In Switzerland they have brotherly love, 500 years of democracy and peace, and what did they produce? – The cuckoo clock.'

All relationships are power relationships

Some people believe (**Karl Marx**) that because it's difficult if not impossible for every need and want to coalesce, all relationships between people and groups are power relationships. Even in a marriage, unless one person is totally dominant, the power between partners will shift back and forth never really reaching equilibrium depending on the issues at hand. The concept of the decision-making unit (DMU) in marketing is about identifying where the consumer decision-making power lies. This is not always easy and will vary from culture to culture. As a retailer, salesperson or a customer service manager there is always the possibility of unpleasant, unsatisfying and, often, irritating situations that sometimes turn into confrontations with the consumer. Good staff training, well-thought out processes and a total commitment to customer satisfaction should lessen the likelihood of such unrewarding conflict.

Groupthink – faulty decision making

Groupthink is a concept that was first identified by Irving Janis (1972) and it refers to faulty decision making that can take place within groups. This can be in a formal group, e.g. a work meeting, or in an informal group, e.g. friends out together. Groupthink occurs when there is pressure of some kind on people to make decisions. It seems that because responsibility seems to be shared some participants can take less trouble or be less critical about issues than they would if making decisions individually.

Characteristics of groupthink

Groupthink can take many forms depending on the characteristics of the individuals involved, e.g. how charismatic, dominant, submissive or interested different members might be in the problem under discussion. Power centres, levels of cohesion and time considerations will influence outcomes. Groupthink can lead to less criticism, fewer ideas and alternatives being examined and the selective use of information. Expert opinion might be ignored or not be sought, feedback and contingency plans not implemented, leaving some group members with a feeling that poor decisions had been rationalised. On occasions some individuals can leave a meeting feeling they have not expressed their true feelings and had been pressurised into agreeing with an answer that they subsequently feel was misguided or wrong.

8.21 Marketing example — Groupthink

Many wrong decisions have been made throughout history due to problems associated with 'groupthink'. There are examples of products being launched on to the markets despite research telling the organisation that consumers are ambivalent about purchase. It's as if new product launch management teams convince themselves through a process of 'groupthink' that success is assured and manipulate the research to come to this conclusion. A major example is the launch and subsequent failure of 'new coke' in 1985. Despite warning signals, including the consumer loyalty and history attached to the existing product, insufficient market testing and feedback and little consideration of alternatives, they launched 'new coke'. Within eight weeks, because of catastrophic falling sales the company re-launched the old product under the name ' Classic Coke'.

Questions

1 Discuss the problems associated with the launch of new coke.
2 Can you identify other occasions when 'groupthink' may have caused wrong decisions to be made?

De-individuation and groupthink

Informal groups, such as gangs of young people or crowds of football supporters can attack one another, set upon innocent bystanders or fight with the police, as group strength appears to give people an illusion of invulnerability. In these situations de-individuation, the loss of self-awareness and restraint can happen and ▶ ethnic groups and others can be attacked. In these situations blame **stereotyping** is magnified and individual morality seems to be subordinated to a kind of group morality (see Case Study 1 at the end of the chapter).

De-humanising and making others anonymous

It's much easier to be unconcerned about others if they seem to be anonymous in some way. An earthquake in China in 1976 killed over 250,000 people yet had very little coverage in the press. The death of President Kennedy in 1963 however had pages of TV and newspaper coverage for weeks. Everybody felt that they knew Kennedy personally but had no knowledge (or interest) in the Chinese. Every US soldier in the Iraq war has been identified but nobody officially even bothers to count the ten of thousands of Iraqis that have suffered the same fate. In fact it's a well-taught adage in war (Knightly 1989) that the first thing that you must do is to make anonymous and/or demonise the enemy. In this way they can easily be killed. Nearer to home, many countries have experienced terrible scenes of violence at high-profile football matches as drink laden supporters have attacked and killed one another in a frenzy of nationalistic and team competition. The 'Portman Group' was formed by a group of UK drinks manufacturers, with the purpose of promoting sensible drinking and avoiding alcohol misuse. Cynics might argue that they act to pre-empt the intervention of the Government with heavier laws.

The suggestibility of groups – following group norms

Group behaviour is contagious. One person laughs and giggles, coughs or yawns then others follow. Canned laughter is still used in TV programmes on comedy shows by producers who know that it will encourage the audience at home to do the same, thus feeling happy in the process. One person staring up into the air, or looking into a building site will soon have others following suit. Many experiments have demonstrated that people can be persuaded into believing the beliefs of the group rather than the reality of their own eyes. Police have long seen that witnesses will often change their description of somebody that they have seen earlier committing a crime, in discussion with others. In one experiment people were shown a stationary light in a darkened room. Some perceived it as moving by as much as 20 cm, others by 5 cm. When discussing together the estimates gradually converged. More startlingly sociologists have shown that copycat suicide rates increase if a suicide is shown in a TV soap opera or after a famous celebrity takes his or her life.

8.11 General example | **Asch's conformity experiment**

Solomon Asch argues how difficult it can be to hold out against the views of the group and most people will bring their behaviour in line with some group standard. In a simple demonstration he drew a line, the standard on the board. He then drew three other lines of differing lengths alongside. Only one of these lines was the same length as the standard line (line2). He then invited a group of students to enter the room and sit down. All persons involved in the experiment were collaborators accept for one naive individual. He went on to ask the group to say which lines were the same length. The collaborators said 3 (untrue) causing the unsuspecting student considerable anxiety and internal conflict as he or she fought to resolve the dilemma (it was 2). In thousands of experiments he found that as many as two-thirds of all unsuspecting participants ended up agreeing with the group collaborators after hearing their opinions offering incorrect estimates.

Group polarisation – similar behaviour attracts

Social researchers have also discovered that individuals with the same or similar views will tend to come together in groups (we seem to like people who think in the same way that we do). If the views held are on a subject where prejudices are deeply held, these views will strengthen and polarise over time especially if there are no moderating influences. This can have helpful consequences where the views held are beneficial to the wellbeing of society but awful consequences where groups come together because of deeply felt grievances, becoming more extreme the more isolated they become (e.g. Palestinians and Israelis). One of the accusations thrown at the American electorate and the growth in Christian fundamentalism is that many Mid-West residents never travel more than a few hundred miles from their home town and only mix with like-minded people. This phenomenon emphasises the importance of dialogue, constant information and travel, so that individuals and groups become more tolerant as they mix and talk with others.

8.22 Marketing example | **Consumer behaviour and word-of-mouth**

Although difficult to measure, the importance of word-of-mouth to most businesses cannot be underestimated. Research has consistently shown that at many as 75 per cent of consumers never complain about shoddy goods or services, they just tell many others and don't come back (Cartwright and Green 1997). Once group consumer views have polarised and become common currency it is very difficult, if not impossible, for this general attitude to be changed. The product Avert Virucidal Tissues, launched (1985) by Kimberly-Clark, lasted ten months because people didn't believe the claims and they were frightened by the name. Gerber's launched (1974) a variety of fruits, vegetables and entrees. However, consumers simply could not relate to adult food products sold in baby food jars and it failed.

Marketing, consumer behaviour and groupthink

▶ The influence that peer group and reference **group pressure** has on consumer purchase behaviour was discussed earlier and experiments and research undertaken into 'groupthink' adds power to these observations. Marketing and salespeople have known for decades that once they can get people buying others will follow, often in an unthinking sheep like manner and the more excitement that can be generated the greater will be the group hysteria. Pictures of large groups waiting outside a departmental store for the start of a grand sale appear in the newspapers every Christmas. When the doors are opened there is mad, undignified collective rush (sometimes even involving fighting known as 'sale rage') to buy the most attractive products. When in a strange town, and looking for a decent place to eat, people will look to see if a restaurant seems full or not and of course that's why the earliest diners are seated in the window. Builders on new housing sites will put sold notices on unsold houses knowing that this will give possible buyers a sense of security feeling that others think the same as themselves.

8.23 Marketing example Persuading purchase

Salespeople the world over know that the hardest thing to do is to persuade customers to make the final decision, that is to purchase. But once the decision is made a weight is taken off the shoulders of the consumer. The foot-in-the-door phenomenon is the idea that if you can persuade the buyer to purchase small amounts, commitment has been given and larger amounts will follow more easily. Similarly offering such things as a free trial, sales promotions, money back, free interest and so on will all help in the decision-making process. One of the oldest scams in the world is for the seller, on a market stall or in an auction room, to have a few collaborators in the audience who will rush eagerly forward to buy as soon as the sales pitch has finished. This will then encourage others (real members of the public) to immediately follow up (at times in an almost hypnotic state) feeling secure in the knowledge that other group members are purchasing. It's only when a purchaser has time to think that regrets about the purchase surface.

Figure 8.4

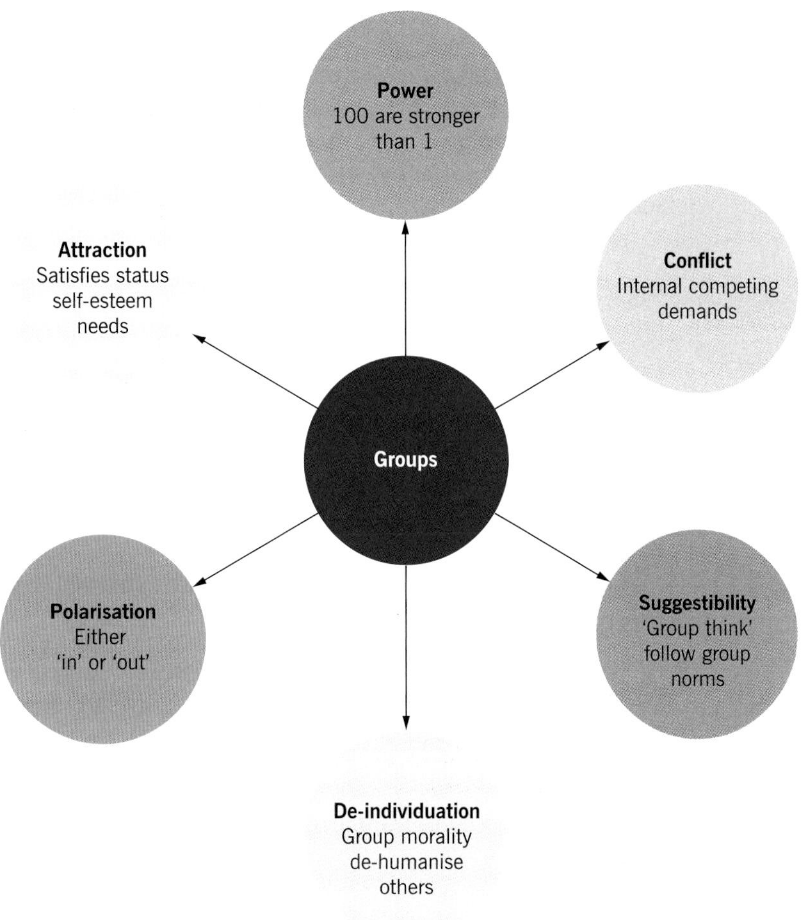

Aspects of group behaviour

Concern for others in society

There are many commentators who argue that unbridled competitive consumerism has led to a selfish non-caring society, where individuals no longer really care for others outside of the family circle and immediate friends (Blackwell Cook and Frank 1995). This general problem and more immediate examples where people have ignored the screams for help and the suffering of others lead many social psychologists to research into levels of altruism (unselfish concern for the welfare of others) to try to discover the truth behind this assumption. Some examples of the experiments conducted included a collaborator lying at the side of the pavement as if unconscious, somebody having a simulated epileptic fit and a stranded motorist, asking somebody to make an emergency phone call (Latane and Darley 1968, 1976). They were all experiments designed to see who would stop and help.

Marketing, consumer behaviour and altruism in society

Many organisations depend on the goodwill of others for resources to be able to continue and research has been undertaken by charities and others on how to encourage people (and companies) to give such things as blood, clothes, time, intellectual resources and money (Walker *et al.* 2002). Some of the conclusions are shown in Table 8.5.

Table 8.5 **Research into charity giving has found that people could give for the following reasons:**

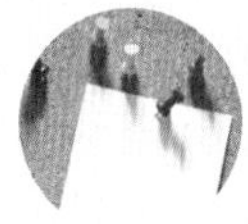

- They are feeling guilty.
- They are able to feel empathy for the plight of the victim.
- They understand the problem.
- They feel the victim is the same as them.
- They enjoy social approval and the feelings associated with being good.
- They observe others responding.
- They feel that their contribution will not be wasted.
- They have beliefs and attitudes about morality, duty and responsibilities.
- They are in a good mood.
- They are not in a hurry.
- They are not preoccupied with own concerns.

Helping others for ulterior motives

Many social psychologists argue that all people weigh (consciously or subconsciously) the cost and benefits involved in helping others. For example if we are to donate blood we will weigh the costs (financial, time, anxiety, discomfort) against the benefits (social approval, good feelings, reduced guilt, entry into Heaven). If the benefits outweigh the costs then people will give, if they don't then they won't. ▶ This leads us on to look at **social exchange theory**.

Social exchange theory

Social exchange theorists (Thibaut and Kelley 1959) argue that individuals make choices in their individual and group social relationships with other people based upon the reward or punishment inherent in the outcome (see Watson's theory on conditioning). The reward can be both financial and/or approval of some kind. It is believed that some individuals undertake a conscious rational cost benefit analysis about membership while others allow emotional or badly thought through reasons to dominate. For example a self-employed builder might want to join the Freemasons because he might get work from other members. They will only let the builder join if they think that he will offer something in return. Neighbours might want to know a person's occupation and social position to see if he or she offers enough associated kudos and is worth cultivating and inviting to dinner. If both agree to the arrangement then joint behaviour develops through mutual reinforcement. In this way all participating members learn to behave in acceptable ways to other individual or group members.

Reciprocal altruism

There are some who argue that all actions are can be viewed in terms of social exchange even where the motives ostensibly seem to be altruistic (Robert Trivers (1998), Rutgers University). For example a person needs help, perhaps he or she is drowning and somebody bravely dives in to execute the rescue; we might think a perfect example of an unselfish act. The theory of reciprocal altruism, however, will not allow for this unselfish humane act. It argues that the reason why individuals risk their lives for others is more selfish and it is in the hope that if a similar thing happened to them somebody would bravely commit himself or herself to the same kind of rescue.

8.24 Marketing example — Exchange theory and marketing

We should remember that marketing is an exchange process. Customers purchase products and services from organisations in return for financial or emotional benefits of some kind. Individuals will join a leisure or sports club, university, the Conservative party, the Chartered Institute of Marketing, buy a particular motor car, eat at the top London Ivy restaurant, take out a financial bond, as long as they get the clear targeted benefits in return. A person will give to charity as long as it is at a public auction and he or she can show off in front of others by paying a large amount of money. The difficulty is that the reward wanted might be easily identified, feeling good when driving a new sports car, or it might be much more complex and deeply hidden by layers of conditioning.

Key point Social exchange theory sees relationships, business and personal, in terms of satisfying (maximising the reward) or non-satisfying (minimising costs) financial or emotional experiences.

Groups and attractiveness

Much thought has been given about the physical and personal characteristics that come together to make one person more or less attractive than another. It seems that beauty for some can mean physical, intellectual and spiritual attractiveness and it can be considered relative and cultural or universal and world-wide. It's of special importance to marketers because people are spending more and more time, energy and money in an attempt to become more attractive to others and to stay younger longer. It's now a multi-billion dollar business around the world.

Is attractiveness universal or relative?

One of the intriguing questions searching for an answer is whether attractiveness and beauty are universal or relative. Is beauty truly in the eye of the beholder or is this just a romantic illusion? Many aspects of attractiveness appear to be relative and film stars of 50 years ago need only be compared to films stars of today to illustrate this point. Both men and women around the world do different things to make themselves attractive. This includes such things as body building (using steroids), body piercing, body painting and hair dying, neck and lip stretching, putting on enormous weight and slimming down to skeletal proportions. Women flatten their breasts by using straps while others make them bigger by silicone implants.

8.25 Marketing example — Consumer behaviour and attractiveness

Producers will want to associate their brands with attractive people. The art is to make certain that the consumer target audience will believe that the association is realistic. For example many years ago an agency advertised a slimming reduction product by showing a super slim model on the front of the box. Unfortunately for the ad agency the target audience could not believe that they would ever be that slim, and so the product did not sell. Realising this they put a bigger rounder woman on the packaging and it sold. Having said this we only have to look at the ads on the TV every evening to see them full of beautiful people selling hair, cosmetic and body products. Other growth areas include breast implants, Botox wrinkle remover, cellulite treatment, tummy tucks, nose jobs, liposuction, eyelid surgery, face and neck lifts. It's big business and almost any area of the body can be cosmetically improved.

Question

1 Discuss your feelings about these sorts of products. Why do some consumers want so much more from body perfection than others?

Key point Not surprisingly it appears we like people who reward rather than punish us in some way, are physically attractive, like us, make us feel good or are around us when good things happen.

Marketing, consumer behaviour and group communications

'I think we risk becoming the best informed society that has ever died of ignorance.' REUBEN BLADES, US cult actor

The impact of social communication can hardly be exaggerated. People talk, listen and come into contact with other people, friends, work colleagues, retailers, salespeople and the media on a constant basis. In this way opinions, beliefs and attitudes about everything they value in life (not least corporate and product brands and services) are formed. Individuals now talk to one another around the world and word-of-mouth opinions can speed across the globe in the blink of an eye. The rise and rise of the Internet and global communications has given all manner of formal and informal groups a tremendous amount of power and group networking is a force that marketers must harness in a beneficial manner if its power is to be controlled. This will be discussed in more detail in the next chapter.

Summary

- In this chapter on social influences on social behaviour we began by describing what we mean by society and the part that the study of sociology and social psychology played in the process.
- We then went on to look at culture, sub-cultures, cultural differences, homogenisation and cultural imperialism, discussing how the whole area impacted on understanding marketing and consumer behaviour around the world.
- Social class, open and closed societies, ascribed and acquired class groups, were identified and examined to see how easy it is to move from one class to another and the affect that all this might have on consumer behaviour.
- The role of social agencies such as the family, schools, religion, the work place, the media and so on were shown to be paramount in socialising and inculcating social norms and value into people so that all members learnt acceptable and unacceptable ways of behaving. We also identified ways that individuals and groups could be made to conform. Social role-playing and the meaning of status were then examined.
- Labelling theory and symbolic interaction theory were briefly touched upon before looking at the whole area associated with group behaviour.
- Beginning with a simple definition of a group, we then identified many different types of groups including ascribed and acquired groups, peer groups, reference groups, primary and secondary groups, informational, normative and identification reference groups and contrived and emergent groups.
- Group power was used as a heading to discuss such things as groupthink, de-individuation, suggestibility and polarisation in groups.
- Finally we looked at social exchange theory, how people care for one another in groups, group communications and the attractiveness of people.

Questions

1. Explain the meaning of society and discuss how it differs around the world. Do you think that society makes people or people make society? Give examples.
2. Sociology is a relatively new discipline. Identify and evaluate the areas that the discipline covers. Compare the differences with social psychology. Relate and give examples on how knowledge of the subject will help marketers in understanding all aspects of consumer behaviour.

3 Discuss the basis and the importance or otherwise of social class and status in society. How might it be different around the world, is it changing and how might it relate to marketing and consumer behaviour?

4 Describe and examine the many different types of groups, for example peer groups and reference groups. Discuss why it is important for marketers and retailers to understand how they operate and give live examples of how this understanding could be used in practical ways.

5 Examine what we mean when we talk about culture and compare and contrast aspects between cultures in the world that are radically different. In what ways might consumer behaviour be the same and in what ways might it be different?

6 Give examples how marketing managers have exploited sub-cultures.

7 Explain the role of socialisation is society and describe how social agencies operate in imposing norms, values and expected ways of behaving on people. Might there be any genetic input into the process?

8 Describe, evaluate and compare labelling theory, symbolic interaction theory and exchange theory and give examples of how knowing these theories can help in understanding retail and the motives behind consumer behaviour.

9 Discuss and examine such concepts as groupthink, de-individuation, polarisation and suggestibility and show how this can affect both group activity in businesses and group buying in consumer markets.

10 Discuss the overall affect that you think that capitalism and unbridled consumption has had on society. Is it a good or bad thing and what worries and hopes might you have for the future?

Case study

Case study 1 Power of obedience

▶ **Stanley Milgram** conducted a remarkable series or experiments in the 1960s that set the academic world alight. He put adverts in the newspaper asking for volunteers to take part in a series of experiments offering them a small amount of money to take part. Participants were invited to a simulated laboratory and introduced to the experimenter who was dressed in a white coat (the dress of a scientist). His research involved leading the volunteers to believe they were administering electric shocks to a person (a collaborator) sitting behind a screen and who was making errors in a learning experiment. They were told to increase the voltage every time a wrong answer was given. Results showed that almost all participants were prepared to keep giving higher and higher shocks although they were aware from the screams and moans coming from the receiver that it must have been extremely painful and highly dangerous. Factors that seemed to contribute to this remarkable inhuman reaction included the authority figure's gradual escalation of the scope of their orders, their visual cues of power (the white lab coat) and the assumptions that the experimenter (not the volunteers) would be responsible for the actions, i.e. abdicating moral responsibility to a higher authority. It's the 'I was only following orders' syndrome that appears to allow people to commit so many cruel outrageous acts on fellow human beings.

Questions

1 Discuss the idea that authority figures are able to manipulate individuals and groups to behave in unexpected ways.

2 How might the ability to manipulate behaviour, suggested in the manner above, be used in marketing, retail and advertising. Do you think that consumers can be persuaded to buy brands and services not really wanted?

Case study

Case study 2 People define themselves by the possessions they have

The concept of status is enormously important for marketers as evidence shows that many people define themselves and their high or low position in society by the possessions they have (Belk 1988). Products and brand ownership come together to build a complex language of emotional symbols that communicate to others beliefs, attitudes and personality. In this way we write messages about ourselves with the things we own and read other people through their possessions. Every time we make a choice about the things we buy we are expressing an identity. In a survey most adults agreed with the statement: 'If I lost all my possessions I would feel stripped of a sense of self'. It also seems to be a fact of life that we judge people by what they have and down deep we really do believe that the more a person has, the better a person is. In one classic experiment, researchers found that people were less likely to yell angrily at an expensive car stopped at a green light than at a more modest auto. In another study, people were given luggage that was 'found' at an airport and bus terminal and asked to describe the person based on the luggage. Consistently, the air traveller whose luggage looked more expensive, was judged to be more likeable, more generous, responsible, attractive and aggressive than the bus rider (Rochberg-Halton and Csikszentimihalyi 1981).

Questions

1 Discuss the premise that people define themselves by the possessions that they have accumulated though life, for example: house, furniture, car, spouse, type of holiday taken and so on.

2 Do you think that we define and judge the value of others in the same way?

Further reading

Books

Bandura, A. (1977) *Social Learning Theory*, New York: General Learning Press.

Bandura, A. and R.H. Walters (1963) *Social Learning and Personality Development*, New York: Holt, Rinehart & Winston.

Blackwell Cook, P.J. and R.H. Frank (1995) *The Winner-Takes-All Society: Why the Few at the Top Get So Much More Than the Rest of Us*, New York: Viking Books.

Blass, Dr Thomas (2004) *The Man who Shocked the World: The Life and Legacy of Stanley Milgram*, New York: Basic Books.

Bordens, Kenneth S. and Irwin A. Horowitz (1991) *Social Psychology*, Mahwah, NJ: Lawrence Erlbaum Associates.

Brown, R. (2000) *Group Processes: Dynamics Within and Between Groups*, 2nd rev edn, Oxford: Blackwell.

Cartwright, R. and G. Green (1997) *In Charge of Customer Satisfaction*, Oxford: Blackwell.

Chodorow, Nancy (1978) *The Reproduction of Mothering*, Berkeley, CA: University of California Press.

Elster, J. (1989) *The Cement of Society*, Cambridge: Cambridge University Press.

Gaulin, S.J.C. and D.H. McBurney (2001) *Psychology: An Evolutionary Approach*: Prentice Hall, New Jersey.

Giddens, A. (1973) *Capitalism and Modern Social Theory: An Analysis of the Writings of Marx, Durkheim and Max Weber*, Cambridge: Cambridge University Press.

Goffman, Ervin (1959) *The Presentation of Self in Everyday Life*, New York: Doubleday.

Haralambos, Micheal, R.M. Heald and Martin Holborn (2004) *Sociology Themes and Perspectives*, London: Collins Education.

Hendon, D. (1992) *Classic Failures in Product Marketing: Marketing Principles Violations and How to Avoid Them*, New York: McGraw-Hill.

Hendry, Joy (1999) *An Introduction to Social Anthropology: Other People's Worlds*, Basingstoke: Palgrave Macmillan.

Hostede, Geert (1991) *Cultures and Organizations: Software of the Mind*, New York: McGraw-Hill.

Janis, Irving (1972) *Victims of Groupthink*, Boston, MA: Houghton Mifflin; 2nd edn. (1982), *Groupthink: Psychological Studies of Policy Decisions and Fiascos*, Boston, MA: Houghton Mifflin.

Jones, P. (2003) *Introducing Social Theory*, Cambridge: Polity Press.

Kelley, Harold H. and John W. Thibaut (1978) *Interpersonal Relationships*, New York: John Wiley & Sons.

Knightly, Phillip (1989) *The First Casualty – From the Crimea to the Falklands: The War Correspondent as Hero, Propagandist and Myth Maker*, London: Pan Books.

Kohn, A. (1992) *The Brighter Side of Human Nature: Altruism and Empathy in Everyday Life*; New York: Basic Books, repr.

Latane, D. and J. Darley (1968) *The Unresponsive Bystander: Why Doesn't He Help?*, New York: Appelton-Centun Crofts.

Magee, B. (2000) *The Great Philosophers: An Introduction to Western Philosophy*, Oxford: Oxford Paperbacks.

McNeilly, F.S. (1968) *The Anatomy of Leviathan*, New York: St Martin's Press.

Mead, George Herbert (1934) *Mind, Self, and Society*. Chicago, IL: University of Chicago Press.

Mead, Margaret (1928) *Coming of Age in Samoa*, New York: William Morrow.
de Mooij, M. (1998) *Global Marketing and Advertising: Understanding Cultural Paradoxes*, Thousand Oaks, CA: Sage Publications.
Morley, D. and K. Robins (1995) *Spaces of Identity: Global Media, Electronic Landscapes and Cultural Boundaries*, London: Routledge.
Myers, D.G. (1986) *Psychology*, 4th edn, New York: Worth Publishers.
Nutt, P. (2000) *Why Decisions Fail: Avoiding the Blunders and Traps that Lead to Debacle*, San Francisco, CA: Berrett-Koehler Publishers.
Packard, Vince (1957) *The Hidden Persuaders*, New York: Pocket Books.
Pendergrast, Mark (2000) *For God, Country, and Coca-Cola: The Definitive History of the Great American Soft Drink and the Company That Makes It*, New York: Basic Books.
Porter, M.E. (1980) *Competitive Advantage*, New York: The Free Press.
Rawls, J. (1971) *A Theory of Justice*, Cambridge, MA: Harvard University Press.
Rijkens, R. (1992) *European Advertising Strategies*, London, Cassell.
Rochberg-Halton, Eugene and Mihaly Csikszentimihalyi (1981) *The Meaning of Things: Symbols in the Development of the Self*, Cambridge: Cambridge University Press.
Rowell, T. (1972) *Social Behaviour of Monkeys*, Baltimore, MD: Penguin.
Stratham, J. (1986) *Daughters and Sons: Experiences of Non-sexist Childraising*, Oxford: Basil Blackwell.
Thibaut, J.W. and H.H. Kelley (1959) *The Social Psychology of Groups*, New York: Wiley.
Ullmann-Margalit, E. (1977) *The Emergence of Norms*, Oxford: Oxford University Press.
Vaughan, G. and M. Hogg (2004) *Social Psychology*, Harlow: Prentice Hall.
Walker, C. and C. Pharoah (eds) (2002) *A Lot of Give – Trends in Charitable Giving for the 21st Century*, London: Hodder & Stoughton.
Zyman, Sergio (1999) *The End of Marketing as We Know It*, New York: Harper Business.

Journals

Belk, R.W. (1988) 'Possessions and the Extended Self', *Journal of Consumer Research*, 15: 139–68.
Benne, Kenneth and Paul Sheats (1948) 'Functional Roles of Group Members', *Journal of Social Issues*, 4: 41–9.
Dutta, S. and A. Segev (1999) 'Business Tansformation on the Internet', *European Management Journal*, 17(5): 466–76.
Emerson, Richard M. (1976) 'Social Exchange Theory', *American Sociological Review*, Vol. 35: 335–62.
Fischer, P.M. and M.P. Schwartz *et al.* (1991) 'Brand Logo Recognition by Children Aged 3 to 6 Years: Mickey Mouse and Old Joe the Camel', *Journal of American Medicine Association*; Vol. 266, December 11, www.jama.ama-assn.org.
Latane, B. and J.M. Darley (1976) 'Help in a Crisis: Bystander Response to an Emergency', in J.W. Thibaut and J.T. Spence (eds), *Contemporary Topics in Social Psychology*, Morrstown, NJ: General Learning Press.
Ruble, T.L. and K.W. Thomas (1976) 'Support for a Two-dimensional Model of Conflict Behavior', *Organizational Behavior and Human Performance*, 16: 143–55.
Smith, A. D. (1990) 'Towards a Global Culture?', *Theory, Culture & Society*, 7: 171–91.
Trivers, R. (1998) 'As They Would Do to You: A Review of *Unto Others: The Evolution and Psychology of Unselfish Behaviour* By Elliot Sober and David Sloan Wilson', *Skeptic*, Vol. 6, No. 4.

Weitzman, L., D. Eifler, E. Hokada and C. Ross (1972) 'Sex-role Socialization in Picture Books for Preschool Children', *American Journal of Sociology*, 77: 1125–50.

Will, J.A., A. Self and N. Datan (1976) 'Maternal Behaviour and Perceived Sex of Infant', *American Journal of Orthopsychiatry*, Jan., 46(1): 135–9.

Website

The Cooperative retail movement, www.cooponline.coop.
Media Watch, www.Medialens.org.
Newproductworks.com.
Portman-group.org.uk.

9 Psychographics, lifestyle and changing customer demands

'Jumping off of the corporate wheel in favour of a self-sufficient lifestyle, is a fantasy shared by many seemingly die-hard businessmen and women.'

Tracey Smith, writer and columnist

Objectives

At the end of this chapter the reader should be able to:

1. Examine the growth of lifestyle segmentation giving particular attention to the development of motivational research and psychographics in the process.
2. Identify and evaluate the part that segmentation and positioning plays in understanding consumer behaviour.
3. Appreciate the importance of innovation and new product development in attracting and holding on to customers.
4. Examine and evaluate customer relationship management programmes.

Introduction

'The forward looking organisation must take its customers skin temperature daily to check and adapt to behavioural changes.' ANON.

Throughout the book we have tried to identify and understand consumer behavioural characteristics so that marketers can construct products and services that have benefits that clearly meet the needs of a company's target market. The problem is that the level of service and benefits demanded are constantly changing upwardly. In a highly competitive market what might have been considered discretionary benefits ten years ago are now demanded as a right by customers. They know that if one store or producer doesn't offer high levels of service another one will. To remain competitive and retain its customers a company such as Ikea, the furniture and household retailer, cannot stand still and expect its customers to do the same. To understand changing consumer behaviour constant communications, talking and listening to the customer and marketing research must be put at the top of the agenda and marketing strategies continually upgraded to match and exceed satisfaction needs.

Key point Customers are constantly demanding more and services considered discretionary a decade ago are now demanded by right.

Markets and customer behaviour at different stages around the world

As more manufacturers and retailers operate in international markets there is the need to understand that consumer behaviour will be different in different parts of the world. This is not only because of all the cultural differences discussed in the preceding chapter. Products and services will often be at different stages in market **life cycles** (introduction, growth, maturity and decline), also causing consumer behaviour to be different. For example cigarettes are in decline in most of the Western world, because of highly publicised health warnings, but they are in the growth stage in other parts of the world such as China. The market for automatic washing machines is in the maturity stage in the UK but in the growth stage in India. Marketing managers must therefore construct appropriate marketing strategies both for different cultures and for different stages of the life cycle (see Figure 9.1).

Figure 9.1

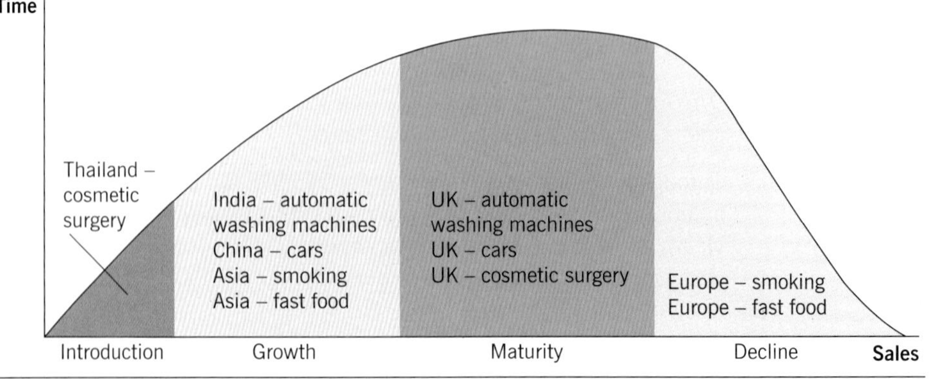

Products and services at different life cycle stages around the world

Asia

Europe

Rickshaws are in the maturity stage of the life cycle in Asia but in the growth stage in many European cities.
Source: Simon Wright

9.1 Marketing example **Customising products for different markets**

The Samsung fully automatic washing machine range has been customised to suit the Indian requirements by being equipped with a new 'memory backup' feature. With the memory backup feature, the programme settings of the washing machine are not disturbed in case of power failure during the wash cycle. The rust proof polypropylene base makes the machines better suited for the Indian weather conditions. These washing machines have also been provided with five wash cycles – fuzzy, heavy, speedy, wool and saree, to take care of the Indian wash requirements.

Key point Marketing managers must implement appropriate marketing and consumer strategies to take into account different cultures and buying behaviours at different stages of the product and market life cycle around the world.

Market segmentation

This leads us into the concept of segmentation, which is at the very heart of marketing. Manufacturers and retailers have known almost instinctively from early times that in most cases they cannot sell the same product in the same way to every customer. This has become increasingly so as consumers become more sophisticated, wealthier and more aware of choice. So men will want different products to women, the young different from the old, the wealthy from the poor, people that enjoy adventure holidays different from those that would rather take a holiday cottage in the country, psychological introverts from extroverts and so on. In fact understanding consumer behaviour becomes more complex and difficult the more markets are segmented into ever smaller and intricate types of consumer groups.

Consumer markets have been traditionally segmented according to the following groupings:

- *Socio-economic* – social class, occupation, income, age, gender, family life cycle stage.
- ***Demographic and geographic*** – where people live, region, country, trading union (e.g. EU).

- ***Behaviour*** – heavy and light users, brand and own label users, past, present or potential users.
- ***Awareness state*** – benefits wanted, outlets used.
- *Personal factors* – **lifestyle** and **psychographics**.

Segmenting markets, more and less sophisticated

The more mature the market and the higher the level the competition the more discerning will be consumer behaviour. Conversely the newer the market and the lower the level of competition the less demanding will be the consumer. This has enormous implications for understanding behaviour, segmenting the market and providing products and services that offer the exact benefits demanded by groups and individuals. For example, selling into third world countries in many parts of Africa, where wages are low for the majority of the population and choice across all products minimal, will demand less intricate understanding of consumer needs and wants. So the same or very similar products can, more or less, be offered to the whole mass of the market, perhaps just segmenting in terms of gender and age. As countries develop economically and groups of people start to earn more (for example in Thailand) they want more choice and better benefits and consumer behaviour becomes more complex, needing more understanding and greater group segmentation. These stages in segmenting markets can be seen in Table 9.1.

Table 9.1 Different stages of segmentations

Markets are at different stages of development around the world. Large sophisticated markets and customers demand increasing amounts of personal service causing evermore deeper consumer understanding about both group and individual needs and wants. Less sophisticated markets less so.

Mass markets
Marketing more or less the same product or service to all, e.g. one type of cigarette across all markets and to all customers (Africa, some parts of China).

Mass segmentation
Marketing different products or services to large groups within the mass markets, e.g. clothes for men and women, the old and young (Eastern Europe).

Narrow segmentation within mass markets
Marketing different products and services selectively to smaller groups of consumers within large markets, e.g. a large range of confectionary products all based on such factors as age, gender, income. Also seen as **niche marketing** (particular products in Western markets).

Mass-customisation or one-to-one micro-marketing
Marketing products and services across large markets specifically geared to meet individual consumer needs, e.g. a motor-car (a Volvo) personalised according to individual desires, by allowing the customer access to a whole range of added extras as it moves through the production line (UK, Switzerland, Scandinavia).

> **Key point** Modern markets have moved from mass segmentation to more personalised micromarketing.

Reasons for purchase could be different

It should be remembered that consumers around the world might also purchase products for different reasons. For example the bicycle in the UK is marketed for health and sports reasons but in China it is predominantly seen as a form of

Dieting and health products.
Source: Bird's Eye Foods

transport. Similarly many food products are marketed using health or dieting benefits in sophisticated markets but not so in developing markets.

9.2 Marketing example — Volvo segmenting in the consumer market

Volvo offers the following models all aimed at different market segments in terms of age, gender, income and lifestyle. These include the following models: Volvo S40, Volvo S60, Volvo S80, Volvo V40, Volvo V70, Volvo XC70, Volvo XC90 and the Volvo C70 convertible. Many hundreds of variations are offered across all the range including the opportunity to have a customised car identified on their website. Personalised benefits (greater choices in leather interiors, body colours, more layers of paint, sound systems and so on) can then be added as the car moves through the production line.

Motivational consumer behaviour

As the level of gross domestic product (GDP) per capita income (PCI) and individual wealth grows in any one nation, consumers are ready to pay for products and services that are customised and more readily match an individual's lifestyle. Functional reasons for purchase (food to satisfy hunger, clothes for warmth and protection) become less important as basic needs are easily satisfied. Consumers begin to demand more from products and brands wanting deeper emotional benefits linked to such things as self-esteem, status, recognition, security and so on (discussed in detail in the preceding chapter).

Key point More emotional and lifestyle benefits, rather than functional, will be wanted by the wealthier consumer.

The development of motivational research

The world of corporate and consumer communications was galvanised into a whole new era in the US in the first part of the twentieth century with the arrival of **Edward Bernays**. He was the first to introduce the Freudian idea of the human subconscious, psychographic segmentation (see Chapter 8) and motivational research into understanding marketing, consumer behaviour and advertising.

Edward Bernays – the father of public relations

In the development of understanding consumer behaviour, Edward Bernays is seen as one of the most influential figures of the twentieth century. Born in Austria in 1891, he was the nephew of Sigmund Freud and he moved to the USA when still a young man. Using the theory of the mind developed by his uncle, he took many of the ideas associated with psychoanalysis and unconscious thought and sought to apply them to the political and commercial world. In this way he sought to control how people (especially consumers) thought and behaved. He founded the first Public Relations firm in the world in 1919 in the US and came to be known as the father of public relations and later the father of spin (Tye and Brody 2002). He was enormously influential for most of his life (he lived to 100) at the highest level in both business and politics and counted presidents (Woodrow Wilson), political leaders and company presidents (Henry Ford) as his clients. Along with other powerful people in the US (who employed him) he believed that democracy was correct in principal but that the uneducated mass of the population could not be relied upon to vote in a sensible way, driven as they were (he thought) by basic emotional instincts resident in the lower levels (subconscious) of the mind (Bernays, *Propaganda*, 2004).

The use of propaganda

'If we understand the mechanism and motives of the group mind, it is now possible to control and regiment the masses according to our will without their knowing it.' EDWARD BERNAYS in Tye and Brody (2002)

Combining sociology, individual and social psychology, market research, public opinion polls, political persuasion and advertising, Bernays set about 'engineering consent' and constructing 'necessary illusions' **(propaganda)** which filtered out to the masses as 'reality'. The overriding belief at the time was that if the population could be manipulated into believing that consumerism and the ownership of products was the ultimate purpose of life they would not think too deeply about other political concerns. In this way they would vote the way that they were told. The objective for Bernays was to provide government and media outlets with the powerful tools for this social persuasion and control. Along with US journalist Walter Lippmann he argued that people were incapable of governing themselves, a job he felt was better suited to an educated elite class (among which he included journalists). He saw the manipulation of news, deciding on what's news and what isn't, as a part of a new discipline he identified as public relations (Lippmann, *Public Opinion*, 1997).

9.3 Marketing example — Manipulating the mass market

Working with Walter Lippmann, Bernays was able to persuade reluctant Americans to sign up and go to war in Europe in 1917 by creating an anti-German frenzy and creating the patriotic war slogan 'Make the World Safe for Democracy'. After the war while working for the Tobacco industry on a marketing and advertising campaign, Bernays had one of his greatest successes in persuading women to take up smoking, always seen as strictly a male prerogative. At this time, women appeared to have less freedoms than men so he hit upon the idea of parading a group of attractive women through the centre of New York smoking and carrying banners bearing the slogan 'March for Freedom'. The cigarette (a symbol of male dominance) became associated with female emancipation, 'the torch of freedom', and the number of women who took up smoking rocketed. He went on to many more successes using psychoanalytical techniques such as product placement and pseudo-scientific endorsement by so called 'experts' to sell all manner of consumer products and services.

Questions

1 How valid do you think that this approach is today?

2 Give examples of this type of manipulation being used in the media.

The legacy of Ernest Dichter

'A sedan is a wife but a convertible is a mistress.' ERNEST DICHTER (1964)

As the US economy expanded and the importance of retail spending in the process was recognised others became interested in investigating the deeper motives behind consumer purchase. One of the most influential was **Ernest Dichter** (1907–91). Born in Vienna in 1907 and heavily influenced by Freud he became well known worldwide through the advertising bestseller *The Hidden Persuaders* by Vance Packard. After jobs in marketing in the US with car giant Chrysler (working on the Plymouth automobile), packaged branded goods manufacturer Procter & Gamble (on Ivory soap) and an advertising agency (on Esquire magazine) he founded the Institute of Motivational Research in New York in 1946.

Qualitative rather than quantitative research

Motivational research (MR) had always interested Dichter and he saw qualitative methods such as focus groups and in-depth interviews, designed as they were to uncover the consumer's subconscious or hidden motivations, as the key to determining buying behaviour. Up to this time more quantitative methods, surveys, asking respondents closed ended questions about such things as age, income occupation and so on were used. Many, however, believed that this kind of research only showed general patterns of consumer behaviour and could not get at the underlying opinions and motives. Along with others, Dichter perceived humans as immature, ruled by irrational insecurity, motivated by erotic desires and only this new type of research could unlock the real reason for purchase. In the 1950s pent-up demand for consumer products exploded and the demand for motivational research grew alongside as manufacturers and retailers realised its worth.

Key point As the starting point of all marketing activities, motivational research shifted the emphasis on to the consumer's innermost needs and desires rather than general patterns of behaviour. MR is now widely acknowledged as the precursor of today's consumer lifestyle studies.

9.4 Marketing example — Motivational research

In the 1960s motivational research showed that the public saw the humble prune (a dried out plum) as a laxative product for the old, a symbol of a dried out life on the point of death with none of the taste and juiciness of plums. An advertising campaign was conducted to change perceptions. Using children in the adverts to counter the image of wrinkly old age, the wretched prune became the 'Californian sunshine fruit' replete with hidden goodness to build both a healthy mind and body. Similarly, for years petrol company Esso (now Exxon) extolled consumers to 'put a tiger in your tank' after Dichter found that people responded favourably to animal symbolism with vaguely sexual undertones. In both cases sales increased, a testimony that hidden consumer motives can be discovered by psychological techniques and used to both change the consumers' view from the negative to the positive and increase sales. Similar methods continue to be used and can be seen in adverts everyday.

Key point Motivational research includes all types of research into human motives. It was particularly concerned with qualitative research into the consumer's subconscious or hidden motives behind the purchase of products and services.

Criticism of motivational research

Many other people involved with research at this time began to question the heavy influence of motivational research and there was a great deal of criticism of Dichter's work (Alfred Politz 1957). Because of its subjective nature, findings could be confusing, complex and open to interpretation. It was costly and time consuming, as researchers needed to spend large amounts of time with individuals and small groups. Others argued that there were also ethical issues related to the improper invasion of people's private thoughts in order to manipulate to persuade the purchase of products. Critics were also unhappy about the tendency with motivational research to constantly impute sexual motivation to rather mundane consumer purchases (Hardy 1990). It was argued that deeply held emotions and feelings were important but not at the expense of a more objective approach using larger samples and more scientific quantitative methods.

Key point Motivational research was considered limited in its uses involving few respondents and requiring expert analysis. Quantitative research was considered to be more objective, more scientific and more wide ranging.

Psychographic personality types and motivation

As a result of many of the criticisms of motivational research, more sophisticated methods were developed. Recognising that qualitative research still had a lot to offer, consumer researchers went on to adapt many of the psychological methods (psychoanalysis, in-depth interviews) used by Freud, Bernays and Dichter so that they were more effective. The problem with motivational research up to this time was that it tended to be applicable to individuals and this made it difficult to use with large groups. So in an attempt to overcome this difficulty **psychographic** profiles of people were built that could be put into distinct personality type clusters. It was hoped that by defining a person's psychological make-up according to deeply embedded cardinal personality traits, group purchase behaviour might be better differentiated and understood.

Customised strategies for each group

Using psychographic profiling, customised marketing and advertising strategies could then be built for each consumer group. Psychographic personality types were categorised according to such traits as feelings of insecurity, shyness, dominance, needing to be in control and so on. A selection of the group categories is identified in Table 9.2.

Table 9.2 Opposite psychographic personality types

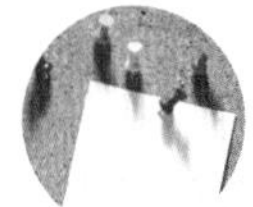

Extrovert	Introvert, inward looking
Sensitive	Insensitive
Secure	Insecure
High achievers	Low achievers
Leaders	Followers
Dominant	Submissive
Guilt laden	Innocence
Gregarious, outward going	Shy
Compulsive, impulsive	Controlled, conservative

9.5 Marketing example — Psychographic personality types and advertising campaigns

Many adverts can be seen that reflect some of the personality types identified above that attempt to satisfy major emotional needs. If the need is security then the major product should reflect this, for example the Volvo automobile is marketed with safety benefits. If the overriding need is compulsive cleanliness then the same would apply, for example 'Domestos kills all known germs'. High achievers might be seduced by the Nike slogan 'Just do it', the guilt laden woman by the L'Oreal slogan 'Because I'm worth it', and the gregarious fun-loving by the Club Med holiday group promise that its holidays are 'The antidote for (the boredom of) civilization'. The usually submissive male becomes dominant and becomes surrounded by submissive women after he uses Lynx aftershave and gets 'the Lynx affect'.

Key point Early psychographics concentrated on a person's psychological make-up. It attempted to categorise groups according to deeply embedded personality traits. Marketing and advertising programmes could then be tested and developed to see which worked best on each group.

Psychographic and lifestyle segmentation

Psychographic personality segmentation, although still in use, has gradually developed into a more sophisticated approach to understanding consumer behaviour. This was because early psychographics, based on cluster analysis and limited consumer personality traits, was demonstrated to be too limiting. Because of this concern it was found to be more helpful if the groups could be broadened to include the way that consumers think, interact and generally live their lives, as it was shown that this could all affect buying behaviour. Consumer lifestyle refers to patterns of behaviour reflecting how a person, or more likely a family, chooses to spend their time and money. It was recognised that people like to associate themselves with others who live in the same or similar ways across a whole range of activities. Most psychographic research now attempts to segment consumers according to three categories of variables, **activities, interests and opinions (AIO)** (plus demographics) first identified by Wells and Tigert in 1971.

Key point Generally the terms psychographic segmentation and lifestyle segmentation now tend to be used interchangeably.

Value of psychographic segmentation

Many commentators argued (Weinstein 1994) that consumers often behave unpredictably in the way that they demonstrate loyalty to one brand over another, blindly following trends and buying according to subjective convictions and aspirations. Individuals might be innovators with one category of product, but not in another. According to other observers (Heath and Chatterjee 1996) consumers also say one thing and then do another. Psychographic research has helped with these problems where more conventional research into segmentation has failed. It allowed marketers to better define and explain the market and provide a more complete profile of the target markets.

Activities, interests and opinions (AIO)

'I consider skateboarding an art form, a lifestyle and a sport.' TONY HAWK

Marketers are interested in the sorts of activities consumers indulge in, their general and specific interests and beliefs, attitudes and opinions held. In conducting this type of psychographic research, respondents are given lists of statements about the opinions they have, the things that they are interested in and the things that they do and asked to indicate how much they agree or disagree with each one. Demographic information is also obtained for information on age, income, family size and so on. Like-minded people can then be segmented and clustered together into the same group. In this way marketing and advertising campaigns can be clearly targeted and customised benefits offered that match researched needs and wants.

Table 9.3 AIO lifestyle variables

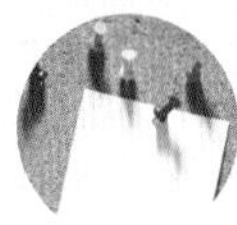

Using the AIO approach, questions are asked across the categories and subjects identified below. Group lifestyle clusters can then be developed that reflect common interests.

Activities undertaken	Interests in	Opinions about	Demographics
Shopping	Family	Social issues	Age
Work	Home	Politics	Education
Playing sports	Watching sports	Education	Income
Club membership	Food	Radical, liberal, conservative	Occupation
Social events	Fashion	Business	Family size
Family	Brands	Economics	Housing type
Home	Media	Environmental issues	Geography
Hobbies	TV, newspapers,	Consumer issues	City size
Entertainment	radio, magazines	Conformist, non-conformist	Stage in life cycle
Holidays	Recreation	Future	
	Films	Themselves	
	Music		
	Reading		

Source: William D. Wells and Douglas J. Tigert, 'Activities, Interests, and Opinions', *Journal of Advertising Research*, 11 (August 1971): 27–35. The Advertising Research Foundation.

Reasons behind product and brand purchase

Participating respondents in lifestyle research will be asked about patterns of product and brand buying so the types of products, names of brands, prices paid and the light, medium and heavy users can be identified. Researchers try to establish reasons behind purchases, for example why people buy bicycles or shoes (fun, exercise, health, fashion, transport). Products can then be branded and marketed to meet changing segmented needs.

The development of lifestyle segmentation

The increase in technical ability and the widespread use of computer power enabled researchers to combine psychological methods, market research and information

9.6 Marketing example — Research into product usage

International research company TNS (www.tns-global.com) has consumer panels of people from sample households in 28 countries reporting continuously on the purchase of FMCG/packaged goods. Each country panel will consist of a representative sample of hundreds of consumer households. Each week, in return for points and prizes, individuals will record their weekly grocery shopping using purchase diaries and barcode scanning equipment. This information can then download to the company. In this way they are able to determine changing buying patterns across products and brands and the prices being paid. Every year the National Readership Survey (NRS) interviews a representative sample of 35,000 people in Britain. It is a non-profit-making but commercial organisation, which sets out to provide estimates of the number and nature of the people who read 250 of Britain's most popular newspapers and consumer magazines. Combined with lifestyle segmentation these two research studies will therefore tell manufacturers and retailers who is buying what brands and products and which magazines and newspapers they need to use for advertising.

Question

1 Investigate the type of lifestyle research described above and evaluate its pros and cons.

technology. In this way they were able to build complex databases looking at personality types and the emotional rather than the rational bonds (often crossing socio-economic barriers such as social class, occupation and income) that consumers develop to the things that they buy.

Marketing agencies and segmentation approaches

Marketing agencies are constantly looking for insights that will allow them to gain competitive advantage by identifying more meaningful ways of using lifestyle segmentation. Although the AIO method has been successful, many felt that it failed at times to get at more complex and deeper reasons behind consumer purchase and was losing its predictive affect. It seems that the more consumer products are purchased the more complex and deep-rooted the reasons for purchase become.

VALS – values and lifestyles

One of the most well-known psychographic methods was the values and lifestyles (VALS) system, developed for commercial reasons by SRI International in California. Searching for more powerful ways to understand consumer lifestyle it came up with groups of questions based around emotional experiences such as 'excitement', 'happiness', 'family values', 'meaning of work', 'social issues', 'loyalty' and so on. Using these questions, SRI came up with a range of variables that they then used to divide US consumers into different groups with distinct characteristics. The company stated that their identified group categories could be used to cover the whole of the US. Using this information they argued that they were able to predict consumer values and motivations so that products could be marketed and promoted in the most effective way to meet the needs of each group (see Table 9.4).

Table 9.4 Values and lifestyles (VALS) types

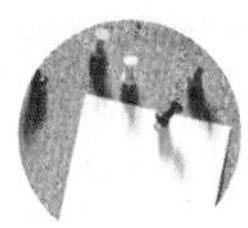

Innovators	Successful, sophisticated, take-charge people with high self-esteem
Thinkers	Organised, self-assured, intellectual, mature, satisfied
Believers	Literal, respectful, loyal, conservative, practical
Achievers	Conventional, brand conscious, realistic, career-oriented
Strivers	Eager, social, trendy, unsure of themselves
Experiencers	Impatient, impulsive, spontaneous, young, enthusiastic
Makers	Self-sufficient, practical, family oriented
Survivors	Cautious, conservative, conformist, poor, ill-educated

(http://www.sric-bi.com/VALS/types.shtml)

(It's worth noting that the groups are not mutually exclusive and individuals can spill over into different groups.)

Key point Affluence and the seemingly limitless availability of products and services appears to have the power to create the need for evermore complex and varied lifestyles.

Family life cycle segmentation

Many agencies have attempted to develop their own models of segmenting the family life cycle. This is because in many cases it is not individuals but households that make consumer decisions. This is why an understanding of the family life cycle concept is so important. It is an attempt to understand consumer behaviour patterns of individuals and groups as they age, marry or live with one another, have children and retire, and how their discretionary income and products and services bought will vary over their life span. The family life cycle is a good example of how marketers need to be constantly revisiting and researching segmentation clusters to update and keep constantly fresh and realistic. Table 9.5 is a general example of the type of categories used with the sorts of products demanded.

Key point In many cases it is not individuals but households that make consumer decisions.

National and cultural lifestyle differences

Although many lifestyles around the world are becoming similar, there are still many differences. This might be because consumers are buying in markets in different stages of the lifecycle or it might because of national, cultural and regional differences. People will eat different food and at different times. In France restaurants are closing at 10 pm, in Spain they are just opening. In the summer in some parts of Australia a lot of the time is spent outside the house having picnics and barbeques and drinking ice-cold lager; in England this is a relatively rare

Table 9.5 **Family life cycle segmentation**

Example of family lifestyle segmentation with product examples.

Tweenies – 9 to 12 year olds between childhood and teens – buying music, magazines.

Young singles – young single people not living with parents (which gave rise to the category of 'Yuppies' or 'young, upwardly-mobile persons') – buying alcohol, fragrances, cosmetics.

People living together – no children (acronym 'Dinkies' meaning 'double income – no kids') – eating out, premium grocery products, adventure holidays.

Full nest I – with the youngest child being under six years of age (acronym 'Orchids' one recent child, heavily in debt) – buying nappies, baby food, economy grocery products.

Full nest II – is where the youngest child is six or over – educational toys, children's clothes, family holidays.

Full nest III – older married couple with older, adult dependent children living at home – home meals, large grocery packs, new car.

Empty nest I – no children living at home, husband and wife working (acronym 'Woopies', well off older persons) – two holidays a year, cruising, theatre. Convenience products.

Empty nest II – both couples retired – two or three holidays a year, eating out regularly, medical products.

Solitary survivor retired (acronym 'Cocoon' meaning 'cheap old child-minder, operating on nothing') – watching TV, listening to the radio, self-prepared dinners.

occurrence. The Swedes do most of their family entertaining in the home while in Italy it's not unusual for the whole family, including small children, to eat together in restaurants. These and other examples illustrate the need for caution when adapting lifestyle segmentation across global markets.

9.7 Marketing example — The psychographic segmentation of the female market in Greater China

The Department of Business Studies at The Hong Kong Polytechnic University, Kowloon, Hong Kong attempted to segment the female consumers' market in Greater China (the People's Republic of China, Taiwan, and Hong Kong) by employing principal component factor analysis and cluster analysis. Psychographic dimensions were generated and the factor scores were computed and used in cluster analysis to develop psychographic segments of the female consumers' market in Greater China. Four distinct segments were identified and these were labelled as 'conventional women' (40.7 per cent of the sample), 'contemporary females' (21.9 per cent), 'searching singles' (19.4 per cent) and 'followers' (18.1 per cent). This enabled unique marketing campaigns to be constructed to meet the needs of each group. (*International Marketing Review*, May 1998, vol. 15, no. 1: 61–77(17)).

Figure 9.2

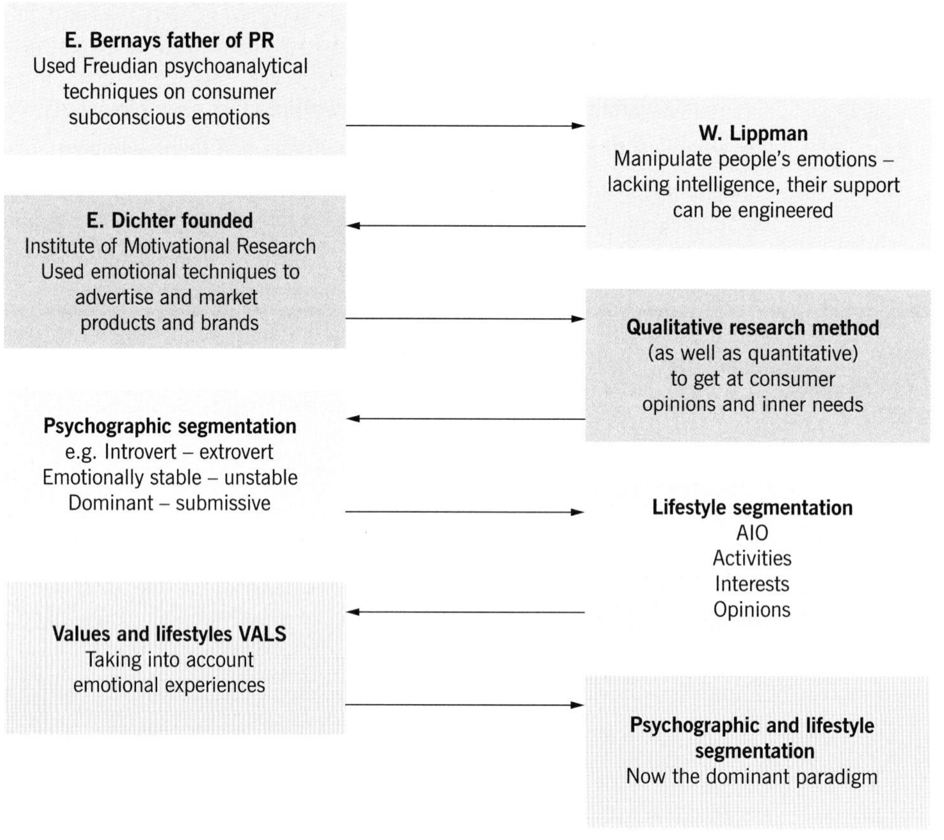

The development of motivational research

Targeting the market

Once an appropriate basis for segmenting the market has been selected, i.e. socio-economic, income, occupation, location, purchasing behaviour, psychographic and lifestyle and the important characteristics determined, the company must choose which segments to **target** and which to ignore.

Evaluating the segments

In the segmentation process each segment needs to be thoroughly researched and analysed so as to evaluate its attractiveness to the organisation.

The fundamental questions that need to be answered would include the following:

The markets: questions to be asked here would include: market size, market growth, potential and cost and profit levels as well as the amount and the size of the competition, the availability of raw material supplies and the role, if any, of the middleman in the supply chain.

Company resources: questions here would focus on internal strengths and weaknesses and include such areas as: availability of capital, skills of the workforce, existing product portfolio synergy and its market fit, price suitability and ability to deliver in the most appropriate way for the target segments.

Factors that make a market segment particularly attractive include the following:

- It has sufficient current profit and sales potential to meet the organisation's aims and objectives.
- Competition in the segment is not too intense.
- There is good potential for future growth.
- The segment has some previously unidentified requirements that the company has recognised and is now in a position to serve especially well.

Selecting the segment

After evaluation, the organisation can select one or more of the most attractive segments at which to target its products. A clear **customer profile** should be developed for each segment so that nobody should be in any doubt about the needs and wants of each market. Below in Table 9.6 are two customer profile examples, a simple one for the clothes industry and a more complex one for the holiday market.

Table 9.6 Examples of customer profiles

Customer profile for a clothes industry segment:
Sex, female; age, 35–50; income, £50,000 a year; family life cycle stage, married with no children; lifestyle, independent business woman; live in a town house in Islington, London N1.

Customer profile for the holiday market:
Male; single; age, 22–35; social class, ABC1; income £40,000–50,000; drives a sports car; works in financial services; large disposable income; lives in the middle of a large town and has own flat; an outgoing extrovert; gregarious; enjoys 'the good life' with both male and female friends; drinks upmarket branded lager; eats out in pubs and clubs; likes popular music; enjoys active adventurous holidays with people of the same age; size of the market in the UK 2 million; market static.

Positioning, brand and customer perception

Market positioning is the 'place' a product/brand occupies in a given market in relationship to the competition in terms of such factors as brand image and personality value. Having identified, evaluated and selected the most attractive segments and spelt out a clear behavioural customer profile for each buyer group, the marketing manager must decide where in the market his or her product should be positioned. Positioning is the 'place' a product/brand occupies in a given market in relationship to the competition, in terms of such factors as brand image and personality, value for money, price, availability and so on. For example the Ford Ka is lower in price and quality than the Mercedes and is perceived to occupy a different position in the car market (lower) by the two separate target markets. Similarly a Rolex watch will be positioned differently (higher) in the market to a Timex watch (lower). Both functional and emotional characteristics are given consideration. Marketers work hard to make certain that the brand being marketed is positioned in the market exactly where a particular customer expects it to be seen. Ultimately the position a product/brand is perceived to occupy in any one marketplace must happen in the mind of the targeted consumer not in the mind of the brand manager.

> **Key point** Product brand positioning is where a consumer expects a particular brand to be in the marketplace in terms of price and value in relationship to the competition. It is an emotional concept and ultimately has to happen in the mind of the consumer not in the minds of the marketing people.

Figure 9.3

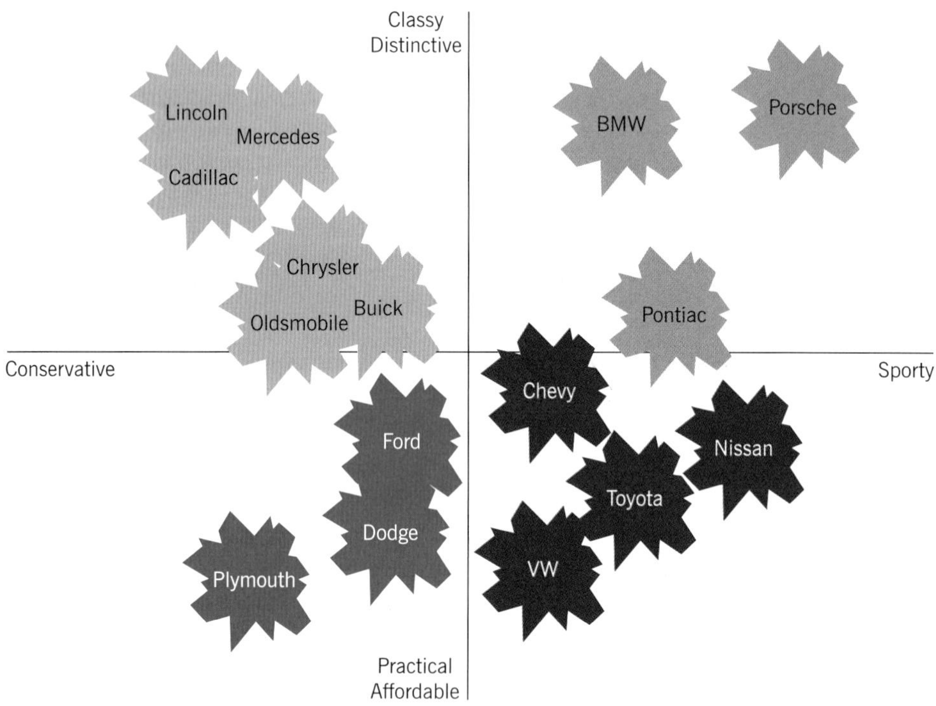

▶ **Product positioning map** – the place in the market occupied by different manufacturers as perceived by the consumer. *Source*: Answers.com

Developing a marketing mix for each segment

With the help of marketing and consumer research a customer profile and product/brand positioning statement can be developed for each individual market. A relevant customised marketing mix (product, price, place and promotion) offering can then be developed for each identified segment. The whole segmentation process can be seen below in Table 9.7.

Table 9.7 The segmentation process

Market segmentation

Stage one

1 Identifying the basis for market segmentation
2 Determine the important characteristics of each segment

Targeting the market

Stage two

3 Evaluating the market attractiveness of each segment
4 Select one or more segment

Product positioning

Stage three

5 Identify where the product will be positioned in the market *and in the mind of the consumer* so as to gain competitive advantage
6 Develop a marketing mix strategy for each targeted segment

Consumer behaviour and the need for product development

'I think one can achieve a very pleasant lifestyle by treating human beings, fellow human beings, very well.' RENE RIVKIN, Australian Entrepreneur

Consumers are now more demanding than ever before about the innovation and value they expect from products and services. Increasing competition from around the world, the growth in technological possibilities, the availability of information and the shortening of product life cycles has forced organisations to constantly innovate so as to build and maintain competitive advantage. Bringing new products to markets, however, is a risky business and many fail (McMath 1998) and organisations have to try to have a clear understanding of consumer behaviour when confronted with new products. The real value of an existing brand is the knowledge, trust and passion built up over the years in the minds of the consumer. Consumers feel safe buying a Mars Bar, Persil soap powder, Maxwell House coffee, Nokia phone, Sony TV etc., anywhere in the world because that know that they have been on the market a while and are well tried and tested. This is not the case with buying new products where every launch has a degree of failure risk. Risk of failure is especially high if the launch is by a company whose name is unknown.

Key point Constant consumer demand for innovation, choice and evermore value has put enormous pressure on companies to be continuously bringing new products and services to the market in order to maintain market share and fight off the global competition.

9.8 Marketing example — New product failure rate

Kellogg's launched Breakfast Mates in the US as a convenience breakfast food. It contained a small box of Kellogg's cereal packaged with a container of milk and a spoon. Ideal for children to serve themselves while their parents were still in bed, for students or for people just in a hurry. After two years of extensive advertising the company announced it was pulling the product because demand hadn't reached the necessary level. Consumers decided they would rather have their breakfast with fresh milk and not have to pay a premium price. This was just another statistic to add to the astonishing 80–95 per cent failure rate for new grocery products (Robert M. McMath, New Product Works).

Questions

1 Why do you think that the failure rate for new products, especially in the FMCG market, is so high?

2 Discuss consumer reaction to new product innovations. Give examples of products that you have tried once and discarded.

Size and scope of NPD programmes

Some organisations will have a larger NPD programme than others and this will depend on the type of products produced, the market structure and the level of the competition. The need for NPD programmes will be higher where:

- Customer demand is for new, progressive, hi-tech products (computers, mobile phones, TVs).
- The company maintains competitive advantage through constantly bringing new products (or existing product updates) to market (Sony, 3 ms, Phillips, Nestlé, P&G).
- There is a tradition in the market for new products (grocery fast-moving-consumer-goods, children's toys).
- There is intense competition (toiletries, airline travel, financial services).

Internal culture of innovative thinking

Companies like 3 ms, Phillips, Nokia, Nestlé and Sony that are heavily involved in constant new product development, have recognised the need to build an innovative business culture into the company. Employees are encouraged to think in a creative and innovative manner so that new product ideas are continuously generated. This can be informally by attempting to create a supportive culture that helps people to think about new ideas and formally by recognising its importance as an integral part of the long-term strategic planning process. This will involve commitment from top management, clear processes and allocation of responsibilities including appointing a 'product champion' at every stage of the new product development process. It will also include making certain that its manufacturing, technical, management and marketing processes and systems are benchmarked and kept continuously up-to-date.

Key point The consumer should be involved in some way or another at most stages in the new product development process

A customised car can now be purchased with changeable side panels to reflect the lifestyle, mood and dress of the owner

Launching new products and services

Marketers need to understand what constitutes a 'new' product from the perspective of the target customer. If consumers have problems understanding the reason behind the launch they will not buy. The behavioural needs of the customer not the organisation should therefore dictate the size and nature of the task to be undertaken.

For example a 'new' product might be any of the following all demanding a different marketing approach:

- A change or replacement to an existing product such as added features or changing benefits, e.g. Kellogg's launching a breakfast variation to cornflakes; Kit-Kat bringing out miniature variations; Mars moving into ice-cream.
- An existing concept (motorbikes, car insurance) but new to the organisation, e.g. Harley Davidson marketing clothes, Virgin selling insurance.
- A totally new concept to the market, e.g. microwave cookers, buying on the Internet, digital cameras.

9.9 Marketing example **Campbell's fresh tasting soups in a glass container**

Innovation and function come together in Campbell Soup Company's new line of quality soups. This product line was the first introduction of soups in glass jars on a national scale. Glass was the perfect choice for Campbell's to highlight the quality of their product.

Consumers loved the convenience afforded by the re-sealable glass jars. Bringing back a bygone era, this package shows a venerable idea in a new light. Glass container supplier was Owens-Brockway Glass Containers. Glass Packaging Institute (www.gpi.org).

Key point The consumer should be the arbiter on what constitutes a 'new' product, not the marketer. In this way launch programmes can be designed that clearly meet the needs of the target market.

Convincing the consumer

The company might need only to reinforce existing customer brand loyalty and inform about the benefits available in the new product extension in the case of Kellogg's, Kit-Kat and Mars. The advertising agency working for Harley Davidson will have to work a little harder as they will need to convince the target market that Harley, known for selling motorbikes, will offer good value in their clothes range. When microwave cooking first came on to the market in the 1970s the customers had first to be educated and then convinced about cooking in this revolutionary way before the company could move on to promoting and selling the brand.

Consumer behaviour and why new products fail include the following:

- Consumer behaviour is misread, needs and wants misunderstood and the wrong marketing mix strategy implemented.
- Consumers fail to see enough relevant benefits in the new product.
- The wrong consumer target group has been targeted.
- The marketing mix was integrated incorrectly and the consumer was unhappy with the relationship between the product value, its price and the channel of distribution.
- A weak or the wrong positioning strategy (e.g. value and price too high or too low) has been used.
- The promotional and advertising campaign generated an insufficient level of new product/new service awareness.

Consumer behaviour and the innovation adoption process

Marketing people are interested in the process of new product adoption including the behaviour of the consumers involved and the time that it takes for the different segments to accept the products (known as the **diffusion of innovation**). The speed of new product adoption equates to product sales revenue and profit returns. Before the onset of a new project, investors will want to know how long it will take before they will get their money back (the payback period). Inevitably one project will be competing with another and this payback period will be an important consideration.

Figure 9.4

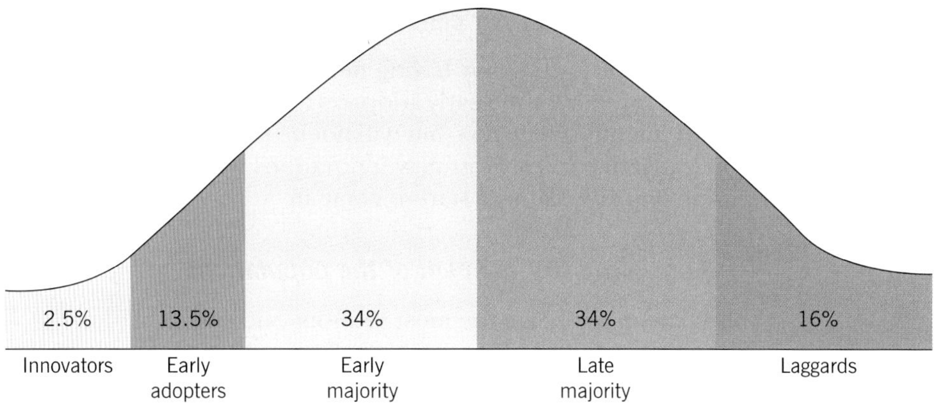

Innovation adoption curve

Different consumer buying behaviour

The new product adoption process (Rogers 1995) will involve different groups of customers at different stages at different times along the adoption curve (see Figure 9.4). Each group will have different behavioural need characteristics that demand specific benefits. It is the marketing department's task to understand and develop marketing mix packages that cater for the separate needs of each group. The aim is to move product/brand/service sales from the beginning to the end so that (in theory) 100 per cent of the target population will have purchased. Of course innovation adoption curves will vary across the world according to technological developments and new product development take-up.

Innovators (2.5 per cent of the population)

Innovators are always first into the market and eager to try new ideas, to the point where it can become an obsession. They enjoy the status and the recognition from others that comes for having the latest and innovative products and services before others. They will have a high income and are prepared to accept the occasional setback when new ideas prove unsuccessful. Marketers will want to use the publicity that comes from opinion leaders adopting their new product and they will often use high-profile celebrities as a catalyst to set the adoption process in motion.

Early adopters (13.5 per cent of population)

Early adopters enjoy the admiration that comes from having the latest products but, unlike the innovators, are willing to wait a small time while the innovators test out whether the product or service will be seen to be successful. The early adopter is usually respected by his or her peers and has a reputation for successful and discrete use of new ideas. They provide advice and information sought by other adopters about an innovation. Because they make up a sizeable minority of the market and act as a gateway to the bulk of the market, it is crucial that they are persuaded to purchase.

Early majority (34 per cent of the population)

The early majority enjoy having new products, will adopt before the average consumer but wait for the early adopters to recommend or to have bought. They interact frequently with peers, but will not be known for taking new initiatives or taking on leadership roles. Most new innovations will not really start to earn good profits until the early majority start to come in.

Late majority (34 per cent of the population)

The late majority are the most cautious and sceptical of the groups, only adopting when the products have been on the market for quite a while and are well tried and tested. Peer-group pressure, the opinion of others, and existing product limitations and breakdown will force this reluctant consumer to purchase.

Laggards (16 per cent of the population)

Laggards are very slow to change, suspicious of new ideas and the last to adopt an innovation. They are fixated on the past, and all decisions must be made in terms of previous generations. They tend to buy when the price is at its lowest and even when the particular model is on its way out. They will just be buying mobile phones and video recorders.

Close relationships with the customer

Many organisations recognise the need to understand consumer behaviour, constantly engage them in a dialogue and try to build close relationships. Experience has shown that most people prefer dealing with companies that offer consistently upgraded value and employ salespeople who are knowledgeable and can be respected and trusted. There are good examples of successful companies that have understood the need to observe, constantly talk, and more importantly listen to their customers on a daily basis (Apple iPod, Google, P&G). The 'share of customer' is now considered just as important as 'share of market'.

Listening and understanding can be a complex task

In some circumstances there are problems in fully understanding needs because consumers will not always be able to articulate what they really want or have deeply ingrained 'not yet realised needs'. This can be a particular problem when a company is thinking about launching a new product to the market. Not having experienced anything similar before can cause research respondents to misinterpret the customer response when the product actually hits the market. And there is more to incorporating customer insights than simply listening to customers more closely. Often, the best innovators not only understand customer behaviour but the reasons behind that behaviour. 'It's not just what they do, but why they do it.' People form different kinds of relationships with products, just as they do with other people. It's important to understand the dynamics of the relationship (e.g., short term versus long term, shared power versus dominant/submissive) consumers have with your product in order to know how to talk to them about it. The problems can be more or less overcome by employing researchers skilled in using a range of qualitative techniques, such as focus groups and psychographic interviewing discussed in detail in Chapter 2 on marketing research.

Key point Listen carefully to what your customers want and why they want it and then respond with new products that meet or exceed their needs.

9.10 Marketing example Keeping close to the customer

Advertising agency Booz Allen based in New York cites Starbucks as a company that has a superb record for anticipating customers' unarticulated desires to create new and better experiences. They say that 'coffee was a commodity and consumption was declining until Starbucks came up with a different concept, meeting a previously unrealized need' (Booz Allen, NY, 'How Companies Turn Customers' Big Ideas into Innovations', taken from www.strategy-business.com). Close attention to customer needs has enabled them to offer a whole range of speciality coffees to the market encouraging consumers to buy more exotic and more expensive options. The coffeehouse has become an exciting new public space where friends and business colleagues alike can meet. They also cite McDonald's saying that they have been able to stay at the top of the fast-food business for so long because they understand what each customer wants and why they want it. They say that the answer lies in using multiple sources of market data and building extremely close relationships with customers.

Questions

1. Analyse and evaluate the success of Starbucks and other similar organisations.
2. Why is research into new products more difficult than research into existing or add-on products?

Customer relationship management (CRM) programmes

It is impossible to say precisely what customer relationship management means to everyone. It developed out of the basic concept that underpins marketing, that of 'staying close to your customer at all times'. Over the decades many companies would have developed customer relationship programmes without describing them as such. For example sending out personal promotional letters with special offers, talking regularly on the telephone, inviting past users in to visit the factory or for a wine and cheese evening in the shop. With the onset of computers the idea of more formal CRM systems gathered apace. In the early days it was little more than a series of simple software programmes specific to sales and support business functions. The applications were lightweight by today's standards and did little more than capture and store, often unconnected, data on customers and markets.

Key point Traditional relationships between customers and marketers were often seen as adversarial in which organisations try to sell their products and customers try to avoid them. On the other hand CRM views the customer as a fully informed participating partner. The relationship should not be seen as cosmetic and the customer must feel valued in a real sense.

Orange understands the importance of customer service.
Source: Orange

More sophisticated techniques

As information technology has developed and techniques become more powerful, software programmes that allow companies to talk to individual customers and adjust elements of their marketing programmes in response to each customer's reactions to elements of the marketing mix have become increasingly more sophisticated and meaningful. This has led to the concept of 'one-to-one' marketing and 'mass customisation' discussed earlier in this chapter. Because it is always easier and many times less expensive to keep an existing customer than to get a new customer (Park and Kim 2000) CRM-oriented firms now realise the value in focusing on increasing their share of customer spend as well as increasing the share of the market (the latter is not always possible in a mature market).

9.11 Marketing example CRM systems

CRM systems are about strategically managing the relationship with the customer. It's about collaboration, talking and listening to the customers and making products and services immediately available. This includes websites that let the customer check his or her account or monthly spend, check a bill, look up questions and answers about products and services, offers or problems (increasingly in real time). There could be an area for observations, compliments and complaints and home deliveries might be tracked to find out delivery times or delay possibilities. When a customer receives a phone message, email or postcard from the dentist reminding him or her about an appointment or when the Ford car dealer phones asking a recent buyer about the new vehicle, or a favourite restaurant sends a birthday or anniversary offer of two meals for the price of one, that is a CRM system. What's important is that everything coming out from the one company should be clearly targeted and offer personalised benefits that are satisfying and welcomed. All subsections of a CRM system should fit neatly together, not be intrusive, offer security when necessary, and make the customer feel special and wanted. In this way loyalty might be engendered.

Questions

1 Discuss how a consumer might react to the type of CRM systems discussed here.

2 Known as 'permission marketing' do you think that the consumer should be asked first before becoming involved in CRM-type programmes?

CRM not be used as an excuse to reduce costs

CRM systems should not be used as an excuse to reduce costs and in doing so offer a much poorer service. To sit on the telephone and be pushed from one recorded voice or piece of music to another is wrong and gives the concept and the company a bad name and will eventually lose customers. Good CRM systems should be used in a focused and an integrated way minimising waiting times, offering constant value upgrades, improving all round service and making every customer contact point a rewarding experience.

9.12 Marketing example CRM strategy

To appreciate the value of a CRM strategy, consider the experience of financial services firms Salomon Smith Barney and Fidelity Investments. In general, an investment banker needs to manage accounts as well as open new ones – often 30 to 50 per month. Just opening the account can take 45 minutes, not a satisfying process for the banker or the customer. But with an automated CRM system, the banker can open an account, issue a welcome letter, and produce an arbitration agreement in 10 minutes. They can create a unique marketing campaign for each client based on that person's life cycle – including such variables as when a person opened an account, the person's annual income, family situation, desired retirement age, and so on. The marketer can generate a happy anniversary letter to clients (to commemorate when they joined the firm, not when they got married) and include an invitation to update their investment objectives.

Managing customer relations

Integrated CRM systems, combined with personal information about age, gender, address (on a loyalty, debit, credit card, from warranty card returns, competition entry, catalogue purchases and so on) will allow an organisation such as American Express, Kraft Foods, Carrefour, Tesco, B&Q, HSBC, to manager customer relations in a productive and effective way. In this way marketers can closely track consumer buying habits and build databases that exploit and reward individual behaviour in an optimum manner.

Successful integrated CRM strategies perform the following functions:

- Identifying customer buying patterns and offering promotions on complementary products.
- Identifying and rewarding the customers who spend the most and those who are the most profitable.
- Encouraging two-way communications about products and services availability and after-sales service and other problems. Feedback should be seen to be valued.
- Gaining information about current and future needs and building complex databases.
- Motivating the consumer to begin a dialogue with the company that ideally will result in a deeper, long-term relationship.

The meaning of consumer loyalty

▶ Many **loyalty** programmes seem to assume that consumers want to have a relationship with the retail organisation. Not all customers, however, want the close type of relationship suggested by the idea of customer relationship management. In reality the idea of what constitutes consumer loyalty is a difficult concept to pin down as consumers will sometimes say one thing about shopping in one store rather than another and then behave in other ways. If behaviour is to be measured, the number of months or years a shopper has been coming to the store should be assessed as well the number of times the store is used in one week and the amount of money spent. Similarly how many other competitor retailers are used might also come into the equation. Research company Taylor Nelson Sofres argue that brand building based on clear customer profiling and insight into the target group's in-depth psychological, social and functional needs is the key to building loyalty.

Research group Mintel have shown that there are consumers who will use the same store on a regular basis and welcome recognition and constant contact. On the other hand they have shown that there are groups of shoppers who hold many loyalty cards, have no allegiance to any one store and will shop wherever they feel the most comfortable at any one time.

Attempting to measure consumer loyalty

Researchers (Backman and Crompton 1991) have attempted to answer some of these questions by identifying different loyalty strengths according to how much respondents said they liked a particular store (psychological attachment) and how often the store was used (behavioural consistency) see Figure 9.5 below.

Figure 9.5

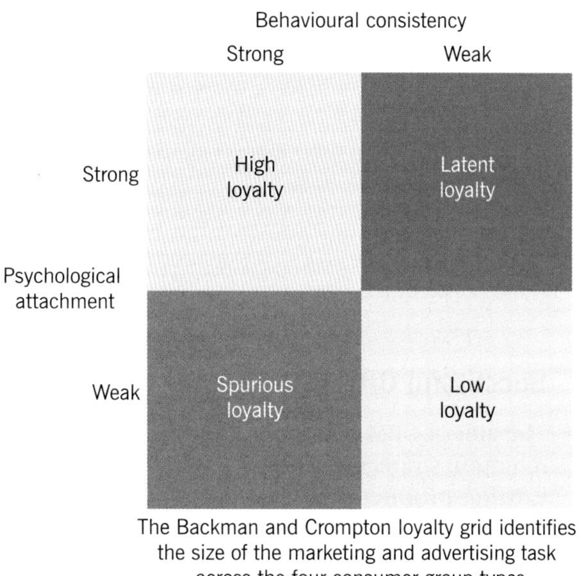

Backman and Crompton consumer loyalty grid

Customers are now in control

Increasingly many people are positively turned off by companies constantly contacting them, for whatever the reason, and do not want a relationship with a manufacturer or retailer. This is especially so if the contact comes from an outsourcing company operating from the other side of the world. Many consumers see CRM as direct marketing by another name, knowing that the retailer or brand owner wants to build a two-way relationship for purely commercial reasons. It also seems that many now recognise the power they have and are prepared to remain loyal to any one company just as long as they get what they want, going elsewhere when better opportunities arise.

9.13 Marketing example Failure of CRM programmes

The secret of successful CRM is building (and managing) an understanding of consumer value and determining how it can be created more effectively through interactive relationships. There are companies, however, that are not even doing direct marketing properly and don't even have a meaningful database. Several research studies in the US (Gartner, Meta Group, and Forrester Research) and around the world claim that anything between 50 per cent and 70 per cent of CRM projects fail and are abandoned. This appears to be because some organisations believe that simply deploying technology is enough. That approach may be right for a production line or logistics process, but it will not work for marketing. For one thing many of the marketing strategy people who start the programmes, will have moved on in the first year and so fail to see the project through over the longer term. Second, consumer needs are always changing and company benefit offerings and processes must be constantly fine-tuned to match expectations.

Questions

1 Discuss the cultural problems associated with CRM implementation and failure.

2 'CRM programmes such as automatic telephone answering services are more to do with cost reduction than increasing customer satisfaction.' Discuss.

Key point Successful CRM programmes must be strategically and tactically driven by the needs of the consumer, not the organisation.

Successful CRM programmes

The aim of CRM programmes is to improve sales by attempting to build long-term retention strategies so that loyal customers will constantly purchase and re-purchase existing products and services as well as being persuaded to buy complimentary offerings. More effective targeting should make it easier to identify, and reward, the heaviest and the most profitable users. Better profiling of customers who have been lost will enable more effective claw-back strategies to be implemented. They should also work to encourage word-of-mouth recommendation and in this way encourage customers to switch from competitor organisations. Eventually more effective and efficient business processes resulting from the productive use of CRM technology and other resources should bring in overall reduced costs.

Successful CRM programmes exhibit the following characteristics:

1 Strategic support from top management
2 Designed by marketing people not IT
3 Listening constantly to the customer
4 Understand consumer behaviour
5 Encourage collaboration
6 Encourage word-of-mouth recommendation
7 Always updating the customer database
8 Expect to change in line with consumer expectations

Figure 9.6

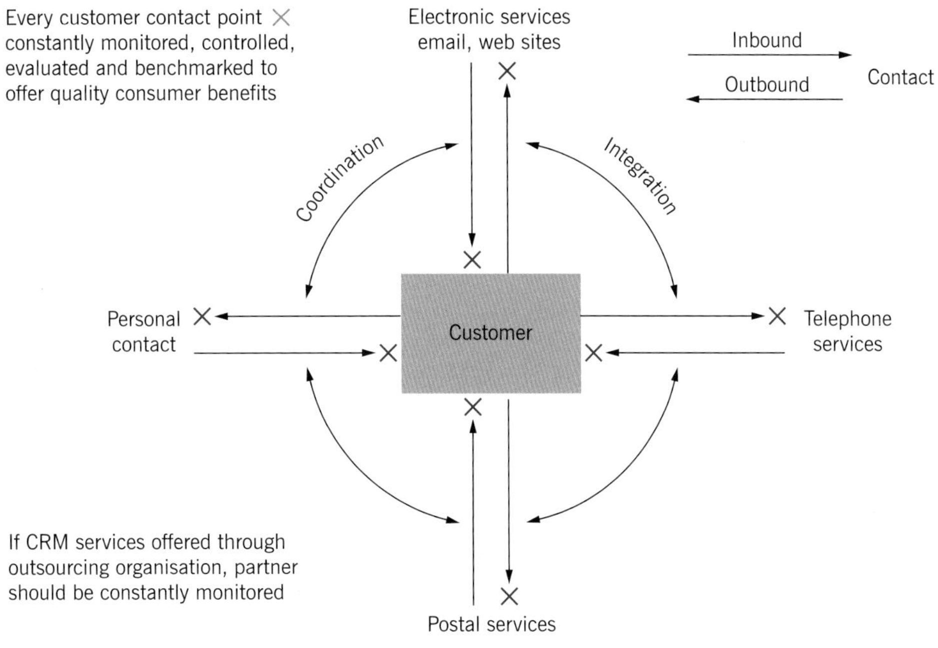

CRM contact points

9 Offering outstanding quality service at every customer contact point
10 Feedback monitoring, control and evaluation mechanisms

> **Key point** Instead of always talking to consumers, organisations have to help consumers talk to each other about their successful products.

Summary

- We began the chapter by looking at how mass marketing, mass segmentation, narrow segmentation and one-to-one marketing developed in modern economies, making the point that markets could be at different stages around the world.
- The role of psychoanalysis and motivational research and its use in understanding and manipulation of consumer behaviour was then examined, looking particularly at the work of Edward Bernays, Ernest Dichter and Walter Lippmann.
- This led on to illustrating how the use of psychographics and personality types as methods of segmenting markets became the forbearers of lifestyle marketing.
- It was then shown how a combination of psychographics, the activities/interests/opinion model and personal and socio-geographic information came together to form the basis of lifestyle segmentation.
- The role of segmentation as the purpose of understanding consumer behaviour and its importance to product positioning and marketing mix development programmes was then demonstrated.

- Examples of how lifestyle markets are segmented were then given before moving on to look at consumer behaviour and the need for product development and an understanding of Roger's new product development innovation adoption process.
- The growth and sophistication of customer relationship management (CRM) programmes were examined in some detail and examples given of good and bad usage.

Questions

1 Shown below is a list of consumer personality psychographic characteristics. Attempt to identify real advertisements in the main media that have produced campaigns that are aimed at groups and individuals that might have one or more of these personality traits.

Introvert – extrovert
Sensitive – insensitive
Secure – insecure
High achiever – low achiever
Leader – follower
Dominant – submissive
Guilt laden – innocence
Gregarious – shy
Compulsive – controlled

2 Examine why traditional methods used to understand consumer behaviour (social class, occupation, age) are of limited use in segmenting some types of customers and markets. Give examples that support your reasoning.

3 Discuss the following statement made by Edward Bernays, known as the father of PR: 'If we understand the mechanism and motives of the group mind, it is now possible to control and regiment the masses according to our will without their knowing it.' How might this idea affect consumer behaviour?

4 Identify and evaluate the role that psychographics played in understanding consumer behaviour. Give live examples of its advantages and disadvantages.

5 Discuss the reason that psychographics and the activity, interests and opinion model came together to develop lifestyle segmentation.

6 Identify the segmentation process and demonstrate how the manufacturer of an FMCG product might use it to clearly identify different target markets for a range of boxed chocolates.

7 Examine the value of clear customer profiling and give real examples of how this has been used across a range of retailers.

8 Discuss the part that the consumer might play in the development and launch of new products. Why is this an important area in the understanding of consumer behaviour? Give live examples to illustrate your answers.

9 Explain and give examples on the use of customer relationship management (CRM) programmes. Discuss their growth and evaluate their advantages and disadvantages.

10 Discuss the moral and ethical issues associated with psychographics and motivational research. Give live examples of its possible misuse and actions that government might have taken to protect the consumer.

Case study

Case study 1 Ikea

Source: IKEA

Founded in Sweden in 1943, Ikea has proved a hit with consumers around the world ever since. In 2004 it had over 200 large stores in 32 countries around the world. Its products are aimed at groups of consumers who are interested in developing particular lifestyles. The retailer has approximately 12,000 different products including kitchen cupboards and equipment, three-piece suites, bedroom furniture, tables, cupboards, household linen, curtains, candle-holders and so on. Its catalogue is available in 34 different languages and it is reputedly to be the second most widely distributed book after the Bible (100 million copies produced every year). Many stores include restaurants serving typically Swedish food. Its lifestyle formats seem to work in most towns where it has a store.

Ikea is so popular that customers are happy to travel many tens of miles to visit one of its stores and there is often pandemonium whenever a new store opens. In 2005 in the UK several people were hurt in the crush as thousands flocked to the midnight opening of an Ikea store in Edmonton, north London. As soon as the doors opened everybody pushed forward and it stayed open for just 30 minutes because of safety fears. Five people had to be taken to hospital for treatment. Bargain-hunters even abandoned their cars on the main road so that they could get to the store. This caused severe traffic problems. The mayhem was blamed on Ikea management for offering first arrivals products at knockdown prices and not having enough security staff to deal with the problems that they must have known would happen. In a similar incident in western Saudi Arabia more than 8000 people pushed for entry and at least three people were crushed to death.

Questions

1 Ikea sees itself as a lifestyle retailer. What do you think that they mean by this and why do you think that they are so successful? Give examples of other so-called lifestyle retailers.

2 Discuss why you think that consumers behave in the way described above.

Case study

Case study 2 Family life changing

Over the last 20 to 30 years many changes have taken place in family life. In many Western countries fewer babies are being born and women are leaving it much later in life to give birth. Children are growing up quicker, recognising brands as early as three years old and staying at home watching TV and playing computer games rather than going outside on the street or into the park to play. Children are becoming fashion conscious as early as eight and nine and regularly using cosmetics and fragrance by eleven and twelve. In the 1960s in the UK very few people lived together before being married (2 per cent) now the majority of young people (75 per cent) say they would rather live together first before getting married (Mori research). Modernised family life cycle models now have to incorporate single parents with children, single people living on their own, childless couples, gay couples and the fact that people are living to an older age, staying healthier longer and demanding brands that reflect lifestyles well into old age. There have been many devastating problems, however, when the old and the new cultures clash. Excess drinking and unseemly behaviour by young people out to enjoy themselves has made some parts of a city a no-go area for older family members. In the UK there have been incidences of young Asian girls being forced to marry Asian men they have never seen and being heavily punished, even killed for refusing to obey the wishes of their parents. Gay marriages are now allowed in some countries while in others homosexuality is still a criminal offence.

Questions

1 Critically examine how changing family life patterns are affecting the marketing of brands and products. Give live examples.

2 Do you think that consumer behaviour around the world, particularly from the young, is becoming more Westernised and standardised in the way that products and brands are bought and used? Again give examples.

Further reading

Books

Aaker, D. (1991) *Managing Brand Equity*, New York: Free Press.
Bernays, E. (2004) *Propaganda*, New York: IG Publishing.
Dichter, E. (1964) *Handbook of Consumer Motivation*, New York: McGraw-Hill.
East, Robert (1990) *Changing Consumer Behavior*, London: Cassell Publishing.
Ewen, Stuart (1996) *PR! A Social History of Spin*, New York: Basic Books.
Gunter, B. and Furnham, A. (1992) *Consumer Profiles: An Introduction to Psychographics*, New York: Routledge.
Hawkins, D.I., R.J. Best and K.A. Coney (1998) *Consumer Behavior: Building Marketing Strategy*, 7th edn, Burr Ridge, IL: Irwin/McGraw-Hill.

Hardy, H.S. (ed.) (1990) *The Politz Papers: Science and Truth in Marketing Research*, Chicago, IL: The American Marketing Association.
Key, Wilson Bryan (1974) *Subliminal Seduction*, New York: Signet Books.
Lippmann, Walter (1997) *Public Opinion*, New York: Free Press, reissue.
MacMath, R. and T. Forbes (1998) *What Were They Thinking*, New York: Crown Business.
Packard, Vance (1991) *The Hidden Persuaders*, London: Penguin Books.
Rogers, Everett M. (1995) *Diffusion of Innovation*, 4th edn, New York: Free Press.
Solomon, R. (2004) *Consumer Behaviour: Buying, Having and Being*, Harlow: Prentice Hall, 6th edn.
Tye, Larry and Deborah Brody (eds) (2002) *The Father of Spin: Edward L. Bernays and the Birth of Public Relations*, New York: Owl Books.
Wheeler, J. and S. Smith (2002) *Managing the Customer Experience: Turning Customers into Advocates*, Harlow: Financial TimesPrentice Hall.
Weinstein, W. (1994) *Using Demographics, Psychographics, and Other Niche Marketing Techniques to Predict and Model Customer Behaviour*, Chicago, IL: Probus Publishing Company.

Journals

Backman, S.J. and J.L. Crompton (1991) 'Differentiating between High, Spurious, Latent and Low Loyalty Participants in Two Leisure Services, *Journal of Park and Recreation Administration*, 9(2): 1–17.
Barnard, S. (1995) 'Generation Games: The Key to a Successful Product is Lifestage Marketing', *Grocer*, Vol. 217 (7): 42.
Belk, Russel W. (1988) 'Posessions and the Extended Self', *Journal of Consumer Research*, Vol. 15 (September): 139–68.
Day, G.S. (1969) 'A Two-dimensional Concept of Brand Loyalty', *Journal of Advertising Research*, 9: 29–35.
Dichter, Ernest (1985) 'What's in an Image?', *Journal of Consumer Marketing*, Vol. 2, Winter: 75–8.
Heath, Timothy B. and Subimal Chatterjee (1996) 'Conflict and Loss Aversion in Multi-Attribute Choice', *Organizational Behavior and Human Decision Processes*, Vol. 67 (August) 144–55.
Park, S.H. and Y.M. Kim (2000) 'Conceptualizing and Measuring the Attitudinal Loyalty Construct in Recreational Sport Contexts', *Journal of Sport Management*, 14: 197–207.
Politz, Alfred (1957) ' "Motivation Research" From a Research Viewpoint', *Public Opinion Quarterly*, Vol. 20: 663.
Sampson, P. (1992) 'People are People the World Over: The Case for Psychological Market Segmentation', *Marketing and Research Today*, 20: 134–48.
Wells, William D. and Douglas J. Tigert (1971) 'Activities, Interests, and Opinions', *Journal of Advertising Research*, 11 (August): 27.
Zablocki, Benjamin D. and Rosabeth Moss Kanter (1976) 'The Differentiation of Life-Styles', *Annual Review of Sociology*, 2: 269–97.

Websites

Advertising Age, Trade journal for marketing and advertising professionals. www.adage.com.
The Association for Qualitative Research, www.aqrp.co.uk.
CACI International Inc, IT and network solutions (including ACORN) www.caci.com.

Creative and innovation website, www.bemorecreative.com.
Forrester Research, www.forrester.com.
Gartner Research Group, www.gartner.com.
Interbrand, www.interbrand.com.
Mind Tools, www.mindtools.com.
New Product Works, www.newproductworks.com.
Qualitative Research Consultants Association, www.qrca.org.

The marketing mix, consumer behaviour and organisational buying behaviour

10

'If you work just for money, you'll never make it, but if you love what you're doing and you always put the customer first, success will be yours.'

Ray Kroc, founder of McDonald's (1992)

Objectives

At the end of this chapter the reader should be able to:

1 Analyse and evaluate how the marketing mix, the product, price, place and promotion, is developed and adapted so as to correspond to an understanding of consumer behaviour.

2 Identify, examine and evaluate the differences between consumer and organisational buying behaviour across the marketing areas.

Introduction

Marketing – anticipating and satisfying (exceeding) customer needs and wants.

Commonly known as the marketing mix or the 4ps, the product, price, place and promotion are shorthand for the controllable tools and techniques that the marketing manager must use to manipulate, hone and shape in order to satisfy the consumer needs that marketing research should have identified. It's important that all elements of the marketing mix come together in an integrated and effective way so that an optimum customer-satisfying solution is achieved. Ideally all the effort put into understanding consumer behaviour discussed throughout this book should come to fruition in the development of an integrated marketing mix that exactly meets the needs of every individual consumer in the target market. Figure 10.1 shows a simple model of the marketing process.

Figure 10.1

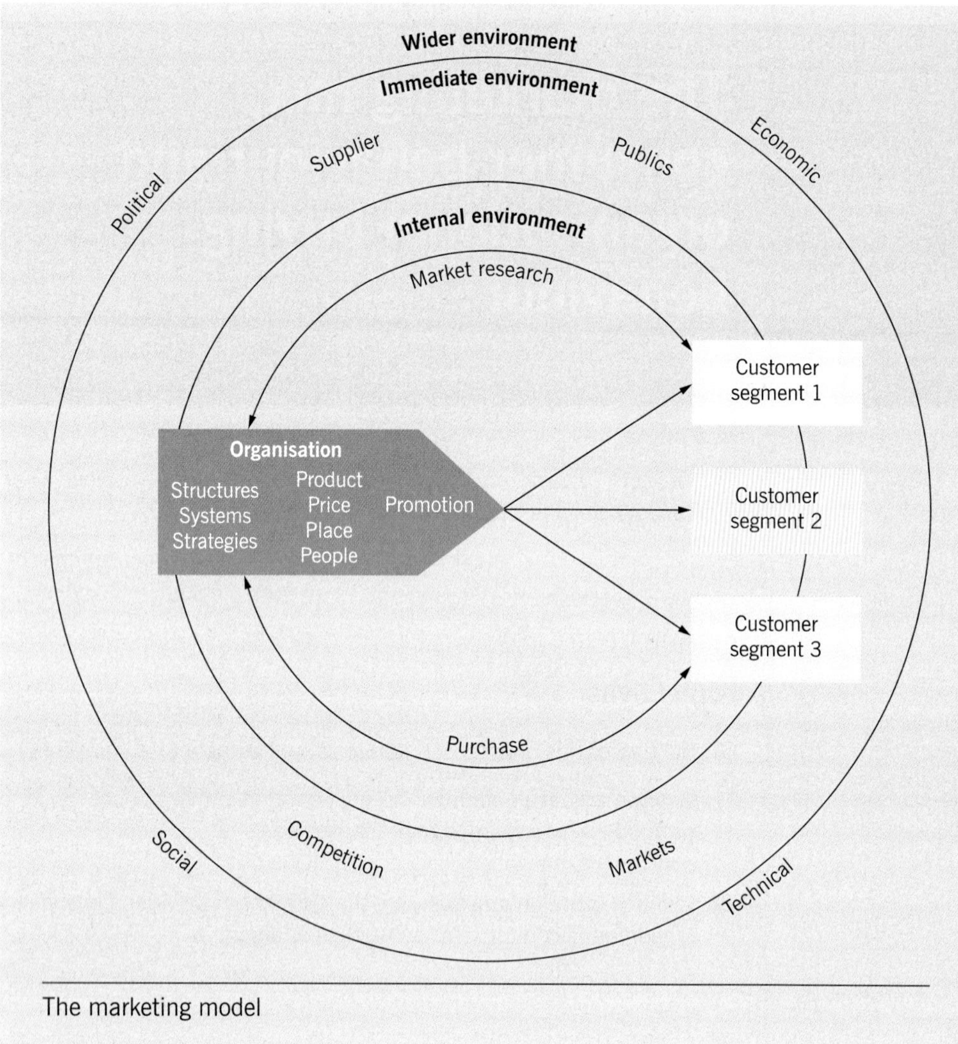

The marketing model

The marketing mix

The part the marketing mix plays in understanding consumer behaviour, developing the 'right product' and the 'right price', making it available in the 'right place' and then 'promoting in the right way' can now be briefly outlined. If the programme is successful and the customer is delighted the product will be purchased and repurchased on a continuous basis, if not the sales will be lost and the company will go out of business.

The product and consumer behaviour

'I'm convinced that my epitaph will one day read, "It all comes down to product!" And that's OK by me,' he quipped. 'That's why the Chrysler Group will continue to develop and launch new vehicles at a brisk pace.' DIETER ZETSCHE, CEO Chrysler

It might arguably be said that the product or service that the organisation offers for sale is the very reason for its existence. Without the product there is no sale, without the sale there is no revenue, no profit and no existence. As marketing puts the customer at the very heart of its activities the product or service must be developed and offered in conjunction with the customer and the market's needs. As we have seen in the many preceding chapters, consumer needs and wants are complex and many ranging from the functional, the rational, the emotional and the psychological. The product on offer has to offer benefits that satisfy some or all of these needs. This truism creates a demanding and exciting challenge for researchers, product innovators and marketers.

Key point Taking a wide definition, a product/service can be anything that satisfies (exceeds) a need or want, functional, rational, emotional, psychological, in exchange for some kind of payment (money or some other benefit other than money).

Building consumer benefits by adding value to the product

People buy products because they hope that the benefit gained in the transaction will satisfy some outstanding need or want (either conscious or subconscious). So another way of looking at a product is as a 'bundle of benefits' put together by the producer to perform this task. As the consumer becomes more sophisticated more personalised benefits are demanded. It was argued that these benefits are predominately symbolic and emotional. To maintain a competitive advantage the organisation must constantly upgrade and offer more. Therefore marketing and selling products and services in the modern market can be seen as a process of constantly adding customised value in response to the ever-changing researched demands for choice and better value. Because of this ever better value, the consumer will often be prepared to pay a higher price.

▶ There are many different ways that an organisation can **add value** to its products in response to customer demands and the progressive and subsequently more successful company will always be looking for innovative ways.

Prioritising added value

▶ **Added value** benefits to the product and other elements of the marketing mix should be prioritised according to individual and consumer group demands. This will vary from product to product and from market to market but continuous consumer and market research should drive the process. In some markets after-sales service might be most important (computer systems, Internet broadband), in others it might be the brand name (clothes, cars, confectionary, fragrances). In one area it might be the functional that might be emphasised (DIY) in another the symbolic (beauty and skin care). Inherent in the concept of good marketing is the realisation that the correct need must be identified and the relevant benefits offered. Get this wrong and the product will not sell.

Figure 10.2

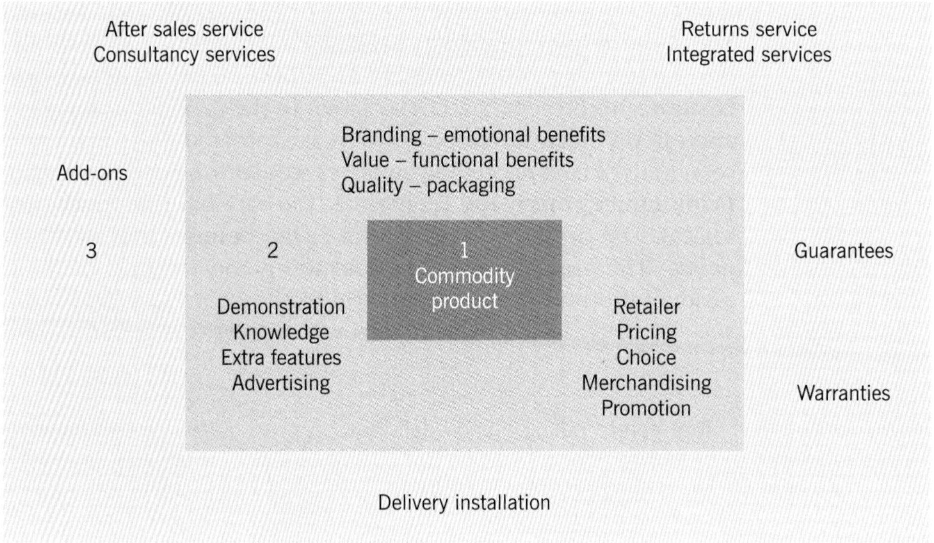

1. Commodity produce – little or no added value
2. Primary added value – before product is sold
3. Secondary added value – after product is sold

The added value process

Added value and change

Organisations cannot afford to become complacent as customer added value priorities change and became evermore demanding over time. This is because people are more affluent, have more information and are more educated about products and services on offer (the growth in information technology). Programmes in the media about food and holiday travel, keeping fit and losing weight, house makeovers, body makeovers, alternative medicines and so on, as well as practical experiences and incessant competition from around the world is constantly opening up possibilities encouraging shoppers to demand more choice and become quickly bored unless they have the latest innovative offering.

The functional and symbolic attributes of the product

Added value can be categorised under two general areas corresponding to the types of benefits demanded by the customer. These two areas can be categorised as:

1 The functional
2 The symbolic

The functional

It can be argued that consumers want products for their functional properties. This is the overt purpose of the product and the reason for purchase seems to be self-evident. As an example we can think of buying a watch to tell the time, bottled water to quench our thirst, a car to use for transport, clothes to keep us warm, food to satisfy hunger and insurance protection in case of a mishap.

The symbolic

Of course we buy a watch to tell the time, water to quench our thirst and food to satisfy our hunger, but continuous in-depth research and practical experience has shown that people buy products and brands for reasons other than the functional – that is for symbolic reasons. By symbolic we mean that the product/brand comes to represent some other, sometimes deeper and less transparent, emotional or instinctive need. For example:

- A gold watch may be bought to inform others how successfully rich we are (status needs), a Mickey Mouse watch to show how fun loving and un-materialistic we are (social needs) and a 'chunky' divers watch with 100 functions operable 100 metres under water gives 'street credibility' to the owner (security needs).
- Scottish highland spring water in a premium priced designer blue bottle at a dinner party informs our guests that we are avant-garde and in the forefront of middle-class activity (status needs).
- An expensive Audi car associates the owner with having knowledge of quality and comfortable wealth (social class and status).

Premium branded bottled water is more expensive per litre than car petrol. Who would have imagined consumers would be prepared to pay a thousand times more for water which many argue tastes the same as tap water. There are over 250 different brands in the UK

A combination of functional and emotional needs

It seems that products are purchased for both functional and emotional needs and it's not always possible to distinguish between the two. So when designing, developing and promoting a product, brand and packaging, both functional and symbolic needs might have to be catered for. The importance of each can be discovered by customer behavioural research. With some products the reason for purchase will lean more toward the functional (basic foodstuffs, building materials) and with others more toward the symbolic (fashion clothes, fragrances).

To a lesser or greater extent most consumer products are bought to satisfy a large emotional need element and so symbolic benefit needs are hugely important. On the other hand, most business-to-business products are bought for functional reasons and these differences should be recognised when developing the marketing mix (B2B products and markets will be discussed in more detail later in the chapter).

Key point Most consumer products are bought for symbolic reasons while most B2B products are bought for functional reasons.

Figure 10.3

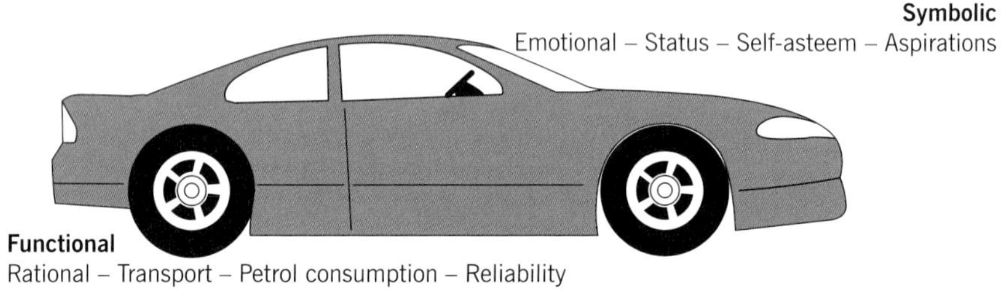

Products – functional and symbolic attributes of a motor car

Gaining competitive advantage

According to Michael Porter (1998) **competitive advantage** can be achieved in three basic ways. By under pricing all others in the market, offering the same products and service but doing it better or differentiating. Only the most powerful can under price all others (through economies of scale, for example Wal-Mart and Carrefour) and product offering and quality of service and differentiation can be copied. There are really only two ways of building an unassailable competitive advantage that nobody else can exactly copy. The first is by having a patent on a product or process (and this finishes after perhaps 20 years). The second is having ownership of a distinctive brand. This is a **USP** or **UEP** (**unique selling proposition, unique emotional proposition**) that is protected by law and that no others may use (except illegally as in some Asian countries).

Key point To keep and maintain competitive advantage a company must make its product/service cheaper, better or different from the competition.

The market leader brand is all

Differentiation through branding has been shown to be the most profitable way for many companies (especially FMCG) to run its business (PIMS-Europe research). A leading market brand perceived by consumers to have unique qualities can never be equalled as long as benefits offered are constantly communicated and in line with customer expectations and the product is always available. Brands enable the owner to charge higher prices and so make more money. This is why brands are worth so much money (often more than the worth of the rest of the company) (see Table 10.1).

Table 10.1 Top brands in the world 2004, by value

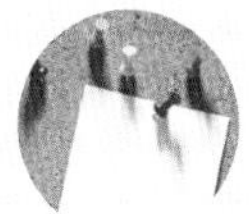

Rank	Brand	Brand value billions
1.	Coca-Cola	$67.39
2.	Microsoft	61.37
3.	IBM	53.79
4.	GE	44.11
5.	Intel	33.50
6.	Disney	27.11
7.	McDonald's	25.11
8.	Nokia	24.04
9.	Toyota	22.67
10.	Marlboro	22.13

Source: Interbrand Corp, J.P. Chase and Co, CIF group, Morgan Stanley

Brand personality

A brand can have great strength and value because of its perceived '**brand personality**' in the minds of the consumer. The brand seems be able to take on human characteristics and consumers begin to think of some products as 'people'. For example many consumers have names for their cars and will even talk to them. In many cases the brand personality will have been built up at great cost, often over years through extensive marketing, advertising and celebrity endorsement. The value of the brand personality is enormous. In fact many companies, known as 'virtual' companies (for example Nike, Sara Lee) outsource everything including purchasing, storage, manufacturing and distribution. They control, however, the most valuable part of the process, marketing and the brands. Brand personality seems to exist across a whole range of companies and products creating bonds of **brand loyalty** that can last for years from one generation to another. The task of the marketing person is to build brand personality characteristics that match lifestyle benefits demanded.

Figure 10.4

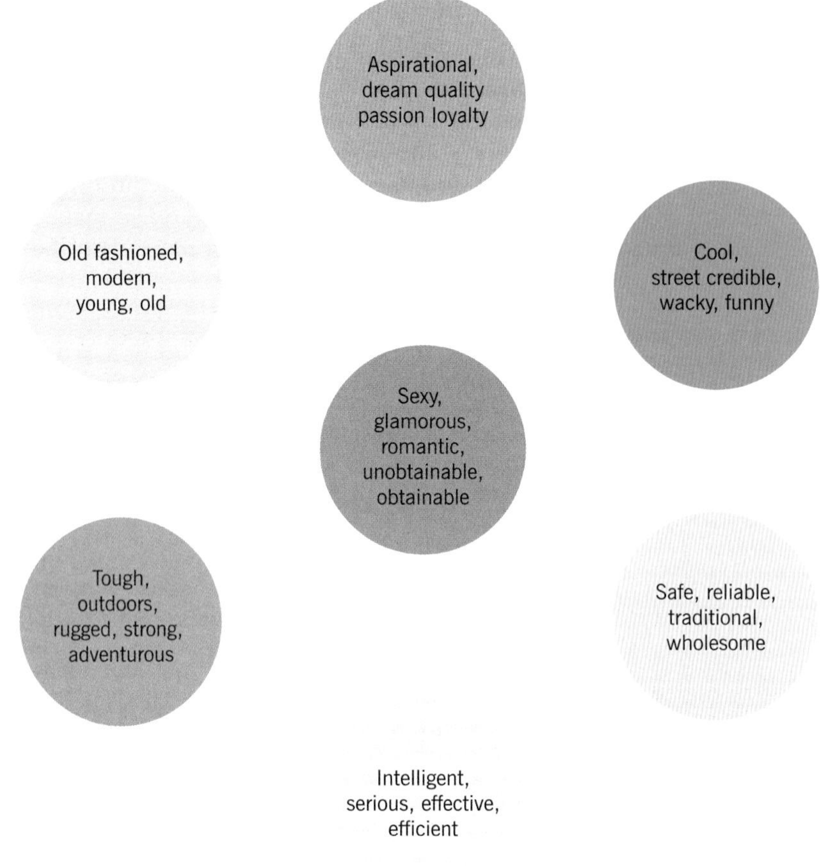

Examples of perceived brand characteristics across different products

10.1 Marketing example — Brand equity

Nike's products are worn by children and adults, not because they are comfortable to run in, but because they want to feel some association with the star athletes used in their advertising campaigns ('be like Mike' – for Michael Jordan). It is not the functional or physical features that drive demand for their products, but the marketing image, the personality, that has been created. Consumers are willing to pay much higher price premiums over brands that are less well known but which may offer the same, or better, product quality and features.

Question

1 Discuss brand equity and examine why brands seem to have such a hold on most consumers around the world.

Key point A brand exists in the mind of the consumer and is the sum of all feelings, thoughts and recognitions, both good and bad, that people have about a company and its products. It is the unique or emotional selling proposition that nobody else can copy.

The benefits of branding

People love brands and they have become an inextricable part of many people's lives and the benefits of branding on both a national and global scale cannot be underestimated. Manufacturers have long since recognised the benefits that can accrue to the customer, to the retailer and to their own company by putting some kind of recognisable name or mark on their products. Over time, through communications, advertising, use and word of mouth, this recognisable name, the brand, its **logo**, colours and personality, becomes the driving force of consumer loyalty repelling competition and satisfying rational and emotional benefits that can be passed on from generation to generation.

Key point A brand engages consumers on the level of senses and emotions. It develops a personality and comes to life for people, forging a deep, lasting, loyal connection.

10.2 Marketing example — Name children after famous brands

Mr Evans, a professor at Bellevue University, Nebraska, has studied baby names in the US for 25 years and he has found that Americans are increasingly using brands to name their children. He found almost 300 girls recorded with the name Armani, six boys called Timberland and seven boys called Denim. Seven boys were found to have the name Del Monte, after the food company and 49 boys were called Canon, after the camera. Six boys were named after Courvoisier cognac. He has found that car models were a popular source of inspiration; 22 girls are registered as having the name Infiniti while 55 boys answer to Chevy or Chevrolet and five girls Celica. *Source*: BBC website.

10.3 Marketing example — Brand definition

The American Marketing Association defines a brand as the following 'A name, term, design, symbol, or any other feature that identifies one seller's good or service as distinct from those of other sellers'. The legal term for brand is trademark. A brand may identify one item, a family of items, or all items of that seller. If used for the firm as a whole, the preferred term is trade name. This might be the Kellogg's cockerel, the Marlboro cowboy, Coca-Cola's white wavy line and bottle shape, Shell's shell, the Guinness harp, the Nike tick.

Critics of branding

Branding has its critics however and there are those who argue that branding is expensive and a waste of money, adding heavily to the price because of advertising

Table 10.2 Why consumers love brands

- *Satisfies emotional and psychological needs*. Brand names such as Porsche, Bacardi, American Express, Tiffany, Apple computers, Cartier, Disney, Harley Davidson, satisfy needs such as status, recognition, self-esteem, nostalgia, companionship, security, spiritual satisfaction etc.
- *Identifies function and meaning*. A well known brand and its function, both real and symbolic, can be immediately recognised. Persil washes clothes whiter, Gillette provides shaving products for 'real men', Kellogg's contributes to 'healthy living', Volvo means 'safety', Apple computers 'simplicity', Duracell 'long life', Oil of Olay 'the promise of beauty' and so on.
- *Recognised quality and consistency*. Having used the product once and liked the experience, the consumer can purchase again secure in the knowledge that quality and value will remain consistent anywhere in the world. A Mars Bar, Heinz beans, McDonald's hamburger, Pepsi-Cola should taste the same whether purchased in Manhatten, Moscow or Manchester.
- *Provides information*. The brand becomes the receptacle for a vast amount of information about the company, its products and its personality.
- *Stress reduction*. Decision making can be highly stressful especially on more expensive items, known brands reduce risk and levels of anxiety.
- *Time saving*. It saves the consumer time by not having to personally seek out and test variable and unknown quality levels.

and promotion. They also argue that it is an offensive waste of scarce resources when there are millions starving in the world.

Others argue that customers want branded products and are prepared to pay extra feeling that they offer real value for money in both functional and symbolic terms. The growth in retailer private own label products has failed to dent the attraction of brands and they still account for approximately 60 per cent (ACNeilsen, 2003) of products sold.

10.4 Marketing example Manufacturers' brands and private own label

According to research company ACNielsen (2003), retailer private label products are on the increase across Europe, representing 41 per cent of sales in the United Kingdom, 31 per cent in Germany and 25 per cent in France. Wal-Mart's private label goods make up half of its sales in Europe compared to a quarter in the US. Private or retailer own label products are now marketed and advertised in a similar way to manufacturers' brands and are building their own brand personalities. There appears to be a limit on the amount of own label penetration because consumers demand the choice of buying well-known manufacturer brands. There is evidence, however, that if manufacturers reduce advertising spend on their brands, retailer's own label products can make inroads into the market (ACNielsen).

The consumer and packaging

Customers' evaluations of products are greatly affected by appearances and design including such things as touch, taste, texture and smell. In many cases the packaging that surrounds the product has become at least as important, if not more so in some cases, than the product itself (e.g. boxed chocolates, children's toys, perfumes) and it continues to be an integral part contributing to the overall attractiveness of the product and becoming a quintessential ingredient in the emotive process of brand building.

Companies will spend a fortune on consumer and packaging research making certain that such things as materials used, colour combinations, wording and overall appropriateness match (or exceed) customer wants and expectations. This is especially so in the fast-moving-consumer-goods market (FMCG). Imagine Kit-Kat without its familiar red and white packaging, or Coca-Cola without the well-known tin or bottle, or Kellogg's cornflakes without the cockerel on the constantly busy box full of information, free gift and games and competition for the children to do.

10.5 Marketing example — Innovative packaging

Research has confirmed that an estimated one to three seconds is all the time that an FMCG company will get to sell its product as the consumer browses the retail marketplace. So the packaging can mean the difference between success and failure in business. With this in mind Fortune 500 Companies (US) will commonly spend 60–80 per cent of the total item cost on B2C packaging knowing this limited attention of a passing shopper (www.signaturebag.com). Many companies have gained competitive advantage through the development of innovative packaging. Examples are toothpaste and whipped cream in push-top containers, a widget injecting gas into a pull-ring beer can, wine in a sealed container in a box, Tetra-Pak for longer life liquids, tea in pyramid shaped tea bags, Pringles in a tube, Jif lemon juice in a lemon shaped container, various glass shapes for coffee. A great deal of information can also be placed on the packaging. This can include pictures, a table of contents and instructions for use, sales promotions, special offers, games and information about other company products.

Questions

1 Discuss and evaluate the importance of packaging in the consumer market. How might it influence consumer behaviour?

2 Identify and evaluate new packaging initiatives you might have seen and analyse why they might or might not be successful.

Packaging, merchandising and making the sale

In many areas of retail, with the advent of self service, it's the packaging that sells the product and it has become known as the 'silent salesman'. Research by research organisation POPAI, Mintel and others has shown that at times over 70 per cent of the brands in the supermarket are chosen on impulse and colours, pictures, words, designs, sales promotions etc. used skilfully on the packaging can 'talk' to the customer and hopefully persuade purchase. A bright, warm, friendly atmosphere backed up by retail merchandising such as video displays, signs, show cards, banners, floor, wall and ceiling adverts, coupon dispensers, electronic shopping trolley advertising, interactive electronic information booths, audio devices and taste exhibitions and so on all add to customer enjoyment and encourage brand and product spending.

Key point In consumer marketing the packaging can be more important that the product in persuading purchase.

How consumers move around the store

A great deal of consumer research (by personal observation and the use of cameras) studies how shoppers move around the shop or supermarket. Which way they go when they first enter (to the left or right) how fast they walk, where they stop and look, how they interact with the merchandise, the way that their eyes scan the shelves and so on. From this information, display racks, width of walkways, merchandise range planning and layout and the area where goods sell the most ('hot spots') can all be evaluated and brought together to optimise satisfaction.

Consumer reaction to services

The service sector is now huge around the world often accounting for as much as 80 per cent of all employment in any one country. Services will include retail, leisure, food and drink, financial, health, medical, communication, energy, transport, household, waste and education. Consumer behaviour will often be different when buying services compared to buying products because the customer cannot see or touch the products. (This is why we often see the 4p acronym of the marketing mix extended to include the 'p' for 'physical attraction'.)

Customers looking for 'physical attraction' or quality clues

Because of its intangible nature, customers will usually look for tangible clues that might offer an idea of the quality/value of the service on offer. The age, appearance and knowledge of the salesman or woman trying to sell financial services in the home of the prospective buyer will come under intense scrutiny. As will the quality and professionalism of the brochures, catalogue and website of a company marketing holidays and the experiences and recommendation of consumer protection groups and friends and acquaintances. If we take, for example, eating out at a new restaurant, customers will examine the restaurant from the outside, how busy it seems and its overall cleanliness (especially the toilets) and warmth on the inside. Of course the quality of the food is important but the consumer will not know this until it's produced and eating begins. If the overall impression is good then the customer will come again and tell others. If it is doubtful or bad the customer will not come again and will tell others, but this time about the bad experience. If a company has many restaurants across the country (Ask, or Pizza Express) maintaining quality consistency can be a real problem, as the service given will begin every time a new meal is served.

10.6 Marketing example **Attacking service variability**

McDonald's, the largest fast-food chain in the world with 47 million customers served daily, have built and applied work systems to every single part of the business. This ensures that employees are following exactly the same service processes and procedures in every one of the thirty thousand plus stores whether in New York or Tokyo, or Hong Kong or Moscow. They say that this will ensure optimum, consistent levels of quality, service and cleanliness (QSC) with friendly people, offering the right product at affordable prices in places that are clean contemporary and welcoming, and creating promotions that resonate with key consumer groups.

Key point Service, before, during and after the sale is an integral part of the consumer benefit offering.

Behaviour and price

'Value is remembered long after price is forgotten.' ANON

In very general terms, the more value that a company can add to its product the more the customer might be prepared to pay. In this way more profit can be made. An example might be a commodity product like frozen chicken. The basic product could be sold on average for 45 p per kilogram. It might be a little cheaper in one supermarket and a little more expensive in another. However, add more value, for example tandori chicken slices or chicken cooked in orange or red wine and offered in eye-catching attractive packaging and double, treble or quadruple the price per kg can then be charged. Consumer behaviour will pitch backwards and forwards between price and added value depending on both functional and emotional concerns. It is mostly in the interest of marketing managers to push consumers toward the added value end of the spectrum where more customer satisfaction can be given, highest prices charged and greater profits made. This is the role of the brand.

Price —— continuous movement → added value (brands)

Psychological pricing

The importance of pricing cannot be underestimated and a great deal of research has been undertaken in trying to discover how it can be used to make consumers buy one product rather than another or more of one product. Psychological pricing is the theory that prices have a psychological, almost subliminal rather than a rational impact on the way that consumers think about retail pricing. Examples are

Table 10.3 Factors affecting price and consumer behaviour

The factors that have been shown to affect the relative importance of price and value will include the following:

- Emotional as well as rational needs
- Advertising and branding at both corporate and product level
- Ease of payment method
- Economic circumstances
- The importance of the decision
- The type of product or service
- The target segment
- Convenience
- Other benefits such as service, delivery, knowledge etc.

the way that retail prices are often expressed as odd prices, e.g. $19.95, £99.95, $999.85, rather than a rounded number, e.g. $20, £100, $1000. The theory is based on the belief that consumers perceive fractional pricing as being lower than whole number pricing and that it also suggests that merchandise is marked at the lowest possible price.

10.7 Marketing example Research supporting odd pricing theory

Kenneth Wisniewski and Robert Blattberg at the University of Chicago's Centre for Research in Marketing showed that when the price of margarine was lowered from 89 cents to 71 cents, sales volume increased a mere 65 per cent, but when it was lowered from 89 to 69 cents, sales volume increased by 222 per cent. In another study, the perceived value of all the numbers between 1 and 100 were studied and 77 was shown to have the lowest perceived value relative to its actual value. Schindler and Kibarian (1996) tested odd pricing using three versions of a direct mail catalogue for women's clothing. The catalogues were identical except for the prices that ended with 00, 99 or 88. The version with prices ending in 99 generated 8 per cent more sales volume and had more purchasers than the 00-ending version. The 88-ending catalogue produced a similar sales volume and number of purchasers to the 00-ending version.
Source: Answers.com (Wikepedia)

Price and sales promotions

Price is seen as an essential ingredient in the promotion of a product. As a form of sales promotion it is used to offer such incentives as short-term discounts and money-off (groceries, alcohol, clothes), easy credit terms and interest free (cars) and 'buy now and pay in six months time' (TVs, furniture).

Care should be taken, however, in using price for promotion purposes. Some practitioners argue that an organisation should be wary about using price as a form of promotion because it encourages the purchaser to concentrate on price rather than value and brand. It might also lead to the customer only being willing to purchase when prices are reduced and for them to view the retail outlet as a cut price operation.

Place and channel of distribution

The producer has two basic ways that it can make the product available to the end consumer, direct or indirect. What is crucial to the sales and marketing success is that the method chosen exactly fits customer expectations. For example the consumer would not expect to see designer clothes such as Armani, Prada, Gucci or Versace for sale in a Carrefour, Wal-Mart or Woolworth. Similarly they would not expect to buy a Rolls Royce from a back street garage, an expensive meal from a transport café, or life insurance from a vending machine. Most selling of consumer products takes place through a retailer and the store location, car parking and ease of access are of the utmost importance. Shoppers now increasingly expect shopping to be exciting and entertaining and retailers will change store design, cosmetically and structurally on a regular basis. Competition among shopping centres (high streets, regional shopping centres, retail parks, factory villages) is rife and retail centre marketing managers have to look constantly at new initiatives to excite and attract the consumer. Technological developments, particularly on the Internet, are creating new challenging methods of distribution causing marketers to constantly research how this affects consumer behaviour and expectations.

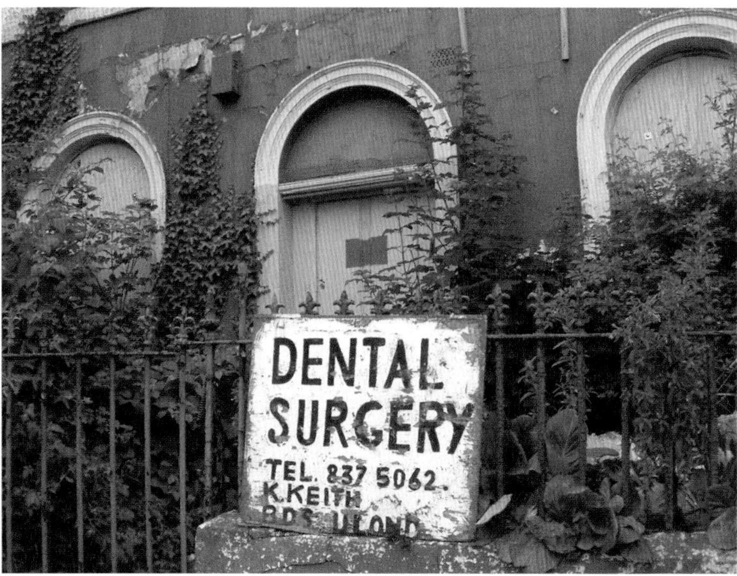

This dentist is unlikely to attract many customers
Source: Simon Wright

Marketing communications

It is by the skilled use of communications techniques that marketing and advertising managers are able to build brand benefits, often over years, which appeal to consumer needs and wants in some way or another. Through the use of advertising campaigns, brand images are created and woven together in ways that will appeal directly to the deeply researched target market creating such loyalty that customers will want constantly to be associated with both the company and the company's products and a bond will be created that the competition will be unable to break. Communications managers have to understand audience reaction to changing circumstances and new methods brought on by technological developments if they are to stay ahead of competitors.

> **Key point** Marketing communications is where all the information gathered on consumer behaviour can be put to use in persuading the consumer to purchase and repurchase the company's products and brands.

Many different promotional techniques

Every day consumers are bombarded with adverts on TV, newspapers, magazines, radio, outdoor billboards, the Internet and direct mail trying to build the attraction of the brand and entice them into buying one product brand rather than another. There are many different marketing promotional strategies because there are many different target markets. Each audience segment might have to be approached in different ways and different promotional techniques are used as they are all good at doing different things. In most cases the consumer cannot be made aware, have interest created and then persuaded to purchase a product with only one promotional technique. Even personal selling, the strongest form of communication, works much better if the customer has been made aware of the company and its

Figure 10.5

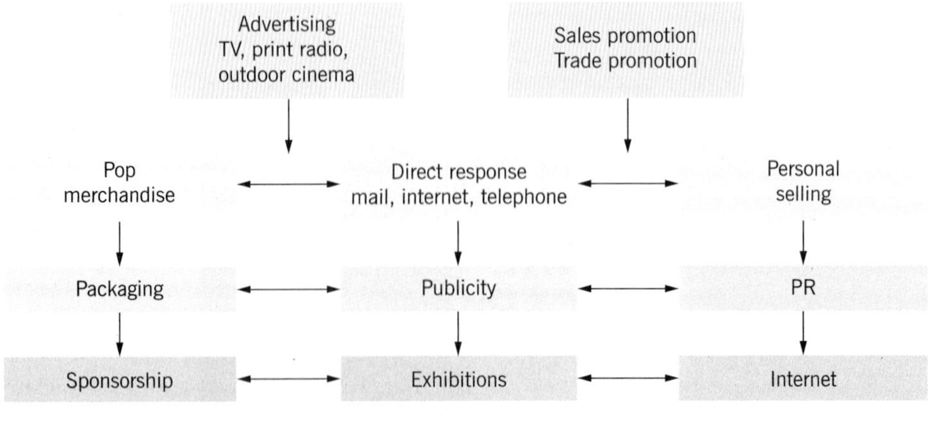

Different promotion strategies

10.8 Marketing example Product placement

There has been an enormous growth in the use of product placement. This is a promotional technique used by marketers in which real commercial products are used in plays, films, television shows, DVDs and books. Typically either the product and logo is shown or favourable product qualities are mentioned. It has been highly successful working on the concept that consumers will think highly of products and brands that are associated with famous celebrities and highly rated films. For example, it has been extensively used in all the James Bond films (BMW, Vodka Martini, Perrier, Rolex, Aston Martin). In *Die Another Day*, 20 companies paid between them $70 m (£44 m) for the privilege of seeing their products on the big screen.

Product placement is often used in movies; James Bond and Aston Martin feed off each other.
Source: Getty Images

products before the salesperson approaches the customer. For example TV advertising is good at creating mass awareness and brand building, often over many years, while sales promotions are good at getting the consumer to try the product.

Understanding consumer audience reaction

There are many barriers that can affect productive consumer communications, not least the fact that thousands of competing companies will be vying for the same customer's attention. These barriers must be overcome if products and services are to be successfully sold. Marketing and advertising communications and message building is a consummate skill and is the reason why most advertising campaigns take place through professional, commercial marketing and advertising agencies, such as Saatchi and Saatchi and Olgilvy and Mather. Agency staff will have spent many hours researching consumer needs and wants, both rational and emotional and translating this into advertising messages that speak the same language and is understood by the target audience, whatever the age, income, nationality, social class, gender, family life cycle and lifestyle.

Integrated communications

The overriding concern for marketing communications managers it to make certain that all the communications strategies and techniques work effectively and economically together in sending coherent benefit messages to a clearly identified target audience. For example using an emotional romantic theme in a TV advertisement for a perfume, having a functional theme in a magazine and placing a humorous message on the website could cause consumer confusion and a dilution of the overall communication. Similarly offering a night out at the opera as a sales promotion on new type of lager advertised in a 'laddish' manner for young men will come across as disjointed and disconnected.

Figure 10.6

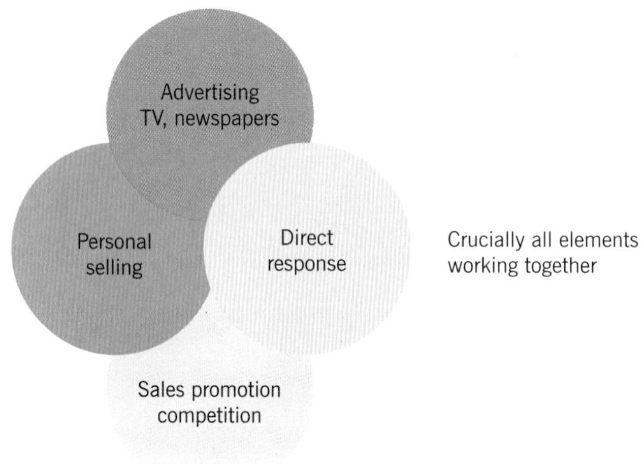

Integrated marketing communications (IMC)

> **Key point** Every element of the **communications mix** must work closely together in an integrated manner so as to put across a seamless message and avoid the chance of any consumer confusion.

People in the marketing mix

It's worth repeating that the role of organisational people (service, admin, sales people etc.) in the marketing mix can never be over emphasised. Almost every sale will involve a 'people service' of some kind that will be seen by the consumer as an essential part of the benefit offering. It's a truism that behaviour begets behaviour and obstructive and unhelpful staff will elicit a negative response. Conversely friendly, knowledgeable and obliging staff will help build and support a positive image of professional customer-centred concern.

The integrated marketing mix

All elements of the marketing mix, the product, price, place and promotion must work together (in the same integrated way as all the elements of promotion) each complementing the other, so as to offer the consumer the 'right' product (e.g. a premium perfume) at the 'right' price (e.g. £100) in the 'right' place (e.g. Harrods department store) while promoting in the 'right' way (e.g. through an expensive magazine such as *Hello*). This is at the very heart of marketing.

> **Key point** It is crucial that marketing mix, product price, place and promotion (plus the other 2 'ps' discussed above, physical attraction and people) work harmoniously together so as to offer the customer quality integrated benefits.

Organisational behaviour

We have spent the whole of the book discussing and analysing consumer rather than organisational behaviour. In this section the balance can be redressed and organisational buying behaviour, known as business-to-business (B2B), can be examined and major differences compared with consumer buying behaviour (B2C).

Business-to-business markets

Business-to-business markets are where goods and services are sold by one organisation to another organisation *for its own use* in some way or another or to be sold on to another organisation for *its own use*. For example Whirlpool, the domestic appliance manufacturer, will buy a component part such as a stainless steel washing drum to go into a consumer product, a washing machine, but it will be bought for use in the running of the business and will be classified as a B2B product. Similarly P&G will

> **Key point** Business-to-business marketing, B2B definition
> Business-to-business marketing is where one business markets products or services to another business for use in that business or to sell on to other businesses for their own use.

10.1 General example — Complex relationships in B2B markets

Supplier–buyer relationships are complex and interdependent. For example, suppliers closely connected to the Jeep markets' factory will not make a vehicle's parts until it starts to move down the assembly line. Eight suppliers, including seven with plants newly built or leased for this purpose near Toledo, are delivering parts and subassemblies not only just in time but also exactly in production line sequence, with each item bearing the VIN (vehicle identification number) of the Jeep for which it was built. Half of these suppliers don't start building parts until they get electronic notification that the painted body of the Jeep for which they're intended is heading into the first assembly-line workstation.

Manufacturing accounts for a large percentage of world output. Car manufacturers will buy in capital equipment, raw materials and component parts from hundreds of B2B suppliers around the world. *Source*: Corbis

want to buy such things as packaging, food flavouring, vegetables, tea and coffee for its one use to go into its branded FMCG products. All can be identified as B2B products and services. In some markets suppliers sell these B2B products to other intermediaries such as agents or wholesalers before being bought by companies such as P&G and Whirlpool. All these examples will still be seen as B2B products.

B2B markets compared to B2C

B2C markets are where producers sell finished products and brands to retailers who then sell them on to the end consumer or where the producer sells the finished product direct to the end consumer, by-passing the retailer. So selling Campbell Soups into Asda for onward sale to the end consumer is B2C selling, but selling shelving for use in shop displays is B2B selling. Selling cars into the showroom for the end consumer is B2C and selling fleet cars for sales staff is B2B.

Reasons for purchasing in B2B and B2C

There will be differences in buying behaviour between the business or industrial buyer and consumer buying.

Table 10.4 Examples of the difference between B2C and B2B

B2B and B2C in retail markets	
B2B marketing	*B2C marketing*
Electronic tills to Curry's for use in the business	Electrolux refrigerators to retailer Curry's for onward sale to consumer
Shelving to supermarket Tesco	Cadbury's chocolate to Tesco
Computer systems for own use in the running of the business	Viglen Computers to PC World for onward sale to consumer
Display racks to Next	Fashion clothes to Next

Rational rather than emotional reasons

The biggest difference between organisational and consumer buying is the reason driving the purchase. The concept that consumers more often than not purchase for complex symbolic and emotional reasons rather than functional and **rational reasons** has been mentioned throughout the book. They will be buying for themselves or for friends and family. This is the reason why branding and advertising plays such an important part in the process. On the other hand, however, the buyer in an organisation will be purchasing goods and services for the organisation and though there may be some element of emotion driving the decision (e.g. liking the salesperson/company, status behind the purchase) the major reasons driving the purchase will be rational and functional.

Professional versus amateur buyers

B2B professional

The person buying for an organisation will, in most cases, be trained and highly professional and he or she will know what benefits they want from **B2B products and services**. This puts enormous pressure on the supplier and the suppliers salespeople, to have intense knowledge about the customer's functional needs and wants, the relevant market and industry and the products and services offered by the competitors. The sales pitch must be based on a rational understanding of the customer and any benefit over emphasis or exaggeration will soon be spotted and the salesman or woman will be quickly shown the door.

B2C amateur

On the other hand the consumers are isolated, buying only for self or family. In relation to the organisation they could be said to be the amateur relying on information from B2C literature, packaging, consumer support associations and the salesperson in the shop. As much as consumers shop around looking for information about product value and safety, ultimately they will only ever garner a small amount of information on brands and so have to rely on the integrity of the selling organisation. Governments have passed many consumer protection laws over the decades because of the lopsided power relationship between individuals and mighty organisations such as Nestlé, Nokia, Mercedes, General Motors, BSkyB, Intercontinental Hotels.

The retail organisation buying behaviour (B2C)

Although a business selling finished branded products into the retailer to sell on to the end consumer is not classified as B2B under our definition, it should be recognised that in B2C marketing benefits wanted by the retail buyer will not necessarily be those wanted by the end consumer. For example the retailer wants bottles of orange juice to stack on to pallets, sell well and to make a decent profit, whereas the end consumer wants a bottle of orange juice to taste like oranges, be energising and to contribute to a healthy lifestyle. The retailer will want to know that if a seller's products are to be stocked they will sit attractively on the shelf, will be profitable and sell-out within a reasonable time to the end customer. Similarly the retail buyer will want to know that products will be delivered promptly when wanted, stock taken back if found to be faulty in some way, and after-sales service undertaken efficiently if this is part of the agreement. Other factors will be different and will more readily mirror B2B than B2C. Marketing mix concerns covering price and promotion will be more like marketing mix concerns in B2B.

Key point The retail buyer in B2C markets wants to buy branded quality products that will sell quickly, are profitable, easy to transport, store and put on the shelves.

Commercial fridges sold to a retailer for use in the running of a business in the B2B market (left) and consumer branded fridges sold to a retailer to sell on to the end consumer in the B2C market (right)

The business-to-business buying behaviour

It has been shown that organisations buy products and services for use in the running of the business and benefits demanded will be functional and rational rather than symbolic and emotional. However, behaviour will often vary in some way or another from one sector and industry to another, from one market to another and from one company to another. As with consumer markets, these behavioural differences must be understood so that the approach by the supplier to the customer is readily understood and accepted.

Key point Organisational buying behaviour will vary according to sector, industry, market and company.

Private, public and not-for-profit organisation behaviour differences

Buying behaviour in the commercial sector will be different from behaviour in both the public and not-for-profit sector because of the differences in ownership, charitable status and aims and objectives.

The private or commercial sector

Companies in the private sector are in business to make money for their owners and shareholders. Their overriding aim is to give value to the customer and in this way makes sales and profits so that there will be a satisfactory return on investment for the company shareholders. This need to make sales and profits drives the organisation's behaviour.

Public sector organisational behaviour

At national level governments and quasi-government organisations buy B2B goods and services for defence, social welfare, administration, education, hospitals, transport and so on. At the local level it could purchase goods and services for police, ambulance and fire services, waste management, schools, road maintenance and so on, according to the national/local responsibility mix. Unlike companies in the private sector these organisations are not in business to make a profit but to provide a cost effective, value-for-money service to the general public. Because they are spending taxpayers' money, they have to be accountable and everything they do has to be open continuously to public scrutiny. Any deviation from acceptable transparent purchasing behaviour could be pounced upon and criticised by politicians, the general public, the media and other stakeholders (see Table 10.5).

Table 10.5 Public sector buying behaviour

Because of constant public scrutiny from many stakeholders, public sector organisations portray the following behaviour:

- Transparency, working practice open to constant scrutiny
- Rule and process driven
- Strict and clear accountability
- Compulsory competitive tendering to ensure best value
- Intense scrutiny to make certain that suppliers are honest and ethical in how they run their business
- Complex purchasing behaviour (DMU, DMP, DMD), with preferred supplier lists, negotiations and strategic partnership relationships

Not-for-profit

Not-for-profit organisations are, as the term suggests, in business for reasons other than making a profit. Of course that will not mean that they cannot earn a return on investments but as the NFP organisation hasn't any shareholders this will not be returned to shareholders as a dividend but used to reinvest or spent to achieve its not-for-profit goals. NFP organisations include charities such as Oxfam, Médecins Sans Frontières, NSPCA, associations such the Scouts and the Girl Guides and pressure groups such as Greenpeace and the Animal Liberation Front. As with buying in the public sector, behaviour must be seen to be transparent because these organisations are spending money contributed voluntarily by individuals, groups, businesses, government (tax benefits and grants) and charitable trusts. NFP organisations will exhibit the following behaviour:

- Administrative transparency.
- Spending as little as possible on running costs.
- Seen to be achieving objectives such as protecting the environment, helping others and generally benefiting society.

The decision-making unit (DMU) differences

The decision-making unit (DMU) is a term that embraces all the people who might be involved in some way or another in the buying process. This was discussed in Chapter 1 and in consumer markets this will be fairly simple, for example consisting of mother, father and the child when buying a child's toy or husband and wife when buying a car. It can be a little more complex when buying more expensive items, e.g. a house where the DMU might consist of a young couple, family and friends, and professionals such as solicitors, estate agents and accountants.

The DMU (or buying centre) in organisations, however, can be much more complex, especially if the product or service being purchased comes to many millions of pounds, euros or dollars. The chances are that lots of people could be involved including managers, product users, directors, as well as accountants, marketers, engineers and consultants and, in the case of the public sector, politicians and civil servants. The make-up of the DMU will reflect the differences between commercial, public and NFP organisations outlined above.

Key point The DMU in organisations is usually larger and more complex than the consumer DMU and could involve employees across the whole of the organisation. They will all be professional people, buying for functional reasons and often spending large amounts of money over long periods of time.

Decision-making process (DMP)

The decision-making process (DMP) for consumer buying behaviour was discussed in some detail in Chapter 1. The DMP for business markets is similar except behaviour can be much more complex and drawn out over long periods of time depending on the value of the goods and services being purchased and its importance to the organisation. It's crucial for suppliers to understand the process, which might vary from one organisation to another, so that purchasing behaviour can be understood and beneficially influenced.

Decision-making difficulty (DMD)

Decision making will vary in levels of difficulty depending on the products and services under purchase consideration. In consumer markets degrees of difficulty and the time taken in decision making will range from the simple, e.g. habitually buying the weekly groceries from Tesco, to the more difficult, e.g. buying a holiday or a new car. Most purchases (except buying a house) will be in relatively small amounts. In business markets, however, the levels of difficulty will range from just sanctioning repeat orders, e.g. ordering more copier paper or component parts, to signing a contract for a new computer system or a road-building contract. Money involved can run into hundreds, thousands, millions or billions of dollars, pounds or euros. The size of the order, contract and consultancy and the importance of the purchase to the successful running of the business will dictate the time taken in contemplation and the number of people involved in making the final decision.

Table 10.6 **DMU in B2B compared to B2C**

The DMU in B2B

- Buying for the organisation, complex structure, many people involved
- Could take a long time to make decisions depending on product value
- Rational reasons for purchase
- Product/services, contacts, projects and consultancies high value
- End user will probably not be the decision maker
- Supplier might get to know DMU members over a long period

The DMU in B2C

- Buying for self or family, simple structure, few people involved
- Short time to make decisions
- Mainly emotional reasons for purchase
- Relatively low value of products
- End user probably the decision maker

Key point Marketers must understand all aspect of decision making so that they will be able to develop marketing programmes to successfully influence the process so that benefit solutions can be offered that will solve buyer problems more effectively than those offered by competitors.

Marketing research in business compared to consumer markets

'Your most unhappy customers are your greatest source of learning.' BILL GATES, Microsoft

Marketing research information needed by marketers about customers and markets will differ when operating in business rather than consumer markets because the markets and customers are entirely different. Some of the major reasons for these differences are highlighted opposite in Table 10.7.

Information needed when looking at B2B markets

Because reasons for purchase are rational and functional rather than symbolic and emotive, there isn't the same need to be constantly examining buyer motivation in business markets as there is in consumer markets. More important are the factors that will have short-, medium and long-term affects on the running of the particular business. This will be macro and micro secondary research looking at areas such as political and legal conditions, economic, industry and market growth, numbers and sizes of competitors and possible competitive advantages, numbers and sizes of business customers, types of products and services wanted, use of technology and so on. It will also include such things as existing partner supply chain relationships, types of distribution channels, cost and profit structures and methods of promotion.

Key point Most information required in B2B markets will be quantitative using statistics and models rather that qualitative, asking opinions.

Secondary research more important than primary research

Most of the information outlined above can be discovered through the use of **secondary research** (information already collected) obtained relatively inexpensively through government, trade and commercial sources. On the other hand, although background secondary research is used in consumer markets, **primary research** (collecting first hand, current information) has an added importance because consumers are more unpredictable, tastes and fashions change at an increasing rate and behavioural reasons for purchase are sometimes multifaceted and difficult to understand. Where primary research is used in business markets, it is easier to collect because fewer customers need to be interviewed as 'rich' information can be obtained from just a few leaders of industry. On the other hand, in consumer markets, the numbers can run into millions across the world in an attempt to identify individual and group buying patterns.

Key point Most information in B2B will be secondary rather than primary.

Table 10.7 **Differences in information needed in B2B and B2C markets**

Information in business markets	Information in consumer markets
More secondary research	More primary research
Quantitative research	Qualitative research
Less primary research	Less secondary research
Small samples needed	Larger samples needed
Primary research, easier and cheaper	Primary research expensive

Customers in business and consumer markets

It is worth repeating that the major difference between organisational customers and end consumers is that consumers buy products and services for own or family use while business buyers buy for company use. The former could be said to be amateurs, buying more for emotive reasons and being relatively uninformed about products on offer in the market. On the other hand, the latter could be said to be professionals buying for their company's use and being highly informed about the benefits wanted and competitor products on the market. Consumers usually approach the retailer to purchase and the supplier will usually approach the organisational buyer. Consumers in any one market could number millions while buying organisations are nowhere near as large. In any one market it might number only one or at the most into the hundreds. The loss of one customer in consumer markets, while regrettable, will not be noticeable but it could be catastrophic for a supplier perhaps having only two or three major customers.

Segmentation in business markets

The importance of segmentation, breaking the market down into like-minded groups of consumers so that behaviour can be understood and clear product benefits offered was discussed earlier. Suppliers will need to do the same in B2B markets. In consumer markets, individuals make personal buying decisions and markets are segmented according to socio-economic, buying behaviour, psychographic and lifestyle methods. In business markets, the industrial sector, type and company size becomes more important in segmenting markets than personal behaviour and psychological needs. As with consumer markets, organisation needs and wants and buying behaviour will vary across industries, markets and from company to company, and suppliers must research and understand these differences. Marketing mix offerings can then be targeted that exactly meet each company's needs and wants.

Key point Unlike B2C markets, B2B markets will not be segmented in terms of individual or group needs and wants. They are more likely to be segmented by industry and individual company need.

Table 10.8 Comparing segmentation methods

Segmenting in business markets

- Geographic segmentation – regional, national or international
- Segmenting by public, private or not-for-profit sector
- Industry segmentation – manufacturer, service or agricultural industries
- Type of industry – steel, car, electronic, engineering, IT, consultancy, energy, waste management, catering, leisure etc.
- Segmenting by small, medium or large company
- Segmenting by products and/or services offered
- Present, past, or non-user; heavy, medium, or light-user; repeat purchaser
- Sales, costs and profits and payment record

Segmenting in consumer market

- Geographic – where people live
- Demographic – the make-up and movement of the population
- Socio-economic – age, sex, religion, social class, occupation, family life cycle etc.
- Behavioural – heavy users, brand switchers, past users, role-play users etc.
- Psychographic and personality – introverts/extroverts, power seekers, high/low achievers etc.
- Lifestyle – grouping attitudes, interests and activities into lifestyle grouping

Products and services in business markets

B2B goods and services are quite different from consumer products because they are bought for use in the running of the business and not for personal consumption. They can be classified under capital goods, material parts and supplies and running services. Of course the categories discussed below are not all mutually exclusive and there is bound to be some overlapping. Buyer behaviour in each product/service area identified above will vary according to the cost of the product, how often it might be purchased and its value in the production of goods and services.

Capital goods

Capital goods are major strategic items that are purchased at both the initial business start-up and at other important times as the business grows and expands. They include the major long-term investment items that are the foundation of the business and the equipment that underpins the manufacturing and service processes. It will inevitably involve large amounts of money. If the company makes the wrong decision at this stage any hope of maintaining competitive advantage will be lost. This will include such permanent things as land, buildings, factories, offices, as well as industrial robotics, power presses, large computer systems, IT, office equipment, transport and so on.

Material and parts

Materials and parts are all those goods that a company will purchase for use in producing the end product. This category can be identified by the stage in the value adding process and consists of raw materials, manufactured materials, accessory goods and component parts. Many of these types of products are purchased in one-off batches (sometimes through an online auction site) or on a yearly contract basis.

Supplies and running services

Supplies and services are all those products and services that will be used by the organisation in the day-to-day, month-by-month running of the business. The categories identified below are fairly arbitrary, not mutually exclusive and could vary in usage from company to company depending on its history, custom and practice and buying predilections. Service examples include: energy and waste services, transport, distribution and storage services, administrative services, management and marketing services and maintenance services.

Integrated solutions

In many instances B2B buyers are looking for solutions to whole problems rather than buying separate products and benefits. It can be more cost effective for a B2B

10.9 Marketing example — Range of products and services demanded in business markets

The range and diversity of products and services bought and sold in B2B across the whole supplier chain is mind-boggling when compared with B2C. It could include anything from iron-ore, wood, oil and petrol to component engine parts, leathers and plastics, road and bridge building materials, computer and biotech services.

Glass Technology Services (GTS) provides a comprehensive range of services related to glass manufacture and use, including: bloom/weathering; decorative coatings; adhesion; surface contamination; delamination; hot-end coating durability; cap/glass interactions. The range of glass products covered are many and varied such as: bottles and jars; glazing (including commercial and automotive); domestic glass; technical glass; and pharmaceutical containers. Related services are: durability testing; compositional analysis and consultancy (www.glass-ts.com on the British Glass website www.britglass.org.uk). Customer needs and wants and behaviour will vary according to the industry. This means that suppliers must have skills and professional knowledge about their buyers if they are to compete against competitors that could now come from any corner of the world.

Questions

1 Discuss the problems associated with selling products such as oil and glass products and services to other businesses.

2 How will behaviour differ when selling products in B2B compared to selling branded products in consumer markets?

organisation to buy in the whole solution to a problem from an expert supplier rather than to atomise and seek out the individual products and services needed to solve the problem. This has led to high business market use of many different kinds of integrated solutions including leasing, renting and outsourcing, all needing detailed and specialist supplier knowledge and skills across a whole operation.

Branding in B2C and B2B markets

There is still uncertainty and disagreement about the real value of branding in the B2B market. There is now no doubt about its enormous worth in consumer markets where the majority of purchases are made for emotional and psychological reasons linked to the brand name. Corporate names such as Nike, Coca-Cola, Mercedes, Gillette, Microsoft, Disney as well as product brands such as Kit-Kat, Persil, Bold, Maxwell House and Pringles are legendary in the attraction they have for the consumer and the worth they bring to their shareholders. The same cannot be said in the business market.

Product branding less important, corporate branding more important

Unlike consumers, however, B2B buyers will be loath to purchase branded products because of the emotional attraction of the name. A large part of the cost in B2C branding is in the promotion and advertising and industrial organisations will not be prepared to pay this premium. Because the purchase is for the company, rather than for own use, the value offered in the product must be seen to be real and functional rather than abstract and symbolic. Not all benefits associated with the brand name are emotional benefits and B2B buyers will be interested in corporate branding (the name of the company) because this can indicate trust and quality, service and long-term value when dealing with a well-respected organisation such as Bosch, Northern Foods, IBM, BAE systems, GlaxoSmithKline and GKN. The corporate brand name thus offers low-risk time-saving advantages to the busy purchasing team.

Key point Corporate business brands (BAE systems, IBM, Dupont Chemicals) are more important in business markets than in consumer markets, while product brands (Persil, Kit-Kat, Birds Eye) are less important in B2B markets than in B2C markets.

Packaging and merchandising

Packaging is used in both B2B and B2C markets but for different reasons. In B2C, although it is used to protect the product, it is seen emotively by the end consumer to be an essential and integral part of the brand. Package/brand ownership brings such things as reassurance, feelings of status, pleasant associations and so on. In some cases the packaging is the brand and is worth more than the content, e.g. boxed chocolates, perfume, cosmetics. Because the overwhelming reason for purchase in B2B markets is rational and for the firm rather than self, packing has

10.10 Marketing example | Packaging in B2B

Packaging in B2B has many, many dimensions and spawns a multi-billion pound industry. The supply chain in B2B packaging can be long and diverse and involve the design, engineering, computer, chemical, biological, paper, metals, adhesives and sealants, glass, crates, printing and labelling, plastics and capital equipment industries to randomly name a few. Organisations involved might be driven by the buyer need for delivery protection, consistency and speed, health and safety, security, recyclability and waste disposal. The imperative might be for the packaging to load efficiently into lorries and containers, to fit efficiently onto delivery pallets or to sit comfortably and attractively on the retail shelf. The overriding issue might be one of ease of use causing designers, engineers and computer experts to work together on new ways to open, use and dispose of cans, bags, bottles, boxes, cartons and crates. Or it might be the constant need for creativity, design, printing, colour combinations and exciting promotions to hold the interest of the consumer in an ever-changing, ever more demanding market environment.

Questions

1 Examine the differences between B2B and B2C packaging.

2 Identify all the B2B functions involved in B2B packaging.

different purposes. These include protection, security and ease of storage and delivery. In many cases, e.g. building materials, packaging will be minimal.

Merchandising

Merchandising (how attractively the product is displayed) is crucial in consumer markets where colour, music, lighting, adverts, displays and packaging, play an important part in creating retail atmosphere and encouraging purchase. This is not the case in B2B markets where display is functional rather than theatrical and emotive.

The interior differences between B2B (left) and B2C (right) display can clearly be seen

Promotion in business compared to consumer markets

'Spend a lot of time talking to customers face to face. You'd be amazed how many companies don't listen to their customers.' ROSS PEROT, www.brainyquote.com

Marketing communications in B2B and B2C are similar in that both use a mixture of tools and techniques to communicate and persuade customers to buy the product or service on offer. The actual process, however, can be very different because of the dissimilar buyers, the reasons for purchase and the use that will be made of the bought product or service. For example, as there are relatively few buyers wanting advice about negotiating large orders in B2B, personal selling backed up by trade advertising will be heavily used. In consumer markets, there are millions of consumers spending relatively small amounts of money and selling personally to each customer would be unrealistic. In this case TV and press advertising will be used. Similarly short-term sales promotions (competitions, two for the price of one) offering added value over a short term to encourage trial will be used in consumer markets for their emotive attraction and less in business markets where functional incentives (bulk order discounts, extended credit) will be more effective.

Table 10.9 B2B and B2C promotional strategies

Promotional strategies are different in B2B compared to B2C

In business markets

- Personal selling (including emails and telephone calls to book appointments) will be more important in business markets because there are fewer but larger important customers that might all need to be seen personally.
- Trade press advertising could be used in a supportive role to build initial corporate awareness before the salesperson calls.
- Trade promotions (extended credit, extra support, sale or return) are sometimes used to encourage purchase, especially of new products.
- Trade exhibitions are important marketplaces to meet existing and new business customers.

In consumer markets

- Millions of customers can only be reached effectively through TV and press advertising used to create brand awareness and interest.
- Sales promotions (BOGOF, competition, value points etc.) can then be used to encourage purchase and trial in the retail outlet.
- Direct response is used to try to build long-term relationships with customers.
- Personal selling is used to sell into the major retailers.

Competition in B2B and in B2C markets

'Competition brings out the best in products and the worst in people.' ANON.

Competition in most B2B markets is as intense as competition in B2C markets but, because consumers want different benefits than business buyers, it tends to be of a different kind. Competition in B2C markets is just as likely to be on product and service brands as it is on price, while in B2B it more likely to be on functional benefits offered and after-sales service as it is on the brand or the price. Although price is important in the latter market, functionality and reliability can be crucial as a dysfunction in some way could be catastrophic in terms of lost production. There are liable to be more competitors in consumer markets because of the possibility of millions of consumers and millions of different kinds of consumer products. Competition can also come about through alternative, substitute choices, e.g. buying a car or a holiday (known as secondary competition as opposed to primary competition). This is very rarely the case with business markets where the product wanted must match a particular solution wanted. In many B2B industries competition will often come from a relative few number of known competitors although this is increasing as world markets shrink.

Competition in B2B markets

- Competition in B2B markets will come from a relatively small number of companies and organisational behaviour will be based on such things as strategic partnerships along the supply chain, product price and value and the quality of delivery and after-sales service.

Competition in B2C markets

- Competition in B2C markets will come from many hundreds of retailers and thousands of different products and brands depending on the consumer's constantly changing choice demands.

B2B and B2C laws

There are national (UK), supranational (EU) and international laws and rules and regulations that affect B2B and B2C organisational behaviour. They are there to encourage good behaviour and prevent unacceptable ways of running a business. They will affect behaviour in the following ways.

Laws in B2B markets

- Anti-competitive activities, customer, local community and employee exploitation as well as monitoring the effects on the working and general environment.
- Organisations can be fined millions of pounds for violations and corporate senior managers can be fined or sent to prison.
- Laws dictate what goods and services can and cannot be offered, what materials and component parts can and cannot go into products and services and what labelling and informational procedures should be followed.

Laws in consumer markets

- Consumer laws are there mainly to protect the individual against the power of the organisation and have grown as products and services grow in complexity.

- They lay down a structure and dictate how companies, retailers and salespeople must act before during and after the sale of a product or service.
- They inform consumers about their rights and spell out what actions to follow if they feel aggrieved in some way or another.
- They limit the claims that manufactures and retailers can make for their products in terms of features and benefits offered.
- They protect the individual against the manufacture and sales of potentially dangerous or defective products, giving authorities the right to force producers to recall products of this kind.

Understanding customer behaviour along the whole supply chain

There will be many B2B organisations buying and selling along the whole supply chain at both the national and international level. This could mean that a supplier

Key point There will be many relationships across the supply chain with suppliers selling to other suppliers and manufacturers selling to manufacturers. Behaviour must be understood at every level.

Table 10.10 **Overall differences in buyer behaviour in B2C and B2B markets affecting behaviour**

- B2C decisions involve thousands and millions of individuals, friends and families buying for own consumption, while B2B decisions involve considerably fewer people buying as a group for the organisation.
- There are many suppliers and many, many buyers in B2C but only a relatively few buyers and sellers in B2B.
- B2B purchases will often run into large amounts of money, often millions of dollars, while B2C purchases usually involve relatively smaller amounts of money.
- B2B decisions can take days, weeks, months or sometimes years to come to fruition. B2C decisions will usually be made much more quickly.
- One B2B decision can affect the very existence of an organisation while this will seldom be the case with most B2C decisions.
- B2B buyers are limited in number and are usually clustered in small geographical areas, while B2C, although concentrated in cities, towns and villages, are widespread and can be found anywhere.
- B2B buyers are now more professional than in the past and a professional supplier approach will be expected. B2C buyers, although more informed than in the past, will generally be at a much lower level of awareness.
- B2B decisions tend, in the main, to be made on strictly rational criteria, while B2C decisions, although having an element of rationality about them, are made on symbolic and emotional criteria.

might have to develop an understanding about organisational behaviour across long supply chains, often across many countries. In some cases a buyer might insist on a partnership and a long-term commitment from a supplier depending on the product or service being marketed. As a condition of the partnership, the supplier might have to purchase expensive equipment, e.g. compatible computer software and be prepared to allow all its processes and systems to be benchmarked according to the buyer's specifications. They might also be asked for a monopoly on all purchases. This can be an expensive risk, especially if the contract offered is only over a short period. Competition is then seen as between one supply chain (e.g. Wal-Mart) against another supply chain (e.g. Tesco) rather than individual company against individual company.

Summary

- In this chapter the marketing mix, product, branding, packaging, price, place, retail outlets and promotion was examined, looking at how this could all alter in response to changing consumer behaviour.
- We then went on to examine organisational buying in some detail showing how buying behaviour in business-to-business (B2B) organisational markets differs from business-to-consumer (B2C) markets.

Questions

1. Describe and evaluate the marketing model and show how it is affected by consumer behaviour.
2. Discuss the elements of the basic marketing mix, product, price, place and promotion and analyse how all parts must integrate so as to offer complete customer satisfaction. How might consumer behaviour differ when marketing combinations are altered? What's the importance of the other 2ps, physical attraction and people?
3. Identify and evaluate the differences in consumer behaviour in marketing programmes when selling services rather than products. Give live examples to illustrate your findings.
4. Take a real product and service and demonstrate how the adding value process before and after purchase can influence consumer behaviour. Discuss and prioritise added value areas that could be the most important.
5. It could be argued that the competition can copy almost any unique selling proposition (USP) except a brand. Discuss this proposition and show how organisations develop and build brand values in the mind of the consumer.
6. Outline the major differences between customers in business-to-business markets compared with customers in business-to-consumer markets. Give examples to illustrate your answers.
7. Discuss and evaluate how products and services are marketed in business-to-business markets compared with business-to-consumer markets. Show how these differences affect the different areas of the marketing mix.

8 Identify and evaluate the major differences between consumer and business markets at both the national and international level.

9 Describe and examine how customer behaviour affects decision making in both business and consumer markets. Show how this might affect customers along the whole of the supply chain.

10 Show how segmentation, targeting and positioning could differ when looking at consumer and business markets. Give reasons why this might be so and illustrate your answer with examples.

11 Select one element of the marketing mix, product, price, place and promotion, and show how it might differ between B2B and B2C. Give real examples.

12 How might B2B and B2C relationship marketing programmes be used effectively? What is the difference between the two markets? How might they be misused?

Case study

Case study 1 Cultural differences in business markets

It could be argued that the degree of cultural diversity is not so important in B2B markets as in B2C. English is now accepted as a common means of business communication in many markets as are Western ways of dressing and behaving. The move to standardise and internationalise all ways of undertaking B2B relationships, including common efficiency systems, international contract law, supply-chain management, shared use of information through **electronic data interchange (EDI)** systems, the Internet and so on, all add to the seemingly irreversible thrust for business sameness in world marketplaces. As companies expand by joint ventures, mergers and acquisitions of foreign companies they bring universal ways of dressing and working as well as giving employees the opportunities to live and work in company divisions elsewhere in the world. On the other hand there are those who argue that there are still distinct differences in business dress and ways of acting and talking to one another when undertaking some form of business negotiation. For example the dress code in Saudi Arabia requires businesswomen to cover everything except the face, hands and feet in public and there will be a long period of formal polite conservation before any negotiation will take place. In Japan a businessman may be expected to take his shoes off in temples and homes, as well as in some restaurants. Extremely personal questions regarding salary, education and family life can also be discussed.

Questions

1 Investigate the importance that culture may, or may not, play in negotiations and business dealings.

2 Give examples and discuss whether you think that globalisation is making business culture less relevant.

Case study

Case study 2 Tetra Pak – business to business

Tetra Pak began in the early 1950s as one of the first packaging companies for liquid milk. Since then, it has become one of the world's largest suppliers of packaging systems for milk, fruit juices and drinks and many other products. The founder of Tetra Pak, Dr Ruben Raising, believed in the driving tenet that 'the packaging should save more than it should cost'. He initiated the development of the tetrahedron shaped package. His fundamental idea was to form a tube from a roll of plastic-coated paper, fill it with the beverage and seal it below the liquid level. In this way the life shelf of the liquid could be increased a hundred fold. Aseptic technology is Tetra Pak's most outstanding innovation. It keeps even the most perishable liquid foods fresh, tasty and nutritious for months, without refrigeration or added preservatives. They invented the technology in the 1960s and have continued to develop it ever since.

In 1991, at the behest of its business customers Tetra Pak expanded from packaging into liquid food processing equipment, plant engineering, and cheese manufacturing equipment. Today, it is an international company able to provide integrated processing, packaging, and distribution line and plant solutions for liquid food manufacturing. The company has 77 marketing companies across the world, 59 packaging material plants including licensees, and 12 packaging machine assembly factories. The company has 20,150 employees and achieved in 2001 net sales of 7.65 billion Euro. Tetra Pak products are now sold in more than 165 markets.

Questions

1 Identify and analyse suppliers that could be selling products and services to Tetra Pak. How might their behaviour differ from consumer marketing?

2 How might relationships between buyers and sellers differ in this business when compared to retailers and end consumers?

Further reading

Books

Bovee, Courtland L., John V. Thill, George P. Dovel and Marian Bunk Wood (1995) *Advertising Excellence*, London: McGraw-Hill.

Brooks, I. and J. Weatherston (2000) *The Business Environment – Challenges and Changes*, Harlow: Pearson Education, 2nd edn.

Butte, F. (1996) *Relationship Marketing: Theory and Practice*, London: Paul Chapman Publishing Ltd.

Foss, B. and M. Stone (2001) *Successful Customer Relationship Marketing: New Thinking, New Strategies, New Tools for Getting Closer to Your Customers*, London: Kogan Page.

Foxall, G.R. (1994) *Consumer Psychology for Marketing*, London: Routledge.

Hutt, Micheal, D. and Thomas W. Hett (1998) *Business Marketing Management*, London: The Dryden Press 6th edn.

Kroc, Ray (1992) *Grinding it Out: The Making of McDonald's*, New York: Saint Martin's Press.

Lovelock, Christopher and Charles Weinberg (1984) *Marketing for Public and Non-profit Managers*, New York: Wiley.

Porter, M. (1998) *Competitive Strategy*, New York: Free Press.

Ries, A. and J. Trout, (1981) *Positioning: The Battle for Your Mind*, New York: Warner Books – McGraw-Hill.

Wright, Ray (1999) *Marketing, Origins, Concepts and Environment*, London: ITBP.

Wright, R. (2000) *Advertising*, Harlow: Pearson Education.

Wright, R. (2002) *Business and Marketing Dictionary*, Chelmsford: Earlybrave Publications.

Wright, Ray (2004) *Business-to-Business Marketing – A Step-by-step Guide*, Harlow: FT/Prentice Hall.

Journals

Dickson, P.R. and J.L. Ginter (1987) 'Market Segmentation, Product Differentiation, and Marketing Strategy', *Journal of Marketing*, Vol. 51 (April): 1–10.

Schindler, R.M. and T.M. Kibarian (1996) 'Increased Consumer Sales Response Through the Use of 99-Ending Prices', *Journal of Retailing*, 72 (Summer): 187–199.

Websites

ACNielen Research, www.acnielsen.com.

Mintel Research, www.mintel.co.uk.

PIMS Europe research, www.pims-europe.com.

Studentshout marketing website, www.studentshout.com.

Superbrands, www.superbrands.com.

11 Present and future developments

'Quality in a product or service is not what the supplier puts in. It is what the customer gets out and is willing to pay for. A product is not quality because it is hard to make and cost a lot of money, as manufacturers typically believe. This is incompetence. Customers pay only for what is of use to them and gives them value. Nothing else constitutes value.'

Peter Drucker, American business writer, http://en.thinkexist.com/

Objectives

At the end of this chapter the reader will be able to:

1 Identify, examine and evaluate many of the demographic and social changes that will affect consumer behaviour in the future.

2 Analyse factors that are driving changes in consumer behaviour and identify markets that are developing as a response.

3 Examine and evaluate the relationship between organisations, legislators and consumers.

Introduction

Trying to understand and predict consumer behaviour is a constant process that must never be forgotten within the organisation. Experience has shown that to become complacent, ignore or misunderstand this fundamental premise will lead to customer desertion and falling sales. A position that then becomes extremely difficult to recover from. Changing retail formats such as edge-of-town retail parks, regional shopping centres and of course the Internet, offer an explosion of new shopping methods that are affecting consumer ways of behaving and threatening more traditional forms of retail. New technology is offering people more information about the range of products on offer around the world as well as developing evermore product options to choose from. This in turn makes individuals bored and dissatisfied with existing benefits, causing them to turn to which ever company is more in tune with their needs and wants. Increased affluence gives them the ability to make these sorts of choices. And this is happening across a wider age range as children have become more brand knowledgeable and mums and dads and grandfathers and grandmothers are living and staying younger longer.

11.1 Marketing example — Failing retailers

Examples of failing retailers are legion, the Dutch retailer C&A, had been operating in the UK for over 80 years when it closed its 109 shops in 2001 because of losses of over £250 million. 4,800 staff lost their jobs because of dramatic changes in consumer behaviour in the high street that C&A where unable to predict. Marks and Spencer, once the favourite and most profitable store on the UK high street is still desperately trying to recover from a disastrous period of falling sales caused by unseen changing consumer behaviour and rejection of its existing product lines.

The changing customer

Customer expectations have risen and continue to rise in both B2C and B2B markets. Everybody now expects a more relevant personalised relationship with an organisation but on their terms. As the pace of innovation explodes and technology life cycles shorten, an increasing number of customers will expect the quality of service to be continually upgraded, they will also expect personalisation and access to more information. With standards of living so high across most developed countries and an excess of material products/services and brands, customers are demanding more all round experiences that satisfy deeper emotional needs. Happiness now comes from doing things, holidays, keeping fit, playing golf, eating out, healthier eating and gardening, rather than just owning more possessions. This is especially so with older consumers as they become less self-indulgent and focus on developing their inner-life.

Socio-demographic changes

Society, culture and ways of living are changing around the world, throwing up new market opportunities, threats and challenges for business organisations. Although there are market variations across the 30 richest countries in the world, both men and women are now living longer (women longer than men), are more active and they are enjoying better and more options in their lives than ever before. Family situations are continually changing. Women are choosing to have fewer children, have them later in life or have no children at all. Men in their fifties are remarrying and starting a new family. More couples are living together before getting married and divorce is much easier than ever before for people in failed marriages. Single households and single parent households are on the increase, causing some to worry about the role of the 'traditional' family in transmitting culture to future generations.

Population ageing

In Europe today those over 50 years old represent 130 million people, i.e. about one third of the population of Belgium, France, Germany, Italy, Netherlands and Spain and the United Kingdom. Over the next 20 years, the over sixties will double, those over 75 will triple and those over 85 will be multiplied by five. It's a world phenomenon with 700 million over fifties in 2005 and 1100 million in 2020. In the UK the over fifties account for 20 million consumers and it's still growing. For many years this segment of the market was ignored while organisations concentrated on selling to younger consumers (www.senioragency.com).

Key point Populations around the world are ageing as more people live to an older age and remain healthy longer. This will have an enormous affect on consumer behaviour as consumer demand shifts and changes to match benefits wanted at different ages.

11.1 General example — Family change is happening at a quickening pace across the world

In common with Western countries where social changes have happened much earlier, South Korea has seen a massive shift in traditional family values, with soaring divorce rates that are now second only to the United States. For every two marriages registered last year, there was one divorce. As South Korean society becomes more Westernised, fewer couples are willing to put up with unhappy marriages. In just 30 years there have been social changes in the family and in the roles of men and women that took centuries in Western societies. If a similar pattern of change happens in China (with its 1.3 billion population) the impact on individual and consumer behaviour will be almost unimaginable (Divorce-online.co.uk).

Questions

1. Discuss and explain the reasons why social changes have happened so quickly in South Korea.
2. What might be the market and consumer results of this change? Consider both China and India in your analysis.

Changing patterns of consumer behaviour

Increased information, wealth and the availability of products and services in many countries across the world is quickening the pace of change and having enormous effects on consumer behaviour across all age segments of the market. Below is just a small example.

Young people

'There is no such thing as "fun for the whole family".' JERRY SEINFELD, US Comedian and television actor

Across many European countries, young people are now more affluent than ever before using their increased purchasing power to live a more pleasure seeking life than the preceding generations. Young men and women are delaying getting married, buying a house and having children for much longer and the single hedonistic lifestyle period is lasting often until people are into their thirties. However, not all are acting in a responsible and healthy manner. According to pressure group AIM (Alcohol in Moderation) young people are 'increasingly likely to be overweight, indulge in binge drinking, have a sexually transmitted infection and suffer mental problems with a risk of dying younger than their parents' (from a presentation given by Helena Conibear, Director of AIM, on 27th October 2004, www.aim-digest.com). (These findings have been mirrored in the US, where obesity is set to overtake tobacco as the biggest cause of premature death). The UK government has threatened to introduce more draconian laws because of unruly, drunken behaviour at night making some of the big cities no-go areas for families and older people (Datamonitor, Mintel).

Teenage activity

'Almost a third of 15 year-old Britains report getting drunk on a regular basis compared to one in ten French and Italian teenagers.' MINTEL REPORT 2004

Pre-teenagers and teenagers also have large amounts of disposable income, spending money on cosmetics, music, clothes and fast food at ages that get younger. They are more sophisticated, materialistic and street-wise at a much earlier age than their parents and demand products and services that relate specifically to them.

The 'grey' consumer

'Consumers don't stop having hopes, aspirations and dreams as they grow older.' ANON.

There seemed to be a general business consensus that the older people got the less concerned they were about personalised products and services. There was a market but only for the extremely wealthy older person and not for the mass **grey market**. Then came the gradual realisation that in some countries over fifties hold as much as 70–80 per cent of the country's wealth and have the largest amount of disposable income. Research has shown that both men and women in this group want personalised products and services and markets must be constantly segmented into ever-smaller groups for both men and women if success is to be attained. Older people are growing users of fashion wear (and this doesn't stop even into the late seventies and early eighties) cosmetics, holidays, cruises travel, eating out, drinking wine etc. (www.ageconcern.org.uk).

11.2 Marketing example — Advertising and the grey market

According to a recent Age Concern survey, two-thirds of elderly consumers felt that advertising portrays them in a negative way and three-quarters simply didn't relate to it at all. When asked, many felt that adverts tended to use the same ageing geriatric actors and other celebrities putting them into situations where being old (and possibly infirm) was unnecessarily emphasised. They also have a tendency to put the messages over in the wrong manner using such things as humour when it's just the facts that are important. The advertising agency 'SeniorAgency', which specialises in campaigns for the grey market argues that most agency people are under the age of 40 and fail to understand the needs of this market. They go on to say that organisations must research this market as diligently as other markets and not talk down to older people if success is to be assured (www.senioragency.com).

Questions

1 Do you think that it is possible for young people in advertising agencies to really understand the needs and wants of older people or should older people be employed?

2 In the same way do you think that older advertising people can understand the needs of very young consumers, especially children when building advertising campaigns?

Wealth and over indulgence

The health and wellbeing of people of all ages is now the concern of social commentators in all wealthy economies. It seems that both young and old are eating too much unhealthy food and some are now seriously overweight and threatened by illness and even premature death. This is particularly worrying among children and social marketing campaigns are used to encourage parents and schools to think more closely about the food that they offer youngsters. Older people, of both sexes, are a problem as well and constant bad publicity has forced fast-food companies such as McDonald's and Burger King to offer healthier products.

Lifestyle and healthier living

Gradually it appears that some age groups are looking to adopt increasingly healthier lifestyles. Television, newspapers, magazines and radio bombard their audiences and readers with health information and messages about the benefits of healthier living. Commercial organisations are opening more fitness clubs, selling health products as well as offering private health protection schemes. Governments are also reinforcing these messages, keen to see that people look after themselves and do not become a burden on the state and more people are taking positive steps that lead to ever-healthier lives. They are starting to take appropriate exercise, joining health and fitness clubs, finding ways of relaxing and eating a balanced, nutritious diet. When millions of people decide to change their lifestyle and their buying habits, market-led companies are certain to notice and to respond. This is because their ability to stay in business depends on providing goods and services that meet customers' needs and to respond to changing requirements.

The demand for healthier foods

Many consumers are now buying organic food and beverages because they feel that it is both healthier and it tastes better. They argue that this is because of the absence of pesticide residues, fewer additives (flavourings, colourings, sugar and salts) and no genetically modified ingredients (GM). They go on say that it causes less pollution, uses less energy, is good for wildlife and encourages high standards of animal welfare. Converts are prepared to pay a premium price for these types of products. Although some market analysts have predicted near saturation, the market for organic continues to grow at approximately 20 per cent a year in the US and at a similar pace across many European countries.

11.3 Marketing example — Healthier food

Social marketing health campaigns in many Western countries are helping to change eating behaviour by persuading overweight people to seek out healthier foods and consume less. Media publicity about obesity, artery-clogging fats, the potential for heart problems and the popularity of low-carbohydrate diets is forcing branded food manufacturers (Kraft, Nestlé, Unilever) and fast-food outlets (McDonald's, Burger King) to rethink the content of their products on offer. More legislation is also forcing manufacturers to put clearer and more enlightening information on the packaging so that people can see what it is that they are eating. This eating revolution is invading schools where marketing and advertising campaigns are being used to try to get children to adopt healthier lifestyles.

Question

1 Investigate the growth in the health market and speculate on the possibility of future markets.

Convenience foods

US research by Marketingresearch.com has shown that 60 per cent of all meals in this country are prepared and eaten in the home, largely because the increasing number of two working parents and single-parent households mean less time to cook. The pressure of modern life and the reluctance of working women to make the evening meal has led to an increase in supermarket, ready-made convenience foods. According to research company Mintel in 2004, using of sample of 25,000,

British consumers now spend £18 billion a year on supermarket meals up 63 per cent on 1993. Seventy per cent of the survey said they eat convenience foods on a regular basis including ethnic meals and pre-sliced and frozen chips.

Key point Time poor consumers are eating ready-made meals on a regular basis and suppliers are offering economy, middle-range and premium offerings.

Media-consumption patterns

The enormous advances in information technology are irreversibly altering the pattern of media consumption. There are now many different ways that people can obtain information from around the world. This has had a great affect on the ways that marketers are able to reach and communicate with their customers. Where there were a few TV and radio channels there are now hundreds, most operating on a 24/7 basis. Newspapers and magazines can be produced more quickly allowing new products to more easily enter the market. The communicative role of the Internet has been staggering and the part that it will play in the future is constantly unfolding. Media fragmentation makes it more difficult for advertisers to reach mass-market segments through one media type and many now have to be strategically considered in any promotional campaign. On the other hand niche markets, e.g. fishing, gardening, computers, DIY, can more readily be reached through specialised media channels.

11.4 Marketing example — Electronic recording

Sophisticated home entertainment technology will continue to cause more problems for advertisers as consumers are able to record and then zip through and ignore the adverts. This could get much worse if recording equipment is sold with the ability to stop recording when the adverts begin and start again when they are finished. This could affect the quality of programmes because ultimately it is advertising money that pays for the programmes. Because of laws on TV advertising, the problem is more acute in some countries rather than others. Advertising companies and advertising agencies are constantly lobbying legislators and looking for more effective ways to promote their brands through such methods as sponsorship and product placement.

Question

1 Examine the problems discussed above. How might sponsorship and product placement work? Give other examples.

Key point Media fragmentation makes it more difficult to reach mass markets with a single selling message. Niche markets can more readily be reached through specialised channels.

Shopping patterns

Shopping patterns have changed enormously over the last decades and this looks to continue (although planning authorities could step in if communities are threatened). Consumers can now choose the high street, shopping malls, edge-of-town retail parks, out of town regional shopping centres, factory village retail outlets, local convenience stores and home shopping. Or they can choose the one-stop shopping offered by the mighty hypermarkets, selling everything from groceries and beverages, clothes and electrical appliances to holidays, insurance, motor cars and funeral services. It seems that consumers will use more than one method depending on need, convenience, choice and personal inclination. In many cases shopping has become a social and emotional experience to be enjoyed alone or with the family for the whole of the day. Themed regional shopping centres can offer ethnic restaurants and takeaways, cinemas and theatres, pleasant picnic areas, swings and roundabouts and in-centre entertainment as well as choices of famous departmental stores and shops. They offer a crèche for the children and special rest and entertainment areas for the men where they could wile away the time while the women shop.

Small independent shops are now rapidly declining, driven out by large corporate retail groups

New technology and innovations

'In the modern world of business, it is useless to be a creative original thinker unless you can also sell what you create. Management cannot be expected to recognise a good idea unless it is presented to them by a good salesperson.'
DAVID OGILVY

According to the market concept of supply and demand as the price of scarce commodities rise, innovation and technology will find more economical resources to use, or present resources will be adapted to using less without lowering standards of living. For example as demand increased for whale oil, used for lighting in lighthouses, factories and the home in the nineteenth century, the number of whales decreased and the price rose. Fortunately, kerosene was discovered as a material that could be extracted from petroleum and the market for whale oil was superseded. Currently car manufacturers are working with concepts such as hydrogen-powered fuel cells and electric motors producing no harmful emissions that could make the internal combustion engine obsolete.

Constant technology upgrade

The world and market are changing at an ever-faster rate and creative, innovative new features and new products, brands and services are constantly coming to the market. Examples given throughout the book include the use of technology in product and packaging development, retail merchandising, range planning and pricing, customer research, communications and promotions and logistics. As fast as some new technological innovation hits the markets, within a few months it seems to be superseded by something else, better and offering more benefits, e.g. retail and entertainment on the Internet, interactive kiosks, mini-discs, DVDs, digital cameras, interactive flat TVs, the list goes on and on.

Key point Technology is being upgraded at an exponential rate causing product and market life cycles to constantly shorten.

Challenges for the consumer

All this technology and incessant materialism has had huge implications and challenges for human behaviour and understanding how consumers have been able to manage such mind-blowing changes. This is especially true with older people who have had to come to terms with concepts that would have been undreamt of in their formative years. The challenge for the manufacturers is to simplify and constantly make user-friendly the new technology that they bring to the market.

11.5 Marketing example — Silver surfers (www.btopenworld.com)

According to a survey by Btopenworld more retired people are spending time online than pursuing any other hobby, with 83 per cent surfing on a regular basis. These 'silver surfers' are finding the Internet an excellent way to socialise and stay in touch with friends and family clocking up an average of four emails a day. Breaking the myth about female techno-phobia, the web is proving particularly popular with older women with nearly half of them going on to the Internet for the first time after retiring from work. Almost two-thirds of them said they felt more open to new experiences and 42 per cent felt they were more tolerant to the way the world was changing.

Question

1 Discuss the idea that older consumers use the Internet. What industries might gain from this large market segment going on-line to look for products and services?

Shortening lead times

To remain competitive both manufacturers and retailers look constantly to shortening the time that it takes for the customer's order to be fulfilled. To hold goods in stock just in case (JIC) it is needed is not viable in a business world that looks to constantly reduce costs. The movement to a 'just-in-time' (JIT) system of stock delivery on the day it is needed was easier in some areas of business than others (e.g. car manufacturer). In fashion retail it has been harder and it could take a year for high fashion to move from the catwalk to the high-street store. Using technology such as CADCAM, fashion retailers such as Zara, the Spanish chain, and H&M, the Swedish group are able to replenish stock as well as offering customised designs within two to four weeks. Increasingly, mid-market and value retailers, including Next and George at Asda are also shortening lead times. This should please consumers and help minimise the amount of stock at the end of each season that has to be discounted.

Key point Customers are unhappy to wait for products unless it happens to be the norm.

Leading edge technologies

New or leading-edge technologies are emerging across a whole range of industries offering the innovative company almost unlimited opportunities for consumer products and services. Below is just a small example.

Biotechnology

This is the medical and industrial application of advanced genetic research in the use of drugs, hormones, and gene manipulation for both agricultural and human uses. Food can be manipulated to last longer and look and taste better. Human diseases can be genetically identified and eradicated. It is also being used for individual identification in credit, debit and other types of personal cards.

Nanotechnology

Nanotechnology is the ability to create materials from building blocks smaller than atoms that will unleash unprecedented capabilities. Pocket-sized super-computers, material 100 times stronger than steel but a sixth the weight, 1000 miles to a gallon of fuel, car batteries the size of small torch batteries are only some of the opportunities.

Information and communications

Technology that will allow the development of products that process increasing amounts of information in shorter periods of time including communications satellites, central processing units, and peripheral units such as disk drives, control units, modems and computer software.

Table 11.1 **Consumer benefits from using web technology**

- Fully customised products and services delivered more quickly.
- In-the-home on-line catalogues, ordering, servicing, payment and settlement.
- Instant information on company, product, price, delivery comparisons.
- Buying, selling, exchange, bartering opportunities across world markets.
- Up-to-date information including electronic newsletters and product updates.
- Transactions and record keeping.
- Reduced processes and delivery costs.
- Constant communications improvements including the Internet, TV, radio, email, mobile phones.
- Entertainment, music, films, books, magazines, newspapers, photography.

The rise and rise of materialism

'Wealth is like drinking sea water – the more we drink the more thirsty we become.' ANON.

Many argue that modern societies have become constantly more materialistic and consumers, never happy with what they have got, are always seeking different and better products and services. They go on to say that this has become for many the main reason for existence and for these consumers there is no doubt that shopping has become their number one pastime. Whether this love affair with all things materialistic comes about by self-motivated wants and desires or, as many argue, is something fuelled by marketers and advertisers is a polemic that will run and run.

The strength of consumerism

In a planned economic system of the type that used to exist in Eastern Europe before the fall of the Russian Empire, it was governments and administrators who planned ahead and decided what should and should not be produced. This was found to be inefficient, often leading to over- and under-production and a shortage and surplus of products. Economists, governments, politicians and regulators now recognise the importance of the consumer to the successful running of a liberal market economy. Under this type of economic system, experience has shown that more growth, effectiveness and success will come about if the consumer is able and allowed to make enlightened free choices about what goods and services will and will not be produced and marketed in a fully competitive marketplace. If customers want a particular product, it will sell and the manufacturer will prosper and survive but if another product has little or no demand, it will not sell and the manufacturer will go out of business.

Key point According to the philosophy of the free market, if the affluent consumer likes the benefits of a product it will sell, otherwise it will not.

Manipulating the consumer

There are many politicians, agencies and consumer groups that stridently argue that, in the relationship between the organisation and the consumer, the organisation is in the stronger position when it comes to understanding and manipulating consumer behaviour.

Unbalanced power relationship

There are many that stridently argue that, in the relationship between the organisation and the consumer, the organisation is in the stronger position when it comes to understanding and manipulating consumer behaviour. They go on to state that informational technological developments now allow managers and marketers to have enormous amounts of information on every individual throughout the land. The ability to use more intensive methods of understanding human nature (especially weaknesses) and in the development and use of communication skills leads to a situation where consumers can be manipulated by marketers and persuaded to buy products and brands that can be harmful to both the user and/or to society as a whole. Those that broadly support this position press for the need for constant government supervision, the setting up of overseeing bodies and, where necessary, the imposition of protective laws and rules and regulations (restrictions on limits and the use of consumer information already exist in many countries).

Less legislation, not more is the answer

On the other hand there are those who take an opposite view and argue consumers must, at some time, take responsibility for their own actions and too much legislation begins to interfere with the smooth and successful running of the marketplace. Most marketers and advertisers argue that, first, they would not want to sell products and services that are harmful or are not what people want (they wouldn't purchase again) and, second, that it is a fallacy to think that people could be persuaded to buy products that are not really wanted. They go on to say that governments should set the overall, fairly loose economic and social market framework within which suppliers and customers could then freely interact.

11.6 Marketing example Food Commission parent survey

In a survey in 2002, the Food Commission asked 800 parents for their views on unhealthy foods. The drink Sunny Delight won the award for 'additive nightmare', with accusations that it had 'pitifully low levels of real fruit juice – just 15 per cent'. The 'pester power' award for manipulative advertising or marketing techniques went to McDonald's Happy Meals for using toys to entice children into the chain. Other products which failed to impress the parents' jury included Dairylea Lunchables which contain ham and cheese slices and wheat crackers. Parents described the snack as 'over-processed rubbish'. Kellogg's Real Fruit Winders, a wound-up length of fruit-flavoured jelly won the 'tooth rot' award (www.foodcomm.org.uk).

Question

1 What's your view on these types of product? Should there be more rules and regulations restricting activities?

Addictive consumption

Scientific research has shown (in some cases beyond any reasonable doubt) that there are products on the market that have a physiological and/or psychological addictive affect creating consumer dependency that can cause ill health and even premature disability and death. We think particularly of cigarette smoking, gambling and over indulgence in the drinking of alcohol. All these areas have been hugely marketed in the past but, despite internal regulation and codes of conduct imposing self-restraint, have now attracted legislation in the UK and across the EU, imposing external limitations on product development and promotion and advertising. Most responsible commentators would accept, to a lesser or greater extent, some kind of proscription in these (proven) health damaging areas.

11.7 Marketing example Acceptable or unacceptable marketing

According to the British Medical Association 'The tobacco industry would have us believe that advertising has no affect on whether people smoke. Yet each year, in the UK alone, they spend over 100 million pounds promoting their products. The truth is that the industry advertises to replace the 550,000 Europeans who die from smoking each year. Every minute of every day, this lethal industry must recruit a new smoker to replace the 550,000 who die each year.' They are now spending vast amounts of money in Asia trying especially to encourage young men and women to take up the habit. The European Union has voted to outlaw tobacco advertising in newspapers and magazines, on the Internet and at international sports events from 2005. This will not, however, affect cinemas, posters, billboards and the print media published outside the EU (www.bma.org.uk).

Question

1 How much responsibility should governments take for the way that people behave?

Compulsive consumption

On the other hand there are other, less noxious products, such as chocolate, soft drinks, tea and coffee, which can also cause some form of compulsive behaviour. Likewise, on a wider scale, there are many people who seem to be addicted to shopping, constantly wanting to buy new things, try different brands, finding in some way therapeutic comfort, the 'feel-good factor' in treating themselves either through home shopping, or more likely by going out, mixing with others, and physically handling the products. In fact this can become so obsessive that many individuals and families spend themselves into enormous amounts of debt that they then become unable to pay back.

> **Key point** Consumers shop for functional, emotional and compulsive reasons.

Consumer protection and encouraging free markets

The importance of free consumer choice, to be able buy from a range of competing products, to the success of an economy has informed and encouraged governments to enact laws and regulations that made certain that the unequal power of the large organisation wasn't used in some way to distort the buyer/seller relationship to the detriment of the customer.

Consumer protective legislation

So over the decades large swathes of protective consumer legislation (e.g. trade description, sale of goods, fair trading) and laws that prevent anti-competitive behaviour (e.g. mergers and acquisitions that create monopolies, price fixing and competition shut-out clauses) have been introduced. Governments have also created overseeing bodies such as the Office of Fair Trading (OFT) and the Competition Commission in the UK, the European Competition Commission in the EU and the Federal Trade Commission in the US. All have the power to stop and prosecute if necessary any anti-consumer, anti-free market legislation. Producers and retailers have also introduced their own codes of conduct that recognise the importance of the consumer by spelling out how well they will treat the customer if a problem in the relationship happens. Many pressure groups have sprung up over the years, coming into being with the expressed purpose of protecting the consumer and taking their side in their relationship with retailers and manufacturers (discussed in more detail on the next page).

> **Key point** Some commentators argue that much legislation goes too far and consumers, when reaching adulthood, must ultimately be responsible for their own behaviour (a case of 'caveat emptor' or 'buyer beware') even if it is foolhardy, reckless or just plain silly.

Table 11.2 **Consumer protection and pressure groups**

Below is a small selection, out of the many that exist, of UK consumer protections groups.

The Consumer Gateway A website of consumer information and protection services, run by the Department of Trade and Industry in the UK.

Card Watch The UK banking industry's body that works with police, retailers and organisations including Crimestoppers to fight plastic card fraud.

Citizens Advice Bureau The Citizens Advice Bureau Service is a UK registered charity and says that they offer free, confidential, impartial and independent advice on consumer issues.

Consumer Complaints A free online service run by the local Trading Standards Office set up to investigate consumer complaints anywhere in the UK.

Consumer Association A consumer protection, not-for-profit commercial organisation, run by 'Which'.

Increased use of legislation

Individuals, groups, organisations are now much more likely to resort to legislation to overcome a problem they feel they have with a business than in the past. Increased knowledge and easy access to lawyers, often with a 'no pay out no fee' clause, encourages all to take this kind of action when a wrongdoing is perceived. Miscreant organisations can now expect customers, communities, employees, regulators and governments around the world to take legal action to recover damages, sometime running into millions of pounds, for actions considered inappropriate or wrong in some way. This might be because of the harmful effect of products and services being sold, the way a company operates in a market or the manner in which employees are treated. Global organisations must be aware of the possible local legislative differences which, coupled with language and geographical barriers, can lead to expensive and protracted problems.

Corporate responsibility and codes of conduct

As news filters through about the damage that is being caused to the environment, people dying of starvation in Africa or companies acting unethically by using child labour, more people join the chorus of protestors angry about free markets and apparently unbridled capitalism. Research (MORI research 2000) has shown that many consumers react much more favourably to companies that seem to act as good corporate citizens and come across as being a friend to their customers. In light of this, more and more large companies now see the public relations (PR) value in having codes of conduct setting out clearly how they intend to treat the customer, the wider public and the general environment. This is over and above the protection that consumer law provides. Some see this as a cynical, self-serving ploy, while others argue that it is because well-behaved firms can have real altruistic feelings about their market behaviour.

Table 11.3 Pros and cons of consumer protection

For greater consumer protection

- Consumers can be manipulated into buying products that are unwanted or unnecessary.
- Companies will market products that are damaging, or have the potential to cause damage, to both the individual and/or the environment if more sales can be made.
- The government must regulate through the use of laws and rules and regulations to protect the consumer.

For less consumer protection

- It is patronising to think that consumers can be persuaded to buy unnecessary or unwanted products and services.
- Consumers must take responsibility for their own decisions.
- Organisations are responsible corporate citizens and would not manufacture and sell harmful products and services.
- Government legislation and interference should be kept to a minimum to ensure the effective and efficient running of the marketplace.

Irresponsible consumerism

There are many commentators, however (see www.ethicalconsumer.org), who are unhappy with the philosophy of free market concepts that underpin the ideas about consumerism. There now seems to be a rising trend around the world in the amount of individuals and groups that are against 'irresponsible consumerism' and who feel that, among other things, that the wealthy countries exploit the poorer countries and large multinational companies use their massive power to get their own way at the expense of others much less powerful. They feel that the rush to more and more materialism is bad for consumers, bad for the country, bad for the poor nations of the world and is ultimately damaging the planet.

11.2 General example Corporate social responsibility (CSR)

Market and Opinion Research International (MORI) and CSR (Corporate Social Responsibility) Europe conducted the first consumer survey of attitudes toward CSR in late 2000. They surveyed 12,000 people, 60 per cent said a company's commitment to social responsibility was important when buying a product or service and 20 per cent said that it would influence their spending behaviour.

(www.mori.com – corporate social responsibility)

Key point Corporate responsibility is important to some customers and will affect the brands that they consider for purchase.

Opening up undeveloped markets

Members of the eight richest countries (G8) come together on a regular basis to discuss social and market problems around the world. In 2005 the overriding issue was poverty across Africa. The need to help individual countries to develop their own markets was top of the agenda involving financial aid and debt relief. Also discussed was the need to curtail the use of subsidies to rich country farmers that caused products to be dumped at below cost price on African markets. The success or otherwise of African markets will have an affect on consumer behaviour across many other markets across the world.

11.8 Marketing example — Fair trade products

Fair trade brand labelling was introduced in the Netherlands in the late 1980s in response to rock bottom prices received for commodity products such as tea, coffee beans, nuts and fresh fruit in poorer countries. Many farmers only grow the one commodity crop and when prices fluctuate and fall dramatically it can have a huge affect on the lives of millions of small-scale producers causing heavy debt levels and loss of livelihood. The Fairtrade foundation is a non-profit making organisation set up to guarantee producers a fair price for their commodity products no matter what the going market rate. They try to encourage large retailers around the world to take in a range of fair trade products, working on the premise that there is a growing segment of consumers prepared to pay a higher price for such things as tea and coffee if this will supplement the living style of poorer families. The $100 million fair trade coffee market (2004) is the fastest-growing sector of the coffee industry (www.fairtrade.org.uk).

Questions

1 Evaluate the success or otherwise of this type of product.

2 Examine the theory that people are ethically driven and are prepared to make sacrifices for the less fortunate.

Key point More consumers are adopting an ethical stance when buying products and services.

Using up the Earth's finite resources

There are constant reminders in the media about the damage happening across the world by the seemingly uncontrolled consumption of goods and services using up the Earth's finite resources. Many governments have enacted legislation (with more to follow) to try to prevent environmental abuse by suppliers, producers, retailers and consumers.

11.3 General example — EU Recycling programme

After a vote in the European parliament, all electrical goods sold in Europe after 2005 will have to be recycled at the manufacturer's expense. Under the new legislation, householders will not be allowed to throw away unwanted electrical goods but will have to sort them out ready for collection and recycling. The legislation will cover TVs, washing machines, stereos, computers, mobile phones, vacuum cleaners, hairdryers or anything considered electrical or electronic. The Directive on Packaging and Packaging Waste aims to reduce the amount of packaging used, to encourage its reuse, enhance recycling and recovery and divert waste from landfill. The End of Life Vehicle (ELV) Directive has set a target for 95 per cent of vehicles by weight to be reused or recovered (including energy recovery) by 2015. The cost of collection, dismantling and recycling will be borne by manufacturers but they are expected to pass it on to consumers. Green groups are delighted with the new rules and believe they will force manufacturers to design more environmentally friendly products. The challenge for manufacturers is to try to produce these goods and services without reducing consumer value in any way (*Official Journal of the European Union*, 2000).

Questions

1 Do you think that it is possible for the recycling programmes to be carried without reducing value in any way as suggested above?

2 Discuss the new products and service markets that might arise because of the EU recycling programmes.

Global warming

Global warming is now a constant issue and looks certain to have a large effect on consumer behaviour in the future. The tourism industry is a major contributor to global warming through transportation. Emissions from aeroplanes are considered by many to be one of the largest contributors to climate change and the industry continues to grow. Environmental campaigners call for economic measures, like tax on air fuel and airline tickets to be introduced and for travel to be reduced (UK Environmental Audit Committee 2003). This is bound to affect the growth of both long-haul and shorter tourist flights. Other sources of carbon dioxide include lorries, buses, cars, power plants, factories, office buildings and homes, all large markets that will have to adapt and change in some way or another. After carbon emissions caused by humans, deforestation, the destruction of the rain forests for the use of the land and the wood, is the second principle cause of atmospheric carbon dioxide (perhaps as much as 25 per cent).

Government commitment to reduce carbon emissions

Although there is little commitment by the US, China and India to reduce carbon emissions (at the time of writing), other countries, particularly in the EU, have agreed to a gradual reduction over the next 40 to 50 years. This will have ramifications across industries and particularly in the use of the motorcar. There are bound to be restrictions on both the type of vehicle being produced and its use by consumers. There is already a congestion charge for using the car in London and other cities are looking to follow suit. There is also talk of introducing general road charges of some kind or another to force drivers to walk, cycle and use public transport and to shop more from home. There is pressure on manufacturers to produce cars that emit less carbon dioxide and are more fuel efficient.

Traffic jams are increasingly the norm around the world

Increase in oil prices

At the same time as politicians were discussing global warming, world oil prices hit a record high of US$58 a barrel in April 2005, and this is expected to top US$100 within two years as demand increases. This is driven particularly by China and India (with over a third of the world's population) as they continue to modernise their economies. This could create problems for conventional private and industrial methods of transport as organisations and consumers have to pay more for petrol or manufacture and use smaller vehicles. This will force industrial prices and costs up affecting all manner of consumer and business products and services. Oil, precious and strategic metals, wood, fish are a few of the many other markets with finite resources that are being used up at an increasing rate.

Environmental concern issues include the following:

- Genetic engineering, genetic modification of food.
- Depletion of the ozone layer.
- Climate change leading to flooding, droughts and unstable and unnatural weather patterns.
- Depletion of natural resources on land, sea and air.
- Damage to ecosystems.

Locally sourced food products

There is a movement by a small but significant number of consumers to buy regionally sourced seasonal products supporting the local community, farms and suppliers. There is a gradual realisation that the cost of 'food miles', transporting many food products, by road, sea and air, from every corner of the world, is another factor contributing to global warming and other environmental costs and this needs to be reduced to protect the environment (research report by Professor Jules Pretty and Professor Tim Lang, University of Essex and City University, UK).

11.4 General example — Food miles

Many vegetables travel unnecessary distances so that consumers can have seasonal products all the year round including apples from South Africa, New Zealand, Chile and the United States. Mange Tout is flown 500 miles by air from Zambia, broccoli or strawberries travel 700 miles from Spain, lamb and apples 11,700 by sea from New Zealand. The local supermarket might have asparagus from Peru (6,300 miles), sugar snap peas from Guatemala (5,400 miles), kiwi fruit, and grapes and wine from Chile (7,200 miles) and advocados, salad potatoes and tomatoes from Israel (2,200 miles). The ethical farming group Sustain (www.sustainweb.org) looked into a sample shopping-basket of 26 imported organic items and found the contents had travelled 150,000 miles – equivalent to six times round the equator. According to Pretty and Lang, these so-called 'food miles' have not been taken into account when looking at the cost to society of the food that is eaten.

Question

1 Examine and evaluate the concept of 'food miles' research by Pretty and Lang. How might the research affect future behaviour?

Global terrorism

Global terrorism continues to pose a clear danger to the international community and no business can afford to be complacent about its effects. Any country and any company can be considered to be vulnerable to an attack of some kind leading to possible loss of life, the destruction of property and heavy costs. Industries such as travel, tourism and insurance are particularly susceptible and business will need to have contingency measures in place for any such attack that may happen. As well as the loss of revenue, a huge rise in the cost of insurance cover for war and terrorism risks could result in heavy losses and even in the ruin of some businesses operating in areas such as the airline and tourism industry.

Pressure groups

There are a number pressure and interest groups that have been set up to promote the wishes and the wellbeing of their members seeking to persuade policy makers and organisations to act in ways that will be beneficial to the cause that they have adopted. Some are formal charitable organisations and include: the Consumer Association, Greenpeace, The Wildlife Fund, Friends of the Earth, Oxfam and so on. Other pressure groups are less formal and come into being in an ad hoc manner including animal rights, anti-hunting, against the use of powdered baby milk in Africa, anti-capitalists and so on. They may lobby politicians, disseminate bad publicity, encourage the widespread boycott of firms and products they consider unethical or harmful in some way or another, march on the streets and even commit acts of sabotage of some kind. The speed of the Internet and mobile phone communications now enables large numbers of people to quickly come together to protest across a myriad number of causes and their power over the next decades will only but grow.

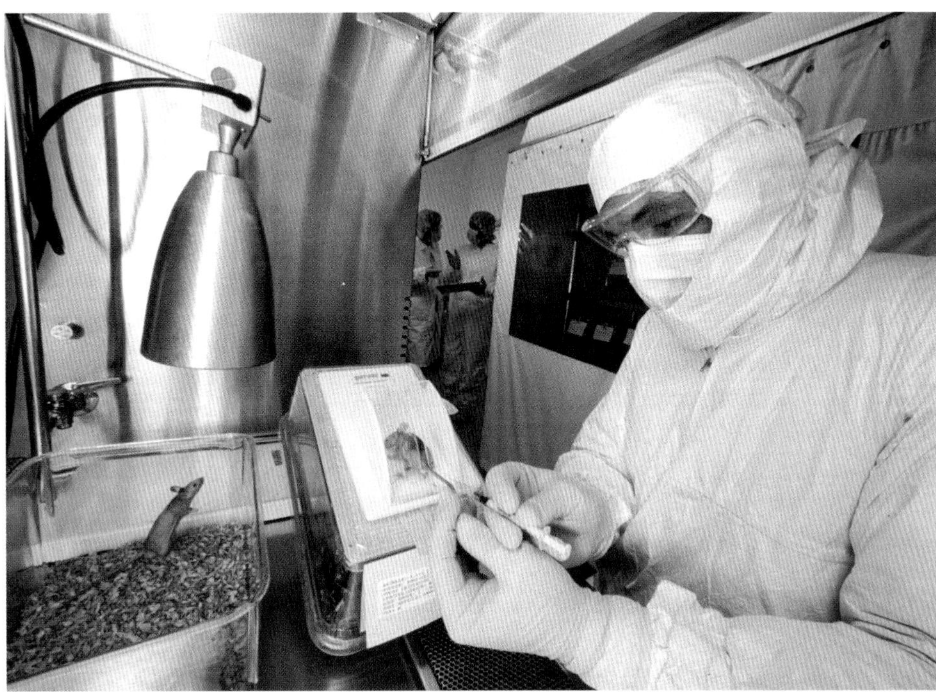

Vivisection and the use of animals in consumer product research upset many consumers. *Source*: Alamy

Key point International issues will continue to play an important part in consumer behaviour.

Summary

- In this chapter some of the changes happening to consumers were discussed including demographic, family and lifestyle.
- Some of the market lifestyle changes now and into the future were also identified covering eating, health and spending patterns.
- The part that innovation and technology plays in retail and the influence that it has on consumer behaviour was outlined.

- Consumer manipulation and the pressure of consumerism were identified, with the arguments for and against government involvement and organisation codes of conduct briefly examined.
- Global problems influencing consumer behaviour in the future were identified, including global warming, the use of finite resources, poverty in the third world and terrorism.

Questions

1 Examine the changing demographic patterns across a country of your choice and illustrate how this could affect market segmentation.

2 Discuss the market opportunities across the 'grey market'. Why do you think that a large segment of the market has been relatively unexploited over the last 20 years?

3 Identify and evaluate a particular market that you think might be ripe for more focused segmentation.

4 Examine how the problems associated with global warming could affect consumer behaviour?

5 Analyse the factors associated with poverty in most African countries. How does it affect consumer behaviour?

6 What needs to happen in the future to ameliorate the situation in underdeveloped countries and cause markets and consumer demand to grow?

7 Discuss the problem of global terrorism and examine the effects that it could have on consumer behaviour and retail.

8 Identify current lifestyle trends and speculate what lifestyles might arise in the future.

9 Examine the proposition that people are victims in a material world where companies, marketers and advertisers manipulate consumers into a state of 'addictive consumption' never satisfied with what it is that they already have and always seeking new experiences.

10 Discuss the whole concept of consumer behaviour and analyse the idea that it can be studied in a meaningful and useful manner.

Case study

Case study 1 Intelligent products

Cars already come equipped with navigation systems, but soon they will become smarter in other ways. Inbuilt computers will diagnose problems with the car and send information about the car's performance back to the factory. Home appliance manufacturers will begin adding intelligence to washers, dryers and refrigerators. It will allow the history of the product to be monitored, faults immediately diagnosed and will even let the user call home and make sure that the cooker has been turned off. Radio identification chips (RFID) in supermarket products will allow shopping trolleys to be scanned at they move through the checkout without taking the goods out. It will also act as a security check preventing goods being stolen. Trolleys can also have plasma screens attached that react to the customer loyalty card and then talk to the customer as he or she moves around the store pointing out products and promotions. A woman picks up a new blouse and an image flashes up of her wearing it, at the same time suggesting matching jacket, skirt and shoes. Pervasive computing means that every device, every appliance, everything we have, including the things that we eat and wear, are going to have computer capability. Products on 'smart shelves' could be individually tagged so that prices can be changed from a central location and whenever one is picked up and taken away, built-in readers alert staff at the back of the store to come forward and re-stock. There is an electronic vision device that recognises shapes and colours so that fruit and vegetables could be recognised and priced immediately they are put on to the scales. It has been predicted that if its suppliers could attach tags to each product vast supermarket chains, such as Wal-Mart in the US, could save up to $7.6 billion (£3 billion) a year by knowing exactly where every single item is along its supply chain. Spare parts can be tagged to prevent counterfeiting and in hospitals, details can be tagged to patients to ensure that they receive the right care and medication.

Questions

1 Examine the use of the new technology discussed above. How do you think that customers will react to the plethora of new concepts coming on to the market?

2 Discuss the opportunities for innovative new products and services that could enhance the consumer experience.

3 What are the security and privacy implications for all the above? Do you think that more legislation is necessary?

Case study

Case study 2 A lifestyle phenomenon

US motorbike maker Harley-Davidson is the only remaining major manufacturer of motorbikes in the US. The company has been producing bikes since 1903 and by 1912 it had over 200 dealers across the country and began exporting to Japan. Over 20,000 of its bikes were used in the First World War and by 1920 it was the largest motorcycle company in the world with 2000 dealerships in 67 countries, and 90,000 of its bikes were in use at the end of the Second World War. By 2000 there were 500,000 members in the Harley Owners Group, including ageing actors and rock stars, and it was selling upwards of 200,000 bikes a year. By now it had taken on an iconic status and there were waiting lists for particular models. However, in early 2005 it had a slight decline in sales (although still selling US$1 billion in 2004) and questions were being asked about a possible loss of cult following. It seems that the average Harley rider is 45–50 years old, has been to college and earns approximately $75,000 a year (Business week online), a great, but ageing customer profile. With the average baby-boomer now reaching 50, the recent drop in Harley sales suggests that this lifestyle phenomenon could be tailing off in the country's largest demographic group and it was suggested that the company had to attract younger users. Others are more optimistic and argue that this baby boomer customer segment is healthier and more active than in the past and will continue to buy the bike well into their sixties. Harley has extended the brand into clothes and fashion accessories.

Questions

1 Evaluate the attraction of Harley-Davidson to its lifestyle segment.

2 How might it reposition the product to attract younger riders?

3 Discuss the dangers involved with attempting to stretch the brand into unassociated product areas. Give live examples where this has been successful and unsuccessful.

Further reading

Books

Bagozzi, Richard, J.R. Priester and Zeynep Gurhan-Canli (2002) *The Social Psychology of Consumer Behaviour (Applying Social Psychology)*, Maidenhead: Open University Press.

Newman, Andrew and Peter Cullen (2002) *Retailing, Environment and Operations*, London: Thomson Learning.

Roberts, S. (1998) *Harness the Future: The 9 Keys to Emerging Consumer Behaviour*, New York: J. Wiley and Sons.

Schiffman, Leon and Leslie Laze Kanuk (2003) *Consumer Behaviour*, Upper Saddle River, NJ: Prentice Hall, 8th edn.

Solomon, Micheal (2002) *Consumer Behaviour: Buying, Having and Being*, 5th edn, International edn, Upper Saddle River, NJ: Prentice-Hall International.

Wright, Ray (1999) Marketing: Origins, Concepts, Environment, London: Thomson Business Press.

Journals and papers

ADAS Consulting (2001) Energy Use in Organic Farming Systems for MAFF, Project OF0182, DEFRA, London, www.adas.co.uk.

Boge, Stefanie (1993) 'Road Transport of Goods and the Effects on the Spatial Environment', Wuppertal, Germany, July (a photocopy of the English summary can be obtained by post from the UK Food Commission).

Cowell, S. and R. Clift (1996) 'Farming for the Future: An Environmental Perspective', paper presented at the Royal Agricultural Society of the Commonwealth, July, CES, University of Surrey.

Lucas, Caroline (2001) 'Stopping the Great Food Swap – Relocalising Europe's Food Supply', Green Party.
Mintel Reports (2005) 'Retail Intelligence'.
Pretty, Professor Jules and Professor Tim Lang (2005) Research report on 'Food Miles', University of Essex and City University, UK.
RCEP (2000) *Energy – The Changing Climate*, The Royal Commission on Environmental Pollution, 22nd Report, June 2000, London: HMSO.
SAFE Alliance (1994) *The Food Miles Report: The Dangers of Long-Distance Food Transport*, London: SAFE Alliance, October.

Websites

British Medical Association, www.bma.org.uk.
British Medical Journal, www.bmj.com.
Btopenworld, www.btopenworld.com.
Datamonitor Business Intelligence, www.datamonitor.com.
The Department for the Environment Food and Rural Affairs (Defra), www.defra.gov.uk.
Divorce online, Divorce-online.co.uk.
Environmental Audit Committee, www.publications.parliament.uk.
Fairtrade Foundation, www.fairtrade.org.uk.
Food Commission parent survey, www.foodcomm.org.uk.
Health Telegraph, www.telegraph.co.uk/health.
Institute of Science in Society, www.i-sis.org.uk.
Marketresearch.com, www.marketresearch.com.
Mintel Research Organisation, www.mintel.co.uk.
Mori research, corporate social responsibility, www.mori.com.
Senioragency.com, www.senioragency.com.
Soil Association, www.soilassocaition.org.
Sustain, ethical farming group, www.sustainweb.org.

Glossary

absolute sensory threshold the point where something first becomes noticeable to the senses

Adams, J. Stacey known for his equity theory of job motivation

added-value customer benefits added to the basic core product, e.g. advertising, branding, delivery, service etc.

Adler, Alfred (1870–1970) individual psychologist, believed that individuals are unique and develop personality through interaction with others. Known for his work on the 'inferiority complex'

advertising jingle a catchy musical refrain delivering an advertising message, frequently used on radio or television

AIDA model (Awareness, Interest, Desire, Action) an acronym and memory aid (mnemonic) used in advertising. The target audience needs to be moved down through the AIDA process usually using more than one promotional technique

AIO, activities, interests and opinions psychographic variables that focus on customer activities, interests and opinions and group them into clusters for use in market segmentation

Allport, Gordon (1897–1967) American social psychologist, postulated the trait theory of personality

analytical psychology the theory that people are unaware of a universal inherited 'collective unconsciousness' that affects all people. Associated with **Carl Jung** (1875–1961)

anger displacement taking out anger on others when the original cause is unapproachable

anthropology study of primitive groups of people

ascribed and acquired groups we are born into ascribed groups and move into acquired groups

aspiration reference group groups to which we would like to belong

attitude the strength of the consumer's belief with regard to an object of some sort, e.g. the company image or brand. It can be positive, negative or neutral. It has three components: beliefs, emotions and behaviour

attitude measurement methods there are three major research types measuring and tracking customer attitudes: Thurstone scale; Likert scale; semantic differential

attribution theory looking for detailed explanation about the person and the situation to explain behaviour. First associated with Fritz Heider's writing in 1958

aversion therapy a method of desensitising harmful conditioning

awareness a measure of the proportion of a target audience who have heard of a particular product or service

balance theory individuals look for consistency between attitudes

Bandura, Albert (1925–) Canadian social psychologist, known for his work on social learning theory

basic consumer communications model simple model that looks at the message sender, message encoding, medium, message decoding, receiver, interference, feedback and control

behaviourism the view that psychology should be an objective science that studies only observable behaviour without reference to mental processes. Generally now disregarded with the realisation of the importance of cognition. Associated with **J. Watson** (1878–1958), **E. Thorndike** (1874–1944), **B.F. Skinner** (1904–90)

behaviouristic segmentation a method of segmenting a market by dividing customers into groups based on their usage, loyalties or buying responses to a product or service

beliefs mental and verbal ideas and assessments we have and we make about the world we inhabit. They will be of varying strengths. Belief × Strength = Attitude

Bernays, Edward (1892–1995) German American opinion former and propagandist; nephew of Freud and the father of public relations

Berne, Eric writer and researcher developed the concept of transactional analysis, 'father', 'parent', 'child'

Binet, Alfred (1857–1911) French scientist, created the first '**intelligence test**' **(IQ)**

biological gene pool biological factors that humans are born with (in the **DNA**) often affecting health, physical abilities and personality

biometrics using the iris of the eye, voice tones, palm print, face outline, as means to access security walls, e.g. ATMs, computers etc.

blind testing the testing of products with potential consumers where brand names, packaging and other identifying items have been removed. Used in experimental research

body language non-verbal forms of communication including, smiling, frowning, body movements, touching etc.

brand a product, service, idea, person etc., identified by a name, symbol, trademark or characteristic that differentiates it from competitor offerings. Usually registered for protection. The way to gain competitive advantage

brand extension build a family of products all trading on the one brand name

brand loyalty degree to which the customer will purchase certain brands without considering the alternatives. Companies try to encourage and measure it

brand personality the sum of all feelings, thoughts and recognitions, both good and bad, that people have about a company and its products. It is the unique or emotional selling proposition that nobody else can copy

brand stretching using the brand name across a whole range of seemingly unconnected products

Burt, Sir Cyril (1883–1971) British educational psychologist accused of fraud in research into intelligence

business-to-business products and services classified as capital equipment, raw and manufactured materials, component parts and services

business-to-business (B2B) markets one business marketing products and services to another business in the running of the business and not passing them on to the end consumer except as part of the end product

business-to-consumer (B2C) markets products and services produced explicitly for end consumer use

buyer behaviour the way in which a customer acts and thinks, and the steps taken in the purchase decision-making process

capitalism an economic system characterised by a market environment where the free market forces of demand and supply determine what will, and will not be produced

Cattell, Raymond (1905–98) American social psychologist, developed trait theory into modern usage; known for his 16 Factor Personality Questionnaire

causal research research that looks for causal relationships between two variables, e.g. loyalty cards and real customer loyalty. (See **exploratory research**; **descriptive research**)

CCTV closed circuit TV. Most large shops, shopping and leisure centres etc. seem to have them. Big brother is watching you

celebrity endorsement endorsement of products by well-known personalities from the field of sport, entertainment, etc.

channel of distribution how and where the producer makes the product available to the customer, i.e. direct or indirect, wholesaler, retailer etc. An essential element in the marketing mix. A path that includes a grower, producer, manufacturer, broker, wholesaler and retailer

classical conditioning a learning process whereby a conditioned stimulus that elicits a response is paired with a neutral stimulus that does not elicit any particular response. Through repeated exposure, the neutral stimulus comes to elicit the same response as the conditioned stimulus. Associated with **Ivan Pavlov** (1849–1936)

closure the perceptual tendency to fill in the gaps in things we observe, thus enabling one to perceive disconnected parts as a whole. The need of the individual to see and organise the world as whole; to have a happy ending. (See **Gestalt**)

cognitive dissonance holding in the mind two or more conflicting and contradictory ideas, beliefs or values (often post purchase). The marketer must resolve this. Associated with **Leon Festinger** (1919–47)

cognitive psychology studying all the mental activities associated with thinking, knowing, remembering and communicating. Looking at the role that the mind plays in behaviour. First associated with **Martin Seligman**

communications mix all the tools and techniques the organisation can use to promote its products and services including: advertising, sales promotions, public relations, publicity, packaging, merchandising, point-of-purchase, direct response, personal selling, sponsorship, exhibitions, word of mouth

competitive advantage an element within a product offering that is particularly attractive to customers and not offered to them by competitors (make it better, cheaper or different)

conditioned response our automatic response (through the nervous system) to a situation built up by repeated exposure

conditioned stimulus a stimulus paired with another stimulus that elicits a known response then serves to produce the same response by itself, e.g. the approach of food causes the dog to salivate – paired with a bell, the sound of the bell then causes the dog to salivate. Associated with **Ivan Pavlov** (1849–1936)

consciousness our awareness of ourselves and our environment

consumer the eventual user of a product, not necessarily the customer (see **customer**)

consumer behaviour how individuals behave when buying goods and services for their own use

consumer buying behaviour information both quantitative and qualitative marketing research into the needs, wants, opinions, attitudes, etc. of consumers

consumer loyalty the measure of how often a customer will purchase from one particular company or purchase one particular brand

consumer needs basic physiological drives, e.g. hunger, thirst, warmth, sex and curiosity, that can be fulfilled by purchase behaviour. (See **consumer wants**)

consumer shadowing a qualitative observation study where an interviewer accompanies a respondent for the day as they go shopping so as to study behaviour. Also known as accompanied shopping

consumer wants emotional demands over and above basic physiological needs e.g. 'I am thirsty and need a drink; but I want a Coke'

consumerism the rise in consumer power, consumer rights and protection through legislation and company codes of conduct

co-operative a wholesaling operation established by a group of retailers to give themselves a buying advantage by being able to buy in bulk and so gain economies of scale

corporate and brand positioning positioning is where a company and/or its brand sits in the market *vis-à-vis* the competition, e.g. Skoda and Mercedes. Positioning is ultimately in the minds of the consumer

corporate culture the shared values emanating from the organisation in terms of beliefs, attitudes, and behaviour

corporate image how an organisation attempts to portray itself to its public. It includes a company's name, logo, typeface, colours, slogan, etc. It can project 3 things, which you are, what you do and how you do it

crystallised and fluid intelligence information, skills and strategies that people have learned through experience and apply to problem-solving situations. Tends to stay even as we get older. Associated with Fluid – reflects reasoning, memory and information processing capabilities. Dissipates with age. **Raymond Cattell** (1905–98)

cultural imperialism 'Western', US cultural values being forced on non-Western societies by mass media and global giants such as McDonald's

culture the ideas, beliefs, values, mores, customs, ways of living, language, infrastructures shared by groups of people passed on from one generation to another. It can differ from area to area and country to country and so may demand a different marketing approach

customer generally any person or organisation who buys a product or service, Not necessarily the end consumer; the most important factor for the company to consider (see **consumer**)

customer profile a detailed description of the customer in a particular market according to certain characteristics, e.g. in terms of their age, gender, life-cycle stage, occupation and lifestyle

customer relationship management (CRM) a more intensive form of relationship marketing. Managing a personalised relationship in an integrated long-term manner designed to optimise profitability, revenue and customer satisfaction. CRM applications focus on relationships, rather than transactions

customer retention maintaining the existing customer base by establishing good relations with all who buy the company's product; it is said it is five times more expensive to gain a new customer than it is to keep the existing one

customer retention programmes loyalty programme created to improve customer retention. It's based on the realisation that it is many times more expensive to look for new customers

customised or one-to-one marketing marketing activity in which a company attempts to satisfy the unique needs of every customer

customised products/brands making different products for different customer segments and different countries

database marketing continually updating, cross-referencing and using the information database to reach existing and new target markets offering added benefits and different products

data mining discovering previously unknown information from the data in a data warehouse, by performing clever searches

Dawkins, Richard English evolutionary psychologist

defence mechanisms methods of dealing with uncomfortable mental thoughts and dilemmas including; rationalisation, intellectualisation, sublimation, compensation, projection, repression, and so on

demographics information relating to the broad population statistics such as age, sex, income, occupation, education level or marital status, as well as movement of people. Often used as a basis for segmentation

descriptive research research that attempts to describe the variables involved in a project

Dichter, Ernest (1907–91) American marketer, founded the Institute of Motivational Research in New York in 1946

diffusion of innovation the process and time rate by which the sale of new products and services spreads among customers. Across the whole market the groups are: innovators 2.5 per cent; early 13.5 per cent; early majority 34 per cent; late majority 34 per cent; laggards 16 per cent. Associated with Everett Rogers (1931–2004).

disassociation reference group groups to which we would not like to belong

disposable income spending money left to buy consumer products and services after essential household spending

DMD (decision-making difficulty) the degree of consumer difficulty involved in making a decision. Classified under routine, limited and extensive

DMP (decision-making process) a model for showing the decision-making process faced by a customer when purchasing a product

DMU (decision-making unit) an acronym used to define those individuals who are involved, or could be involved, in a particular purchase decision

DNA hereditary genetic system consisting of genes and chromosomes

drive reduction theory the idea that all organisms are genetically programmed to maintain a state of equilibrium

Ebbinghaus, Herman (1850–1909) German scientist, seen as a pioneer in the study of memory

economics the study of how scarce resources and infinite human needs and wants are best reconciled

efficient consumer response (ECR) all distribution channel members cooperatively working together to make cost savings that will benefit the end consumer

ego according to Freud, thinking based on the reality principle balancing the primitive needs of the id with the moral demands of the superego (see also the **id** and the **superego**)

ego-defensive to protect self-esteem

ego states a proposition in **transactional analysis** that every person has three mental conditions – parent ego state, child ego state and adult ego state, and that at any particular time one of these states is dominant in the personality

electronic data interchange (EDI) standardising and optimising information flows along the distribution chain (between suppliers, producers and retailers) through the use of standardised computer hardware and software

emotional reasons feeling: anger, love, jealousy, happiness etc. All will affect reasons for purchasing particular products and services

empirical knowledge knowledge through observation and experience

empty nesters people whose children have left or are about to leave the family home. Used in market segmentation

equity theory motivational theory that argues that unequal rewards for the same work will de-motivate. Associated with **J. Stacey-Adams** writing in 1965

Erickson, Erick (1902–94) German social psychologist, believed that personality developed through a series of psychosocial stages in life

ethical consumerism concern that companies are conducting business according to some set of ethical principles, such as not harming the environment, not testing on animals and treating their employees properly

ethical problems moral principles (what is right and wrong), and values that govern the actions and decisions of an individual or group or organisation

evolutionary psychology a reductionism theory that says that if we want to know reasons for present-day human behaviour, we should study the animal world, e.g. baboons

existentialism there are many types but basically the idea that people come to the world with nothing and must decide their own values and morals throughout life. Associated with

M. Heidegger (1889–1976), **J.P. Sartre** (1905–80), **Erich Fromm** (1900–80)

expectancy theory motivation is dependent on the balance between the value of the reward or goal and the difficulty of obtainment; associated with **Victor Vroom**

explanatory research research that looks for cause and effect between variables

explicit memory includes semantic memories about words, ideas and concepts; episodic or autobiographic memories of things that have happened; and skill memories, how to do things

exploratory research initial marketing research looking into the nature of a problem, trying to identify all the possible intervening factors, in general terms, before committing larger expenditure

extended self this consists of our actual self and the external objects that we gather around us that we consider part of our self

extranet external private Internet system available only to a selective group of companies

extrinsic coming from outside, external, not essential, foreign: the opposite of 'intrinsic'

extrinsic rewards rewards for doing a job which are external to the individual, such as wages, bonuses, incentives, job promotions, and so on

eye-tracking research in qualitative research, this involves the use of various mechanical devices to record consumers' eye movements when they are looking at some form of stimulus

Eysenck, Hans (1916–97) British psychological theorist and writer, argued for the importance of inherited intelligence

factory village retail stores that sell the products of a manufacturer at very low prices

family life cycle used in segmentation: baby, toddler, teenybopper, tweenie, teenager, single, with partner, living with partner, married, child under 6 years, children over 6 years, single parent, married with grown-up children, married children left home, retired. All can be offered different types of products

fast-moving-consumer-goods (FMCG) products with a quick turnover, i.e. anything sold at e.g. Tesco

feminine psychology the idea that gender personality differences are determined by society rather than genetics. Associated with **Karen Horney** (1885–1952)

Festinger, Leon (1919–90) American psychologist, most widely known for his theory on 'cognitive dissonance'

four Ps (4Ps) the four major controllable variables of the marketing mix - product, price, promotion and place

Freud, Sigmund (1856–1939) developed a universal theory of the mind, especially the concept of subconscious motives for certain behaviour. In marketing we try to understand how these subconscious drives affect behaviour

Fromm, Erich (1900–80) German writer and existentialist

Gall, Franz Joseph (1758–1828) inventor of phrenology, defining personality through bumps on the head

Galton, Sir Francis (1822–1911) psychologist, postulated that intelligence was all genetics ('nature') and only loosely influenced by social interaction ('nurture') in a very limited way

galvanometer a scientific instrument used in qualitative marketing research to measure the emotional reaction (skin response) of a consumer to a particular stimulus such as an advertisement or product packaging

garbology examining rubbish for information on consumer lifestyle

Gestalt the theory that individuals are born with the perceptual need to organise the world in whole images using techniques such as: closure, grouping, figure and ground, proximity, continuity and similarity

goal-setting theory states that people will perform better if they are working toward some type of known goal or objective they would like to achieve

grey market consumers over 50

group dynamics the interaction between people in a group of two or more

group pressure members of a family, peers, fellow workers, opinion leaders, etc. have an effect on a consumer's purchase behaviour

groupthink faulty decision making that can take place in groups of people. Associated with Irving Janis writing in 1972

habituation a situation where the stimulus is no longer noticed

Harlow, Harry (1905–81) American psychologist, worked with monkeys developing the concept of cognitive learning, memory and emotional attachments

Hertzberg, Frederick (1923–2000) American social psychologist known by marketing students for his work on motivation and 'hygiene factors'

Hertzberg (F) motivation theory certain factors, money, work conditions, security (hygiene factors), will only maintain normal motivational levels, e.g. 70 per cent of effort or attention. To get 100 per cent effort, other motivational factors are needed, e.g. achievement, recognition and responsibility (**Frederick Hertzberg** 1923–2000)

Hobbes, Thomas (1588–1679) English philosopher and political writer argued that society protects individuals

home shopping a customer buying products from home, e.g. using television (QVC), catalogues, Internet

homeostasis internal, genetically programmed method of maintaining and bringing back to equilibrium

Horney, Karen (1885–1952) neo-Freudian psychologist, believed that gender differences are determined by society

humanistic personality development the theory that most humans are driven to achieve their maximum potential in life and will always do so unless obstacles are placed in their way. Associated with **Abraham Maslow** (1908–70) and **Carl Rogers** (1902–87)

id inherited, instinctive primitive ways of thinking driven by sexuality, aggression and the need for instant gratification. Associated with **Sigmund Freud**. Part of the unconscious mind (see also the **ego** and the **superego**)

implicit memory includes faintly remembered memories and memories in the subconscious

individual psychology each person is unique and adjusts differently to the environment (**Alfred Adler** 1870–1970)

innate knowledge knowledge we are born with

insight learning learning by sitting back and thinking about a problem and then the answer suddenly arises in the mind. Associated with Harry Harlow (1905–81)

instinctive behaviour acting, seemingly without thought; also compulsive behaviour

intangible product a product/service that has no physical substance and cannot be touched, e.g. a mortgage

integrated marketing mix all the 4Ps (or more Ps depending on the model you use) working in an optimum way to achieve customer satisfaction

intellectual development of personality children develop through a series of intellectual stages. Associated with **Jean Piaget** (1896–1980)

intelligence: IQ tests an attempt to measure levels of intelligence. Thought to be inherited. Associated with **Alfred Binet** (1857–1911)

Intranet a private internal organisation Internet system

intrinsic inherent feelings and emotions that come from within the mind of the customer

Jung, Carl (1875–1961) Swiss neo-Freudian and analytical psychologist; developed the idea of the 'universal collective unconscious'

justification principle individuals look to constantly justify attitudes adopted

just noticeable difference: sensory the per centage change needed before individuals can notice a particular difference. Known as Weber's Law

knowledge function adopted through knowledge and understanding

Kohler, Wolfgang (1887–1967) German/American psychologist, identified the concept of insight learning while working with animals (chimps)

labelling theory classify an individual or group as deviant and they act in a deviant manner

latent learning used in trying to understand customer behaviour. Learning that occurs at one time but not apparent until later when there is an incentive to demonstrate it. Associated with **Edward Toleman** (1886–1959)

learned helplessness the hopelessness and passive resignation learned when an animal or human is unable to avoid repeated aversive events

learning a relatively permanent change in organism/human behaviour due to experience

Lewin, Kurt (1890–1947) American social psychologist, researched into mental motivational conflict

liberal or free market economy allowing the economic laws of consumer supply and demand to decide what should and should not be produced. The economic system that now dominates world political thinking

life cycle stages from birth, growth, maturity, saturation, decline and death. It can be applied to people, products, brands, markets and industries

lifestyle segmentation segmenting the market according to values, opinions, interests, attitudes and lifestyle

Likert scale a scale measuring a respondent's strength of attitude about a particular issue, e.g. strongly agree, agree, neither, disagree, strongly disagree

linguistics the study of the structure, nature, meaning and development of language

Locke, John (1632–1704) English philosopher, argues that all learning comes about through the senses and experience

logo usually, a small image, consisting of graphics and text, that represents a business. A logo provides a distinctive 'signature' and helps to establish recognition of the advertiser's name and product. The 'Michelin Man' uses the concept in its tyre advertisements

Lombroso, Cesare (1836–1909) Italian physicist, believed that criminal types could be identified by the make-up and structure of the face

loyalty the extent to which customers repurchase a particular product or brand

macro-environment uncontrollable factors that constitute the external environment of marketing including political/legal, economic/demographic, social/cultural and technological/physical

market positioning marketing activity that attempts to create a particular image for the company and its products in the marketplace compared to the competition, e.g. Mercedes is positioned at a higher status level than Fords

market segmentation splitting the market into groups of customers with similar features. Segmentation methods include splitting the market by: industrial or consumer markets, geographic, socio-economic, behavioural, psycho-graphic and lifestyle

marketing information system (MIS) a set of formal procedures for collecting and analysing data from all sources (identified as: internal reports; marketing intelligence system; marketing research; data storage and analysis), and disseminating information regularly to marketing decision makers

Marx, Karl (Heinrich) (1818–83) philosopher, sociologist, economist and founder of international Communism

Maslow, Abraham (1908–70) American humanist psychologist (remembered by students for the 'Maslow Triangle')

Maslow's hierarchy of needs a motivational theory, it argues that people's needs are satisfied in an ascending order from: physiological, safety, social, status and finally self-actualisation needs

mass marketing treating the market as a homogenous whole. Making no allowances for ethnic, cultural or national differences

materialism a preoccupation with material things rather than intellectual or spiritual concerns

McClelland, David (1917–98) American psychologist known for his theory on the need for achievement and power

McGregor, Douglas (1906–64) American social psychologist, is mostly known by students for his work on theory x and theory y theory of motivation

Mead, George H. (1863–1931) American sociologist, major theorist of symbolic interactionism, how the individual mind and self arises out of the social process

Mead, Margaret (1901–78) anthropologist and scientist. Her major work was *Coming of Age in Samoa*

memory where knowledge is used and stored. It includes sensory and short and long-term memory. Associated with **Herman Ebbinghaus** (1850–1909)

memory process involves encoding, storage and retrieval

merchandising making certain that everything surrounding the product on display adds value to its appearance, e.g. position, cleanliness, POP, staff knowledge

metaphysics might be described as the study of the mind and consciousness rather than the study of matter

microenvironment the specific external (nearer or immediate) business environment in which an organisation operates. (Acronym SPICC: Suppliers; Publics; Intermediaries; Customers and markets; Competition)

Milgram, Stanley American psychologist, known for his work on power and obedience

Mill, John Stuart (1806–73) English philosopher, theorised it was socialisation and the nurture of others that made the difference in defining levels of intelligence and learning

mind-set a way of viewing the world

models artificial constructions that are used to simplify complex problems

motivation the basic process that involves needs (internal or external), which set drives in motion to accomplish goals to satisfy these needs

motivational research qualitative research using psychological techniques getting at underlying (unconscious) perceptions, beliefs and attitudes that might drive motivation. Associated with **Ernest Dichter** who founded The Institute of Motivational Research in New York in 1946

MRI and PET scanners machines that measure the electrical impulses in the brain; sometimes used as a measure of reactions to advertising

nature versus nurture argument are we born with intelligence (or other attributes) or do we learn through social interaction?
need for achievement associated with David McClelland (1917–98) this theory argues that the need for achievement and success is an important motivator
neuromarketing using brain-scanning techniques to measure consumer reactions to marketing stimuli
Newton, Isaac (1642–1727) British scientist. Was able to predict the path of planets and comets with little or no observation, using mathematics and reason
niche marketing marketing to a small highly targeted group of individuals who are most likely to need or want what you have to offer
norms (group) the accepted ways of behaving in society. Norms are learnt from parents, peer groups and others

observation research a research study where data is collected by watching/videoing consumer behaviour or events taking place without becoming involved, e.g. customers moving around a supermarket
ontology the study of what exists (or doesn't exist) on the Earth or in the universe
operant conditioning learning in which voluntary behaviour is strengthened or weakened by consequences (events that follow actions) or antecedents (events that precede an action). (Also known as instrumental conditioning)
own label products a product made for a retailer by a manufacturer but branded with the retailer name

paradigm a basic theory, a conceptual framework within which theories (scientific) are constructed, e.g. Freud's theory of the subconscious
Pareto 80/20 rule used in many ways, e.g. 80 per cent of your business comes from 20 per cent of your customers
Pavlov, Ivan (1849–1936) Russian scientist, seen as the father of classical conditioning form of involuntary learning
peer group friends and people that we associate with. We buy products and brands that conform to their approval, e.g. family, friends, colleagues and fellow students
perception the process of selecting, organising, and interpreting sensory data into usable mental representations of the world
perceptual sets mental categories of products and brands that are liked and disliked by a consumer
personality genetics, emotions, experiences, traits, beliefs, attitudes, behaviour that make us different. Used in segmentation and understanding customer behaviour
personality trait theory see **trait personality theory**
personality type theory for example, happy people, sad people, angry people, natural criminals and so on
phenomenological or interpretative research looking for information about individual and group feelings and opinions
Piaget, Jean (1896–1980) French educational psychologist, researched into early intellectual development stages
planned economy an economy where supply and price are regulated by the government
political science studies power relations and forms of government in societies
Popper, Karl (1902–94) a philosopher of science who promoted the theory that science moves forward by attempting to falsify hypotheses and theories
positive and negative reinforcement reinforcement that motivates and encourages or discourages behaviour
positivism epistemological approach that rejects theology and metaphysics for observation and uses experiment and an empirical scientific approach
post purchase evaluation how the customer acts and feels after purchase. Also know as post purchase evaluation
pressure groups groups of people who come together to promote some special interest or other, e.g. Greenpeace, anti-hunt protesters
primary needs inner feelings of psychological deprivation related to our mental well-being, e.g. wanting to be loved
primary research new research undertaken to collect specific information
product driven markets products and services produced because of the inclination of the producer, not the consumer
product positioning mapping an analysis technique plotting a product/brand's perceived value against the competition on a visual map, e.g. high value and low value on one axis, and high quality and low quality on another
propaganda spreading and gaining support for an idea, opinion, cause or belief; usually one-sided in its demands, often bending the truth and not to be confused with publicity

psyche the mind
psychoanalytic theory an approach to the study of human motivations and behaviours pioneered by **Sigmund Freud** (1856–1939)
psychodynamic conflicting forces the theory that the mind is made up of conscious, pre-conscious and unconscious parts and is driven by conflicting forces, the id, ego and superego. All affect personality development. Associated with **Sigmund Freud** (1856–1939)
psychographics a means of segmenting consumers based on personality, attitude, beliefs and lifestyle characteristics
psychology the study of the mind
psychosexual stages the theory that personality develops through a series of interactive sexual stages from birth to adulthood. Associated with **Sigmund Freud** (1856–1939)
psychosocial stages the theory that personality developed through a series of interactive social stages from birth to adulthood; associated with **Erick Erickson** (1902–94)

qualitative marketing research research which produces non-statistical feedback (opinions) from customers, suppliers, experts, etc. It gets at the opinions of customers unattainable through quantitative research. Methods used include: focus groups, interviews, psychological tests, etc.
quantitative research research that produces numerical data that can be statistically analysed, often from large samples. More 'scientific' than qualitative data

radio frequency identification (RFID) tags silcon chips built into products that contain information that can be used to trace and react to product movement and usage of some kind
rational reasons customer motivations for buying that are based on logic or judgement rather than on emotion
rationalism knowledge obtained about the world through mental reasoning
received knowledge knowledge about the world obtained from a deity
reference groups those groups of people we respect and often want to copy when buying products; also categorised as membership groups and affinity groups
regional shopping centres purpose built retail villages usually in an out-of-town facility
representative sample the statistical selection of a group of respondents to represent the opinions of many within a particular universe
repressed emotional memories memories in the unconscious part of the mind
retail aromatics distinctive aromas, e.g. bread baking, coffee beans cooking, are pumped into the store at different spots so as to interest the consumer
retail atmospherics designing buying environments to produce specific customer emotional reactions that enhance purchase probability. It includes point-of-purchase (POP), layout, colour, smells, music, lighting, materials etc.
retail audits examining, noting, counting, purchasing and stock movements in the store
Rogers, Carl (1902–87) humanist social psychologist believed the basic normal motivation for all humans was to develop their potential to the highest possible level
role model an admired person that others might want to use to model their behaviour
role play the concept that people role play many different parts in life, e.g. husband, son, father, lover, mother, daughter, student, etc. Some argue that life is nothing other than role play with no core 'self'
Rorschach inkblot test used in qualitative motivational research. Subjects are shown a figure that looks like a large ink blot on a piece of paper and asked what they see. Inadequacies and conflicts can be revealed in the different interpretations
Rousseau, Jacques (1712–78) French philosopher and political writer argued that society corrupts individuals

safety needs the desire of humans for safety, shelter, security and warmth
sales promotion below the line activity such as competitions, discounts, two for the price of one etc.; used to get the customer to try the product
Sartre, Jean Paul (1905–80) French existentialist writer
Saussure, Ferdinand de (1857–1913) widely considered to be the founder of modern linguistics and semiotics
scapegoating blaming someone or something else to ease our frustration and/or anger
Schacter, Daniel and Endel Tulving psychologists, introduced the terms explicit and implicit memory
schemata a concept or framework that we use to organise and interpret information
scientific method the 'scientific' way to search for the facts. Acronym POACHER

secondary research research already in existence. Sometimes known as 'second-hand research' or 'desk research'

segmentation breaking an amorphous diverse market up into relatively similar units so that products can be customised, positioned and promoted to meet each groups' exact needs

selective retention when we retain information that fits into own existing beliefs and attitudes

self-actualisation fulfilling one's full spiritual, intellectual potential

self-concept theory looking at personality from the beliefs that individuals hold about their own attributes and characteristics. Associated with **Henry Stack Sullivan** (1892–1949)

self-esteem one's feelings of high or low self-worth operating at both the conscious and unconscious level

self-perception theory individuals will alter the facts to fit personal concepts and behaviour

Seligman, Martin American psychologist, worked on the part that the concept of mental thought and reasoning might play in the learning process

semantic differential extreme opposite statements (e.g. strong/weak; modern/old fashioned; good service/poor service), are presented to the respondent and they are asked to grade between each statement on a scale of, say, 1–10

semiotics the use of signs, symbols and images in language. Used by advertisers, e.g. the Marlboro cowboy is a sign for a romantic, heroic lifestyle. (Swiss linguist **Ferdinand de Saussure**)

sensation the immediate and direct response of the senses to a stimulus such as an advertisement, package, brand name or point-of-purchase display

senses how we perceive the world, i.e. taste, smell, sight, touch, and hearing

sensory defence mind mechanisms that are used to protect against unwelcoming stimuli

sensory deprivation when animals and humans have been deprived of one or more of the senses

sensory evaluation tries to measure, analyse and interpret consumer levels of sensory reaction to a whole range of products, brands and services

sensory overload more information than the mind is able to cope with

sensory threshold the level at which individuals are able to detect or to lose the presence of a sensory stimulus

services intangible 'products', e.g. retail, leisure, financial, medical, communication, energy, household, education

shaping the reinforcement of successive acts that lead to a desired animal or human behaviour pattern or response. Associated with **B.F. Skinner** (1904–90)

Sheldon, William (1898–1977) American psychologist, believed that personality could be known through body types

Skinner, B.F. (1904–90) American behavioural psychologist, used more complex trial and error and reward and punishment techniques (notably the 'Skinner Box') relating animal experiments to how humans learn

Smith, Adam (1723–90) born in Scotland and seen as the father of modern economics, Adams wrote *The Wealth of Nations*

social agencies socialising institutions e.g. family, school, work, government etc.

social class grouping the population according to occupation, income and lifestyle; in simple terms, upper, middle and lower class. It can be ascribed or acquired. Associated with **Max Weber** (1864–1920)

social diversity a mixed, multi-ethnic group of people

social exchange theory the theory that our social behaviour is an exchange process based on maximising benefits and minimising costs (reward and punishment)

social judgement theory perceptions about the world are interpreted in terms of existing mind sets

social learning learning through watching, listening and copying others. Associated with **Albert Bandura** (1925–)

social marketing seeks to influence social behaviours not to benefit the marketer, but to benefit the target audience and society in general

social psychology the scientific study into how individuals and groups think, behave and interact with each other

socialisation society institutions indoctrinating citizens to behave in acceptable ways

socialisation process the process by which an individual acquires the skills needed to function in the marketplace as a consumer, usually from parents and peer groups

socially excluded members of society who have less access to resources than the average

society people coming together to live in groups including language, systems, institutions, organisations and infrastructures
sociology the study of society including people, organisations and structures
status power relationship that one group or individual has with others, e.g. high and low status
status needs the desire to feel important through the eyes of others
stereotype a generalised (often over-generalised) belief about a group of people, e.g. all men drink too much!
sub-cultures smaller groups within a culture that possesses similar beliefs, values, norms and patterns of behaviour, which differentiate them from the larger cultural mainstream
subliminal advertising television or cinema commercials containing too few frames for the eye to record, but sufficient for the subconscious mind to capture the message
subliminal perception the ability of an individual to perceive a stimulus below the level of conscious awareness
Sullivan, Henry Stack (1892–1949) American social psychologist, developed self-concept theory
superego in Freudian theory, that part of the personality that reflects society's moral and ethical codes of conduct. Our parents give it to us
symbolic interaction how subjectively humans interact and continually adjust their behaviour to the action of other 'actors' in life. Associated with **Max Weber** (1864–1920) and **George H. Mead** (1863–1931)
symbolic reasons for purchase buying brands for emotional rather than rational reasons

targeting identifying, analysing and selecting particularly attractive market segments in which to market products
theory X and Y theory X people are lazy, manipulative and will only work under threats and punishment; Theory Y people will work better if they are encouraged and praised. Associated with **Douglas McGregor** (1906–64)
Thorndike, Edward (1874–1949) American behavioural psychologist, used basic trial and error and reward and punishment techniques on animals to try to understand the learning process
Toleman, Edward (1886–1959) American psychologist, introduced the idea of latent cognitive mapping and learning into the behavioural process
trait personality theory the theory that personality is built up through a combination of different characteristics or traits (inherited and/or acquired) and each personality could be unique. Associated with **Gordon Allport** (1897–1967), **Raymond Cattell** (1905–98) and **Hans Eysenck** (1916–97)
transactional analysis the idea that personality is made up of three interacting 'ego states' (mind sets) the 'parent', 'adult' and 'child' and we switch back and forth between each one. Associated with **Eric Berne** (1910–70)

unique emotional proposition (UEP) similar to USP but a unique emotional benefit is used, e.g. nostalgia, social inclusion, sex appeal, family wholeness
unique selling proposition (USP) having a distinctive product feature or unique element in the marketing mix, such as a brand, excellent service, a unique feature etc.
universal law of effect a given behaviour is learned by trial-and-error, and those actions we find rewarding we will repeat, and those we don't, we will not. Associated with the behavioural theorists
utilitarian purpose to gain reward and avoid punishment

value-expressive purpose to fit into an individual's life values
value systems enduring moral beliefs shared by people living in a society and becoming an essential part of the culture
Vroom, Victor known for his expectancy theory of motivation published in 1964

Watson, John (1878–1958) American psychologist, argued that human learning behaviour could only be understood by observing and experimenting with animals; it came to be known as '**behaviourism**'
Weber, Max (1864–1920) German sociologist and philosopher

Index